Microsoft Project 2013

the missing manual®

The book that should have been in the box®

Bonnie Biafore

O'REILLY®

Beijing | Cambridge | Farnham | Köln | Sebastopol | Tokyo

Microsoft Project 2013: The Missing Manual

by Bonnie Biafore

Published by O'Reilly Media, Inc.,
1005 Gravenstein Highway North, Sebastopol, CA 95472.

O'Reilly books may be purchased for educational, business, or sales promotional use. Online editions are also available for most titles (*http://my.safaribooksonline.com*). For more information, contact our corporate/institutional sales department: (800) 998-9938 or *corporate@oreilly.com*.

April 2013:   First Edition.

Revision History for the First Edition:

2013-04-09   First release

See *http://oreilly.com/catalog/errata.csp?isbn=9781449357962* for release details.

ISBN-13: 978-1-449-35796-2

[LSI]

Contents

Part Three: **Projects in Action**

Part Four: **Project Power Tools**

Part Five: **Customizing Project**

Part Six: **Appendixes**

> **NOTE** You can download one additional chapter—Chapter 25: Collaborating on Projects with SharePoint—from this book's Missing CD page at *www.missingmanuals.com/cds*. See page xxii for more about the Missing CD page.

The Missing Credits

ABOUT THE AUTHOR

 **Bonnie Biafore** has always been a zealous organizer of everything from software demos to gourmet meals, with the occasional vacation trip to test the waters of spontaneity. As an engineer, she's fascinated by how things work and how to make things work better. Ironically, fate, not planning, turned these obsessions into a career as a project manager. When Bonnie realized she was managing projects, her penchant for planning and follow-through kicked in and she earned a Project Management Professional certification from the Project Management Institute.

When she isn't managing projects for clients, Bonnie writes about and teaches project management, personal finance and investing, and technology. She has a knack for mincing these dry subjects into easy-to-understand morsels and then spices them to perfection with her warped sense of humor.

Bonnie is also the author of *Successful Project Management*, which won an International Award of Merit from the Society of Technical Communication, *QuickBooks 2013: The Missing Manual* (now Intuit's Official Guide to QuickBooks), and several other award-winning books. She has recorded several courses on project management, Microsoft Project, and QuickBooks for Lynda.com. In addition, she writes and presents frequently for the Microsoft Project Users Group.

When unshackled from her computer, she hikes in the mountains with her dogs, cycles, cooks gourmet food, and mostly tries not to act her age. She has also published her first novel, *Fresh Squeezed*, featuring hit men, stupid criminals, and much political incorrectness. You can learn more at her website, *www.bonniebiafore.com*, or email her at *bonnie.biafore@gmail.com*.

ABOUT THE CREATIVE TEAM

Dawn Mann (editor) is associate editor for the Missing Manual series. When not reading about Microsoft Project, she beads, plays soccer, and causes trouble. Email: *dawn@oreilly.com*.

Melanie Yarbrough (production editor) lives and works in Cambridge, MA. When she's not ushering books through production, she bakes, writes, and sews whatever she can think up.

Sean Earp (technical reviewer), CISSP, MCITP, is Program Manager at a large software company in Redmond, WA, specializing in Project, Project Server, and SharePoint technologies. Trained in the school of hard knocks, Sean has experienced nearly every project-management pitfall outlined in this book. When not in front of his computer, Sean likes spending time with his wife and three wonderful kids, being a Cub Scout leader, and training for a marathon.

Michael Wharton (technical reviewer), MVP, MBA, PMP, MCT, MCITP, MCTS, MCSD, MCSE+I, MCDBA, MCC 2012, has been a Project/SharePoint Consultant since 2003. He has implemented project server in over twenty-five PMO organizations, trained hundreds of project managers, migrated many organizations from project server 2003 and has passed over 40 Microsoft certification exams. He is active in the local PMI chapter, MPUG community, MS Project Forums, PASS and many local technical user groups. Michael lives in North Carolina and is happily married to his wife Gwen and loves spending time with his family when not working on project. Michael's field notes can be found in his blog at *http://MyProjectExpert.com*, and you can reach him at *mwharton@WhartonComputer.com*.

Julie Van Keuren (proofreader) quit her newspaper job in 2006 to move to Montana and live the freelancing dream. She and her husband, M.H. (who is living the novel-writing dream), have two sons, Dexter and Michael. Email: *little_media@yahoo.com*.

ACKNOWLEDGMENTS

No O'Reilly book that I author can go to print without me acknowledging the awesome team at O'Reilly. Dawn Mann is editor extraordinaire. She can spot potential points of confusion in my writing from a mile away and usually comes up with a wonderfully clear alternative. If she's stumped, she asks for clarification in a way that even a diva (oh, I so hope I haven't become one) wouldn't mind. She stays on top of details, so they're taken care of before anyone even thinks to ask. She has earned my gratitude for keeping me company via email as we both worked weekend after weekend to complete this book. My thanks go to Melanie Yarbrough and the rest of the O'Reilly folks for shepherding my book through the publication process. I am grateful for the eagle eye of Julie Van Keuren, the proofreader, for wrangling punctuation, capitalization, and ungainly sentences into submission.

The technical reviewers Sean Earp and Michael Wharton caught my mistakes and shared their knowledge of the finer points of project management, Microsoft Project, and SharePoint. I was fortunate to have them as guinea pigs for the many sections that I ripped apart and put back together. Fortunately, my rewrites successfully passed their gimlet-eyed scrutiny.

I also want to thank a few old friends and several new ones in the project-management community. Teresa Stover is a wonderful writer, a good friend, and a trusted colleague who is always willing to pitch in to dissect gnarly Project features despite her deadlines. Ellen Lehnert is a fabulous trainer and another one of my go-to people for Project questions. I've also had the great fortune to befriend and, in some cases, collaborate with other incredible Project educators: Sam Huffman, Larry Christofaro, John Riopel, Eric Uyttewaal, and Eric Verzuh.

I am fortunate to have more good friends than my prickly personality deserves. Special thanks go to all of them—who leave me alone when I'm under deadlines, go out with me when I need a break, and still speak to me after another trying winter of work. A shout-out to everyone in Rocky Mountain Fiction Writers and the Rocky Mountain chapter of the Mystery Writers of America for letting me be part of the tribe.

Finally, I thank my agent, Neil Salkind, for his hard work, support, and friendship over the past (is it really?) 13 years. He recently retired, and I'd like to think I helped him realize that dream. Neil, you haven't heard the last from me!

— Bonnie Biafore

Introduction

People have been managing projects for centuries. The construction of the mountaintop city of Machu Picchu was a project—although no one's really sure whether the ancient Inca had a word for "project manager." In fact, you may not have realized you were a project manager when you were assigned your first project to manage. Sure, you're organized and good at making sure people get things done, but consistently managing projects to successful conclusions requires specific skills and know-how. Whether you're building a shining city on a hill or aiming for something more mundane, Microsoft Project helps you document project tasks, build a schedule, assign resources, track progress, and make changes until your project is complete.

Perhaps you've launched Project, and now you're staring at the screen, wondering about the meaning of the program's Gantt Chart and Resource Usage views. Or maybe you already have dozens of Project schedules under your belt. Either way, some Project features can be mystifying. You know what you want to do, but you can't find the magic combination that makes Project do it.

This book addresses the double whammy of learning your way around project management and Microsoft Project at the same time. It provides an introduction to managing projects and shows you how to use Project to do so. For more experienced project managers, this book can help you take your Project prowess to a new level with tips, time saving tricks, and mastery of features that never quite behaved the way you wanted.

■ What's New in Project 2013

Microsoft Project comes in several flavors: Project Standard is good if you want to save some bucks; Project Professional can handle most of your project-scheduling needs; Project Pro for Office 365 gives you the convenience of an always-up-to-date version of the program; and Project Server is great if your organization wants to manage an entire portfolio of projects. (This book focuses on Project Standard and Project Professional.) Since its introduction, Project Server has often gotten most of Microsoft's attention and cool new features, and Project 2013 is no exception. However, Project 2013 Standard and Professional have some new and improved features that could quickly grow on you.

Perhaps the biggest news is that Project is now part of the Office 365 suite of applications. You can install Project 2013 the way you've installed earlier versions (from a CD or downloaded file), or you can download and install Project Pro for Office 365, a subscription-based version of Project, which means you'll always have the most up-to-date version. Project's reporting features also got an overhaul—you can now produce graphical reports so you and the rest of the project team can see what's going on.

Here's an overview of the new Project 2013 features and where to learn about them in this book:

- **Project Pro for Office 365.** If you have an Office 365 account, you can purchase and download Project Pro for Windows. With this subscription version of Project, you can set things up so that the program automatically updates when a software update is available. See page 732 to learn how to install Project Pro for Office 365.

- **The Get Started template.** Project 2013 offers this template to help you learn your way around the program and meet some of its new features. When you launch Project 2013 for the very first time, the Get Started template appears. Click the Start button to start the tour. As you follow along, you can dig deeper on any topic by clicking "Learn more" links. Jump to page 85 for more info on this template.

- **Access to the cloud.** Project's Backstage view now makes it easier to work with files stored in the cloud, whether you use Microsoft's SkyDrive or another cloud-storage service. When you choose File→Open or File→Save As, the Open and Save As screens list locations, such as Computer or SkyDrive. You choose the location where your file is stored, and then choose the folder and file. Chapter 5 provides the full scoop on opening and saving files, on or off the cloud.

- **Improved reporting.** Projects seem to be all about communication, although people spend a lot of time with their heads down working. When it's time to communicate, Project 2013 offers easy-to-digest reports that make it easier to communicate status to stakeholders and other team members. These reports can include dashboards with charts and tables, instead of row after row of numbers. The program comes with a bunch of reports to help you get started, but you can build and customize reports to your heart's content. Or your team members can set up their own reports to see project information in a way that makes sense to them. Chapter 16 is all about project reports.

- **Task path.** If you work on large or complex projects, you know how tough it can be to keep track of task dependencies and how tasks affect one another. Project's Task Path feature (page 312) helps you view the path of tasks linked to a specific task. For example, if a crucial task is running late, Task Path can show you the task's predecessors and driving predecessors (the ones that determine the task's start date). In addition, you can watch the downstream effects by looking at successors and driven successors.

- **Integration with SharePoint and Office 365.** Project 2013 is a lot chummier with SharePoint and other collaborative tools than earlier versions of Project were. You can now easily share Project data on a SharePoint team site. For small projects, a SharePoint Tasks List might be enough. If your scheduling needs grow, you can share tasks between Project and a SharePoint Tasks List, and vice versa. In addition, team members can provide task updates via SharePoint. Chapter 25 (available from this book's Missing CD page—see page xxii for details) shows you how to get Project and SharePoint to play well together.

◼ Where Microsoft Project Fits In

Any project manager who has calculated task start and finish dates by hand knows how helpful Project is. By calculating dates, costs, and total assigned work, the program eliminates a *mountain* of grunt work and helps prevent carpal tunnel syndrome, so you'll have time and stamina left over to actually manage your projects.

In the planning stage, Project helps you develop a project schedule. You add the tasks and people to a Project file, link the tasks together in sequence, assign workers and other resources to those tasks, and poof!—you have a schedule. Project calculates when tasks start and finish, how much they cost, and how many hours each person needs to work each day. The program even helps you develop *better* project plans, because you can revise the schedule quickly to try other strategies until the plan really works. Views and reports help you spot problems, like too many tasks assigned to the same beleaguered team member.

Once your project is under way, you can add actual dates, hours, and costs to the Project file. With actual values, you can use Project to track progress to see how actual progress and cost compare to the project plan. If problems arise—like tasks running late or over budget—you can use Project's tools, views, and reports to look for solutions and quickly make changes until you find a way to get the project back on track.

Of course, plenty of project-management work goes on outside Project. Touchy-feely tasks like identifying project objectives, negotiating with vendors, and building stakeholder buy-in are all about people skills (although Project's reports can certainly *help* you communicate status with these folks). And projects typically require a lot of documents besides the project schedule. For example, a project plan may include financial-analysis spreadsheets, requirements and specifications documents, change request databases, and diagrams to show how the change-management process works. In addition, thousands of email messages, memos, and other correspondence could change hands before a project finishes.

Communication, change management, and risk management are essential to successful project management, but they don't occur in Project, either. For example, you may have a risk-management plan that identifies the risks your project faces and what you plan to do if they occur. You may also develop a spreadsheet to track those risks and your response if they become reality. In Project, you can link the risk-tracking spreadsheet or risk-response document to the corresponding tasks, but that's about it.

NOTE The enterprise features in Project Server combined with SharePoint help you track risks, issues, changes, and more. But smaller teams can collaborate on topics like these on an Office 365 team site. Chapter 25 (available from this book's Missing CD page) describes Office 365 and SharePoint collaboration features in more detail.

■ Choosing the Right Edition

This book covers Project Standard and Project Professional, which have about the same capabilities if you manage projects independently and aren't trying to work closely with other project managers, teams, and projects. It doesn't cover the enterprise features available in Project Professional and Project Server. (The box on page xvii describes some of Project's enterprise features so you can see whether they make sense for your organization.)

NOTE This book also covers Project Pro for Office 365 as that edition stood at the time this book was written. However, because Project Pro for Office 365 will update more frequently than the desktop versions, differences between that edition and this book will increase over time.

Project Standard works for most one-person shows, even if you manage several projects at the same time. It lets you communicate with your team via email and share documents on a network drive, or the cloud (page 93).

Project Professional adds Team Planner view, and the abilities to inactivate tasks and synchronize Project tasks to a task list in SharePoint 2013. If you manage project teams with hundreds of resources, share a pool of resources with other project managers, or manage your project as one of many in your organization's project portfolio, then you need Project Professional, along with Microsoft Enterprise Project Management Solutions. (You can set up your own Project Server environment or subscribe to a hosted solution, such as Project Online.)

COMPLEMENTARY SOFTWARE

UP TO SPEED

Enterprise Project Management

The main difference between Project Standard and Project Professional is that you can turn on the enterprise features in Project Professional and connect it to Project Server to collaborate, communicate, and share across hundreds of projects and people. Setting up an enterprise-wide project-management (EPM) system takes some planning and effort, depending on the size and complexity of your organization. Fortunately, Microsoft and several of its partners offer hosted solutions that make it much easier to set up and use enterprise project-management tools. Here are some of the advantages that Project Professional and the enterprise project-management tools offer:

- **Track all projects in one place.** If you build Project schedules with Project Professional, then when a project is ready for prime time, you can publish it to Project Server to add it to the overall project portfolio. That way, the status for all projects appears in a single view.

- **Share resources enterprise-wide.** Instead of playing phone tag with other project managers about when resources are available, Project Server keeps track of all resources and when they work on which project. You

can look for the right kind of resources using multilevel resource skill characteristics, and then see who's available for your projects.

- **Communicate with resources.** Project Web App makes it easy for you to communicate with your team, requesting statuses, sending messages, and so on. It also makes it easy for your team to communicate with you, reply with statuses, accept assignments, and provide time worked.

- **Timesheets.** With Project Professional, team members can fill out timesheets for project work. The time they submit shoots straight into the Project Server database to update progress on your projects.

- **Track issues, risks, and documents.** Projects are more than schedules. Issues crop up that need to be resolved; risks lurk that you have to watch and manage; and there's no end to the additional documents produced, like specifications, plans, work packages, and so on. Using SharePoint websites and Project Web App, team members can collaborate on these elements online.

NOTE Project Standard and Project Professional are both available for purchase in retail stores like Office-Max and Amazon.com. However, Project Server or a hosted EPM solution are available for purchase only through Microsoft and Microsoft partners and solution providers.

■ Complementary Software

Managing a project requires other programs in addition to Project. Word and Excel are great for working with the documents and financial-analysis data you produce. PowerPoint is ideal for project presentations and status meetings. And Outlook keeps project communication flowing. This book includes instructions for using these programs in some of your project-management duties.

Office 2013 Home and Business includes Word, Excel, PowerPoint, OneNote, and Outlook. You can purchase Office at stores like Staples or websites like *www.bestbuy.com*. Office 2013 Professional adds Office Web Apps, Publisher, and Access to the Office Home and Business suite. (Office 2013 Professional Plus adds Lync to the Office Professional lineup so your team members can communicate via instant messaging, voice, and video.) Here are some of the ways you might use these products in project management:

- **Word.** Producing documents like the overall project plan, work-package descriptions, requirements, specifications, status reports, and so on.

- **Excel.** Creating spreadsheets for financial analysis or tracking change requests, risks, issues, and defects reported.

- **PowerPoint.** Putting together presentations for project proposals, project kickoff, status, change control board meetings, and so on.

- **Outlook.** Emailing everyone who's on the project team.

- **Publisher.** Publishing newsletters, fliers, invitations to meetings, and so on.

- **Access.** Tracking change requests, requirements, risks, and issues. Access is a database program that's a more robust alternative to Excel.

Visio 2013 Professional is another program that comes in handy, whether you want to document project processes in flowcharts or to generate Visio-based visual reports from within Project. Visio isn't part of the Office suite, so if you want to use Visio, you have to purchase it separately.

■ About This Book

Over the years and versions, Project has collected improvements the way sailboat keels attract barnacles. To use Project successfully, you need to understand something about project management, but that's an exercise Microsoft leaves to its customers. The program's Help feature is at least organized around the activities that project managers perform, but Help still focuses on what *Project* does rather than what *you're* trying to do.

Project Help is optimistically named, because it often lacks troubleshooting tips or meaningful examples. In many cases, the topic you want simply isn't there. Help rarely tells you what you *really* need to know, like *when* and *why* to use a certain feature. And with Help, highlighting key points, jotting notes in the margins, or reading about Project after your laptop's battery is dead are all out of the question.

The purpose of this book is to serve as the manual that should have come with Project 2013. It focuses on managing projects with Project Standard or Project Professional, with the aid of a few other Microsoft programs like Word and Excel. The book points out some of the power tools that come with Microsoft's enterprise project-management software, but it doesn't explain how to set up or use Project

Server and Project Web App. (To learn how to work with Project Server, check out *Microsoft Office Project 2013 Inside Out* by Teresa Stover [Microsoft Press] or *Microsoft Project Server 2013 Install and Wire-up* by Gary L. Chefetz and Bill Raymond [MSProjectExperts]).

> **NOTE** Although each version of Project adds new features and enhancements, you can still use this book if you're managing projects with earlier versions of Project. Of course, the older your version of the program, the more discrepancies you'll run across.

In these pages, you'll find step-by-step instructions for using Project Standard and Professional features (minus the ones that require Project Server), including those you might not quite understand: choosing the right type of task dependency, assigning resources, assigning overtime, leveling resources, producing reports, and so on. This book helps you be productive by explaining which features are useful and when to use them. From time to time, this book also includes instructions for using other programs—like Word and Excel—in your project-management duties.

Although this book is primarily a guide to Project 2013, it comes with a healthy dose of project-management guidance. The chapters walk you through managing a project from start to finish: getting a project off the ground (initiating), figuring out who needs to do what when and more (planning), doing the project work (executing), keeping the project on track (managing and controlling), and tying up loose ends (closing). You'll find practical advice about what project managers do and how those activities help make projects a success.

Microsoft Project 2013: The Missing Manual is designed to accommodate readers at every level of technical and project-management expertise. The primary discussions are written for advanced-beginner or intermediate Project users. First-time Project users can look for special boxes labeled "Up to Speed" to get introductory information on the topic at hand. Advanced users should watch for similar boxes labeled "Power Users' Clinic," which offer more technical tips, tricks, and shortcuts for the experienced Project fan. Boxes called "Tools of the Trade" provide more background on project-management tools and techniques (Gantt Charts, for example). And if you've ever wondered how to extract yourself from a gnarly project-management situation, look for boxes called "Reality Check" for techniques you can try when project-management textbooks fail you.

About the Outline

Microsoft Project 2013: The Missing Manual is divided into six parts, each containing several chapters:

- **Part One: Project Management: The Missing Manual** is like a mini-manual on project management. It explains what projects are and why managing them is such a good idea. These chapters explain how to pick the right projects to perform, obtain support for them, and start them off on the right foot. You also get a whirlwind tour of planning a project, which Part Two tackles in detail.

- **Part Two: Project Planning: More Than Creating a Schedule** starts by introducing you to Project 2013 and creating a simple project schedule to whet your appetite. These chapters then take you through each aspect of planning a project, including breaking work down into manageable pieces, estimating work and duration, building a schedule, assembling a team, assigning resources to tasks, and setting up a budget. The remaining chapters explain how to refine your plan until everyone is (mostly) happy with it, and then how to prepare it for the execution phase of the project.

- **Part Three: Projects in Action** takes you from an approved project plan to the end of a project. These chapters explain how to track progress once work gets under way, evaluate that progress, correct course, and manage changes. Other chapters explain how to use Project's reports and complete important steps at the end of a project.

- **Part Four: Project Power Tools** helps you get the most out of Project. These chapters talk about how to work on more than one project at a time, share data with other programs, and collaborate on projects with colleagues.

- **Part Five: Customizing Project** explains how to customize every aspect of Project to fit your needs—even the ribbon. After all, every organization is unique, and so is every project. Other chapters show you how to save time by reusing Project elements (in templates) and boost productivity by recording macros.

- **Part Six: Appendixes.** At the end of the book, three appendixes provide a guide to installing and upgrading Project, a reference to help resources for Project, and a quick review of the most helpful keyboard shortcuts.

> **NOTE** You can download one additional chapter—Chapter 25: Collaborating on Projects with SharePoint—from this book's Missing CD page at *www.missingmanuals.com/cds*. See page xxii for more about the Missing CD page.

The Very Basics

To use this book—and Project—you need to know a few computer basics. Like other Microsoft programs, Project responds to several types of mouse clicks, menu commands, and keystroke combinations. Here's a quick overview of a few terms and concepts this book uses:

- **Clicking.** This book gives you three kinds of instructions that require you to use your computer's mouse or trackpad. To *click* means to point the arrow pointer at something on the screen, and then—without moving the pointer at all—press and release the left button on the mouse (or laptop trackpad). To *right-click* means the same thing, but using the right mouse button instead. To *double-click* means to click the left mouse button twice in rapid succession, again without moving the pointer at all. And to *drag* means to move the pointer while holding down the left mouse button the entire time.

When you're told to *Shift-click* something, press and hold the Shift key, and then click; then release both the key and the mouse button. Related procedures, such as *Ctrl-clicking*, work the same way—just click while pressing the corresponding key.

- **Keyboard shortcuts.** Nothing is faster than keeping your fingers on your keyboard—entering data, choosing names, and triggering commands, all without losing time by reaching for the mouse. That's why many experienced Project fans prefer to trigger commands by pressing combinations of keys on the keyboard. For example, when you read an instruction like "Press Ctrl+C to copy the selection to the Clipboard," start by pressing the Ctrl key; while it's down, type the letter *C*, and then release both keys.

About→These→Arrows

Throughout this book and the Missing Manual series, you'll find sentences like this one: "In the Gantt Chart Tools | Format tab's Bar Styles section, choose Format→Bar Styles." That's shorthand for selecting the Gantt Chart Tool contextual Format tab on the ribbon, navigating to the tab's Bar Styles section, clicking Format, and then clicking Bar Styles. Figure I-1 shows what this looks like.

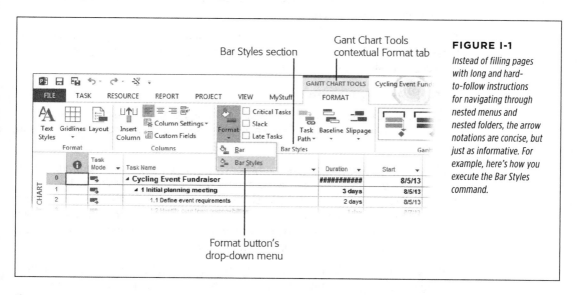

FIGURE I-1

Instead of filling pages with long and hard-to-follow instructions for navigating through nested menus and nested folders, the arrow notations are concise, but just as informative. For example, here's how you execute the Bar Styles command.

If you see an instruction that includes arrows but starts with the word File, it's telling you to go to Project's Backstage view. For example, the sentence "Choose File→New" means to select the File tab to switch to Backstage view, and then click the New command (which appears in the narrow list on the left).

About MissingManuals.com

At *www.missingmanuals.com*, you'll find news, articles, and updates to the books in this series. The website also offers corrections and updates to this book (to see them, click the book's title, and then click Errata). In fact, you're invited and encouraged to submit such corrections and updates yourself. In an effort to keep this book as up to date and accurate as possible, each time we print more copies, we'll make any confirmed corrections you suggest. We'll also note such changes on the website so that you can mark important corrections into your own copy of the book.

In the meantime, we'd love to hear your suggestions for new books in the Missing Manual line. There's a place for that on the website, too, as well as a place to sign up for free email notification of new titles in the series.

About the Missing CD

As you read through this book, you'll find references to files that you can use to help you manage your projects. To download these files, you need to hop online and visit this book's Missing CD page. This book also mentions websites that offer additional resources. Each reference includes the site's URL, but you can save yourself some typing by going to this book's Missing CD page, where you'll find clickable links to all the sites mentioned here.

To get to this book's Missing CD page, go to *www.missingmanuals.com*, click the Missing CDs link, scroll down to *Microsoft Project 2013: The Missing Manual*, and then click the Missing CD-ROM link.

Safari® Books Online

Safari® Books Online is an on-demand digital library that lets you easily search over 7,500 technology and creative reference books and videos to find the answers you need quickly.

With a subscription, you can read any page and watch any video from our library online. Read books on your cellphone and mobile devices. Access new titles before they're available for print, and get exclusive access to manuscripts in development and post feedback for the authors. Copy and paste code samples, organize your favorites, download chapters, bookmark key sections, create notes, print out pages, and benefit from tons of other timesaving features.

O'Reilly Media has uploaded this book to the Safari Books Online service. To have full digital access to this book and others on similar topics from O'Reilly and other publishers, sign up for free at *http://my.safaribooksonline.com*.

> **NOTE** If one of your goals is to pass the Microsoft Project MCTS Exam, including the upcoming exam for Project 2013, this Missing Manual includes all the Microsoft Project information you need.

Project Management: The Missing Manual

Projects: In the Beginning

Microsoft Project 2013 is brimming with features to help you manage any kind of project, but you have to know something about project management to make those features sing. If your boss hands you a project to manage and you ask what she means by "project" and "manage," this chapter is for you.

A project is different from day-to-day work, and this chapter explains how. You'll learn what project management is at a high level—and why it's worth the effort. Project management helps you deliver the right results on time, within budget, and without going into crisis mode. When a project falters, project-management techniques also help you get it headed back in the right direction.

But before it even begins, a project has to make it through a selection process. Just like a major-league baseball player waiting for a good pitch before he swings, you'll learn what to look for in potential projects. (Even if your boss currently mandates which projects you manage, learning to prioritize and select projects may increase your influence in the future.)

The chapter concludes by covering the one skill that no project manager can afford to ignore: gaining and maintaining the support of *stakeholders*—the folks who care about the project's success. You'll learn how to identify stakeholders and their expectations, and how to keep them on board so they're ready and willing to pitch in when the project needs their help.

■ What's So Special About Projects?

Projects come in all shapes and sizes, from a child's birthday party to the inauguration of a new president of the United States. What's the common thread that unites all projects and makes them different from other kinds of work? Here's one definition: *A project is a unique endeavor with clear-cut objectives, a starting point, an ending point, and (usually) a budget.* Here's a breakdown of the definition's main points:

- **Unique** is the most important word in that definition, because every project is different in some way. Charity bike rides in different cities, over different routes, during different weather conditions, and organized by different teams constitute different projects. The event's venue, site conditions, weather, and team members make every event unique, even if they have the same basic structure. In contrast, a crew that makes fundraising phone calls or mails requests for donations performs the *same* work every day; this kind of work is typically called *operations*.

- **Clear-cut objectives** are necessary if you want any hope of reaching the end, staying within budget, and making customers happy. Whether you call them specific, quantifiable, or unambiguous, objectives define what the project is supposed to accomplish so everyone knows when it's done. "Train the cat" isn't a good objective. It doesn't specify what you're trying to train the cat to do—or not do. (In this case, the objective may not even be feasible.) On the other hand, an objective that you *can* complete (albeit with some physical risk) is "Remove the cat from the Thanksgiving turkey carcass." For a fundraiser, you might have objectives like raising a million dollars and retaining a specific percentage of the top fundraisers.

- A project **begins** at one point in time and **ends** when it achieves its objectives (although some projects *seem* interminable). When the cleanup crew hauls off the last of the trash and the money raised is put to work, the fundraising project team is ready to move on to the next project. However, if the end of the project always seems just out of reach, poorly defined objectives are usually to blame. You'll learn how to define objectives in Chapter 2.

- **Budgets** play a role in most projects, because few people consider money irrelevant. In addition to achieving the objectives within the desired timeframe, you also have to keep the price tag within an acceptable range. For example, donors want to know that their money is earmarked for good works, not consumed by excessive administration. So the fundraiser's budget might be set to 10 percent of the fundraising goal. In addition, time may be as important as money for some projects, so you might budget time as well.

NOTE   Dr. Joseph M. Juran, best known for his work on quality management, was the impetus for today's Six Sigma process-improvement methodology; he described a project as a *problem scheduled for solution*. The concept is the same as the definition described in the preceding list: Working with stakeholders to identify and agree upon the problem that needs solving helps identify the project's objectives. When you schedule the problem for solution, you determine the project's start and end dates.

◼ What Is Project Management?

Project management is the art of balancing project objectives against the constraints of time, budget, resource availability, and quality. Achieving that balance requires skill, experience, and a boatload of techniques. This section gives you a glimpse of what happens from a project's infancy to its old age.

Novices sometimes think of project management as building a sequence of tasks, but those in the know recognize that project management starts *before* a project officially begins and doesn't end for a while after the project's objectives are achieved. There's no one "right" way to manage projects (the box on page 7 identifies a few different project-management methodologies), but most methodologies cover the following five phases (illustrated in Figure 1-1):

- **Getting started.** Often called *initiating*, this first phase of project management is short but important. It's your only opportunity to get the project off to a good start. In this phase, you answer questions like "Why are we doing this project?" and "Do we really want to do it?" The initial attempts to describe the purpose of a project may produce vague results like "Hold an event to raise money." But as you identify the stakeholders (page 17), you learn what the project is about and what the stakeholders hope to achieve. The more specific you are when you describe a project's objectives, the greater your chances for success.

  Neglecting to line up support for a project (page 16) is all too common, and it's *always* a big mistake. A project needs buy-in from an executive sponsor (page 18) and the stakeholders to survive challenges like contradictory objectives, resource shortages, funding issues, and so on. What's more, *you*, the project manager, need official support, too, so everyone knows the extent of your authority.

- **Planning.** This phase, which Chapter 2 covers in greater detail, is where you draw your road map: the objectives to achieve; the work to perform; who's going to do that work, when; and how much the whole thing will cost. Moreover, you set out the rules of the game, including how people will communicate with one another, who has to approve what, how you'll manage changes and risks, and so on.

- **Performing the project.** Also referred to as *executing*, this part of project management lasts a long time, but it boils down to following the plan. As the project manager, your job is to keep the project team working on the right things at the right times.

- **Keeping things under control.** In a perfect world, performing the project would be enough, because things would always run according to plan. But because the world isn't perfect, project managers have to monitor projects to see whether they're on schedule, within budget, and achieving their objectives. Whether someone gets sick, a storm washes out a bike path on the ride route, or your data center is plagued with locusts, something is bound to push your project off course. In the *controlling* phase, you measure project performance against the plan, decide what to do if the project is off track, make the necessary adjustments, and then measure again. Chapter 14 explains how to use Project 2013 to control things.

- **Gaining closure.** Like personal relationships, projects need closure. Before you can call a project complete, you have to tie up loose ends like closing out contracts, transitioning resources to their new assignments, and documenting the overall project performance (page 503). The *closing* phase is when you ask for official acceptance that the project is complete—your sign that your job is done. Chapter 17 describes the information to collect in this phase and different ways to archive a project.

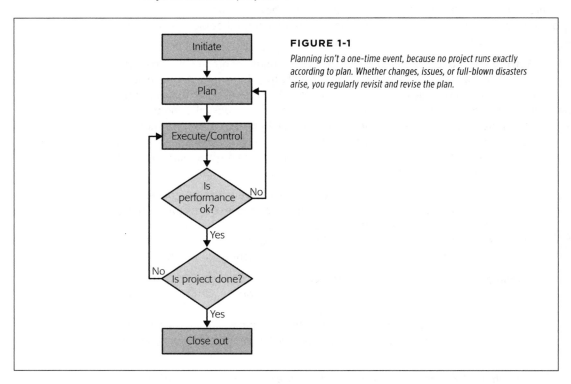

FIGURE 1-1

Planning isn't a one-time event, because no project runs exactly according to plan. Whether changes, issues, or full-blown disasters arise, you regularly revisit and revise the plan.

TOOLS OF THE TRADE

Picking a Project-Management Methodology

Companies that perform project after project usually pick a project-management methodology, such as PRINCE2 or Agile, and stick with it. That way, all their projects follow approximately the same project-management processes. Teams learn what works and what doesn't, and everyone learns what to do and expect.

The approach you choose depends a lot on the environment in which you work. Complex environments with large projects, widely distributed teams, or multiple vendors usually need a robust project-management methodology with formal, well-documented procedures, standardized forms and documents, and project-management software like Microsoft's Enterprise Project Management Solutions to keep track of everything. Simpler, smaller projects would bog down with that kind of overhead but run just fine with a more informal approach.

This book introduces the basic steps of project management, which you can use as a starting point. If you want a ready-made methodology to adopt, check out the following resources:

- Many organizations have developed methodologies based on the project-management principles outlined in the Project Management Institute's (PMI) **Project Management Body of Knowledge** (affectionately known as PMBOK).

- **PRINCE2** (PRojects IN Controlled Environments) is a methodology used to manage government projects in the United Kingdom as well as private-sector projects around the world.

- **Iterative and agile methodologies** work well when the solution for the project isn't clearly defined. You use iterations to gradually identify the solution as you work on the project.

- **TenStep, Inc.** offers a project-management approach that (predictably) takes 10 steps from start to finish. This approach can be adapted to projects large and small. If you register with the website *www.tenstep.com* (for free), you can mine a mother lode of additional project-management wisdom.

- *Project Planning, Scheduling & Control* by James P. Lewis (McGraw-Hill) bucks the trend in project-management books by providing an easy-to-read, and even amusing, description of one way to manage projects.

- *A Management Framework for Project, Program, and Portfolio Integration* by R. Max Wideman (Trafford Publishing) tries to simplify project management—and for the most part succeeds.

■ Why Manage Projects?

The five phases of an *unmanaged* project go something like this: wild enthusiasm, dejected disillusionment, search for the guilty, punishment of the innocent, and promotion of those not involved. An unmanaged project is like a black hole that sucks up every person, resource, and dollar—and still doesn't deliver what it's supposed to. Despite all that, many organizations fear that project management requires bureaucratic and inflexible procedures and will make projects take longer. On the contrary, planning projects and managing the plan provides many benefits, including the following:

- **Happy customers.** Whether a project is for outside customers or groups within your organization, customers like to get *what* they want *when* they want it. Because the first step in project management is finding out what your customers and stakeholders want to accomplish with the project, your customers are more likely to get the results they expect. And by keeping the project under control, you're also more likely to deliver those results on time and at the right price.

- **Achieved objectives.** Without a plan, projects tend to cultivate their own agendas, and people tend to forget the point of their work. A project plan ties a project to specific objectives, so everyone stays focused on those goals. Documented objectives also help you rein in the renegades who try to expand the scope of the project.

- **Timely completion.** Finishing a project on time is important for more than just morale. As work goes on for a longer duration, costs increase and budgets get blown to bits. In addition, you may lose the resources you need or prevent other projects from starting. Sometimes, on-time completion is one of your objectives, like when you're trying to get a product to market before the competition.

- **Flexibility.** Contrary to many people's beliefs, project management makes teams *more* flexible. Project management doesn't prevent every problem, but it makes the problems that occur easier to resolve. When something goes wrong, you can evaluate your plan to quickly develop alternatives—now that's flexibility! More importantly, keeping track of progress means you learn about bad news when you still have time to recover.

- **Better financial performance.** Most executives are obsessed with financial performance, so many projects have financial objectives—increasing income, lowering costs, reducing expensive recalls, and so on. Project management is an executive-pleaser because it can produce more satisfying financial results.

- **Happier, more productive workers.** Skilled workers are hard to come by and usually cost a bundle. People get more done when they can work without drama, stress, and painfully long hours. Moreover, they don't abandon ship, so you spend less on recruiting and training replacements.

◼ Picking the Right Projects

There's never a shortage of projects, but there's not enough time, money, and staff in the world to complete them all. Before you begin managing a project, make sure it earns its place in your organization's project portfolio. Throwing darts or pulling petals off daisies isn't the answer; you're better off knowing what's important to your organization and picking projects that support those objectives.

Project-selection criteria are just as helpful once projects are under way, because projects don't always deliver what they promise. If a project isn't meeting expectations, the management team can decide whether to give it time to recover or cut it loose. Similarly, if a juicy new project appears, you can compare its potential results to those of projects already in progress to see if it makes sense to swap it for a project that's partially complete.

NOTE Selection criteria can save time and effort *before* the selection process even starts. People thinking about proposing a project can evaluate potential results before facing the selection committee. If the results don't pass the test, there's little point in presenting the project to management.

To make good decisions, you need some kind of consistent selection process, whether you're a small-business owner allocating limited resources or a committee setting up a multiproject portfolio. (The box below provides an example of how a committee might evaluate and select projects.) You can then evaluate the candidates and choose the projects with the most compelling results. When you run out of money and resources, you can put any remaining projects that meet your selection criteria on the waiting list.

UP TO SPEED

Picking by Committee

Management by consensus has a bad reputation, but a *project-review board* is a good way to make sure your organization selects the right projects. An effective project-review board includes decision makers from every area of your organization with a variety of skillsets, and it applies agreed-upon selection criteria to choose projects as objectively as possible. Without an impartial jury, project sponsors and their project managers may choose projects for less compelling reasons: They find the project intriguing, the work is relatively risk-free, or they simply grow attached to the projects they propose.

A project-review board doesn't doom you to a bureaucratic selection process. With documented selection criteria, the steps are pretty simple:

1. **Someone proposes a project.** Project sponsors or project managers usually prepare proposals to sell the projects to the review board—why the projects are worthwhile, what benefits they provide, and how they fare against the selection criteria.

2. **The project-review board evaluates proposals.** The board meets regularly to evaluate proposed projects. People who propose projects get a chance to make their pitches, which usually include rigorous Q&A sessions with the board members to clarify ambiguous points. After the presentations, the board discusses the merits of the projects, how the projects fit with the organization's objectives, as well as any conflicts or issues they see.

3. **The board approves or rejects project proposals.** The board decides which projects get to move forward and then notifies proposers of the fate of their projects (and, preferably, explains the reasons for these decisions).

The Importance of Business Objectives

Some projects are no-brainers, like the ones needed to satisfy government regulations. For example, American companies that want to stay in business have to conform to the accounting requirements of the Sarbanes-Oxley Act. On the other hand, you can cull projects from your list by picking only the ones that support the organization's mission and business objectives. If your company dabbles in widgetry, the goal might be getting your tools to market before the competition. But in the healthcare industry, safety trumps speed, because recalling devices already implanted in people is going to hurt the patients *and* the company's pocketbook.

Any time you begin to describe a project by saying, "It would be nice…" you may as well stop right there—unless you can link the project to quantifiable business objectives. Here are some common objectives that trigger projects:

- Increase revenue
- Improve profitability
- Increase market share
- Reduce prices to stay competitive
- Reduce costs
- Reduce time to market
- Increase customer satisfaction
- Increase product quality and/or safety
- Reduce waste
- Satisfy regulations
- Increase productivity

Common Selection Criteria

Although some projects get a free pass due to regulatory requirements or because the CEO says so, most have to earn their spot in the project lineup. Because business objectives vary, you need some sort of common denominator for measuring results—which often comes down to money. This section describes the most common financial measures that executives use, and the pros and cons of each. (The box on page 11 explains what you can do if your organization doesn't *have* selection criteria.)

Whether you're trying to increase revenue, reduce costs, or improve product quality, you can usually present a project's benefits in dollars. The winner is the project that makes the most of the money spent on it. Of course, to calculate financial results, you need numbers; and to get numbers, you have to do some prep work and estimating (page 162). You don't need a full-blown project plan (page 24) to propose a project, but you do need a rough idea of the project's potential benefits and costs. That's why many organizations start with *feasibility studies*—small efforts specifically for determining whether the project delivers the financial benefits described in the following sections and, therefore, makes sense to pursue.

NOTE If some business objectives are way more important than others, you may want to evaluate the projects that support those key objectives first. Then, if you have money and resources left over, you can look at projects in other areas of the business. Risk is another consideration in selecting projects. Suppose a project has mouthwatering financial prospects *and* heart-stopping risks. Project proposals should include a high-level analysis of risks (page 38) so the selection committee can make informed decisions.

REALITY CHECK

Surviving Without Selection Criteria

Why should you care about project-selection criteria if you typically learn about projects only when you're assigned to manage them? What if the selection process is nonexistent, and obtaining resources and support is always a battle? If you know what makes a good project (and have some time and patience), you can turn these trials and tribulations to your advantage.

When executives seem to want everything with equal desperation, it's up to you to learn what's *really* important. Ask managers what their priorities are, and find out what the CEO always inquires about. Listen closely to executives in company meetings.

Once you've identified the key business objectives, manage your projects to deliver the results that count. The more often you hit the target, the easier it'll be to get the resources and help you need. You can't give everyone everything they want, so focus on the most important objectives.

After you've made an impression with a few successful projects, you can pitch a project-selection process to the executive team.

■ PAYBACK PERIOD

Payback period is the time a project takes to earn back what it cost. Consider a project that reduces warranty repairs by $10,000 each month and costs $200,000 to implement. The payback period is the cost of the project divided by the money earned or saved each month:

```
Payback period = $200,000 / $10,000 per month = 20 months
```

Payback period has simplicity on its side: The data you need is relatively easy to obtain, and even non-financial types can follow the math. But if you get really finicky about it, payback period has several limitations:

- **It assumes enough earnings to pay back the cost.** If your company stops selling the product that the warranty-repair project supports, the monthly savings may not continue for the calculated payback period, which ends up costing money.

- **It ignores cash flows after the payback period ends.** When you compare projects based on their payback periods, projects that generate money early beat out projects that generate more money over a longer period. Consider two projects that each cost $100,000 to complete. Project #1 saves $20,000 each month for 5 months. Project #2 saves $10,000 each month for 24 months. Project #1's payback period is 5 months compared to Project #2's 10 months. However, Project #2 saves $240,000, whereas Project #1 saves only $100,000.

- **It ignores the time value of money.** There's a price to pay for using money over a period of time. Payback period doesn't account for the *time value* of money, because it uses the project cost as a lump sum, regardless of how long the project takes and when you spend the money. The measures explained in the next sections are more accurate when a project spends and receives money over time.

■ NET PRESENT VALUE

Net present value (NPV) takes the time value of money into account, so it provides a more accurate picture of financial performance than payback period does. The *time value* of money is the idea that money isn't always worth the same amount—money you earn in the future isn't as valuable as money you earn today. For example, the value of your salary goes down as inflation reduces what each dollar of your paycheck can buy each year. The time value of money is a factor in the NPV measure because you pay a price for using money, like the interest you pay on a home mortgage. The longer you borrow money, the more interest you pay. If you pay for a project with cash on hand, you don't pay interest. However, organizations want to earn a return on the money they invest, so the project must deliver enough earnings to balance out (or exceed) the price you pay for that money.

NPV starts by combining a project's income (earnings or savings) and costs into *cash flows*. (For instance, if you earn $4,000 a month and spend $3,000 on living expenses, then your net cash flow is $1,000.) Then, NPV uses a rate of return to translate the cash flows into a single value in today's dollars. If NPV is greater than zero, then the project earns more than that rate of return. If NPV is less than zero, then the project's return is lower. Where does this magical rate of return come from? In most cases, you use the rate of return that your company requires on money it invests. For example, if your company demands a 10 percent return to invest in a project, you use 10 percent in the NPV calculation. If the NPV is greater than zero, then the project passes the company's investment test. Figure 1-2 shows the NPV of a project that costs $10,000 each month for a year and then earns $15,000 each month for a year after it's finished.

NPV has two drawbacks. First, it doesn't tell you the return that the project provides, only whether the project exceeds the rate of return you use. You can compare NPV for several projects and pick the one with the highest value, but executives typically like to see an *annual* return. One way to overcome this issue is with a *profitability index*, which is NPV divided by the initial investment. This ratio basically tells you what bang you get for your buck from each project. The higher the profitability index, the better. The second drawback is that NPV is hard to explain to non-financial folks. (Luckily, however, most people whose jobs involve picking projects are well versed in financial measures.)

To avoid frenetic finger work calculating NPV on a handheld calculator, try Microsoft Excel's XNPV function. You provide the required rate of return, the cash flows the investment delivers, and the dates on which they occur (remember, the value of money changes over time), and Excel does the rest.

NOTE If cash flows occur on a regular schedule like once a month, you can use Excel's NPV function, which doesn't require dates. This function assumes a regular schedule, and you simply input the rate of return for each time period. If the annual rate is 10 percent and you have monthly cash flows, you enter the rate as 10 percent divided by 12, or 0.833 percent. The NPV function accepts up to 254 values, which is enough for monthly cash flows for more than 10 years.

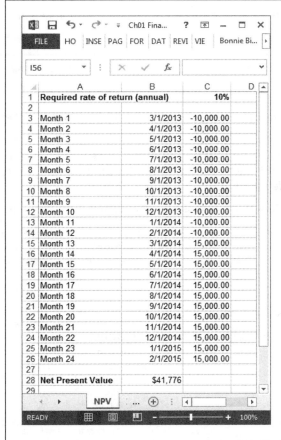

FIGURE 1-2

In Excel, the XNPV function interprets negative numbers as money spent—like $120,000 for a project. Positive numbers represent money coming in (as a result of the project's outcome). If you spend and earn money on the same date, simply enter the net amount (the income minus the expense). Because NPV in this example is greater than zero, the project provides a return greater than the required annual 10 percent return.

Here's how to use the XNPV function:

1. **In an Excel workbook, fill in one cell with the annual rate of return you want to use, and then enter the cash flows and dates in two of the workbook columns, as shown in Figure 1-2.**

   The dates and cash flows don't have to be side by side, but you can read the workbook more easily if they are.

2. **Select a blank cell where you want to insert the function (like cell B28 in Figure 1-2), and then click the Formulas tab. On the left side of the ribbon, click Insert Function.**

   The Insert Function dialog box opens with the "Search for a function" box selected.

3. **In the "Search for a function" box, type *XNPV*, and then click Go.**

   In the "Select a function" list, Excel displays and chooses the XNPV function. It also lists related financial functions.

> **TIP** You can also locate the XNPV function and its siblings in the "Or select a category" box by choosing Financial and then picking the financial function you want.

4. **Click OK to insert the function into the cell, and then fill in the boxes for the function's arguments.**

   In addition to adding the function to the cell, Excel opens the Function Arguments dialog box, shown in Figure 1-3, which presents the function's three arguments with hints and feedback.

5. **Click OK to complete the function and close the dialog box.**

> **TIP** If you're an old hand at Excel functions, you can type the entire function into a cell: Select the cell and then type =XNPV(, and Excel shows you the arguments it requires. You can select a cell for the first argument, type a comma, and then select the cells for the next argument.

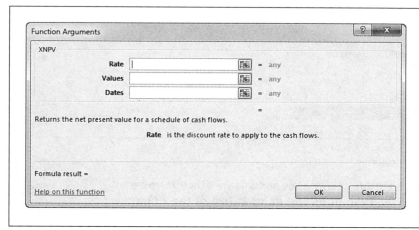

FIGURE 1-3

To fill in an argument, click a box, such as Rate. Then, in the worksheet, click the cell (or cells) that contain the input. For example, for Values, you can drag over all the cells that contain the cash flows (in Figure 1-2, that's cells C3-C26).

■ INTERNAL RATE OF RETURN

A project's *internal rate of return* (IRR) tells you the *annual* return it delivers, taking into account the time value of money. IRR is like the annual percentage yield (APY) you earn on a savings account, which includes the compounded interest you earn during the year. If your project delivers an IRR greater than the return your company requires, you're golden.

Just like NPV, IRR depends on *when* cash flows in or out. For example, money you spend up front drags the IRR down more than money you spend later on. Likewise, if a project brings money in early, the IRR is higher than if the income arrives later.

Like payback period and NPV, IRR has its drawbacks. The big one is that it can give the wrong answer in some situations! It works like a charm when you have money going out for a while (negative numbers) and then the rest of the cash flows are money coming in. However, if the series of cash flows switches between positive and negative numbers, several rates of return can produce a zero NPV, so, mathematically, there are several correct answers. If you calculate IRR in Excel, the program stops as soon as it gets an answer. But if you run the function again, you might get a different result.

Another issue arises if you borrow money for your project. In that situation, the first cash flow is positive (money coming in) and the later cash flows are negative (money flowing out to pay project costs). Because of that, you have to switch the way you evaluate IRR: In such situations, you (counterintuitively) want to reject a project if its IRR is greater than your company's required rate of return and accept a project if its IRR is *less than* the required rate of return.

Excel's XIRR function calculates IRR based on cash flows and the dates on which they occur, as shown in Figure 1-4. The steps for inserting the XIRR function into a worksheet are similar to those for XNPV in the previous section. (For the mathematicians in the audience, IRR doesn't have a formula of its own. The way you calculate IRR by hand is by running the NPV calculation with different rates of return until the answer is zero—*that* return is the IRR.)

NOTE If the XIRR function doesn't find an answer after 100 tries, it displays the #NUM error in the cell. You also see the #NUM error if your series of cash flows doesn't include at least one positive and one negative cash flow.

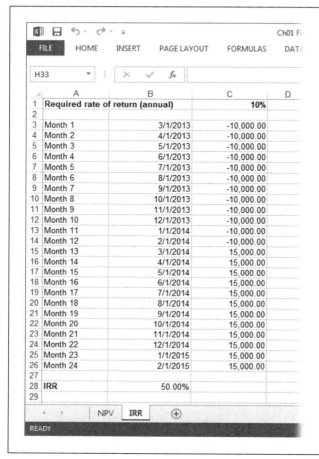

FIGURE 1-4

In this example, the project costs $10,000 per month for the first 12 months. Then, once the project outcome is reached, it earns $15,000 per month for the next 12 months. The resulting IRR is 50%.

	A	B	C	D
1	Required rate of return (annual)		10%	
2				
3	Month 1	3/1/2013	-10,000.00	
4	Month 2	4/1/2013	-10,000.00	
5	Month 3	5/1/2013	-10,000.00	
6	Month 4	6/1/2013	-10,000.00	
7	Month 5	7/1/2013	-10,000.00	
8	Month 6	8/1/2013	-10,000.00	
9	Month 7	9/1/2013	-10,000.00	
10	Month 8	10/1/2013	-10,000.00	
11	Month 9	11/1/2013	-10,000.00	
12	Month 10	12/1/2013	-10,000.00	
13	Month 11	1/1/2014	-10,000.00	
14	Month 12	2/1/2014	-10,000.00	
15	Month 13	3/1/2014	15,000.00	
16	Month 14	4/1/2014	15,000.00	
17	Month 15	5/1/2014	15,000.00	
18	Month 16	6/1/2014	15,000.00	
19	Month 17	7/1/2014	15,000.00	
20	Month 18	8/1/2014	15,000.00	
21	Month 19	9/1/2014	15,000.00	
22	Month 20	10/1/2014	15,000.00	
23	Month 21	11/1/2014	15,000.00	
24	Month 22	12/1/2014	15,000.00	
25	Month 23	1/1/2015	15,000.00	
26	Month 24	2/1/2015	15,000.00	
27				
28	IRR	50.00%		
29				

NPV **IRR** ⊕

READY

NOTE XIRR includes a third argument called "guess," which is the first return you use in the search for the IRR. If you leave the guess argument blank, Excel uses 10%. Depending on whether the resulting NPV is positive or negative, the XIRR function tries a different value until NPV equals zero.

Gaining Support for a Project

Sponsorship is important during the selection process, but support becomes *crucial* once projects start up. Projects rarely finish without running into some kind of trouble, and you often need help digging them out. Alas, many people lend a hand only if there's something in it for them, which is why identifying the people who care about a project (the *stakeholders*) is so important.

Stakeholders can play a part in projects from proposal to the final closeout. During the planning phase, stakeholders help define the project and evaluate the project plan. A few lucky stakeholders then cough up the money to fund the project. During the execution phase, stakeholders help resolve problems and make decisions about changes, risk strategies, and (if necessary) whether to fork over more money. At the end of a project, some of the stakeholders get to declare the project complete so everyone can move on to another project.

Identify Who Has a Stake in the Project

Commitment comes from all levels of an organization, from the executive-level project sponsor to the people who work on the project every day. Project stakeholders get their name because they have a *stake* in the project's outcome. They either give something to your project—like the managers who provide the resources you use—or they want something from it, like the sponsors who support your fundraiser in exchange for publicity. (If your stakeholders aren't providing the support you expect, read the box on page 19 for ways to get them on board.)

Identifying stakeholders can be tough. Some people don't realize they're stakeholders, like the development team that learns about a project when they receive a list of requirements for a new website. Other people *pretend* to be stakeholders but aren't, like a department that gets chummy because they see your project as an inexpensive way to get their new database. If you're not careful, your project can gain extraneous requirements but no additional money.

Here are the main types of stakeholders, tips for identifying them, and some hints on keeping them happy:

- **Project customers** are easy to spot, because they're the ones with the checkbooks. Pleasing the stakeholders who fund your project is a matter of delivering the results they expect (page 33). Stay on top of financial performance (page 305) so you can explain financial shortfalls and your plan to get back on track. The people who control the pocketbook can be formidable allies if other groups are trying to expand the project.

  Because customers foot the bill, they usually have a lot to say about the project's objectives, requirements, and deliverables. Of course, the person who cuts the check isn't often the person who defines requirements, but they both represent the project's customer. (For instance, with a fundraising event, the customer sets the fundraising goal and the event budget, while the event director defines the event's features.) Customers also approve documents, intermediate results, and the final outcome. Approvals are much easier to come by if you work closely with customers during planning to identify their objectives and what they consider success.

NOTE When you manage a project that produces a product to sell, you don't interact with the *final* customers—the ones who buy the product. Instead, you work with intermediaries like sales reps, marketing departments, and focus groups.

- **Project sponsors** are the folks who want the project to succeed and have the authority to make things happen, like the regional director who's backing the fundraising project. If you, the project manager, don't have that kind of authority, you may depend on sponsors to confer some of their authority to you. A sponsor's role is to support the project manager and the project team to make the project a success. After guiding a project through the selection process, the sponsor's next task is to sign and distribute a project charter (page 21), which publicizes the new project and your authority as the project manager.

  A sponsor can help you prioritize objectives, tell you which performance measures are critical, and guide you through the rapids of organizational politics. She can also recommend ways to build commitment or fix problems. Sometimes, project sponsors are also project customers, whether for internal projects or for those that deliver products to external customers.

  If you don't have enough authority to make a crucial call or the project hits serious obstacles, the sponsor can step in. While sponsors want their projects to succeed, they expect *you* to manage the project. Dropping problems at their doorstep every few minutes won't win their hearts, but neither will hiding problems until it's too late. If you need help, don't be afraid to get your sponsor involved.

- **Functional managers** (also called *line managers*) run departments like marketing, finance, and IT. They have quotas and performance measures to meet in addition to supervising the resources in their departments. Project resources almost always come from these departments, so you have to learn to work with these folks.

  The easiest way to win over functional managers is to let them do their jobs. Don't tell them who you need (unless you already have a great working relationship). Instead, specify the skills you need and the constraints you face, like cost, availability, or experience. Then, after the managers provide you with resources, do your best to stick to the assignment dates you requested. When schedules slip, notify functional managers quickly so you can work out an alternative.

TIP Functional managers spend time listening to employees complain about being overworked, overwhelmed, or bored. So if you can demonstrate why you need the resources you request, when you need them, and that the schedule is feasible, managers are more likely to commit their people.

- **Team members** who do project work are stakeholders, too, because they perform the tasks that make up the project. Other types of stakeholders often do double duty as team members, like when a customer defines requirements.

  Keeping team members happy requires a combination of a reasonable workload, meaningful work, and a pleasant work environment. Communication is as important with team members as it is with every other type of stakeholder: Team members want to know how their tasks support the big picture, what their tasks represent, and when they're scheduled to perform them.

- You already know that **project managers** are stakeholders, because your reputation and livelihood depend on the success of your projects. The project manager is easy to identify when it's you. How to make *yourself* happy is something you have to figure out on your own.

- **End users** of the project result are also stakeholders. For example, a project to streamline your organization's business processes will affect the employees, so you should include a representative from the department or role that's affected.

   If your project's goal is a new product for your company to sell, it's too early to assign stakeholder status to the customers who will purchase the product. In this situation, you might include a small group of *potential* customers to provide feedback on your plan.

The process of building a project plan (page 25) helps you identify stakeholders. For instance, the purpose of the project and who benefits from it tell you who the customer and sponsor are. Project objectives help you identify which groups participate in achieving those objectives. The responsibility matrix (page 196) identifies the groups involved in a project and their level of involvement, so it acts as a checklist of stakeholder groups. Of course, you still have to identify the specific people to work with within those groups. When you start to build your project team, the list of functional managers and team members falls into place.

When Stakeholders Aren't Supportive

Some projects are good for the organization as a whole but cause problems for a few stakeholders. For example, a process-improvement project may save your company tons of money but spell layoffs for one group. Unsupportive stakeholders can actively undermine your project by doing things like withholding resources or raising issue after issue.

Project management isn't as ruthless as a career in organized crime, but Michael Corleone provided sound advice for winning over stakeholders in the movie *The Godfather Part II*: "Keep your friends close, and your enemies closer." Find out what stakeholders' issues are, and you may find ways to appease them.

Sometimes, the project sponsor or other stakeholders can help you bring reluctant stakeholders onboard. But politics and relationships that outlast your project often leave you to muddle through on your own. If winning people over is out of the question, be sure to identify the risks that this logjam raises. Then you can communicate those risks and potential workarounds to all the stakeholders and let them decide what to do. Still, the outcome isn't always a success, and the conflicts may permanently damage your project.

Documenting Stakeholders

As projects pick up momentum, their details quickly become too numerous for you to remember them *all*. Stakeholders are so important to projects that you can't afford to forget them. As you identify stakeholders during planning, create a *stakeholder analysis table*. Merely listing names and types of stakeholders in this table isn't enough. Also include information about people's roles, which objectives matter most to them, and whom they listen to.

Figure 1-5 shows a sample stakeholder analysis table, which you can download from this book's Missing CD page at *www.missingmanuals.com/cds*. Look for the Word file *Ch01_Stakeholder_Analysis.doc*.

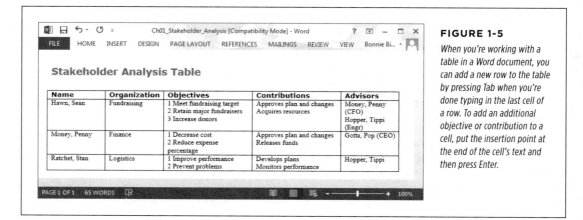

FIGURE 1-5

When you're working with a table in a Word document, you can add a new row to the table by pressing Tab when you're done typing in the last cell of a row. To add an additional objective or contribution to a cell, put the insertion point at the end of the cell's text and then press Enter.

Here's some info that's helpful to collect about each stakeholder:

- **Organization or department.** Knowing where a stakeholder works helps you remember the objectives they care about, and helps you decide whether they should participate in different activities. For instance, if your company wants to keep strategy sessions confidential, you don't want to invite external stakeholders to them.

- **Objectives.** List the objectives that each stakeholder cares about—from her hottest button to her coolest. If you need help rallying stakeholders around an objective, this info helps you find allies.

- **Contributions.** List what the stakeholder does for the project. Contributions you list here are different from the responsibilities you put in a responsibility matrix (page 197). In the stakeholder table, you specify the contributions that individuals make to the project in their roles as stakeholders.

- **Advisors.** The people to whom stakeholders listen are great sources for tips on presenting information effectively and deciding which options a stakeholder might prefer.

■ Publicizing a Project and Its Manager

A project that gets the go-ahead needs publicity just like movies do. You want people to know the project is starting and why it's vital. Most important, you want the entire team to get fired up over their new assignments.

The project manager needs some publicity, too. Your authority comes from your project and its sponsor, not your position in the organization, so people need to know how far your authority goes. The *project charter* is like a project's press release—it announces the project itself, as well as your responsibilities and authority as its manager.

A project charter doesn't impress anyone unless it comes from someone powerful enough to grant you authority, like the project's sponsor or its customer. On the other hand, don't have the biggest kahuna distribute the charter unless that person actually *knows* something about the project—you need authority, but credibility is important, too. You may have to tactfully suggest that the project's customer or sponsor develop and distribute the charter.

TIP You can often get the charter out more quickly by writing it yourself so the sponsor has only to sign and send it.

A project charter is pretty simple, as Figure 1-6 shows. (You can download a sample charter, *Ch01_Project_Charter.doc*, from *www.missingmanuals.com/cds*.)

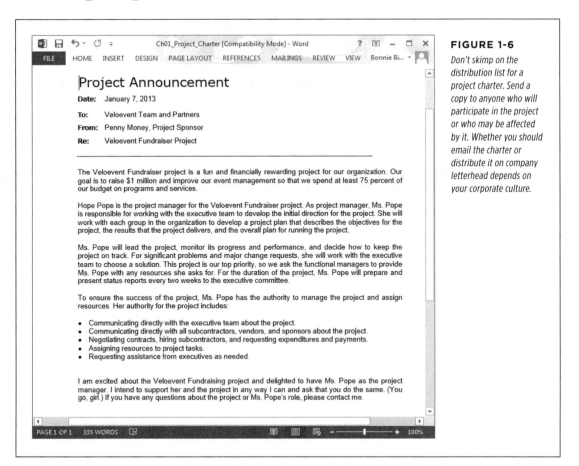

FIGURE 1-6

Don't skimp on the distribution list for a project charter. Send a copy to anyone who will participate in the project or who may be affected by it. Whether you should email the charter or distribute it on company letterhead depends on your corporate culture.

Here are typical elements of a charter:

- **Project name.** A catchy name that rolls off everyone's tongue is wonderful, but a brief name that identifies the project will do.

- **Purpose.** The mission statement works well as the purpose, because it's a high-level overview of the reason for the project. If you haven't crafted a mission statement yet, simply summarize what the project is supposed to achieve.

- **Project manager.** Announce who will manage the project. If you're writing the project charter for a sponsor to sign, don't be afraid to blow your own horn. Stakeholders need to know who you are and why you're the person who's going to make sure this project is a success.

- **Project manager's duties.** Summarize the manager's responsibilities. This brief introduction to the project manager's tasks can warn people about what the project manager may expect from them—and educate people about the mysterious activities that project managers perform.

- **Project manager's authority.** Here's where the sponsor or customer sprinkles authoritative fairy dust on you. Much like a power of attorney, this section tells everyone that the sponsor or customer authorizes you to perform certain activities, like hiring contractors or dipping into the project's emergency fund.

- **The official commitment to the project.** Don't forget to include a brief bullet point that confirms in writing that the sponsor or customer supports the project *and* the project manager.

Now that the introductions are out of the way, it's time to start planning your project. The next chapter provides an overview of a project plan—all the pieces that go into one and why they're important. After that, you'll learn the finer points of using Project 2013 and other programs to build and manage a project schedule.

Planning a Project

I f you're out for a leisurely drive, you can take any road and see where it takes you. But when you're heading to scary Aunt Edith's house for Sunday lunch, you'd better know where you're going. No matter how fast you drive, if you're on the wrong road, you're not going to get there on time. If you want to make Aunt Edith happy, you need to plan how you're going to get to her house—when you're supposed to and with what you're supposed to bring.

You've probably worked at a few places where people think they don't have *time* to plan (see the box on page 28). Managers breathe down your neck asking how much you've finished while you're still wondering what you're supposed to do. You may have to do work over because no one agreed on how to do it right in the first place. Critical deadlines slip by, and the pressure to finish increases.

Fortunately, there's a better way. Planning ahead helps you do the right things the right way the first time around. A project plan acts as the road map to your destination. The less time, money, or resources you have, the more you need to plan. Think, for example, about those time-share presentations where a company rambles on for a few hours about the benefits of "owning the dream." Then, think about the 30-second commercial selling the same dream. Squeezing the message into a brief commercial actually requires far more planning than putting together a 2-hour sales pitch.

This chapter provides a quick introduction to project planning. You'll see what goes into a project plan. You'll also learn how to create a document for stakeholders to approve before you begin executing the project, along with tips and tricks for getting the information you need.

■ Project Planning in a Nutshell

Project planning is like other types of planning—you figure out what you're going to do before you do it. And like other types of plans, project plans are destined to change, because the projects they guide never happen exactly as planned. But the inevitability of change shouldn't scare you off planning. What you learn during the planning process can help you keep a project on course even when changes occur.

Project planning involves two main elements: *why* you're doing the project, and *how* you're going to do it. You begin by identifying what the project is supposed to accomplish. Only then can you start planning how to achieve the project's goals.

Veteran project managers have official names for each part of a project plan, but any plan boils down to a series of questions. The rest of this chapter describes the components of a project plan in more detail, but here are the basics:

- **Why are we going to perform this project?** The answer to this question describes the point of the project. You can also rephrase this question as "What's the problem we want to solve or the opportunity we want to leverage?" You describe the problem that the project is supposed to solve in the *problem statement* (page 29).

- **What are we going to achieve?** By definition, a project eventually ends. You have to know what the project is supposed to achieve so you can tell when it's done. The first step is to spell out all the goals, or *project objectives* (page 29). Projects usually have several goals, which can fall into different categories. For example, a fundraising event may have a financial objective to raise a minimum amount of money, a business objective to raise awareness of the organization and its mission, and a performance objective to improve how the event is run so that more of the money raised can benefit charitable programs.

- **What approach are we going to take?** The problems that projects solve usually have more than one solution. Part of project planning is figuring out which solution—or *project strategy*—is best. Then, the project plan documents the strategy you're going to use to address the problem and why you chose it.

- **What are we going to do?** Based on the strategy that's selected, the project plan describes how the project will achieve its objectives in a few other forms, each of which plays a specific role. The *project scope statement* (page 34) lists what is and isn't part of the project. It delineates the boundaries of the project so stakeholders know what to expect. The scope statement also helps you rein in pressures to expand the project (*scope creep*).

  Intimately linked to project scope are *deliverables*—the tangible results the project needs to produce (page 33)—and the *success criteria* you use to judge whether the deliverables are acceptable. Every section listed in the project scope statement has corresponding deliverables and success criteria, and vice versa.

With the scope, deliverables, and success criteria in hand, you're ready to describe the work that needs to be performed. As its name implies, a *work breakdown structure* or *WBS* breaks down the work that people do on a project into manageable pieces. (This major part of the plan is the sole topic of Chapter 6.)

In addition to the work specific to achieving project objectives, projects need a few project-management processes (for things like managing risk, controlling changes, communicating, and managing quality, which are explained on page 36) to keep the project under control. A project plan outlines how these processes will work.

• **When will the project start and finish?** Projects have starting and ending points, so the plan documents these dates. In addition, the *project schedule* (page 161) actually shows the sequence of tasks and when each one starts and finishes.

• **Who will work on the project?** People and other resources actually do the work, so the project plan includes a *responsibility assignment matrix* and a *project organization chart* (page 201) to identify the team. Depending on the size of the project and where resources come from, the plan might also include a detailed staffing plan.

• **How much will it cost?** Blank checks are rare in any environment, so the project plan includes a budget (page 264) showing where all the money goes.

• **How good do the results need to be?** Given constraints on time, money, and resources, you usually don't have the luxury of doing a spectacularly better job than required. The project plan outlines how you intend to achieve the level of quality the project requires, and how you'll measure that quality.

• **How do we know when we're done?** Part of project planning is to clearly define success. For each objective and deliverable you identify, specify how you're going to determine whether they're done. Otherwise, you could have trouble bringing closure to your project.

Project planning is an iterative process, not a one-time deal. You may run through the planning steps several times just to get a plan that the stakeholders approve. Then, once you begin to execute the plan, you'll have to rework it to accommodate the changes and glitches that come up. In addition, for projects with goals that aren't clear-cut, you might use an even more iterative approach: planning and executing small portions of the project until the entire solution is complete. Figure 2-1 shows the project-planning steps and the path you take the first time through.

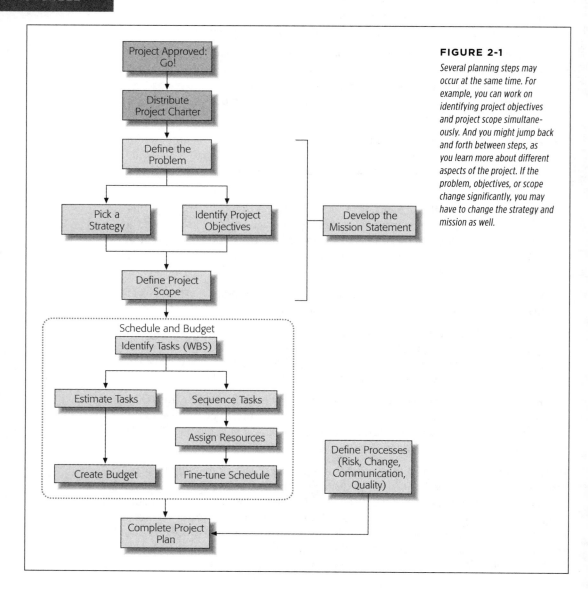

FIGURE 2-1

Several planning steps may occur at the same time. For example, you can work on identifying project objectives and project scope simultaneously. And you might jump back and forth between steps, as you learn more about different aspects of the project. If the problem, objectives, or scope change significantly, you may have to change the strategy and mission as well.

TIP Not every project plan requires detailed write-ups for every component described in this chapter. For example, a small project may need only a sentence or two about how you're going to communicate with your two other team members. Use your judgment to decide how much detail to include.

The Benefits of Project Plans

A project plan is the road map you use to guide a project toward completion. But it helps you in many other ways, too, from the very beginning to the very end of the project. Here are some of the other benefits such a plan provides:

- **Getting buy-in.** When your project passes your organization's selection process, you've got a commitment from the customer or project sponsor. But you need buy-in from all the other stakeholders and team members, too. Parts of the project plan—like the mission statement, objectives, and deliverables—help people understand *why* the project deserves their commitment and what's in it for them.

  Having stakeholders and team members help you develop the plan is invaluable. People tend to back away from efforts they didn't help define, and rightly so. In addition, without input from the trenches, your estimates of time and cost could be way off, and the expectations of results impossibly high. Asking for feedback during planning makes people more willing to pull together when they're working on the project.

- **Focusing on the goal.** A project plan tells team members what they're supposed to do and where they're headed. In addition to communicating assignments, the plan gives people the background they need to make the right decisions as they work. This focus is good for the project, the team members, *and* the project manager—you can spend less time on day-to-day supervision, and more time proactively managing the project.

- **Tracking progress.** You can't tell how close you are to your destination if you don't know where you are or even where you're going. A project plan tells you where you're supposed to be at every point in a project so you can compare your actual progress (explained in Chapter 13) to what you estimated. If the road gets bumpy, these comparisons can help you figure out how to get back on track.

- **Improving performance.** The project plan is the baseline to which you compare your actual performance (you'll learn how in Chapter 14). It helps you see where you went wrong and what went right. If you communicate how things went to everyone involved in the project, they can do better the next time. Then, archive the final performance information so other project managers can benefit from it as well.

NOTE For a project-plan template, download *Ch02_Project_Plan.dot* from this book's Missing CD page at *www.missingmanuals.com/cds*.

Get Enough Planning Time

A well-known cartoon shows a manager telling programmers to start coding while he finds out what the customers want. You can see disaster coming: The ill-fated programmers are about to do hundreds of hours of work that the customer will reject as useless.

With everyone on the go these days, the temptation to *do* something is hard to resist, especially when customers or executives are watching impatiently over your shoulder. But if you cave in to the pressure to skip planning, the failed project ends up on your résumé, not theirs.

To persuade customers and other stakeholders to give you time to plan, you have to speak their language. You can compare project planning to the planning activities that executives perform—preparing a strategic business plan, setting up a product launch, or planning the company's IPO.

After you wrangle planning time into the schedule, don't forget to document project performance and lessons learned when the project is complete (page 508). Publicize the reports showing how planning contributed to success, and you'll have an easier time getting the planning time you need in the future.

■ Defining the Project

As Yogi Berra once said, "You've got to be very careful if you don't know where you're going, because you might not get there." Projects usually get the go-ahead for good reasons, but the motivation for a project may be barely sketched out when the project begins. Before you can work out the details of how you'll perform the project, you need to identify what the project is supposed to achieve.

Dr. Joseph M. Juran's definition of a project is a problem scheduled for solution, so identifying the problem you want to solve is usually the first step. A project's mission statement presents the problem in a way that makes people care. Because most problems have more than one possible solution, the project strategy outlines the solution you've picked. From there, you identify all the project's goals, the results it'll deliver, and the assumptions you've made in preparing the plan. The following sections give you an overview of each of those steps.

What's the Problem?

When you start to identify the problem that needs solving, your colleagues turn into hypochondriacs, overwhelmed with symptoms and making wild guesses at the underlying problem. Just like antibiotics don't help when you have a virus, the right solution to the wrong problem is still wrong. As project manager, your job is to tease out the *real* problem from the project's sponsor, customer, and other stakeholders.

Most people offer solutions instead of describing the actual problem. For example, suppose your director says the organization needs a TV ad campaign. You could start planning a series of TV commercials, but does that project have a point? To get to the problem, start asking "Why?" For example, why TV ads? If the director says that donations are drying up, a commercial might help, but it also might not be the best solution. Asking "Why?" a few more times may uncover that the economy has affected charitable giving and competition for donations is at an all-time high—and no amount of TV advertising will correct those problems.

In a project plan, a problem statement describes the problem to solve or the opportunity to take advantage of—not the symptoms or a solution. You might be able to flesh out the problem statement by asking, "What will happen if we *don't* do this project?"

Here's an example of the right way and the wrong way to state the problem:

- **Right way:** Donations have dropped 25 percent in the last year, and a donor survey identifies the poor economy and increased requests from charities as the top two reasons. If we don't increase the money raised, we will have to cut some of our programs.

- **Wrong way:** We need a TV commercial to advertise our organization.

A problem statement shouldn't include solutions, but sometimes you have to bend the rules. Maybe your organization bet big money on a database, so your project had better use it. For situations like these, include those constraints in the problem statement, and add them to the assumptions section (page 34) for good measure. That way, when you choose a project strategy, you can be sure to take those constraints into account.

TIP   Different stakeholders often see different problems and want different results. Your job as project manager is to guide the stakeholders to agreement (however tenuous) on what the project will achieve. When you work on the problem statement, you're bound to hear a combination of solutions, objectives, and expectations. Write everything down. You may not need this info at the moment, but you will soon enough for the sections on objectives, strategies, and success criteria.

Defining the Project's Goal and Objectives

People often don't know what they want, have trouble putting what they want into words, or simply want everything they see (after all, everyone was once a 3-year-old at an ice cream shop). To make matters worse, different people want different things. Identifying project objectives and getting everyone to agree on them is hard work, as the box on page 31 explains. Regrettably, if you try to shortcut this step, your stakeholders will be quick to tell you if they get something they *don't* want.

The project goal is a high-level description of what the project is supposed to achieve. For example, the goal of the cycling fundraiser is to raise $1,000,000 while minimizing the percentage of management and administrative expenses so more money can go to the charity's programs.

Even if its goal fits in a few short sentences, a project can have all kinds of objectives. The main objective might be to increase money raised, but the organization might have other objectives, such as streamlining work to save money in other ways or implementing new systems so improvements can be shared with other regions. Project objectives fall into one (or more) of the following categories:

- **Business.** These objectives relate to business strategies and tactics. Whether your executives fixate on increasing sales or extending product life, business objectives are usually the initial impetus for a project.

- **Financial.** These are usually distinct from business objectives but closely related. Financial objectives can apply to the entire business or just the project. For example, a project's business objective may be achieving a 10 percent profit margin on sales, while its financial objective might be delivering an 8 percent return on investment. The fundraiser's financial objective is to raise $1,000,000. Another objective that is part financial and part performance (performance objectives are discussed in a sec) is limiting expenses to no more than 25 percent, so that 75 percent of the money raised goes to funding programs.

- **Regulatory.** Many projects have to conform to regulations, and they all have to obey the law. For example, a project to automate electronic distribution of investment info has to follow SEC guidelines.

- **Performance.** Schedule and budget quickly come to mind when you think of performance objectives—finishing before a crucial deadline or keeping costs low to earn a performance bonus, for example. Meeting requirements and matching specifications are other types of performance objectives.

- **Technical.** These objectives may be the type and amount of technology that a solution uses. For example, an emergency broadcast system requires equipment with highly dependable and redundant systems. Or a project may have internal technical requirements like using software that the company already owns.

- **Quality.** When you talk about decreasing the number of errors or increasing customer survey ratings, you're identifying quality objectives—how good results must be. These objectives also give the project quality plan (page 37) targets to shoot for.

You also have to prioritize objectives, because a project is a balance between scope, time, cost, and quality. You're almost guaranteed to find that you can't achieve all the objectives with the time and budget you're given. An overabundance of objectives dooms projects to failure. By prioritizing objectives, you can figure out the best ones to eliminate—or at least scale back. For example, the financial objectives are top priority for the fundraising project, so you can't eliminate them. The project stakeholders can help you choose the ones to eliminate. For instance, the director might tell you to wait until next year to work on making the fundraiser applicable to other regions.

Well-Defined Objectives

How can I tell whether objectives will help me successfully complete a project?

Vague objectives are the main source of difficulty in obtaining approval for a project plan. You need solid objectives to build a project plan and to complete a project to everyone's satisfaction. Here are the characteristics of well-defined objectives:

- **Realistic.** What's the point of setting an objective that no one can reach? Set attainable goals. Challenging objectives are OK, but people stop trying when goals are too far out of reach.

- **Clear.** If you've ever worked with someone who does exactly what you say, you know how hard it is to clearly specify what you want. For example, saying you want "an attention-grabbing TV commercial that'll increase market share" could translate into a guy with a loud voice (and plaid jacket to match) selling your product at half the price of your competitors. It'll grab attention and increase market share...and decimate your profits.

- **Measurable or verifiable.** Make objectives as measurable or provable as you can. For example, how do you measure whether a training class is effective? When you use subjective goals, be sure to define how you'll know whether you've succeeded. For example, you may decide that an average evaluation score of 8 means the class will improve productivity when the trainees get back to the office.

What Strategy Will You Use to Solve the Problem?

Every project solves a problem, but most problems have more than one right answer. You want the solution that does the best job of achieving the project's goal and objectives. You might work on identifying objectives and studying strategies at the same time. When the objectives gel, the stakeholders can evaluate the strategies and make their choice.

Remember those solutions people tried to pass off as the project's problem? Now that you know the *actual* problem the project is supposed to solve, you can ask stakeholders about potential solutions or review the solutions they gave you earlier. Brainstorming with stakeholders is a good way to start evaluating strategies. The back and forth between different stakeholders can also help you clarify must-have and nice-to-have objectives.

These discussions can also give you insight into which strategies are likely to work for your stakeholders (or not). A winning strategy satisfies the must-have objectives and most of the nice-to-have objectives (page 32). A strategy also has to pass a few additional tests to be a success. Here are a few questions to ask while evaluating project strategies:

- **Is it feasible?** If the strategy won't work, the project won't either. If you're considering an untested or rarely used solution, run a feasibility study that looks at whether the solution will work before you commit the entire project to it.

- **Are the risks acceptable?** Part of a project plan is risk analysis (page 38). Project *risk management* analyzes the hazards and windfalls in the selected strategy and the plan that goes with it to minimize the chance of failure. Before you choose a strategy, you need to perform a mini risk analysis to eliminate the "We'd be crazy to do that" solutions.

- **Does the strategy fit the culture?** Cultural factors are touchy-feely, but they're also almost impossible to overcome. For example, if your company emphasizes its connection with its customers, an outsourcing solution isn't likely to work. Strategies that run counter to the corporate culture aren't completely out of the question, but if you pick one, you'll need to spend extra time getting—and keeping—commitment from the stakeholders.

Choosing a project strategy isn't an exact process because you have to estimate the potential results for each option. Besides, some project objectives are simply hard to quantify. A *decision matrix* pits project objectives against project strategies. As you can see in Figure 2-2, you can evaluate strategies as quantitatively or qualitatively as you like.

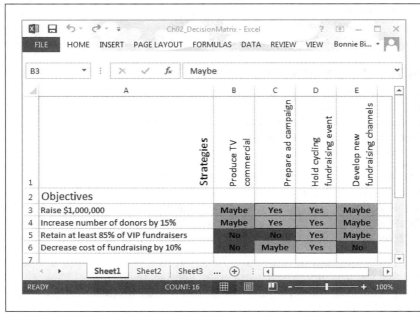

FIGURE 2-2

One way to highlight passing or failing grades in Excel is with conditional formatting, which applies different formatting depending on which condition a cell meets. For example, if you rate strategies with values like Yes, No, and Maybe, you can shade cells based on their values. Download the Excel workbook, Ch02_DecisionMatrix.xlsx, complete with sample conditional formatting, from this book's Missing CD page at www.missingmanuals.com/cds.

TIP Consider placing the must-have project objectives at the top of the decision matrix and nice-to-have objectives below that. If a strategy doesn't satisfy the must-have objectives, then don't bother rating the other objectives. Or, you can begin evaluating strategies by their must-have performance. Then, when you've shortened the list, you can evaluate the full list of objectives.

Identifying Project Results

Deliverables are the tangible results a project produces—like the money raised for a charity, a bridge you can drive across, or the incriminating pictures you were hired to shoot. Projects churn out a major deliverable at the end, but smaller deliverables surface throughout the projects' lifetimes—like blueprints for a bridge, the fabricated steel girders that support it, and even the project plan itself.

Each major deliverable represents a component of the project, which, in turn, appears as a bullet point in the project scope statement (page 34). If you find an item in the project scope statement that doesn't correspond to a deliverable, you've either missed a deliverable or you need to move that item to the "Out of scope" column.

Because deliverables don't appear out of thin air, you need tasks to produce them. You can use the list of deliverables you develop to double-check that you've identified all the tasks in the work breakdown structure (page 127). Although documentation is a deliverable that people tend to overlook, government projects (to name one example) are known for significant documentation deliverables that are also contractual requirements. If documentation is a deliverable, be sure to include tasks to produce it.

> **NOTE** The goal of a project, its scope, and its deliverables provide a high-level view of what the project is supposed to accomplish. These components of the project plan often come packaged as a document called the *statement of work*, a project synopsis that's perfect for including in legal contracts.

Interim deliverables that appear during the course of a project don't always go to the project's customer. For instance, you need contracts with all the vendors for your event, but the director or the charity doesn't need to see them.

Interim deliverables are great for keeping everyone on course. Team members use them as short-term targets to shoot for. And you can use deliverables as milestones in your project schedule to gauge the project's progress.

Gauging Success

There's nothing quite as disheartening as reaching the end of a project only to find out that some people think you aren't done yet. The best way to prevent such disappointment is to clearly define what constitutes success during project planning. As you document objectives and deliverables, be sure to specify how you're going to determine whether they've been achieved. For the fundraiser, you might include the accounting report that shows the net income and the percentage of total income. Other projects might require more detailed (and subjective) criteria, such as software acceptance based on successfully completing a set of test transactions, eliminating all critical and serious bugs, or completing test transactions in a timed test.

Being specific about success criteria is crucial and requires persistence. You have to make sure that you clearly define every aspect of your criteria. For instance, if acceptance depends on eliminating critical bugs, you also need to carefully define what you mean by "critical bug."

TIP   If success criteria aren't clear-cut, you might consider building a worksheet that correlates objectives, deliverables, and success criteria to ensure that you can obtain acceptance of each deliverable and the entire project.

Defining Project Boundaries

Project scope is the delineation of what a project includes and what it doesn't. For example, once you have the fundraiser's objectives and deliverables confirmed, you know that the project scope revolves around this year's bicycling event and doesn't include planning for a national program of cycling events. A *scope statement* describes a project's boundaries.

Project scope can derive from the project objectives, deliverables, requirements, and specifications. And you can play these components off one another to ensure that you've clearly defined the scope.

Like an inexorably spreading waistline, *scope creep* is a dreaded scourge for projects. Without a well-defined scope statement, you're likely to find requests nibbling away at your project's limited budget and time. To document project scope clearly, you identify items that are out of scope; that way, stakeholders don't assume that you simply forgot their pet deliverables. Then you can fire up your change-management process (page 456) to estimate the effects of adding changes to the budget and schedule. Then the customer can decide whether the request is worth the price or should be moved to a follow-up project instead.

Documenting Project Assumptions

You've probably heard that the word "assume" makes an *ass* out of *u* and *me*. While all clichés have a grain of truth, assumptions are dangerous only when people make them without telling anyone else. A customer might assume that some work is part of the project's scope even though it doesn't appear in the scope statement. Or you may assume that people from the customer team will turn their reviews around in one week. As you plan a project, you can uncover hidden assumptions by continually asking about what people expect. Then add the assumptions you find to the project plan.

Assumptions can affect every part of your project plan. Sometimes, they clarify the meaning of a project's objectives or end up as items in the scope statement. They can also crop up as expectations about resources, how processes run, or who's responsible for what.

■ Documenting How You'll Run the Project

Scheduling and budgeting a project takes a lot of time and effort, but the results of that work take up little space in the project plan. You don't have to document *all* the planning that goes into building a schedule and budget, just the end results. This section gives you an overview of project documentation. Other chapters in this book explain in detail how to develop the work breakdown structure, project team, schedule, and budget.

Here's a quick introduction to the sections of a project plan that make up the *project implementation plan*, which maps out how you expect to perform the project:

- **Identifying the work to do.** A *work breakdown structure* or WBS (page 124) breaks up work into small tasks that you then put into sequence and assign resources to when you build your schedule. The lowest-level tasks are called *work packages* because they contain the work that people have to perform. All the higher-level tasks merely summarize groups of lower-level tasks. Chapter 6 focuses on building a WBS and getting it into Microsoft Project.

- **Laying out the project's schedule.** With the WBS complete, you can estimate the effort required to perform each task and its duration and then put tasks into the sequence in which they need to happen. The result is a schedule that approximates how long the project will take and when tasks should start and finish. Chapter 7 talks about estimating task effort and duration; Chapter 7 also explains how to turn a WBS into a schedule.

  As you manage the project, its schedule tells you how far you've come and whether it's still on track to finish on time. In Project, you can compare the original schedule with what's actually happening (page 431) to see where you may have to make adjustments.

- **Building a project team.** You can estimate work hours and duration all you want, but you won't really know what the schedule looks like until you know how many resources can work on tasks, and when those resources are available. Building a project team begins with identifying the skillsets you need for tasks and other resources such as equipment and materials. You can assign these generic resources to tasks to get an idea of the schedule. Once you know who's working on the project, you can replace the generic resources with people's names, and finally identify when tasks start and finish. Chapter 8 explains how to put a project team together and add the team to your Project file; Chapter 9 shows how you assign resources to tasks.

- **Setting the project's budget.** Whether the customer has a set amount of money to spend or your company's executives require a minimum return on investment (page 15), money matters. The cost of a project is a combination of labor costs, equipment and material costs, and other expenses like travel or training. As you assign resources to tasks in Project, you can see how all these costs add up. (Chapter 8 explains how to assign costs to different types of resources.) Then, you can use these costs to calculate the project's budget and cash flow. Chapter 1 explains some of the financial measures used to evaluate projects, and Chapter 10 describes how to use Project's budgeting features and Excel workbooks to build budgets.

NOTE Sometimes, the budget is expressed in resource hours rather than currency, particularly for projects that use internal employees who are paid whether or not they work on a project. For projects like these, financial measures don't apply. However, you can still compare your planned hours to actual hours to evaluate performance (page 438).

◼ Laying Out Project Processes

As you manage a project, some activities keep running for as long as the project does. For example, you have to keep an eye on changes that people ask for and run them through a change-management process to prevent scope creep. A change-manage-ment process includes steps for requesting changes, deciding whether to include changes in the project, and tracking the changes. Similarly, risk-management, com-munication, and quality-management processes also run until the project is complete. Defining these processes has to occur while you're still planning the project, or your team will mill about like sheep without a border collie. This section introduces the four processes you define and document in the project plan.

TIP How you approach change management, risk management, and other processes depends on your project. Small projects can survive with relatively informal procedures, whereas large, global projects require more rigor. Moreover, corporate culture has an effect on how team members view the processes you define.

Communicating

As a project manager, you already know that most of your job is communicating with people. But everyone else working on a project communicates, too. A *communication plan* describes the rules for sharing information on a project, like whether people should email status updates, post them on a website, or scratch them into banana leaves. Chapters 19, 20, and online-only Chapter 25 (available from this book's Missing CD page at *www.missingmanuals.com/cds*) talk about ways to share project information, but you need to document your choices in the communication plan section of the project plan. A communication plan answers the following questions:

- **Who needs to know?** For instance, who should receive the list of pending change requests?

- **What do they need to know?** The change control board may receive the full documentation of change requests, whereas a team leader receives only info about the associated work tasks and when the work is due.

- **When do they need to know it?** Do status reports come out every week, every other week, or once a month? And do they come out on Friday or a different weekday?

- **How should they receive it?** The methods for distributing information depend on what your organization has available, as well as how people like to communicate. Some organizations place more weight on paper documents, while others prefer the convenience of email or collaboration websites.

Managing Change

When you plan a project, you define its scope, the deliverables it will produce, and the objectives it will achieve. Inevitably, when the project starts, someone remembers one more thing they need, and someone else finds a better way to tackle a problem. These changes can dramatically affect the plan you so carefully prepared, so you need to evaluate requested changes to decide whether they belong in the project. If they do, then you adjust the project plan accordingly.

A *change management plan* describes how you handle change requests: how people submit them, who reviews them, the steps for approving them, and how you incorporate them into your plan. (It doesn't, however, describe how you manage the extra work that those change requests entail.) For modest projects, an Excel workbook and email may be enough to handle change-management activities. But most projects need a *change control board*—a group of people who decide the fate of change requests. Chapter 15 gets into the nitty-gritty of managing changes, but here are the basic activities involved:

- Submit change requests
- Receive and record change requests
- Evaluate the effects of change requests on cost, schedule, and quality
- Decide whether change requests become part of the project
- Update project documents to incorporate accepted changes
- Track changes as you do other project task work

Managing Quality

Most projects have objectives that relate to quality, whether you need to attain satisfaction ratings from sponsors or hit a particular decibel level of audience applause. A *quality management plan* starts with a project's quality objectives. Then, for each objective, you define how you plan to achieve those quality levels, which is called *quality assurance*. Finally, you describe how you plan to monitor and measure quality performance, which is called *quality control*.

Managing Risk

Things can and will go wrong on your projects. It's easier and faster to recover from troublesome events if you anticipate them and have a plan for how to respond. Risk management starts with identifying what could go wrong. Then you analyze those risks and decide what you'll do if they actually happen. As the project progresses, you monitor risks to see whether they're getting more threatening or going away. Finally, if a risk does become reality, you launch your counter-attack and monitor the results. This section introduces the different aspects of risk management.

NOTE This section is merely an introduction to the robust field of risk management. If you want to learn more, consider reading *Project and Program Risk Management: A Guide to Managing Project Risks and Opportunities* by R. Max Wideman (PMI) or *Risk Management: Tricks of the Trade for Project Managers* by Rita Mulcahy (RMC Publications).

■ IDENTIFYING RISKS

A *risk management plan* begins with imagining what could go wrong (and what could go much better than expected). For example, materials could get lost in transit, a key resource might be unavailable, or price hikes could put the project's budget in jeopardy. On the other hand, sponsors could be incredibly generous, and the permits could come in record time. For the hopelessly optimistic, identifying risks can be difficult. Here are some questions that can help you uncover potential problems:

- **Are there uncertainties in the plan?** If you don't know whether you'll get a key resource, you have more risk of things going awry. Similarly, the risk to success is high if you don't have a good idea of what the project is supposed to do or you have little contact with key stakeholders. Scrutinize your project for anything that isn't clearly spelled out.

- **Are your choices limited?** A single person with critical skills or a single vendor for key ingredients increases the risk of something going wrong. When you don't have many options, it's more difficult to find alternatives to recover from a problem.

- **Are constraints significant?** Tight budgets, fixed finish dates, and limited resources give you little leeway when things go wrong.

- **What level of experience do people have?** Whether one or two resources are new to what you're doing or the project is breaking new ground, lack of experience spells risk.

- **Does the project depend on factors out of your control?** Weather and politics are just a couple of factors that can affect projects. Because you can't control them, you have to work harder to plan for a workaround.

NOTE Most people think of risk as the possibility of bad things happening. However, risk actually represents uncertainty—that is, bad things *or* good things that might happen. If you're relatively new to risk management, you can focus on handling the bad things that might occur. Then, as your risk-management skills grow, you can add in planning for how you'll make the most of positive risk.

■ ASSESSING RISKS

Projects can face an overwhelming number of risks. If you try to manage them all, you may not have time for anything else. The good news is you can put aside risks that have little impact on your project or are highly unlikely. You make this distinction by drawing an imaginary line based on a combination of impact and probability called *risk value*.

For example, low probability and minimal impact probably means you can ignore the risk and accept the consequences. Why spend time planning a response to something that isn't likely to happen and won't hurt much even if it does? On the other hand, high probability and high impact is a combination you can't afford to ignore. You can decide what other combinations of probability and impact to include in your risk assessments.

You don't have to quantify impact as dollars or time, nor do you have to calculate probabilities to one tenth of one percent. For risk assessment, *high, medium,* and *low* are often enough. However, estimates of dollars and time can help you figure out how much of both to spend responding to a risk. The spreadsheet in Figure 2-3 places risks on a graph to visually show the risks you want to manage.

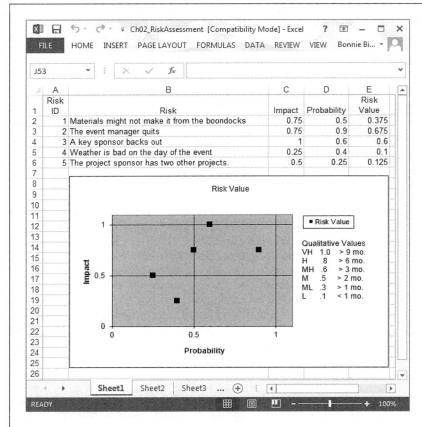

FIGURE 2-3

To add risks to an Excel graph, assign numbers to the impact and probability for each risk. Use a simple conversion like 1.0 for Very High and 0.5 for Medium.

■ PLANNING RISK RESPONSE

For each risk you intend to manage, you need to decide what you're going to do if it happens. The best responses prevent bad things from occurring in the first place. However, that's not always possible, so here are other ways to respond to risks:

- **Accept.** If the risk won't cause noticeable damage, you can just accept the consequences. For example, you can forgo putting money in a parking meter if you don't mind paying $20 if you get caught.

- **Avoid.** Avoidance is one way to handle a risk if the risk doesn't affect the project's ability to achieve its objectives. For instance, if you have two ways to get home and one of them is a narrow, windy road with no guardrails, take the highway.

- **Control the pain.** The formal name for this approach is *risk mitigation*: You take action to reduce the consequences if you can't completely eliminate them. For example, insurance companies share humongous risks with one another. They all accept some of the cost if a big claim comes in, but none of them go bankrupt.

- **Give the risk to someone else.** Transferring risk means that you let someone else take on the risk—but you pay a price. For example, you pay homeowners and auto insurance premiums so that the insurance company covers the cost if something bad happens. Fixed-price bids are another example of risk transfer; you pay a bit more than you would for just time and materials, but the vendor handles the risk if the task takes longer or costs more than expected.

- **Give yourself options.** Contingency plans are another option. They typically make use of funds set aside (called *contingency funds*) to handle the additional cost, as described in the box on page 41.

> **TIP** In your risk-response documentation, specify how you plan to measure the success of a response to something bad that occurs during your project. For instance, you might plan to review the cost or the schedule variance to see whether the response keeps the project's schedule and budget where they should be.

■ TRACKING RISKS

Risk is at its highest in the beginning of a project when you have the least certainty about what will happen and the most time for things to go wrong. Fortunately, the amount of risk you face decreases as the project progresses. Risk management includes tracking risks that have occurred and keeping an eye on those that are still potential problems.

A *risk log* documents the status of each risk you've decided to manage. For risks you monitor, include a summary of the risk and your planned response. Also, identify the person who's monitoring each risk. You have to stay on top of risks and update the log regularly. For example, when you monitor the success of your response, update the risk log with the results.

Saved by Contingency Funds

Risks you identify are called *known unknowns* because you know they may occur but you don't know whether they will. For example, bad weather is a given during the winter, but you don't know when the snowstorms are going to hit. Unfortunately, there are also *unknown unknowns*—risks you don't even know you should worry about. For example, if you don't buy into extraterrestrial intelligence, you won't anticipate the resource crisis when people-eating aliens arrive.

Organizations often set aside contingency funds to spend if known risks occur. One problem is figuring out how much money you need. People often use a percentage of the project's budget to choose the level of contingency funds. You can start with 15 percent. Then, as you gain experience with projects, you can use the performance of past projects to set a percentage.

If the project uses only internal resources, you can also set aside time that you can allocate to deal with any unknown unknowns that arise.

Project managers usually have the authority to spend some amount of the contingency fund without asking permission. However, when you exceed that limit, you need to go to management or other stakeholders with hat in hand to ask for more money.

Management reserve is another bucket of money that stakeholders set aside to deal with risks they don't expect. It's usually a fixed percentage of the project's budget. Besides using it to deal with risks, management can apply reserve money, at its discretion, to a project to cover change requests.

Project Planning: More Than Creating a Schedule

Getting to Know Microsoft Project

L earning how to manage projects while also learning how to use Project 2013 is too much for most mortals. So this chapter starts with a simple map to show you around the program. The journey begins with launching Project 2013. After that, the chapter takes you on a tour of Project's ribbon tabs and the Quick Access toolbar. Then you'll wander through the panes that appear in the Project window.

This chapter wraps up with an explanation of Project's two modes for scheduling tasks. Some project managers want a simple tool they can use to craft a list of tasks and set the dates when they should occur. Other project managers want a scheduling engine that digests all the information they provide and spits out schedules. Project's *task modes* enable you to work whichever way you prefer. Manually Scheduled tasks wait for you to tell them when to start and finish. In contrast, with Auto Scheduled tasks, Project calculates your schedule using the task links, resource assignments, working calendars, and other details you specify. It's easy to set which task mode Project uses if you always use one or the other. But you can switch back and forth anytime you want or change a task's setting at any time.

■ Launching Project 2013

All you have to do to launch Project is choose Start→All Programs→Microsoft Office 2013→Project 2013 (for standard Microsoft Office installations). Unlike earlier versions, Project 2013 opens to Backstage view, which is where you create new Project files, open existing ones, and perform a few other actions. If you've opened Project files before, you see them listed under the Recent heading on the left side of the view.

For the purposes of this tour, simply click Blank Project on the right side of the view to create a new, blank project. Chapter 5 provides the full scoop on creating and opening Project files.

■ Getting Around Project

The Project window is chockablock with panes and other parts that either display the information you want to see or help you work faster. Some features—like the ribbon, the main Project view, and the status bar—are always available, while others—like the Task Inspector pane—stay hidden until you need them. This section shows you all the components within the Project window and how to make them work for you.

Navigating the Ribbon and the Quick Access Toolbar

Project's ribbon is like a cyber border collie, herding related features onto tabs to make them easier to find, as shown in Figure 3-1. As you plan and manage a project, you shift your focus from tasks to the resources who work on them to the big picture of the entire project, so the Task tab, Resource tab, and Project tab make perfect sense. You'll also turn to a few other tabs as you work with your Project files and look at your projects in different ways. This section steps through the seven tabs that appear when you launch Project 2013 for the first time and explains how to use and customize the Quick Access toolbar. (See page 686 to learn how to add other tabs to the ribbon or to create your own custom tabs.)

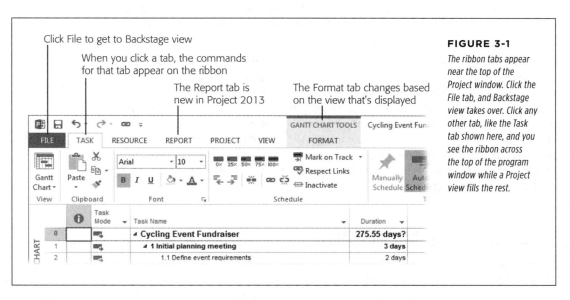

Click File to get to Backstage view

When you click a tab, the commands for that tab appear on the ribbon

The Report tab is new in Project 2013

The Format tab changes based on the view that's displayed

FIGURE 3-1

The ribbon tabs appear near the top of the Project window. Click the File tab, and Backstage view takes over. Click any other tab, like the Task tab shown here, and you see the ribbon across the top of the program window while a Project view fills the rest.

■ MANAGING FILES IN BACKSTAGE VIEW

The File menu from Project 2007 and earlier versions is now the File tab on the ribbon. When you click this tab, Project opens *Backstage view*. When you click a command on the left side of the Backstage view screen, it takes over the entire Project window, as you can see in Figure 3-2. For example, when you click New, Backstage view presents several ways to create a new file (page 87).

FIGURE 3-2

When you click the File tab, the ribbon tabs disappear and Backstage view takes over. After you finish working in Backstage view, you can return to the Project ribbon by clicking the arrow at the top left of the screen.

Some of the commands listed in Backstage view should be familiar: Save, Save As, Open, Close, and Exit. For the most part, they do what they've always done. (Chapter 5 describes the new tricks they've learned for Project 2013.) The other entries in Backstage view let you do even more. You'll learn about them in other chapters of the book, but here's a quick intro:

- **Info.** Clicking this entry opens the Info page, which displays information about the active Project file, such as its start and finish date, on the right side of this page. Click Project Information and choose Project Statistics to see the project's scheduled, baseline, and actual values. This page also includes an Organizer button that lets you copy project elements between files (page 702). And if you use Project Server and Project Web App, you can access Project Web App accounts, assign permissions, and publish project progress to Project Web App from this page.

- **New.** This page offers several ways to create a new file (page 87), including starting from scratch with a blank project; using a template; or creating a file from an existing project, an Excel workbook, or a SharePoint task list. If you want some serious handholding to get started, in the page's list of templates, click the "Welcome to Project" icon. Page 85 describes this step-by-step template in detail.

- **Open.** The Open page, shown in Figure 3-3, has been revamped in Project 2013, so it's easy to access your Project files, whether they're stored on your computer or in the cloud. Click Recent Projects to see a list of all the projects you've opened lately. If you open a lot of Project files—say, as you write a book about Project—this is the quickest way to reopen a file. File locations in the cloud, such as SkyDrive or Office 365 SharePoint, appear below the Recent Projects entry. You can add other storage locations by clicking "Add a Place." If you use Project Server or subscribe to Project Online (an online Microsoft service for managing project portfolios and collaborating with project teams), you can also share your file to Project Server or Project Online. For files stored on your trusty computer, click Computer.

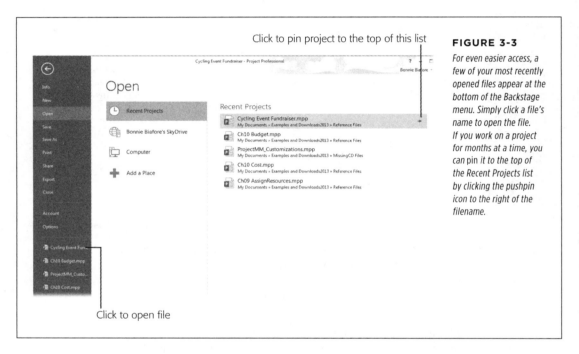

Click to pin project to the top of this list

Click to open file

FIGURE 3-3

For even easier access, a few of your most recently opened files appear at the bottom of the Backstage menu. Simply click a file's name to open the file. If you work on a project for months at a time, you can pin it to the top of the Recent Projects list by clicking the pushpin icon to the right of the filename.

> **TIP** To change how many projects appear at the bottom of the Backstage menu, display Backstage view by clicking the File tab, and then click Options. On the left side of the Project Options dialog box, click Advanced, and then scroll to the Display section. Turn on the "Quickly access this number of Recent Projects" checkbox and then, in the box to its right, type the number you want.

- **Print.** The Print page looks like a spiffed-up version of the familiar Print dialog box. This page lets you select a printer, specify print settings like paper orientation, and choose page setup options like margins (page 484). If you rarely touch any of those settings, you can simply choose the number of copies and click the big Print button at the top of the page. If you don't have a widescreen monitor, the Print page leaves little room for a preview of what you're printing, and you can't shrink the print options area. See page 502 to learn how to work around this limitation.

- **Share.** As its name implies, this page offers features for sharing Project files. You can synchronize your Project file with a SharePoint Tasks List (see online-only Chapter 25, available from this book's Missing CD page at *www.missingmanuals. com/cds*) or send it as an email attachment (page 562).

- **Options.** Click Options to open the Project Options dialog box and choose settings to tell the program how you'd like it to behave.

- **Export.** Despite its name, this page offers several methods for saving a project in other file formats, such as PDF, XPS, older Project formats, project templates, Excel, XML, and so on.

- **Close.** Click this command to close the active Project file.

- **Account.** This page displays the information about the Microsoft account you use to log into Project 2013 and access connected services like SkyDrive. (You set up a Microsoft account during installation, if you don't already have one.) Click the About Project button on this page to see which version of the program you have.

■ A TOUR OF THE OTHER RIBBON TABS

Project management's focus on projects, tasks, and resources is a natural fit for tabs on the ribbon. The ribbon groups features into tabs that, for the most part, are logically organized. Here's a quick introduction to the rest of the tabs on the Project ribbon besides the File tab (you'll learn about each one in detail throughout this book).

- The **Task tab** is your first stop after creating a Project file. It's home to commands for creating tasks (subtasks, summary tasks, and milestones), linking them to one another, and rearranging them into an outline. The first section on this tab lets you choose popular task-oriented views like Gantt Chart. You can also use this tab to format tasks, copy and paste them, or look at their details. This tab also includes the incredibly useful "Scroll to Task" command, which scrolls the view timescale (page 337) until the selected task's task bar is visible. While the project is under way, you can use commands on this tab to move tasks to new dates, to update task progress, and to investigate scheduling issues.

- The **Resource tab** is next up in the project-scheduling lineup, because you need resources to complete the work. This tab has a section for choosing popular resource-oriented views, like Resource Sheet and Team Planner (page 240). Whether you're adding resources to a project, assigning them to tasks, or leveling them to remove overallocations, this is the tab you want. It also contains commands for setting up, refreshing, and updating a resource pool (page 525) so you can share resources among several projects. If you use Project Server, this tab has the commands for accessing the Enterprise Resource Pool and substituting resources.

- The **Report tab** is new in Project 2013 and was added to go along with the new reports that the program provides. (Text reports are no longer available in Project 2013.) This tab includes several categories of built-in reports, such as Dashboards, Resources, and Costs. You can also create visual reports, create your own customized reports, or compare two Project files. Chapter 16 has the complete details on running and customizing reports.

- The **Project tab** is a catch-all for commands to fine-tune your project: viewing project information, defining work calendars, setting project baselines, inserting subprojects, creating links between projects, and so on. This is also the tab to select if you want to work on custom fields or your WBS codes. In addition, you can find commands here to set the project's status date and to update the project in certain situations (page 422).

- The **View tab** starts with buttons for the most popular task and resource views, but you can also access the More Views dialog box to choose any view you want. This tab has commands for controlling what information you see in a view: how many levels in the outline; the table applied; highlighting; how the view's contents are filtered, grouped, or sorted; and the time periods used in the timescale. You can turn the Timeline pane and the Details pane on and off and choose the view that appears in the Details pane (page 189). You can also switch between windows and arrange windows from this tab. The only command that doesn't seem to belong on this tab is in the last section: You choose Macros to run macros.

- The **Format tab** is a chameleon that offers different formatting commands depending on the view that's active. For example, when Gantt Chart view is applied, the Gantt Chart Tools | Format tab lets you insert columns in the table, format task bars and text styles, display elements like summary tasks or critical tasks, and so on. When you switch to Timeline view, the Timeline Tools | Format tab lets you add tasks to the timeline and format them. For Resource Usage view, the Resource Usage Tools | Format tab has checkboxes that let you control which fields you see in the time-phased data grid.

■ FINDING COMMANDS ON THE RIBBON

If you can't find the command you want on the ribbon, you may be looking in the wrong place—or the command simply might not *be* on the ribbon. To see where a command resides on the ribbon, do the following:

1. **Right-click anywhere on the ribbon, and then choose "Customize the Ribbon" on the drop-down menu.**

   The Project Options dialog box opens to the Customize Ribbon screen.

2. **Click the down arrow to the right of the "Choose commands from" box, and then choose All Commands.**

   The list box below the "Choose commands from" box displays the complete list of Project commands.

TIP To determine whether you can't find a command because it isn't on the ribbon, in the "Choose commands from" drop-down list, choose "Commands Not in the Ribbon." If you find the command you're looking for in the list, you have to add it to a custom group (page 689) to use it.

3. **Scroll to the command you're looking for and position your pointer over the command's name.**

   A tooltip appears that tells you the ribbon tab, group, and name of the command. For example, if you point at the Assign Resources command, the tooltip reads "Resource tab | Assignments | Assign Resources (ResourcesAssign)," which means that the command is on the Resource tab in the Assignments section, and the command is labeled Assign Resources. The text in parentheses ("ResourcesAssign" in this example) is the name of the command if you're using Visual Basic.

TIP Chapter 22 explains how you can customize the ribbon to add tabs, sections (technically called custom groups), and commands.

■ TAMING THE PROJECT RIBBON

The ribbon takes up a broader swath at the top of the main Project window than the menu bar used to. If you want to reserve your screen real estate for your project schedule, the ribbon will obligingly take up less space. This section describes a couple of methods for reducing the size of the ribbon.

Once you're familiar with which commands reside on which tabs, you can collapse the ribbon to a trimmer profile. To collapse the ribbon to something more like the old menu bar, use any of these methods:

- Double-click the active ribbon tab.

- Right-click the ribbon and then choose "Collapse the Ribbon."

- Click the up arrow at the bottom right of the ribbon.

Choosing commands when the ribbon is collapsed is almost the same as choosing them when the ribbon is visible. To choose a feature on a tab, click the tab's name (the tab appears). Choose the command you want, and the tab disappears. The only difference is that you have to click the tab to open it each time you want to choose a command on it, even if you want to use two commands in a row that are on the same tab. For example, to change the task mode to Auto Scheduled and then insert a new task, you would first click the Task tab, and then, in the Tasks section, click Auto Schedule. Project would then collapse the ribbon, so you'd have to click the Task tab again, and in the Insert section, click Task.

To switch back to keeping the ribbon in view, double-click anywhere on the collapsed ribbon, or right-click any tab name, and then choose "Collapse the Ribbon."

The ribbon also contorts itself to fit as you resize the Project window (see Figure 3-4). For example, if you narrow the window, the ribbon makes some buttons smaller by shrinking their icons or leaving out the icons' text. If you narrow the window dramatically, an entire section may be replaced by a single button. When you click the button, a drop-down panel displays all the hidden commands.

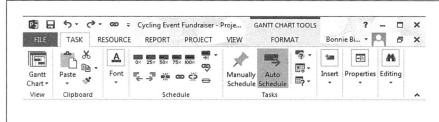

FIGURE 3-4

When you shrink the Project window, the ribbon rearranges sections and buttons to fit. Some buttons just get smaller. If the window is very narrow, sections turn into buttons (like Insert in this example). Click this button and the hidden commands appear in a drop-down panel.

TIP If you prefer to keep your fingers on the keyboard, you can trigger ribbon commands without the mouse. To unlock these nifty shortcuts, press the Alt key. Letters appear below each tab on the ribbon. Press a key to pick a tab, and Project then displays letters under every button on that tab. Continue pressing the corresponding keys until you trigger the command you want. For example, to insert a task with the Insert Task command, press Alt, and then press the H key to open the Task tab. You see the letters "TA" below the Task button in the Insert section, so press the T key followed by the A key to display the drop-down menu. To insert a task, press T again. See page 745 to get the full scoop on keyboard accelerators.

■ WORK QUICKER WITH THE QUICK ACCESS TOOLBAR

The Quick Access toolbar is so small that you might not notice it above the File and Task tabs (see Figure 3-5). But it's always visible, so it's a handy place for your favorite commands. (In addition, it keeps you from having to jump from tab to tab to get to your favorites.) Out of the box, it has icons for Save, Undo, and Redo, because people use these commands so often. To add more commands, click the down arrow on the right end of the toolbar, and then, on the drop-down menu (shown in Figure 3-5), choose the command you want to add. For example, to make views easy to select, choose View on the drop-down menu. Then you can click the down arrow in the View box and choose the view you want to display.

TIP To make the Quick Access toolbar even easier to reach, click the down arrow on the right end of the toolbar, and then, on the drop-down menu, choose "Show Below the Ribbon." When you do that, the toolbar snuggles up underneath the left side of the ribbon.

FIGURE 3-5

To add a command to the Quick Access toolbar, click the down arrow at the right end of the toolbar. Click the command you want to add to turn on its checkmark. For example, the View checkmark is turned on here, so the View box appears in the toolbar. (In this example, it indicates that Gantt Chart view is displayed.) To position the Quick Access toolbar below the ribbon instead of above it, choose "Show Below the Ribbon."

NOTE You can add any command you want to the Quick Access toolbar. On the ribbon, right-click the command you want to add to the Quick Access toolbar, and then choose "Add to Quick Access Toolbar."

Working with Views

Managing projects means looking at information in many different ways, which explains all the built-in views Project offers. These views come with a lot of moving parts. This section explains what each one does and how to choose the view you want.

■ CHOOSING A VIEW

Over the life of a project, you need to look at its data in different ways, so it's no surprise that you frequently change the view you're looking at. For that reason, Project has buttons for choosing views in several locations on the ribbon. Here are your choices:

- **The Task tab.** To choose a view in this tab, head to the View section, click the bottom half of the Gantt Chart button, and then choose the view you want from the drop-down menu. If the view you want isn't listed, then choose More Views at the bottom of the menu. In the More Views dialog box, double-click the view you want to apply.

- **The Resource tab.** In this tab's View section, click the bottom half of the Team Planner button, and then choose the view you want from the drop-down menu. You can also choose More Views at the bottom of the menu to open the More View dialog box so you can choose *any* view that's in your Project file or global template (page 697).

- **The View tab.** This tab (shown in Figure 3-6) has two sections devoted to choosing views. The Task Views section contains buttons to display Gantt Chart view, Task Usage view, Network Diagram view, Calendar view, and Task Form view. In the Resource Views section, click the appropriate button to apply Team Planner view, Resource Usage view, or Resource Sheet view. If you want to apply a view that doesn't have a button, click the down arrow on any of these buttons, and then choose More Views on the drop-down menu that appears.

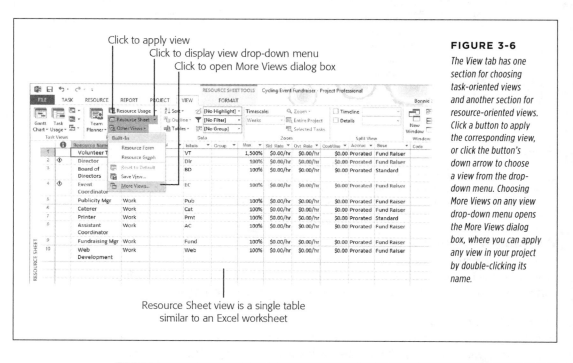

FIGURE 3-6

The View tab has one section for choosing task-oriented views and another section for resource-oriented views. Click a button to apply the corresponding view, or click the button's down arrow to choose a view from the drop-down menu. Choosing More Views on any view drop-down menu opens the More Views dialog box, where you can apply any view in your project by double-clicking its name.

NOTE If you've created any custom views (page 598), the view drop-down menus on the Task, Resource, and View tabs include two headings: Custom and Built-In. (If you haven't created any custom views, you see only the Built-In heading.) The views listed below the Custom heading are custom views that you've created or copied into your Project file from another file. The views listed below the Built-In heading are the views that come with Project.

- **The Quick Access toolbar.** You can add a view drop-down list to this toolbar so you can choose a view without switching tabs. To do this, click the down arrow to the right of the toolbar and then click View to turn on its checkmark.

The View box appears in the toolbar. Click the down arrow to the right of the View box, and then choose the view you want from the drop-down list. To apply a view that's not listed there, choose More Views at the bottom of the menu.

■ THE ANATOMY OF PROJECT VIEWS

Some views, like Resource Sheet view and Task Sheet view, are like giant tables, similar to Excel worksheets, as you can see in Figure 3-6. But most views have a left and a right pane. For views like Gantt Chart and Task Usage, the left side of the view is a table with field values in the columns, as shown in Figure 3-7. The rows show tasks, resources, or assignments. You can add or edit values directly in the table or use it simply for reviewing. The pane on the right side is called the *timescale* and shows values by time period. In a Gantt Chart view, task bars in the timescale show when tasks begin and end. Task Usage view's timescale uses a time-phased table instead, in which the columns represent time periods.

A Gantt Chart timescale displays task bars that show when tasks start and finish

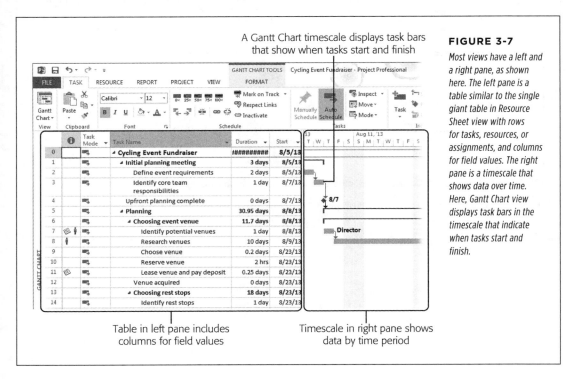

Table in left pane includes columns for field values

Timescale in right pane shows data by time period

FIGURE 3-7

Most views have a left and a right pane, as shown here. The left pane is a table similar to the single giant table in Resource Sheet view with rows for tasks, resources, or assignments, and columns for field values. The right pane is a timescale that shows data over time. Here, Gantt Chart view displays task bars in the timescale that indicate when tasks start and finish.

But that's not all! You can tell Project to display *two* views, one above the other. The top pane of this double-decker arrangement is called the primary pane, whereas the bottom pane is called the Details pane. Figure 3-8 shows Gantt Chart view in the primary pane and Resource Graph view in the Details pane. The Details pane shows detailed information about the task, resource, or assignment that's selected in the top pane. To display the Details pane, in the View tab's Split View section, turn on the Details checkbox, and then choose the view you want in the Details pane from the drop-down list.

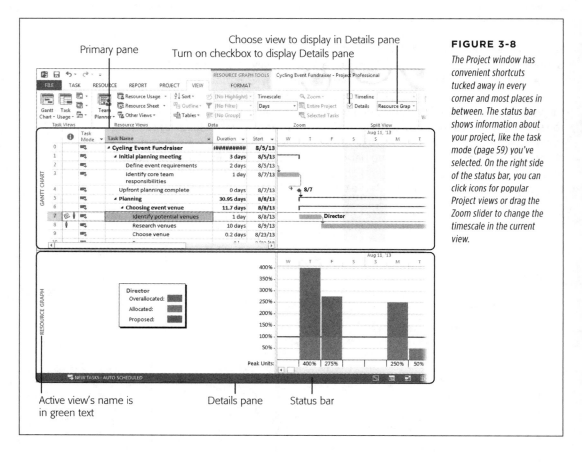

Primary pane

Choose view to display in Details pane
Turn on checkbox to display Details pane

Active view's name is in green text

Details pane

Status bar

FIGURE 3-8

The Project window has convenient shortcuts tucked away in every corner and most places in between. The status bar shows information about your project, like the task mode (page 59) you've selected. On the right side of the status bar, you can click icons for popular Project views or drag the Zoom slider to change the timescale in the current view.

Project's views come in single and combination variations. A single view is simply one Project view that you can choose to display in the primary pane or the Details pane. Combination views, on the other hand, contain *two* single views: one on top and one in the Details pane. The built-in Task Entry view, for example, has Gantt Chart view (a single view) on top and Task Form view (another single view) in the Details pane. The box on page 57 explains how to apply views and switch between one and two panes.

NOTE The actions you can perform in Project depend on whether the primary or Details pane is active. If you select a new view, then Project replaces the view in the active pane with the one you selected. You can tell which pane is currently active because its name is displayed to the left of the pane in green text (see Figure 3-8); the inactive pane's name is displayed in gray text.

Just to keep life interesting, Project also has *task panes* (no relation to view panes) for different project-related activities. For example, when you choose Task→Tasks→ Inspect, the Task Inspector pane appears to the left of your views (see page 307).

UP TO SPEED

One Pane or Two?

Even if you apply a combination view that comes with one view in the primary pane and another view in the Details pane, you can tell Project whether you want to see both the primary pane and the Details pane, or only the primary pane. For example, if you're using a combination view like Task Entry (Gantt Chart on top and Task Form in the Details pane), you can hide the Details pane to concentrate on task dependencies in Gantt Chart view or restore the Details pane to simplify editing tasks. When both panes are visible and you select a single view, Project applies the view to the active pane and keeps the other pane as it is.

To show or hide the Details pane, in the View tab's Split View section, turn the Details checkbox on or off. When you turn the checkbox on, in the drop-down list, choose the view you want to see in the Details pane. (Less obvious controls are also available to hide and show panes. If both panes are visible, you can hide the Details pane by double-clicking the horizontal divider between the two panes. To bring the Details pane back, you can double-click the box immediately below the vertical scroll bar on the right side of the Project window, shown in Figure 3-9. You can also adjust the height of the panes by moving your cursor over the horizontal divider; when the cursor turns into a two-headed arrow, drag up or down until the panes are the height you want.)

As if the primary pane and the Details pane weren't sufficiently overwhelming, there's another pane you can display: Timeline view (in the view tab's Split View section, turn on the Timeline checkbox), which appears in its own special pane above the primary pane. (See page 619 to get the full story on Timeline view.) However, you can see only two panes at a time, which means you have to choose between Timeline view's pane and the Details pane. If the Details pane is visible and you turn on the Timeline checkbox, then Project automatically hides the Details pane (and turns off the Details checkbox). Similarly, if Timeline view's pane is visible and you turn on the Details checkbox, Project hides Timeline view's pane.

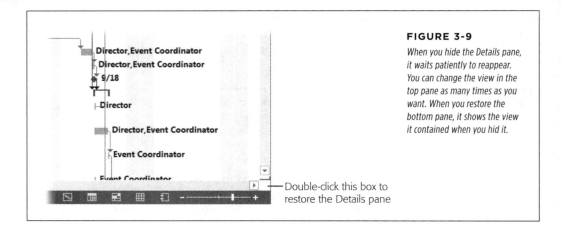

FIGURE 3-9

When you hide the Details pane, it waits patiently to reappear. You can change the view in the top pane as many times as you want. When you restore the bottom pane, it shows the view it contained when you hid it.

ScreenTips and Smart Tags

ScreenTips and Smart Tags are two Project features that make only temporary appearances. ScreenTips blossom into view when you position the mouse pointer over certain items onscreen, like the icons in the Indicators column in a table (that's the column whose header is an i in a blue circle). The ScreenTip for a date constraint icon tells you the type of constraint and the date. A Task Note icon displays a ScreenTip with part of the note. When you put your pointer over a button on the ribbon, a ScreenTip appears with a description of the command and the keyboard shortcut for triggering it. To learn about the purpose of a Project field or how it's calculated, position the pointer over a column header and read the ScreenTip that appears.

Smart Tags, on the other hand, appear when you perform certain Project actions that have a reputation for confusing beginners. For example, if you select a Task Name cell in a table and then press the Delete key, a Smart Tag appears to the left of the cell. When you click the Smart Tag's down arrow, Project displays options for deleting just the task name or the entire task, as illustrated in Figure 3-10. The Smart Tag icon you see depends on what you're trying to do. For example, if you edit a task's duration, then the icon is an exclamation point inside a yellow diamond.

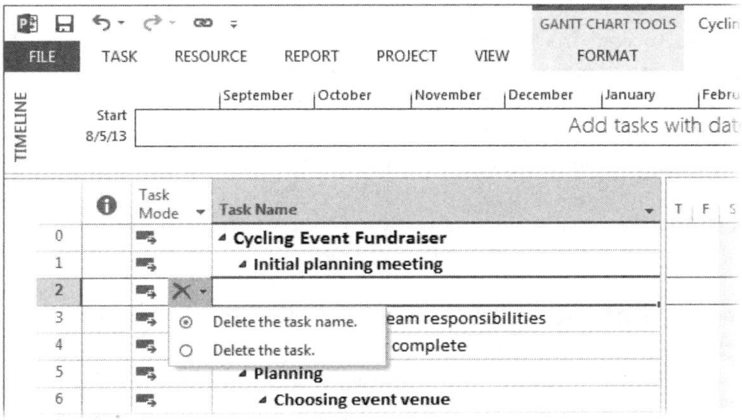

FIGURE 3-10

Smart Tags also appear when you edit a task's start or finish date, asking if you want to set a date constraint for the task (page 189). Similarly, if you change the duration, work, units, or resources assigned to a task, Smart Tags help you tell Project the results you want.

TIP Once you know Project inside and out, you probably don't need the help that Smart Tags offer. In that case, you can turn off different types of Smart Tags. To do that, click the File tab, and then choose Options. On the left side of the Project Options dialog box, choose Display. In the "Show indicators and options buttons for" section, turn off the checkboxes for the Smart Tags you don't want. Turning off the "Resource assignments" checkbox removes the Smart Tags that appear when Project needs more info about how to adjust a task when you change its resource assignments (such as shortening duration or increasing work). Turning off the "Edits to work, units, or duration" checkbox hides the Smart Tags that appear when you change a task's work, duration, or units and Project needs to know what you're trying to accomplish. Similarly, the "Edits to start and finish date" checkbox controls whether Smart Tags prompt you for more info when you change a task's date. And the "Deletions in the Name column" controls the Smart Tag that asks if you want to delete the task name or the entire task when you select a Task Name cell and then press the Delete key.

■ Scheduling Manually or Automatically

In Project 2010, Microsoft introduced *task modes*, which let you choose whether *you* want to control when tasks start and finish (Manually Scheduled) or whether you want Project to calculate start and finish dates automatically (Auto Scheduled). Before that feature was introduced, all tasks were automatically scheduled. Although automatic scheduling is a huge help for projects with lots of tasks and resources, manual scheduling can help in several ways. This section describes what both task modes can do and how to decide which one you want.

Manually Scheduling Tasks

Out of the box, Project comes with Manually Scheduled mode turned on for all new tasks. If you're new to project management, you can leave that option alone and merrily set the dates for the tasks in your project.

But to seasoned project managers, manual scheduling sounds like heresy. After all, the point of using project-management software is to let a computer calculate the project schedule and adjust the schedule automatically as you change tasks, resource assignments, and so on. But manually scheduled tasks come in handy for several common project-management situations, like at the beginning of a project when you have a paucity of info, or when you're planning from the top down with timeframes handed down from management. This section describes the different ways you can put manually scheduled tasks to work.

■ SETTING THE START AND FINISH DATE FOR A TASK

Every so often, you run into a task that *must* occur on a specific date—for example, a training class for team members or a company-wide meeting. With a manually scheduled task, you can pin the start or finish date, or both, to the calendar dates you want; page 187 tells you how. (Project's date constraint feature [page 189] is another method for setting either a task's start or finish date—but not both.)

■ CREATING TASKS WITH INCOMPLETE INFORMATION

One challenge early in project planning is trying to define tasks and build a schedule when you don't have all the information you need. For example, you may not know how long some tasks will take or when other tasks must occur. With manually scheduled tasks, you can fill in the information you *do* know and leave the rest blank without Project complaining. For example, you might know that a task has to start on January 14, but you don't know how long it will take. In situations like this, you can type notes in the date or duration fields to jog your memory when you fill in the missing information later. As you can see in Figure 3-11, Project 2013 uses colors, task-bar formats, and end-caps on task bars to indicate what information a task includes.

Pushpin with question mark indicates
incomplete information

Task bar is teal with end caps when
duration and both dates are set

FIGURE 3-11

*Out of the box, Manually
Scheduled task bars are
teal with darker end-caps
for dates that you specify.
Manually scheduled sum-
mary tasks use black
brackets to indicate the
durations you enter. If
the subtasks take longer
than their summary task's
duration, the rolled-up
summary task bar that
shows the duration of all
the subtasks turns red.*

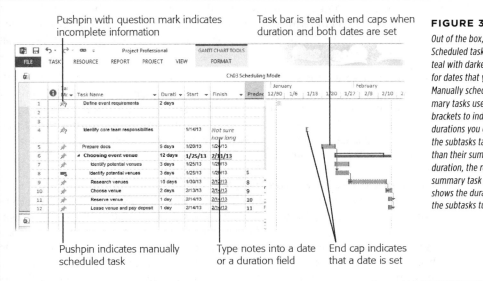

Pushpin indicates manually
scheduled task

Type notes into a date
or a duration field

End cap indicates
that a date is set

Here's what happens when you create manually scheduled tasks with different
types of information:

- **Set task duration.** If you set the duration for a manually scheduled task without
  setting either the task's start or finish date (as is the case for the first task listed in
  Figure 3-11), Project draws a task bar starting at the project's start date with the
  duration you specify. The task bar doesn't have end-caps because you haven't
  defined either date. In addition, the task bar is a light blue and faded at each end.

TIP As you find out more about project tasks, you can filter your task list to display only the tasks without
dates. To filter the list for tasks without a start or finish date, in the View tab's Data section, click the Filter down
arrow and then choose More Filters. In the More Filters dialog box, double-click the Tasks Without Dates filter (or
select the Tasks Without Dates filter and then click Apply).

- **One date set.** When you specify a date (either Start or Finish) for a manually
  scheduled task, Project draws an end-cap at that end of the task bar, as you
  can see with the second task listed in Figure 3-11.

- **Notes entered in a date or duration field.** If you don't know the value for a date or duration field but you have some information about the value, you can type placeholder notes in the field. For example, in the second task in Figure 3-11, the start date is set, but the duration is uncertain, so there's a note about that. When you determine the task's duration or finish date, simply fill in the value, and Project adds end-caps or colors to the task bar to indicate that the value is now present.

- **Two of three values set.** If you specify two of the three values Project needs to schedule a task (Start, Finish, and Duration), it calculates the third value. For example, if you set the Start and Finish dates, Project calculates the duration. Or you can set one date and the duration and let Project calculate the other date. In this case, the task bar is teal with darker end-caps, as shown for the third task listed in Figure 3-11.

■ PLANNING FROM THE TOP DOWN

Executives and project customers have a habit of telling you how long you have to complete a project long before you know whether that length of time is sufficient. If you're planning a project based on timeframes you've been given by someone else, you can use manually scheduled tasks to schedule from the top down. To do this, you create manually scheduled summary tasks with the duration and dates you're trying to meet. Then you create subtasks within those summary tasks. As you add the subtasks for all the project work, you can see whether they fit within the summary-task duration or run over the allotted time (see Figure 3-12).

Here's how you plan from the top down:

1. **Set Project's task mode to Manually Scheduled by clicking New Tasks in the status bar at the bottom of the Project window and then choosing Manually Scheduled.**

   Project will now create all new tasks as manually scheduled until you change the task mode (page 64).

2. **To add a new summary task, click the table row below where you want the new task to go, and then, in the Task tab's Insert section, click Summary.**

   Project inserts two new rows, one for the summary task (and gives it the place-holder name "<New summary task>") and one for a subtask ("<New Task>"). The program selects the Task Name cell for the new summary task. Type the summary task's name, and then press Enter. Project selects the Task Name cell for the new subtask. Type the name of the subtask.

3. **In the summary task's Duration cell, type the duration you've been given for the summary task.**

   In the timescale pane, Project draws an elongated black bracket the length of the duration that starts at the project's start date (the current date or the start date you specify, as described on page 90). If you type a date in the Start field, the bracket moves to start at that date.

4. Add subtasks to the summary task.

You can create subtasks as manually scheduled or auto-scheduled and create task dependencies between them. Project keeps track of the duration you specified for the summary task and the total duration of all the subtasks, as you can see in Figure 3-12. The task bar immediately below the summary-task bracket shows the rolled-up duration of all the subtasks, which is drawn between the Scheduled Start and Scheduled Finish dates, although these fields don't appear in the view's table. (For a manually scheduled task, the Scheduled Start and Scheduled Finish fields are read-only and contain the dates that Project recommends for the task's start and finish. Most of the time, the Scheduled Start and Scheduled Finish values are the same as the task's Start and Finish values.)

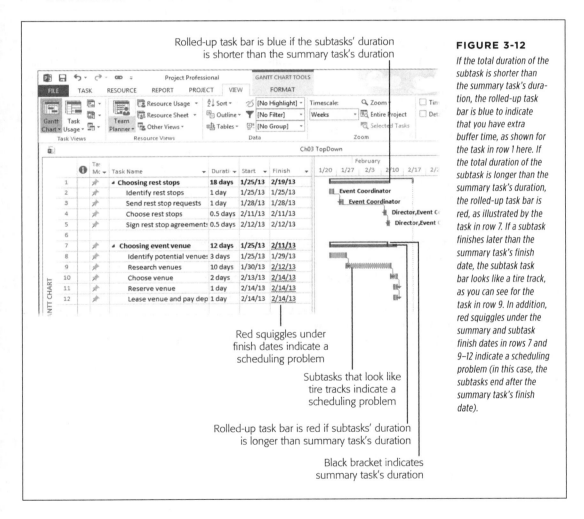

Rolled-up task bar is blue if the subtasks' duration
is shorter than the summary task's duration

Red squiggles under
finish dates indicate a
scheduling problem

Subtasks that look like
tire tracks indicate a
scheduling problem

Rolled-up task bar is red if subtasks' duration
is longer than summary task's duration

Black bracket indicates
summary task's duration

FIGURE 3-12

If the total duration of the subtask is shorter than the summary task's duration, the rolled-up task bar is blue to indicate that you have extra buffer time, as shown for the task in row 1 here. If the total duration of the subtask is longer than the summary task's duration, the rolled-up task bar is red, as illustrated by the task in row 7. If a subtask finishes later than the summary task's finish date, the subtask task bar looks like a tire track, as you can see for the task in row 9. In addition, red squiggles under the summary and subtask finish dates in rows 7 and 9–12 indicate a scheduling problem (in this case, the subtasks end after the summary task's finish date).

Automatically Scheduling Tasks

If you're a project-management veteran, you'll probably want to change the Project's task mode to Auto Scheduled. That way, Project takes care of calculating when tasks start and finish. With auto-scheduled tasks, Project automatically makes the first task's start date the same as the project's start date. When you specify the task's duration, Project calculates its finish date. Then, as you link tasks, assign resources, and add the occasional date constraint (page 189), Project recalculates the schedule for you.

> **TIP** You can specify whether auto-scheduled tasks start on the project's start date or the date on which you create the task. To do that, choose File→Options. On the left side of the Project Options dialog box, choose Schedule. In the "Auto scheduled tasks scheduled on" drop-down list, choose Project Start Date or Current Date.

If you use Project's automatic scheduling, resist the temptation to specify start or finish dates for tasks, or you'll lose one of the advantages of using Project's scheduling engine in the first place. Project calculates dates for you based on the sequence and duration of tasks. If you enter dates for tasks, the resulting date constraints (page 189) make your schedule inflexible and difficult to maintain.

Setting the Task Mode

Depending on whether you usually work on small informal projects or monster schedules, you'll probably work primarily in one task mode or the other. But you can also mix and match manually scheduled tasks and auto-scheduled tasks to your heart's content, as you'll soon see. This section tells you how to set the task mode you want to use.

■ SETTING THE TASK MODE FOR NEW TASKS

By default, Project's task mode option for new tasks is set to Manually Scheduled. The fastest way to change the mode Project uses for new tasks is to head to the status bar at the bottom of the Project window, click "New Tasks: [task mode]" (where [task mode] is the task mode that's currently set), and then choose either Auto Scheduled or Manually Scheduled. If you have other settings you want to change, you can change the mode Project uses for new tasks in the Project Options dialog box.

Here's how:

1. **Choose File→Options. On the left side of the Project Options dialog box, choose Schedule.**

   The scheduling options you can control appear in the Project Options dialog box.

2. **Next to the "Scheduling options for this project" heading (Figure 3-13), choose which project(s) you want this task-mode setting to apply to.**

   You can choose any Project file that's currently open or All New Projects.

3. **Below the "Scheduling options for this project" heading, in the "New tasks created" drop-down list, choose the task mode you want Project to assign to new tasks.**

   Initially, this box is set to Manually Scheduled, as shown in Figure 3-13. If you want new tasks to be automatically scheduled, then choose Auto Scheduled instead.

4. **If you chose Auto Scheduled, then in the "Auto scheduled tasks scheduled on" drop-down list, choose the date you want Project to use for new auto-scheduled tasks.**

   Choose Project Start Date if you want new auto-scheduled tasks to start on the project's start date (page 90). Choose Current Date to create auto-scheduled tasks starting on today's date.

5. **Click OK.**

   The Project Options dialog box closes, and the task mode appears at the bottom of the Project window (Figure 3-13).

First, choose the project whose options you want to change

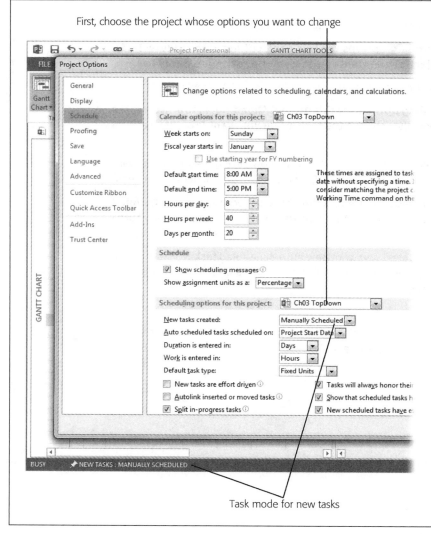

Task mode for new tasks

FIGURE 3-13

The "Scheduling options for this project" drop-down list contains all the files currently open in Project. Before you change any options below this drop-down list, choose the project whose options you want to change. If you want your future projects to use a specific task mode, then create a template (page 708) with Project options set the way you want.

■ SWITCHING THE TASK MODE AS YOU WORK

You don't have to open the Project Options dialog box every time you want to switch between Manually Scheduled and Auto Scheduled mode. You can change the mode as you work. In the status bar at the bottom of the Project window (see Figure 3-13), simply click New Tasks, and then choose either Auto Scheduled or Manually Scheduled. Project sets all new tasks to the mode you choose until you change the mode again.

■ CHANGING THE MODE OF AN EXISTING TASK

If you're in the early planning stages of a project, you may want tasks set to Manually Scheduled because you don't have all the info you need. As the project picture becomes clearer, many of those manually scheduled tasks will fall into place in your overall schedule, and you'll likely want them to be auto-scheduled. On the other hand, if you usually work with auto-scheduled tasks but have one task that occurs on a specific date, then you can switch it to Manually Scheduled mode. Happily, you can change a task's task mode anytime you want.

NOTE You can change tasks' task modes only in Project files saved in the Project 2010 file format or later. If you open a file from an earlier version in Compatibility Mode, you can click the Task Mode cell but you can't change its value. In addition, if you save a Project file containing manually scheduled tasks in an earlier file format, those tasks revert to being automatically scheduled.

The Entry, Schedule, and Summary tables automatically include the Task Mode column, so they're your ticket to switching modes. To change a task's task mode, follow these steps:

1. **In the View tab's Data section, click Tables, and then choose Entry, Schedule, or Summary to display the corresponding table.**

   To show the Task Mode column in another table, right-click the column heading to the right of where you want to insert the column, and then choose Insert Column. In the drop-down list, choose Task Mode.

2. **Click the task's Task Mode cell, click the down arrow that appears, and then choose Auto Scheduled or Manually Scheduled.**

   The Manually Scheduled icon looks like a pushpin. The Auto Scheduled icon looks like a task bar with an arrow pointing to the right. In addition, the task bar style in the timescale changes to indicate whether the task is manually or automatically scheduled, as described on page 61.

Creating a Simple Project

I n the first few chapters of this book, you've gotten a brief introduction to projects and project management, and taken a quick tour of the program. Maybe you're intimidated by all the commands you've seen on the ribbon, the shortcut menus, the status bar, and so on. And you've probably noticed just how many moving parts the Project window has. If you're wondering whether you need to master *all* of these things before you can do anything in Project, rest easy because you don't.

This chapter shows you just how easy building a project can be. It starts with creating a new Project file and creating a list of tasks for the work that has to be done. Then you'll learn how to tell Project how long tasks should take. After that, you'll do a little organizing: creating summary tasks to keep related tasks together. The next step is linking tasks to build a sequence of work, which results in a schedule that takes you from project start to finish. Finally, you'll add resources to tasks. And voilà—you have your first project schedule!

The rest of this book uses organizing and running a bike-ride fundraising event as a sample project. This chapter sticks to the charitable theme, but on a much smaller scale. Suppose you want to support your favorite charity by riding in its cycling fundraiser with a small team of your cycling compatriots. Your team goal is to raise $5,000, so you decide that you need to treat this undertaking as a project. In this chapter, you'll learn how to put together a simple schedule for your fundraising endeavor.

■ Creating a New Project File

To get this test drive going, you need a new Project file. Here's how to create a new Project file and set it up for your project:

1. **Launch Project. Then, in Backstage view (page 47), click the Blank Project icon on the right side of the screen (see Figure 4-1).**

   Project creates a new blank file, called something like Project1.

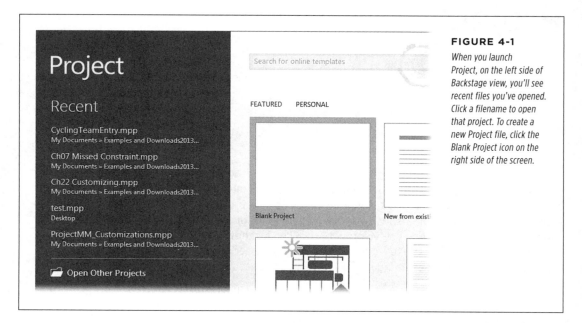

FIGURE 4-1

When you launch Project, on the left side of Backstage view, you'll see recent files you've opened. Click a filename to open that project. To create a new Project file, click the Blank Project icon on the right side of the screen.

TIP If Project is already running and you see the ribbon tabs (Task, Resource, and so on) instead of Backstage view, you can create a new blank Project file simply by pressing Ctrl+N, or by choosing File→New, and then, on the New page, clicking the Blank Project icon.

---

2. **To change your project's start date, in the Project tab's Properties section, click Project Information.**

   The Project Information dialog box opens.

3. **In the Start Date box, select the starting date, such as 2/10/2013, and then click OK.**

   Your project typically doesn't start the same day you build your project schedule, so change the project's start date to when you expect work to begin. Setting an accurate start date is important, since Project schedules new tasks to start as soon as possible—initially, the project start date.

For this sample project, the rest of the settings in the Project Information dialog box are fine. (You'll learn all about the Project Information dialog box in Chapter 5.)

You're ready to add the tasks for your project, as described in the next section.

◼ Creating a Task List

The foundation of any schedule is the work that needs to be done to achieve the project's objectives and to deliver the desired results. Before you can do anything else, you need a list of the tasks to perform, from beginning the project to sweeping up the confetti at the end. This section describes how to build a list of individual tasks.

Creating Work Tasks

In this test drive, you'll create the first few tasks for the project—getting your team signed up for the fundraising event. After that, you can practice by filling in the rest of the tasks on your own.

> **NOTE** If you want to jump ahead and see the finished schedule, you can download the sample project *CyclingTeamEntry.mpp* from this book's Missing CD page at *www.missingmanuals.com/cds*.

Here are the steps for adding tasks to your project:

1. **Click the first cell in the Task Name column on the left side of the screen, type *Research entry requirements*, and then press Enter.**

   Project automatically selects the blank Task Name cell below the one you just filled in.

   The Task Name cell is the only one you *have* to fill in. Because Project initially creates new tasks as manually scheduled, it leaves the Duration cell for your first task blank. The icon in the Task Mode cell (a pushpin with a question mark next to it) indicates that more information is needed. (You'll fill that in later.)

> **TIP** Your project schedule will be easier to understand if the task names you use describe the work that the tasks represent. Start with a verb that identifies the work to be performed, and then add a noun for the item the work is performed *on*—for example, "Submit entry form."

2. **In the selected Task Name cell, type the next task's name, and then press Enter to add the following tasks:**

   - Line up team members
   - Submit entry form
   - Receive fundraising materials
   - Fill out online team profile

Figure 4-2 shows what the task list looks like when you're done.

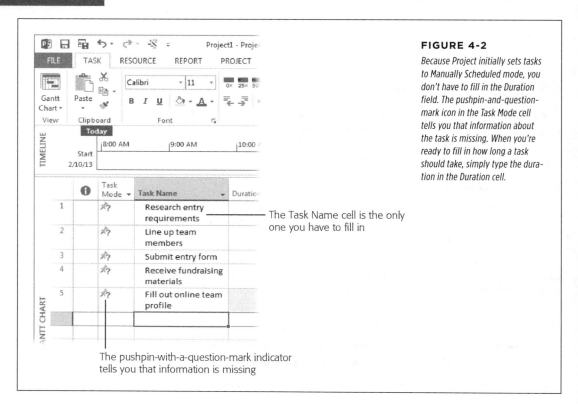

FIGURE 4-2

Because Project initially sets tasks to Manually Scheduled mode, you don't have to fill in the Duration field. The pushpin-and-question-mark icon in the Task Mode cell tells you that information about the task is missing. When you're ready to fill in how long a task should take, simply type the duration in the Duration cell.

The Task Name cell is the only one you have to fill in

The pushpin-with-a-question-mark indicator tells you that information is missing

Defining How Long Tasks Should Take

Estimating how long tasks should take can be the most difficult part of scheduling. You need to look into your crystal ball and give your best guess—er, informed estimate—of each task's duration. You can find entire books on this subject alone, but Chapter 7 provides a brief introduction to estimating. For now, you'll simply fill in a few task durations in the test-drive project. Here's how:

1. **Click the Duration cell for the "Research entry requirements" task.**

   Manually scheduled tasks don't need to have a duration initially. However, to complete your schedule, every task needs a duration. Project sets the duration of Auto Scheduled tasks to one day unless you fill in a different value.

2. **Enter the duration (the length of working time from start to finish) you think it will take to complete this task (Figure 4-3).**

   You can enter durations in minutes (m), hours (h), days (d), weeks (w), or months (mo). Type the number followed by the abbreviation for the unit you want to use. For example, type *3d* for 3 days or *6h* for 6 hours.

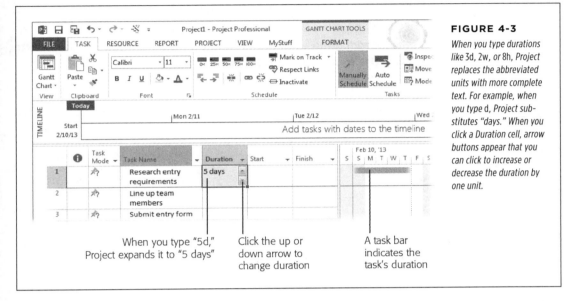

FIGURE 4-3

When you type durations like 3d, 2w, or 8h, Project replaces the abbreviated units with more complete text. For example, when you type d, Project substitutes "days." When you click a Duration cell, arrow buttons appear that you can click to increase or decrease the duration by one unit.

When you type "5d," Project expands it to "5 days"

Click the up or down arrow to change duration

A task bar indicates the task's duration

3. **Repeat step 2 for each task in your task list.**

When you fill in a duration, you'll see a task bar appear on the right side of the screen; its length represents the task's duration. In Figure 4-3, the ends of the task bar are faded, because the task doesn't have a start or finish date yet. You'll see how to define task dates on page 76.

Adding Milestones

Milestones are markers you can use to indicate progress in your project. They're perfect for identifying crucial decisions that affect the project, like a go/no-go decision, or the completion of a significant portion of the project, like your team's profile being published on the charity's donation website. Completing a milestone is like crossing off an item on your to-do list. Because milestones usually mark some type of goal, they're set to zero duration. (For more about milestones, see page 133.)

Here's how you add a milestone:

1. **Click the blank Task Name cell below the "Fill out online team profile" task. Then, in the Task tab's Insert section, click Milestone.**

Project names the task <New Milestone> and puts "0 days" in the Duration cell. On the right side of the screen, the task bar symbol is a diamond, as shown in Figure 4-4. (Don't worry about the milestone's date just yet.)

2. **In the Task Name cell, type *Team signup complete.***

You'll learn more about task naming in Chapter 6. A good way to differentiate milestones from work tasks is to name the milestone based on what was accomplished.

As you practice adding more tasks to your Project file, be sure to add milestones to mark the end of each portion of the project.

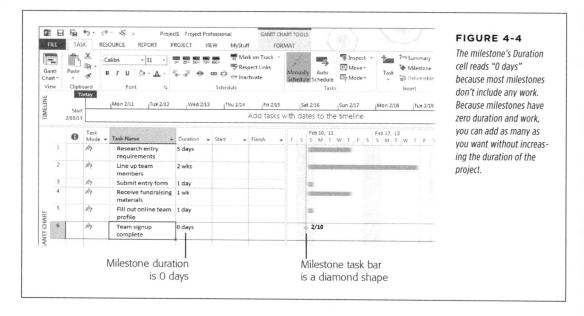

FIGURE 4-4

The milestone's Duration cell reads "0 days" because most milestones don't include any work. Because milestones have zero duration and work, you can add as many as you want without increasing the duration of the project.

Milestone duration is 0 days

Milestone task bar is a diamond shape

■ Organizing Work

When all you have is a long list of tasks, you can lose sight of the project's big picture. Organizing related tasks makes major portions of the project and the overall schedule easier to grasp. By creating *summary tasks* to keep related subtasks together, you turn your long task list into what looks like an outline. (Chapter 7 provides a detailed description of how to break work down and group it into related chunks.)

Here's how to organize a few related tasks under one summary task:

1. **Drag over the Task Name cells of all the tasks you've added so far to select them. Then in the Task tab's Insert section, click Summary.**

Project inserts a new summary task above the selected tasks, named <New Summary Task>. The program indents the selected tasks to make them subtasks, as shown in Figure 4-5. You can see that the summary task is set to Auto Scheduled, which means Project calculates the values for the task from the earliest start date to the latest finish date of its subtasks. It also sets the summary task's start date to the project start date. If you type a value in the summary task's Duration cell, Project changes the task to Manually Scheduled mode.

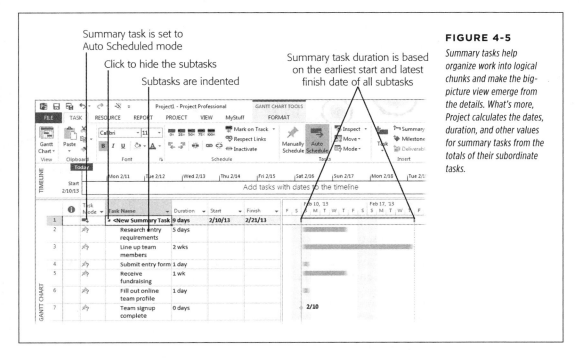

Summary task is set to Auto Scheduled mode

Click to hide the subtasks

Subtasks are indented

Summary task duration is based on the earliest start and latest finish date of all subtasks

FIGURE 4-5

Summary tasks help organize work into logical chunks and make the big-picture view emerge from the details. What's more, Project calculates the dates, duration, and other values for summary tasks from the totals of their subordinate tasks.

2. **Type a name for the summary task, like *Sign up cycling team*, and press Enter.**

   When Project inserts the new summary task, it selects the Task Name cell, so you can immediately type the summary task's name.

3. **To create a summary task and subtasks at the same time, click anywhere in a blank row in the task list and then, in the Task tab's Insert section, click Summary.**

   Project inserts a new summary task with one subtask, named <New Summary Task> and <New Task>, respectively.

4. **In the <New Summary Task> cell, type *Raise money*, and then press Enter. In the <New Task> cell, type *Send donation requests*, and then press Enter.**

   Project selects the next cell in the Task Name column.

5. **In the next two blank Task Name cells, add the following tasks:**

   • Send donation reminders

   • Send thank-you messages for donations

   Just like the "Send donation requests" task you created in the previous step, these new tasks are subtasks of the "Raise money" summary task.

TIP   To move tasks inward or outward in the outline at any time, select the tasks and then, in the Task tab's Schedule section, click Indent Task or Outdent Task. Indent Task is a green arrow pointing to the right; Outdent Task is a green arrow pointing to the left. (*Outdent* is Microsoft-ese for the opposite of indent. That is, outdenting moves a task out to the next higher level in the outline.)

All the tasks you've created so far start on the same day, which isn't the way work will actually occur. The next section gets your project tasks into the right order.

Putting Tasks in the Right Order

Albert Einstein said, "The only reason for time is so that everything doesn't happen at once." The people who work on your project can't do everything at once, so you have to obey the rules of time and put tasks into a sequence. In Project, a relationship between two tasks is known as a *task dependency* or a *task link*. Defining the dependencies between tasks helps you determine which tasks start when, as well as when the project might finish.

To link the tasks for your cycling team, do the following:

1. **Select the tasks related to signing up the team ("Research entry requirements" through "Team signup complete").**

   You can select tasks in any number of ways. You can drag your mouse over the several rows to select the tasks. (You can drag over any cells in the rows.) To select individual tasks, Ctrl-click anywhere in each individual task's row. To select adjacent tasks, click the first task, and then Shift-click the last task.

   No matter which method you use, Project highlights the selected tasks.

2. **To create links between the selected tasks, in the Task tab's Schedule section, click the Link Tasks icon, which looks like links of chain (shown in Figure 4-6).**

   The tasks automatically cascade with Finish-to-Start dependencies (page 177) so one occurs after the other. If you want to remove the dependencies, simply click Unlink Tasks, which looks like a broken link.

3. **Select all the subtasks under the "Raise money" summary task, and link them as explained in the previous step.**

   Sending reminders and thank-you messages occur at the same time, so in the next step, you'll modify a task dependency to show those tasks starting at the same time.

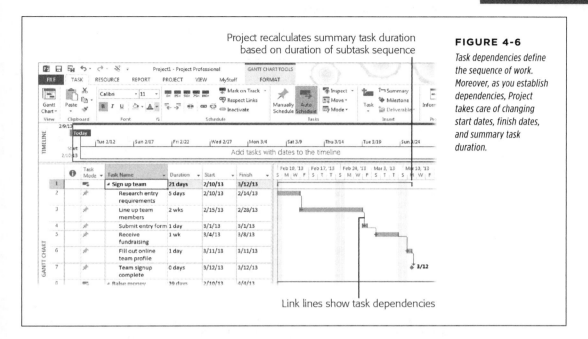

Project recalculates summary task duration
based on duration of subtask sequence

FIGURE 4-6

*Task dependencies define
the sequence of work.
Moreover, as you establish
dependencies, Project
takes care of changing
start dates, finish dates,
and summary task
duration.*

Link lines show task dependencies

NOTE If a summary task is manually scheduled, it'll have two task bars, because Project keeps track of the
duration you specify for the summary task (the task bar looks like a horizontal bracket), as well as the duration
of all its subtasks (a solid task bar as described on page 63). That way, you can see whether your estimate for
the summary task duration is long enough for all the subtasks.

---

4. **Click the "Send thank-you messages for donations" Task Name cell, and
   then, in the Task tab's Properties section, click Information.**

   The Task Information dialog box opens.

5. **Click the Predecessors tab.**

   Predecessors determine when the selected task starts or finishes. The Predecessor tab's table shows the predecessors linked to the selected task. The Type cell
   shows the type of task dependency; in this example, it's Finish-to-Start (FS).

6. **Click the first Type cell (the one that reads "Finish-to-Start (FS)" in this example), click the down arrow that appears, and then choose Start-to-Start (SS). Then click OK.**

   The two tasks now start on the same day, as shown in Figure 4-7.

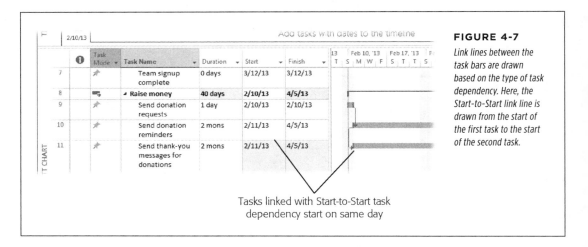

FIGURE 4-7

Link lines between the task bars are drawn based on the type of task dependency. Here, the Start-to-Start link line is drawn from the start of the first task to the start of the second task.

Tasks linked with Start-to-Start task dependency start on same day

---

NOTE Relationships between tasks come in several flavors, with the most common being Finish-to-Start, as illustrated in the previous steps. See page 178 to learn about the other types of task dependencies.

Switching Tasks to Auto Scheduled Mode

So far, the work tasks in your project (but not the summary tasks) have been set to Manually Scheduled mode. If you want Project to calculate your schedule for you (see page 64), you need to switch some or all of your tasks to Auto Scheduled mode. That way, Project can take care of recalculating start dates, finish dates, and durations as you add more details to your plan.

Here's how to change the tasks in the sample project to Auto Scheduled mode:

1. **Click the Task Mode cell for the first summary task (which is already set to Auto Scheduled mode).**

   A down arrow appears, which you can click if you want to choose either Manually Scheduled or Auto Scheduled from a drop-down menu. In addition, a *fill handle* (a green square), appears at the bottom right of the cell.

2. **Position your cursor over the fill handle. When it changes to a + sign, drag over the Task Mode cells of all the tasks in the list.**

   The icons in the Task Mode cells change to indicate that the tasks are Auto Scheduled.

Assigning People and Other Resources

People and their availability (when folks are scheduled to work, and when they're taking vacation) ultimately control when tasks get done and how long the project takes. In Project, *resources* are any people, equipment, or materials needed to complete tasks in your project. Chapters 8 and 9 provide the full scoop on how to create and manage all types of project resources. This section provides a quick introduction to adding people to your project as resources and assigning them to tasks.

Add People to Your Project

Work could still be up for grabs when you create your schedule. Even if you don't know resource names, you probably know what skills are required to do the work. You can use a person's name if you have a lucky team member lined up, or fill in generic names when all you know is the type of work or skill required.

Project's Resource Sheet view is specifically for listing resources. Here's how to display it and fill it in:

1. **In the View tab's Resource Views section, click Resource Sheet.**

   A new spreadsheet-like view appears with fields for recording information about your resources.

2. **To add yourself as a resource, click the first Resource Name cell, type your name (in Figure 4-8, it's Chris), and then press Enter.**

   Project selects the next Resource Name cell.

3. **Repeat step 2 for the colleagues you've corralled into cycling.**

   If you don't know who else will work on your project, then in the Resource Name cell, type a name that indicates the skill required of the resource, like Rider2, Rider3, and Rider4 in Figure 4-8.

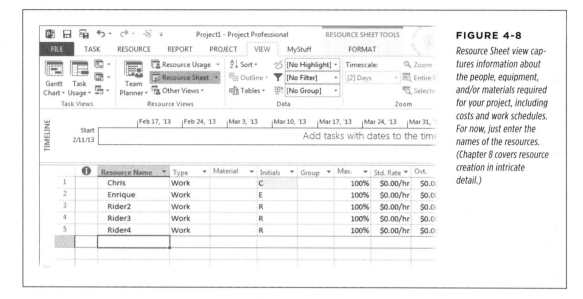

FIGURE 4-8

Resource Sheet view captures information about the people, equipment, and/or materials required for your project, including costs and work schedules. For now, just enter the names of the resources. (Chapter 8 covers resource creation in intricate detail.)

Assign Resources to Tasks

At this point, you have a list of all the people who are pitching in. If you handed them your schedule now and told them to get to work, you'd have a free-for-all on your hands. To get the work done on time with a minimum of chaos, all team members need to know which tasks are theirs to do. Here's how to assign your project's resources to tasks:

1. **In the View tab's Task Views section, click the top half of the Gantt Chart button (where the chart icon is).**

   Project switches to Gantt Chart view. The table on the left side of this view lists tasks with fields for details, such as Duration, Start, Finish, Predecessors, and Resource Names. The right side is the Gantt Chart timescale.

   Make sure you can see the Resource Names column. If necessary, adjust the Gantt Chart's two panes to display it: Position the mouse pointer over the vertical bar between the panes. When the pointer changes to double arrows, drag the divider bar to the right until the Resource Names column is visible.

2. **Click the Resource Names field for the "Research entry requirements" task.**

   Project displays a box around the cell and displays a down arrow for the resource drop-down list.

NOTE Summary tasks don't get resource assignments, because the resources are already assigned to the individual tasks that belong to summary tasks. Likewise, don't assign resources to milestones, because their zero duration means there's no work to perform.

3. **To select a name, click the down arrow, turn on the checkbox for a name in the list, and then press Enter.**

   The name you selected appears in the task's Resource Names cell. It also shows up in the timescale next to the task's task bar (Figure 4-9). For other ways to assign resources to tasks, see page 228.

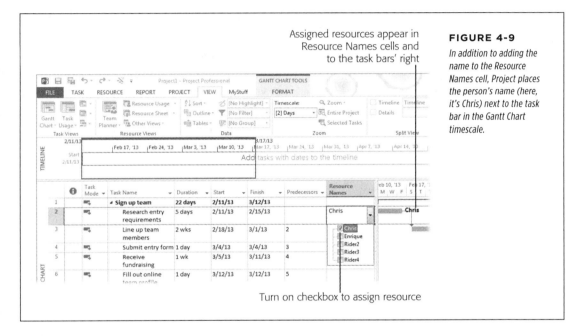

Assigned resources appear in Resource Names cells and to the task bars' right

FIGURE 4-9

In addition to adding the name to the Resource Names cell, Project places the person's name (here, it's Chris) next to the task bar in the Gantt Chart timescale.

Turn on checkbox to assign resource

4. **Repeat steps 2 and 3 until you've assigned resources to all the tasks.**

   Or not. If you don't know who to assign and can't determine a generic resource, then leave the Resource Names field blank. You can come back and assign resources later.

NOTE After you assign resources to tasks in the sample project, you'll probably notice red icons in the Indicators column (the icon looks like a person). That icon represents a resource overallocation. You'll learn how to balance resource workloads to eliminate resource overallocations in Chapter 11.

You're now ready to proceed to the last step of the test drive.

■ Saving Your Project

The final step is saving your hard work so you can come back to it later:

1. **Choose File→Save As.**

   Backstage view's Save As screen appears.

2. **In the "Save and Sync" list, click Computer. Then, on the right side of the screen, click Browse.**

   The Save As dialog box opens.

3. **Navigate to the folder where you want to store the file. In the "File name" field, type a name, and then click Save.**

   Project saves the file in the location you specified.

As you work on your project, remember to save early and save often. Pressing Ctrl+S to save a Project file is so fast that you can make it a habit in no time. Chapter 5 explains other ways to save projects (page 92).

Congratulations! You've created your first project.

Setting Up a Project File

For days, weeks, sometimes months, you build the foundation of your project plan—the project's goal, objectives, scope, requirements, and so on. At long last, you're ready to build the project schedule, the map that guides the project from beginning to end. It tells everyone what work is required, who's supposed to do it, when it should be done, and how much it should cost. Something this fundamental to project management takes some preparation—and the next several chapters of this book—to construct.

The project schedule is where Microsoft Project becomes indispensable. In Project, you build a list of project tasks, link them to define their sequence, and assign resources and costs. This chapter is the first leg of this schedule-building marathon. It begins with creating and saving a new Project file, whether you make one from scratch or start from an existing project or template.

This chapter continues with a few key elements of every project schedule. You learn the pros and cons of scheduling from the project start or finish date, as well as how to tell Project which method you want to use. You'll also learn how to define working days and times for your overall project and for project resources. As you proceed to the remaining chapters in this section, you'll learn the rest of the process for building a project schedule.

▇ Creating a New Project File

Before you can create that schedule you're itching to get started on, you have to create a new Project file. This file is like a container that holds the project's tasks, its resources, and the relationships between them. You can even attach other project documents to it (page 154), like your scope statement or requirements. This section describes several ways to create a new Microsoft Project file: from scratch, using predefined templates, from an existing Project file, or from an Excel workbook. The box on page 85 describes the guided tour offered by Project's Get Started template.

> **NOTE** If you have tasks set up in SharePoint, Project can also create a new project from a SharePoint task list. On Backstage view's New page (to display it, click File→New), click the "New from SharePoint Tasks List" icon. Online-only Chapter 25 (available from this book's Missing CD page at *www.missingmanuals.com/cds*) shows you how this works.

Creating a Blank Project File

If you're starting an unconventional project or want to unleash your maximum creativity, a new blank Project file is like an empty canvas. Here are two easy ways to create a blank file:

- **From Backstage view.** Choose File→New. On the New page, at the top left of the set of template icons, click "Blank project," and voilà—Project creates a new blank file, called something like Project1.

- **With a keyboard shortcut.** Anytime the ribbon tabs are visible, simply press Ctrl+N to create a blank Project file.

> **NOTE** Backstage view contains many of the same commands that appeared on the File menu in Project 2007 and earlier versions (New, Open, Save, and so on). It also includes the Options command, which opens the Project Options dialog box, where you can tell the program how you want it to behave. The online-only Project Options reference (go to this book's Missing CD page at *www.missingmanuals.com/cds*) describes several options you might want to set for new projects you create.

Project's Get Started Template

Previous versions of Project used to throw you into the pool without water wings: The first time you launched Project, all the program did was open a blank Project file. In Project 2013, the Get Started template helps you ease into the water. When you launch Project 2013 for the first time, the Get Started template (Figure 5-1) greets you, assuring you that you can get your project started in four simple steps. (If you skipped the Get Started template the first time you opened the program, you can get back to it anytime you want. In Backstage view's New page, click the Get Started template in the list of featured templates, and then click Create.) To take the tour, simply click the Start button.

When you click Start, the "Schedule your work" screen appears, highlighting the first three steps to getting your schedule started: adding tasks, organizing them, and linking them to create a sequence. If you're itching to learn the details of any of these steps, click the "Learn more" link below the graphic. When you're done with scheduling, click the Next button at the screen's top right. (You might have to scroll to see the Next button, depending on the size of your monitor.)

The next three screens cover creating a timeline, creating reports, and sharing Project information with your team using SharePoint. Click the Next button on each screen to proceed to the next one. On the "Collaborate with your team" screen, clicking the Next button takes you to a final screen with a few links to places where you can learn even more: the Project 2013 Getting Started Center, and the Project blog. Click the "Try out the new features" link to open a small, pre-built project to practice with.

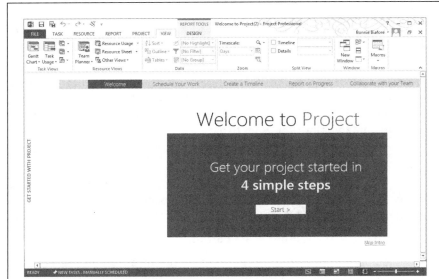

FIGURE 5-1

The Get Started template steps you through the basics of creating a Project schedule and introduces several Project features. It appears when you launch Project 2013 for the first time, but you can go back for a refresher by choosing the Get Started template on Backstage view's New page.

Using a Template to Create a Project File

Projects, by definition, are unique endeavors, so you might think that a template won't be much help for creating a new Project file. But it turns out that the basic tasks for similar projects are often pretty much the same, even if the dates, team members, and results are different.

Templates are often great to use as the basis for a new file, because they contain elements that are common to many other projects. Just edit the tasks, names, dates, and so on to match your current project. Templates usually include typical tasks linked to one another in a logical sequence. Sometimes, they include durations if the work almost always takes the same length of time.

Microsoft Project displays several templates on Backstage view's New page (File→New). If you don't see a template that sounds like your project, you can search Office.com for additional templates, as the box on page 87 explains.

TIP If your projects tend to follow a regular approach, you can create your own templates. In addition to a sequence of tasks with estimated durations, you can include resources and resource assignments if you always use the same team. If you customize elements like your company's working calendar, views, tables, reports, and so on, those are all fair game to include in your own templates. See page 708 for instructions on creating templates. (To learn how to create a new project based on the Project file for a project you've done before, see the box on page 89.)

No matter where you get the template you want to use, the steps for creating a new project file from a template are similar:

1. **Click File→New.**

   Backstage view's New page appears with commands for creating Project files in different ways and choosing featured templates, as shown in Figure 5-2.

2. **If a template's name sounds like it describes your project, click its icon. If you've created your own templates and set up a folder for them (page 88), click the Personal heading below the search box, and then click the icon for the personal template you want to use.**

   If you choose a featured template, a dialog box opens, showing a thumbnail of the project, the name of the person or company that developed it, and a brief description. For personal templates, the dialog box displays only the template name and the Create button. If the featured templates aren't what you're looking for, the box on page 87 tells you how to search online for more templates.

3. **In the dialog box, click the Create button.**

   If the template is a featured template, Project downloads it and then creates a new file from it. With personal templates, Project simply creates a new file from the template—no download required.

Presto! You're ready to work on or save your new file (page 92).

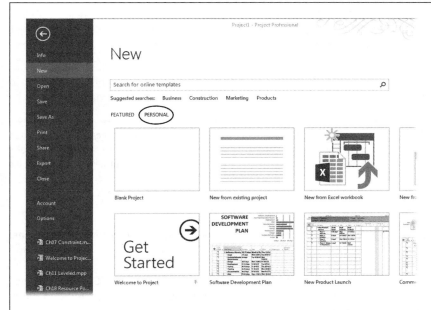

FIGURE 5-2

The first several icons on the New page represent different ways to create a new project: a blank Project file, from an existing project, from an Excel workbook, and from a SharePoint Tasks List. Below those choices, the New page initially lists several templates it thinks might interest you. If you want to use your own templates, click the word "Personal" (circled) below the Search box. Your templates appear only if you tell Project which folder holds them, as described in the steps on page 88.

Searching for Templates Online

Project 2013 makes it easy to search Office.com for just the right template. After you choose File→New, type keywords in the "Search for online templates" box, and then click the magnifying glass icon. For example, if you're planning to start a new business, type a keyword like "startup." Project displays a list of the templates it finds. To start a new Project file from one of these templates, click its icon and then click Create.

You can also search Office.com using your web browser. Go to *http://office.microsoft.com* and then click Templates at the top of the page. The quickest way to find project templates is to type keywords in the "Search all templates" box, and then click the magnifying glass icon. Because Office.com has templates for several Microsoft Office programs, be sure to include "project" as one of your keywords. The results identify the program and version that the template was created with, such as Project 2010, Project 2013, or Excel 2010.

If you find a template you want, put your pointer over the template's icon, and then click the Download link. In the dialog box that appears, select the Save File option and then click OK. In the Save dialog box that opens, navigate to the folder where you want to save the template, type a name for the template in the "File name" box, and then click Save. If you save it in your personal template folder (page 88), you can easily select the template right from the New page (page 86).

Specifying a Template Folder

If you've invested time and effort in creating templates (page 708), you want them to be easy to find. It's a good idea to store the templates you create in a folder that your backup procedure saves along with your other data. If you share templates with other project managers, then keep your project templates where all the project managers in your organization can reach them, so everyone can take advantage of the work others have done.

Project has an option for specifying your template folder. The templates you store in this folder appear when you click the Personal heading on the New page (Figure 5-2).

> **TIP** Another way to keep your templates close by is to *pin* them to the template list on the New page. To do so, point your cursor at the template you want to pin to the New page. When the horizontal pushpin icon appears at the bottom-right of the template icon, click it. The pushpin rotates to vertical and the template appears at the top of the template list.

Here's how to specify your template folder:

1. **Click the File tab. On the left side of the Backstage view screen, click Options.**

   The Project Options dialog box opens.

2. **On the left side of the dialog box, click Save. Head to the "Save templates" section, and, to the right of the "Default personal templates location" box, click Browse (Figure 5-3).**

   The Modify Location dialog box appears.

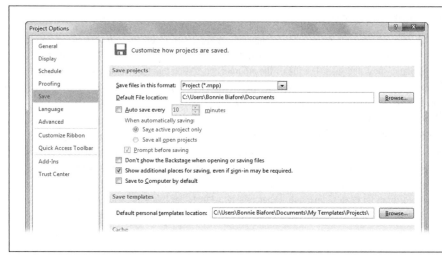

FIGURE 5-3

The "Default personal templates location" box specifies where Project should go to find the templates that you create or download (the filenames of templates end in .mpt). Below the "Save projects" heading, the "Default File location" option tells Project where you save the regular Project files you create (.mpp files).

3. **In the Modify Location dialog box, choose the folder where you store your templates, and then click OK.**

   When you click OK, the Modify Location dialog box closes and the path to the folder you chose appears in the "Default personal templates location" box.

4. **To tell Project which folder to open for your Project *schedule* files (*.mpp* files), under the "Save projects" heading, click Browse to the right of the "Default File location" box, navigate to the folder with your schedules, and then click OK.**

   When you specify a default file location, Project will point the Open and Save As dialog boxes to this folder whenever you choose Computer on Backstage view's Open or Save As page and then click the Browse button.

5. **Click OK to close the Project Options dialog box.**

   The next time you click the Personal heading in the New page, you'll see the templates in your personal templates folder. If you store your templates in sub-folders within your personal templates folder, you'll see a folder icon for each subfolder. Click one of these icons to see the templates stored within that folder.

GEM IN THE ROUGH

Creating a New Project from an Existing Project

If you're planning a project similar to one you've done in the past, you may long to borrow those ready-made tasks and dependencies. But you might not use the same people, monetary values, and other details of that old project. You could clear the values from all those fields, but that would take just as long as creating the new project from scratch. Although Project's New page contains a "New from existing project" command, clicking it simply opens the file you select so you can save it as a new file with a different name. This command doesn't remove any of the old values you want to leave behind.

The best way to turn an existing project into a *clean* new project is to create a template from the existing project. Here's what you do:

1. Open the existing project, and then immediately choose File→Save As.

2. Choose a location for the new file. (For example, choose Computer or your SkyDrive location, and then choose the folder where you want to store the file.) If you plan to use the file as a new project *and* a template for future projects, then choose your personal templates folder (page 88).

3. In the Save As dialog box's "File name" box, type a new name.

4. In the "Save as type" drop-down list, choose Project Template ("Project Template (*.mpt*)" if you have Windows Explorer set to show file extensions), and then click Save.

5. In the Save As Template dialog box that opens, turn on the checkboxes for the data you want to *remove* from the project (not the data you want to keep). You can remove baseline values, actual values, resource rates, and fixed costs—typically, you want to remove all of those.

6. Click Save to close the dialog box. Project creates a template file, which uses an *.mpt* file extension, and opens it.

7. Now, to save that template as a new squeaky-clean Project file, choose File→Save As. Choose the location for the new Project file. In the Save As dialog box, make sure that the "Save as type" box is set to Project, and then save the file in the folder you want, with the name you want.

Creating a Project File from an Excel Workbook

If you define tasks in an Excel workbook, you can import those tasks into Project. Here's the easiest way to do it:

1. **Choose File→New.**

   The New page displays commands for creating a new project in several ways.

2. **Click the "New from Excel Workbook" icon.**

   The Open dialog box appears. In the box to the right of the "File name" box, choose the file type for your Excel file: Excel Workbook, Excel Binary Workbook, or Excel 97-2003 Workbook. You can also choose Text (Tab delimited), CSV (Comma delimited), and XML Format, if the data is in one of those formats.

3. **Double-click the name of the workbook.**

   The Import Wizard opens. See page 540 to learn how to use it to bring tasks into Project from Excel.

You can also create a Project file from an Excel workbook with the Open command. Choose File→Open, and then select the location where you stored the Excel workbook (such as Computer and the folder). When the Open dialog box appears, in the file type drop-down list to the right of the "File name" box, choose Excel Workbook, and then click Open. The Import Wizard launches to help you import tasks into Project (page 541).

■ Setting the Project Start Date

Projects rarely start on the day you create your Microsoft Project file. You usually have some business to take care of before the work begins, like obtaining project plan approvals or lining up funding. The date on which you plan to start the project is the setting you're most likely to change in any Project file.

> **TIP** To ensure that you set the project start date and other key file options, you can tell Project to ask you for that information when you create a new file. Choose File→Options, and then, on the left side of the Project Options dialog box, choose Advanced. In the General section, turn on the "Prompt for project info for new projects" checkbox, and then click OK to close the dialog box. Exit and restart Project. After that, as soon as you create a new project, the Project Information dialog box appears.

Here are the steps:

1. **With the Project file open and active, in the Project tab's Properties section, click Project Information.**

   The Project Information dialog box opens, as shown in Figure 5-4. If you created the file from scratch, Project sets the "Start date" box to today's date. If you create a new Project file from a template or an existing project, the "Start date" box contains the start date that was set in the original file.

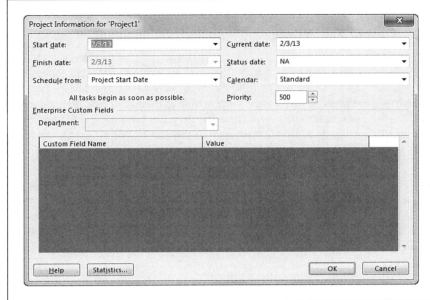

FIGURE 5-4

Out of the box, the "Schedule from" box is set to Project Start Date, which is almost always what you want. When you set the start date, Project calculates the finish date for you. Even if you know the end date you want, you're better off scheduling from the start date, as the box on page 92 explains.

2. **In the "Start date" box, type or choose the date on which you plan to start the project, and then click OK.**

   If you choose a weekend day or other non-workday, Project adjusts the start date you entered to the next business day.

   The "Finish date" box shows the date Project calculates for when the project will finish. If the Project file doesn't have any tasks yet, then the "Finish date" value is the same as the "Start date" value. The date in the "Finish date" box isn't meaningful until you've completely defined your project schedule.

NOTE You can also add information about the project, like a subject and keywords, to the Project file's properties as you can with files for other Office programs. With the Project file open and active, choose File→Info. Click the down arrow next to the Project Information heading, and then choose Advanced Properties. In the "[project name] Properties" dialog box ([project name] is the filename prefix), fill in a title for the project. If you want, fill in other fields like Author, Manager, Company, Category, and Keywords. (You can include the Title and Author fields in Project report headers; then, if this information changes, your report headers use the current values automatically.) Any text in the Comments box appears in a note attached to the project summary task (page 156), so this box is a good place to write a brief summary of what the project is about. You can also search these fields in Windows Explorer (type keywords in the Search box).

Scheduling from the Start or Finish Date

You can schedule a project in two ways: by entering a start date and working forward, or by entering an end date and working backward. Although customers and executives always seem to have a finish date in mind, scheduling projects from the start date is usually the best approach. Entering a specific end date cripples one of Project's most powerful features—the ability to calculate a realistic end date based on tasks, resources, and work time.

If you know when the project can start and how long tasks should take, Project spits out when the project should end. With a calculated end date, the first advantage is that you can show the stakeholders when the project can realistically finish. Armed with this information, you may be able to negotiate for a different deadline.

If the end date *can't* move—as in the case of the cycling fundraiser, which has a fixed event date for the race—schedule from the start date anyway. If the project deadline date is earlier than the finish date that Project calculates, you can evaluate whether techniques like crashing or fast-tracking (both of which are described in Chapter 14) can shorten the schedule sufficiently.

Another reason to avoid scheduling from a finish date is that, when you do that, Project sets all the task constraint types to As Late As Possible (page 188). As the name implies, this constraint type means that tasks are scheduled to start as late as possible, which removes any wiggle room that you might need to respond to problems.

■ Saving a New Project

Whether you created a file with a blank project or a template, the first time you save it by choosing File→Save, Project opens Backstage view's Save As page instead so you're sure to save a new file. That's Project's way of protecting you from saving blank projects named Project1. Project, like other Microsoft programs, automatically uses the Save As command whenever you save a file created from a template, so you can name the new file whatever you want. Most of the time, you choose a location, folder, and filename, and you're done. But Project mavens know that there are other handy tools for saving files in special ways, which are described on pages 96 and 98.

> **TIP** To bypass Backstage view's Save As page and open the Save As dialog box directly, press F12. If you want Ctrl+S to open the Save As dialog box the way it did in earlier versions of Project, choose File→Options, and then, on the left side of the Project Options dialog box, choose Save. Turn on the "Don't show the Backstage when opening or saving files" checkbox, and then click OK.

Here are the steps for saving a new project, whether you store your files on your computer or in the cloud:

1. **Choose File→Save.**

   Backstage view's Save As page appears (Figure 5-5).

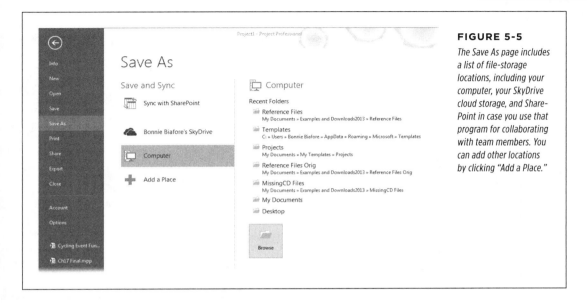

FIGURE 5-5

The Save As page includes a list of file-storage locations, including your computer, your SkyDrive cloud storage, and Share-Point in case you use that program for collaborating with team members. You can add other locations by clicking "Add a Place."

TIP If you opened an existing project and want to save it as a new one, then choose File→Save As instead of File→Save. Otherwise, all Project will do is save any changes you made to the existing project.

2. **On the left side of the Save As page, select where you want to save the new file, such as Computer or <your name>'s SkyDrive, where <your name> is the name on the Microsoft account you use to log into Project (page 732).**

   When you select a location, a list of recent folders appears on the right side of the page below the Recent Folders heading. (In case you grow weary of clicking a bunch of times to save files, the section "File Saving Shortcuts" on page 94 offers several timesavers for saving files.)

3. **Select the location where you want to save your file.**

   If the name of the folder you want appears in the Recent Folders list, simply click its name, and the Save As dialog box opens to that folder.

   If the folder where you want to save the project *isn't* in the Recent Folders list, then click Browse to open the Save As dialog box. Then navigate to the folder.

4. **In the "File name" box, type a name for the project.**

   Short but meaningful filenames—like *CyclingEventFundraiser*—help you and your colleagues find the right files.

5. **Leave the "Save as type" drop-down list set to Project to create a regular Project .mpp file, and then click Save.**

   If Windows Explorer is set up to show file extensions, the "Save as type" drop-down list includes the file extension, such as "Project (*.mpp)." See page 96 to learn about the different file formats in which you can save Project files, and when to use them.

If you want to specify how Project both saves and opens the file that's specified in the Save As dialog box's "File name" box, click Tools→General Options. The Save Options dialog box opens (Figure 5-6).

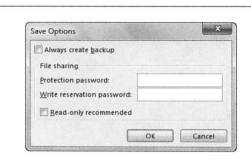

FIGURE 5-6

To open this dialog box with options for saving and opening files, click the Tools button in the Save dialog box, and then select General Options. These settings are described in detail on page 98.

TIP To automatically associate your name and initials with files you create, in Project, choose File→Options. In the Project Options dialog box, choose General. Under "Personalize your copy of Microsoft Office," type your name and initials in the "User name" and Initials boxes.

File-Saving Shortcuts

After you save a file for the first time, you can prevent untold grief by getting into the habit of frequently pressing Ctrl+S to save your file as you work. The old adage "Save early, save often" applies just as much to Project as it does to old favorites like Word and Excel. This section describes options and keyboard shortcuts that can help you save files in no time. To access the settings described in this section, choose File→Options, and then on the left side of the Project Options dialog box, choose Save.

■ SETTING FILE FORMAT AND LOCATION

You can tell Project the file format and storage location to use when you create and save your projects. These settings are located below the "Save projects" heading:

- **File format.** Initially, Project is set up to save files using the Project (*.mpp) format. However, you can specify another file format if, for example, your colleagues still use Project 2003 or Project 2007. In the "Save files in this format" drop-down list, choose the format you want, such as Microsoft Project 2007

(*.mpp) or Microsoft Project 2000 - 2003 (*.mpp). You can also choose Project Template (*.mpt) if, for instance, it's your job to create template files for the project managers in your organization.

- **File location.** If you specify a folder in the "Default File location" box, Project automatically opens the Save As dialog box to that folder.

SETTING UP PROJECT TO SAVE AUTOMATICALLY

If you've lost work in the past because you forgot to save files often enough, you'll be happy to know that Project can automatically save your work every so often. You can tell the program to ask you whether you want to save, as well as which projects to save. Use these options (below the "Save projects" heading) to control how Project automatically saves projects:

- **Auto save frequency.** To tell Project to save your files automatically without any action on your part, turn on the "Auto save every __ minutes" checkbox, and then type a number of minutes in the box. For example, 45 minutes is a good trade-off between security and interruption.

NOTE Auto Save saves your Project files with any changes you've made. That means that if you're playing what-if with a schedule, Auto Save could make the current scenario permanent. However, Auto Save is indispensable if you get lost in schedule work and forget to save for hours.

- **Active or all files.** Unless you change it, Project selects the option to save only the *active* file (the one you're currently working on). If you work on several files simultaneously, select the "Save all open projects" option instead.

- **Prompt before saving.** If you want Project to ask your permission before saving a file, keep the "Prompt before saving" checkbox turned on so the program doesn't save files without your knowledge.

SETTINGS FOR SAVING TO YOUR COMPUTER AND THE CLOUD

Project 2013 makes it easy to work with files whether they're stored on your computer or in the cloud. So it's no surprise that the program has a few new options related to opening and saving files. Here's what the options at the end of the "Save projects" section do:

- **Open the Open and Save As dialog boxes directly.** If you store files on your computer, you don't need more steps for opening and saving files. Initially, the "Don't show the Backstage when opening or saving files" checkbox is turned off, which means that choosing File→Open takes you to the Open page of Backstage view, and choosing File→Save As displays the Save As page of Backstage view. To open the Open and Save As dialog boxes with a single keyboard shortcut, turn this checkbox off. Then, you can press Ctrl+O to jump straight to the Open dialog box, and press F12 or Ctrl+S to jump right to the Save As dialog box.

- **Show all storage locations.** Out of the box, the "Show additional places for saving, even if sign-in may be required" checkbox is turned on. With this setting on, the Save As page shows *every* location you've set up for file storage, even if you have to sign in to access it. If you're working offline and don't want to be distracted by file locations you can't use, then turn this checkbox off.

- **Save to your computer.** Initially, when you try to open or save a file, Project 2013 selects your SkyDrive location automatically. If you store your files on your computer, turn on the "Save to Computer by default" checkbox to make Backstage view's Save As page automatically select Computer instead and show the recent folders you've used to save files.

> **NOTE** The Cache section includes two additional settings, which let you save projects locally to a cache in case you're disconnected from Project Server or SharePoint, for example. When you're back online, you can publish your updates from the cache to Project Server or SharePoint. You can specify the size of the cache and where it's stored.

Saving Projects to Other File Formats

The most common file format for a Project file is the .mpp file extension, which stands for Microsoft Project Plan. Project 2013 can open .mpp files created in Project 2010, 2007, 2003, 2002, 2000, and 1998. However, people with earlier versions of Project can't open Project 2013 .mpp files, so you have to save your files in these *legacy formats* (Microsoft's term for earlier file formats). In addition, you can save Project files in other formats to do things like use Excel to analyze costs, or to publish project information to the Web. (Chapter 19 covers exporting from and importing to Project using different file formats.)

To save a Project file in another format, choose File→Save As, and then select the location and folder (page 93) in which you want to save the file. Then, from the "Save as type" drop-down list, choose the format you want. Here are some occasions when you might choose other formats:

- **Working with earlier versions of Project.** If a colleague uses an earlier version of Project, you can save a Project 2013 file that opens in those versions by choosing Microsoft Project 2007 or Microsoft Project 2000-2003. Project warns that you may lose data from Project 2013's new enhanced features and lists the changes or omissions that come with saving to the earlier format. If you use Project 2013 to open files created in Project 2007 or earlier, you can edit them, although with reduced functionality.

- **Exporting data to Excel.** If you want to export data from Project fields to a spreadsheet (to create a budget from estimated costs, say), then choose Excel Workbook, Excel Binary Workbook, or Excel 97-2003 Workbook. When you save in these formats, Project launches the Export Wizard (page 548), which steps you through selecting and exporting the data you want in the way you want. You can also *import* Excel spreadsheets into Project (page 551).

- **Exporting Project data to use in other programs.** As you manage projects, other programs are sometimes better tools for working with data—creating a WBS, estimating, or managing risk, for example. Depending on the format that the other program reads, choose "Text (Tab delimited)" or "CSV (Comma delimited)" to create a file in a generic text format (page 545). When you save in these formats, Project saves just the active table (the table area in the left pane of the view), not the entire project.

- **Publishing to the Web or interchanging data.** If you want to publish a project online or use extensible markup language (XML) to exchange structured data, choose "XML format."

Project 2013's factory settings don't let you open or save files in older (legacy) Project file formats or to other formats like database-file formats (called *non-default formats*). So if your and your compatriots' files are in older formats, one of the first actions to take after installing Project 2013 is to tell it to work with these older files. To save and open legacy and non-default formats, do the following:

1. **Click File→Options→Trust Center.**

   The Trust Center opens, containing several links related to privacy and security.

2. **Click the Trust Center Settings button.**

   The Trust Center lets you sprinkle your trust onto publishers, add-ins, macros, legacy formats, and more. In addition to the options for working with file formats, you can clear a few file properties when you save a file. On the left side of the Trust Center, click Privacy Options and then turn on the "Remove personal information from file properties on save" checkbox. This setting removes Author, Manager, Company, and Last Save By, presumably to cover your tracks when distributing a project to others.

3. **Click Legacy Formats, and then select the Legacy Format option you want, as shown in Figure 5-7. Then click OK.**

   Project automatically selects "Do not open/save file with legacy or non-default file formats in Project," but this option means that you can't work with existing files in older formats. If you have lots of files in legacy or non-default formats, then the most sensible option is "Allow loading files with legacy or non-default file formats," although this choice lowers your security level and increases the chance of your computer becoming infected by a virus embedded in a file. However, it lets you open and save legacy and non-default file formats without any interruptions. Otherwise, select the "Prompt when loading files with legacy or non-default file format" option so Project will ask if you want to open or save a file with an older or non-default format.

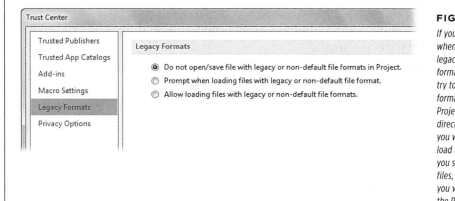

FIGURE 5-7

If you select the "Prompt when loading files with legacy or non-default file format" option and then try to open an older file format or a file format that Project doesn't work with directly, a dialog box asks you whether you want to load the file. And when you save these types of files, Project asks whether you want to save them in the Project 2013 format.

Protecting Your Project Files

Your investment of time and brainpower grows as you build your project schedule. At some point, you've probably been devastated by the disappearance of an important file. You can protect the work in your Project files from inadvertent changes by creating backup copies. Moreover, passwords can protect files from unauthorized editing by a desperate team member trying to obtain more time for a task.

Some security options don't appear in the Project Options dialog box. Instead, they're tucked away in the Save and Save As dialog boxes. If you choose File→Save while you're working on a Project file that you've already saved, the program immediately saves the file without opening a dialog box. So if you want to add security options to an existing file, choose File→Save As instead, and then select the location and folder in which you want to save the file. In the Save As dialog box, click Tools→General Options; the Save Options dialog box (shown back in Figure 5-6) opens. After you choose the security options you want (they're described below), click OK, and then click Save.

> **TIP** Even if you open the Save As dialog box, you can save the file with the same name.

Here's what the settings in Project's Save Options dialog box can do for you:

- **Always create backup.** Creates a backup copy of a file when you first open it, so you can quickly eliminate all the changes from the current session. The file extension for a backup is .bak. To open a backup file, choose File→Open. In the Open dialog box, in the "Files of type" box, choose All Files. Select the backup file, which looks like *FileName.BAK*, and then click Open.

- **Protection password.** Sets a password that you have to type before Project will open the file. Without the password, the file can't be opened for editing or even viewed as read-only. When you type a password in this text box and then click OK to close the Security Options dialog box, a Confirm Password dialog box opens, so you don't end up with a file you can't open due to a typo in the password. Retype the password, and then click OK.

  When you open a file with a protection password, a Password dialog box opens. In the Password box, type the password, and then click OK. Project opens the file.

WARNING　There's no way to remove passwords once you add them, so be sure to store your passwords in a safe place.

- **Write reservation password.** Sets a password that you have to type if you want to *edit* the file. (You can open the file as read-only without a password.) Type a password in this box and, when you click OK to close the Security Options dialog box, a Confirm Password dialog box opens so you can retype the password.

  When you open a file with a write reservation password, a Password dialog box opens. To open the file for editing, in the Password box, type the password, and then click OK. If you want to open the file as read-only, click Read Only instead.

- **Read-only recommended.** When you open a file that has this setting turned on, a message box appears that tells you to open the file as read-only unless you need to write to it. To take Project's advice, click Yes; the file opens as read-only. To write to the file, click No.

◾ Opening a Project File

Project 2013 has new features to help you open Project files, whether you store them on your computer or in the cloud. This section explains how to open files in Backstage view and also tells you about some shortcuts for opening files.

TIP　To bypass Backstage view's Open page and jump straight to the Open dialog box, press Ctrl+F12.

Here's how you open files using Project 2013's Backstage view:

1. **Choose File→Open.**

   Backstage view's Open page appears and displays a list of recent projects, as shown in Figure 5-8.

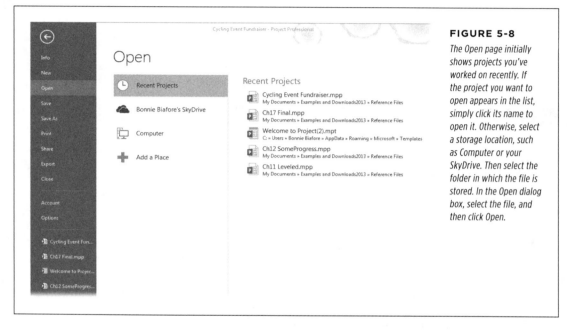

FIGURE 5-8

The Open page initially
shows projects you've
worked on recently. If
the project you want to
open appears in the list,
simply click its name to
open it. Otherwise, select
a storage location, such
as Computer or your
SkyDrive. Then select the
folder in which the file is
stored. In the Open dialog
box, select the file, and
then click Open.

2. **If you recently worked on the project you want to open, click its name below the Recent Projects heading.**

   Project immediately opens the file, so you can skip the rest of the steps in this list.

3. **If the project you want to open doesn't appear in the Recent Projects list, then on the left side of the Open page, select where you stored the file, such as Computer or <your name>'s SkyDrive, where <your name> is the name on the Microsoft account you use to log into Project (page 732).**

   When you select a location, a list of recent folders appears on the right side of the Open page below the Recent Folders heading.

4. **Choose the folder where the file is stored.**

   If the folder that contains the file you want appears in the Recent Folders list, click its name. The Open dialog box opens to that folder.

   If the folder *isn't* in the Recent Folders list, click Browse. In the Open dialog box, navigate to the folder.

5. **In the file list on the right side of the dialog box, click the name of the project you want to open, and then click Open.**

The file type drop-down list to the right of the "File name" box is initially set to Projects. If you want to open a different file format, click the Projects down arrow, and then choose the format you want, such as Project Templates or Excel Workbook.

File-Opening Shortcuts

Although File→Open is the tried and true method for opening Project files, the program offers several shortcuts for opening a file:

- **Choose recent projects on the Start page.** When you launch Project, it opens to the Start page, which is like Backstage view's New and Open pages rolled into one. On the left side of the page, you'll see files you've worked on recently, starting with any files you pinned to the Recent Files list (page 48). To select a recent project, click its name. To open other projects, click Open Other Projects at the bottom of the menu.

- **Jump directly to the Open dialog box.** Pressing Ctrl+F12 bypasses Backstage view and opens the Open dialog box. If you want Ctrl+O to open the Open dialog box the way it did in earlier versions of Project, then choose File→Options, and then, on the left side of the Project Options dialog box, choose Save. Turn on the "Don't show the Backstage when opening or saving files" checkbox and then click OK.

- **Open recent projects.** When you choose File→Open, Backstage view's Open page selects the Recent Projects category and displays several recent projects, as shown in Figure 5-8. Simply click a filename in this list to open it.

To specify how many recent projects appear in this list, choose File→Options. In the Project Options dialog box, choose Advanced. Scroll to the Display section. Change the value in the "Show this number of Recent Projects" box to control how many projects appear on Backstage view's Open page.

TIP   If you work on a few projects for months at a time, you can pin projects to the top of the Recent Projects list so they won't be replaced by other files. Point to the filename in the Recent Projects list, and then click the horizontal pushpin icon that appears to the right of the filename. The pushpin rotates to vertical, and the project name leaps to the top of the list.

- **Display projects on Backstage view's menu.** When you click the File tab, Backstage view opens with a menu on its left side. You can display projects on that menu (also shown in Figure 5-8) so you don't have to choose Open in the menu. To set this shortcut up, choose File→Options. In the Project Options dialog box, choose Advanced. Scroll to the Display section, and then turn on the "Quickly access this number of Recent Projects" checkbox and type the number you want. Project displays that number of recent projects, starting with projects that are pinned to the Recent Projects list. Click a filename to open that Project file.

- **Open the last file you worked on when Project launches.** If you work on only one project at a time, a slick shortcut is to have Project open the last file you worked on automatically. That way, each time you launch Project, your latest project is waiting for you. Choose File→Options. In the Project Options dialog box, choose Advanced. In the General section, turn on the "Open last file on startup" checkbox and then click OK.

Setting Standard Workdays

The amount of available working time has a big impact on how quickly a project finishes. A mission-critical project to beat the competition to market might opt for longer workdays during the week with some weekend overtime as well. On the other hand, if you're building a vacation house on a tropical isle, you might have to adjust the working time for the more relaxed work schedules that hot sun and siestas induce. You need a calendar to indicate which days and times are available for work.

In Microsoft Project, *calendars* have working and nonworking days and times blocked out. You can use one of the program's built-in calendars, modify existing calendars, or build brand-new ones for unusual work schedules. Then you can apply a calendar to an entire project to set the standard working times, which is perfect for specifying the holidays for your organization or telling Project that Fridays are half-days for your company. You can also define and apply calendars to individual people—for instance, to specify luxuriously long scheduled vacations—or to tasks—for example, to schedule a task to run around the clock until it's done. (See the box on page 103 for more details.)

To keep Project's work and duration calculations accurate, it's important that the number of hours Project assumes for duration match the hours those durations represent in your organization's typical work schedules. Project's calendar options control how the program converts durations (page 105) into hours of work.

This section shows you how to select the project calendar you want to use and to set calendar options to match your project's working times. If you want to set up customized calendars, jump to "Defining Work Times with Calendars" on page 107.

Choosing a Project Calendar

Project uses the project calendar to schedule tasks and resources that don't have their own special calendars. For most projects, the project calendar looks a lot like your organization's work schedule—its standard workdays, the official start and end of the workday, the time off for lunch, and official holidays. But some projects follow a different drummer. For instance, construction work on a busy highway might take place from 9 p.m. to 5 a.m. to minimize agonizing gridlock during rush hour.

Project comes with three built-in *base calendars*, which are calendar templates you can use as-is or modify to represent your organization's work schedule:

- **Standard.** Sets working time to Monday through Friday from 8 a.m. to 5 p.m. with an hour for lunch from 12 p.m. to 1 p.m., shown in Figure 5-9.

- **Night Shift.** Sets working times from Monday through Friday from 11 p.m. to 8 a.m. with lunch from 3 a.m. to 4 a.m.

- **24 Hours.** Schedules work 24 hours a day, 7 days a week. Although many high-pressure projects *feel* like they run on 24-hour schedules, this calendar is suitable for projects that *actually* run three shifts or tasks that run 24 hours a day.

UP TO SPEED

How Calendars Control Schedules

Calendars can affect different aspects of a Project file with dramatically different scheduling results. Calendars can apply to entire projects, resources, and tasks. Here are the three kinds of calendars Project offers and how to apply them:

- **Project calendar.** Assigning a calendar to a project sets the standard working days and times for the entire project. If tasks or resources don't use special calendars, then your calendar work is done. If all your projects follow your organization's work schedule, you can modify the built-in Standard calendar with your company's standard workdays, work times, and holidays (page 109). When you create new project files, Project automatically assigns the Standard calendar from your *Global.mpt* file as their calendar, and your working times are set. If, on the other hand, you work with other companies and subcontractors who don't have the same work schedules and holidays, you can copy the Standard calendar give it a copy to reflect your organization's work schedule. Then you can apply the modified copy to your projects.

- **Resource calendar.** A resource calendar is ideal when an individual or a group of resources work specialized schedules. If your project spans multiple shifts, then you can define a calendar for each shift and apply the shift calendar to the folks who work that shift. For the ultimate in schedule accuracy, you can set up a resource calendar for each person to reserve dates for scheduled vacations. Individual resource calendars help you see whether your schedule needs tweaking to deliver a deadline before a key resource heads off on a Tahitian honeymoon. See page 214 to learn how to assign a calendar to a resource.

- **Task calendar.** Most tasks run according to the project calendar and any resource calendars applied to the assigned resources. But occasionally, tasks follow their own schedules, in cases like installing new security cameras only when the bank vault is open. Applying a calendar to a task is ideal to specify offbeat work times that apply only to that task.

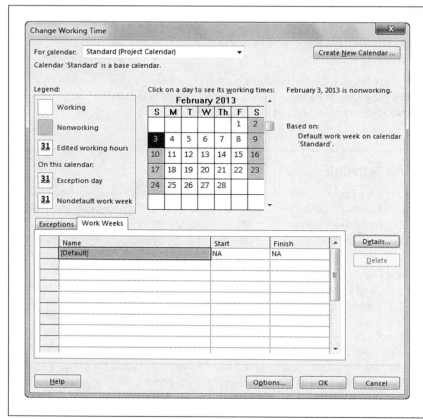

FIGURE 5-9

The Standard calendar comes without any days off for holidays, but you can—and should—change this calendar to add holidays or tweak working times. Project automatically assigns this calendar to new projects you create.

TIP Whether you modify the Standard calendar to mirror your organization's work schedule or create a brand-new calendar for that purpose, you can tell Project to use that calendar for every new project file you create. To do so, first, use the Organizer to copy that calendar to the *Global.mpt* template, as described on page 702. Then apply the calendar to a new project by following the steps in this section.

Once the Standard calendar (or a customized copy of it) reflects your working and nonworking times, you're all set. When you create a new project, Project automatically assigns the Standard calendar to it. To use a different project calendar, follow these simple steps:

1. **With the project open, in the Project tab's Properties section, click Project Information.**

   The Project Information dialog box opens.

2. **In the Calendar drop-down menu, shown in Figure 5-4 on page 91, choose the calendar you want, whether it's a built-in calendar or one you've customized (page 109), and then click OK.**

   If you open the Change Working Time dialog box described on page 109, then in the "For calendar" box, you see "(Project Calendar)" to the right of the name of the calendar that the entire project uses. The working and nonworking time for all tasks and resources without special calendars conform to the project calendar work schedule.

Setting Calendar Options

Calendars, like the project calendar you assigned in the previous section, specify working days and times. But calendar options, stored in the Project Options dialog box, tell Project how to translate durations for those working times into hours of work. For example, if the "Hours per week" option is set to 40, a task with a 2-week duration represents 80 work hours. But if "Hours per week" is set to 35, then a 2-week task represents only 70 hours of work. Because calendar options and calendar work times have to match, calendar options can be different for each project, as Figure 5-10 shows. (The box on page 107 describes some of the problems created by mismatched calendars and calendar options.)

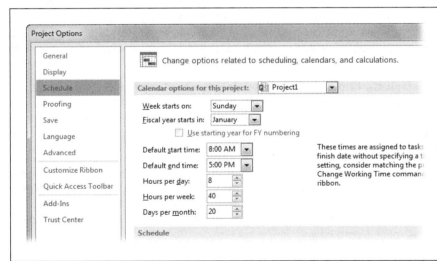

FIGURE 5-10

The label "Calendar options for this project" means that the option settings in the section apply to the project whose name appears in the box. You can modify these options without affecting the calendar options in other projects. When more than one project is open, you can choose a different project name in this box to assign calendar options to that project.

Project's out-of-the-box calendar options are perfect for your typical 8-to-5 operation. Usually, a quick glance at these options confirms that they fit your organization's schedule, and you can move on to other project-management duties. To view Project's calendar options, choose File→Options. In the Project Options dialog box, click Schedule. Here are the options you can set and what each one does:

- **Week starts on.** This option specifies the first day of the week in your schedule and is initially set to Sunday, which is usually fine. You might change this option when you exchange actual project values with your corporate time-tracking system, for example, so both programs start work weeks on the same day of the week.

> **TIP** If your organization uses an unusual work schedule for *all* its projects and you want to adjust the calendar options to follow suit, then in the drop-down list to the right of the "Calendar options for this project" label, choose All New Projects to apply the current calendar options to all *new* (not existing) projects. If you want to change the settings for existing projects, you have to open each project and follow the instructions in this section to change the calendar options.

- **Fiscal year starts in.** You need to change this option only when your corporate fiscal year starts in a month other than January *and* you want to produce fiscal-period reports in Project. When you set the month for the fiscal year, the Gantt Chart timescale displays the fiscal year. For example, if the fiscal year begins in July, then September 30, 2013, appears under the 2014 fiscal year. If you set the "Fiscal year starts in" box to a month other than January, the "Use starting year for FY numbering" checkbox springs to life. Turning on this checkbox sets the fiscal year to the calendar year in which the fiscal year begins. For example, with this checkbox turned on and the fiscal year set to start in July, July 2013 is in fiscal year 2013. With this checkbox turned *off* and the fiscal year set to start in July, July 2013 is the beginning of fiscal year 2014.

- **Default start time.** For most tasks, the start time depends on when predecessor tasks finish. The time in this box affects a task's start time only when you create a task and specify a start date without a start time. This option is set to 8:00 a.m. initially. If your workday starts earlier or later, adjust the value of this box accordingly.

- **Default end time.** The finish time for most tasks depends on when the task begins and how long it takes. The time in this box becomes the finish time for a task only when you specify a task's finish date without specifying a finish time. This box is set to 5:00 p.m. initially. If your workday ends earlier or later, adjust this value accordingly.

- **Hours per day.** Sets the number of working hours for a single workday. For example, with the standard setting of 8.00, one workday represents 8 hours of work.

- **Hours per week.** Defines the number of working hours in one week and is set to 40.00 initially.

- **Days per month.** This option is the conversion between days and months and is set to 20 workdays (4 weeks each with 5 workdays) per month initially.

Calendars and Calendar Options

Project doesn't warn you when your calendar options and project calendar don't jibe, so it's a good idea to make sure they do. Project uses the calendar options to convert one time period into another—for instance, to calculate the work hours that correspond to a duration you enter in weeks. If the calendar options and the calendar disagree, then duration and work estimates don't agree, and resource assignments may not make sense.

Suppose the Hours Per Day option is set to 6 hours. For a task with a 5-day duration, Project multiplies the 5 days by 6 hours per day to get task work of 30 hours. Someone assigned to the task at 100 percent may work 8-hour days according to the project calendar. But when Project converts workdays into work hours, it thinks he's working only 6 hours a day because of the Hours Per Day option. The solution to this brainteaser is to set the same number of work hours per day in your calendar options *and* the calendar.

■ Defining Work Times with Calendars

Resources aren't at your beck and call 24/7. Team members take vacations, attend training and conferences, and get sick. They may also work part time or work 4 long days and take Fridays off. Incorporating nonworking time and specialized work arrangements makes a Project schedule more likely to forecast how the project will actually play out. In Project, *calendars* carve out working and nonworking times.

Calendars are multitalented: You can apply a calendar to an entire project, individual resources (page 120), or specific tasks (page 120). For instance, you can set up a calendar to reflect your organization's standard working times, corporate holidays, and factory closures, and use that calendar for all your projects. On the other hand, a resource calendar can represent a shift-work schedule or a team member's particular work schedule and time off.

Project comes with a few built-in calendars (page 103) and automatically applies the built-in Standard calendar to new projects you create. However, you can modify existing calendars or build completely new ones and then apply them to custom-fit your projects' and resources' work hours.

This section explains creating and customizing calendars in Project. You'll also find a quick review of how to apply calendars to projects, resources, and tasks. See page 213 to learn how to integrate calendars, resource units, and resource availability to resolve common resource-scheduling issues.

TIP You can copy calendars you create using the Organizer so they're available to other projects. If you create a copy of the Standard calendar in one Project file to include company holidays, for example, then copy that calendar into the Project global template (page 703) to share that calendar with all new projects.

Creating New Calendars

You can create as many calendars as you need. Whether you want to create a calendar for a project, a resource, or a task, the steps are the same: Create the new calendar, edit it to reflect the working and nonworking times, and then apply it. Here are the steps for creating a new calendar:

1. **In the Project tab's Properties section, click Change Working Time.**

   The Change Working Time dialog box opens. The "For calendar" box shows the calendar you've applied to this project. For example, "Standard (Project Calendar)" indicates that the Standard calendar is set as the project calendar for the current Project file.

2. **Click Create New Calendar.**

   The Create New Base Calendar dialog box appears, as shown in Figure 5-11 (foreground). *Base calendar* is Project's name for calendars that act as templates for other calendars. For example, the Standard calendar is a base calendar because you can use it as the foundation for customized project calendars and resource calendars.

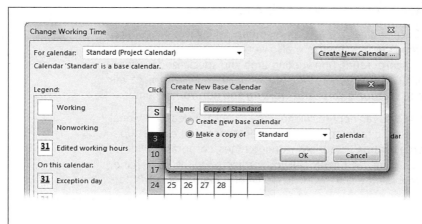

FIGURE 5-11

Project suggests that copying an existing calendar is the preferred way to create a new base calendar by automatically selecting the "Make a copy of" option. Although you can modify the built-in Standard calendar to represent your organization's customized work schedule, it's better to copy the Standard calendar instead and give the copy a meaningful name like Fundraiser or Half Time Schedule.

3. **In the Name box, type a new name for the calendar.**

   If you copy an existing calendar, Project adds "Copy of" in front of the calendar's name. If you create a new calendar, Project fills in the box with a name like Calendar 1. The best names are short but give you a good idea of the working time they represent, like Night Shift.

4. **Tell Project whether you want to make a copy of an existing calendar or create a brand-new one.**

To use an existing calendar as your starting point, leave the "Make a copy of" option selected, and then, in the "Make a copy of _ calendar" drop-down list, choose the calendar you want.

For a calendar that's very different from any you have already, you can create one from scratch by selecting the "Create new base calendar" option.

5. **Click OK.**

The Create New Base Calendar dialog box closes, and the new calendar's name appears in the "For calendar" box. Because this new calendar isn't assigned as the project calendar for the current project, only the calendar name appears in the box [it doesn't have "(Project Calendar)" after it]. (Page 120 shows how to make a calendar the project calendar.) Now you're ready to set the calendar's working times, which the next section describes in detail.

Modifying Calendars

Any calendar in a Project file, whether it's built-in or one of yours, is fair game for modification. Although you can modify the built-in Standard calendar, copying it to create a separate calendar for your organization's work and holiday schedule makes it easy to tell which calendar defines your organization's work time and days off. Then, if you store that custom calendar in the Project global template (page 703) and apply it as the project calendar for new projects (page 120), every new Project file knows about your work weeks and time off.

Setting up work schedules for people and tasks is another reason to modify calendars. You could create a "Half time" calendar for the people who work the company's part-time schedule and specify the work times as 8 a.m. to 12 p.m. Then you apply that calendar to every resource who works half time.

If you create a brand-new calendar as explained in the previous section, Project selects it in the Change Working Time dialog box's "For calendar" box as soon as you create it. However, if you want to modify an existing calendar, you have to select it first by performing the following steps:

1. **In the Project tab's Properties section, click Change Working Time.**

The Change Working Time dialog box opens, showing the current project calendar in the "For calendar" box.

2. **In the "For calendar" drop-down list, choose the calendar you want to modify, as illustrated in Figure 5-12.**

The "For calendar" drop-down list starts with built-in calendars and any new calendars you've created. Calendars for each resource in the Project file appear at the end of the list.

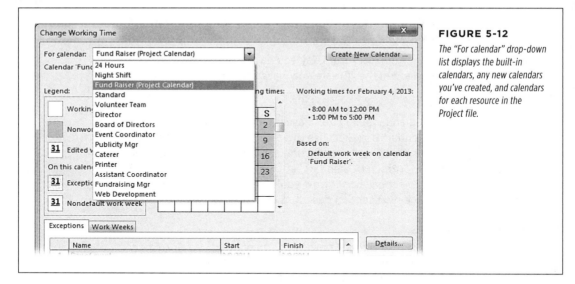

FIGURE 5-12

The "For calendar" drop-down list displays the built-in calendars, any new calendars you've created, and calendars for each resource in the Project file.

Now you're ready to modify the selected calendar as described in the following sections.

Defining Work Weeks and Exceptions

Project calendars offer two features for defining working and nonworking time: work weeks and exceptions. This section explains what each one does and how to use them to specify workdays and non-workdays and times.

■ UNDERSTANDING WORK WEEKS

Work weeks identify the workdays and non-workdays in a 7-day week, as well as the work hours for each workday. Set up an additional work week when a work schedule lasts several weeks or months, with different workdays and times—like a stint of 10-hour days Monday through Saturday to meet a critical deadline. You tell Project the date range within which that work week schedule applies and define the work week (by clicking the Details button in the Change Working Time dialog box). Project then modifies the current calendar to use that work week between the start and stop dates you specified.

You can set up more than one work week within the same Project calendar, which is great if your organization has different work schedules at different times during the year. Here are some examples of why you might create additional work weeks:

- **Company-wide work schedules.** Create additional work weeks when your company has a summer-schedule work week, a winter-schedule work week, and the standard work week in force the rest of the year.

- **Extended company-wide nonworking time.** You can also set up a work week for company-wide *nonworking* time that lasts one or more weeks—for example, a factory shutdown for the last two weeks of the year.

> **NOTE** You can't create a work week and apply it to several different time periods. So if you set up a summer-schedule work week, you have to create separate work weeks for *each* summer.

- **Resource work schedules.** Work weeks in a resource calendar are great when someone works an altered schedule for a few weeks or months; for example, when someone works half-days for two months while recuperating from an illness. You simply select the resource calendar and then create a work week for the recuperation schedule.

■ UNDERSTANDING EXCEPTIONS

Exceptions are primarily for nonworking time, like company holidays, but you can also use them for alternate work schedules that run for a shorter period of time. In a Project calendar, you create a separate exception for each company holiday or other special day. You can also set up recurring exceptions—for example, to schedule a non-workday once a quarter for the ever-popular all-hands meeting.

Consider using calendar exceptions for the following situations:

- **Single days with a different schedule.** A company holiday and a half-day for a corporate meeting are perfect examples of single-day exceptions.

- **Multiple days with a different schedule.** For example, you can set a modified schedule for a multiday training class that someone attends, a conference, or a series of short days when the auditors are in town.

- **Recurring changes.** Use exceptions to specify altered work times that occur on a regular schedule, like company meetings or the monthly ice cream social.

- **Altered work schedules longer than a week.** You can use an exception for a schedule change that lasts longer than a week as long as all the days of the exception are either nonworking days or have the same working times. (For that reason, work weeks and exceptions work equally well for factory shutdowns and people's vacations.)

■ DEFINING WORK WEEKS FOR A CALENDAR

Every calendar in a Project file comes with one work week. When you select a calendar and select the Work Weeks tab, the name of the first entry is [Default]. The Start and Finish cells are set to NA, which means that the work week applies to all dates.

NOTE   Initially, the [Default] work week considers weekdays as workdays and weekends as non-workdays. To set different work times on specific days, you have to specify those work times in either calendar work weeks or exceptions. Also, when you specify start and end times for work hours for calendar days, make sure the start and end work times you specify in Project's calendar options (page 106) are set to the same times.

If you need an additional work week (see page 110 for why you might need one), it needs a name as well as start and stop dates for the modified work schedule. Here are the steps for creating a new work week:

1. **In the Change Working Time dialog box, in the "For calendar" drop-down list, select the calendar, and then click the Work Weeks tab.**

   "[Default]" appears in the table's first row with any other work weeks you've defined in rows 2 and higher.

2. **On the Work Weeks tab, click the first blank Name cell, and then type a name for the work week schedule.**

   Use a meaningful name, like Summer2014, for the summer work week. If you create a work week in a resource calendar, you might call the work week Spring Vacation or Medical Leave.

3. **Click the Start cell in the same row, click the down arrow that appears in the cell, and then choose the first date to which the work week applies, as shown in Figure 5-13. Click the Finish cell in the same row, and then choose the last date to which the work week applies.**

   When you click the down arrow in a Start or Finish cell, a calendar drop-down appears. Click the left arrow or right arrow to move one month into the past or future, respectively. To select a date, click the date in the monthly calendar. If the date is several months in the future, typing the date (like *6/1/14*) may be faster.

4. **To specify workdays and times, click Details. Then specify the workdays and times as described in the next section. Click OK when you're done.**

   When you set up additional work weeks with alternate work schedules, the calendar in the top half of the Change Working Time dialog box underlines the dates with non-standard workdays, as you can see for June 2014 in Figure 5-13.

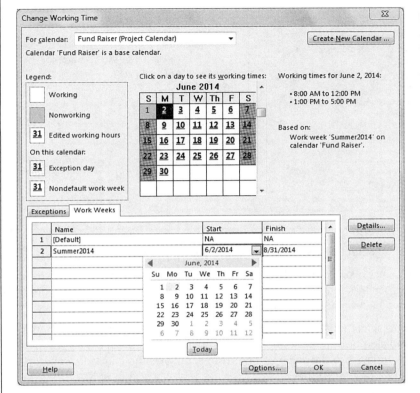

FIGURE 5-13

If you click a day in the calendar at the top of the Change Working Time dialog box, Project displays the working times for that day, and the work week that applies to that day.

■ **DEFINING A WORK WEEK'S WORKING AND NONWORKING DAYS AND TIMES**

Here's how you define workdays and work hours for a work week, whether you want to change a calendar's standard work week or modify a special work week you created:

1. **In the Change Working Time dialog box, select the calendar, and then click the Work Weeks tab. In the Work Weeks table, click the cell that contains the name of the work week you want to modify.**

   If you haven't added any additional work weeks, the only entry you see in the Work Weeks tab is "[Default]" in the Name cell of Row 1.

2. **To specify the workdays and times, click Details.**

The Details dialog box appears with the heading "Details for <work week name>" as shown in Figure 5-14.

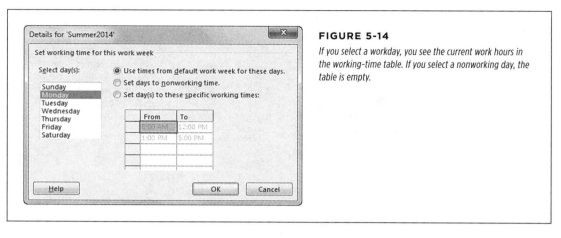

FIGURE 5-14

If you select a workday, you see the current work hours in the working-time table. If you select a nonworking day, the table is empty.

3. **In the "Select day(s)" list, select the day(s) you want to modify.**

To select a single day, click it. To select several adjacent days, drag over the days (or click the first day and Shift-click the last). To select nonadjacent days, Ctrl-click each day you want to select.

If you select multiple days that use different settings, none of the options in the dialog box are selected and the working-time table is blank. When all selected days use the same settings, Project shows the common work times in the working-time table.

4. **Select the appropriate working-time option.**

The initial setting for every day of the week is "Use times from the default work week times for these days," which sets weekdays as workdays and weekends as non-workdays. (If you're modifying the [Default] work week, the label reads "Use Project default times for these days.") To change a workday to a non-workday (for example, to change Friday to a non-workday), select the "Set days to nonworking time" option.

To change the work hours for any workday, select the "Set day(s) to these specific working times" option. This option makes the working-time table editable, so you can change the work hours for the selected days. In addition to changing work hours, use this option to change a non-workday (like a weekend day) to a workday.

5. **To change the work hours in an existing entry in the table, click the cell, and then type the new time.**

   When you click a cell in the working-time table, Project selects the cell's entire contents, so you can simply start typing to change the value.

   Working-time text boxes behave like all other text boxes. You can edit times by clicking to position the insertion point, or by dragging to select the text you want to edit. The box on page 115 provides some shortcuts for editing times.

6. **To add a new row of working times, click the first blank From cell, and then type the starting time.**

   Suppose you switch to 14-hour days and add a second break in the late afternoon. You can add a new row for the third set of work hours.

7. **To remove a row of work times, click in either the From or To cell, and then press Delete.**

   Project removes the times in both the From and To cell. For example, to change a full workday to a half workday, you can delete the after-lunch work hours.

8. **To specify working times for other days, repeat steps 3–7.**

   When you're done, click OK to close the dialog box.

UP TO SPEED

Telling Project Time

Project recognizes a few shortcuts in the working-time table. For example, if you type *8* in a cell, Project fills in 8:00 AM. In fact, Project switches to an a.m. time whenever you type a number from 7 to 11. Project changes the number 12 and the numbers from 1 to 6 to p.m. times; for instance, *12* becomes 12:00 PM. To enter a time including a.m. or p.m., simply type a value like *8 pm*.

Project double-checks the times you enter and tries to be helpful. If you type a time in a From cell that's later than the To time, Project automatically adjusts the To time to be one hour later than the From time. For example, suppose the first set of work times run from 8:00 a.m. to 12:00 p.m. If you change the From cell to 1:00 PM, then Project changes the To cell to 2:00 PM.

Overlapping times in different rows are a problem. For instance, suppose you enter work times of 1:00 PM to 5:00 PM in the first row and 4:00 to 5:00 PM in the second row. Project doesn't complain until you click OK, when it warns you that the start of one shift has to be later than the end of the previous shift. Click OK and remove the overlap.

■ SETTING ASIDE HOLIDAYS AND OTHER EXCEPTIONS TO THE WORK SCHEDULE

Work weeks assign the same schedule of workdays and times over a specific period of time. As their name implies, calendar *exceptions* are better for shorter changes to the work schedule. Here are the steps for defining an exception in a calendar:

1. **In the Change Working Time dialog box, in the "For calendar" drop-down list, select the calendar, and then click the Exceptions tab.**

   Project doesn't set up any exceptions automatically, so all the rows in the Exceptions table start out blank.

2. **On the Exceptions tab, click the first blank Name cell, and then type a name for the exception, like *Day of event* for the cycling fundraiser race day.**

   You can create as many exceptions in a calendar as you need—to set each company holiday in the year or to reserve vacation time for someone who frequently flits around the world, for example.

3. **Click the Start cell in the same row, click the down arrow that appears in the cell, and then choose the first date to which the exception applies. Click the Finish cell in the same row, and then choose the last date for the exception.**

   Start and finish dates can be the same day, a few days apart, or any two dates you want. The only restriction is that all the days within that date range must be either non-workdays or have the same working times.

4. **To define the days and times for the exception, click Details.**

   The "Details for <calendar name>" dialog box opens. Because many exceptions are holidays and other days off, Project automatically selects the Nonworking option at the top of the dialog box. If the exception is for nonworking time, just click OK. However, if you're creating an exception for a few days of altered work times, select the "Working times" option instead, as shown in Figure 5-15.

   For one or more adjacent days, you can ignore the settings in the "Recurrence pattern" and "Range of recurrence" sections. (The next section of this chapter explains how to create recurring exceptions.)

5. **If the exception represents modified working times, set the working times in the "Working times" table (see the box on page 115 for time-setting shortcuts). Click OK when you're done.**

   The Details dialog box closes, and the exception is waiting for you on the Exceptions tab.

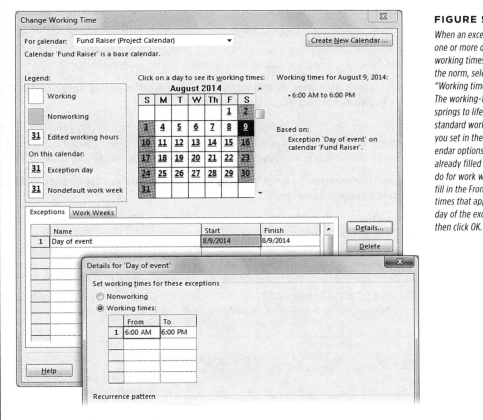

FIGURE 5-15

When an exception is for one or more days with working times outside the norm, select the "Working times" option. The working-time table springs to life, with the standard working times you set in the Project calendar options (page 106) already filled in. As you do for work week details, fill in the From and To times that apply to every day of the exception, and then click OK.

■ DEFINING RECURRING EXCEPTIONS

Sometimes, exceptions to the work week occur on a regular schedule—like the quarterly half-days of nonworking time for all-hands meetings. Recurring tasks and recurring exceptions have the same types of frequency settings, as the box on page 119 explains. However, recurring tasks represent project work that repeats, while recurring exceptions represent repeating special work times.

The details for a calendar exception specify whether exception days are nonworking or working days (along with the work hours). The lower part of the "Details for <calendar name>" dialog box has options to set a frequency for the exception and when it starts or ends. Here are the steps for defining a recurring exception in a calendar:

1. **In the Change Working Time dialog box, select the calendar from the "For calendar" drop-down list, and then click the Exceptions tab.**

2. **In the table, enter the name, start date, and finish date as you would for a regular exception (page 116).**

   Recurring exceptions tend to span longer periods of time than exceptions for holidays or training classes. For example, you might set up the start and finish dates for the charity's national board meetings to span two years.

3. **Click Details and specify the nonworking or working time settings for the days in the recurring exception.**

   The section "Defining a work week's working and nonworking days and times" on page 113 describes how to specify nonworking and working times for days. With a Project calendar exception, every day of the exception must use the same settings.

4. **In the "Recurrence pattern" section, select the correct frequency option, as demonstrated in Figure 5-16.**

   The options include Daily, Weekly, Monthly, and Yearly. The other settings that appear depend on which frequency option you select. For example, the Weekly option has a checkbox for specifying the number of weeks between occurrences (1 represents every week, 2 represents every other week, and so on) and checkboxes for the days of the week on which the event occurs. The Monthly option has one option for specifying the day of the month, and another for specifying the week and day of the week (like first Monday).

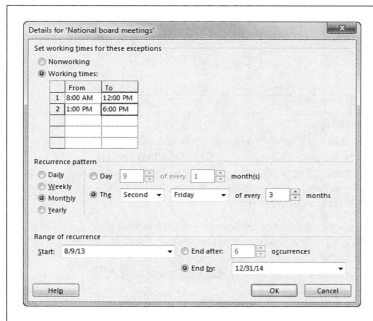

FIGURE 5-16

For a recurring exception, you specify the recurrence pattern as well as how long the pattern lasts. Project initially sets the pattern to every day by selecting the Daily option and filling in the "Every _ days" box with 1. Project also fills in the Start and "End by" dates with the exception's start and end dates.

5. **In the "Range of recurrence" section, specify the date range or the number of occurrences.**

Project fills in the "Range of recurrence" Start box with the start date from the Exceptions tab—basically, the first date of the first exception. It also selects the "End after" option. Because the exception is initially set to Daily, it fills in the "End after" box with the number of days between the exception's start and finish date (from the Exceptions tab).

Suppose you want to carve out time from your project for a national board meeting every 3 months starting in August 2013 until the end of 2014. In the "Recurrence pattern" section, select the Monthly option and specify the frequency, as described in the previous step. Then, in the "occurrences" box, type the appropriate number (*6* in this example). If the Finish date you set on the Exceptions tab is too early to fit all the occurrences, Project automatically changes that date. For example, if the Finish date were set to 6/1/14, Project would change it to 11/14/14 to accommodate the six quarterly meetings.

The other approach tells Project to set up as many exceptions as fit between the start and "End by" dates. In this case, select the "End by" option and then fill in the date in the box. Project uses the recurrence pattern to set up exceptions, with the last exception occurring before the "End by" date.

6. **Click OK.**

Whether you set dates or a number of occurrences, a recurring exception can repeat up to 999 times. If your recurrence pattern results in 1,000 occurrences or more, then Project displays a warning when you click OK.

UP TO SPEED

Recurring Tasks vs. Recurring Exceptions

The settings for recurring calendar exceptions look like the ones for recurring tasks (page 136). However, recurring exceptions and recurring tasks do very different things.

A recurring *task* is project work that occurs on a regular schedule, like a biweekly status meeting. When you add these tasks to your schedule as recurring tasks, you can track the work hours and meeting costs.

A recurring *exception* specifies a work or nonwork schedule that repeats regularly, like a half-day the last Friday of every month. Project takes the exception days and times into account when it schedules project work for any project that uses that calendar. When you copy a calendar from one file to another (page 702), the calendar's exceptions and work weeks copy over, too.

Applying Calendars

Sometimes, entire projects follow a different work schedule, like a subproject with a partner who has an enviable number of holidays. More often, one or more resources need their own work calendars to reflect work shifts, vacations, or unique working hours (like those of the token vampire on your team). And the occasional task may have its own calendar, like the server maintenance task that has to run from 9 p.m. to 5 a.m.

To apply a calendar to a *project*, follow these steps:

1. **With the project open, in the Project tab's Properties section, click Project Information.**

   The Project Information dialog box opens.

2. **In the Calendar box, choose the calendar you want, and then click OK.**

   Project uses this calendar for the project's working and nonworking time (except where you've applied a special calendar to any resource or task).

Applying a calendar to a *resource* is even easier:

1. **In the Resource Sheet (in the View tab's Resource Views section, click Resource Sheet), on the right side of the table, click the resource's Base Calendar cell (the column heading might say "Base" if the column is narrow).**

   A down arrow appears on the right side of the cell.

2. **In the drop-down list, choose the calendar you want to apply.**

   Project uses that calendar whenever you assign that resource to tasks. (If you add exceptions or additional workweeks to the calendar specific to the resource, Project goes by the resource's calendar if it differs from the resource's base calendar.)

TIP　Resources start out using the calendar you apply to the project, unless you tell Project otherwise. If you want to define a resource's vacation time, for example, you make those changes in the resource's calendar: In the Project tab's Properties section, click Change Working Time. In the "For calendar" drop-down list, choose the resource's name. Now you can define the work weeks or exceptions for that resource. (Alternatively, if you double-click a resource's name in the Resource Sheet, the Resource Information dialog box opens. On the General tab, click Change Working Time. The Change Working Time dialog box opens right to that resource's calendar.)

Sometimes tasks need to run at specific times, like a planned outage that has to take place in the middle of the night. Although task calendars aren't that common, you *can* apply a calendar directly to a task. Here's how:

1. **Create the calendar you want to apply to the task (page 108).**

2. **In the table area of a task-oriented view like Gantt Chart, select the task(s) that require a special calendar, and then in the Task tab's Properties section, click Information.**

   If you select only one task, then the Task Information dialog box opens. If you select more than one task, then the Multiple Task Information dialog box opens instead. The fields in these two dialog boxes are identical.

3. **Click the Advanced tab and, in the Calendar drop-down list, choose the one you want to apply. Click OK to close the dialog box and apply the task calendar.**

The "Scheduling ignores resource calendars" checkbox is initially turned off, which means that Project schedules work only during working hours common to both the assigned resources and the task. If the task calendar and resource calendars for the assigned resources don't have any mutual work time, a message box warns you that the calendars don't jibe. You can change either the task calendar or the resource calendar to create some common time. Another approach is to schedule work by the task calendar only—by turning on the "Scheduling ignores resource calendars" checkbox. Project then assumes that the assigned resources work during the task's work time.

Identifying the Work to Be Done

When you organize a simple activity like seeing a movie with friends, you probably don't bother writing out the steps. You just call your friends, pick a movie, get tickets, and buy popcorn without a formal plan. But for more complex projects—like holding a fundraiser or launching a new product line—identifying the work involved is key to planning how and when to get it done. For example, you have to get all the prep work for the fundraiser done *before* the big day, or your event and the donations it generates will be a bust. And that new product may make a profit only if you get it on store shelves before Thanksgiving and keep costs below $100,000. In cases like these, delivery dates, costs, and other objectives are important.

That's where a WBS (*work breakdown structure*) comes in. Carving up the project's work into a hierarchy of progressively smaller chunks until you get to bite-sized pieces is the first step toward figuring out how and when everything will get done. If you're new to managing projects, don't panic—you've built a WBS before. The movie example in the previous paragraph is actually a simple WBS.

The structure of a WBS is much like the circulatory system in your body. You can think of the circulatory system itself as the entire project (its goal is to distribute blood throughout your body), and the smaller blood vessels as progressively smaller chunks of the overall work at each level (*summary tasks*). The hordes of tiny capillaries that deliver blood to every part of your body correspond to the individual tasks (called *work packages*) at the bottom of the WBS, which are the small chunks of work that you assign to people to complete the project.

This chapter begins with an overview of how to create a WBS that successfully communicates the work within a project, and how to tell when the WBS is broken down enough. The rest of the chapter helps you get your tasks and WBS into Microsoft Project so you can move on to constructing a project schedule as described in Chapter 7.

If you're working on a small, informal project, you can jump straight to this chapter's sections on creating tasks (page 131). If you and your team members love working in Microsoft Word, Outlook, and Excel, you can build task lists in any of those programs and transfer the results into Project. (When you copy an indented list of tasks from Word or Outlook, Project 2013 automatically transforms them into a hierarchy of summary tasks and subtasks.)

This chapter continues with how to organize tasks. You might start by creating summary tasks to structure low-level tasks into a WBS. Or you can change tasks' outline levels to fine-tune your WBS hierarchy. This chapter describes the steps for building a WBS from the top down in Project. Then you'll learn how to rearrange your task list, whether you want to insert, copy, move, or delete tasks. Finally, you'll learn how to add more detail to tasks, both in Word documents and in your Project file.

■ Breaking Down Work into Manageable Chunks

Knowing the high-level tasks that make up your project is important, but it's tough to estimate hours, line up resources, schedule work, or track progress when all you have are huge chunks like Build Bridge, Raise Money, and Hold Fundraising Race. You need to get much more specific about the work your project is going to take.

The point of a WBS is to break down the work into small enough pieces (called work packages) so that you can do the following:

- **Improve estimates.** Smaller tasks are not only less intimidating than big tasks, but they also make it much easier to figure out the type (and number) of people you need to perform each portion of work, how long it'll take, and how much it'll cost.

- **Keep the team focused.** Because the WBS spells out exactly what's needed to achieve the project's objectives, it acts as a checklist for the work on the project team's plate. It also gently guides team members *away* from doing things outside the project's scope.

- **Assign work to resources.** When work is broken down into discrete tasks, it's easier to identify the skills needed to complete the assignments, so the project manager can clearly determine who's responsible for what. Also, team members are more likely to understand their individual assignments, which makes them more productive and helps keep the project on track.

  On the other hand, don't go overboard by dissecting work into minuscule assignments. Productivity drops when team members keep switching to new assignments. In addition, smaller assignments could increase your temptation to micromanage. (The section "When Is Enough Enough" on page 129 describes how to choose the appropriate size for a work package.)

- **Keep the project on track.** Shorter tasks give you frequent checkpoints for tracking costs, effort, and completion dates. Moreover, if tasks have strayed off course, you can take corrective action before things get out of hand.

NOTE In the PMI project-management methodology, introduced briefly in Chapter 1, a WBS is the result of the scope-definition process. The starting point is a scope statement (page 34) in which you define what's within the boundaries of the project and, just as important, what *isn't*. For example, knowing whether the cleaning service you hire takes on teenagers' rooms could be essential to success. For many projects, especially those performed for government agencies, the WBS is a contractually binding document, making the correct inclusion and exclusion of work essential.

Like Goldilocks, you have to find the right size for the work packages—not too big, not too small, but just right. Large work packages can be so vague that team members aren't sure what they're supposed to do. Moreover, your team could reassure you for weeks that a large chunk of work is running smoothly, only to beg for a schedule-busting extension just when you thought they'd be done. Too-small work packages, on the other hand, carry all the disadvantages of micromanagement: excessive communication, unending status reporting, lost productivity, and so on. So how do you build a WBS with work packages that are just right?

Each project is unique, so don't expect the same approach to work for every project you manage. Identifying work can run the gamut from invigoratingly informal to scrupulously methodical, depending on whether you're planning a small project for a close-knit group or wrestling with a multi-year, multi-vendor project. (Whatever the project, a sure-fire shortcut is to borrow from existing sources, as described in the box on page 126.)

A WBS has only two types of elements: summary tasks and work packages. As you saw in Chapter 4, the lowest-level tasks in a WBS are work-package tasks—hunks of actual work that you assign to team members. Anything else in a WBS is simply some level of summary of that work, which can nest to as many levels as you need, as shown in Figure 6-1. As the following sections explain, you can build a WBS from whichever direction you prefer—top down, bottom up, or side to side.

Borrowing a WBS

Even with input from all the project's stakeholders, a blank WBS can be as daunting as the first blank page of that novel you want to write. Fortunately, several methods of developing a WBS let you learn—or even borrow outright—from the ideas and work of project managers who've walked this path before:

- **Similar projects.** If you know of a project that's similar to the one you're working on, the fastest way to create a WBS is to start with one that's already finished, whether it's stored in Project or another program. Be sure to check that project's final schedule and its closeout documents (page 505) to identify work that was added during that project's execution.

- **Experienced resources.** If people in your organization (or outside consultants and contractors, for that matter) have experience with your kind of project, they can help flesh out a WBS or identify work you've missed. Write up the WBS as best you can, and then ask those folks to provide feedback.

- **Microsoft Project templates.** When you install Project, you automatically get access to templates for different types of projects—everything from business-oriented plans to residential construction (page 86). Start with one of these templates to launch your WBS, and tweak it until it fits your project like a glove.

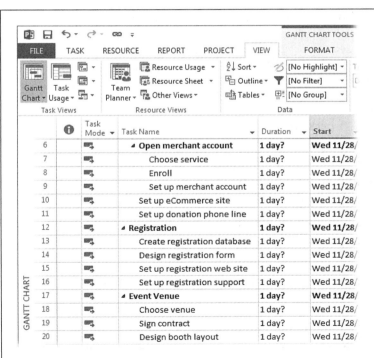

FIGURE 6-1

The organization of a WBS can vary, but the work packages usually remain the same. For example, you might track a project by phases (planning, acquisition, setup, and delivery) or by completed components (accounting system, registration, venue, food, and so on). As you build a WBS, you can change summary tasks and move work packages around.

TIP Don't forget to include project-initiation and project-management tasks in your WBS. Sure, some of your work goes on behind the scenes without obvious deliverables, but project management is essential to keeping projects within budget and on schedule. Besides, project management *does* have deliverables, since most customers and stakeholders sign off on project plans and want to see status reports, documents, and expenditures.

Identifying Work from the Top Down

As the name "work breakdown structure" implies, the most common way to build a WBS is to start with the entire project and break it down until you reach assignable work packages. (The box on page 127 describes how to show a top-down view of a WBS in Project.) The most common way to *decompose* (that is, break down) a project is by the deliverables that you want it to produce and the milestones you want it to attain. (See pages 33 and 73 for detailed definitions of *deliverables* and *milestones*.) This top-down approach is as easy as 1-2-3 (although sometimes, the levels might continue to 4, 5, and 6). If you work with a team of people, see the box on page 129 for hints on building the WBS without a computer.

POWER USERS' CLINIC

Displaying a WBS in a Hierarchy

The outline you see in Project's Gantt Chart view (see Figure 6-1) shows the levels of the WBS hierarchy, but you might prefer to view the WBS as a hierarchy similar to an organization chart, for example, when you're presenting the WBS to audiences unfamiliar with Project.

In Microsoft Project 2003, the Visio WBS Chart Wizard transformed a task list in Project into a tree diagram in Visio, but that tool went the way of the dodo bird in Project 2007.

Nowadays, you can use a *visual report* (page 485) to turn a task list into a tree. Although Project doesn't include a built-in visual report for displaying a WBS, you can head to this book's Missing CD page at *www.missingmanuals.com/cds* and download a visual report template for a WBS. This template uses only the Task Name, WBS, Work, and Duration fields, and sets up a tree structure. (See page 496 to learn how to generate a visual report from a template.) When you work with visual reports, you can specify which folders to search for customized templates, as described on page 498. Project then displays the templates in that folder in the visual report list.

If the WBS visual report isn't what you hoped for, a third-party WBS tool might be the answer. WBS Chart Pro (*www.criticaltools.com/wbsmain.htm*) is a popular Windows-based program for creating a WBS in a hierarchical format. It isn't free, but it does offer a 30-day limited trial. Alternatively, for a free online tool, go to *www.wbstool.com*.

Here are the steps for working on a WBS from the top down:

1. **Define the top level.**

   A project scope statement (page 34) usually lists a set of deliverables that the project's customer and other stakeholders expect to receive. One of the best ways to identify project work is to create high-level tasks for every deliverable. For example, if you're planning a big fundraiser, you might create summary tasks for donations, sponsorship, event registration, website, venue, food, and so on.

2. **Break down work into lower levels.**

   Once you've defined the top-level tasks, take another pass at decomposition by identifying intermediate deliverables and critical milestones, like completing the fundraiser's website or finalizing the contracts for all the vendors. For each intermediate deliverable and milestone, ask yourself what work it entails. For instance, the donation aspect of the fundraiser requires an accounting system, a merchant account for accepting payments, as well as an e-commerce website, so add lower-level summary tasks for each of those. Then simply repeat this process for each deliverable until you have work packages that you can assign to your people, third-party vendors, and other folks you hire.

3. **Verify the WBS.**

   Make sure all the items in the scope statement have corresponding work in the WBS. Look out for work packages that don't support the scope. Add missing summary tasks and work packages or remove those that don't belong. If you think of a deliverable that isn't in the scope statement, add the work to the WBS and revise the scope statement. (Keep in mind, though, that if you're doing projects for customers, you probably need their approval to change the scope statement.)

Developing a WBS from Start to Finish

Another way to slice and dice a project is to identify what you have to do from the beginning of the project until the end. This approach isn't all that different from the top-down decomposition described in the previous section, except that you decompose each branch of the tree until you reach its work packages. Then you go back to the top and work your way to the bottom of the next branch.

This variation on the top-down method is ideal when different teams or groups work on a project. Once you identify top-level tasks, you can assign their decomposition to the groups that do the work. (See page 137 for instructions on assembling WBSs from several groups.)

Assembling a WBS Without a Computer

Sticky notes and an empty wall or whiteboard might be the best solution for capturing tasks when a team is tossing around ideas. In fact, sticky notes offer enough advantages that you might use them even when WBS sessions proceed at a more leisurely pace.

Sticky notes are a democratic way to collect tasks when several people collaborate on a WBS. Team members can have their own pens and pads of sticky notes so no one is stuck being the sole scribe. Moreover, anyone can walk up to the sticky-note WBS and move summary tasks and work packages around. The hardest part of the sticky-note approach could be too *much* enthusiasm. If disagreements begin to break out over added or relocated tasks, then it's time to jump in and take over sticky note maintenance until things calm down.

Sticky notes are slick when you're searching for the ideal project organization. You can peel a note off the wall and move it to wherever you want without mouse clicks or keyboard shortcuts. And if you buy sticky flip charts, you can use them to represent summary tasks and attach sticky notes representing work packages to them.

One drawback to sticky notes is that they lose their stickiness over time. The safest approach is to record the contents of a sticky-note WBS in Project or another program before you leave the meeting room. If your room reservation has expired, fold the pages carefully and transport them to your office. For sticky notes stuck directly to the wall or whiteboard, post a polite note asking others to leave your masterpiece alone until you can come back and transcribe it—and snap a photo of it with your smartphone to be safe.

Constructing a WBS from the Bottom Up

Identifying work packages and then organizing them into summary tasks usually works only for small projects, but small projects occur often enough to make this a popular approach. Whether you write tasks on sticky notes or type them into Project, you and your team can identify every iota of work you can think of. Then you can head to a quiet spot to organize it into higher-level tasks (page 142).

When Is Enough Enough?

Most people can keep track of up to five things at once, although stress and age increase forgetfulness. If you're a juggler extraordinaire, you might be able to absorb eight items, but, beyond that, all bets are off. Between three and seven levels of summary tasks is ideal for a WBS that audiences can digest. For example, you can divide the entire project at the top level into phases like defining requirements, designing systems, and developing components. Then, within each phase, you can create lower levels to identify work in more detail.

For monster projects, though, you can maintain focus by breaking the behemoth into subprojects. If the overall project is a nationwide fundraising initiative, you can have a few levels of decomposition to reach a set of subprojects, each of which contributes major deliverables (corporate sponsorship initiative, individual donation campaign, bicycle race program, and so on). Then you can create a separate three- to seven-level WBS for each subproject. (If vendors or subcontractors are performing subprojects, ask them to develop the WBSs for their subprojects.)

TIP If you have a bunch of folks helping you create the WBS, see the box below for advice on working together effectively.

WORD TO THE WISE

Too Many Cooks Can Spoil the WBS

If you're a team of one but tend to argue with yourself, asking another person to act as a tiebreaker can save time and frustration. In most cases, however, the problem is too *many* people with their own convictions about the correct way to break down the project. You'll end up reorganizing your WBS, rearranging summary tasks, and revising work packages with little progress toward a completed WBS.

A better approach is to start with a small group of renaissance folks—people knowledgeable in one or more sections of the project and familiar with the overall goal. For example, you could work with the managers of each department involved in the project to craft the top two or three levels of the WBS. Then, you can assign the decomposition of the lowest summary tasks of this initial WBS to work teams that have experience with the type of work involved. For example, the event manager can handle the tasks related to race day, and the fundraising manager can identify the tasks involved in raising money.

As with almost any endeavor, the last 20 percent is the most difficult. The first several levels of the WBS might appear almost effortlessly, but then the decomposition can slow to a crawl as you try to decide whether something represents a work package or not. Here are some ideas for how to decide what constitutes a work package:

- **To estimate work.** Break tasks down into work packages that represent chunks of work you know how to estimate. That way, estimating the overall project is as easy as adding up estimates for all the chunks. For example, you may not have a clue how long it will take to deploy Windows 8 throughout your organization, but you know that it takes 3 hours to reconfigure one computer.

- **To track progress.** One rule of thumb for defining work packages is to keep task duration between 8 and 80 hours (in other words, anywhere from one workday to two work weeks). These durations give you early warning when tasks overrun their estimates. Another approach is to break work down into durations no longer than the time between status reports, so you're likely to have concrete progress to report. To use this method, you need a clear idea of how long various tasks take, so this approach works well only for projects similar to those you've performed in the past.

- **To maintain focus.** Guidelines aside, simply decompose work to the level of detail that you can handle. If you're a keep-things-simple type, you can keep your WBS at a high level and let team leaders manage details. On the other hand, if you can remember details the way a Starbucks barista remembers coffee orders, you can break down the work to your heart's content. Just remember that dividing work into portions that take less than a day can reduce productivity and morale (with certain exceptions, as discussed in the box on page 131).

GEM IN THE ROUGH

When Short Is Sweet

Most of the time, you don't want to break down your WBS into tasks that take less than a day. Most people can handle a task like sending out invitations without reporting back to their boss after they buy the postage stamps. But suppose your project's goal is replacing a mission-critical software system. When it's time to switch to the new system, you probably have only a few hours or even *minutes* to make the change. For a short, crucial period like that, you don't have time to manage a project schedule. All you need is a detailed checklist of steps each person needs to perform.

Fortunately, situations like this are few and far between. But here's an example of how the WBS for this type of project

might work: The months of work preparing for the changeover is broken into day- or week-long chunks. Then, the changeover work that has to be done over a single night (before the staff comes in the next morning) can be checklists in Word documents that describe what each person does. These checklists help you line up the people you need (because you won't have time to call them in at the last minute) and spot potential delays. If you create a single task in your project schedule called something like "Mission-critical changeover," you can attach all these Word documents to a note for that task (page 583) for easy reference.

■ Adding Tasks to Your Project File

Don't worry about getting tasks in the right order or giving them the correct structure when you add them to your Project file. You can add additional tasks as you think of them or rearrange tasks (page 144) anytime after you create them. This section shows you how to create different types of tasks in Project and bring in tasks you've documented in another program. To learn how to add summary tasks to your list, see the section "Inserting Summary Tasks" on page 143.

NOTE   If you have a handwritten WBS ready to go, flip to the section "Building a WBS from the Top Down" (page 145) to learn how to quickly enter your summary tasks and work packages.

Creating Tasks

In Project, the table on the left side of Gantt Chart view is the place to be for fast task entry. Here's how to add tasks in this view:

1. **If you're not already in Gantt Chart view, then on the ribbon's Task tab, click the bottom half of the Gantt Chart button (Figure 6-2), and then click Gantt Chart on the drop-down menu that appears.**

   Alternatively, on the View tab, click Gantt Chart, and then choose Gantt Chart.

2. **In the table on the left side of the view, click a blank Task Name cell, and
then type the name of the task. Press Enter or the down-arrow key to save
the task and move to the Task Name cell in the next row.**

   After you name your task (see the box on page 134 for task-naming tips) but
   before you press Enter or the down-arrow key, the task name isn't saved and
   most commands on Project's menus are inactive. So if Project menus are awash
   with grayed-out commands, that might be the culprit. To make most commands
   available, simply press Enter to save the current task.

3. **Repeat step 2 to create as many tasks as you want.**

   If the task mode isn't set the way you want, then in the status bar, click New Tasks and then choose the task mode you want. (See page 67 to learn more about switching task modes.)

That's all you have to do for the moment. Page 149 tells you how to insert a task between existing tasks in a task list.

TIP To edit a task's name, click its Task Name cell in the table area, and then click it *again* until the text-insertion point appears in the name. Then make your changes. You can also double-click the Task Name cell and edit the task name in the Task Information dialog box.

Another way to edit a task name is in the Entry bar, which appears between the ribbon and the current view—*if* you tell Project to display it: Choose File→Options; on the left side of the Project Options dialog box, choose Display, and then turn on the "Entry bar" checkbox. When you edit the text in the Entry bar, press Enter to save the changes or press Esc to cancel them.

Creating Milestones

In bygone days, a milestone was literally a stone that marked a distance of one mile from the last stone. In projects, milestones typically measure work progress, not distance. However, milestones can represent all kinds of progress: events (like receiving a payment), deliveries (like delivering a requirements document), or achievements (like completing a phase). And because milestones have no duration, you can add as many as you want without extending the project's finish date.

Creating tasks for milestones couldn't be easier:

1. **Select the task below where you want to insert a milestone by clicking anywhere in its row. In the Task tab's Insert section, click Milestone.**

   Project inserts a new task with the name "<New Milestone>" and sets its Duration cell to "0 days."

2. **Give the milestone a name.**

   The Task Name cell is selected automatically, so you can simply start typing the milestone's name. In the Gantt Chart timescale, the task's task bar is a black diamond to indicate its milestone status. Even better, because the milestone's duration is zero, you don't have to assign any resources to it.

Good Task Names

Like poetry, the best task names communicate the work they represent in a few well-chosen words. The better a task name conveys the work it represents, the less you have to worry about whether you're managing the work you're supposed to.

Most importantly, task names should be unique. Duplicate task names can cause problems when you generate reports, group tasks with similar characteristics using the Group command, or hide summary tasks. In those cases, duplicate task names might appear side by side with no indication of which is which. The simple fix is to add a word or two to make task names unique: "Set up registration website" and "Set up donation website," for example.

In addition, it's helpful to include a verb and a noun in task names—the action you want people to take and the result you expect. You can help your audience interpret tasks by differentiating summary tasks, work packages, and milestones with different grammatical forms:

- Because summary tasks represent a series of activities that span time, change the verbs for summary tasks to gerunds (verbs with "ing" at the end), like "Setting up registration."

- Using the present tense of a verb presents the task as a command or a directive, which is perfect for work packages. For example, "Write instructions" clearly identifies the type of work and which deliverable the work applies to. "Instructions" alone doesn't tell the assigned resources whether they are writing, editing, or posting the instructions to the website. Unambiguous verbs help clarify work.

- Milestones (which represent goals or states) typically have names that include the deliverable and its state, such as "Registration website design approved" or "Registration website operational."

TIP You can designate tasks with durations as milestones. To appoint any task to milestone-hood, double-click the task in the task table to open the Task Information dialog box. (Or select the task and then, on the Task tab, click Information.) Then select the Advanced tab and turn on the "Mark task as milestone" checkbox.

Here are several ways to put milestones to use:

- **Project start or project phase.** Using a milestone as the first task in a project or phase makes it easy to reschedule an entire project or a portion of one. For example, if your customer doesn't send in the deposit payment you require to begin work, you can delay the entire schedule by changing the date for the deposit-payment milestone. Once a project is under way, you can delay a section of it by modifying the date of the section's starting milestone.

- **Project completion.** By adding a milestone as the last task in a project schedule and linking the project's final tasks to it, you make it easy to see the current estimated finish date.

- **Decisions and approvals.** High-risk, big-budget projects often use feasibility studies to determine whether the project (and its funding) will continue. Milestone tasks are perfect for representing go/no-go decisions, approvals required before work can continue, or other decisions that affect the tasks that follow. For example, a go/no-go milestone might turn into the last milestone if the project is canceled, but it controls when successor tasks begin if the project gets the OK to continue. Milestones can also delay work that hinges on other types of decisions. For instance, the choice of programming language for your website determines who you hire, how the site is designed, and what code is written.

- **Progress.** Actual progress is stored within your project's work-package tasks, but you can gauge progress by adding milestones at significant points during the project, such as the completion of deliverables, be they documents, programs, tents, or cooked food. You can add a milestone after any summary task, for example, to show that all its work is complete.

- **Handoffs and deliveries.** A milestone can document when the responsibility for work transfers to a new group (for instance, when the registration website is turned over to the people who will record event registrations). Milestones also work for deliveries you expect from subcontractors or vendors. When you place an order for tents, tables, and chairs for an event, you don't manage the rental company employees who assemble the order and load the delivery truck; you simply plan for the goods to arrive on the day they're promised. Thus, all you need is a milestone for that delivery date.

> **TIP** Unlike the names of work tasks and summary tasks, *don't* include action verbs in milestone names. Nouns and adjectives (or verbs in past tense) are all you need to identify the deliverable and the state it's in: "Rental supplies delivered."

Creating Repeating Tasks

Some tasks occur on a regular schedule—for example, monthly meetings of the change control board, biweekly status meetings, or nightly backups of project files. Fortunately, you don't have to create each occurrence separately in Project. Instead, you can create a *recurring task*, and Project then takes care of creating individual tasks for each occurrence and a *summary task* for all the occurrences.

To create a recurring task, do the following:

1. **Click anywhere in the row *below* where you want the new recurring task. Then, in the Task tab's Insert section, click the Task down arrow, and then choose Recurring Task.**

   The Recurring Task Information dialog box appears.

2. **In the Task Name box, type the name for the recurring task, such as *Stakeholder Status Meeting*.**

   Project automatically sets the value in the Duration box to 1 day (abbreviated as 1d). This box sets the duration for one occurrence of this task—that is, one status meeting. If the occurrence takes less than a day, then in the Duration box, type the correct duration, such as *2h* to reflect a 2-hour meeting.

3. **In the "Recurrence pattern" section, specify the frequency of the task.**

   Choose from Daily, Weekly, Monthly, or Yearly. For each option, you see additional settings that let you add more detail about the timing, as illustrated in Figure 6-3. To schedule occurrences for more than one day a week, you can turn on the checkbox for each day of the week on which occurrences are scheduled, such as Monday and Thursday. Occurrences for other periods have different frequency settings. For example, when you select the Monthly option, you can specify when the tasks occur each month, such as on the 15th or on the first Monday.

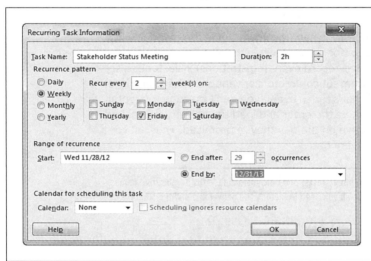

FIGURE 6-3

If the occurrences don't happen every single period, choose the number of periods, like 2 to schedule a meeting every 2 weeks. The "Range of recurrence" section lets you set the starting date and either the number of occurrences or the finish date.

4. **In the "Range of recurrence" section's Start box, choose the date you want the occurrences to begin.**

   Project initially sets this box to the project's start date.

5. **To specify when the occurrences end, select the "End after" option, and then type a number of occurrences. Alternatively, select the "End by" option if you want to set the end date.**

   Project initially selects the "End by" option and sets the date to the project's end date. With either option, you'll have to edit this recurring task later if the project runs longer than you anticipated—Project doesn't automatically extend recurring tasks to conform to a new end date.

6. **Click OK to close the dialog box and add the recurring task to the project, as shown in Figure 6-4.**

   In the Indicator column, a circular icon with arrows indicates that the task has multiple occurrences. To view the task's frequency and range, position your pointer over this icon.

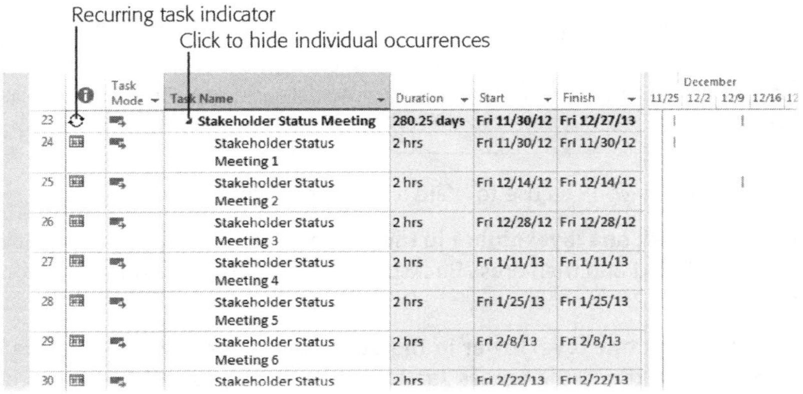

Recurring task indicator

Click to hide individual occurrences

FIGURE 6-4

A recurring task includes both individual occurrences and a summary task to shepherd all the occurrences into one spot. To hide the individual occurrences, click the outline symbol to the left of the summary task's name. (The outline symbol is a black triangle when the subtasks are visible, as shown here. It changes to a white right-pointing triangle when the occurrences are hidden.) To open the Recurring Task Information dialog box for a recurring task, double-click the summary task's name.

		Task Mode	Task Name	Duration	Start	Finish	December 11/25 12/2 12/9 12/16 12
23			**Stakeholder Status Meeting**	**280.25 days**	**Fri 11/30/12**	**Fri 12/27/13**	
24			Stakeholder Status Meeting 1	2 hrs	Fri 11/30/12	Fri 11/30/12	
25			Stakeholder Status Meeting 2	2 hrs	Fri 12/14/12	Fri 12/14/12	
26			Stakeholder Status Meeting 3	2 hrs	Fri 12/28/12	Fri 12/28/12	
27			Stakeholder Status Meeting 4	2 hrs	Fri 1/11/13	Fri 1/11/13	
28			Stakeholder Status Meeting 5	2 hrs	Fri 1/25/13	Fri 1/25/13	
29			Stakeholder Status Meeting 6	2 hrs	Fri 2/8/13	Fri 2/8/13	
30			Stakeholder Status	2 hrs	Fri 2/22/13	Fri 2/22/13	

The summary task for a recurring task is always set to be automatically scheduled. That's because it calculates the total duration, work, and other values of all the occurrences. The subtasks for the individual occurrences use whichever task mode (page 59) is currently selected. (See page 64 to learn how to set the task mode for new tasks or new projects. Page 67 describes how to change task modes as you work.)

NOTE Because recurring tasks are scheduled to take place on specific dates, occurrences that are automatically scheduled use Start No Earlier Than date constraints (page 188) to pin the occurrences' dates. Whether an occurrence is auto-scheduled or manually scheduled, you can edit an occurrence if, for example, you need to reschedule one status meeting because of a scheduling conflict.

Importing Tasks from Another Office Program

You and your teammates can also whip up a list of tasks in Microsoft Word, Outlook, or Excel. More of your team members are likely to be familiar with these programs than with Project, so documents, emails, and spreadsheets are a great way to get task info from them. If your team members prefer Excel, you can take advantage of the Excel templates that Microsoft provides. When you use the Project Task List Import Template or Microsoft Project Plan Import Export Template, the Excel worksheet is set up to make importing a snap. This section explains how to import tasks from Word, Outlook, and Excel.

■ IMPORTING TASKS FROM WORD OR OUTLOOK

In Word and Outlook, it's easy to indent, outdent, insert, move, and delete tasks. Then all you have to do is copy the text in either of those programs and paste it into Project. This section describes methods you can use to build your task list in Word or Outlook and then outlines the steps for getting those tasks into Project.

> **NOTE** Project is smart enough to transform the indents in Word documents and Outlook emails into outline levels in Project.

Here are techniques you can use to build a task list in Word or Outlook:

- **Promote a task one level higher in the outline.** Position the cursor to the left of the task's text and then press Backspace to, for example, change a task from level 3 to level 2.

- **Demote a task one level lower in the outline.** Position the cursor to the left of the task's text and then press Tab to, for example, push the task from level 3 down to level 4.

- **Move tasks.** Select any tasks you want to move, and then drag them to a new position. Or, use Ctrl+X and Ctrl+V (respectively) to cut and paste the tasks from one position to another. If need be, promote or demote the tasks to the correct level.

- **Delete tasks.** Select the task(s) you want to delete, and then press Delete or Ctrl+X.

- **Import Outlook tasks into Project.** If you create tasks in Outlook (in the Home tab's New section, click the down arrow next to New Items, and then choose Task on the drop-down menu), you can import them into Project. In Project, in the Task tab's Insert section, click the down arrow below Task, and then choose Import Outlook Tasks. In the Import Outlook Tasks dialog box that appears, turn on the checkboxes for the tasks you want to import, and then click OK. See page 560 for the full scoop on importing Outlook tasks into Project.

Once you have a task list in Word or Outlook, here's how to paste it into Project:

1. **Open the document in Word or the email in Outlook.**

2. **Select the tasks you want to paste into Project, as shown in Figure 6-5 (top), and then press Ctrl+C.**

3. **Switch over to Project and click the first blank Task Name cell where you want to paste the tasks; then press Ctrl+V.**

   Project inserts the task names into the Task Name cells and indents the tasks to the same levels they were at in the Word document or Outlook email, as shown in Figure 6-5 (bottom).

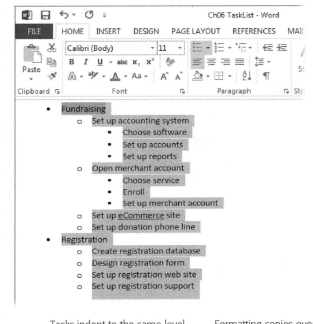

FIGURE 6-5

Top: Type each task name on a separate line in a Microsoft Word document. To make a line a subtask, select it and then press Tab. To promote an item to a higher level, position the cursor to the left of the task name's text, and then press Backspace.

Bottom: When you paste tasks into Project, it figures out the correct outline level and keeps the formatting from the Word document or Outlook email.

■ USING AN EXCEL TEMPLATE TO IMPORT DATA

If you have both Project and Excel installed on your computer, Excel includes two templates tailored to work perfectly with Project's Import Wizard. (The box on page 140 describes how to add these templates to your personal templates location in Office.) The columns in the Excel worksheets map to Project fields so task info slips into the right slots in your Project file:

- The **Microsoft Project Task List Import Template** is an Excel template with columns for basic task fields, perfect for importing your initial task list. It contains a Task_Table worksheet with columns for ID, Name, Duration, Start, Deadline, Resource Names, and Notes. It also includes an Info_Table worksheet that explains how to use the template. (You don't enter any information in that one.)

- The **Microsoft Project Plan Import Export Template** has four worksheets: Task_Table, Resource_Table, Assignment_Table, and Info_Table. The Task_ Table worksheet includes columns for ID, Name, Duration, Start, Finish, Predecessors, Outline Level, and Notes. The Resource_Table worksheet mimics the field you see in the Project Resource Sheet. The Assignment_Table includes columns for Task Name, Resource, Name, % Work Complete, Work, and Units.

If you don't see these two templates, the box below explains where to find them.

WORKAROUND WORKSHOP

Where Are My Templates?

If you don't see the Project Import and Project Export templates in Excel's Backstage view, don't be alarmed. For unknown reasons, the templates may not appear in your initial list of Excel templates. The easiest solution is to copy them to the folder where you keep your other templates—or to create a folder for your favorite templates and store them there.

If you're using the 64-bit version of Microsoft Office, you'll find the templates in *C:/Program Files/Microsoft Office/Templates/1033* (if you installed the 32-bit version of Office instead, they're in *C:/Program Files (x86)/Microsoft Office/Templates/1033*). Remember, Excel and Project must both be installed on your computer for the task-list and project-plan templates to appear.

In Windows Explorer, copy these files to your personal templates folder. For example, in Windows 7, when you create a user, Windows automatically creates a My Templates folder located at *C:/User/<your username>/My Documents/My Templates*, which is perfect for storing templates you use often. But, if you prefer, you can create your own folder for templates wherever you want.

Then you can tell Excel where to find your personal templates. Click File, and then choose Excel Options. On the left side of the Excel Options dialog box, click Save. In the "Default personal templates location" box, fill in the path to the folder that holds your templates, such as *C:\Users\<your username>\Documents\Custom Office Templates*.

The overall process is simple: First, create a new Excel file from either of the templates. Then give the Excel files to others to fill out. When your colleagues send the filled-in files back, import them into Project using the Import Wizard. Here are the steps:

1. **In Excel, click File→New.**

   Backstage view opens to the New page and displays available templates.

2. **If you stored the templates in your personal templates folder, then tell Excel where to find them.**

In Excel 2013, below the Search box, click Personal. Excel displays the Excel templates in the folder you designated as your default personal templates location, as described in the box on page 140.

In Excel 2010, click "Sample templates" to see built-in templates. If you stored the templates in your personal templates folder, below the Available Templates heading, click "My templates."

3. **Double-click the template you want to use.**

Excel creates a new workbook, which contains two worksheets. The Info_Table worksheet merely explains what the template can do, not how to fill it in.

The Microsoft Project Task List Import Template is ideal for building a task list because it's simple. However, you can also fill in task names and import your task list using the Microsoft Project Plan Import Export Template. (Page 209 describes the other things you can do with the project plan import template.)

4. **Click the Task_Table worksheet tab (at the bottom-left corner of the Excel window) to view the fields that the template contains.**

Be sure to tell your team members that they *don't* have to enter dates despite the presence of the Start and Finish columns. If tasks have critical finish dates, team members can enter them in the Deadline column.

5. **Choose File→Save. Navigate to the place or folder where you want to save the file.**

The Save As dialog box appears.

6. **In the "File name" box, type a filename, such as MyTaskListforImport, and then click Save.**

Excel automatically selects Excel Workbook in the "Save as type" drop-down list. If you want to save the workbook in a different format, click the down arrow in the "Save as type" box and then choose a format on the drop-down list.

7. **Distribute the file to team members, so they can open the file and enter data.**

The first row in the file displays Project field names, so people know which columns contain which fields. They don't have to fill in every cell; they should just fill in what they can. When team members finish entering data, they simply save the file and send it back to you.

> **NOTE** The Excel files based on these templates don't apply specific formatting to the columns, so whoever fills in the files must enter the values correctly (or you'll have to edit the values so Project can understand them). For example, duration is a length of time like 5d or 3w. If the values aren't valid, then the Project Import Wizard displays an error message (page 536).

8. **When you're ready to import the tasks that people sent you, in Project, choose File→Open, and then navigate to where you saved the filled-out Excel workbooks.**

   The Open dialog box is automatically set to look only for Project files, so you have to tell it which type of file you want to import. You'll do that in the next step.

9. **In the box to the right of the "File name" box, click the down arrow, and then choose the file format you want to import: Excel Workbook for Excel 2013 or Excel Workbook (*.xslx) in Excel 2010.**

   The Open dialog box shows only the files of the type you selected. So if the file you want is conspicuously absent, it might be a different format than you think.

10. **In the file list, double-click the name of the workbook file (or click its file-name, and then click Open).**

    The Import Wizard appears. Click Next to bypass the welcome screen, which does nothing but explain the process.

11. **On the "Import Wizard - Map" screen, keep the "New map" option selected and click Next. On the "Import Wizard - Import Mode" screen, select the "Append the data to the active project" option if you're going to import several files of tasks into the same project.**

    Appended data appears in the current Project table after the existing rows.

12. **On the "Import Wizard - Map Options" screen, turn on the Tasks checkbox and then click Next.**

    The "Import Wizard - Task Mapping" screen appears.

13. **Click Finish to import the Excel data into the Project file.**

    Because the mapping between Excel columns and Project fields is already done, Project takes care of the heavy lifting and imports the data.

NOTE   See page 540 to learn more about importing, exporting, and using these Excel templates.

■ Organizing Tasks

If you're in high gear churning out project tasks, you can gleefully insert, delete, and rearrange tasks in the WBS outline as you go—and the resulting WBS looks exactly the same as one methodically typed from the top down. The methods for adding, moving, and changing outline levels for tasks are the same whether you're creating or modifying a WBS. This section covers all the options from adjusting the outline of tasks to adding, removing, and rearranging tasks. If you're building a formal WBS, you'll also learn how to customize the WBS code format to your liking (or your company's standard).

Inserting Summary Tasks

Summary tasks help you plan, track, and manage project work, as described in the section "Breaking Down Work into Manageable Chunks" on page 124. If you entered all your WBS tasks into Project in one fell swoop, you can turn existing tasks into summary tasks by changing their outline level as described in the next section. But, if you want to insert a *new* summary task (in any Gantt Chart view), you can choose from the following three methods:

- **Insert a new summary task with a new subtask.** This method is perfect if you want to add an entirely new batch of work, so you need to insert a new summary task and a new subtask. Click a blank Task Name cell, and then, in the Task tab's Insert section, click Summary. Project selects the Task Name cell, which now contains the text "<New Summary Task>," as shown in Figure 6-6, so you can simply start typing to name the new summary task. Press Enter to move to the new subtask's Task Name cell. Type the name for the subtask and press Enter. Now you can move these tasks to another location (page 151), change their level in the outline (page 144), or insert additional subtasks (page 149).

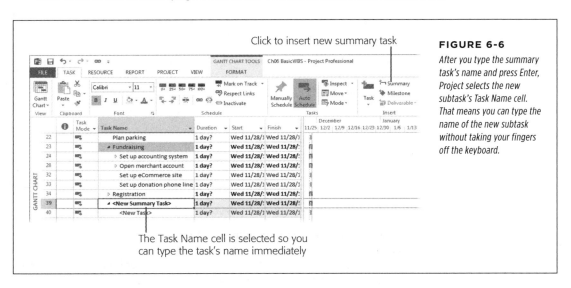

Click to insert new summary task

FIGURE 6-6

After you type the summary task's name and press Enter, Project selects the new subtask's Task Name cell. That means you can type the name of the new subtask without taking your fingers off the keyboard.

The Task Name cell is selected so you can type the task's name immediately

- **Insert a new summary task for selected subtasks.** If you want to summarize several existing tasks, the Summary command is still the answer. First, select tasks that you want as subtasks. Then, in the Task tab's Insert section, click Summary. Then type the name of the summary task and press Enter.

- **Insert a new task and make it a summary task.** If you want to insert several new summary tasks in the middle of your task list, the easiest approach is to insert regular tasks and then change them into summary tasks. Select the row below the new task and then, in the Task tab's Insert section, click the Task icon (the blue bar with a green + sign). In the Task Name cell, type the new summary task's name, and then press Enter. Reselect the new task and then either press Alt+Shift+left arrow or, in the Task tab's Schedule section, click Outdent Task (the green, left-pointing arrow) until the summary task is at the level you want.

Reorganizing the Task List Outline

Changing a task's level in the outline is easy, although the results depend on what type of task you modify and whether you move it lower or higher in the outline. You can use the following techniques to develop a WBS in any order. The table in Gantt Chart view indicates outline level in several ways, as shown in Figure 6-7. (The box on page 145 explains additional methods for choosing which tasks appear in this view.)

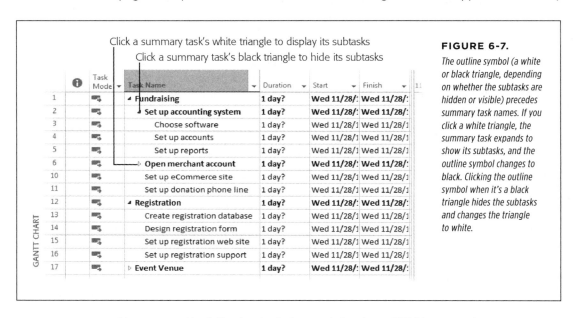

FIGURE 6-7.

The outline symbol (a white or black triangle, depending on whether the subtasks are hidden or visible) precedes summary task names. If you click a white triangle, the summary task expands to show its subtasks, and the outline symbol changes to black. Clicking the outline symbol when it's a black triangle hides the subtasks and changes the triangle to white.

You can use the following techniques to develop a WBS in any order:

- **Make a summary task into a nonsummary task.** Select the first subtask for the summary task, and then either press Alt+Shift+left arrow or, in the Task tab's Schedule section, click Outdent Task (the green, left-pointing arrow). When you outdent the subtask, the summary task turns into a regular task, and its summary-task triangle disappears.

- **Elevate a summary task to a higher level.** Select the summary task, and then either press Alt+Shift+left arrow or, in the Task tab's Schedule section, click Outdent Task (the green, left-pointing arrow).

- **Indent a task to the next lower level.** If you add several tasks in a row, they all start out at the same level. To turn them into summary tasks and subtasks, you indent the subtasks. To do that, select the soon-to-be subtask(s), and then press

Alt+Shift+right arrow or, in the Task tab's Schedule section, click Indent Task (the green, right-pointing arrow). If the task was at the same level as the task above it, then the task indents to the next-lower level in the outline, while the task above it turns into a summary task. If the task you indented was at a higher level than the task above it, the task above doesn't become a summary task.

TIP To select several adjacent tasks, click the first task's ID cell and then Shift-click the last task's ID cell. You can also drag over the ID cells of the tasks you want to select. To select several nonadjacent tasks, Ctrl-click the ID cell of each task.

- **Elevate a subtask to the next higher level.** Moving a task higher in the outline comes in handy when you want to disconnect a task from its summary task (for example, when you want to delete a summary task without deleting its subtasks). Select the subtask(s), and then press Alt+Shift+left arrow or, in the Task tab's Schedule section, click Outdent Task. If the outdented task was one of several at the same level, it turns into a summary task.

- **Indent or outdent several tasks at once.** If you want to indent or outdent several tasks, select them all, and then use the techniques in this section. To select adjoining tasks in the outline, drag across them. To select several separate tasks, Ctrl-click each one.

UP TO SPEED

Hiding and Showing Tasks in the Outline

As you work on one part of the WBS, tasks in other parts of the project might get in your way. Or your stakeholder team might be interested in only the first few levels of the WBS. Regardless of the reason, you can choose which tasks and subtasks to show or hide at any time. Here are several techniques for displaying only the tasks you want to see:

- **To display only non-summary tasks** (work packages), in the Gantt Chart Tools | Format tab's Show/Hide section, turn off the Summary Tasks checkbox. If you want to see the outline level for each task, then in that same section, turn on the Outline Number checkbox.

- **To display summary tasks,** in the Format tab's Show/Hide section, turn on the Summary Tasks checkbox.

- **To hide or show subtasks for a specific summary task,** click the outline symbol to the left of the summary task's name. You can also select the summary task in the outline and then, in the View tab's Data section, choose Outline→"Show Subtasks or Outline"→Hide Subtasks.

- **To show all tasks down to a specific outline level,** in the View tab's Data section, click Outline and then, from the drop-down list, choose the lowest level you want to display. For example, if you want to view the top three levels of the WBS, choose Level 3.

- **To display all the tasks in the project,** in the View tab's Data section, choose Outline→All Subtasks.

Building a WBS from the Top Down

Your WBS may not start out in Project—maybe you scribbled it on a whiteboard, scrawled it on sticky notes pasted to flip charts, or it's just rattling around in your head. Regardless of where your ideas are, you can make short work of getting them into Project. Now that you're familiar with outlining tasks (described in the previous section), you can quickly build your WBS in Project from the top down. Because Project creates each new task at the same outline level as the previous task, this approach keeps indenting and outdenting to a minimum.

For maximum efficiency, when you flesh out a lowest-level summary task, insert as many rows as there are work packages for that summary task, and then type the names of the work packages in the Task Name cells. The following steps show you exactly how to work your way down a WBS one level at a time:

1. **Create a new blank file (page 84).**

   Gantt Chart view appears with the Entry table on the left and the Gantt Chart timescale on the right. (If you don't see Gantt Chart view, in the Task tab's View section, click Gantt Chart.)

2. **If you don't see a WBS column in the Entry table, right-click the Task Name heading and, from the shortcut menu, choose Insert Column.**

   Project inserts a new column to the left of the Task Name column with "[Type Column Name]" in the heading cell.

3. **Type WBS, and then press Enter.**

   You could also scroll in the drop-down list that appears, as shown in Figure 6-8, and then click WBS, but in this case, typing is quicker.

> **NOTE** The WBS code format that Project uses out of the box is a number at each level, with levels separated by periods. If your organization has a custom WBS format, you can set up your own WBS code (see page 157).

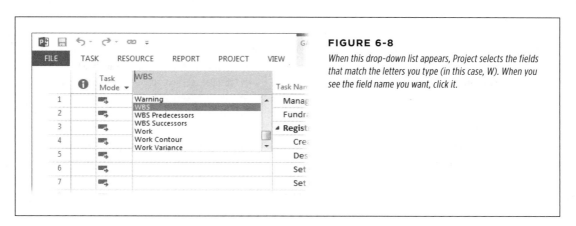

FIGURE 6-8

When this drop-down list appears, Project selects the fields that match the letters you type (in this case, W). When you see the field name you want, click it.

4. **In the Entry table, click the first Task Name cell, type the name of the summary task, and then press Enter.**

   Project selects the Task Name cell in the next row, so you're ready to enter the next task.

NOTE You don't have to create a top-level task for the overall project. Behind the scenes, Project has a *project summary task* that sits in the exalted position of Row 0 and rolls up the values for all the other tasks in the schedule. To display the project summary task, in the Gantt Chart Tools | Format tab's Show/Hide section, turn on the Project Summary Task checkbox. To *always* show project summary tasks for your projects, click File→Options. On the left side of the Project Options dialog box, click Advanced. Finally, scroll to the "Display options for this project" section, and then, in the "Display options for this project" box, choose All New Projects. Then turn on the "Show project summary task" checkbox. By doing that, the project summary task will appear automatically for every new project you create. You can hide the project summary task at any time by turning off the Project Summary Task checkbox on the Gantt Chart Tools | Format tab.

5. **Repeat step 4 for each top-level task in the WBS.**

   Project creates the next task at the same level in the WBS outline as the previous task, so you're ready to enter the next top-level task. As you'll see shortly, this behavior makes it easy to add several tasks at the same level, no matter which level of the WBS you're creating. Once the top-level tasks are in place, you're ready to add tasks at the next level of the WBS.

6. **To add subtasks to a summary task, click the Task Name cell immediately below the summary task you're fleshing out, and then press the Insert key on your keyboard as many times as there are subtasks, as demonstrated in Figure 6-9.**

   This step is the secret to speedy outlining because it works in the same way at every level of the WBS: second-level, third-level, and lowest-level summary tasks. When you insert rows for a lowest-level summary task, insert as many rows as there are work packages for that summary task. Then you can type away and fill them all in quickly.

FIGURE 6-9

You can insert blank task rows by clicking anywhere in the row below the summary task and pressing the Insert key. But if you click the Task Name cell in the row below the summary task, then when you press Insert, the blank task's Task Name cell becomes the active cell—ready for you to type the name of the first subtask.

7. **With the top blank Task Name cell beckoning you, type the name of the subtask, and then press Enter to save the task.**

Pressing Enter moves the active cell to the next Task Name cell. However, the first subtask isn't at the right level—it's still at the same level as the summary task.

8. **To indent the subtask, press the up-arrow key, and then press Alt+Shift+right arrow or, in the Task tab's Schedule section, click Indent Task (the green, right-pointing arrow).**

Project indents the subtask and indicates its subordinate position in two ways: with a WBS number and a summary-task outline symbol—both shown in Figure 6-10.

9. **Press the down-arrow key to move to the next Task Name cell, type the name, and then press Enter.**

Because the first subtask now is at the correct level, the remaining subtasks come in at the right level for their summary task.

10. **Repeat steps 6–9 for every summary task in the WBS, ultimately filling in each level of the WBS.**

Your initial draft of the WBS is complete!

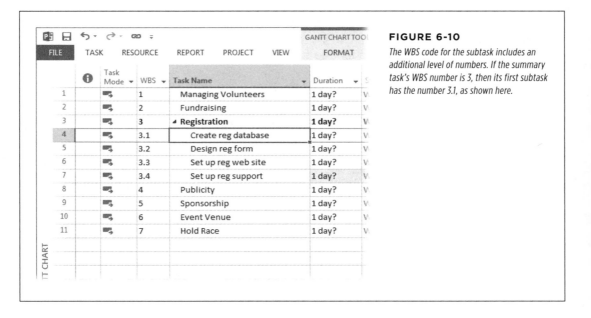

FIGURE 6-10

The WBS code for the subtask includes an additional level of numbers. If the summary task's WBS number is 3, then its first subtask has the number 3.1, as shown here.

Rearranging Tasks

You can organize tasks as you create them, or come back later and change their order. Summary tasks, work-package tasks, milestones, and repeating tasks all respond to Project's organizational techniques. The following sections describe different ways you can arrange tasks in your Project file.

■ INSERTING ADDITIONAL TASKS

Sometimes your project planning uncovers more work than you originally estimated, and you need to add tasks to your existing list. Other times, you might decide to change the way you summarize work or to decompose work further, which means creating new summary tasks.

Here's how to insert tasks in an existing list:

- **Insert a summary task.** Click the row below where you want the new summary task to go and then, in the Task tab's Insert section, click Summary. Project inserts the new summary task at the same outline level as the task above it, fills in the Task Name cell with the text "<New Summary Task>," and turns the task below it into its first subtask. Type the new summary task's name, and then press Enter to save it.

- **Insert a new summary task for several existing tasks.** First, select the soon-to-be subtasks. Then, in the Task tab's Insert section, click Summary. Project inserts the new summary task *and* transforms all the selected tasks into subtasks.

- **Insert a task at any level.** To insert a new task between two existing ones, click the lower of the two existing task rows, and then press the Insert key. In the Task Name cell of the blank task row that appears, type the new task's name, and then press Enter. If the task isn't at the correct outline level, press Alt+Shift+right arrow or Alt+Shift+left arrow to indent or outdent it, respectively.

- **Insert a new subtask.** In the row below an existing subtask, click the Task Name cell, and then press the Insert key. A new, blank task row appears at the same outline level as the existing subtask.

■ COPYING TASKS

If your project plan includes similar tasks in several areas of the project, it's often easier to create a set of tasks and copy them to each place you use them. Or, if you have a task that already has values you want in a new task (such as hours, assigned resources, and deadlines), you can copy it so that the new task includes the same values. (You should, of course, rename the new, copied task to avoid confusion; the box on page 151 explains a shortcut for renaming tasks.) You can copy just task names or entire tasks.

Here are different methods for copying tasks and when to use each one:

- **Copy task names.** When you copy only task name cells, be sure to paste them only into *blank* rows, so you create new tasks. If you paste the task names into rows that contain values, you'll overwrite the current contents of the task name cells instead of creating new tasks. To copy one or more task names, select the Task Name cells you want to copy and then press Ctrl+C (or, in the Task tab's Clipboard section, click Copy). Next, click the first blank Task Name cell, and then press Ctrl+V (or, on the Task tab, click Paste).

> **TIP** To select several adjacent Task Name cells, click the first one and then Shift-click the last one. (You can also drag over the Task Name cells you want to select.) To select several nonadjacent Task Name cells, Ctrl-click each one you want to select.

- **Repeat a set of task names.** Say you have a set of task names that you want to repeat several times, such as the steps for setting up several websites for a project. In this case, Project's *fill handle* is just the ticket. The fill handle is the little green box at the lower right of a selected cell (or range of cells); it lets you copy the content of cells to adjacent cells in your task list. First, select the Task Name cells you want to copy. Then position your mouse pointer over the lower-right corner of the last Task Name cell; you can tell when the pointer is over the fill handle because the pointer turns into a + sign, as shown in Figure 6-11 (left). Then drag the fill handle over the Task Name cells into which you want to copy the selected names. When you let go of the mouse, Project repeats the existing task names in the blank Task Name cells you dragged over, as shown in Figure 6-11 (right).

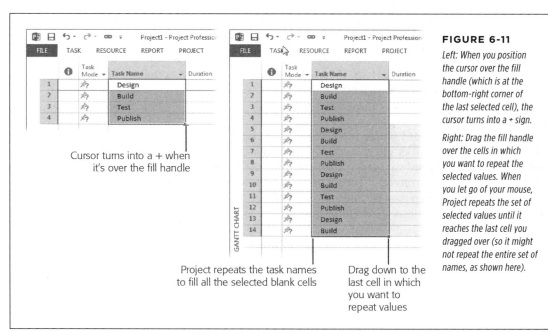

FIGURE 6-11

Left: When you position the cursor over the fill handle (which is at the bottom-right corner of the last selected cell), the cursor turns into a + sign.

Right: Drag the fill handle over the cells in which you want to repeat the selected values. When you let go of your mouse, Project repeats the set of selected values until it reaches the last cell you dragged over (so it might not repeat the entire set of names, as shown here).

Cursor turns into a + when it's over the fill handle

Project repeats the task names to fill all the selected blank cells

Drag down to the last cell in which you want to repeat values

- **Copy whole tasks.** When you copy and paste an *entire* task, Project inserts the task into new rows in the task list, so you don't need blank rows to paste into. First, select the entire task you want to copy by clicking its ID cell. (If you want to select more than one task, then drag the pointer across adjacent task ID cells. You can also Shift-click the first and last ID cells to select adjacent tasks, or Ctrl-click each task's ID cell to select nonadjacent tasks.) Then press Ctrl+C or, in the Task tab's Clipboard section, click Copy. Finally, click the ID cell of the task above which you want to insert the copied tasks, and then press Ctrl+V (or, on the Task tab, click Paste).

WORKAROUND WORKSHOP

Renaming Copied Task Names

If you work hard to keep task names unique, copying tasks raises an issue: The copied tasks have the same names as the originals. Don't despair—the Replace command can come to the rescue and replace the adjectives for each phase or deliverable. Here's how it works:

1. Select the tasks you want to rename that use the same adjectives or qualifiers. For example, say you've copied tasks called "Design reg website," "Code reg website," and "Test reg website," and you want to change the word "reg" to "fundraising."

2. To open the Replace dialog box, press Ctrl+H or, in the Task tab's Editing section, click the down arrow next to the Find button (it looks like a pair of binoculars), and then choose Replace.

3. In the Replace dialog box, be sure that the Search box is set to Down, indicating that Project will begin at the

first selected task and search in *all* subsequent tasks in the list.

4. In the "Find what" box, type the word(s) you want to replace—*reg* in this example.

5. In the "Replace with" box, type the new term for the copied tasks, for instance, *fundraising* to change the name from "Design reg website" to "Design fundraising website."

6. Click Replace to replace the first occurrence of the term. Continue to click Replace once for each selected task. To skip an occurrence, click Find Next.

   It's tempting to click Replace All, but don't do it. Otherwise, Project will replace that word in *all* tasks in the schedule—including the ones you want to leave as is.

■ MOVING TASKS

If you decide that tasks belong in another section of the WBS, you can move them in the Project task list. For example, you might move a subtask to a different summary task to change how you decompose work. Or you can move a subtask to a position before or after another subtask so the subtasks are in the sequence they'll occur.

To move one or more tasks, do the following:

1. **In Gantt Chart view's table area, select the entire task you want to copy by clicking its *ID cell*, as shown in Figure 6-12.**

   If you want to select more than one task, drag the pointer across adjacent task ID cells. If you want to select nonadjacent tasks, then Ctrl-click each task's ID cell.

When it's in the ID column, the pointer turns into a four-headed arrow to indicate that you can move the selected task(s).

ID column

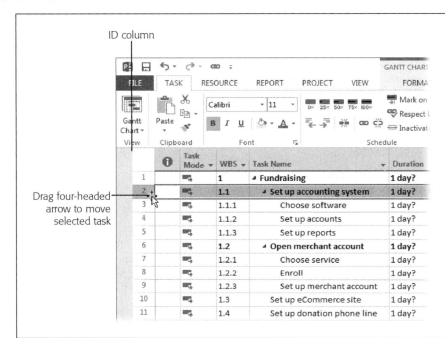

Drag four-headed arrow to move selected task

FIGURE 6-12

Unlike other columns, the ID column doesn't have any text in its column heading; it's the first column in the table area. The ID numbers are a single sequence of integers, unlike the WBS codes, which can have multi-level values of numbers, letters, or both (page 157) to correspond to the outline levels of your tasks. When the four-headed arrow shown here appears, you can drag the selected task(s) to a new spot in the task list.

2. **Drag the task(s) to the new location.**

   As you drag, a gray line appears in the border between rows, showing where the task(s) will end up when you release the mouse button.

TIP   Project used to scroll like lightning, which made dragging tasks accurately beyond the visible rows all but impossible. Although Project's scrolling has slowed to a manageable pace, cutting and pasting tasks is still a more convenient way to move them when their new location is several pages away. To cut and paste tasks, select the tasks, and then press Ctrl+X. Then select the row below where you want to paste them, and then press Ctrl+V.

---

3. **If the task isn't at the correct outline level, press Alt+Shift+right arrow or Alt+Shift+left arrow to indent or outdent the task, respectively.**

   You can also click Indent Task or Outdent Task in the Task tab's Schedule section (the icons with the green left and right arrows) to change the outline level.

■ **DELETING TASKS**

Although work rarely disappears in real life, you may sometimes need to delete tasks in Project. Perhaps you've decided to decompose work differently, or the customer has chosen to reduce the project's scope to fit the budget.

TIP See page 364 to learn how to inactivate tasks instead of deleting them. Inactivating tasks has several advantages: The tasks remain in your plan for historical purposes, and they're easy to reactivate if the stakeholders change their mind about what they want.

Here are the various ways to delete tasks:

- **Delete a subtask.** Select the subtask by clicking the row's ID number, and then press Delete.

TIP If you press Delete when an automatically scheduled Task Name cell is selected, Project displays an indicator (a box containing an X) to the left of that cell. You can click the indicator's down arrow and select the "Delete the task name" option to delete the name or the "Delete the task" option to delete the *whole* task. To hide the delete indicator, choose File→Options. On the left side of the Project Options dialog box, choose Display, and then turn off the "Deletions in the Name columns" checkbox.

- **Delete a summary task and all its subtasks.** To delete a summary task and all its subtasks, select the summary task's ID cell, and then press Delete, or right-click anywhere in the summary task's row and then choose Delete Task from the shortcut menu.

- **Delete a summary task but not its subtasks.** If you're moving subtasks to a different summary task, relocate the subtasks to their new home and then delete the summary task as described in the previous bullet point. If you're not sure where you want the orphaned subtasks to end up, simply change them to the same outline level as the summary task *before* deleting the summary task. To do that, select the subtasks and then press Alt+Shift+left arrow to move them to the same outline level as their summary task. Then select their former summary task by clicking its ID cell and press Delete.

TIP If you want to delete other aspects of a task, the Clear command is at your service. In the Task tab's Editing section, click the down arrow to the right of the Clear button and then choose what you want to delete from the drop-down menu: hyperlinks, notes, or formatting. Choose Clear All to clear all three types of elements. The Entire Row option clears *all* the cells in the row, including the task name, leaving you with a blank row.

■ Documenting Task Details

Providing team members with clear guidance about the work they need to perform and the results you expect is important, but task names aren't the place to get into detail. You need a place to store all the details that explain how to perform tasks completely and correctly. Fortunately, you don't have to worry about keeping track of lots of loose documents: You can link external documents to tasks or add details to notes attached to tasks. This section describes both options.

Documenting Work Details in Word

Ideally, a work-package document describes the work to perform, how to know when it's done, and how to tell whether it's done right. A work package for creating an online-donation mechanism might include the steps for designing the online form, linking to the merchant account, and sending a confirmation. The document could specify the information the donor has to provide and the methods of payments to accept. The document could also describe the desired results, including the transactions processed and the notifications that are sent for both successful and rejected transactions.

After you create work-package documents that spell out the details of tasks (the box on page 155 describes one way to simplify this chore), you're likely to refer to those documents as you work on your Project schedule. There's no need to open them by hand or to try to remember where they are. Instead, you can insert a hyperlink from a task in the Project schedule to the corresponding work-package document. With the hyperlink in place, opening the work-package document is a simple matter of a quick click in Project.

To create a hyperlink in a Project task, do the following:

1. **In Project, right-click anywhere in the row for the task you want to link to a work-package document, and then choose Hyperlink from the shortcut menu.**

   The Insert Hyperlink dialog box appears.

2. **In the "Link to" column, click "Existing File or Web Page" (if it's not already selected).**

   Selecting this option is how you tell Project that you want to link to a document that's already stored on your computer.

3. **Use the options in the center of the dialog box to navigate to the folder that contains the work-package document, and then click the name of the work-package file.**

   The "Look in" box shows the name of the current folder, and the Address box displays the current filename.

4. **Click OK.**

   In the Indicators column (its heading is an i in a blue circle), a hyperlink icon appears, as shown in Figure 6-13.

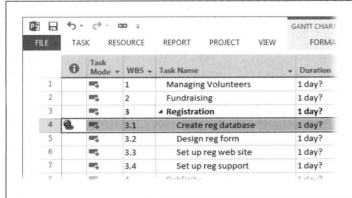

FIGURE 6-13

The hyperlink icon looks like a globe with a link of chain, a not-so-subtle commentary that hyperlinks connect the world. If the Indicators column isn't visible, then right-click a column heading in the table and choose Insert Column on the shortcut menu. In the Field Name drop-down list that appears, choose Indicators.

5. **To access a hyperlinked file, simply click the hyperlink icon in the Indicator cell.**

   The program associated with the file launches and opens the file.

Creating a Reusable Work Package

Even small projects require a multitude of work-package documents. You can speed up your work by creating a Word template for work packages that's as basic or as fancy as your knowledge of Word. That way, you create a new document from the template and have everything labeled and ready for you to fill in. For example, you might set up a basic work-package template with the following information:

- **WBS number.** This is the WBS number that Project assigned to the task in your project schedule.

- **Work-package name.** The task name from the Project schedule.

- **Description of work.** You can use paragraphs or bullet points and provide as much detail as you need to ensure success. If you know an experienced resource is going to

do the work, the document can be brief. For trainees, on the other hand, you can provide detailed checklists of steps or the name of the person who can mentor them.

- **Result.** Describe the final state when the work is done, as well as how to verify that it was done correctly. In a work package for creating a form, for example, you might include who needs to receive the completed form and a list of valid values for each field.

- **Reference materials.** Projects use many types of documents to specify deliverables: requirements, specifications, blueprints, and so on. If other detailed documentation exists, list where to find those documents, like the project notebook or the folder on the network drive.

Adding Details in Task Notes

Project can store supplementary information right with the tasks in your Project file in the form of *notes*. The downside to this approach is that your team members need to be able to open the Project file (or a copy of it) to view the details.

To attach a note to a task, follow these steps:

1. **In a task-oriented view (such as Gantt Chart view or Task Usage view), right-click anywhere in the task's row and then choose Notes from the shortcut menu.**

   The Task Information dialog box opens to the Notes tab.

2. **In the Notes box, type the details of the task.**

   The toolbar within the Notes box includes buttons for changing the font, setting the justification, creating bulleted lists, and inserting objects from another program (like an Excel spreadsheet, an email message, or a specifications document).

3. **When you're done writing, click OK.**

   A notepad icon appears in the task's Indicators cell. To see the beginning of the note (as in Figure 6-14), position your pointer over this icon. To see the entire note, double-click this icon; Project opens the Task Information dialog box to the Notes tab.

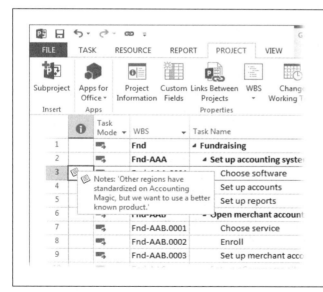

FIGURE 6-14

Once you add a note to a task, the task's Indicator cell displays an icon that looks like a sticky note. To see a preview of the note (like the one shown here), put your pointer over the icon.

■ Setting Up a Custom WBS Code

The WBS codes built into Project are simple outline codes with a number for each level in the outline hierarchy. For instance, a WBS code of 2.1.3 might represent the second phase of the project, the first summary task in that phase, and the third work package for that summary task. If your organization uses custom codes, you can build a tailored numbering system—called a *code mask*—to specify each level of your WBS code. For example, if you use abbreviations for phases, numbers for summary tasks, and letters for work packages, a customized WBS for the design phase of a project might look like this: Dsn.1.a.

To define a custom WBS code, follow these steps:

1. **On the Project tab, click WBS→Define Code.**

   The WBS Code Definition dialog box appears. Without a custom WBS code, Project automatically assigns WBS codes using numbers for each outline level with a period as a separator. (The fields in this dialog box don't show this out-of-the-box format. The fields remain empty unless you specify a custom scheme for your WBS codes.)

NOTE   If you assemble several projects into a single master project (page 516), you can make WBS codes unique for each project, even if they use the same code mask. If you work with multiple projects, set up the code mask for a new project before you get too deep into defining the project's tasks. That way you don't have to renumber all the tasks later. In the WBS Code Definition dialog box's Project Code Prefix field, type a prefix for the current project, like "Colo." Project then inserts this prefix at the beginning of the WBS codes for all the tasks in that project; for instance, Colo.1.4.1.

---

2. **In the dialog box's "Code mask" section, in the first Sequence cell, choose the type of characters you want to use for the top level of the hierarchy, as shown in Figure 6-15.**

   You can choose from Numbers (ordered), Uppercase Letters (ordered), Lowercase Letters (ordered), and—for the most flexible coding—Characters (unordered). With ordered numbers and letters, Project automatically increments the numbers or letters as you add tasks to the WBS, proceeding, for example, from 1.1 to 1.2. to 1.3.

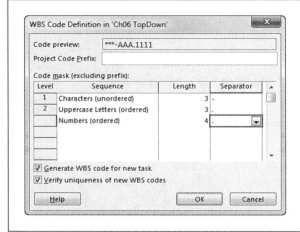

FIGURE 6-15

As you specify the code mask for each level, the "Code preview" field at the top of the dialog box displays a sample of your new WBS code. The choices for characters, length, and separators are limited. If you use unordered characters, you have to type the characters you want for each code, such as Reg.1, Pub.3, or Acc.7, in each summary task's WBS cell.

3. **In the first Length cell, choose a number (from 1 to 10) for the length of the top level's mask.**

   Project initially selects Any here, which means the entry for the level can be of any length. If the level uses a number, then Project increments the number beginning at 1 and continuing to 10, 100, or 1,000, if necessary. If the level uses letters, then you can type a code of any number of characters at that level.

   Choosing a number limits the entry to between one character and the length you specify. For example, if you limit a numeric entry to one character, Project cycles through the numbers 1 through 9, moves to 0, and then repeats.

4. **In the first Separator cell, choose the character that separates the top level from the next level.**

   Your only choices for separators are periods (.), minus signs (–), plus signs (+), or slashes (/).

5. **Repeat steps 2–4 for each additional level of the code mask.**

   A WBS code can be as long as 255 characters, so you can specify dozens of levels in a code mask. But as you learned on page 129, limiting the number of WBS levels makes the schedule (and WBS codes) easier to comprehend.

6. **After you've defined all the levels in the code mask, be sure that the "Generate WBS code for new task" checkbox is turned on so Project will automatically assign a WBS code to new tasks you create. Click OK, and then review the refreshed WBS codes in the task list, as shown in Figure 6-16.**

The only time you might want to turn this checkbox off is when you plan to renumber all the WBS codes after you've organized your tasks and don't want to be distracted by the interim codes that Project assigns.

To ensure that you don't create any duplicate WBS codes, keep the "Verify uniqueness of new WBS codes" checkbox turned on, too. Although Project adds WBS codes to tasks when the "Generate WBS code for new task" checkbox is turned on, you might type some WBS codes manually, and that can lead to duplicate values. The only time you might turn off the "Verify uniqueness of new WBS codes" checkbox is if you're planning to renumber tasks later and you get tired of the warnings Project displays. As the box on page 160 explains, you can renumber the WBS codes for tasks to correct or reorder your project.

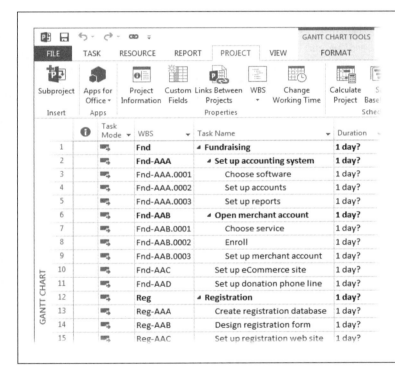

FIGURE 6-16

When you click OK, Project automatically applies the new code mask to all the tasks in the schedule. If you use unordered characters in your WBS, then you need to edit the WBS value for each task using unordered characters to specify the code for that part of the WBS, such as "Fnd" and "Reg" in this example.

7. **If the WBS column isn't visible in the current view, add it so you can verify that the code is set up the way you want.**

   Right-click the Task Name heading and, from the shortcut menu, choose Insert Column. In the new column's heading cell, type *WBS* and then press Enter.

Congratulations! You've customized your WBS codes.

Renumbering Task WBS Codes

When you customize WBS codes, the WBS Code Definition dialog box's "Generate WBS code for new task" checkbox tells Project to automatically assign WBS codes to new tasks you create, whether you insert tasks within the outline or add tasks at the end. With this checkbox turned on, as soon as you press Enter to save a new task, the WBS code pops into the WBS cell, maintaining the sequence you've defined. If you rearrange and re-outline your tasks, your WBS sequence can turn into a mess.

The alternative is to turn *off* this checkbox, and then, after a heated session of adding or modifying the task order, renumber the WBS codes all at once. Fortunately, that's pretty easy to do. When your tasks are organized the way you want them, do the following to renumber the tasks' WBS codes:

1. If you want to renumber only some of the tasks in the Project file, select them.

2. On the Project tab, click WBS→Renumber.

3. If you selected tasks, in the WBS Renumber dialog box, keep the "Selected tasks" option selected. To renumber the whole project, select the "Entire project" option instead. (If you didn't select tasks, Project automatically selects the "Entire project" option.)

4. Click OK. Project reapplies the WBS code scheme to the tasks, alphabetizing ordered letters and incrementing ordered numbers.

When you start to build other documents that reference your WBS codes (like work-package Word files), you don't want Project to change the existing codes. That's another time to turn off the "Generate WBS code for new task" checkbox. Before you type in new WBS codes manually, make sure the WBS Code Definition dialog box's "Verify uniqueness of new WBS codes" checkbox is turned on so Project will warn you if you've duplicated an existing WBS code.

Building a Schedule

O nce you've identified the tasks that comprise a project, the next step is figuring out how many hours or days of work those tasks entail—and the length of time to allocate for that work. For example, you need to know how long it takes to repair and paint the front of a '67 Mustang Fastback to figure out whether you can hide the evidence before your parents get home from vacation.

In Project, as in life, building good relationships is a key to success. When you define relationships between tasks in a Project file—called *task dependencies* or *task links*—the program calculates task start and finish dates based on those relationships. Some tasks have to finish before others can start. For example, the law of gravity requires that you finish a building's foundation before you start pouring the concrete for the first floor's walls. With all the task dependencies in place, tasks nestle into sequence, and you can finally see the entire project schedule from the start date for the first task to the finish date of the last task. Placing tasks in sequence is what turns a task list into a project schedule.

In this chapter, you'll learn different ways to estimate time and duration, how to improve estimates, and how to avoid estimation landmines. You'll also learn how to create spreadsheets for collecting estimated numbers from team members, and how to import those numbers into Microsoft Project.

Once your Project file includes tasks with estimated values, you can start transforming the file into a true schedule. This chapter describes the different types of task dependencies, the pros and cons of each one, and how to create and modify these links. Also, although task dependencies let Project adjust task start and finish dates automatically, some situations call for specific dates for tasks. In this chapter, you'll learn two ways to specify when tasks can start or finish: manual scheduling and date constraints. More importantly, you'll find out how to use date constraints and deadlines to handle specific dates *without* limiting Project's ability to calculate the schedule.

> **NOTE** *Before* you dig into defining the relationships between tasks, you should build a list of all project tasks and milestones (and, ideally, organize those tasks into a work breakdown structure), as described in the previous chapters. Otherwise, you won't have all the information you need to put tasks into a logical sequence.

■ Estimating Task Work and Duration

You'll never predict project duration with total accuracy. However, estimating work time and task duration as closely as you can is the goal, because both high and low estimates can cause problems. Overestimate how long your project will take, and the project might get squelched before it begins. Underestimate, and you might run into disappointment, extensions, and financial consequences. This section explains the difference between work and duration and then describes several methods for obtaining estimates.

Understanding Work and Duration

In Project, *work* and *duration* are both ways of measuring time, but each term has a specific meaning:

- **Work.** The number of person-hours (or equipment-hours) a task requires. For example, setting up a website may take you (that is, one person) 40 hours.

- **Duration.** The span of work time from the start of a task to the finish. Duration varies according to how many resources (people or equipment) you use, and when those resources are available. If you have other things to do and can't spend more than 4 hours each day on the website, you may need 10 workdays for that 40-hour task. On the other hand, if you convince three colleagues to help (and they share your skills), the duration decreases to a little more than one workday, but the four of you still devote 40 hours of work to the task.

Whether you estimate work, duration, or both depends on whether you know how many people are available to work on tasks. If you don't know how many resources are available, then estimate the hours of work (or days of work for very large projects) and use that work estimate as the duration estimate. When one person is assigned to work full time on a task, the number of hours of work equals the hours of duration. However, if you have multiple resources in mind, you can estimate a duration that differs from hours of work. Up to a point, you can shorten task duration by adding additional resources, as in the website example. Either way, when you assign resources to a task, Project adjusts the task's work and duration accordingly (page 251).

Getting Good Estimates

"Guesswork" is the more candid name for estimating, but important project decisions hinge on guesses being good. Project stakeholders care deeply about financial measures like return on investment, cash flow, payback period, and so on. Because time *is* money, the time you estimate for project work translates into the financial measures that make or break your project. Too-high and too-low estimates of time—and therefore costs—can both jeopardize a project, albeit for different reasons, as the box on page 163 explains.

Estimating is part science, part sorcery, so it takes some time to master. You're trying to forecast the future as accurately as possible. Fortunately, you can choose from several methods to make your estimates more precise. This section describes several commonly used estimating methods and one simple technique for improving future estimates.

UP TO SPEED

Why Not to Over- or Underestimate

The temptation to tell people what they want to hear is almost irresistible. Lowering your initial time and cost estimates might make stakeholders happy for a while. Invariably, though, underestimated projects come in late and over budget. The projects don't meet their targets, but worse than that, the money may have been better spent on other projects.

On the other hand, being too pessimistic can be just as bad. Ironically, high estimates tend to come true, even though their lowball relatives hardly ever do. Lavish estimates sometimes lead stakeholders to expect—or demand—more features

or higher quality. Moreover, team members feel flush with time and might embellish their assignments beyond what is required or work at a more leisurely pace. The result could be an unacceptable return on the money invested, which may persuade the stakeholders to can the project—or worse, pass over a good project.

Overly padded estimates can also limit an organization's productivity. When bloated projects commandeer the budget and resources, other worthy projects and their benefits get squeezed out.

■ HOW ACCURATE DO ESTIMATES NEED TO BE?

Before you launch into estimating, find out how good your estimates have to be. If your clients for a custom-built home tell you their budget is $5 million, give or take a million, you have some room to maneuver. On the other hand, the harried parents who are building an addition to house their triplets probably have a tight budget and want the estimate right on the nose.

Objectives, requirements, specifications, and other project-planning details affect the estimates you develop, so accurate estimates require research and planning—and those take time and effort. No one wants to spend a lot of time or money estimating a project that's going to cost too much or finish too late, so sometimes a quick-and-dirty estimate can help determine whether a detailed estimate is called for. There are a couple of ways to trade off up-front effort for accuracy:

- **Estimate based on the required level of accuracy.** If a rough estimate is fine—for example, plus or minus 50 to 75 percent—you can produce a high-level estimate in almost no time. This type of estimate is called a *rough order of magnitude estimate* (also known as SWAG, which stands for "scientific wild-assed guess") and works well for selecting projects. Typically, a second round of estimates for organization-wide budgeting strives for plus or minus 25 percent.

  For the final project budget, you have to spend time up front clarifying project details in order to produce a more accurate estimate (for instance, plus or minus 10 percent).

- **Estimate more accurately as you progress.** Big projects often use *feasibility studies*, small projects whose sole purpose is to determine whether it makes sense to pursue the full-blown project any further. For example, a small team could develop a prototype system to see whether the time savings are sufficient. The time and money spent early on can save the organization from spending orders of magnitude more on a dead-end project. You can use order-of-magnitude estimates to make go/no-go decisions for projects. If a project gets approval to proceed, you perform another round of estimating with more detail. Then, at the end of each project phase, you can review performance and refine your estimate for the next phase to see if the project should continue.

Finally, give yourself enough time to come up with an estimate you feel confident in, even if you have to stall a little while, as the box on page 164 explains. After you complete your initial estimate, look at it with a more critical eye. Does the estimate seem ridiculously high or optimistically low? Either way, dive back in and tweak the estimate until you think it's realistic. Because stakeholders usually hope for good news and balk at higher time and cost estimates, document your reasoning and assumptions. Not only will you be able to defend your results, but you'll also know to rework your estimates if any of your assumptions change.

REALITY CHECK

Know When to Hold 'Em

Managing stakeholders' expectations would be a breeze if they patiently waited for your thoroughly analyzed estimates. But stakeholders and management are an impatient bunch, so the pressure is on for estimates before you're ready. Don't cave in to that pressure, or you may end up making promises you can't keep. Innocent questions like, "What's the finish date looking like?" don't call for a specific, set-in-stone answer on the spot. Indeed, the people asking don't expect you to answer right away (but they are sure to remember your answer if you give them one). And if you provide a date prematurely, your answer may come back to haunt you. (If you're like most people, your off-the-cuff estimates are almost always overly optimistic.)

Without the project plan in hand, it's easy to forget details or even major components. Instead of caving, you're better off saying something like, "I'll have the analysis done by tomorrow (or next week, or next month) and can give you a better answer then."

Of course, if a bigwig is asking for an answer, you might feel queasy about stonewalling. If you feel compelled to give an answer, then deliver a document called a *basis of estimate* (BOE), which documents the elements that go into your current estimate: assumptions, risks, risk mitigation, constraints, and so on.

■ WAYS TO ESTIMATE WORK

Estimating is an art form because there are so many ways to approach it. And identifying the best method for estimating a specific project is a matter of experience. Here are a few of the approaches you're most likely to use:

- **Estimating from the bottom up.** With this approach, you estimate each work package for a project; the estimates for work packages total up to produce the estimated numbers for their summary tasks. In turn, the estimates for summary tasks roll up until you have an estimate for the entire project. Microsoft Project is the perfect tool for bottom-up estimating, because summary tasks automatically calculate totals from the values of lower-level tasks.

- **Estimating from the top down.** This approach works best if you have experience with similar projects, because you estimate the project at higher levels (like phases), and then progressively allocate the estimated time to lower levels of work.

TIP   Whether you estimate from the bottom up or the top down, don't forget to include time for rework. Deliverables aren't always right the first time around, but most people estimate how long it takes for the first delivery. Be sure to add time to your estimates for correcting first-round shortcomings. Likewise, include time for communication and administrative activities.

- **Parametric estimating.** This method of estimating using historical data along with project variables is common in construction; an example is when your contractor tells you that your home addition will cost $200 per square foot and take 4 months. This approach is helpful only when you have a significant history of documented performance (page 511), so you know what the duration and cost should be for a given unit of output—for example, a square foot of construction, a module of software development, or a page of documentation. In the construction industry, estimating programs use typical construction costs and times to develop estimates, but you can use Microsoft Excel to develop estimating formulas as well. For an example of a parametric estimating tool, check out the software-development tool at *www.costxpert.com*.

TIP   Groups of people almost always produce better estimates than any one person. This estimating approach is called the Delphi method. Learn why it works so well by reading the following Wikipedia articles:

- *http://en.wikipedia.org/wiki/The_Wisdom_of_Crowds*

- *http://en.wikipedia.org/wiki/Delphi_method*

- *http://en.wikipedia.org/wiki/Wideband_delphi*

GETTING ESTIMATES FROM THE RIGHT PEOPLE

Estimates are better when the person estimating has experience in the work involved. (You wouldn't ask your auto mechanic to estimate the time for building an addition to your house, for instance.) Regardless of the type of project you manage, you can track down experts to help you estimate what the work is going to take.

If you know who's likely to work on your project, those resources can produce even better estimates, because they know their strengths and limitations. Besides, when people set targets for themselves, they're often more motivated to meet those targets.

TIP When several people provide estimates, you have to make sure you know what their numbers represent. Suppose someone tells you that developing a brochure takes 2 weeks. Is that 80 hours of work, or is it a 2-week duration for a writer, a copy editor, and a graphic artist? Spelling out tasks in work-package documents (page 154) is one way to obtain clarity.

Duration estimates can be dramatically different from the estimated work hours if team members plan to work on tasks during their "spare time"—that is, when they get time away from their regular work duties. They might estimate the work to be only 8 hours, but they give you an estimated 2-week duration. Unfortunately, spare time often doesn't materialize, which means they may end up cranking the work out at the last possible moment or finish later than planned. If you suspect that team members are counting on spare time in their estimates, negotiate with them and their managers to get *dedicated* time for your project tasks. That way, the duration and work estimates you get are more realistic. In addition, when work starts, team members are more likely to get their tasks done when they're supposed to.

DON'T ASK FOR ONLY ONE NUMBER

In project-management circles, the Program Evaluation and Review Technique (PERT) uses *best*, *worst*, and *most-probable* estimates to get a better idea of how projects might play out. Packing the contents of a house might usually (that is, most probably) take 3 days. But if the owners live with Zen simplicity or reminisce over every tchotchke, then packing could take only a day (best) or weeks (worst). You can borrow the concept of PERT to get better estimates from your team members, even if you don't use PERT to manage the project.

TIP PERT is a statistical approach that uses Monte Carlo simulation, a mathematical technique that helps analyze risk by calculating numerous possible project outcomes using sets of randomly generated values (in this case, task durations). The result is a probability of a project finishing on time given combinations of optimistic, pessimistic, and expected values. If you want to use PERT, consider a third-party program that integrates with Project, such as @RISK for Project (*www.palisade.com*).

Simply by asking for best, worst, and most-probable estimates, as shown in Figure 7-1, you start your estimators thinking about what could go wrong, what could go right, and what's happened most often during similar efforts. You still use the most-probable estimate in Project, but PERT can increase your confidence in that number.

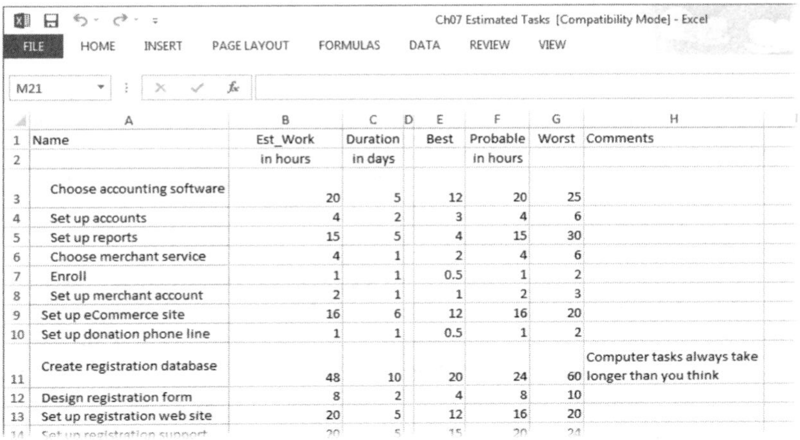

	A	B	C	D	E	F	G	H
1	Name	Est_Work	Duration		Best	Probable	Worst	Comments
2		in hours	in days			in hours		
3	Choose accounting software	20	5		12	20	25	
4	Set up accounts	4	2		3	4	6	
5	Set up reports	15	5		4	15	30	
6	Choose merchant service	4	1		2	4	6	
7	Enroll	1	1		0.5	1	2	
8	Set up merchant account	2	1		1	2	3	
9	Set up eCommerce site	16	6		12	16	20	
10	Set up donation phone line	1	1		0.5	1	2	
11	Create registration database	48	10		20	24	60	Computer tasks always take longer than you think
12	Design registration form	8	2		4	8	10	
13	Set up registration web site	20	5		12	16	20	
14	Set up registration support	20	5		15	20	24	

FIGURE 7-1

Giving people a chance to explain their estimates helps you understand the project better. Pessimistic numbers could be red flags for risks you need to manage. Or people might give optimistic estimates because they've found shortcuts that work in some situations.

DON'T PAD ESTIMATES

People want to look good and deliver results that match their estimates, so they often decide to build in extra time (known as *padding*) to cover problems that might arise with their work. This hidden padding happens all too often and is tough to get rid of because it's hard to see. But padding can lead to some problems:

- **Bloated estimates.** If everyone slips in some padding, estimates get bigger as they move up the food chain. By the time estimates get to the top-level management, they're as engorged as well-fed ticks and so inaccurate that no one knows how long the project will really take.
- **Padding games.** Some project managers try to eliminate hidden padding by trimming each of the estimates they get. If team members see their estimates cut, they simply plump their padding more the next time. With games like these, no one knows whether they can trust one another's estimates, and the relationship between the project manager and the team members worsens each time around.
- **Lack of feedback.** Without feedback, the estimators never get to find out whether their estimates were high, low, or somewhere in between. As you'll learn on page 169, estimators need feedback if you want them to improve.

That said, you need *some* kind of insurance to protect your project's finish date and cost. Rather than having individuals slip padding into their estimates, a better approach is to create a *safety margin* that the entire team can share. That way, if something goes seriously wrong, you can dole out some of that margin to the tasks that need it. (The box below explains different ways to handle time for administrative tasks.)

Adding Admin Time to Estimates

Project team members spend time on a variety of administrative tasks, like preparing status reports, attending meetings, and so on. Although you can add admin work to a Project schedule in several ways, each method has its pros and cons.

The *easiest* way to include admin work in a Project schedule is to increase tasks' estimated hours by a small percentage. The hard part of this approach is figuring out the average percentage of time people spend on admin work. The percentage you choose depends on your organization, the amount of admin work in your project, where team members are located, and so on. If you don't know how to choose a percentage, then ask other project managers what number they use.

Another approach is to create recurring tasks (page 135) in Project for admin time. However, those short, repeating tasks make a schedule hard to manage. If you schedule admin work with recurring tasks, your resources will end up with overallocations whenever their work and admin tasks overlap. Adding splits to work tasks to remove the overallocations becomes a recurring chore, keeping you from more important project-management duties.

You might think about adding one long task for admin work to your project. But this approach gets in the way if you try to use Project's resource leveling feature (page 339). The program can't figure out how to eliminate the resource overallocations that the long task creates. So don't use this method if you plan to do any resource leveling in Project.

As you learned in Chapter 2 (page 41), *contingency funds* and *management reserve* are two types of safety margins that produce a more honest and cooperative scenario. Instead of pockets of personal padding throughout the project, everyone shares a communal pot of time and money and receives something from the pot only if they need it. This way, the project is likely to contain less padding, and the leeway is more likely to go to the people who need it most. Because the safety margins are public, people must ask permission to draw on them.

Savvy project managers and management teams use two types of safety margins:

- **Contingency funds and hours.** Project contingency funds and hours are set aside to cover problems and risks that might crop up (page 38), so you can dip into the pot if something goes wrong. If it's smooth sailing, then the project might come in early or under budget. For example, banks make construction companies set aside money for problems so that buildings don't end up half-built because the companies ran out of money.

  The amount of contingency padding is based on the risks involved. If you're estimating a project that isn't well defined or represents unfamiliar work, then the contingency could be 50 to 75 percent or more. For projects you can perform with your eyes closed, the contingency might be only 5 to 10 percent. Contingency funds and hours are part of the project plan, so you, as project manager, can hand them out as you see fit.

- **Management reserve.** A second level of public padding is management reserve. As its name implies, this safety margin *isn't* at the project manager's discretion. It's a pool of time and money that management can distribute if unexpected events occur—risks that aren't in the risk management plan (page 41). While you have to ask management for a piece of management reserve, the benefit is that you don't have to beg the project's sponsor or customer for time or money.

■ GIVE FEEDBACK ON ESTIMATES

In a common scenario, you ask people for estimates. You use those estimates, perform the project, and then discover that the tasks take more or (occasionally) less time than the estimate. If you don't tell the estimators how their estimates compared to what actually happened, then you'll get the same incorrect estimate the next time you ask. If you want estimates that keep getting better, you have to track actual results (page 401) *and* share the comparisons of estimated vs. actual performance (page 431) with the people who estimate. In addition, these results go into a project archive (page 511) so managers of future projects can learn from previous projects and achieve more accurate estimates. As the box on page 169 describes, accounting systems don't always track a project's actual performance the way you need to see it, so you need to track that detail within your projects.

REALITY CHECK

The Problem with Accounting Numbers

Some companies juggle numbers in corporate accounting systems—sometimes to keep costs for different parts of a project within the limits set by a customer or to satisfy some esoteric financial requirement. Moving numbers between parts of a project means you have no idea what the actual performance was. To make matters worse, timesheet categories might not gather the project data you need.

If you work in an organization that uses SharePoint or Project Server, you can use those products' timesheet and status-update features to collect the information you need and update your projects. For small organizations with only a few

projects, you might have to ask team members to fill out a second timesheet.

No one likes filling out extra forms, so it's best to minimize your imposition on team members. For instance, you can request time at a summary-task level instead of individual work packages, or request weekly totals instead of daily ones. When you ask for team members' time, collect not only the hours worked, but also the hours that the people estimate are remaining (page 393). If their numbers don't match your plan, you can act on that early warning sign to figure out how to bring the tasks back on track (page 429).

Getting Estimates into Project

Although you *can* type estimates directly into task fields in Project, using an Excel spreadsheet to compile estimates instead has several advantages. First of all, many people who estimate tasks are familiar with Excel but not Project. (In fact, estimators may not even have Project on their computers, but they almost certainly have Excel.) And Excel makes it easier to adjust estimates than Project; for instance, it can calculate the average of several estimates.

The first step in compiling estimates in Excel is to export work-package tasks from Project to build a simple estimating spreadsheet in Excel. Because WBS codes are unique, export the WBS field *and* the task name so you have a link between tasks in the Excel spreadsheet and the corresponding tasks in Project. If you ask for three estimates (page 166), you can then use Excel functions to calculate your estimated values or simply choose the value that seems most realistic. You can divvy up the tasks for each estimator into a separate Excel workbook and then reassemble the results in one master spreadsheet that you import back into Project. This section guides you through the steps.

> **NOTE** If you create Auto Scheduled tasks without filling in their Duration fields, Project sets the duration to "1 day?" to indicate that it's an *estimated* duration. That question mark rolls up to summary tasks, so your project duration will contain a question mark if even one task has an estimated duration. (To quickly track down the tasks with estimated durations, in the View tab's Data section, click the Filter down arrow, and then choose Tasks With Estimated Durations. Project displays only tasks with question marks in their Duration fields.) If you like, you can tell Project to fill in regular durations instead of estimated ones when you create an Auto Scheduled task without a Duration. Choose File→Options. On the left side of the Project Options dialog box, choose Schedule. In the "Scheduling options for this project" section, turn off the "New scheduled tasks have estimated durations" checkbox. With this setting, Project sets the duration to "1 day." The downside to this setting is that you have to remember which tasks' durations you still need to fill in with your estimated values.

■ EXPORTING WORK PACKAGES TO EXCEL

If you're estimating from the bottom up, the only tasks you estimate are the work packages—the lowest-level tasks in the Project outline. You don't have to export summary tasks because Project calculates their values from the tasks below them. In Project, you use a *filter* (page 642) to display only the tasks that pass the tests you specify—in this case, work-package tasks for a project. Then you load those tasks into an Excel spreadsheet, using a set of instructions called an *export map* to set up the column names. This section shows you how to export tasks to an Excel estimating spreadsheet. In the next section, you'll learn how to import the estimates back into Project. (If you're estimating a small project, the box on page 171 describes a simpler way to get a few estimated values into your Project file.)

Here are the steps for exporting work-package tasks to Excel, assuming that you've copied the export map from *ProjectMM_Customizations.mpp* into your Project global template, as explained in the box on page 141 (the following steps also explain how to use a new map):

1. **Open the Project file you want to estimate and then choose File→Save As.**

   On the Save As screen, select where you want to save the file. When you click a folder, the Save As dialog box opens.

2. **In the "Save as type" drop-down list, choose Excel Workbook. In the "File name" box, type the name for the file, and then click Save.**

   Project launches the Export Wizard.

The Easy Way to Export Tasks

If you're finding the terms *filter* and *export map* hard to grasp, fear not. These tools will make much more sense when you see them in action in the following steps. In fact, there's a ready-made filter and export map you can download from this book's Missing CD page at *www.missingmanuals.com/cds*. The *ProjectMM_Customizations.mpp* file contains a filter called "Work packages," which shows only work-package tasks (see Figure 7-2). The export map called "Estimate worksheet" exports the Name, Work, and Scheduled Duration fields from Project to Excel—just the ones you need for estimates. After you download the file, use the Organizer to copy the maps into your Project *global.mpt* file. (Why? Because, for maps to appear in the Export Wizard or Import Wizard—which you'll use in the following sections—they have to be in your Project global template, not your Project file.)

Here's how to copy the map and filter into your global template:

1. With the *ProjectMM_Customizations.mpp* file already open, choose File→Info, and then click the Organizer button on the Info page.

2. Select the Maps tab.

3. In the list on the right, select the "Estimate worksheet" map, and then click Copy to copy the map to your global template.

4. Select the Filters tab.

5. In the list on the right, select the "Work packages" filter, and then click Copy to copy the filter to your global template.

6. Click the Close button.

3. **Click Next to start the wizard.**

   On the "Export Wizard - Data" screen, the wizard automatically chooses the Selected Data option, which means you can define the export map you want to use. That's what you want to do, so simply click Next to continue.

4. **On the "Export Wizard - Map" screen, select the "Use existing map" option, and then click Next.**

   If you *haven't* copied the export map from the *ProjectMM_Customizations.mpp* file into your global template, select the "New map" option instead, click Next, and then skip to step 6 to define the export mapping.

5. **On the "Export Wizard - Map Selection" screen, select the "Estimate worksheet" map, and then click Next.**

   Stepping through the next few screens lets you review or change the map's settings before you export.

6. **On the "Export Wizard - Map Options" screen, review the checkboxes that specify the data you're exporting, and then click Next.**

   Because your Project file is still in its infancy, the only checkbox that should be turned on is Tasks. In this example (like most of the time), you want the Project field names to become column names in Excel, so make sure the "Export includes headers" checkbox is also turned on.

7. **On the "Export Wizard - Task Mapping" screen, in the "Export filter" drop-down list, choose "Work packages," as shown in Figure 7-2. If you *haven't* copied the "Work packages" filter from the *ProjectMM_Customizations.mpp* file into your global template, leave the "Export filter" box set to All Tasks.)**

The "Destination worksheet name" box automatically names the Excel worksheet you're about to create *Task_Table1*. You can stick with that or change the name to something more meaningful.

The fields you export include WBS (which uniquely identifies each task), Name (so you know which task you're estimating), Work, and Scheduled Duration. Because WBS codes are unique, exporting the WBS field to the estimate spreadsheet simplifies importing your estimates, as you will learn on page 176.

As you can see in this example, you can name the columns in Excel whatever you want. For example, to clearly show that the workbook is for estimating, change the field's name in the "To: Excel Field" column corresponding to Work to *Estimated_Work*. For extra credit, you can also export a text field, such as *Text1*, which you can use to capture estimating comments in your Excel workbook. That way, when you import estimates back into Project, your assumptions and reasoning will be readily accessible in the Text1 field in your Project file.

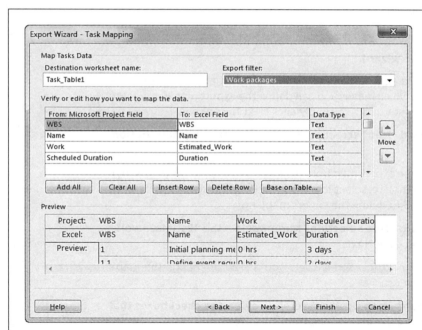

FIGURE 7-2

The "Work packages" filter hides both summary tasks (whose Summary field values equal No) and milestones (whose Scheduled Durations equal 0d). Summary tasks obtain their values by rolling up the values of their subtasks, so you don't have to estimate them. Tasks that represent milestones have a duration of zero, so they, too, require no estimating. (The Preview area shows all the tasks in your project, not just the filtered list. It isn't an accurate preview of the tasks that will be exported, but you can look at the preview to make sure that the mapping between the Project and Excel fields is correct.)

8. **Click Finish.**

Project exports the tasks into a new workbook, shown in Figure 7-3, but you have to launch Excel and then open the file to see it. (The workbook is saved wherever you told Project to save it in step 1.)

If clicking Finish displays a message about trying to save a file in an older file format, then you haven't set up Project to work with older Microsoft file formats. To instruct Project to play nicely with older Microsoft file formats (as well as other file formats Project doesn't initially recognize), choose File→Options. On the left side of the Project Options dialog box, click Trust Center and then click Trust Center Settings. Click Legacy Formats on the left side of the dialog box, select the "Prompt when loading files with legacy or non-default file format" option or the "Allow loading files with legacy or non-default file formats" option, and then click OK.

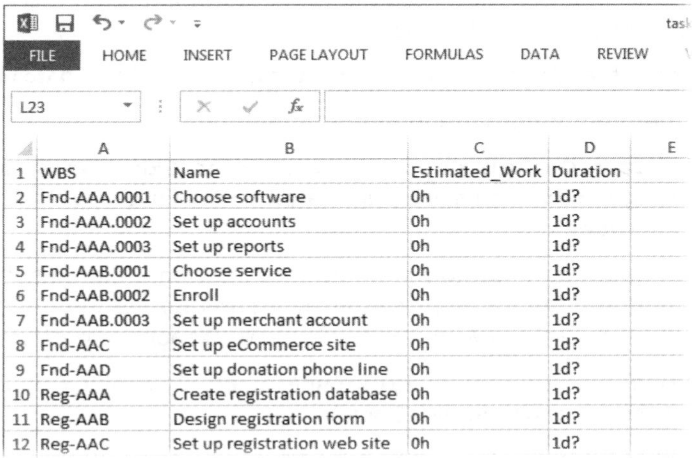

FIGURE 7-3

You can add additional columns in the Excel workbook for best- and worst-case estimates, or a column for the name of the person responsible for estimating the task. Add whatever columns you need to make your work in Excel easier: You don't have to import those columns back into your Project file.

The workbook shown in Figure 7-3:

	A	B	C	D	E
1	WBS	Name	Estimated_Work	Duration	
2	Fnd-AAA.0001	Choose software	0h	1d?	
3	Fnd-AAA.0002	Set up accounts	0h	1d?	
4	Fnd-AAA.0003	Set up reports	0h	1d?	
5	Fnd-AAB.0001	Choose service	0h	1d?	
6	Fnd-AAB.0002	Enroll	0h	1d?	
7	Fnd-AAB.0003	Set up merchant account	0h	1d?	
8	Fnd-AAC	Set up eCommerce site	0h	1d?	
9	Fnd-AAD	Set up donation phone line	0h	1d?	
10	Reg-AAA	Create registration database	0h	1d?	
11	Reg-AAB	Design registration form	0h	1d?	
12	Reg-AAC	Set up registration web site	0h	1d?	

WORKAROUND WORKSHOP

Copying Estimates from Excel to Project

If you're estimating a small project and tasks employ only one resource, then you can copy estimate cells in an Excel spreadsheet directly into cells in the Work or Duration column in the Project table area. To copy cells from a spreadsheet into cells in a Project file, follow these steps:

1. Open the Excel spreadsheet and select the cells that contain your work estimates (work or duration).

2. Press Ctrl+C to copy the cells to the Clipboard.

3. Switch to Project, and click the first blank cell in the Work or Duration column in the table area. (If the Work column isn't visible, right-click the table heading area, and then choose Insert Column. In the drop-down menu that appears, choose Work, and then click OK.)

4. Press Ctrl+V to paste the estimated values. Project copies each cell from the spreadsheet into the selected cell and the ones below it.

■ IMPORTING ESTIMATES INTO PROJECT

Unlike importing a WBS (page 140), when you import estimates into a Project file, the tasks already exist. So instead of adding new tasks to the project, you want your estimated values to slip into the fields for the appropriate tasks. The Import Wizard includes an option to do just that.

The following steps show you how to create a map to import estimates into Project. These steps also tell you where to find the instructions for using the existing map from the *ProjectMM_Customizations.mpp* file. Here's how you import estimated effort into the tasks already in your Project file:

1. **If you want to use an existing import map, download the *ProjectMM_ Customizations.mpp* file from this book's Missing CD page at *www. missingmanuals.com/cds*.**

   This Project file contains a map called "Import estimates" that maps fields in an Excel workbook to Project fields. You can use the Organizer to copy that map into Project's *global.mpt* template (page 703).

2. **In Project, open the Project file that you want to import the Excel data into.**

   The Project file must be open to import estimates into it.

3. **Choose File→Open. On the Open page, navigate to the folder that contains your estimating workbook (the one you created in the previous section, for example), and click it.**

   The Open dialog box opens set to open Projects (the button to the right of the "File name" box), which represents Microsoft Project files. But you want to open an Excel file, so choose "Excel Workbook" or "Excel Workbook (*.xslx)" instead.

4. **In the file list, double-click the name of your estimate workbook. (Alternatively, select the file, and then click Open.)**

   Project launches the Import Wizard. Click Next to get started.

5. **On the "Import Wizard - Map" screen, the wizard automatically selects the New Map option, which is what you want if you don't have a map defined. Click Next.**

   If you've saved a map to import estimates into Project, select the "Use existing map" option instead, as described on page 547.

6. **On the "Import Wizard - Import Mode" screen, select the "Merge the data into the active project" option, and then click Next.**

   This option will stuff the values from your Excel workbook into fields in existing tasks in Project.

7. **On the "Import Wizard - Map Options" screen, turn on the Tasks checkbox and then click Next.**

If the first row of the workbook includes column names, as the Excel spreadsheet exported in the previous section does, then make sure the "Import includes headers" checkbox is also turned on.

8. **On the "Import Wizard - Task Mapping" screen, in the "Source worksheet name" drop-down list, choose the worksheet that contains the information you want to import.**

If the Excel file contains only one worksheet, Project selects it automatically. If the file contains multiple worksheets, you can choose a specific worksheet if Project doesn't select the one you want.

9. **On the same wizard screen, match the values in the workbook to Project fields, as shown in Figure 7-4.**

In addition to WBS and Name, you want to map the columns for work and duration in the workbook to the Work and Duration fields in Project.

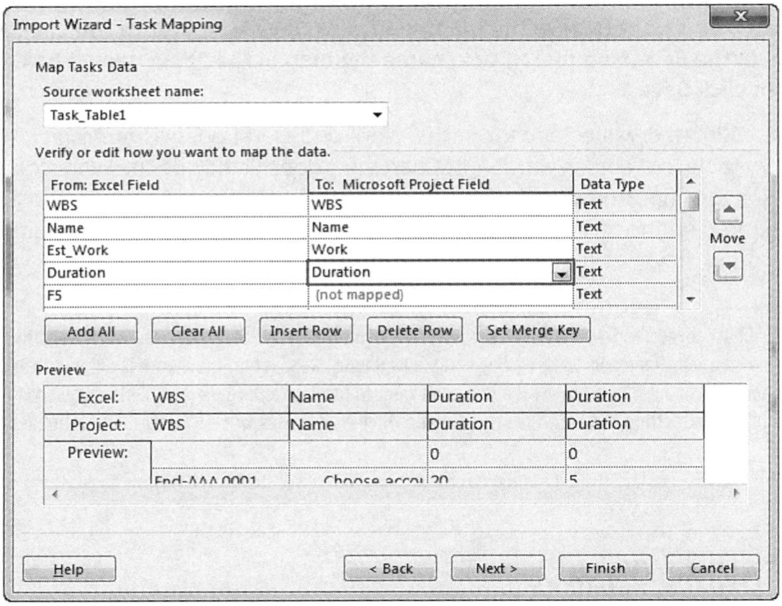

FIGURE 7-4

After you open an exported spreadsheet in Excel, you can add additional columns for best- and worst-case estimates. If you added other columns to your Excel workbook, such as Best and Worst, you might see the words "(not mapped)" in the "To: Microsoft Project Field" column. That's Project's way of saying that the information in those columns will remain in the workbook instead of transferring over to Project (which may be exactly what you want).

10. **When all the fields you want to import are mapped and the Preview area shows values coming into the correct Project fields, click Next.**

A message box might appear telling you that Project needs a primary key before it can merge the data. (If you don't see that message box, then skip to step 12.) In English, this means you have to tell Project which fields in the Excel workbook and the Project file contain unique identifiers for tasks. WBS codes make a perfect primary key, since each task has one code and no two codes are alike. Click OK to close the message box.

> **NOTE** If you didn't export the WBS field with the tasks when you created the estimate worksheet, you may be able to use the Name field, which contains task names. (The one caveat for using the Name field as a merge key is that your task names must be unique.)

11. **On the "Import Wizard - Task Mapping" page, in the table of matched fields, select the first WBS cell, and then click Set Merge Key.**

In the table, both WBS cell values change to MERGE KEY:WBS to indicate that the import process will use the WBS values to match up tasks.

12. **Click Next, and then click Finish to merge the estimates into your Project file. (If you want to save the map, then click Save Map *before* you click Finish. In the Save Map dialog box, name the map in the "Map name" box, and then click Save.)**

The estimated values appear in the Work and Duration cells in Project. (The Entry table that comes with Gantt Chart view doesn't include the Work column. To see the imported Work values in the Gantt Chart table area, insert the Work column by right-clicking a table heading and then choosing Insert Column. In the drop-down list that appears, choose Work, and then click OK.)

> **NOTE** Sharp-eyed readers may notice that Project imports work estimates as hours, regardless of whether you create estimates in days, weeks, hours, or minutes. Remember, the "Work is entered in" option (File→Options→Schedule) tells Project the units you want to use for work (page 234). Unless you change the "Work is entered in" setting, it's set to hours, so that's what Project uses when it imports the estimates from Excel.

■ Linking Tasks

Task dependencies (a.k.a. *task links* or *task relationships*) are what transform a ragtag group of tasks into a well-mannered project schedule, so Project offers several ways to create and modify all types of task dependencies. This section describes your options and the pros and cons of each one, and then walks you through several methods for creating task dependencies, starting with the most common type—finish-to-start.

How Tasks Affect One Another

Clearly defined task dependencies are essential to creating an easy-to-maintain schedule. Like a baton passed from one relay runner to the next, the start or finish date of one task (the *predecessor*) determines when the second task (the *successor*) starts or finishes. (That doesn't necessarily mean the predecessor task starts *before* the successor—the predecessor task is just the one that triggers the start or finish of the successor.)

When you get your task dependencies in place (and use Project's automatic scheduling), project tasks snuggle cozily into sequence, and the program can automatically calculate task start and finish dates—and from those, the end date of the entire project.

As Figure 7-5 illustrates, Project indicates task dependencies with small arrows showing how the start or end point of each task relates to the start or end of another.

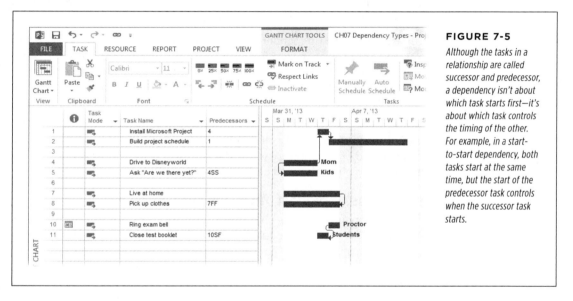

FIGURE 7-5

Although the tasks in a relationship are called successor and predecessor, a dependency isn't about which task starts first—it's about which task controls the timing of the other. For example, in a start-to-start dependency, both tasks start at the same time, but the start of the predecessor task controls when the successor task starts.

Task dependencies come in four flavors, listed here from the most to least common:

- **Finish-to-start (FS)** dependencies are the most common by far. In this relationship, the predecessor task comes first. When it finishes, the successor task begins—for example, when you finish installing a program on your computer, you can start using the program to do your real work.

- **Start-to-start (SS)** dependencies come in handy when the start of one task triggers the start of another. For instance, as soon as you start driving to your vacation destination (the predecessor task), your kids start asking, "Are we there yet?" (the successor task).

  Start-to-start dependencies often come with a delay (called a *lag*) between the predecessor and successor tasks (page 184). On that vacation drive, if your son starts poking his sister (the predecessor), she might not start crying (the successor) until 2 minutes have passed.

- **Finish-to-finish (FF)** dependencies are the mirror image of start-to-start relationships. The successor task continues only as long as the predecessor does. For instance, as long as your teenagers live at home (the predecessor), you pick up their clothes from the bathroom floor (the successor).

  These dependencies also tend to come with lag between the tasks. When a road crew inches along painting the lines on a highway, the folks who pick up the traffic cones finish a little while after the paint has dried.

- **Start-to-finish (SF)** dependencies are rare, which is for the best, since this relationship can be confusing. To better grasp the relationship, avoid the terms "predecessor" and "successor," and simply remember that the start of one task controls the finish of another. For example, when an exam proctor rings the bell (the predecessor) to indicate that time is up, the students have to close their test booklets (the successor), whether or not they've answered all the questions.

All of these examples are pretty straightforward. In real life, it may not always be so clear what kind of dependency you're dealing with. See the box on page 179 for advice on figuring out which kind of dependency you should use.

Creating Finish-to-Start Task Dependencies

Finish-to-start dependencies are so common that the Task tab's "Link the Selected Tasks" command (it's in the Schedule section) is dedicated to creating them. When your tasks follow one another like elephants, with one's trunk connecting to the next one's tail, this "Link the Selected Tasks" command is the fastest way to create those finish-to-start links. It's also the easiest way to link two tasks when you can't see both task bars in the Gantt Chart simultaneously.

Choosing the Right Relationship

For your project schedule to be accurate, you have to use the right type of dependency to link tasks. Simply put, if you don't connect tasks in the right way, the schedule won't reflect how work really proceeds once the project begins. Fortunately, the relationships between tasks are usually easy to identify. Most of the time, you're dealing with finish-to-start dependencies. But if you have trouble figuring out which relationship to use, ask yourself the following questions:

1. **Does the start or finish of one task control the other task?** When you answer this question, you know which task is the predecessor and which is the successor. You also know whether the dependency begins with "finish-to" or "start-to," in the list on page 177.

2. **Does the predecessor control the start or finish of the successor?** The answer to this question settles the type of dependency. Simply add the answer to this question to the answer to question 1. For example, if the predecessor determines when the successor task *starts*, then "finish-to" becomes "finish-to-start."

Another way to sort out the relationship is to complete the following sentence: This task must (start/finish) before I can (start/finish) that task.

In addition to choosing the right type of dependency, it's important to identify *all* the dependencies between tasks. Find relationships you missed by reviewing each task and asking yourself which other tasks affect it. Once you've identified all the predecessor tasks, you can identify the relationship between those tasks and the current task.

Here's how to create a finish-to-start task dependency:

1. **Select the predecessor task, and then select the successor task you want to link it to.**

   If the predecessor and successor aren't adjacent, click the predecessor first, and then Ctrl-click the successor.

   If the predecessor and successor appear one after the other in the table area of the Gantt Chart, simply drag across the two tasks to select both. When you link the tasks, the one higher in the list will become the predecessor to the one immediately following it.

2. **In the Task tab's Schedule section, click the "Link the Selected Tasks" icon (which looks like links of chain) to create the relationship.**

   Project creates finish-to-start dependencies between the selected tasks. The timescale of the Gantt Chart shows the link lines, as illustrated back in Figure 7-5, but you can also see predecessors and successors in Task Form view, the table area of the Gantt Chart, and the Task Information dialog box, as you'll learn shortly.

TIP You can link more than two tasks at once. If several adjacent tasks link with finish-to-start dependencies, drag from the first to the last. If the order of the tasks in the table doesn't match their sequence, click the very first predecessor, and then Ctrl-click each task in the order you want Project to link them. Then click the "Link the Selected Tasks" icon.

When the task bars for two related tasks are visible in the Gantt Chart timescale, you can also create a finish-to-start link by dragging from the predecessor task bar to the successor task bar. This approach can be a perilous path and is advisable only if you pay close attention to what you're doing. If you don't select the first task correctly, you'll move the task instead of linking it, which creates an unintended date constraint (page 190). When you position the pointer over the first task, make sure you see a four-headed arrow. Then, as you drag the pointer to the second task, make sure the pointer changes to a link of a chain, as illustrated in Figure 7-6.

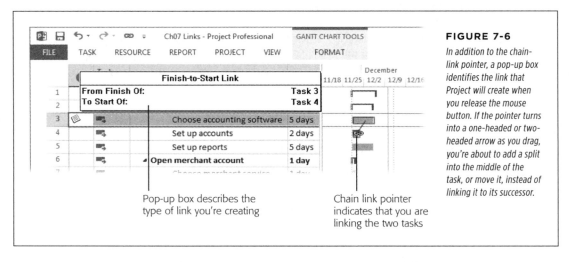

FIGURE 7-6

In addition to the chain-link pointer, a pop-up box identifies the link that Project will create when you release the mouse button. If the pointer turns into a one-headed or two-headed arrow as you drag, you're about to add a split into the middle of the task, or move it, instead of linking it to its successor.

Pop-up box describes the type of link you're creating

Chain link pointer indicates that you are linking the two tasks

Creating and Modifying All Types of Task Links

When you want to create, modify, or delete any kind of task dependency, you can take your pick from several locations in Project. This section is your guide to where you can define task links in Project, and the advantages or drawbacks of each. If Project automatically adds links you don't want, see the box on page 185 to learn how to prevent them.

■ FILLING IN LINKS IN GANTT CHART VIEW

Project's Task Form (to display it in the Details pane, in the View tab's Split View section, turn on the Details checkbox) includes fields for specifying predecessors, successors, types of links, and lag (page 184). It shows the values for the task that you select in the top view pane, so you can define, modify, or delete a task link.

NOTE Out of the box, Project turns on the "Update Manually Scheduled tasks when editing links" setting, which tells Project to change the dates for manually scheduled tasks if you link auto-scheduled tasks to them as predecessors. This setting is great when you create manually scheduled tasks because you don't know their durations but you want their dates scheduled based on their predecessors. (If you link manually scheduled tasks, Project creates the task link but doesn't change the task dates.) But if you want manually scheduled tasks to stay put, regardless of how you link them to other tasks (for example, for a training class that's scheduled for specific dates), turn this setting off. To do so, choose File→Options. On the left side of the Project Options dialog box, choose Schedule, and then look in the "Scheduling options for this project" section.

To link the selected task to its predecessor, do the following:

1. **Display Gantt Chart view in the top pane and Task Form view in the Details pane.**

   In the View tab's Task Views section, click the top half of the Gantt Chart button. In the View tab's Split View section, turn on the Details checkbox. The Details box automatically chooses Task Form.

2. **In Gantt Chart view in the top pane, select the successor task.**

   Task Form view shows the values for the selected task.

3. **In Task Form view, click a blank Predecessor Name cell and then, from the drop-down list, choose the predecessor task, as demonstrated in Figure 7-7.**

   If the Details pane contains a different view, you can switch it to Task Form view by clicking the View tab and then, in the Split View section, choosing Task Form in the Details drop-down list. If you don't see the Predecessor or Successor tables in Task Form view, right-click the form's heading, and then choose Predecessors & Successors.

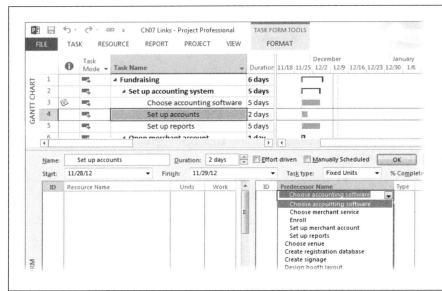

FIGURE 7-7

Task Form view has several different tables you can display, such as Resources & Predecessors, Resources & Successors, Work, Cost, and so on. If you're on a task-dependency tear, Task Form view can set both predecessors and successors at the same time. Right-click the Task Form and then, from the shortcut menu, choose Predecessors & Successors.

4. **In the Type cell's drop-down list, choose the task dependency.**

   The names are abbreviated to initials: FS for finish-to-start, SS for start-to-start, FF for finish-to-finish, and SF for start-to-finish.

TIP If you want to introduce a delay or overlap the tasks, then enter a time value or a percentage in the Lag box. (For more details on how lag time works, see page 184.)

---

5. **Click OK to create the link. (If you don't want the link, press Esc or click Cancel.)**

   The link lines for the dependency appear between the task bars in the Gantt Chart timescale.

Task Form view is a great timesaver, because you can use it to add, modify, or remove links with equal ease:

- **Add a link.** First, select a task in the table area of the top view pane. Then, in a blank predecessor row of Task Form view, specify the predecessor task's ID (or name), the type of dependency, and the lag duration (if any); then click OK.

- **Modify a link.** In Task Form view, click the cell you want to change, and then choose a different value. For example, if you created a task as start-to-start and it should be finish-to-finish, then click the link's Type cell and choose FF. You can modify the predecessor task and the lag, as well. When you're done, click OK.

- **Delete a link.** In Task Form view, click anywhere in the link's row, and then press Delete. Then click OK to confirm the deletion.

■ WORKING ON TASK LINKS IN THE TASK INFORMATION DIALOG BOX

The Task Information dialog box is full of information about the currently selected task. To use it to create links, first select the successor task and then open the dialog box by pressing Shift+F2; in the Task tab's Properties section, clicking Information; or simply double-clicking the successor task. In the dialog box, select the Predecessors tab to define links between the selected task and its predecessors, as shown in Figure 7-8.

Although the Task Information dialog box is great when you want to see or edit everything about a task, it has a few limitations compared with setting dependencies in the Task Form:

- To work on links, you have to open the dialog box, as opposed to seeing the fields at all times in Task Form view.

- The Task Information dialog box lets you define only predecessors to the selected task, not successors.

- To work on links for another task, you have to close the dialog box, select the other task, and then reopen the Task Information dialog box.

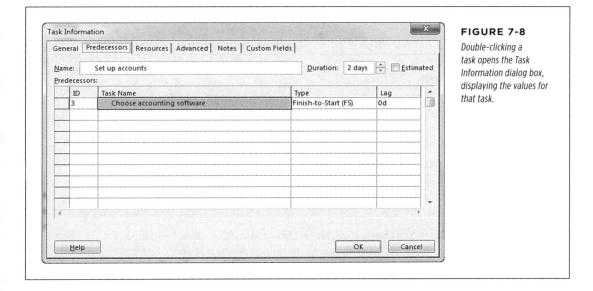

FIGURE 7-8

Double-clicking a task opens the Task Information dialog box, displaying the values for that task.

■ DEFINING TASK DEPENDENCIES IN THE TABLE AREA

The Entry table, which Gantt Chart view displays out of the box, includes the Predecessors column, which is great if you prefer typing to mousing. You can specify everything about a link in a task's Predecessor cell—as long as you know the code:

- **Create a single finish-to-start link.** All you do is type the ID number (the first column in the table area) of the predecessor and then press Enter.

- **Create several finish-to-start links to the selected task.** Separate each ID number with a comma, like this: *1,2,5,10*. Then press Enter.

- **Create a link other than finish-to-start.** Type the dependency abbreviation immediately after the ID number. For instance, to create a start-to-start link with task number 3, type *3SS*. (The abbreviations for the dependency types are the first letters of each half of the relationship: FS, SS, FF, SF.)

- **Designate the lag or lead time (page 185).** Type a plus sign (+) followed by the length of the delay or a minus sign (–) followed by the length of the lead, such as *3SS+5days*.

■ EDITING LINKS BY DOUBLE-CLICKING THEM

Double-clicking a link line in the Gantt Chart timescale opens a small dialog box, shown in Figure 7-9, for modifying or deleting the link. Needless to say, you can't use the double-click method to *create* a task dependency, because you need a link to double-click. Double-clicking a link is easy, unless you've got link lines splattered all over the Gantt Chart timescale, making finding the right link line a challenge.

FIGURE 7-9

Before you change any values, make sure that the From and To tasks represent the link you want to modify. Then, in the Type drop-down list, choose the new dependency. The Lag box is where you specify the lag or lead time. If you want to delete the link, click Delete.

Removing Task Links

The Task tab's Unlink Tasks icon (which lives in the Schedule section and looks like a broken link of chain) does different things depending on what's selected when you click it:

- **Remove the link between two tasks.** If you select two linked tasks, then clicking Unlink Tasks removes the dependency between them.

- **Remove all links to a task.** If you select a single task and then click Unlink Tasks, then Project removes *all* the links to that task, not just the task link you probably had in mind.

You can also delete a link by double-clicking its link line in a Gantt Chart timescale (page 183), removing a predecessor in the Task Information dialog box (page 182), or deleting the link in the Predecessor cell in the Entry table (page 183).

Delaying or Overlapping Tasks

Tasks don't always occur in rapid-fire succession. When a company submits an invoice, for example, it usually has to wait 30 days to receive payment. In casual conversation, the delay between linked tasks is called "lag time," because the second task lags for a while before it starts (or finishes). When tasks overlap, the overlap is often called "lead time"—like giving someone a 30-minute head start because you're faster than they are. In Project, the term *lag* refers to both delays *and* overlaps. Typing a positive number in the Lag field creates a delay between dependent tasks, while a negative number overlaps the two tasks.

> **NOTE** Lag is a delay (or overlap) between tasks that comes about no matter what happens. Project also includes a field called Assignment Delay (page 338), which delays a task until an assigned resource is available to work on it.

Automated Dependencies

How can I prevent Project from automatically creating links between tasks?

Sometimes, Project's attempts to be helpful are annoying. One way it may try to help is by automatically modifying task dependencies as you add, move, and delete tasks. For example, if you insert a new task (page 149) between two existing linked tasks, Project removes the existing link and then creates finish-to-start dependencies between all three tasks. Likewise, if you delete a linked task, Project links the tasks above and below the deleted task. And if you move a task, Project deletes the links at the old spot and then links the task to the tasks above and below it in its new location.

Project doesn't automatically link tasks by default. However, if it is adjusting links automatically, the setting that makes it behave that way could be turned on in the Project file you're working on. To regain control of linking, simply turn the setting off in the Project Options dialog box:

1. Choose File→Options, and then, on the left side of the Project Options dialog box, click Schedule.

2. Find the "Scheduling options for this project" heading. If you have more than one project file open, then to the right of this heading, choose the project for which you want to change the setting.

3. Turn off the "Autolink inserted or moved tasks" checkbox. (Because this checkbox sits underneath the heading that specifies a project file, you can rest assured that this setting applies only to the project you chose.)

These automated links can save time when you're building your initial schedule. Turn on this checkbox and you can insert, rearrange, or remove tasks, while Project manages the dependencies. Once the task links are arranged the way you want, go back and turn off the checkbox, so the links are completely under your control.

In Project, you use the Lag field to specify delays and overlaps, which can be durations or percentages:

- **Add a time delay.** If you have to wait 30 minutes after eating to get in the pool, enter *30min* in the Lag field.

- **Add an overlap.** Enter a negative value, such as *–2d* to start testing a website before all the pages are complete.

- **Add a percentage delay or overlap.** Using a percentage tells Project to adjust the length of the delay or overlap if the duration of the predecessor changes—for instance, to increase the amount of overlap based on the length of a design task. To define a delay or overlap as a percentage, simply type a percentage like *75%* in the Lag field.

TIP Whether you use a delay or an overlap depends on the type of task dependency. If you link tasks with a start-to-start link, entering *50%* in the Lag field tells Project to start the second task when 50 percent of the first one is complete. If you link the tasks as finish-to-start, you can obtain the same results by entering *-50%* in the Lag field. For example, consider a task for raking leaves and another for mowing the lawn. You can create a start-to-start link from raking leaves to mowing with a 50 percent delay so your spouse doesn't start mowing until you've raked half the yard. If you create a finish-to-start link between these two tasks instead and enter *−50%* in the Lag field, the yard-mowing task *still* starts halfway through raking leaves.

All methods for creating and modifying task dependencies, except for the "Link the Selected Tasks" command, include a place to specify the delay or overlap. (If you link tasks with the "Link the Selected Tasks" command, you can edit those links later to add a delay or an overlap.) Here's how you set a delay or overlap using each method of defining task links:

- **Task Form.** When you display predecessors or successors in the Task Form, each link includes four fields: ID, Predecessor Name (or Successor Name), Type, and Lag. In the Lag cell, enter the delay (a positive number) or overlap (a negative number).

- **Task Information dialog box.** When you display the Predecessors tab in the Task Information dialog box, the last column is Lag. As in the Task Form, type the duration or percentage you want in the Lag cell.

- **Table area.** In the table area's Predecessor cells, you append the delay or overlap lead to the link information. If the successor task starts 3 days after the end of the predecessor task (whose task ID is 6), the Predecessor cell would read *6FS+3day*.

- **Double-clicking a link line.** The Task Dependency dialog box includes a Lag box for the delay or overlap value (see Figure 7-9).

■ Scheduling Tasks to Accommodate Specific Dates

Anyone who's taken a project-management course knows the monumental tedium of manually calculating start dates, finish dates, slack time, and other schedule values. Letting Project calculate a schedule frees up your time for more important project-management activities, so normally you don't want to hobble the program's scheduling capabilities. From time to time, though, you need more control over task dates. (See Chapter 3 to learn when it makes sense to take control of scheduling and how to do so with Project's manual scheduling feature.) Suppose the backhoe you need isn't available to dig the foundation until after June 1. Or the new database guru you just hired will start work on October 12 so won't start her tasks before that date. Or the tradeshow your company is attending takes place from July 8–12 whether your booth is ready or not.

To keep your schedule low maintenance, let Project calculate it as much as possible. That way, the program recalculates dates automatically when predecessors get delayed or take more (or less) time than planned. However, when you want tasks to occur on or around specific dates, you can make that happen in two ways:

- **Set a task's schedule mode to Manually Scheduled.** When tasks are set to Auto Scheduled mode, Project does what you expect project-management software to do: It calculates when tasks start and finish based on predecessors, resource availability, and so on. Setting a task to Manually Scheduled mode instead (which is the default setting unless you change it) means Project quietly steps aside as you change the task dates to your heart's content. Manually scheduling tasks is perfect when you want to specify both start and finish dates.

- **Add a date constraint to a task.** A *date constraint* (or simply *constraint*) limits when a task either starts or finishes. Every task has a constraint, even if it's the completely flexible As Soon As Possible constraint. On the other hand, completely inflexible constraints like Must Start On make tasks behave a lot like manually scheduled tasks, except that you can specify a date constraint on only one of a task's dates. (For a complete list of Project's date constraints, see page 188.) One reason to use a date constraint instead of manual scheduling is if you want a constraint that's partially flexible—for example, when you want a task to start before a specific date, but you don't care how much before.

This section explains how to use manual scheduling and date constraints to set task dates. You'll learn about the types of date constraints at your disposal and how to use them without forfeiting schedule flexibility. In addition, you'll find out how to use deadlines to spotlight key dates without applying inflexible date constraints.

Manually Scheduling Task Dates

If a task occurs on specific dates—for example, a safety training course scheduled for October 10 and 11—Project's Manually Scheduled mode helps you set task dates in a jiffy. When a task is set to this mode, you're in the driver's seat date-wise. (To learn everything manual scheduling can do, see page 60.)

Here's how to set task dates with manual scheduling:

1. **Select the task whose dates you want to control. Then, in the Task tab's Tasks section, click Manually Schedule.**

   You can also right-click the task and choose Manually Schedule from the shortcut menu. If you display the Entry, Schedule, or Summary table on the left side of Gantt Chart view, click the task's Task Mode cell, click the down arrow that appears, and then choose Manually Scheduled.

2. **In the task table, type the dates you want in the task's Start and Finish cells.**

   In the Gantt Chart timescale, Project places brackets on each end of the task's bar, as shown in Figure 7-10, and changes the bar's color to teal to indicate that the task is manually scheduled (auto-scheduled tasks have blue bars). If the manually scheduled task's predecessors are delayed, then Project draws a red squiggle below the task's dates to flag that there's a problem. See page 307 to learn what your options are when that happens.

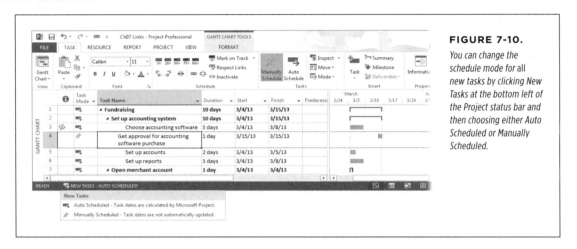

FIGURE 7-10.

You can change the schedule mode for all new tasks by clicking New Tasks at the bottom left of the Project status bar and then choosing either Auto Scheduled or Manually Scheduled.

Types of Constraints

Date constraints run the gamut from totally flexible to totally firm, and each type has its place. Unless a task is associated with a specific date, stick to the most flexible constraints—As Soon As Possible or As Late As Possible. Here are all of Project's constraint types (from most flexible to least flexible) and when to use them:

- **As Soon As Possible.** When you schedule a project from its start date (page 90), Project automatically assigns the As Soon As Possible date constraint to tasks, because this constraint doesn't determine when a task occurs. The start and finish date for the task are scheduled as soon as possible given its task dependencies, duration, assigned resources, and work times.

- **As Late As Possible.** Project automatically applies this constraint to every task when you schedule a project from its finish date (page 92). It's just as flexible as As Soon As Possible. The one problem with As Late As Possible tasks is that they don't leave any wiggle room for delays if something goes wrong. So if you have to delay a task with this type of constraint, its successors (and in many cases, the project's finish date) get delayed as well.

- **Start No Earlier Than.** You use this partly flexible date constraint for tasks that can start only after a certain date. For example, you can't buy concert tickets until they go on sale, but you can buy them any time after that date (until they sell out, that is). If you type a date in a task's Start field in a project that's scheduled from its start date, then Project sets the task to this constraint type.

- **Finish No Earlier Than.** This is another date constraint with some built-in flexibility, and it's ideal for tasks that have to continue until a specific date—for instance, processing event registrations until the cutoff date. If you type a date in a task's Finish field in a project that's scheduled from its start date, Project changes the task's constraint type to this one.

- **Start No Later Than.** This date constraint sets the latest date that a task can begin. You might use this constraint to make sure that construction begins early enough to enclose a house before winter hits, for example. However, construction can begin earlier if everything goes smoothly. If you schedule a project from its finish date, Project uses this constraint type when you type a date in a task's Start field.

- **Finish No Later Than.** You can apply this date constraint to control the latest date for a task to finish. For example, if payments have to be recorded before a specific date, then you can schedule your registration task to finish a few days earlier than that to leave time for processing. If you schedule a project from its finish date, then Project uses this constraint type when you type a date in a task's Finish field.

- **Must Start On.** This date constraint is completely inflexible. It specifies when a task starts—no ifs, ands, or buts. Moreover, this constraint's inflexibility overrides any task dependencies you set, as explained in the box on page 191. Because of that, avoid using this type of constraint unless it's absolutely necessary.

- **Must Finish On.** A control freak when it comes to the finish date, this date constraint specifies the exact date when a task ends. Like Must Start On, it also overrides task dependencies and is best left unused unless absolutely necessary.

NOTE   You can only apply one date constraint to a task at a time—for example, Must Start On or Must Finish On. If you change a task's mode to Manually Scheduled, you set both the start and finish date for the task, so it's like applying a Must Start On *and* a Must Finish On date constraint. If you edit task dependencies connected to manually scheduled tasks, Project recalculates the tasks' start and finish dates. However, you can tell Project to leave manually scheduled tasks' dates as they are, regardless of edits you make to task dependencies. To do so, choose File→Options. On the left side of the Project Options dialog box, choose Schedule. Scroll to the "Scheduling options for this project" section and turn off the "Update Manually Scheduled task when editing links" checkbox. Then click OK.

Setting and Changing Constraints

Microsoft has been called a lot of things, but *minimalist* isn't one of them. As with most of its features, Project lets you work with constraints in several locations:

- **Task Details view.** Task Details view includes a Constraint box and a Date box. To set or change a single task's constraint, select the task in the table area of a view like the Gantt Chart. Then, in Task Details view in the Details pane, in the Constraint drop-down list, choose the type of constraint you want. If you select a constraint other than As Soon As Possible or As Late As Possible, choose a date in the Date box, too.

NOTE   To display Task Details Form view in the Details pane, head to the View tab's Split View section and turn on the Details checkbox. Next, click the down arrow to the right of the Details box and choose More Views in the drop-down list. In the More Views dialog box, click Task Details Form, and then click Apply.

- **Task Information dialog box.** In the Task Information dialog box, click the Advanced tab. In the "Constraint type" and "Constraint date" boxes, choose the type and date for the constraint. (If you select a manually scheduled task, these two boxes are grayed out.)

- **Table area.** The table area is ideal when you want to change the constraints for many tasks at once. If you've just learned about the evils of inflexible constraints, you may want to change all tasks back to As Soon As Possible. To do so, right-click a column heading, and then choose Insert Column from the shortcut menu. In the drop-down list that appears for the new column, choose Constraint Type. In a Constraint Type cell, choose the new constraint type (As Soon As Possible, in this case). To copy that type to additional tasks, position the pointer over the cell's *fill handle* (the small square in the cell's bottom-right corner) until the pointer changes to a + sign. Then drag down through the Constraint Type cells you want to change.

Preventing Unwanted Date Constraints

Because Project automatically assigns the most flexible constraint to auto-scheduled tasks (As Soon As Possible if you schedule from the start date, As Late As Possible if you schedule from the finish date), the golden rule is to leave the constraint alone unless you have a very good reason to change it. But date constraints have an exasperating way of appearing when you're sure you didn't set them. It turns out that a few seemingly innocent actions on your part can create date constraints in Project.

To make sure your schedule doesn't gain date constraints you didn't intend, heed the following guidelines:

- **Don't type a specific date in a Start or Finish cell for an auto-scheduled task.** If you type a date in one of these cells, Project changes the date constraint to Start No Earlier Than in a project scheduled from its start date or Start No Later Than in a project scheduled from its finish date.

- **Don't set the finish date for a task just because that's the deadline.** The whole point of using Project is to find out ahead of time that a task won't finish on time, so you can adjust your plan to bring the finish date back in line.

TIP For a better way to indicate deadlines without adding inappropriate date constraints, read the next section.

- **Don't drag a task bar horizontally in the Gantt Chart timeline.** This action tells Project to change the constraint to Start No Earlier Than or Start No Later Than, depending on whether you've scheduled the project from its start date or finish date. Dragging task bars incorrectly can also link tasks you don't want connected, or split a task into two pieces. Avoid editing tasks in the timescale unless you're completely fastidious and a maestro with the mouse.

NOTE If you set a task's mode to Manually Scheduled, you can safely drag its task bar horizontally to change when it occurs. Project doesn't change the Constraint Type field when tasks are set to Manually Scheduled mode.

When Constraints and Dependencies Clash

Setting a Must Finish On constraint sounds definite, but that constraint doesn't guarantee on-time completion. Moreover, inflexible constraints, such as Finish No Later Than or Must Start On, can generate subtle and dangerous behavior on Project's part. Suppose a predecessor task runs late and pushes a successor past its must-finish-on date. Project can't keep both the Must Finish On constraint and the finish-to-start task dependency, so it has to pick one. Out of the box, Project honors the date constraint, which seems fine until you notice that the two tasks now overlap instead of following each other, as shown in Figure 7-11, top. When you execute the project, those tasks aren't likely to overlap, which will push the tasks' dates beyond the constraint you see in the Project schedule.

Most of the time, you want Project to warn you when your schedule might miss an important date. To get this type of warning, you have to tell Project to honor task dependencies, *not* date constraints. That way, predecessors and successors interact the way they should, but a task that blows past its constraint date displays a Missed Constraint indicator (shown in Figure 7-11, bottom).

To honor task dependencies over date constraints, click File→Options. On the left side of the Project Options dialog box, click Schedule, and then turn off the "Tasks will always honor their constraint dates" checkbox. If you want this setting to apply to all future projects, then in the "Scheduling options for this project" drop-down list, choose All New Projects, and *then* turn off the checkbox.

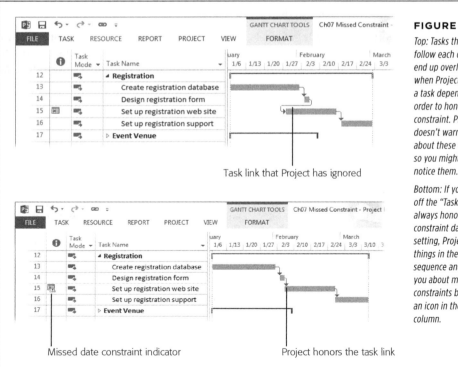

Task link that Project has ignored

Missed date constraint indicator

Project honors the task link

FIGURE 7-11

Top: Tasks that should follow each other can end up overlapping when Project ignores a task dependency in order to honor a date constraint. Project doesn't warn you about these overlaps, so you might not notice them.

Bottom: If you turn off the "Tasks will always honor their constraint dates" setting, Project keeps things in the correct sequence and warns you about missed date constraints by putting an icon in the Indicator column.

Setting Deadline Reminders

As their name implies, deadlines are dates that usually have ghastly consequences if you miss them. Yet Project's date constraints don't guarantee that you'll meet your deadlines and, as explained in the previous section, setting constraints can have serious drawbacks. The best way to stay on top of deadlines in Project is to define the deadline date in a task's Deadline field. Meanwhile, schedule the project as you would normally. That way, with the deadlines set for various tasks, you keep on the lookout for Project indicators that a deadline is in jeopardy. If you spot a missed-deadline indicator, you can investigate the issue and develop a plan to pull the task dates in earlier.

> **TIP** As you execute your project plan, remember to check regularly for missed date constraints and missed deadlines.

Here are the steps for setting and tracking a deadline for a task:

1. **Double-click the task to open the Task Information dialog box.**

   You can also select the task, and then, in the Task tab's Properties section, click Information.

2. **In the Task Information dialog box, click the Advanced tab. In the Deadline box, click the arrow to display a calendar, and then choose the deadline date. Then click OK to close the dialog box.**

   In Gantt Chart view's timescale, Project displays a green down-pointing arrow at the task's deadline date. If the task's bar ends before or at this arrow, the task is ahead of its deadline. If the task's bar ends to the right of this arrow, as shown in Figure 7-12, the task is running late.

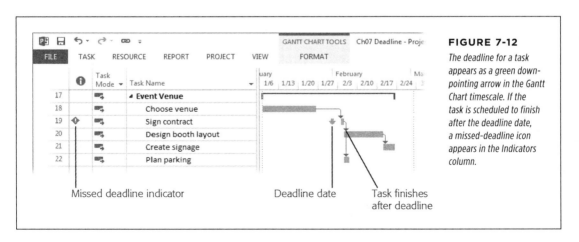

FIGURE 7-12

The deadline for a task appears as a green down-pointing arrow in the Gantt Chart timescale. If the task is scheduled to finish after the deadline date, a missed-deadline icon appears in the Indicators column.

Missed deadline indicator   Deadline date   Task finishes after deadline

3. **To see whether any tasks have missed their deadlines, review the Indicators column for red diamonds with exclamation points inside.**

   To make missed deadlines easier to see, you can filter the task list to show only tasks with Deadline dates assigned. To do that, in the View tab's Data section, click the Filter drop-down list (its icon looks like a funnel), and then choose More Filters. In the More Filters dialog box, double-click Tasks With Deadlines. Project displays tasks with deadlines assigned, along with the summary tasks to which those tasks belong. If you want to hide the summary tasks, in the Gantt Chart Tools | Format tab's Show/Hide section, turn off the Summary Tasks checkbox.

Scheduling Task Work Time with a Task Calendar

Sometimes tasks must run at specific times of the day or on certain days of the week. For example, scheduling computer maintenance during off-hours keeps complaints from information workers to a minimum. Microsoft Project calendars let you specify working and nonworking time to help schedule tasks on the days and times you want. By applying a calendar to a task, you can specify the hours when the task's work should occur.

You can easily assign a calendar to a task. Here are the steps:

1. **In a view's table area, select the task(s) to which you want to assign a calendar, and then, in the Task tab's Properties section, click Information.**

   If you select only one task, the Task Information dialog box opens. If you select more than one task, you see the Multiple Task Information dialog box, which is identical to the Task Information dialog box, except that fields unique to individual tasks are disabled.

2. **Click the dialog box's Advanced tab and, in the Calendar drop-down list, choose the calendar you want to apply, as illustrated in Figure 7-13.**

   Project comes with three built-in calendars: Standard for an 8-to-5 work schedule, Night Shift for the 11 p.m. to 8 a.m. grind, and 24 Hours for the gerbils on treadmills in your organization. If you want a different calendar, you have to create it (page 108) before opening the Task Information dialog box.

3. **Click OK to close the dialog box and apply the calendar to the task.**

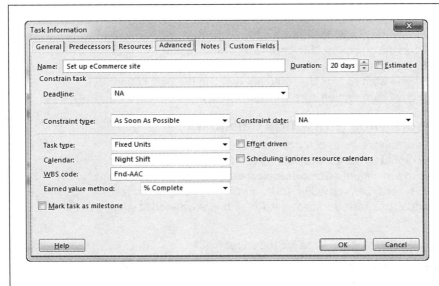

FIGURE 7-13

After you select a calendar in the Calendar drop-down list, the "Scheduling ignores resource calendars" checkbox comes to life, but it's not turned on. With this checkbox turned off, Project schedules work for the working hours shared by the task calendar and calendars for the assigned resources. If the task calendar and resource calendars don't have any mutual work time, a message box warns you that the calendars don't jibe. You can then change the task calendar or the resource calendar to make them overlap. If you want Project to schedule work only by the task calendar (and ignore the resource calendar), turn on this checkbox.

Building a Team for Your Project

Without people, projects wouldn't start and certainly wouldn't finish. To keep projects running smoothly in between the start and finish, you need the right people, and *they* need to know the parts they play. Otherwise, collaboration and communication is like a rousing rendition of Abbott and Costello's "Who's On First?"

You can start building your project team once you've identified the project tasks. You analyze the work and identify the skills and other resources required. Then you're ready to look for resources that are both suitable and available. Whether you add generic resources or real people to your Project file, you can assign them to tasks so Project can calculate the schedule and the cost.

In this chapter, you'll learn the difference between Project's work, material, and cost resources, and when to use each one. People are almost always a project's most important resource, and when this book says "resource," that usually means "person." However, projects also rely on help from nonhuman team members, such as equipment, materials, and training. In Project, *work resources* represent anything you assign by time—people, a conference room you reserve by the hour, a paper shredder you rent by the day, and so on. *Material resources* come in other units, like gallons of sports drinks or cubic yards of gravel. *Cost resources* (introduced in Project 2007) cover expenses that aren't work or material, like travel or fees.

In this chapter, you'll learn how to identify and organize your resources (which may involve help from another program). Then you'll get down to the nitty-gritty of adding resources in Project and filling in fields for availability, costs, and so on. You'll learn how to set up generic resources if you don't know who your team members are just yet. Finally, you'll see how to add even more detail to your resources.

■ Identifying Project Resources

For small projects and tight-knit organizations, a list of skills might be enough to identify Bob and Jan as the people you need. But in most cases, *some* resource planning is needed before you start working on resources in Project. Early on, you identify which groups are involved in the project, which portions of the project they participate in, and the level to which they're engaged in goings-on. After you identify the project work and estimate what it will take to complete it, you identify the skills you need to get it done—and other resources, such as materials, equipment, and money. Part of resource planning is figuring out how many resources you need and when you need them. Then you can begin to line up specific people to staff your project. At long last, a project organization chart shows who reports to whom on your project, so everyone knows whom to ask to resolve resource issues. This section introduces each aspect of resource planning.

Who's Responsible for What

Just as too many cooks spoil the broth, too many groups claiming responsibility for the same work is a recipe for disaster. Turf wars waste time and money because tasks get weighed down with extraneous requirements from fringe groups. Far more dangerous is when *no one* takes responsibility for work, because the work doesn't get done, or isn't done on time and within budget. The project's *responsibility matrix* (sometimes called the *responsibility assignment matrix* or *RACI matrix*, which gets its name from the four levels of responsibility described in the box on page 197) prevents these gaffes by spelling out who's in charge, who's responsible for performing work, who can offer opinions, and who simply needs to know something about some part of the project, like which strategy you're going to use. It's a great tool for settling those "I thought somebody else was doing that" arguments.

The responsibility matrix is a compact document that identifies groups and their responsibilities. The list of project stakeholders is a great place to start identifying groups involved in the project, such as departments, business units, or even external groups like third-party vendors and subcontractors. Knowing what those stakeholders want out of the project can provide hints about their level of involvement—do they have to approve decisions, do they do the work, or do they just need to be told what's going on?

> **NOTE** Because the responsibility matrix comes early in project planning, it doesn't identify every person assigned to a project.

You review the responsibility matrix with stakeholders to sort out the following items:

- **Who's in charge?** You've probably seen those cop movies where the local police and the FBI eye each other warily and grouse about the other group doing everything wrong. The responsibility matrix helps you dispel ownership disagreements *before* you need urgent and crucial decisions.

- **Is any work orphaned?** Like the pop-fly ball that drops to the ground as the third baseman and shortstop stare at each other, project work can fall between the cracks. If you notice work without an owner in the responsibility matrix, you can track down stakeholders until someone accepts responsibility.

- **How do groups interact?** Most of the time, groups have to work together to get things done. The responsibility matrix identifies the level of involvement each group has for each part of a project, so groups know what they have to do *and* what they can expect from others. Clarifying involvement is important when groups all belong to the same organization, but it's *essential* when a project uses contractors, partners, and outsourcing vendors. No doubt you've experienced a tech-support nightmare: You call a company and get bounced from group to group, retelling your plight each time. A responsibility matrix can show who's on the hook until the issue is resolved.

TOOLS OF THE TRADE

Levels of Responsibility

A responsibility matrix shows levels of responsibility, from the group that's in charge to those who just need to know what's going on. Here are the levels you'll find in most responsibility matrices:

- **Accountable** means a group can make decisions, delegate work, and approve deliverables or other groups' decisions. For example, if a director is accountable for a major fundraising project, she decides whom to hire, delegates work to subcontractors, and supervises and approves work. For any given portion of a project, only one group is accountable.

- **Responsible** represents the people who perform the work for a section of the project. For example, the catering subcontractor is responsible for preparing the food, delivering it to the event, and serving it to attendees.

- **Consulted** indicates that the group participates in discussions about a topic or a decision but isn't accountable for the outcome. The event manager might consult with the caterer about where to put the food tent, but the event manager is still accountable for the results of the chosen solution.

- **Informed** means the group receives information. The publicity manager needs to know about event details so she can prepare press releases and advertising for the event.

■ CREATING A RESPONSIBILITY MATRIX IN EXCEL

Project doesn't have a built-in responsibility matrix, but Microsoft Excel makes an ideal tool for creating one, since an Excel worksheet is nothing more than a matrix of cells. As stated above, a responsibility matrix links groups to major sections of a project. Because project sections usually outnumber the groups involved, the groups usually go in the columns and the project sections in the rows, as shown in Figure 8-1.

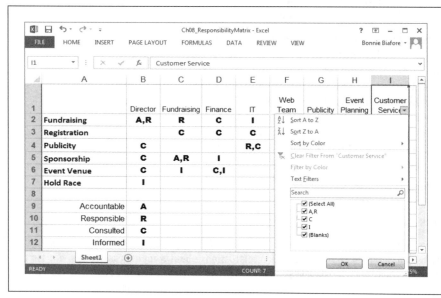

FIGURE 8-1

Because a group might have more than one type of responsibility for a project section, use abbreviations to fit them all in. Here, the levels of responsibility (page 197) are indicated by their first letters and separated by commas.

You can use Excel's AutoFilter feature to apply filters to one or more columns. Each time you apply another filter, Excel displays only the rows that satisfy every filter you've applied.

Don't worry if your Excel skills are rusty—a responsibility matrix relies mainly on plain old spreadsheet columns and rows. Creating a responsibility matrix in Excel requires only a few simple steps. First, create a blank Excel workbook (File→New→Blank workbook), and then do the following:

1. **In the cells in the worksheet's first row, enter headings for each group.**

   After you add the groups, you can select those cells and press Ctrl+B to bold the headings so they're easier to see.

2. **In the cells in the first column, add the names of the project sections.**

   When you type a section's name and press Enter, Excel selects the cell in the next row immediately below the one you just filled in, so you're ready to enter the next project section.

3. **For each cell at the intersection of a group column and project section row, fill in all the levels of responsibility the group has for that part of the project.**

   Groups can have more than one type of responsibility, so some cells might contain more than one entry. You may be both *accountable* for the family vacation (paying the bill, for instance) and *responsible* for making the reservations. Your teenagers are *consulted* on the destination (to reduce complaining), and are also *responsible* for packing their gear. On the other hand, your neighbors are *informed* that you'll be away and that they should keep an eye on your house.

NOTE Remember, a responsibility matrix is a high-level overview—it documents major sections of a project, not each individual task, and groups involved, not individuals. Later on, as you create resources to represent your project team in Project, you can use the Group resource field (page 225) to categorize resources.

■ FILTERING A RESPONSIBILITY MATRIX IN EXCEL

For huge projects, you can filter the Excel responsibility matrix worksheet to see only the sections that a particular group works on. Suppose you've decided to ditch a subpar subcontractor, and you want to know how that subcontractor is involved in the project so you can get the replacement up to speed ASAP. Here's how to filter an Excel responsibility matrix to find a group's involvement:

1. **With the responsibility matrix file open in Excel, click the column heading for the group in question, such as the label "C" above Fundraising in Figure 8-1.**

    If you plan to filter the responsibility matrix group by group, then select all the groups by dragging across the cells that contain the group headings or Excel's letter headings.

2. **To apply Excel's AutoFilter feature to the selected columns, head to the Data tab's Sort & Filter section and click Filter, or head to the Home tab's Editing section and click Sort & Filter→Filter.**

    A small down-pointing arrow appears in the selected columns.

3. **To display the drop-down menu of filters you can apply, shown in Figure 8-1, click the arrow in the heading cell for the group you want to look at first.**

    The drop-down menu suggests several filters based on the data in the column. However, you can create a custom filter by choosing Text Filters→Custom Filter and, in the Custom AutoFilter dialog box, specifying the *filter tests* (criteria).

4. **To display all the rows that contain any level of responsibility for the group, at the bottom of the drop-down menu, turn off the "(Blanks)" checkbox, and then click OK.**

    Excel hides any rows that have an empty cell for that group. The remaining rows contain at least one responsibility level for the group.

5. **To remove the filter, click the down arrow in the group's heading cell, turn on the "(Select All)" checkbox, and then click OK.**

    All the rows in the worksheet reappear. Repeat steps 3–5 to look at a different group.

    To turn off AutoFilter completely, head to the Data tab's Sort & Filter section and click Filter.

Resource Planning

When your project requires a large team, you need a formal process for managing resources. That's where a resource plan comes into play. Your resource plan is where you document your resource-related processes: how you'll bring team members on board, manage them, and then release them from the project when their assignments are over.

Another big part of the resource plan is a staffing plan. After you identify the project work and estimate the effort required to complete that work, you can plan the types and numbers of resources you'll need and when you'll need them. Here are the elements you develop for a staffing plan:

- **Skills matrix.** You identify the skills needed to perform each task. The skills matrix gives you an idea of the types and quantities of people you need.

- **Other resource requirements.** You also identify other resources the project needs, such as materials, facilities, equipment, and money.

- **Initial procurement plan.** Early in project planning, you map out where you plan to obtain project resources—for example, assigning in-house resources, hiring contractors, or using vendor resources.

- **Resource schedules.** As you develop your project schedule, the timing of when you need different resources begins to come into focus. At the same time, you might learn more about when people are available, which could require adjustments to your schedule. If the schedule doesn't meet the target finish date or runs over budget, you have to revise your plan until it meets all the objectives. For that reason, the final staffing plan might take several iterations.

- **Training requirements.** People don't always have all the skills or knowledge your project needs. In that case, you have to identify the training you must provide, because that may add costs to your project and affect when work can occur.

- **Release plans.** In addition to identifying when you need resources for your project, you also need to spell out when they'll be finished and released to their managers for their next assignments.

- **Human resource processes.** Your HR department might have processes in place for compensation, regulatory compliance, rewards, and so on. However, your staffing plan should include any resource processes specific to your project.

Once the schedule and cost are where they need to be, you can provide your draft resource plan to line managers, vendors, and so on, and ask them to commit the resources they manage. (The box on page 201 provides some tips for obtaining and retaining resources.) After that, you'll probably adjust your project plan and staffing plan to include the people assigned to your project, when they're available, and the training they require.

Getting and Holding onto Resources

In this downsized, competitive world, there are never enough resources to go around. Looking for resources with the right skills or characteristics just increases the challenge. Some resources are scarce due to their unusual combination of skills—like a web developer with a financial background who also speaks Japanese. Other resources are scarce because everyone needs them—like a bulldozer after a seven-foot snowstorm.

To complicate matters, projects don't have resources to call their own. People assigned to projects usually work for other departments, vendors, the customer, and so on. The perfect person for the job might sit across from you, but rather than going straight to her and asking if she can work on your project, the approach that works more consistently is to give work-package and assignment information to the people in charge of the resources you covet, and let *them* pick the right

ones based on skills and availability. Providing thorough descriptions and having a realistic schedule help you build good relationships with these resource managers. The time that this relationship-building takes is worth it—especially if you need favors later on.

Resourcing efforts aren't complete when you've finished assigning resources. You have to keep the resources on the project, and that means keeping workloads as consistent as you can (page 327). If resources sit idle, you're likely to lose them to other projects; or worse, the resources may get laid off. On the other end of the scale, pushing people to work long hours incurs overtime costs, increases errors, and generates rework. With a reputation as a bad project manager, you'll have trouble finding people for future projects.

Who Reports to Whom

As you identify the people who work on your project, you can start building a *project organization chart*, which shows the chain of command within your project (not your organization as a whole). Just like a regular org chart, a project organization chart helps people figure out whom to ask if an issue needs escalating, a decision needs deciding, or any other situation requires higher authority.

The project organization chart is especially important for projects with all sorts of partners—internal, external, third party, outsourced, and so on—because it identifies the go-to person when a decision is needed. Does the project sponsor have the final say, or is it an external customer who's picking up the check? If you'd like to clarify these relationships in a chart, you can create one in Microsoft Word, although Microsoft Visio is the better tool. The Visio Organization Chart template works for companies and projects alike, and this section shows you how to use it.

NOTE In Microsoft Project, you can associate resources to groups with the Group resource field (page 225) and use outline codes (page 675) to link resources to an organizational structure. However, creating a project organization chart is best left to Microsoft Visio—or whatever tool your organization uses to document the companywide hierarchy.

■ **CREATING A PROJECT ORGANIZATION CHART IN MICROSOFT VISIO**

With Visio, you can build a project organization chart using the Organization Chart template. In Visio, click File→New→Organization Chart→Create. This template contains shapes that create reporting relationships when you drop them onto manager shapes on a drawing. Even better, this template offers an Org Chart tab that includes an Import command for importing resource information from Excel and other sources like databases.

> **NOTE** In most organizations, people report to functional managers. Then, when these people work on projects, they end up with two bosses—the functional manager, and their supervisor within the project. A project organization chart *isn't* the place to track both sets of bosses. Rely on the companywide org chart or the corporate HR system to track functional managers.

■ Understanding Project's Resource Types

Microsoft Project offers three types of resources for projects, each with its own purpose and idiosyncrasies. Here are the various types, what each one represents, and how it can affect your project (the box on page 204 describes different ways resources of *all* types can affect projects):

- **Work.** Time is what distinguishes work resources from other resource types in Project. For example, people and equipment are work resources, because you track their participation by the amount of time they spend on the project. Whether you're assigning people to direct traffic or renting equipment for an event, your project's tasks depend on when those work resources are available, how much time they have, and how much they cost for a period of time, as shown in Figure 8-2.

> **TIP** Because you usually don't want people's salaries in the public eye, you can fill in pay rates with the *averaged burdened cost* (an employee's hourly wages or salary, plus benefits, taxes, equipment, and so on, which you can get from your HR department) for someone in a given role.

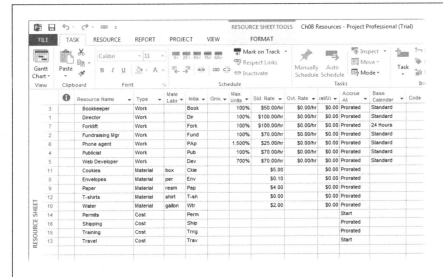

FIGURE 8-2

Fields in Project's Resource Sheet view (page 205) may be blank or contain different kinds of information depending on the type of resource. For example, a work resource doesn't have a Material label, and costs are calculated initially as dollars per hour. Material resources have a cost per unit—per pound, gallon, or piece—and the Material label field defines the units. Cost resources receive a cost value only when you assign them to tasks.

NOTE   Regardless of whether you only know the skills required for tasks or you have the specific names of warm bodies, you can create resources in Project to assign to tasks. See page 222 to learn how to use generic resources to act as placeholders until you identify real resources.

- **Material.** Materials are supplies that are consumed during the course of a project. Suppose you have a task to stuff envelopes to send to potential sponsors. That task requires envelopes and printed materials, as well as people to stuff the envelopes. You assign the people based on the time it will take, but you assign material resources by the quantity you need: 10,000 envelopes, for instance. Because materials aren't measured by time, they affect only the cost of your project (based on the quantities you need and the cost per unit). Materials affect dates or duration only when you have to wait for them to become available. For example, you can't begin setting up tents until they're delivered.

- **Cost.** Cost resources came on the scene in Project 2007, and they represent *only* costs—not time, not quantities. These resources are perfect for ancillary costs that aren't directly associated with the people, equipment, and materials you assign to tasks. For example, expenses such as travel or fees increase the project's price tag, but they aren't associated with work or material resources.

The advantage of this resource type is that you can track different types of costs separately. For instance, you might set up cost resources for travel, building permits, rental expenses, and shipping, as illustrated in Figure 8-2. You can then assign those cost resources to each task they apply to (page 248), and then total what you spend on different types of costs for the entire project (page 249). A kickoff meeting might have, say, $20,000 in travel costs and $5,000 in communications costs for the people who attend in person and via videoconference. And the change control board might have $1,000 in travel costs and $2,000 for videoconferencing. When you see the $21,000 for travel vs. $7,000 for videoconferencing, you might consider changing your approach to meetings.

UP TO SPEED

How Resources Affect Project Schedules

For a quick-and-dirty project schedule, all you need are tasks, estimated task durations, and links between the tasks. Project shows a start date and a finish date for the project, but how do you know whether these dates are any good without resources assigned to do the work? And as you begin the work, how can you tell whether the project is proceeding according to plan?

Assigning resources to tasks in Project provides the information you need to answer these questions. Resource assignments help you manage the project in several ways:

- **Defining the project's schedule.** Because you can specify when resources work and how much they're available (page 213), your project schedule is more accurate, since it calculates task durations based on when resources work.

- **Managing resources.** Resource assignments tell you whether resources have too much work or too little. As you plan the project, you can balance people's workloads to make the schedule more realistic (and make team members happier). In addition, you can play what-if

games with time versus money. For example, you might decide to use less-expensive resources when the budget is more important than the finish date.

- **Preventing ownership problems.** Resource assignments also ensure that someone is working on every project task. At the same time, assignments can prevent overly enthusiastic team members from sticking their noses into someone else's work.

- **Tracking progress.** By updating your schedule with the actual progress people make, you can see whether or not the project is on track. This information is indispensable later on when you want to evaluate your estimating prowess and do better the next time.

- **Tracking spending.** When you track the costs of work, material, and cost resources, you can not only estimate the budget for the project (page 266), but also see actual costs as the project progresses.

■ Adding Resources to Your Project File

Before you can play matchmaker between project tasks and resources, you have to tell Project about the resources you're using. You can get started by filling in a few basic fields, such as the resource names and types. (The box on page 205 explains what you can do if you don't *know* resource names.) As you identify detailed information, such as work schedules, availability, and costs, you can add that information to Project, as described in other sections in this chapter. In turn, Project uses that information to more accurately calculate your project schedule and price tag.

Project offers two methods for entering resource data directly. The Resource Sheet is ideal for specifying values for every resource—you can either copy and paste values, or simply drag values (even into several cells at once). Or, if you have resource information stored in a company directory or other database, importing information into Project makes short work of data entry. This section explains each approach.

TOOLS OF THE TRADE

When to Tell Microsoft Project About the Team

Some project managers identify required skills and resources as they define project work packages. Others focus on completing the work breakdown structure, and *then* go back to identify the required resources. Either way, project managers typically start out by identifying work resources as skillsets (crane operator, financial analyst with nonprofit expertise, or JavaScript developer) and major equipment (computer server, forklift, or printing press). That's because you can't identify specific resources until you know the required skills and the specific task dates.

Fortunately, Microsoft Project can handle this iterative approach. *Generic resources* (page 222) act as placeholders for the skillsets and people you need. (Of course, if you have only a few employees, you can add all their names to Project, so they're fair game for task assignments.)

For example, say you don't know the number of people you need for a task. In that situation, you can assign generic resources to tasks in Project to get an estimate of task durations. If the schedule is too long or too costly, you can make changes, perhaps adding resources to shorten duration, or assume lower pay rates to reduce cost. When you're satisfied with the schedule and resource requirements, you have the information you need to hit up the management team for specific resources. Then, as you obtain specific people or equipment, you can replace the generic resources with the resources that represent the warm bodies you're allocated (page 320). You can also filter your project for tasks with generic resources assigned to see where you have holes in your team.

Adding Resources in Resource Sheet View

Resource Sheet view is a quick way to get resources' names, ranks, and serial numbers into Project. In fact, you can specify most information about resources simply by adding columns to the table (page 633) and filling in the additional cells. (For resources that require more detail, like variable cost rates or availability, you have to use the Resource Information dialog box described on page 216.)

Adding resources in Resource Sheet view is similar to adding task information in the Gantt Chart's table area. Here's how to enter the essential 411 for resources:

1. **In the View tab's Resource Views section, click Resource Sheet.**

    The Resource Sheet (Figure 8-3) lists all existing resources in the Entry table, which initially contains fields for both work, material, and cost resources.

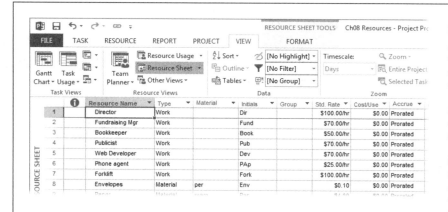

FIGURE 8-3

Resource Sheet view opens with the Entry table, which contains fields you fill in for work, material, and cost resources. To apply a table specific to work or material resources, in the View tab's Data section, click Tables, and then choose "Entry - Work Resources" or "Entry - Material Resources," respectively.

2. **In the first Resource Name cell, type the name of a resource.**

   To make resources easy to find later on, follow a standard naming convention. Commas and brackets are verboten in resource names, so consider something like "Smith J" for people. For generic resources, the job description (like Web Developer) works well. Similarly, a brief description is fine for equipment and materials.

3. **To save the resource and move to the next row, press Enter.**

   Project saves the resource (and automatically assigns it the Work resource type, because that's the most common type) and moves to the Resource Name cell in the next row, so you can type the next resource name. The fastest way to create lots of resources is to type a name and press Enter until you've created and named all your resources. *Then* you can specify other values, if necessary.

4. **For each material and cost resource in the list, click its Type cell and type *m* for material or *c* for cost. Or click the down arrow on the right side of the cell, and then, in the drop-down list, choose Material or Cost.**

   When you choose Material or Cost, Project removes values in columns that don't apply to that type of resource (like the Std. Rate field for a Cost resource).

   TIP If all your material or cost resources are grouped together, you can change the Type cell for the first resource in the group. Then position the pointer over the fill handle (the small square in the cell's lower-right corner), and drag to copy that value to the other cells.

5. **Change other values—such as Initials or Max. Units—by clicking a cell and then entering the value.**

You'll learn how to fill in other resource cells in the remaining sections of this chapter. The box on page 208 shows you how to sort resources to help make them easy to spot.

TIP Say you type a resource name that doesn't exist in the current project file into a Resource Name cell in the Resource Sheet or into an assignment in the Task Form. Project is happy to automatically add a new resource with default values for you. At times, this behavior is a tremendous timesaver, because you can simply type a resource name in the Task Form or in a Resource Name cell without having to detour to the Resource Sheet to create the resource. However, if a typo sneaks in, your project can acquire resources that don't actually exist.

Fortunately, you can make Project notify you when it creates a new resource as it assigns the resource to a task: A message box opens and tells you the resource doesn't exist in the resource pool. If you want to add it, click Yes. If the resource represents a typo so you don't want to add it, click No. To tell Project to do this, choose File→Options. On the left side of the Project Options dialog box, click Advanced. In the "General options for this project" drop-down list, choose the project you want to work on (or select All New Projects), and then turn off the "Automatically add new resources and tasks" checkbox. Doing so also tells the program to notify you in a similar fashion when it creates a *task* if you type a *task name* that doesn't exist while assigning a resource to a task, for example, in a new row in Resource Usage view.

Adding Resources from Excel

Getting resource information from an Excel workbook into Project is easy. For simple resource lists, you can copy and paste values from Excel into your Project file. Alternatively, if you want to import several resources fields, the Microsoft Project Plan Import Export Template, which comes with Excel, might be even easier. This template maps columns in an Excel worksheet to Project resource fields so information slides into the right slots almost effortlessly. (The only catch is that both Excel and Project have to be installed on the same computer for the template to appear in Excel. Page 140 tells you how to locate this template if you don't see it in Backstage view's template list.) In this section, you'll learn both methods for getting resource info from Excel into Project.

Sorting Resources by Names and More

After an invigorating session of resource creation, your Resource Sheet might be a hodgepodge of resources in no particular order. An unsorted list not only makes it hard to see what resources you've got, but it also increases the likelihood of inadvertently duplicating them.

Removing duplicate resources prevents confusion and scheduling problems. If you accidentally create two or more resources with the same name, such as John Smith and john smith, Project considers those resources separate entities. So if you assign some tasks to one resource and other tasks to its doppelganger, your schedule will be wrong. For example, tasks might look like they can run simultaneously and workloads might seem reasonable—but in reality, those tasks might have to run in sequence, or you might have double-booked a resource. Sorting your resource list by name places duplicate names next to each other, so you can delete the duplicates and assign the remaining ones to the correct tasks.

Project makes it easy to sort your resource list by name: Simply click the down arrow to the right of the Resource Name column heading and then, in the drop-down menu, choose "Sort A to Z" or "Sort Z to A." If you want to sort the list by more than one field, here's what you do:

1. In Resource Sheet view (View→Resource Sheet), head to the View tab's Data section and click Sort→Sort By.

2. In the Sort dialog box's "Sort by" box, choose the field you want to use to sort the resources, and then select the Ascending or Descending option. For example, choose Type to separate each type of resource. (Project selects the Ascending option automatically, which is perfect for alphabetical order.)

3. In the "Then by" box, choose the next field to sort by, such as Name. Then pick the Ascending or Descending option, if necessary.

4. If you want to sort by another field, then in the *second* "Then by" box, choose the final sort field.

5. To make this order permanent, turn on the "Permanently renumber resources" checkbox. With this setting turned on, when you complete the sort, Project reassigns the ID numbers that uniquely identify the resources.

6. Click Sort to rearrange the resources.

7. If you chose to renumber the resources permanently (step 5), you should tell Project *not* to renumber resources the next time you sort (in case there is a next time), since that would mess up the numbering scheme for all the resources you've already assigned. To do that, simply reopen the Sort dialog box, click Reset to turn off the "Permanently renumber resources" checkbox, and then click Cancel to close the dialog box without resorting the list.

■ COPYING AND PASTING RESOURCE DATA

Suppose the HR department sent you an Excel workbook containing a list of resources. You can paste values from that spreadsheet directly into the table in Project's Resource Sheet view. Here's how:

1. **In the Excel workbook that contains resource information, select the cells that you want to paste into Project, and then press Ctrl+C (or, on the Home tab, click Copy).**

   For example, if the resource names are in the first column, you can select just the cells in that column. If you want to copy several columns of data from Excel, such as names and standard pay rates, be sure that the data in the Excel worksheet is in the same columns as the columns in the Resource Sheet table.

For example, in the Resource Sheet Entry table, the Standard Rate field is in the seventh column, so you want your pay-rate data in the seventh column in the Excel worksheet.

2. **Switch over to Project and, if necessary, display the Resource Sheet by clicking View→Resource Sheet.**

   Resource Sheet view is one big table, so it's easy to copy Excel data into it.

3. **Click the first blank Resource Name cell where you want to paste the tasks, and then press Ctrl+V.**

   Project inserts the values into the Resource Sheet table, filling in cells below and to the right of the cell you clicked.

■ IMPORTING RESOURCE DATA USING AN EXCEL TEMPLATE

Although you can import data from *any* Excel workbook, the Microsoft Project Plan Import Export Template is already set up to play well with Project. The template's Resource_Table worksheet comes with column headings that match Project's resource fields. All you have to do is put your resource values in the appropriate columns. Then, when you import the workbook, the data goes where it belongs in resource records.

Here's how to import resource information from the Microsoft Project Plan Import Export Template spreadsheet into Project:

1. **In Excel, click File→New.**

   Backstage view opens to the New page and displays the available templates.

2. **Double-click the Microsoft Project Plan Import Export Template.**

   Excel creates a new workbook named ProjPlan1 with separate worksheets for tasks, resources, and assignments.

NOTE This template appears in Excel only if Project is installed on the same computer. (If you want others to fill in the workbook created by this template, send them a copy of it. Or you can create a workbook from the template and add the project's name and the recipient's name to the workbook's filename to help you keep track of things.) If you don't see the template in Excel, see the box on page 140 to learn how to get to it.

---

3. **At the bottom of the Excel window, click the Resource_Table tab, shown in Figure 8-4.**

   If you're importing only resources, you can ignore the worksheets for tasks and assignments.

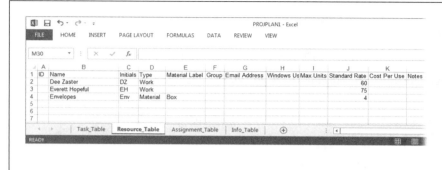

FIGURE 8-4

The Resource_Table worksheet contains columns with headings that correspond to resource fields in Project, such as Name and Type. Don't be concerned that the columns aren't in the same order as the columns in the Resource Sheet's Entry table—you'll map the columns during the import process.

4. **Type or paste resource information into the appropriate cells, and then save the Excel workbook when you're done.**

   Type information into cells if you don't have an existing file with resource data. If you already have a spreadsheet that contains resource information, you can use it to import your resources—with a few additions to the spreadsheet. Copy and paste the column headings in the Project template file to the corresponding column heading cells in your resource Excel workbook. For example, paste the Name heading into the first cell in the column that contains your resource names. Project imports this data based on the column headings in the template, so make sure your information is in the columns with the correct headings.

5. **To import the resources into Project, switch over to Project.**

6. **In Project, click File→Open, click the location where you saved the Excel workbook (like Computer or [your name] Skydrive), and then click Browse.**

   The Open dialog box appears.

7. **In the Open dialog box's unlabeled "Files of type" drop-down list, choose "Excel Workbook (*.xlsx)." Navigate to the folder that contains the Excel workbook with your resource information, and then double-click its filename.**

   The Import Wizard appears. On the first screen of the wizard, click Next.

8. **On the "Import Wizard - Map" screen, select the "New map" option and then click Next.**

   The "Import Wizard - Import Mode" screen appears.

9. **To import the resources into the active project at the end of the existing resource list, select the "Append the data to the active project" option, and then click Next.**

If you select the "Merge the data into the active project" option instead, Project imports resource information into existing resource records, which is perfect if you want to import updated info about your existing resources. The "As a new project" option is *not* the one you want, because it imports the resources into a brand-new project.

10. **On the "Import Wizard - Map" Options screen, turn on the Resources checkbox, and then click Next.**

    The "Import Wizard - Resource Mapping" screen appears. Project automatically chooses Resource_Table in the "Source worksheet name" box. In the table below that, the Excel fields and the Project fields should match up perfectly. If they don't, simply choose the correct Excel field to go with a Project field, or vice versa.

11. **Click Finish.**

    Project imports the resources to your project file, and they appear in Resource Sheet view.

Adding Work Resources from Your Email Address Book

Chances are you have resource information for people in Outlook or on a Microsoft Exchange Server. If so, you can import that information into a Project file. (Project needs to be installed on the same computer as Outlook.)

To import resources from an address book, do the following:

1. **With the Resource Sheet visible (View→Resource Sheet), on the Resource tab, click Add Resources.**

    A drop-down menu appears with commands for creating and importing resources. (If you're using a view other than Resource Sheet, the Add Resources command is disabled.)

2. **Choose Address Book.**

    The Select Resources dialog box appears. If you see the Choose Profile dialog box instead, then choose the profile name for the email system you want to use. For example, if you have a profile for your business email and one for your personal email, choose the business profile.

NOTE   If your organization uses Active Directory to store information, then on the Add Resources drop-down menu, choose Active Directory to import resources from that data source. Then search through the Active Directory for resources instead of browsing as you do with an address book.

---

3. **In the Select Resources dialog box, choose the resources you want to import, and then click Add at the bottom of the dialog box.**

    Ctrl-click to select resources that aren't adjacent. For adjacent resources, simply click the first resource, and then Shift-click the last one. You can also select resources in batches and then click Add to append each batch to the import list.

4. **When all the resources you want to import appear in the Add box, click OK.**

   Project adds the resources to the Resource Sheet. Any information you store in your address book that applies to Project fields transfers over. For example, Project imports email addresses into its own Email Address field.

■ Removing Resources from Your Project

If you've created duplicate resources or lost someone to another project, you might want to delete those resources in Project. However, deleting a resource in Project means any assignments you've made are gone as well. That's right—when you delete a resource, you run the risk of orphaning tasks without anyone to perform them. One way to prevent this issue is to replace the resource (page 333) on task assignments before you delete it.

To simplify resource replacements, first filter the task list to show only the tasks to which the resource is assigned; then you can edit each task to replace that resource. To see the tasks to which a resource is assigned, do the following:

1. **Select a task-oriented view like Gantt Chart and hide the summary tasks (in the Format tab's Show/Hide section, turn off the Summary Tasks checkbox).**

   The task list shows only work tasks and milestones.

2. **In the View tab's Data section, click the Filter drop-down list, and then choose Using Resource.**

   The Using Resource dialog box opens with a "Show tasks using" drop-down list.

3. **In the "Show tasks using" drop-down list, choose the resource you want to delete, and then click OK.**

   Project displays any tasks that have that resource assigned.

4. **To replace the resource with someone else, in the Resource tab's Assignments section, choose Assign Resources. In the table, select the task you want to reassign, and then, in the Assign Resources dialog box, select the resource you want to replace and click Replace. (Page 333 describes replacing resources in detail.)**

   You can also make simple replacements in the Resource Names column by clicking each cell and picking a different resource for each task.

5. **After you finish editing resource assignments, click the Format tab and turn the "Show summary tasks" checkbox back on.**

   The task list is back to its full complement of summary tasks, work packages, and milestones.

6. **In the View tab's Resource Views section, click Resource Sheet.**

   Now you're ready to delete the resource.

7. **In Resource Sheet view, click the row number of the no-longer-available resource, and then press Delete. Or right-click anywhere in the resource's row and choose Delete Resource from the shortcut menu.**

   Project removes the resource from the resource list.

Defining When Work Resources Are Available

You may have already assigned a calendar for your project, as described on page 119, to indicate when work usually takes place. But even if your office is open from 8:00 a.m. to 5:00 p.m., not everybody works the same hours. Creating separate calendars for people whose schedules don't follow the norm tells Project when people are available to work on their assigned tasks. The schedule is more accurate when Project knows about people's vacations, days off, and odd work hours. Project has two ways to specify when resources work, but each method approaches working time differently:

- A **resource calendar** comes in handy for setting aside days off and spelling out specific hours that a resource works—for example, Monday through Thursday from 8:00 a.m. to 7:00 p.m. with an hour at 12:00 p.m. for lunch. You can also use a resource calendar to specify part-time work schedules like Monday through Friday, 8:00 a.m. to 12:00 p.m.

- **Availability,** specified by resource *units*, tells Project what percentage of time the resource is available. For example, most resources work full time during normal working hours. You can alter a resource's units (in the Maximum Units field, which is usually abbreviated to Max. Units) to tell Project that someone works part time, or that a resource is really a three-person team. For example, the folks who work part time could have Max. Units of 60 percent if they work 3 days a week. If you use a resource calendar to define a part-time schedule, then you set Max. Units to 100 percent for the resources who work that schedule. Alternatively, the Max. Units for the three-person team that works on the project full time would be 300 percent.

NOTE When it comes to resource availability, Project's terminology is downright confusing. First, resource units are expressed as percentages or decimal values, not time units you'd expect, like hours or days. Units get more confusing when you assign resources to tasks. Assignments have their own Units field, which is the percentage of time the resource is assigned to the task. (See page 233 for a more detailed description of how units and assignment units work together.)

Resource calendars and units apply only to work resources, because these are the only ones assigned by time. You can use a calendar and units separately or together to identify how much a resource works, as described in detail on page 215.

Project automatically sets a resource's maximum units to 100 percent for full time and uses the calendar that applies to the entire project. However, in reality, people aren't productive 100 percent of the time. They check email, attend non-project meetings, and take breaks. Page 216 describes how you can model productive time in Project.

Specifying a Resource's Work Schedule

If someone doesn't work according to the overall project's calendar, then you can specify a special work schedule by defining a calendar for that resource. Resource calendars come in handy for a variety of special situations like the following:

- Your project spans multiple shifts, and you want to assign people to the shifts that they work.

- Your resources work in different time zones, and you want to assign working times according to their local times.

- A resource will be away from work for an extended period of time—for instance, your star developer is recuperating from carpal-tunnel surgery.

- Your company offers the option to work either 4-day or 5-day work weeks, and you want to assign separate calendars to the people who choose each option.

- Equipment resources often require preventive maintenance, such as a computer server that's shut down for software patch installations once a month.

You can create a custom calendar for an individual resource or apply the same calendar to several resources. (To learn how to create and fine-tune calendars, see Chapter 5.) Here are the different methods for assigning a calendar to a resource:

- **Define a calendar for a resource.** In Resource Sheet view, double-click the resource with the custom work schedule. In the Resource Information dialog box, on the General tab, click Change Working Time. The label at the top of the Change Working Time dialog box reads "Resource calendar for '[resource name].'" Define work weeks and exceptions for that resource (see page 110), and then click OK to save the resource calendar.

- **Apply an existing calendar using the Resource Information dialog box.** Suppose you create a calendar that represents the working time for a group of resources, such as the folks who work the night shift or your part-time contractors. You can apply a shift calendar like this to the people who work that schedule. In Resource Sheet view, double-click the resource to which you want to apply the calendar. In the Resource Information dialog box, on the General tab, click Change Working Time. In the Change Working Time dialog box's "Base calendar" field, choose the calendar you want to apply (for example, a shift calendar like the Night Shift calendar that comes with Project), and then click OK.

- **Apply a calendar in Resource Sheet view.** Click the resource's Base Calendar cell (if the column is narrow, then you may see only the word "Base") and then, in the drop-down list, choose the calendar you want to apply, as shown in Figure 8-5.

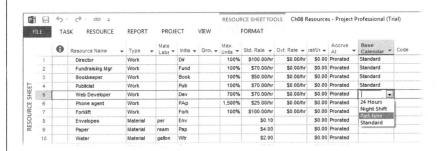

FIGURE 8-5

The fastest way to apply a calendar to several resources is to apply the calendar to one resource and then copy and paste that value to other cells in the Resource Sheet. You can also drag the fill handle (the green square in the Base Calendar cell's bottom-right corner) to copy the value to several adjacent resources.

Specifying How Much Your Resources Are Available

Availability is the percentage of time a resource is available during the resource's work schedule, whether it's the standard calendar or a special one. Here's how availability works:

- If the resource doesn't have a special calendar assigned, then Max. Units set to 100 percent represents full time during regular working hours according to the project's calendar.

- If the resource has a resource calendar with Monday through Thursday as 8-hour workdays, then Max. Units set to 100 percent represents all the time the resource works—that is, 32 hours a week.

- If the resource has a Monday-through-Friday 6-hour workday calendar (that's 30 work hours each week), then Max. Units of 50 percent means the resource is available half of the calendar's working time, or 15 hours a week.

TIP Units aren't limited to 100 percent or less. In fact, if you have a 15-person customer service team, you can set up one work resource for the entire team and set the maximum units to 1,500 percent.

Resource Sheet view is the fastest way to specify maximum units. Simply click the Max. Units cell for a work resource, type the number for the maximum units, and then press Enter. Project adds "%" automatically.

NOTE Project Server uses an administrative project to account for nonproject work time.

Plan for Downtime

No one is productive every minute of every day. Even workaholics spend *some* work time on tasks that aren't a part of your project. An alarming amount of time is spent on unrelated meetings and administrative tasks like filling out health insurance forms. Moreover, the workdays just prior to holiday weekends are renowned for their low productivity. (For more about the importance of building slack time into a schedule, read *Slack* by Tom De Marco [Broadway, 2002]). You can make your Project schedules reflect this downtime:

• **Change the working time for your project.** For example, if experience tells you that 2 hours of every workday are spent on administrative tasks, you can shorten the workdays in your project calendar or resource calendars. This approach can also take into account corporate

holidays and vacation time. One issue with this approach is that the working times you define don't match the start time and end time of your real-world workdays, which might create scheduling issues if a meeting should take place during a time that Project considers nonworking time.

• **Adjust Project's calendar options (page 105) to reflect shorter workdays.** After you change the working time in the project calendar, you need to adjust Project's calendar options to match. In the Project Options dialog box (File→Options→Schedule), you can tell Project that workdays are shorter by changing the values for "Hours per day," "Hours per week," and "Hours per month."

When Availability Varies

What do you do when availability changes over time? Suppose you're working in Kansas duplicating a few of the geoglyphs found in Peru. Carving the giant lizards takes at least a year with everyone working full time, but the number of people on your team varies with the seasons: You have a dozen helpers during the summer and only four people the rest of the year. To help you figure out how long a project like this would take, the Resource Information dialog box's General tab includes a table for setting varying availability levels.

NOTE When the work *calendar* changes over time—for example, a resource switches to 4-day work weeks in the summer—set up different work weeks in a resource calendar (page 111).

Here are the steps for setting up different levels of availability for different time periods:

1. **In Resource Sheet view, double-click the resource you want to edit.**

   The Resource Information dialog box opens. In the General tab's lower-left corner, look for the Resource Availability section (Figure 8-6).

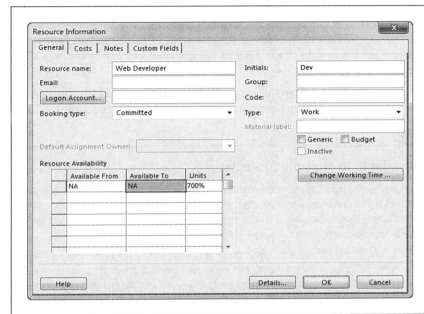

2. **In the Available From column's first cell, choose the date on which the level of availability begins.**

   Any time periods you don't explicitly cover use the value from the Resource Sheet's Max. Units cell.

3. **In the Available To column's first cell, choose the end date.**

   The units you specify in the next step will apply to all assignments that occur between the Available From and Available To dates.

4. **In the Units cell, type the percentage value for the maximum units (such as *50* for 50 percent), and then press Enter.**

   If you omit the percentage sign, Project adds it.

5. **Repeat steps 2–4 in additional rows to specify levels of availability for other timeframes.**

   The dates in each row must be later than the dates in previous rows. For example, if the first row specifies the availability from 6/1/2013 to 8/31/2013, then the dates in the second row must be later than 8/31/2013.

6. **When you finish entering availability, click OK to close the dialog box.**

If you look closely at the Resource sheet, you'll notice that the Max. Units for the resource now appear as 0%. To see the resource's availability, you have to select the resource and open the Resource Information dialog box. Because Max. Units of 0 percent are bound to raise questions from others, you might consider adding a note (page 226) to the resource explaining the reason for this unusual value.

From now on, when you assign this resource to tasks, Project uses the availability percentages that apply for the timeframe during which the task occurs.

POWER USERS' CLINIC

Making Resources Available to Multiple Projects

More often than not, the same resources work on more than one project, whether the projects all occur at once or conveniently follow one after the other. You don't have to recreate the same resources for every project file. It's more efficient to create a *resource pool* for the resources you use time and again, and then apply that resource pool to various projects.

When your projects don't occur simultaneously, a resource pool simply saves you the drudgery of defining the same resources over and over. But if you manage several projects at once (page 516) without the benefit of Project Server, a Project resource pool can help you see who's available, who's already booked, or who's overloaded and needs some assistance.

Creating a resource pool is almost identical to creating a regular Project file. In Project, create a new blank project, and then add (or import) your resources. The difference is that you save the file *after* creating the resources but *before* creating any tasks. To learn how to connect a resource pool to projects and share pooled resources, see page 524.

If your organization manages lots of projects all the time, even a resource pool is unwieldy. Microsoft Enterprise Project Management Solutions provides the tools for mega-project operations. (Project Online is a hosted solution that offers the same capabilities [page xvii].) You can categorize resources by skillsets to locate the right resources, coordinate multiple projects, and view project performance and status for your entire portfolio of projects.

■ Defining Costs for Resources

Unless money is no object (yeah, right), you need to keep a close eye on project costs. Labor and materials usually represent the bulk of the cost for a project. When you assign costs to work and material resources, Project calculates project costs as well as the schedule. The cost fields are available in both the Resource Sheet and the Resource Information dialog box, but the Resource Sheet is usually the quickest option. This section describes how to enter costs for all three types of resources.

Setting Up Work and Material Costs

Work and material resources use the same cost fields, although they don't always represent the same thing. The rate for a work resource is the cost per period of time, whereas a rate for materials is the cost per unit. Here are the cost fields for resources and what they do:

- **Std. Rate** (Standard Rate) is the typical pay rate for a work resource, the cost per time period for a piece of equipment, or the cost per unit for material. For example, a contractor's pay rate of $50 per hour shows up as $50.00/hr. Because work resources are assigned by time, Project automatically adds "/hr" to the number you type. If you pay a contractor a flat rate per month, you can use a different unit of time, for instance, "$5000/mon."

TIP Project includes options for setting the standard rate and overtime rate (discussed in a sec) for resources. Initially, these options are set to $0.00/hr ($0 per hour). However, if most of your resources cost the same amount per hour, you can save a few steps when you're creating resources by setting a default standard or overtime rate. Choose File→Options and on the left side of the Project Options dialog box, click Advanced. In the "General options for this project" drop-down list, choose the project for which you want to set default resource rates, and then type values in the "Default standard rate" and "Default overtime rate" boxes.

Material resources are allocated by units other than time, such as gallons of sports drink, reams of paper, or rolls of shipping tape. For material resources, Std. Rate represents the price per unit. How do you enter the unit for a material resource? The unit is whatever you type into the Material Label cell (if the column is narrow, this columns heading just reads "Material"). For example, for paper, the Material Label unit might be ream. When you type *4.25* in the Std. Rate cell, Project calculates cost as $4.25 per ream. In reality, Project doesn't care what the unit is. The Material Label field is just there to remind you of the units you're using for a particular material so you assign the correct quantity to tasks. Project simply multiplies the quantity assigned by the material's Std. Rate.

- **Ovt. Rate** (Overtime Rate) applies only to work resources. You don't have to fill in this field unless the person earns a premium for overtime and you specifically assign overtime hours to the resource in Project (page 450). People who work for a salary don't cost extra, so their Ovt. Rate is zero. If someone gets the same hourly rate regardless of how many hours he works, you don't have to bother with overtime. (In that situation, you could create an exception with long hours in the resource's calendar.)

NOTE When you assign resources to tasks, Project *doesn't* automatically use the overtime rate for hours assigned beyond the standard workday. To designate overtime hours, you have to modify the resource assignment (page 451) to tell Project to apply the overtime rate.

- **Cost/Use** applies only when you pay an amount each time you use the resource. For example, if you pay a flat $50 each time the network technician comes on site, then enter *50* in the Cost/Use field. That way, every time you assign the network technician to a task, the task's cost includes the hourly rate for the technician *and* his $50 appearance fee. Similarly, you can fill in the Cost/Use field with the cost of delivering rental goods to your event.

- **Accrue At** is important only if someone cares *when* money is spent. For example, if cash flow is tight, knowing whether you pay up front, after the work is done, or spread out over time can make or break a budget. The Accrue At cell offers three settings: Start, Prorated, and End. Start means the cost occurs as soon as the task begins—like paying for a package delivered COD. End represents cost that occurs at the end of a task, such as paying your neighbor's kid when he finishes mowing your lawn. And Prorated spreads the cost over the duration of the task, such as the wages you pay to employees assigned to long tasks.

NOTE Project includes several options for specifying currency. To see them, choose File→Options, and then, on the left side of the Project Options dialog box, choose Display. Below the "Currency options for this project" heading, you can specify the currency symbol you want to use, such as $ for dollars. Type the number of decimal digits you want to see (for example, *2* for cents) in the "Decimal digits" box. Choose the currency in the Currency drop-down list. The Placement setting specifies whether the currency symbol appears before or after the currency value with or without a space between the symbol and the value.

When Pay Rates Vary

The Resource Information dialog box comes in handy for setting costs when a resource has different pay rates or when rates change over time, like if you hire a hermit who charges $50 per hour for work performed at his cave, and $300 per hour for work performed onsite. Here's how you define different or variable pay rates:

1. **Double-click the resource you want to edit.**

   The Resource Information dialog box opens.

TIP If you want to make the same changes to *several* resources, select them all and then, on the Resource tab, click Information. The Multiple Resource Information dialog box opens. Any changes you make in the dialog box are applied to all the resources you selected.

2. **In the Resource Information dialog box, select the Costs tab.**

   The Costs tab contains a cost-rate table with five tabs of its own, labeled A through E (shown in Figure 8-7) so you can define up to five different pay rates for a resource. (If only Project let you assign names to each table so you could tell what each one is for...) Confusingly, Microsoft calls each tab of this table a "cost-rate table." The "A (Default)" tab contains the original values that you entered for this resource.

NOTE After you define a cost-rate table, you can apply it to a resource assignment. Switch to Task Usage or Resource Usage view (on the Task tab, click the bottom half of the Gantt Chart button, and then choose Task Usage or Resource Usage), and then double-click an assignment (in Task Usage view, that's a row containing a resource name; in Resource Usage view, that's a row containing a task name) to open the Assignment Information dialog box. On the General tab, in the "Cost rate table" drop-down list, choose the letter that corresponds to the rate table you want to apply.

3. **To set a second pay rate for the resource, click tab B (shown in Figure 8-7) and then, in its first Standard Rate cell, type the second pay rate.**

To remind yourself what each pay rate is for, select the dialog box's Notes tab, and then type the kind of work and the pay rate that applies.

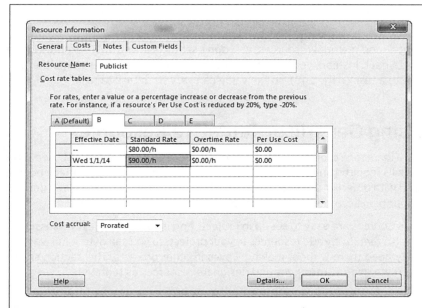

FIGURE 8-7

If you know the dollar amount of the future rate, type it in the appropriate cell (Standard Rate, Overtime Rate, or Per Use Cost cell). You can also specify a rate change with a percentage. If a consultant tells you rates are going up 10 percent, then type 10% in the Standard Rate field. When you press Enter, Project calculates the new rate and replaces the percentage with the new dollar value.

4. **If the pay rate changes over time, select the second cell in the Effective Date column, and then choose the starting date for the new rate.**

The pay rate in the first row applies to any assignments that occur before the first effective date. For example, if the hermit is raising rates on January 1 of the next year, choose that date in the second Effective Date cell.

5. **Repeat step 4 to define additional pay-rate changes and when they take effect.**

6. **To set additional pay rates, select the less-than-helpfully-named tab C, D, or E, and then repeat steps 3–5.**

For each task that uses this resource and cost rate table, Project now applies the pay rate that's in effect when the task occurs.

Specifying Cost for Cost Resources

The Cost resource type is perfect for costs that aren't based on time or any sort of material. Unlike the Fixed Cost field that you had to use in pre-2007 versions of Project, more than one cost resource can apply to a task, like travel, videoconferencing costs, and fees. If you look at cost resources in Resource Usage view, you can review the total cost for each cost resource to see what those categories of costs add up to for the entire project.

To create a cost resource in Resource Sheet view, all you have to do is type its name in the Resource Name cell and then choose Cost in the Type cell. When you press Enter, the standard values for a work resource disappear. The only other fields with values are Initials and Accrue At. To change either the resource's initials or when the cost occurs, click the appropriate cell and then type the new value.

Unlike work and material resources, you *don't* set a cost for a cost resource in the Resource Sheet. Instead, you specify its monetary value when you assign the cost resource to a task (page 248), so the value can vary from task to task.

■ Using Generic or Tentative Resources

Building a team for a project is often an iterative process. You might start by identifying the skills required and craft your initial schedule to determine how many people you need with different skillsets. Then, you find out what resources you can get and revise your plan accordingly. Project can handle both resourcing steps.

Generic resources are easy to set up in Project. And if you use Project Professional, you can also *tentatively* add resources to your project, so you can determine whether you really need them without making waves in other projects. This section shows how to create generic resources and designate resources as tentative.

> **NOTE** If you look closely at the General tab of the Resource Information dialog box, you'll notice the Budget checkbox. With budget resources (page 274), you can record amounts budgeted for different categories of expenses and compare your project's cost performance to the budget. To designate a resource as a budget resource, turn on the Budget checkbox. In addition to turning on the Budget checkbox, it's a good idea to name the budget resource in a way that indicates its budget status. For example, you can add a prefix like "Budget" or "B-." Chapter 10 (page 273) describes how to use Project's budgeting features.

Using Generic Resources

The easiest way to create generic resources is to use job descriptions for resource names, such as Publicist or Web Developer. By creating work resources based on skillsets, you can assign those resources to tasks without worrying about overallocating them. If you need to assign a web developer at 300 percent to make the schedule work, you'll know you need at least three developers to finish on time.

Once you start building your real team, you replace the generic resources with real ones. (See page 333 for the full scoop on replacing resources in assignments.) If you have a cast of thousands, finding assignments that are still using generic resources can take time. The Generic field in Project can simplify finding all your placeholder resources. All you do is filter your project (page 643) for assignments that still have generic resources assigned to them and track down real people to fill those slots until your entire project is staffed.

The easiest way to flag resources as generic is by inserting the Generic column into the table in Resource Sheet view. To do so, right-click a column heading and choose Insert Column; type *g* and then choose Generic from the drop-down list. Then, for each generic resource, change the Generic cell to Yes. When you do, the resource's Indicator column displays an icon of two heads to represent its generic status (Figure 8-8).

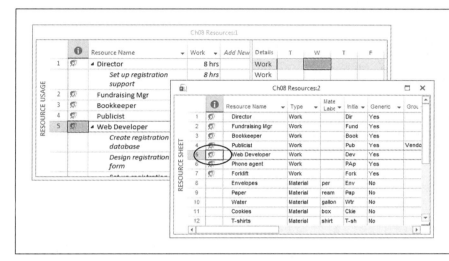

FIGURE 8-8

Resources with Generic fields set to Yes are easy to spot in the Resource Sheet, because the Indicator column displays a generic icon (circled). The same icon appears in the rows for generic resources in Resource Usage view (background) so it's easy to see which assignments you need to edit to assign real people.

Working with Proposed Resources

Project also includes the Booking Type field, which lets you designate resources as Committed or Proposed. If you don't share resources with other projects, you don't have to bother with this field at all. If you do, add this column in Resource Sheet view by right-clicking a column heading, selecting Insert Column, and then choosing Booking Type in the drop-down menu.

This column offers two settings: Committed and Proposed. Project automatically sets new resources to Committed, which means any resource assignment you make reduces the resource's available hours so you can see the person's workload (page 239). The Proposed value lets you *tentatively* assign resources to tasks without locking up their time. Suppose you want to work out a project schedule and budget based on resources that aren't yet officially assigned to your project. Creating them as Proposed means you can calculate dates and costs without taking away any of their available time. When a resource officially becomes yours, you can change its booking type to Committed.

NOTE When you set a resource that's stored in a resource pool to Proposed, the resource shows up as Proposed in every project attached to the resource pool, which probably isn't what you want. So if you're using a resource pool, assign a generic resource instead, and then assign the real resource later.

Adding More Resource Information

The resource fields you change most often appear in the table in Resource Sheet view, so you might never have to give up the convenience and familiarity of entering values in table cells. Besides, if you have other resource fields that you always fill in, then you can insert those columns in the resource table (page 633). This section describes additional resource fields you might want to use and how to specify their values.

> **TIP** If you don't want to change Resource Sheet view's table, use the Resource Information dialog box instead. It contains all the resource fields you can set, and it's the only easy way to add a few of the more intricate resource settings.

Resource Sheet view (View→Resource Sheet) shows the fields most project managers fill in: name, resource type, initials, and workgroup. In the Resource Information dialog box (Resource→Information), the General tab, shown in Figure 8-9, includes these fields and a few more.

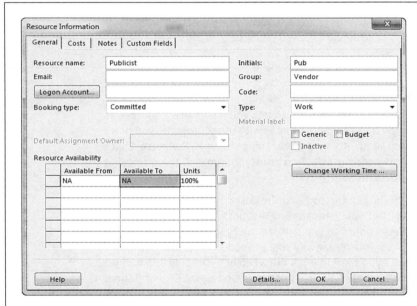

FIGURE 8-9

If the table in Resource Sheet view doesn't show all the fields you want, then the General tab of the Resource Information dialog box is the next place to look. If you don't work with costs, you might not have to venture beyond the General tab.

Filling in Other Resource Fields

Here are the additional resource fields (found on the Resource Information dialog box's General tab) that you might want to fill in, along with their uses:

- **Initials.** The usefulness of this field might not be obvious at first. When you view a schedule in the Gantt Chart timescale, displaying the resources assigned to tasks on the task bars is a quick way to see who does what or to spot tasks without resources. Full names take up too much room and cover up task-link lines, especially when several resources work on the same tasks. Fortunately, you can see who's assigned to tasks without the clutter by displaying resources' *initials* instead of names.

  Project initially sets the Initials field to the first letter of the resource's name. With all but the tiniest teams, that approach doesn't help. You can change the value in this field to whatever you want, like a person's first and last initial or an abbreviated job description.

- **Group.** This field can represent any type of category you want—departments, subcontractors and vendors, or skillsets. In addition to grouping resources in Resource Sheet view, you can also use the Group field to filter the task list to tasks performed by specific work groups, or group tasks by the type of resource required.

- **Code.** This field provides another way to categorize resources, which you can then use to sort, filter, or group tasks and resources. If your organization assigns job codes, you can enter them in this field and then filter for tasks that require a specific job code. (For more on job codes and what you can do with them, see the box on page 226.)

- **Email.** If you distribute information via email directly from Project, then be sure to enter the person's email address here.

NOTE The Resource Information dialog box's Logon Account button applies only if you use Project Server to manage a portfolio of projects. Clicking this button tells Project to fill in the Logon Account box with the person's Windows account information. Then Project uses that info to log into Project Server.

Categorizing Resources in Detail

For a project with a cast of thousands, the Resource Information dialog box's Group and Code fields might not be enough to express all the categories you have. For excruciating detail, *resource outline codes* are a better approach. Similar to WBS codes (page 157), resource outline codes are hierarchical identifiers that can reflect the organizational structure of your company or employee skillsets. For example, you might change a custom outline field like Outline Code1 (page 675) to something that represents the job levels within your organization, like "Eng. Net. Sr." for a senior-level network engineer.

To assign a custom outline code to a resource, in the Resource Information dialog box, select the Custom Fields tab. Any resource outline codes that you've set up appear in the list. In the Value cell, type the code for this resource.

Whether you use a resource outline code, the Group field, or the Code field to categorize resources, you can filter the list of resources in the Assign Resources dialog box to find resources that match your desired characteristics (page 235).

Adding a Note to a Resource

If you want to enter additional information about a resource, head to the Resource Information dialog box. Project calls such additional info *notes*, which can include text, images, and documents. Keep in mind that the information you add to a note is available to *anyone* you share the file with, so don't include anything confidential.

To attach a note to a resource, follow these steps:

1. **In Resource Sheet view, right-click the resource and then choose Notes from the shortcut menu.**

   The Resource Information dialog box opens to the Notes tab.

2. **In the Notes box, type or paste the text you want to add.**

   To format text, select it and then click the buttons on the toolbar above the Notes box, which let you change the font, set the justification, and create bulleted lists. Click the rightmost button (its icon looks like a landscape) to insert an object from another program (such as a document or a photo).

3. **Click OK.**

   A notepad icon appears in the resource's Indicators cell. To see the beginning of the note, position your pointer over this icon. To see the entire note, double-click the Notes icon, and Project opens the Resource Information dialog box to the Notes tab.

Assigning Resources to Tasks

So far, you've created tasks in Project (Chapter 6), put them in the correct sequence (Chapter 7), and told Project about the resources you need (Chapter 8). Now all that hard work is about to pay off. You're ready to turn that Project file into a real schedule that shows when tasks should start and finish—and whether they're scheduled to finish on time.

Although you may estimate hours of work or task durations early on (page 162), you don't see the whole timing picture until you assign resources to auto-scheduled tasks (page 64) in your project. The number of resources you use, how much time those resources devote to their assignments, and when they're available to work all affect how long tasks take and when they occur. And if you've set up your Project resources with costs and labor rates, resource assignments generate a price tag for the project, too.

If you manually schedule tasks (page 60), you're in complete control over when they start and finish. Team Planner view (available in Project Professional) shows who's doing what and when, which tasks aren't assigned, or who's overallocated. With manually scheduled tasks, you can change any of these situations in Team Planner view by dragging tasks to a resource or moving the tasks in the timescale.

This chapter clarifies how duration, work, and units interact, and explains how to use this information to create and modify resource assignments. Assigning resources isn't just picking a task team. You also specify how much time those lucky folks devote to their tasks. For example, once a giant construction crane is on a building site, it's available 100 percent of the time until you move it to another site. However, when you need an attorney for a few days to resolve a legal fiasco, you don't want 100 percent of her working time—or the monumental invoice that comes with it.

■ Assigning Work Resources to Tasks

Project lets you assign work resources in most of the usual places that you set up other task information. Once you've created resources as described in the previous chapter, all you have to do is match them up with the tasks they'll work on. The best way to do that depends on how much assignment detail you want to specify. Here are the methods and when to choose each one:

- **Using the Assign Resources dialog box.** This dialog box is the Swiss Army knife of resource-assignment tools, teeming with indispensable features. Assigning a resource to a task is as simple as clicking a resource's name, but you can also use it to search for specific types of resources, or for resources that have enough available time. This dialog box lets you assign several resources to a task, or assign a resource to several tasks at once. Moreover, you can use it to add, remove, or replace resources you've already assigned.

- **Using Team Planner view.** Team Planner view, available in Project Professional, is a slick way to assign resources, whether you want to assign them to as-yet-unassigned tasks or you want to *reassign* them to get rid of overallocations. This view shows each resource in the project and the tasks they're working on in a timescale. Unassigned tasks appear at the bottom of the view. All you have to do to assign a resource is drag an unassigned task to the resource's row. To reassign a resource, simply drag a task from one resource to another. Page 244 gives you the full scoop.

- **Filling in a task form.** When you already know the resource you want, Task Form view has all the fields you need to craft precise resource assignments. It's easy to display this view in the Details pane as a companion to almost any view. Task Form view also helps when you want to make surgically precise modifications to existing assignments (page 261).

- **Entering names in a task table.** Choosing a resource in a table like the Entry table is good only for the simplest of resource-assigning chores—assigning one or two full-time resources to a task, for example. On the other hand, such a table is ideal for dragging and copying resource assignments to several tasks (page 235).

- **Using the Task Information dialog box.** The Resource tab of this dialog box is another place you can assign resources. But since you have to open and close the dialog box for each task you want to edit, you may want to use it for assignments only when you've already opened the dialog box to make other changes to a task.

Assigning Resources with the Dialog Box

Whether you're assigning one resource to a task full time, assigning several resources to multiple tasks, or searching for the most qualified resources, the Assign Resources dialog box is the place to be. This dialog box can even remain open while you perform other actions in Project. For example, you can assign a few resources and then filter the schedule to evaluate what you've done. If you spot a problem, then you can jump right back to the dialog box to make the fix.

To assign resources in the Assign Resources dialog box, follow these steps:

1. **In the Resource tab's Assignments section, click Assign Resources.**

   When the Assign Resources dialog box opens, drag it out of the way of what you're doing. It stays put and remains open until you move it or click its Close button.

2. **In Gantt Chart view or any other task-oriented view, select the task to which you want to assign resources.**

   If any resources are already assigned to the task, they appear at the top of the list in the Assign Resources dialog box, preceded by a checkmark.

WARNING Project doesn't stop you from assigning resources to summary tasks, but doing so is more confusing than it is helpful. If you assign resources to summary tasks, the rolled-up values (like cost and work) of summary tasks won't equal the totals from all the subtasks because the rolled-up values include values from the summary task's resource assignment. Moreover, summary-task bars in the timescale area of Gantt Chart view don't show assigned resource names at the right end of the bar, so unless you customize the view, you don't even see the resources assigned to summary tasks. (You can see the names in the Entry table, though.)

---

3. **In the dialog box's Resource Name column, click the name of the resource you want to assign.**

   If you want to assign several resources at the same time, click the first resource's name, and then Ctrl-click additional names. If the resources you want are adjacent to one another in the list, click the first resource you want, and then Shift-click the last one.

4. **After you select all the resources you want to assign to the task, click Assign.**

   When you click Assign, Project provides several visual cues for the new resource assignment, as Figure 9-1 shows.

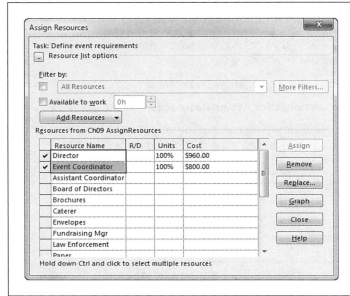

FIGURE 9-1

When you click Assign, the selected resource(s) shoot to the top of the list, above the unassigned resources. A checkmark appears to the left of the assigned resource's name and, in its Units cell, Project automatically enters either the resource's Maximum Units value (page 215) or 100% if the maximum units are greater than 100% (as they are for a team). The cost of using the resource for the time involved appears in the Cost cell.

5. **To change the units for an assignment, type the unitspercentage in the Units cell, and then press Enter or click another field to save the change.**

   To allocate half of the resource's time, type *50* (Project adds the % sign for you). Or click the up and down arrows that appear when you click the Units cell to jump to commonly used percentages. For example, if the Units value is 100%, clicking the down arrow once changes the Units to 50% and clicking it a second time changes the units to 0%. (See the box on page 231 for more about what the term "unit" means in Project.)

   NOTE Units can appear as percentages or decimal values (50% and .5 represent the same allocation), but you have to stick with one format or the other. To switch to decimal units, choose File→Options. On the left side of the Project Options dialog box, click Schedule, and then, in the "Show assignments as a" drop-down list, choose Decimal.

6. **To assign another resource to the same task, repeat steps 3–5.**

7. **To assign resources to another task, select the task, and then repeat steps 3–5.**

   When you're finished assigning resources, click Close to close the dialog box.

You don't have to assign resources to only one task at a time. The Assign Resources dialog box can add assignments to several tasks, as you can see in Figure 9-2. Simply select all the tasks you want to staff by dragging across them or using Shift-click and Ctrl-click. Then use the Assign Resources dialog box as you would for a single task.

UP TO SPEED

What Project Calls a Unit

You'll see the term "units" in a couple of different places in Project: There's a Max. Units (Maximum Units) field in Resource Sheet view's Entry table, and a Units field that's located in the Assign Resources dialog box and Task Form view. It's important to understand that Project uses the term loosely. These are a couple of different types of units in Project, though they're related. Each type is a percentage of time (or the equivalent decimal). The Max. Units field applies to resources, while the Units field (and the related Peak field, which you'll learn about in a sec) apply to the assignments you give those resources. Here's how to keep them straight:

- A resource's **Max. Units** field (page 213), which appears in Resource Sheet view's Entry table and the Resource Information dialog box, is where you indicate the highest percentage of time that resource is available to work on your project. For example, 100 percent means all the resource's time is dedicated to your project; part-time availability can be any value between 1 percent and 99 percent. If you define a resource for a team of interchangeable workers, its Max. Units can even be a value like 300 percent, for three full-time workers.

- The **Units** field in the Assign Resources dialog box and Task Form view is where you record the percentage of time that the resource works on a specific assignment. This field is technically the *Assignment Units* field (even though its label simply reads "Units"), and it represents how much time you initially allocate the resource to the task. For example, a resource working on two concurrent tasks may dedicate 75 percent of his time to one task and the remaining 25 percent to the other.

- Project calculates the highest units assigned at any time during a resource's assignment in the **Peak** field, while keeping the value in the Assignment Units field set to the original value you entered for Assignment Units, as described on page 253. (The Peak field doesn't appear in any tables or forms out of the box. To see it, insert it into a table by right-clicking the table's header row, and then choosing Insert Column→Peak.)

Project flags a resource as overallocated if either the Assignment Units or Peak field value is greater than the resource's Max. Units value.

TIP If a nasty paper-cut accident puts your top assistant out of commission and you need to reassign his tasks to someone else, you can turn to the Replace button in the Assign Resources dialog box. Click the name of the resource you want to replace, and then click Replace. In the Replace Resource dialog box, select the new resource(s), and then click OK. Project removes the original resource from the task and then assigns the replacements.

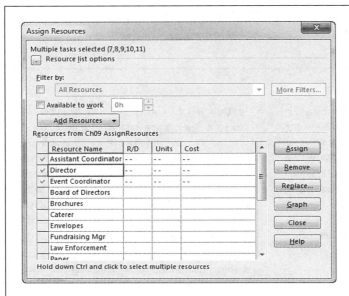

FIGURE 9-2

When you select several tasks, the label at the top of the Assign Resources box changes to "Multiple tasks selected (x,y)," where x and y are the ID numbers of the selected tasks. In addition, gray checkmarks identify all the resources that are assigned to at least one of the selected tasks.

Creating and Assigning Resources at the Same Time

Suppose the resource you want to assign to a task is absent from the list of resources in the Assign Resources dialog box. This omission means that the person (or equipment) doesn't exist in your Project file. Happily, you can create the resource *and* assign it to a task without leaving the Assign Resources dialog box. Here are the steps:

1. In the dialog box's Resources table, click the first blank Resource Name cell, and then type the resource's name.

2. To save the new resource and select it, press Tab.

3. Click Assign. Project moves the resource to the top of the list, puts a checkmark next to it to indicate that it's been assigned, and changes its Units value to 100%.

4. If necessary, adjust the Units value.

After you've completed your assignments, you can add the rest of the information about the resources you added on the fly. To do so, double-click a resource name in the Assign Resources dialog box to see its values in the Resource Information dialog box. Or work on resources in Resource Sheet view. You can use any of the techniques described in Chapter 8 to edit or add to resource records.

The Assign Resources dialog box can also import resources from your email address book or Active Directory (if your computer is connected to an Active Directory domain). To do either, click Add Resources, and then choose either From Active Directory or From Address Book. (If you don't see the Add Resources button, click the + to the left of the "Resource list options" label to display it.)

Assigning Resources in Task Form View

Task Form view and its sibling, Task Details Form view, don't have the fancy features of the Assign Resources dialog box, but they make it easy to assign resources you've identified. The main limitation of these two views is that they let you work with only one task at a time—the one that's currently selected in Gantt Chart or another task view. (But selecting another task is as easy as clicking it.)

Here's how you assign resources in Task Form or Task Details Form view:

1. **In the Task tab's View section, choose Gantt Chart or another task-related view.**

    Task Form view is the standard view that appears in Gantt Chart view's Details pane. If you don't see Task Form view there, in the View tab's Split View section, turn on the Details checkbox (if it's not already on) and choose Task Form from the drop-down list next to it.

2. **In the table in the top pane, select the task that needs resources.**

    Task Form view displays the information for the selected task.

3. **In Task Form view, click the first blank Resource Name cell, and then, from the drop-down list, choose the resource you want to assign.**

    Clicking the down arrow on the right end of the Resource Name cell displays the drop-down list of resources. For large project teams, scrolling through this list can be tedious. When the list is open, you can begin typing a resource's name, and Project jumps to the closest matching name in the list. For example, to skip right to "Smith Brian," type *S*. If Project hasn't located the exact resource, keep typing the resource's name until it does, and then click the resource's name as soon as you see it in the list.

NOTE   Out of the box, Project automatically adds new resources to your file when you type a resource name that doesn't already exist, so a typographical error may create a new—and nonexistent—resource. To prevent these phantom resources from joining your project team, choose File→Options. On the left side of the Project Options dialog box, choose Advanced. In the "General options for this project" drop-down list, make sure the project you want is selected, and then turn off the "Automatically add new resources and tasks" checkbox.

---

4. **To specify the percentage of time the resource devotes to the task, click the Units cell in the same row and type the appropriate number—for example, *50* for 50 percent, as shown in Figure 9-3.**

    If you want to assign the resource at 100 percent (or the resource's maximum units from the Resource Sheet), simply leave the Units cell blank. Project sets Units to 100% or the resource's maximum units automatically when you click OK. The only exception is group resources. If the group resource's maximum units are more than 100 percent, Project still fills in 100%.

The percentage in the Units cell is the percentage of the resource's work schedule, whether it's your organization's standard schedule or a special one. For example, for resources working typical full-time work schedules, 50 percent represents half time (20 hours a week for the typical 40-hour week).

FIGURE 9-3

To assign work instead of units, click the Work cell, and then type the hours, days, or other time units. Project calculates the units based on the work and the task's duration. If you set Project's "Work is entered in" setting to the time unit you use most often (for example, "h" for hours or "d" for days), then you can simply type a number and Project will add the time unit. To set the standard time unit for work, choose File→Options→Schedule.

5. **To assign another resource to the task, click the next blank Resource Name cell, and then repeat steps 3 and 4.**

   After you assign all the resources, click OK. Project calculates the work hours for each resource based on the Units percentage and the task duration, as described in the section "Understanding Duration, Work, and Units" on page 251.

Assigning Resources in a Gantt Chart Table

The Assign Resources dialog box and Task Form view described so far give you the power to enter varying percentages in the Units field, create new resources on the fly, and so on. But if all you need to do is assign all of a resource's available time to one task, then working directly in a table in Gantt Chart view is fast and convenient. Here are the steps:

1. **In the Task tab's View section, choose Gantt Chart.**

   The standard table applied to Gantt Chart view is the Entry table, which includes columns for the task's mode, name, duration, start and finish, predecessors, and resources. If you see different columns, right-click the Select All cell (the one in the table's upper-left corner) and then choose Entry. (You can also apply a table from the View tab's Data section. Click the Tables down arrow and then choose the table you want.)

The Resource Names column is the last column in the Entry table, but it's typically out of sight (covered up by the timescale). Rather than scroll to display the column, make the table area wider so that it displays the columns for both task names and resource names. To do so, position the mouse pointer over the vertical bar between the table and the timescale. When the pointer changes to double arrows, drag the divider bar to the right until the Resource Names column is visible.

2. **In the table, click the Resource Names cell for the task.**

   Project encloses the cell in a heavy green border and displays a down arrow for the resource drop-down list.

3. **To assign a resource, click the down arrow, and then, in the list, turn on the checkboxes for the resource name(s) you want to assign.**

   The name(s) you choose appear in the Resource Names cell. Project automatically assigns the resource at the resource's maximum units (page 213) or 100% for a team resource. If the resource's Max. Units value is 100%, then the Resource Names cell shows only the resource name. However, if the resource's Max. Units value is something other than 100%, then the cell's contents look something like "Bob[50%]."

■ **COPYING A RESOURCE TO MULTIPLE TASKS**

Suppose your able assistant can handle all the tasks required to obtain the proper permits for your event, so you want to assign all those tasks to her. A table makes copying assignments between tasks easy. When you want to apply the same resource and units to several tasks, follow these steps:

1. **Click the Resource Names cell that contains the resources and units you want, and then press Ctrl+C (or in the Task tab's Clipboard section, click Copy).**

   Project copies the values from the Resource Names cell to the Clipboard.

2. **Select the other Resource Names cells into which you want to copy the assignment, and then press Ctrl+V (or in the Task tab's Clipboard section, click Paste).**

TIP   If several consecutive tasks use the same resources, select the Resource Names cell with the value you want to copy. Then position the pointer over the fill handle in the lower-right corner of that cell. When the pointer changes to a + symbol, drag over the rows that use the same resources.

Finding the Right Resources

When resources are plentiful, scrolling through a long list of names to find the resource you want to assign could take a while. You can reduce scrolling by telling the Assign Resources dialog box to list only the resources appropriate for the current assignment. All you have to do is tell it what you're looking for. You can apply a resource filter to find people who possess the right skills, belong to a specific group, or have the job code you're looking for. If you use resource outline codes (page 675) to categorize resources, you can filter by those codes, too. But even the most qualified resources don't help at all if they aren't available. Fortunately, the Assign Resources dialog box also helps you find resources with enough available time.

These filtering features may not appear when you first open the Assign Resources dialog box. To coax the Resource list options into view, click the + sign to the left of the "Resource list options" label, shown in Figure 9-4.

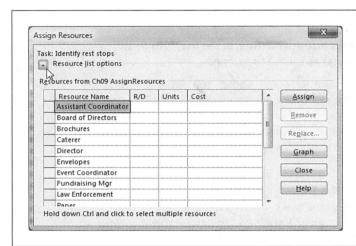

FIGURE 9-4

When the filtering options are visible (which they're not here), the + button to the left of the "Resource list options" label changes to a –, which you can click when you want to hide the options once more. The Assign Resources dialog box remembers whether you had the filtering options expanded or hidden the last time you used it, and it reopens with that same setting the next time you use it.

■ FINDING RESOURCES BY CRITERIA

You can use the Assign Resources dialog box's resource filters to restrict what appears in the Resources table. For example, you can filter the resource list with a built-in resource filter like Group to see only the resources that belong to a specific group. If you've created custom resource filters (page 642), for instance to filter by the Code resource field, then you can filter the Resources table with those, too. (The box on page 191 describes another way to categorize resources so you can find them by filtering the list in the Assign Resources dialog box.)

To filter the resource list by criteria, follow these steps:

1. **With the "Resource list options" visible, turn on the top "Filter by" checkbox.**

   In the "Filter by" box, Project automatically selects the All Resources filter, so the Resources table continues to show all available resources. If the filter options are grayed out, make sure the first "Filter by" checkbox is turned on.

2. **In the "Filter by" drop-down list, choose the filter you want to apply.**

   The Resources table displays only the resources that pass the filter, as illustrated in Figure 9-5.

If a filter's name ends with an ellipsis (...), then the filter requires some input from you. For example, if you select the "Group..." filter, a dialog box opens so you can type the name of the group you're interested in. Enter the value, and then click OK.

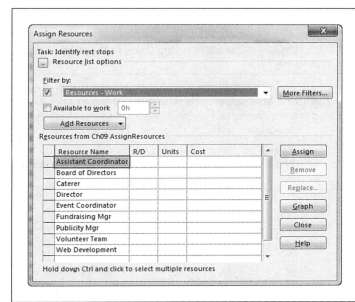

FIGURE 9-5

The "Filter by" drop-down list includes all existing resource filters. If none of these filters suit your needs, click More Filters to open the More Filters dialog box. There, you can create a new filter, edit an existing filter, or copy a filter to obtain exactly the resource filter you want—for example, to search for resources based on their Outline Code values, or to view only Confirmed resources.

3. **Once the Resources table is filtered, assign resources as you would normally (page 229).**

    To view the entire resource list again, in the "Filter by" drop-down list, either choose All Resources or turn off the "Filter by" checkbox.

■ FINDING RESOURCES WITH AVAILABLE TIME

Resources with the right skills aren't any help if they don't have enough time to complete an assignment. Suppose you've added some customer change requests to your schedule, and you want to find people with the spare time to complete these shorter tasks. The Assign Resources dialog box's "Available to work" checkbox is just the ticket for finding folks who are available when the task is scheduled. When you turn it on, Project searches for the resources that have the amount of time you specify available between the task's start and finish dates.

To find people who have enough hours available, do the following:

1. **Select the task to which you want to assign resources.**

    If the Assign Resources dialog box isn't open, then, in the Resource tab's Assignments section, click Assign Resources.

2. **With the Assign Resources dialog box's "Resource list options" visible, turn on the "Available to work" checkbox.**

   The box to the right of the "Available to work" label becomes active.

3. **In the "Available to work" box, type the amount of time the assignment requires, such as *4d* or *32h*, as illustrated in Figure 9-6.**

   Project updates the dialog box's Resources table to include only the resources who have that amount of time available between the task's start and finish dates.

NOTE If you don't type a time unit, Project uses the standard units for work, which is one of the program's settings. (Choose File→Options, and then choose Schedule. The "Work is entered in" box specifies the standard time units for work.) For example, if work units are hours and you type *5*, Project converts the value to 5h. If you type *5d*, Project converts the "Available to work" value to 40h.

---

4. **Choose and assign resources from the filtered list as you would normally.**

   To view resources regardless of availability, turn off the "Available to work" checkbox.

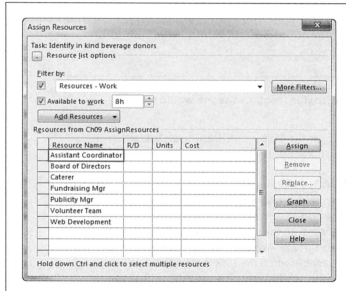

FIGURE 9-6

Although you can filter the list of resources by available time alone, filtering by type of resource and available time (as shown here) shows you the resources that are both qualified and available. In the "Resource list options" section, simply turn on both the "Filter by" and "Available to work" checkboxes. Then choose a resource filter and specify the time required.

POWER USERS' CLINIC

Building Teams with Project Server

If you use Project Server or Project Online to manage your project portfolio, you can classify resources by skillsets with *enterprise resource outline codes* and *resource breakdown structure codes*. These products also offer *multi-value resource outline codes*, which means you can assign more than one skillset to extraordinarily talented resources.

The Team Builder tool in Project Server searches the enterprise resource pool for available resources with the skills you need. If you have to replace someone on a task, Project Server's Resource Substitution Wizard looks for resources with the same skills as the resource you're replacing. For more information on these tools, see the recommended books on Microsoft Enterprise Project Management Solutions (page xix).

■ REVIEWING AVAILABILITY IN DETAIL

The Assign Resources dialog box doesn't see shades of gray when it filters resources by availability: Resources either have enough time available or they don't. But you can use Resource Graph view to get a better idea of whom to assign to a task. For example, if one resource is almost completely booked, then someone with more available time would give you more wiggle room should task dates slip. Or you may see that the perfect resource has *almost* enough time available and realize that the assignment may work if you simply delay it by a day or increase its duration.

Resource Graph view (Figure 9-7) shows the number of hours the resource has available during each time period. For instance, if you have a change request that requires 8 hours of work during a week, you can look for 8 available hours on a resource's graph. You can also use the graph to evaluate the work assigned to proposed resources to see how many more real resources you have to round up, as described in the box on page 240.

You can display Resource Graph view in the following ways:

- In the Assign Resources dialog box, select the resource you want to evaluate, and then click Graphs.

- In the View tab's Split View section, turn on the Details checkbox. Then, in the drop-down list, choose Resource Graph.

To see a graph of the resource's *available* time, which is usually what you want when you have an assignment to fill, right-click the background of the Resource Graph's timescale and then choose Remaining Availability on the shortcut menu. See page 623 for other ways to customize Resource Graph view.

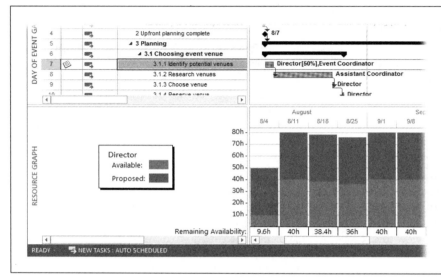

FIGURE 9-7

When you set Resource Graph view to display Remaining Availability, the graph shows available work hours and proposed hours for the selected resource during each time period. Because the graph shows availability over time, it applies only to work resources, not material or cost resources.

Viewing Proposed Bookings

As described in Chapter 8, when you add resources to your Project file, you can specify that they're either committed or proposed resources (page 223). Committed resources are those you know are in your roster, whereas proposed resources represent resources you'd *like* to get but don't have for sure. The Resource Graph shows work you've assigned to both com-mitted *and* proposed resources—the only difference is that the vertical bars for proposed work are purple. (Be careful about changing the status if you use a resource pool. Changing a resource to "Proposed" in a resource pool changes the resource's status to "Proposed" in *every* project to which the resource is assigned.)

Quickly Assigning Resources with Team Planner

Team Planner view is perfect for more informal assignments, when you have several tasks (manually or automatically scheduled) that you want to fling resources at in a jiffy. (To display it, in the View tab's Resource Views section, click Team Planner.) The anatomy of Team Planner view makes it easy to see which tasks are currently orphaned without resources. Then you can drag a task onto a resource's row and—poof!—you've got a resource assignment.

In addition to initial assignments, Team Planner view also helps you spot unassigned tasks or overallocated resources. You can drag a task to a resource who doesn't have anything to do or move a task in the timeline to even out workloads—without messing with Project's fancier leveling features (page 339).

WARNING Moving tasks around in Team Planner is easy—maybe *too* easy. If you're working with manually scheduled tasks, dragging a task to a new date is often exactly what you want to do—for example, to nudge the task one day later so the assigned resource isn't overallocated. However, if your tasks are auto-scheduled, then dragging them around in the timeline creates date constraints (page 190), which limit Project's ability to calculate start and finish dates. So if you use Team Planner to assign or swap resources on auto-scheduled tasks, make sure you don't drag auto-scheduled tasks to different dates.

■ ANATOMY OF TEAM PLANNER VIEW

Team Planner view is divided into four quadrants, each with its own story to tell, as shown in Figure 9-8:

- **Resources.** The upper-left part of the view lists resources assigned to the project itself, one resource per row. If a resource is assigned to tasks that don't have start or finish dates, then those tasks appear in this quadrant's Unscheduled Tasks column.

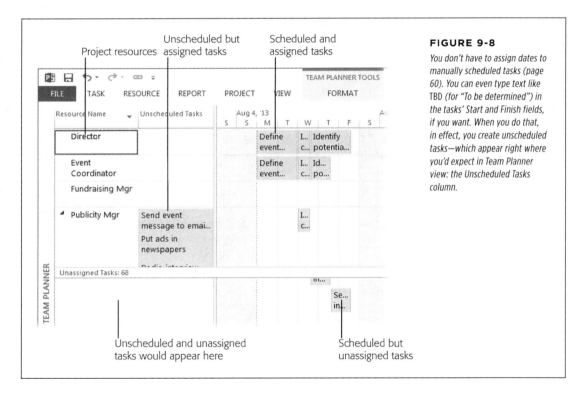

FIGURE 9-8

You don't have to assign dates to manually scheduled tasks (page 60). You can even type text like TBD (for "To be determined") in the tasks' Start and Finish fields, if you want. When you do that, in effect, you create unscheduled tasks—which appear right where you'd expect in Team Planner view: the Unscheduled Tasks column.

- **Assigned task timescale.** Similar to the timescale in a Gantt Chart view, the upper-right part of the view shows a timescale that positions bars based on tasks' start and finish dates. However, these bars are *assignment* bars, not task bars. If a task has more than one resource assigned to it, you see a bar for the task in the row for each assigned resource. The tasks in this quadrant are both assigned to resources and scheduled in time.

- **Unassigned but scheduled tasks.** The timescale in the bottom-right part of Team Planner view shows scheduled tasks that have no resources assigned. If you're trying to tie up the last loose unassigned tasks, look no further than this quadrant.

- **Unassigned and unscheduled tasks.** The lower-left quadrant is reserved for the least-defined tasks of all: ones that don't have start or finish dates, or assigned resources.

TIP You can format Team Planner view to control the information you see or to change the size of the bars. For example, after you assign all the tasks to resources, you can hide the Unassigned Tasks pane. Simply head to the Team Planner Tools | Format tab and turn off the Unassigned Tasks checkbox. To hide the Unscheduled column, turn off the Unscheduled Tasks checkbox. Or, to display a single row for each resource, turn off the Expand Resource Rows checkbox.

■ ASSIGNING TASKS WITH TEAM PLANNER

If a task sits forlornly unassigned in the bottom half of Team Planner, you can assign a resource to it in no time. Just drag the task from its place in the Unassigned Tasks portion of the view to the row for the resource you want to assign it to, as Figure 9-9 shows.

This technique works just as well if you want to reassign a task from one resource to another. Simply drag the task's assignment bar from the assigned resource to the row for the resource you want to assign the task to. When you reassign a task in this way, be sure to drag the bar vertically in the timescale so you don't change the task's dates.

NOTE If you drag a manually scheduled task to different dates, the only things that change are the task's start and finish dates. However, if you drag an auto-scheduled task to different dates, you add a date constraint to the task, which limits Project's ability to calculate the schedule. See page 317 to learn how to find and remove date constraints.

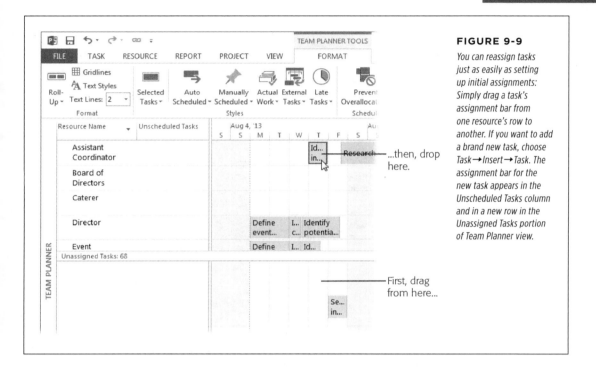

FIGURE 9-9

You can reassign tasks just as easily as setting up initial assignments: Simply drag a task's assignment bar from one resource's row to another. If you want to add a brand new task, choose Task→Insert→Task. The assignment bar for the new task appears in the Unscheduled Tasks column and in a new row in the Unassigned Tasks portion of Team Planner view.

SCHEDULING TASKS WITH TEAM PLANNER

When you figure out when you want an unscheduled task to occur (whether or not it's assigned to a resource), you can drag it to the correct date in the timescale. If it's still unassigned, simply drag it to the date you want in the unassigned portion of the timescale. If you know who will perform the task, drag the bar to the row for the resource and to the date you want in the timescale.

ELIMINATING OVERALLOCATIONS WITH TEAM PLANNER

A resource can work on two tasks at the same time without a problem, as long as neither task is full time. In such cases, each task appears in its own row, as Figure 9-10 shows. However, if the concurrent tasks take up more time than the resource has available, a red box or bracket appears around the timeframe over which the resource is overallocated. Although Team Planner view has a Prevent Overallocations feature, you're better off resolving overallocations yourself, as the box on page 245 explains.

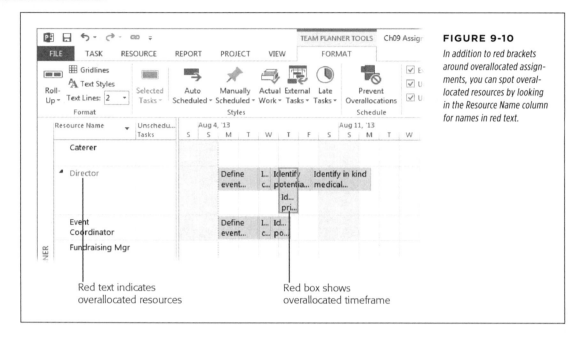

FIGURE 9-10

In addition to red brackets around overallocated assignments, you can spot overallocated resources by looking in the Resource Name column for names in red text.

Red text indicates overallocated resources

Red box shows overallocated timeframe

Resolving overallocations in Team Planner is as simple as assigning resources in the first place. Here are the methods you can use:

- **Reassign a task to another resource.** To reassign a task to a resource who has time available, simply drag the assignment bar to the row for the new resource or right-click the assignment bar and point to Reassign To on the shortcut menu. Then, on the submenu, choose the appropriate resource.

- **Move the task to a different date.** If the resource has a short backlog, you can bump the task further into the future or move it earlier. You can reschedule a task by dragging its bar to a new date in the timescale, or you can use a Move Task Forward or Move Task Backward command. For example, to push the task ahead by a week, click the task's assignment bar to select it and then, on the Task tab, in the Tasks section, choose Move→1 Week.

- **Reschedule the task to when a resource is available.** If a resource works on a hodgepodge of short assignments, finding adjacent timeslots for a longer assignment is almost impossible. Instead, you can tell Project to chop the assignment up and slide it into a resource's open slots. To do so, select the assignment you want to reschedule. Then on the Task tab, in the Tasks section, choose Move→When Resources Are Available.

Don't Let Team Planner Resolve Overallocations

When Team Planner view is visible (in the View tab's Resource Views section, click Team Planner) and you click the Team Planner Tools | Format tab, you might have noticed the Prevent Overallocations button. Telling Project to prevent resource overallocations might sound like a free lunch. But, of course, it isn't.

If you click the Prevent Overallocations button to turn on that setting (you know it's on because "Prevent Overallocations: On" appears in the status bar) and then try to assign a task to an already-allocated resource, Project prevents the overallocation by delaying the assignment until the resource *is* available. However, delaying an assignment isn't the only way to eliminate an overallocation, and it might not be the one you would choose.

The other disadvantage to this feature is that Project could make changes when you aren't looking. Say you display Team Planner view and turn on Prevent Overallocations. Then you switch to a different view and make schedule changes that overallocate some resources. If you switch back to Team Planner view, the Prevent Overallocations feature immediately delays any overallocated assignments to remove the overallocations. But you might not notice that the program made the changes, which makes them tough to find and undo.

■ Assigning Material Resources to Tasks

Assigning material resources is similar to assigning work resources—with one exception: When you assign material resources, you fill in the quantity of material the task will consume instead of the time a work resource spends.

Work resources are always allocated by some unit of time, but you can dole out material resources by whatever unit of measurement makes sense: milligrams of medication, reams of paper, or gallons of water. Truth be told, Project couldn't care less about a material resource's unit of measurement. It calculates cost by multiplying the material resource's Standard Rate (page 219) by the quantity you enter in the assignment. It's your responsibility to define the unit of measurement in the resource's Material Label cell and the Standard Rate as the cost of one unit of the material. Figure 9-11 shows how the material resource fields produce cost in an assignment. (The box on page 248 explains what to do when the amount of material consumed varies with time.)

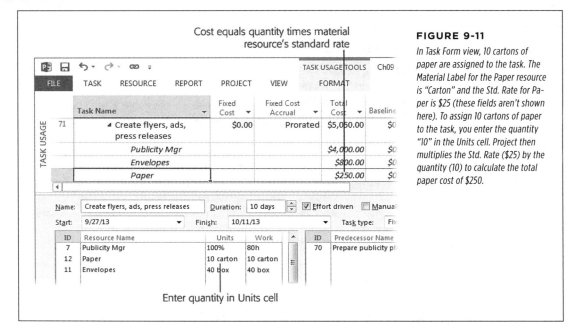

Cost equals quantity times material resource's standard rate

Enter quantity in Units cell

FIGURE 9-11

In Task Form view, 10 cartons of paper are assigned to the task. The Material Label for the Paper resource is "Carton" and the Std. Rate for Paper is $25 (these fields aren't shown here). To assign 10 cartons of paper to the task, you enter the quantity "10" in the Units cell. Project then multiplies the Std. Rate ($25) by the quantity (10) to calculate the total paper cost of $250.

You can assign material resources using any of the methods described in "Assigning Work Resources to Tasks" (page 228). To assign a material resource to a task using the Assign Resources dialog box, do the following:

1. **On Project's Resource tab, in the Assignments section, click Assign Resources.**

   The Assign Resources dialog box opens.

2. **In Gantt Chart view or any other task-oriented view, select the task to which you want to assign a material resource.**

   Any resources already assigned to the task appear at the top of the list, preceded by a checkmark. (At this point, you can add either work or material resources to the task.)

3. **In the dialog box's Resource Name column, click the name of the material resource, and then click Assign.**

   The material resource moves to the top of the list (just like assigned work resources do), as shown in Figure 9-12.

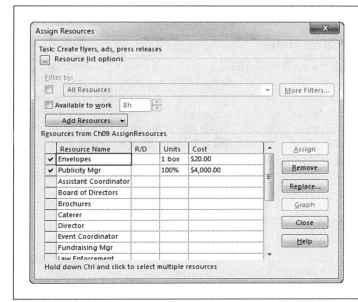

FIGURE 9-12

In the Assign Resources dialog box, Project initially fills in the Units cell automatically with the quantity "1," followed by whatever you typed in the Material cell in Resource Sheet view. To specify the quantity, type a number in the Units cell.

4. **In the Units cell, type the correct quantity. Press Enter or click another cell to complete the change.**

   Project automatically recalculates the Cost field by multiplying the quantity by the material's Std. Rate.

5. **To assign another resource, select the resource name, and then click Assign.**

   To assign resources to another task, in Gantt Chart view, select the next task. Close the Assign Resources dialog box when you're done assigning resources.

When Material Quantity Depends on Time

With some material resources, the quantity assigned to a task is the same regardless of how long the task takes. In other words, that resource has a *fixed consumption rate*. If your task is to put up signs, the quantity of signs is 50, whether the task takes 2 hours or 8 hours. A *variable consumption rate*, by contrast, means the quantity of material varies based on the duration of the task. Say your Hummer chugs 5 gallons of gas each hour you drive around putting up signs. If you complete the job in 2 hours, you use 10 gallons of gas, whereas an 8-hour escapade guzzles 40 gallons.

You specify the units of measurement for a material resource in the Resource Sheet view's Material Label field, and the cost

per unit in the Std. Rate field. But after that, entering variable consumption rates in Project gets a little tricky. Typing *gallons/ day* into the Material Label cell *doesn't* tell Project to calculate quantity based on task duration. The solution—and it's a bit obscure—is to type the quantity per unit of time in the Units field when you assign the material resource to a task. For example, assign the Gasoline resource to the "Post course signs" task. Then, in the Units cell, type *5 gallons/h*. Project calculates the total cost of gasoline by multiplying the standard rate (the price per gallon) from the Resource Sheet's table by the duration in hours.

■ Assigning Cost Resources to Tasks

Cost resources differ from work and material resources in that you don't specify how much they cost until you assign them to tasks. Although you can use any of the methods described in "Assigning Work Resources to Tasks" (page 228) to assign a cost resource, you have one additional step to perform. To assign a cost resource to a task using the Assign Resources dialog box, do the following:

1. **In the Resource tab's Assignments section, click Assign Resources.**

   The Assign Resources dialog box opens.

2. **In Gantt Chart view or any other task-oriented view, select the task to which you want to assign a cost resource.**

3. **In the dialog box's Resource Name column, click the name of the cost resource.**

   Project displays a green border around the resource you click.

4. **In the Cost cell, type the cost for this use of the cost resource. Press Enter or click another cell to complete the assignment.**

   Unlike work and material resources, you specify the cost each time you assign a cost resource to a task, so its cost can differ for each assignment, as shown in Figure 9-13.

FIGURE 9-13

When you assign a cost resource (such as Permits) to a task, you specify the cost for that assignment. For that reason, the cost can differ for each assignment, such as $50 for a county permit and $25 for a law-enforcement permit. Project shows you the total you've spent on each type of cost resource, such as the $120 for permits shown here.

Reviewing Resource Assignments

In earlier sections you learned how to use different views to create resource assignments. However, those initial assignments might not produce the schedule you want. If that's the case, you need to examine the assignments you've made to see what tweaks might be required. Here are several methods for looking at resource assignments:

- **View assignment details as you work on your task list.** Task Form view (page 234) can show you who's assigned to a task, the units they're assigned, and the hours of work they're allocated. This view works equally well for creating, reviewing, and modifying resource assignments. To display this view below any task-oriented view, in the View tab's Split View section, turn on the Details checkbox, and then choose Task Form in the drop-down menu.

- **View assignments grouped by task or resource.** Task Usage view displays a summary row for each task and additional rows for each assignment, which is helpful when you want to see assignment details for all the resources assigned to tasks. However, you might find *Resource Usage* view handier when you're trying to smooth out the workload for an overworked resource. Resource Usage view displays a summary row for each resource and additional rows for the resource's assignments, as shown in Figure 9-14. Another advantage to usage views is that the right side of the view is a time-phased grid that shows when work occurs over time.

- **View assignment details.** The Assignment Information dialog box lets you dig even deeper into an assignment to, for example, see a work contour (page 335) or a cost rate table (page 220) that's applied. When you're in Task Usage or Resource Usage view, double-click an assignment's row to open the Assignment Information dialog box. (If you double-click a task-summary row instead, the Task Information dialog box appears. Similarly, double-clicking a resource-summary row displays the Resource Information dialog box.)

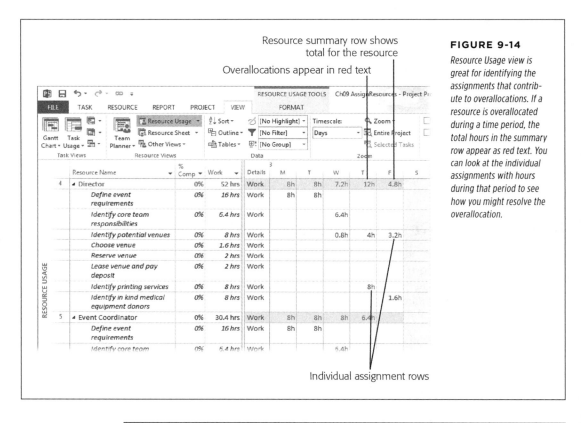

Resource summary row shows total for the resource
Overallocations appear in red text

FIGURE 9-14

Resource Usage view is great for identifying the assignments that contribute to overallocations. If a resource is overallocated during a time period, the total hours in the summary row appear as red text. You can look at the individual assignments with hours during that period to see how you might resolve the overallocation.

Individual assignment rows

TIP Resource Usage view is also helpful for seeing whether you're utilizing your resources fully. To do that, click the black triangle to the left of a resource's name to hide its assignments. That way, you see only the resource's summary row. Then, in the View tab's Zoom section, choose a time unit like Weeks or Months. If you choose Weeks, scan the columns in the time-scaled portion of the view. If the Work cells for most weeks are close to or equal to 40, you're all set. On the other hand, if the assigned work hours vary widely from week to week, you may want to see if you can modify your schedule to keep your resources' workloads more stable over time.

■ Understanding Duration, Work, and Units

Assigning one resource to a task and obtaining the results you want is relatively easy, but modifying existing assignments can be a puzzle. For example, if you assign two more people to attend a meeting in Project, the program makes the meeting shorter (as if that would happen) instead of adding those people's time to the total hours. Understanding how duration, work, and units interact is the first step toward getting the right assignment results the first time—and every time.

Project has built-in rules about which values it changes. To give you a fighting chance, it also offers features that let you control which variables hold steady and which ones change. Task duration, work (think person-hours), and resource units (the proportion of time that resources work on a task) are like three people playing Twister—when one of these variables changes, the others must change to keep things balanced.

When you first assign resources to a task, the task's duration is inextricably connected to the work and units of that resource assignment. The formula is simple no matter which variable you want to calculate. The basic algebra you learned in high school is all you need: Duration = Work ÷ Units, so Work = Duration × Units. Project calculates one of these three variables when you set the other two, as you can see in Figure 9-15:

- **Work = Duration × Units.** If you estimate task duration and specify the units that a resource devotes to that task, then Project calculates the hours of work the resource must perform. For example, a 5-day duration with a resource assigned at 100% (which, as a decimal, is 1) results in 40 hours of work for a typical workday: 40 hours = 5 days (× 8 hours/day) × 1.

- **Duration = Work ÷ Units.** If you estimate the amount of work a task requires, Project calculates the task's duration based on the resource units. For instance, 40 hours of work with a resource assigned at 50% (or .5) produces a 10-day duration based on 8-hour workdays: 10 days = 40 hours ÷ .5.

- **Units = Work ÷ Duration.** If you estimate the work involved and also know how long you want the task to take, Project calculates the units that a resource must spend on it. Eight hours of work over 4 days is 2 hours a day, or a resource assigned 25% based on 8-hour workdays. Project would prefer to not calculate units, as Table 9-1 shows. If you specify work and duration, it might look like Project is ignoring your instructions. See page 253 to learn what's really going on with units in that situation.

TIP Project includes several options for defining the standard number of work hours for different durations. See page 105 for the full scoop on telling Project how to convert different units of time.

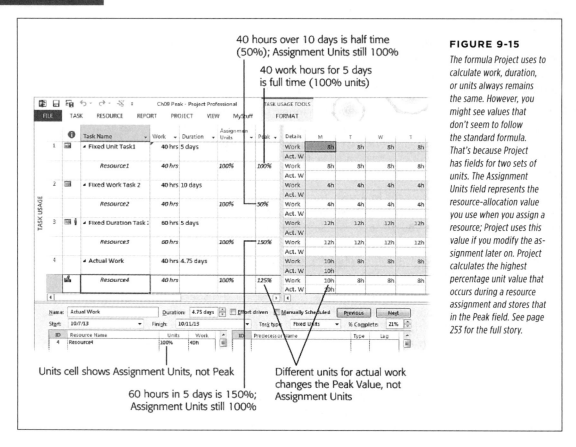

40 hours over 10 days is half time
(50%); Assignment Units still 100%

40 work hours for 5 days
is full time (100% units)

FIGURE 9-15

The formula Project uses to calculate work, duration, or units always remains the same. However, you might see values that don't seem to follow the standard formula. That's because Project has fields for two sets of units. The Assignment Units field represents the resource-allocation value you use when you assign a resource; Project uses this value if you modify the as-signment later on. Project calculates the highest percentage unit value that occurs during a resource assignment and stores that in the Peak field. See page 253 for the full story.

Units cell shows Assignment Units, not Peak

60 hours in 5 days is 150%;
Assignment Units still 100%

Different units for actual work
changes the Peak Value, not
Assignment Units

If you leave some of the assignment fields blank, Project plays favorites when it decides whether to calculate duration, work, or units. Unless you tell Project otherwise, it first tries to change duration, then work, and, as the last resort, units. So the only time Project calculates units is when you specify both task duration and the amount of work. Table 9-1 shows how this favoritism works depending on the values you enter.

TABLE 9-1 *Project calculates duration, work, or units depending on which values you enter*

DURATION	WORK	UNITS
Project calculates	Your input	Your input
Project calculates	Your input	If blank, Project uses 100% or Max. Units.
Your input	*Project calculates*	Your input
Your input	*Project calculates*	If blank, Project uses 100% or Max. Units.
Your input	Your input	*Project calculates*
If blank, Project uses 1 day.	*Project calculates*	Your input

TIP You can download Table 9-1 from this book's Missing CD page at *www.missingmanuals.com/cds.*

Assignment Units vs. Peak

Prior to Project 2010, the program could keep track of only one value for assignment units, which often led to resource assignments that didn't do what you wanted. These days, Project can keep track of the workload you originally assigned to a resource as well as any changes made to that workload. It does that by using two sets of units for assignments: the Assignment Units field and the Peak field. Although those two fields help Project do a better job of assigning resources the way you want, they won't win any awards for most-intuitive feature. For example, you may have noticed that Project doesn't seem to follow the formula Units = Work ÷ Duration when changing a resource assignment. This section explains how Assignment Units and Peak work together to handle resource assignments.

Here's what the Assignment Units and Peak fields do:

- The **Assignment Units** field represents the units you set when you first assign a resource to a task—and the units Project uses if you later reschedule the task. For example, say you assign an 8-hour-a-day resource to a task at 100%, so a 4-day task represents 32 hours of work. If you later increase the task's duration because there's more work to do, Project assigns the resource at 100% for those days as well.

- The **Peak** field, on the other hand, represents the maximum allocation for the resource on the assignment. For example, the third task in Figure 9-15 shows that the resource's maximum allocation to the assignment is only 25%, because the resource works 8 hours over 4 days, even though the initial assignment units were 100%.

TIP It's hard to follow the Assignment Units and Peak action with Project's built-in views and tables. To see what's going on with the Assignment Units and Peak values as you work on assignments, switch to Task Usage view (in the View tab's Task Views section, click Task Usage) and insert an Assignment Unit column and a Peak column into the table, as shown in Figure 9-15.

Consider the task named Actual Work in Figure 9-15 (it's in row 4). Suppose you assign the resource to work 100% of the time on the task, but he works 10 hours the first day. If Project didn't have the Peak field, it would recalculate the resource's Assignment Units to be 125%, based on the duration and work. Then, suppose you add another 40 hours of work to the task. Project would divide the additional work by the 125% Assignment Units value and add another 4 days to the task's duration.

That's where the Peak field comes in. It records the 125% allocation for posterity, while the Assignment Units field value remains 100%. That way, when you increase the task work by 40 hours, Project divides the 40 hours by 100% units and adds 5 more days to the task—just as you intended.

The Peak field also comes into play if you change assignments on tasks set to either the Fixed Duration or Fixed Work task type. Tasks set to the Fixed Units task type don't affect the Peak field. If you use Fixed Work or Fixed Duration tasks to achieve the assignment adjustments you want, you need to understand how the Peak field fits into the picture. Figure 9-15 shows the result of changing tasks set to Fixed Units, Fixed Work, and Fixed Duration task types. They're named Fixed Unit Task 1, Fixed Work Task 2, and Fixed Duration Task 3, respectively. Here's what happens if you change each type of task:

- **Changing a Fixed Units task.** If a 5-day task is assigned full time (100%), the work hours equal 40 hours. If you increase the task's duration to 10 days, Project keeps 100% units and recalculates the work to be 80 hours. Assignment Units and Peak are still both equal to 100%.

- **Changing a Fixed Work task.** Suppose you start with the same 5-day task assigned at 100%. You set the task to Fixed Work so the amount of work doesn't change. If you change the task's duration to 10 days, the work is still 40 hours, so the resource works half time. Project changes the Peak value to 50%, but Assignment Units still equals 100%.

- **Changing a Fixed Duration task.** Using the same 5-day task assigned at 100%, you set the task to Fixed Duration. If you increase the work hours to 60, Project calculates the Peak value to be 150%.

TIP Project calculates an assignment's Peak values minute by minute, so a 1-minute overallocation will flag the resource as overallocated (by displaying the red overallocation icon in a table's Indicators column). If an overallocation is short and you have your timescale set to show longer time periods like months, you won't see the overallocation—for example, in Resource Graph view or the time-phased pane of Task Usage view. However, if you expand the timescale to hours or minutes, the overallocated time period eventually comes out of hiding.

■ Modifying Resource Assignments

Sometimes you want to control how Project calculates resource assignments because the built-in calculations described in the previous section don't quite fit your situation. For example, if you assign two people to a 3-day task, Project initially assigns each person full time for all 3 days. Suppose what you really want is the 3-day task collapsed into 1.5 12-hour days. Using the "Task type" field, you can tell Project that you want to adjust the duration, not the work hours or assigned units.

Another factor to consider when modifying resource assignments is Project's *effort-driven scheduling*, which means that the total amount of work required for a task drives the changes that Project makes. Effort-driven scheduling keeps a task's total amount of work the same when you add or remove resources to the task by reducing or increasing the work each resource performs. But effort-driven scheduling doesn't always hold true, particularly for tasks like diabolical project meetings that refuse to grow shorter no matter how many people attend. This section explains how to integrate task types and effort-driven scheduling with duration, work, and units to modify resource assignments exactly the way you want.

> **TIP** If you're planning to use Project's resource leveling feature, the best method for handling project admin time is to add additional time (for example, 5% or 10%) for it to your tasks. For example, if a task's estimated hours are equal to 40, you might assign the resource to work 44 hours instead. That way, Project's resource leveling feature won't have to struggle with numerous short tasks or one long task for admin time (both of which make it hard for the leveling feature to do its job).

You can modify resource assignments in all manner of ways, as described in the rest of this section: add resources to a task or remove them, modify task duration or work time, or modify a resource's allocated units (the percentage of time devoted to a task).

> **TIP** When you change your project in certain ways, Project may ask you to clarify what you're trying to accomplish. For example, if you change the duration of a task, Project displays an *indicator* (a small triangle in the corner of the cell whose value changed—Duration, in this example). When you point your cursor at this triangle, a yellow diamond with an exclamation point appears. Clicking this diamond opens a shortcut menu with options that let you specify how to complete the change: Decrease work but keep the resources working the same amount each day, or keep the work the same while increasing the hours the resources work each day. If you don't want to see these indicators, choose File→Options. On the left side of the Project Options dialog box, choose Display, and then turn off the "Edits to work, units, or duration" checkbox. Similarly, you can turn off messages about schedule inconsistencies, like a successor that starts before the predecessor. In the Project Options dialog box, click Schedule, and then turn off the "Show scheduling messages" checkbox.

Adding and Removing Resources from Tasks

When it comes to quick assignment changes, the Assign Resources dialog box is (once again) your best friend. After you add or remove resources, Project asks you what you're trying to do and then modifies the appropriate values. Here's how to add and remove resources with the Assign Resources dialog box:

1. **Choose Resource→Assign Resources.**

   The Assign Resources dialog box opens.

2. **In Gantt Chart view or any other task-oriented view, select the task you want to modify.**

   The resources already assigned to the task appear at the top of the dialog box's list, preceded by a checkmark.

3. **To assign another resource to the task, in the dialog box's Resource Name column, click the name of the resource, and then click Assign.**

   To remove an existing resource from the task, click the name of the resource, and then click Remove. The assigned checkmark disappears, and the resource takes its place back in the alphabetical list of unassigned resources.

4. **To change the units for the new assignment, in the Units cell, type the percentage.**

   If you remove a resource, Project automatically clears the resource's Units cell.

5. **Repeat steps 3 and 4 to add or remove other resources.**

   You can add or remove several resources before you close the dialog box or select another task.

6. **When you're done, either select another task in the Gantt Chart table or close the Assign Resources dialog box.**

   In the Gantt Chart table, a green feedback triangle may appear in the upper-left corner of the Task Name cell to indicate that Project needs you to clarify what you're trying to accomplish so it can complete your change. If that happens, move the cursor over the indicator, and then click the Smart Tag indicator (a yellow diamond with an exclamation point) that appears, as shown in Figure 9-16. Then you can choose how you want Project to adjust work, duration, or units.

7. **In the Smart Tag menu, select the option for what you want Project to change.**

   If you've added resources, the first option is "Reduce duration but keep the same amount of work." This option keeps the amount of work the same, and recalculates the task's duration based on the units you specified. (Project selects this option automatically, because shortening duration is the most common reason for adding resources.)

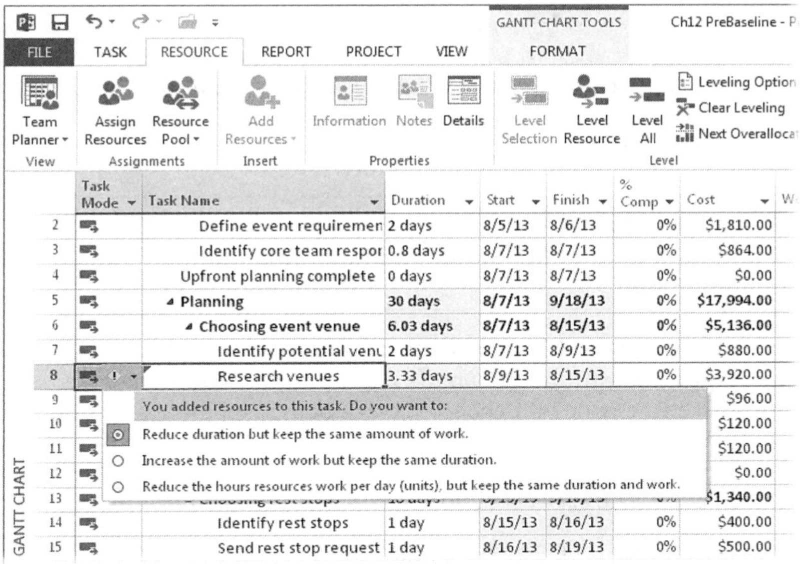

FIGURE 9-16

To tell Project what adjustments to make when you've added or removed resources, click the Smart Tag indicator (a yellow diamond with an exclamation mark inside) to the left of the task's name. Project displays a list of the changes you're most likely to make; simply select the appropriate one.

Selecting "Increase the amount of work but keep the same duration" keeps the same duration but recalculates the amount of work based on the units you specified. This option is perfect when you add resources to a task because the client asked for more features.

The "Reduce the hours that resources work per day (units), but keep the same duration and work" option calculates the units that resources work based on the duration and amount of work. This choice keeps the same duration and total work, while redistributing work to all the assigned resources.

If you remove resources, the three options are similar: The first option increases duration because you have fewer resources; the second option decreases the total amount of work; and the third option increases the units that the remaining resources work each day to compensate for the missing resources.

TIP Sometimes you don't have to add or take away resources, just replace one assigned resource with another. To do that, in the Assign Resources dialog box, select the resource you want to replace, and then click Replace. In the Replace Resource dialog box, select the new resource, and then click OK. To replace a resource in the Task Form, in the Resource Name drop-down list, just click the new resource.

When Effort Drives the Schedule

When does the amount of work control the schedule? Almost always. Project managers typically add resources to finish the same amount of work in less time. If resources disappear, the sad fact is that the work doesn't. Tasks take longer as the remaining resources shoulder the work. Project's term for this conservation of total work is *effort-driven scheduling*, because the effort (the total amount of work) drives the schedule (how long the task takes). With effort-driven scheduling, adding resources reduces the work each resource performs, and removing resources increases the work assigned to each remaining resource.

> **NOTE** Effort-driven scheduling kicks in only when you add or remove resources from a task. Project doesn't apply effort-driven scheduling when you change resources already assigned to a task. If you modify the duration of a task, the task type determines whether the amount of work or the units change (page 259).

Although you typically add resources to shorten duration, out of the box, Project's effort-driven setting is turned off. So the first thing you want to do is turn effort-driven scheduling on. To do that, choose File→Options. On the left side of the Project Options dialog box, choose Schedule. In the "Scheduling options for this project" drop-down list, choose All New Projects, and then turn on the "New tasks are effort driven" checkbox. Then click OK to apply this setting.

Once effort-driven scheduling is turned on, Project automatically turns on the "Effort driven" checkbox for new tasks you create, but you don't have to leave it turned on. (The "Effort driven" checkbox is located in Task Form view and in the Task Information dialog box; the following list explains how to turn it on and off.) Some tasks take the same amount of time no matter how many people you add. For example, adding attendees to a meeting doesn't shorten the meeting's duration—each attendee has to suffer through the same number of hours. For these uncompressible tasks, the total work *grows* with each resource you add. (As you watch the alarming increase in cost, you see why it's so important to keep meetings focused.) Consider a 2-hour status meeting. If you meet with two other people, the total amount of work is 6 hours—2 hours for each attendee. If you decide to invite the entire 10-person team, the total work expands to 20 hours.

Work can also increase because of things like change requests or unforeseen problems. For example, if you want to add resources to complete the change requests the client just delivered, turn off the "Effort driven" checkbox. That way, as you add resources, Project adds work based on the units you specify. Table 9-2 shows how Project adds resources with or without effort-driven scheduling.

TABLE 9-2 *How Project adds resources with the effort-driven scheduling setting on vs. off*

TASK TYPE	EFFORT-DRIVEN SCHEDULING TURNED ON	EFFORT-DRIVEN SCHEDULING TURNED OFF
Fixed units	Adding resources shortens duration.	Adding resources increases total work but keeps units and duration the same.
Fixed duration	Adding resources decreases units for each resource.	Adding resources increases total work but keeps the units and duration the same.
Fixed work	Adding resources shortens duration.	Doesn't apply. Fixed work is the same as effort-driven scheduling turned on.

TIP You can download Table 9-2 from this book's Missing CD page at *www.missingmanuals.com/cds*.

To turn off effort-driven scheduling for a task, do the following:

1. **In Gantt Chart view or another task-oriented view, select the task.**

   Task Form view in the Details pane displays the values for the selected task. (If the Details pane isn't visible, in the View tab's Split View section, turn on the Details checkbox, and then choose Task Form in the drop-down menu.)

2. **In Task Form view, turn off the "Effort driven" checkbox.**

   If you edit a task in the Task Information dialog box (which you open by double-clicking the task in Gantt Chart view or another task-oriented view), select the Advanced tab, and then turn off the "Effort driven" checkbox.

3. **Click OK.**

   Now, when you add resources to the task, its duration remains the same and each new resource represents additional person-hours. If you remove resources, the task's duration remains the same, but the task represents fewer total person-hours.

After you finish adding or removing resources, restore the "Effort driven" checkbox to its original setting.

Controlling Assignment Changes with Task Types

Depending on the assignment change you're trying to make, you may want a task's duration, work, or units to stay the same. Say you want to reduce a task's duration by adding another resource to take on some of the estimated work hours. Or perhaps you want to keep its units the same as you add more work. The "Task type" field tells Project which variable you want to anchor.

You already know that duration, work, and units are inseparable, so you won't be surprised to learn that Project has three task types: Fixed Units, Fixed Work, and Fixed Duration. This section explains how to use all three.

> **TIP** Although the Assign Resources dialog box is a powerful tool for initial resource assignments, Task Form view and Task Usage view are better for changing assignments with precision.

■ KEEPING RESOURCES ASSIGNED WITH THE SAME UNITS

The Fixed Units task type tells Project to keep the same units for each assigned resource regardless of the changes you make to the task's duration or work amount. Out of the box, Project automatically sets the Task Type field to Fixed Units (you can set it in Task Form view or in the Task Information dialog box), because a resource's availability is usually the limiting factor. For example, if you add work to a task, you shouldn't expect a resource assigned at 100 percent to work 200 percent to finish in the same timeframe.

The Fixed Units task type keeps units constant. Here's what Project does to a task assigned this type, depending on whether you change its duration, work, or units:

- **Duration.** If you change the task's duration, then Project adjusts the amount of work based on the set units.

- **Work.** If you change the amount of work, then Project adjusts the task's duration based on the set units.

- **Units.** If you change the units in a Fixed Units task, then Project adjusts the task's duration and keeps the amount of work the same, because of the program's built-in bias toward changing duration before work (page 252).

■ MAINTAINING TASK DURATION

Suppose you lose a resource assigned to a task, and you want the remaining resources to step up to complete the work without increasing the task's duration. The Fixed Duration task type helps you do just that. Here's how a fixed-duration task behaves:

- **Work.** If you change the task's amount of work, then Project adjusts the task's Peak units to keep the set duration. (See page 253 for the skinny on the Peak field and Assignment Units field.)

- **Units.** If you change the task's units, then Project adjusts its amount of work to keep the same duration.

- **Duration.** If you change the duration in a fixed-duration task, then Project adjusts the amount of work, because of the program's bias toward changing work before units (page 252).

Here's how to modify assignments without affecting task duration:

1. **In Gantt Chart view, select the task you want to modify.**

   The values for the selected task appear in Task Form view, in the Details pane.

2. **In Task Form view, in the "Task type" drop-down list, choose Fixed Duration, as shown in Figure 9-17, top.**

   Project will keep the task's duration the same until you change the "Task type" to another value or type a new value in the task's Duration field.

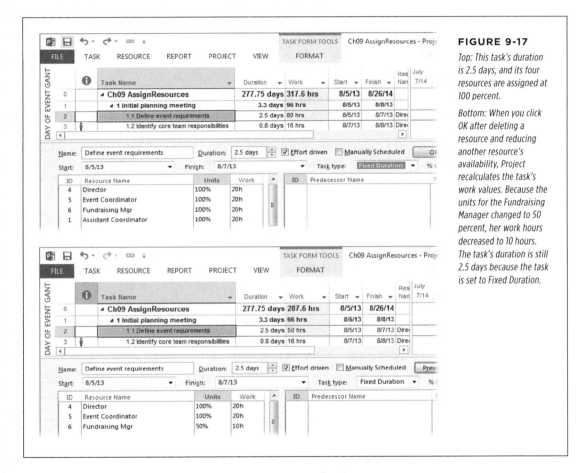

FIGURE 9-17

Top: This task's duration is 2.5 days, and its four resources are assigned at 100 percent.

Bottom: When you click OK after deleting a resource and reducing another resource's availability, Project recalculates the task's work values. Because the units for the Fundraising Manager changed to 50 percent, her work hours decreased to 10 hours. The task's duration is still 2.5 days because the task is set to Fixed Duration.

3. **To remove a resource from the task, select the resource name in the Task Form and then press Delete. If you want to reduce the percentage of time that a resource works on the task, select that resource's Units cell, and then type the new value, for example, changing units from 100% to 50%.**

   The values in the Work cells don't change just yet. The recalculations will occur when you click OK in the next step.

TIP If you add resources to the task, you can't specify their units. Project automatically fills in the Task Form's Units cell with 100% or the resource's Maximum Units. After you add the resources and click OK, *then* you can edit the assignments to modify the units.

4. **After you've made the changes you want, click OK.**

   The task's duration remains the same, and Project calculates the work assigned to each resource, as shown in Figure 9-17, bottom.

5. **In the Task Form's "Task type" drop-down list, choose Fixed Units to reset the task to its standard task type, and then click OK.**

   Restoring the task type to Fixed Units ensures that every task will behave consistently. Whenever you choose a different task type for a specific assignment change, remember to choose Fixed Units when the modification is complete.

■ MAINTAINING THE SAME AMOUNT OF WORK

If you've estimated the amount of work that tasks involve, you don't want Project messing with tasks' work values. Using the Fixed Work task type means you can adjust a task's duration or units without modifying the amount of time a resource spends working on it. For example, if you discover that a resource is available only 50 percent of the time, then Project can keep the amount of work the same while changing the task's duration.

Here's how a fixed-work task behaves:

- **Duration.** If you change the task's duration, Project adjusts the task's Peak units to keep the amount of work the same. For example, if a resource is assigned 40 hours of work in a week, the initial Assignment Units are 100%. If you change the task's duration to 10 days, its Assignment Units are still 100% but its Peak units drop to 50% (see Figure 9-15).

- **Units.** If you change the task's units, then Project adjusts its duration. If a resource is assigned to work 40 hours in 5 days and you change the units to 50%, the task's duration increases to 10 days.

- **Work.** If you change the amount of work in a fixed-work task, Project adjusts the task's duration, because of the program's bias against changing units (page 252).

NOTE You can change the standard task type if you typically keep a different variable steady. Suppose you estimate the work for project tasks, and you don't want Project changing those values as you adjust resource units or change task durations. To change the standard task type, choose File→Options→Schedule. Below "Scheduling options for this project" in the "Default task type" box, choose Fixed Duration or Fixed Work.

Setting Up a Project Budget

P rojects cost money. Whether you're planning a small department retreat or building a new airport, the project's budget will be a key factor in the planning and managing decisions you make.

The budget is a benchmark—a line in the sand that project costs should not overstep. Initially, the cost of your project is the total of all your forecasted costs for scheduled tasks and their assigned resources. Once the project begins and you start tracking progress on tasks, Project adjusts these forecasts to reflect actual and remaining work and costs. One of your jobs as project manager is to make sure project costs don't exceed your allocated budget.

This chapter starts with a brief introduction to some methods that organizations use to develop project budgets. You'll focus on setting up your project so Project calculates costs appropriately—for example, identifying resource costs as well as any additional costs associated with tasks. With this cost and budget information in place, you can analyze whether your project is within budget or in need of belt-tightening.

This chapter also explains how to look at project costs from different points of view, depending on the level of detail you want. You'll learn how to compare project costs against your budget using the budget resource feature. And in case Project gives you bad (but realistic) news that costs are outrunning the budget, this chapter provides specific cost-cutting measures you can pull from your project manager's arsenal. Finally, you'll learn how to set up accounting codes at the task or resource level so that your project costs can work with your organization's financial systems.

TIP This chapter focuses primarily on costs and budgeting during the planning stage, although some of the techniques discussed here work just as well during project execution. Other chapters delve into detail on monitoring project costs after your project is under way. For example, Chapter 12 describes setting a *baseline*, which is the snapshot of the approved project plan. Chapter 13 talks about entering progress information, or *actuals*, into your project. And Chapter 14 describes how to evaluate project performance and the techniques you can use to bring a project back on track.

■ Putting a Price Tag on Your Project

It's the old chicken-and-egg scenario—which comes first, the project's budget or its cost estimates? Either way, your organization wants to know how much the project will cost. Or, looking at it from the other direction, what's the maximum this project *should* cost to get the financial benefit the organization requires?

The financial benefit comes down to whether the project is worth the effort. How much money will the project make or how much will it save? What will it cost to get that result? For example, suppose your boss has an idea for a new product. The bean counters think it could earn more than $3,000,000 over the product's life cycle. The company has to decide how much it's willing to spend on the development project and how much profit it needs to earn to make the project worthwhile. As the project manager, you're expected to provide cost estimates based on the agreed-upon project scope. The hard part is making your project cost estimate agree with the budget the company has in mind.

One approach to calculating the price tag is to develop your schedule, assign resources to tasks, and let Project calculate the resulting costs. You can then use that cost figure as you go, hat in hand, to present the budget. The powers that be often reduce that number, although they also set aside contingency funds and management reserve (page 168) as insurance.

Another method for setting the project budget is *capital budgeting*, which is a set of financial calculations that help determine a project's potential rate of return, return on investment, and payback period (page 11). Capital budgeting can also show the impact of not taking on *other* projects while the organization's resources are busy with the current project. Thus, capital budgeting analysis can help an organization determine whether a project is in line with its financial and other strategic goals—with the result of a go/no-go decision for that project.

For an example, you can download an Excel capital-budgeting template from Microsoft Office Online (*http://tinyurl.com/ROIWorksheet*). Enter your data, and the spreadsheet calculates the rate of return on an investment, the net present value of the investment, and the payback period, as shown in Figure 10-1.

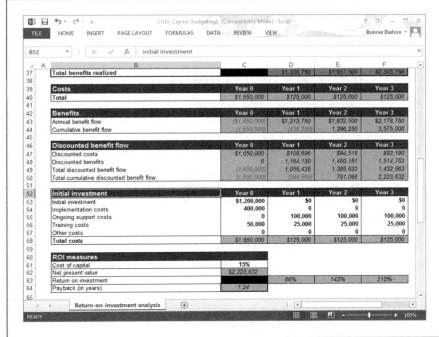

FIGURE 10-1

Capital-budgeting analysis shows the financial benefit of a project based on your estimated costs and can also determine the highest project cost that still achieves those financial benefits. When you plug your numbers into this Excel capital-budgeting spreadsheet, it shows you the project's return on investment, the years required to pay back the investment, and much more.

You can use Project to develop cost estimates to feed into the capital-budgeting spreadsheet. In Project, if you specify costs for your project resources and then assign resources to tasks, the program can give you a total cost estimate for the project. You can look at this cost estimate from different angles—total costs for a resource, total costs for a phase, costs for different time periods, and even costs for an individual task.

When you feed your project's cost estimates into the capital-budgeting analysis, you can see whether the project is even feasible. For example, suppose the capital-budgeting analysis shows that the project is worth doing as long as the cost doesn't exceed $50,000. If your project cost estimate sits steadfastly at $200,000, chances are good that the project won't fly, because trimming 75 percent from the estimate isn't likely.

Project budgeting is an iterative process. The project's customer may have a ballpark number in mind, but you can give the budget a basis in reality with your project cost estimate. Explanations and negotiations may ensue, along with further analysis, until finally you obtain a realistic project budget figure that everyone is willing to accept.

Remember that you need to do everything in your power to not exceed that budget once the project gets under way. If you overshoot the budget, you may have to pay dearly, in unpopular schedule adjustments, reduced scope, cost overruns—not to mention your own reputation. In the end, people say two things about successful projects: "It came in on time and under budget."

▇ Reviewing Cost Information

Suppose the project's customer makes it very clear that the maximum price tag for the fundraising event project is $150,000, and she hints more than once that less than $120,000 would be even better. Now that you've entered tasks, resources, and any associated costs in Project, it's time to see what the event is likely to cost.

In this section, you'll learn how to review total planned costs for all project tasks. By extension, you get a handy forecast of your overall project costs. You'll also learn how to review planned costs for tasks, resources, and assignments, so you can analyze costs at whatever level of granularity you need.

Seeing Overall Project Costs

When you first compare your project plan's performance against the budget, start with a quick bottom-line snapshot. A single number for your project's planned cost tells you whether you need to delve into cost containment or whether you can sit back and relax. This section shows a few ways to come up with that top-level number.

Remember the old garbage in/garbage out maxim? Your total project cost forecast is only as reliable as the information you provide. At this stage of the game, many costs and durations are merely estimates. Still, because these estimates affect your budget, it pays to be as accurate as possible. To forecast the project's total cost reliably, make sure you have the following information in your project plan:

- Costs, including hourly rates and per-use costs, for all work resources assigned to tasks

- Costs for all material resources assigned to tasks

- Costs for all cost resources assigned to tasks

- Any additional fixed costs for tasks

- All resource assignments for tasks

■ VIEWING THE TOTAL PROJECT COST IN THE PROJECT SUMMARY TASK

The project summary task is a great place to spot the total planned project cost, because it rolls up the totals for all tasks and you can keep it visible in the first row of the project task list. To use the project summary task to see rolled-up cost values, follow these steps:

1. **With a task-oriented view like the Gantt Chart visible, head to the Gantt Chart Tools | Format tab's Show/Hide section and turn on the Project Summary Task checkbox.**

   A new row appears at the very top of the table in most views. A project summary node also appears in Network Diagram view. The project summary task rolls up the column values in the current table. For example, in the Entry table (the typical table shown in Gantt Chart view), you can see the total duration, the start date, and the finish date for the entire project.

   For columns that don't roll up, like the Predecessor and Resource Names columns, the corresponding project summary cells remain blank.

2. **Apply the Cost table by clicking the View tab. In the Data section, click the Tables button and then, from the drop-down list, choose Cost.**

   The project summary task displays the total cost of the project in its Total Cost cell. It also shows rolled-up values for Baseline Cost, Cost Variance, Actual Cost, and Remaining Cost in other columns.

   Values in the Fixed Cost column don't roll up into the Fixed Cost field for outline summary tasks or the project summary task. There's a reason for this behavior: so you can enter a fixed cost for a project phase or the project as a whole. (The box on page 268 tells you whether it makes sense to use Project's Fixed Cost field and, if so, where fixed costs you enter there show up in your overall project costs.)

TIP If you spend most of your time in Gantt Chart view and its sidekick, the Entry table, consider adding the Cost column to the Entry table. Right-click one of the table's column headers, and then, on the shortcut menu, choose Insert Column. In the field name drop-down list that appears, choose Cost.

Fixed Costs or Cost Resources

Should I ever use the Fixed Cost field instead of a cost resource?

Cost resources have several advantages over the Fixed Cost field. You can assign multiple cost resources to a single task (page 248), making different types of costs easier to see and track; and you can assign the same cost resource to multiple tasks, even if they have different cost amounts. In addition, if you use budget resources to compare budgeted and planned costs, budget resources take cost resources into account, but they *don't* take values in the Fixed Cost field into account.

A fixed-cost contract is one situation in which the Fixed Cost field might make sense. (A fixed-cost contract means someone commits to delivering a chunk of work for a set price, so you don't have to track work hours or assign resources to a task for such a contract.) If you want to include that cost in your budget comparisons (page 273), a Cost resource still makes sense. You create a cost resource for fixed-price contracts, assign the cost resource to the corresponding task, and fill in the contract cost.

However, if you don't use budget resources to evaluate your project price, you can forgo cost resource assignments and simply fill in the Fixed Cost field with the contracted amount.

1. To assign a value to the Fixed Cost field, display Gantt Chart view or another task-oriented view.

2. In the View tab's Data section, click the Tables button, and then choose Cost from the drop-down menu.

3. In the Fixed Cost cell for the task, fill in the value of the fixed-cost contract.

4. If necessary, select the Fixed Cost Accrual field for the task, and then select Prorated, Start, or End to indicate when the cost should be incurred during the task duration. The typical accrual for fixed costs is Prorated, which means the fixed cost is divided into equal portions across the task's duration—perfect if you make several payments over the course of the contract.

Project adds the value in the Fixed Cost field to the Total Cost field, so it represents work, material, cost-resource costs, and any fixed costs.

Entering a fixed cost for a summary task is helpful when a cost corresponds to a project *phase* rather than an individual task. You add fixed costs to a summary task the same way you add them to regular tasks. Project doesn't roll up the Fixed Cost field to summary tasks, so you can fill in a value in a summary task's Fixed Cost field.

TIP The Fixed Cost field is just a value; it doesn't describe what the cost is for. You can add a note to a task (page 156) to identify the source of the fixed cost.

■ VIEWING THE TOTAL PROJECT COST IN PROJECT STATISTICS

To get to the single number that indicates your project's total costs, use the Project Statistics dialog box as follows:

1. **In the Project tab's Properties section, click Project Information.**

   The Project Information dialog box appears.

2. **At the bottom of the dialog box, click the Statistics button.**

   The Project Statistics dialog box appears, as shown in Figure 10-2.

3. **In the Cost column, review the value in the Current field, which is the forecasted cost for the project as currently planned.**

After you set a baseline (page 375) the Baseline fields are also filled in. And when you start tracking status (page 391), the Actual and Remaining fields have values, too.

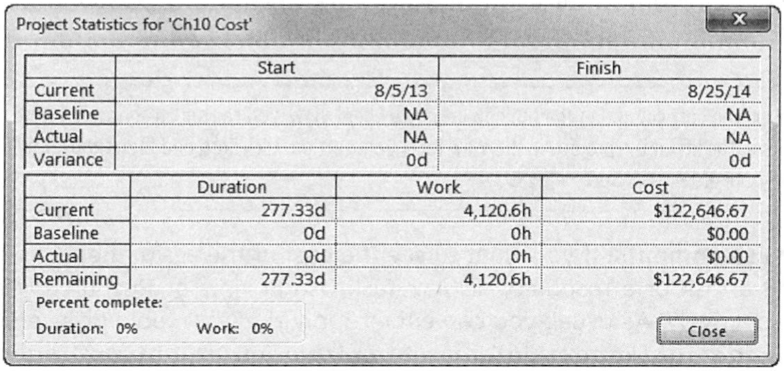

FIGURE 10-2

The Project Statistics dialog box includes bottom-line project information that lets you and others gauge the most important aspects of the project as a whole: when the project starts, when it's scheduled to finish, how much work is involved, and how much it's forecast to cost.

NOTE You can get overall project cost information in a report, too. On the Report tab, click the Dashboards button, and then choose Cost Overview. The Cost Overview report shows the total cost for the project, the remaining cost, and details about the costs of individual tasks. For more about generating reports, see Chapter 16.

Seeing Costs for Tasks, Resources, and Assignments

Now that you've seen the big picture of forecasted costs, you're probably champing at the bit to learn how to find task costs when all resources are assigned and where to look for the total cost of one resource's assignments. This section shows how to break costs down to individual assignments—that is, how much it costs for one particular resource working on one particular task. Use one of the following methods to drill down into costs:

- **Total cost for a task.** First apply the Cost table to a task view (View→Tables→ Cost), and then, in the Total Cost column, check the value. Or insert the Cost column into any task view (right-click a column heading in the table and choose Insert Column), and then check the Cost value for the task. In both cases, the Cost value is the scheduled (planned) cost for the task, including all assigned resources (work, material, and cost) and any fixed costs. See Chapter 14 (page 429) to learn the difference between baseline, scheduled, and actual values.

NOTE Depending on the table you display, you may see the Total Cost or the Cost column. However, both columns show the same information. The Cost table simply uses "Total Cost" as the column heading.

- **Total cost for a resource.** Display Resource Sheet view (View→Resource Sheet), and then insert the Cost column somewhere in the table (right-click a column heading in the table and choose Insert Column). The Cost value for a given resource is the total cost for the resource for all its assigned tasks, based on the standard rate, overtime rate, cost/use, or other specified resource cost. This technique is perfect when you want to see how much you're spending for a specific work resource, such as a contractor, or a specific cost resource, such as travel or training. You can also see the cost for a resource in Resource Usage view in the resource's summary row, as shown in Figure 10-3.

> **TIP** If you insert the Cost column in the table in Resource Sheet view, you can sort resources by how much you pay for them over the life of the project. In the View tab's Data section, click Sort, and then choose "by Cost." To revert to the original order, click Sort→"by ID."

- **Cost for assignments.** If you want to see the cost of the assignments associated with a task or a resource, display Task Usage view or Resource Usage view, respectively. As usual, you can either apply the Cost table or insert the Cost column in the Usage table (or whatever table you want to use), as shown in Figure 10-3.

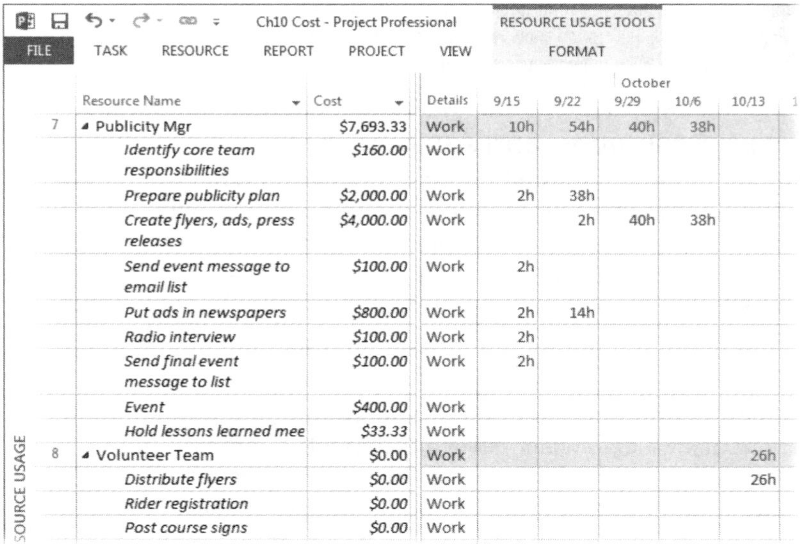

FIGURE 10-3

In Resource Usage view, the Cost field in a task-assignment row represents the cost for that individual assignment. The cost in a resource-name row represents all assignment costs rolled up to give you a total for all tasks assigned to that resource.

Resource Name	Cost	Details	9/15	9/22	9/29	10/6	10/13	1
7 ◢ Publicity Mgr	$7,693.33	Work	10h	54h	40h	38h		
Identify core team responsibilities	$160.00	Work						
Prepare publicity plan	$2,000.00	Work	2h	38h				
Create flyers, ads, press releases	$4,000.00	Work		2h	40h	38h		
Send event message to email list	$100.00	Work	2h					
Put ads in newspapers	$800.00	Work	2h	14h				
Radio interview	$100.00	Work	2h					
Send final event message to list	$100.00	Work	2h					
Event	$400.00	Work						
Hold lessons learned mee	$33.33	Work						
8 ◢ Volunteer Team	$0.00	Work					26h	
Distribute flyers	$0.00	Work					26h	
Rider registration	$0.00	Work						
Post course signs	$0.00	Work						

In Task Usage view, the cost in a resource-name row represents the cost for that individual assignment—what it costs to have that resource assigned to that task. The cost in a task-name row represents all assignment costs rolled up to give you a total for that task.

TIP You can transfer cost information from your Project file to an Excel file for further analysis (page 549).
Whether you copy and paste fields from Project into Excel or export Project information into an Excel spreadsheet,
you can apply formulas, crunch numbers, and create whiz-bang charts and graphs until the cows (or stakeholders)
come home.

Adding Custom Budget Information

The Cost field is great while you're in the planning phase and want to forecast what
the project might cost. In this section, you'll learn how to create your very own
type of cost field. You may want to do this if you have specialized cost or budget
information you'd like to see in your project, like budget targets for key tasks and
phases. To create a custom cost field for these types of figures, follow these steps:

1. **Decide whether you want to add the custom field to the table in the current
   view, and then, depending on what you decide, use the appropriate method
   of opening the Custom Fields dialog box.**

   The steps for opening the dialog box differ depending on whether you want to
   add the custom field to the current table:

   - To create a custom cost field *without* adding it to the table, in the Project
     tab's Properties section, click Custom Fields.

   - To insert a custom cost field into the table, right-click a heading in the
     table and choose Insert Column on the shortcut menu. In the field name
     drop-down list, choose a field name, such as Cost2. Then right-click the
     new column and, on the shortcut menu, choose Custom Fields.

   Either way, the Custom Fields dialog box appears.

2. **At the top of the dialog box, select the Task option if you want to create
   a custom cost field that you can use in task-oriented views, or select the
   Resource option if the new field is for resource-oriented views.**

   A task-cost field represents just task costs, while a resource-cost field works
   only with resource costs. If you opened the Custom Field dialog box using
   the method described in step 1 for adding the custom field to the table, then
   Project automatically selects the Task or Resource option here, depending on
   whether a task or resource view is visible. If, on the other hand, you opened
   the Custom Fields dialog box via the Project tab, the program automatically
   selects the Task option, so you have to choose the Resource option if that's
   what you'd like to create.

3. **In the Type box at the top of the Custom Fields dialog box, select Cost, and
   then in the Fields box below that, select one of the Cost fields that isn't
   already in use.**

   The Field box lists all the custom cost fields—Cost1 through Cost10—along with
   any aliases you define for them (which you'll learn about in the next step), as
   shown in Figure 10-4.

4. **Optionally, click the Rename button to give the custom field a new name so you can easily tell what it's for.**

You don't *have* to rename custom fields, but it's a good idea. The name you assign to a custom field (called an *alias*) appears as the column title when you insert the field into a table. The alias and built-in name both appear together in other places. For example, if you rename the Cost2 field to "Approved Cost Target," then the field appears in field name drop-down menus as "Approved Cost Target (Cost2)" as well as "Cost2 (Approved Cost Target)."

5. **In the Custom Fields dialog box, click OK.**

The cost field is ready for you to use in tables. If you haven't already added the custom cost field to the table, to insert it, simply right-click a column heading in the table, choose Insert Column, and then pick the name of your new custom field. The box on page 273 explains ways you can make cost fields do tricks with values.

FIGURE 10-4

Although Project doesn't force you to rename custom fields, in the Custom Fields dialog box, an alias is your only indication that a field is spoken for. To rename the custom cost field something like Approved Cost Target, select the task, and then click Rename.

Programming Your Custom Cost Fields

Custom fields can do more than go by a different name. You can tell them to calculate values in certain ways or provide hints about valid values. The section "Customizing a Field" on page 664 provides the details, but here's a quick overview of what you can do:

1. **Calculate values with formulas.** You can create a formula to calculate the contents of other fields and display the result in a custom cost field—for example, the variance between the planned cost and the target cost.

2. **Provide values with lookup tables.** You can create a lookup table (page 666) with a list of cost values to choose from when entering values in a custom cost field.

3. **Roll up values.** You can tell Project how it should roll up values in a custom cost field into task- or group-summary rows—for example, by taking the maximum amount of the group, averaging the amounts, or adding together all the amounts in the group.

4. **Roll down values.** You can specify whether Project should distribute the value in a custom cost field in the time-phased portion of assignment rows in a usage-oriented view.

Comparing Costs to Your Budget

Suppose your project plan has budget targets for different cost categories: $90,000 for labor costs, $2,500 for travel expenses, and $500 for permits. Using Project's *budget resource* feature, you can define your budget for different cost categories. You can then group resources to compare your budgeted costs with your planned costs. That way, you can view your travel budget of $2,500 side by side with your planned costs of, say, $3,700, and immediately see that your next goal is to find a way to trim those travel costs. The box on page 274 describes another method for tracking project costs based on your organization's accounting system.

Budget resources are great for comparing budgeted costs against the planned costs for *cost* resources. Budgeted costs for *work* and *material* resources, however, are a different story. For labor and equipment costs (work resources), you can enter only budgeted work amounts, not costs. So instead of a labor budget of $10,000, you have to enter an overall work amount like 200 hours. Knowing what amount of work to enter can be tricky when different work resources have different cost rates. Similarly, for material resources, you have to extrapolate a budgeted work amount based on the quantity of materials you need. The box on page 280 provides a workaround for this situation.

This section describes how to set up budget resources that you can compare with your planned costs and work. It's a five-step process:

1. **Create and designate budget resources.**

2. **Assign those budget resources to the project summary task.**

3. **Enter budgeted cost and work amounts for budget resources.**

4. **Associate work, material, and cost resources with their budget types.**

5. **Group resources to compare budgeted costs and work alongside the planned values.**

The whole process isn't quite as bad as it sounds. If your project is highly cost driven, then budget resources may give you the budget-performance information you need. Take budget resources for a test drive to see if they help.

After you've done the first four steps, everything is in place for you to compare budget values and planned values (step 5) as you monitor and adjust your project plan to keep it in line with the budget. To make comparing values even easier, you can create a custom view (page 592) with the columns and grouping you want. Then for step 5, all you have to do is display your custom view.

POWER USERS' CLINIC

Assigning Accounting Codes

Sometimes it takes more than a handful of chocolate-covered peanuts to keep the accountants happy. Project data that maps to the organization's accounting codes may be just the ticket. Fortunately, it's easy to include accounting codes in Project, whether it's just a simple account number or a hierarchical structure of multilevel codes. Either way, you can enter accounting codes that map to resources, tasks, or project phases. For the full scoop on setting up a flat or multilevel list of codes, see page 675.

First, create a custom accounting-code field, and then add a column for it to the table of your choice (right-click a table

heading and then choose Insert Column). Remember, you can add a task field only to task-oriented views and tables. Likewise, you can add a resource field only to resource-oriented views and tables. With the new column in place, enter the appropriate accounting codes for your tasks or resources.

After you've applied the accounting codes, you can sort, group, and filter information by accounting code, as described in Chapter 21. You can also create reports that use the accounting codes. For more information about generating reports, see Chapter 16.

Step 1: Create and Designate Budget Resources

Creating budget resources is the first step in the budget-resource process. These resources should correspond with the budget line items you want to track in your project (for example, line items that the accounting department uses). You can make them as broad or as detailed as you want, from Labor Budget, Materials Budget, and Travel Budget to Employees, Vendors, Contractors, Equipment Rental, Publications, Lodging, Airfare, Mileage, and Meals.

Budget resources apply to a project as a whole—you can't assign them to tasks, as you do regular resources. Here's how to create budget resources:

1. **In the Resource Sheet (View→Resource Sheet), in a blank Resource Name cell, type the name of a budget resource.**

   It's a good idea to use names that differentiate budget resources from regular resources, as shown in Figure 10-5, so you can more easily pick the right fields for your budget comparisons. For example, if your budget line items are numbered to match your accounting department's account numbers, you could include those line-item numbers in your budget-resource names, such as 8020 TRAVEL.

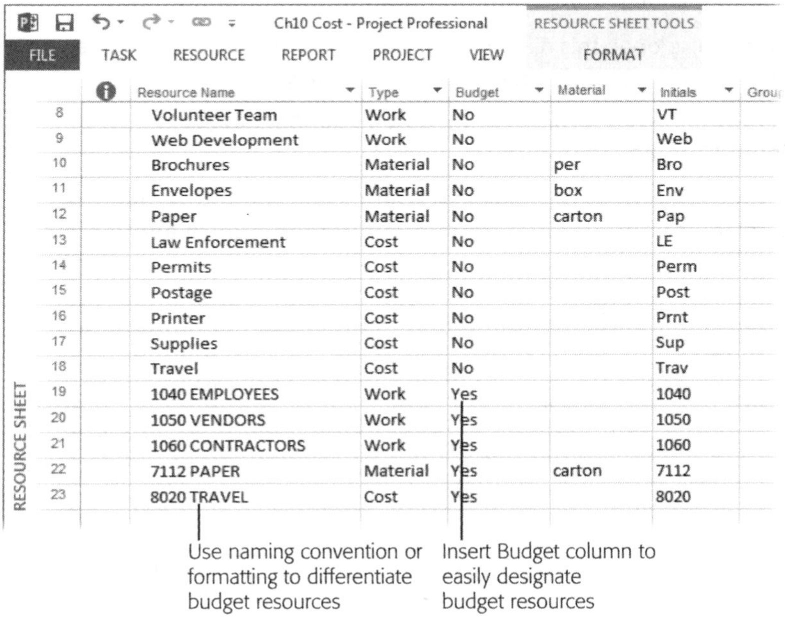

	Resource Name	Type	Budget	Material	Initials	Grou
8	Volunteer Team	Work	No		VT	
9	Web Development	Work	No		Web	
10	Brochures	Material	No	per	Bro	
11	Envelopes	Material	No	box	Env	
12	Paper	Material	No	carton	Pap	
13	Law Enforcement	Cost	No		LE	
14	Permits	Cost	No		Perm	
15	Postage	Cost	No		Post	
16	Printer	Cost	No		Prnt	
17	Supplies	Cost	No		Sup	
18	Travel	Cost	No		Trav	
19	1040 EMPLOYEES	Work	Yes		1040	
20	1050 VENDORS	Work	Yes		1050	
21	1060 CONTRACTORS	Work	Yes		1060	
22	7112 PAPER	Material	Yes	carton	7112	
23	8020 TRAVEL	Cost	Yes		8020	

FIGURE 10-5

Name budget resources so they're easy to identify. For example, you could start their names with the word "Budget" (such as Budget-Travel), put them in all caps (TRAVEL BUDGET), or start their names with the corresponding budget account number (8020 TRAVEL). One advantage to starting them with numbers is that budget resources appear together at the top of a resource list that's sorted alphabetically from A to Z, which is helpful because they're summary numbers.

2. **In the Type field, choose Work, Material, or Cost, depending on the type of cost.**

   For example, a budget resource named 8020 TRAVEL would be a cost resource, while a budget resource named 1040 EMPLOYEES would likely be a work resource.

   For a material budget resource, in the Material Label field, type the unit of measurement, like *cubic yards* or *boxes*. To specify your target budget for material, you enter the number of units you use based on the unit of measurement, so you need to create a separate budget resource for each material resource you want to track against the budget.

You can lump different types of labor together under a single labor budget item (regular employees, contractors, and so on). However, since labor costs often represent a big chunk of the budget, you might want to create a separate budget resource for each resource category whose budget you want to track, such as employees, contractors, and vendors.

> **TIP** If you want to express your labor budget in dollars rather than hours, then identify the budget resources for it as a cost resource rather than a work resource. The box on page 280 explains how to account for different labor rates.

3. **Double-click the ID cell of the new budget resource to open the Resource Information dialog box.**

   You can also open this dialog box by selecting the budget resource and then, in the Resource tab's Properties section, clicking Information.

4. **On the dialog box's General tab, turn on the Budget checkbox, as shown in Figure 10-6, and then click OK.**

   Turning on this checkbox means you can assign this resource only to the project summary task, making it, in effect, a kind of project summary resource.

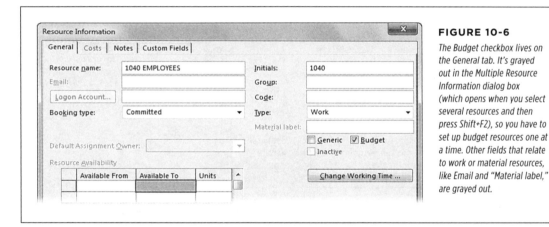

FIGURE 10-6

The Budget checkbox lives on the General tab. It's grayed out in the Multiple Resource Information dialog box (which opens when you select several resources and then press Shift+F2), so you have to set up budget resources one at a time. Other fields that relate to work or material resources, like Email and "Material label," are grayed out.

5. **Repeat steps 1–4 to create additional budget resources.**

   The box on page 278 describes a shortcut for creating several budget resources at once.

Step 2: Assign Budget Resources to the Project Summary Task

With your budget resources created, you're now ready to assign them to your project. A budget resource is meant to convey the total amount allocated to a budget category for an entire project, which is why you assign budget resources to the project summary task, not to individual tasks. In fact, a budget resource can't be assigned to anything *except* the project summary task.

In a task-oriented view like Gantt Chart, if you can't see the project summary task (the one at the top of the view's table in row 0), choose Gantt Chart Tools | Format. In the tab's Show/Hide section, turn on the Project Summary Task checkbox. Then assign budget resources to your project summary task by following these steps:

1. **Select the project summary task, and then in the Resource tab's Assignments section, click Assign Resources.**

   The Assign Resources dialog box appears. If your resource list is long, your budget-resource naming convention comes in handy. For example, by starting all the budget-resource names with a number, as shown in Figure 10-7, budget resources are grouped together at the top of the resource list.

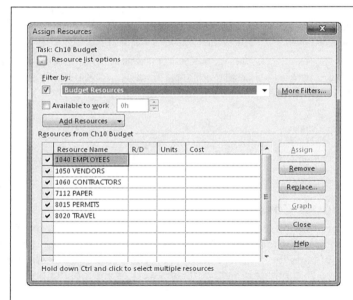

FIGURE 10-7

To display only budget resources in the Assign Resources dialog box, expand the "Resource list options" section by clicking the + button (here, the button has a – sign on it because the section is already expanded). Next, turn on the "Filter by" checkbox, and then, in the drop-down list, choose Budget Resources.

2. **Ctrl-click each of the budget resources you want to assign, and then click Assign.**

   Budget resources are the only kind of resource you can assign to the project summary task. So if you select one resource and the Assign button is grayed out, then the resource you selected isn't a budget resource. Perhaps you gave the resource a budget-resource name but forgot to turn on its Budget checkbox in the Resource Information dialog box (see step 4 on page 276).

3. **Repeat the previous step for any additional budget resources you want to assign to the project summary task.**

   When you're done, you can close the Assign Resource dialog box if you want to see more of the screen.

WORKAROUND WORKSHOP

Creating Several Budget Resources at Once

Most project managers create their budget resources in one fell swoop. Even so, the Multiple Resource Information dialog box doesn't let you turn on the Budget checkbox for all selected resources. Since you have lots of important things to do, here's a shortcut for designating several budget resources at once: Add the Budget column to Resource Sheet view, and then change the value there. Here are the steps:

1. In Resource Sheet view (View→Resource Sheet), right-click the column heading next to where you want to add the Budget column, and then choose Insert Column.

2. In the "Field name" drop-down list, choose Budget. Project inserts the Budget column to the left of the selected column and (usually) displays the value No in it.

3. Select the cell for the first budget resource and, in the Budget field's drop-down list, choose Yes. If budget resources are grouped together, position the pointer over the fill handle in the bottom-left corner of the Budget cell. When the pointer changes to a +, copy "Yes" into the other Budget cells by dragging over them.

4. When you're done, hide the column by right-clicking the Budget column's heading and then choosing Hide Column.

Step 3: Enter Budget Cost and Work Values

With budget resources assigned to the project summary task, you're ready to add budget cost amounts for cost resources, budget work amounts for work resources, and the total number of units for material resources. These budget values are the targets against which you'll compare project costs and work as you monitor project progress.

You can enter budget amounts either as a project total or as incremental totals by time period. This section explains how to do both.

ENTERING BUDGET TOTALS FOR THE PROJECT

If time isn't a factor in your budget, you can add budget cost and work amounts to the entire project. Here are the steps:

1. **Display Task Usage view (in the View tab's Task Views section, choose Task Usage).**

   Task Usage view is ideal for entering budget values because the project summary task sits at the very top with its assigned budget resources below it like fawning admirers, as shown in Figure 10-8.

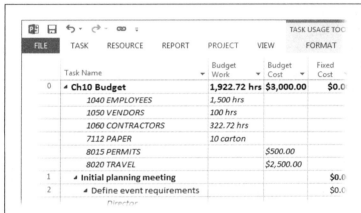

FIGURE 10-8

In Task Usage view, the Budget Work column in the project summary row (row 0) sums up the hours or days for all the budget resources for work. If you want to see separate totals for each budget resource, so you can see quantities for material resources, use Resource Usage view instead.

2. **Insert the Budget Cost and Budget Work columns into the table.**

   Right-click the column heading next to where you want to insert the Budget Cost column, and then choose Insert Column; in the "Field name" drop-down list, choose Budget Cost. Repeat these steps for the Budget Work column.

3. **Select the Budget Cost or Budget Work cell for an assigned budget resource, and then type the overall project budget value for that resource.**

   For a budget resource that's a *cost* resource, type the budget value in dollars into the Budget Cost cell.

   For a budget resource that's a *work* resource, type the budget value as work (hours or days) in the Budget Work cell. (As mentioned earlier, chances are your budgeted target amount is in dollars, not hours or days. The box on page 280 describes one way to resolve this issue.) The Budget Work cell is also where you type the total number of units (cubic yards, tons, packages, each, and so on) for a budget resource that's a *material* resource.

NOTE If you use Resource Usage view (see Figure 10-9) instead of Task Usage view, select the project summary task assignment under the budget resource, and then type its budget value.

Comparing Budgeted Labor Costs

Project calculates labor costs for work resources (people and equipment) by multiplying rates by hours. However, you can't compare these labor costs to the budgeted costs from the program's budget resource feature. Frustratingly, you can compare only budgeted *work* amounts to the work amounts in tasks—that is, the number of hours, days, and so on.

You can work around this problem by creating a single representative rate for work resources. For example, you could use an average or a weighted average based on how your labor costs are distributed and whether you expect to pay overtime. If you have a labor budget of, say, $75,000, and your average

standard rate is $50 per hour, you could divide $75,000 by $50 for a resulting work budget of 1,500 hours.

On the other hand, if you insist on seeing your budgeted labor costs in dollars, not work, a little sleight of hand is in order. Instead of setting up the budget resource that relates to work resources as a work resource itself (like you're supposed to), you can set it up as a *cost* resource instead. Then you can enter the budgeted labor cost and compare it with the rolled-up labor costs from tasks. This trick works equally well for material cost budgets.

■ ENTERING BUDGET TOTALS BY TIME PERIOD

The budget amounts you enter for a project summary task are the total project amounts for those budget items. Unless you tell it otherwise, Project spreads that budget amount equally over the duration of the project. To divvy up the overall budget amounts into the time periods when you expect them to be spent, you can edit budget amounts in the time-phased portion of a task- or resource-usage view.

Follow these steps to add the Budget Cost and Budget Work rows to the time-phased portion of a usage view:

1. **With Resource Usage view displayed (View→Resource Usage), click the Resource Usage Tools | Format tab. In the tab's Details section, click Add Details.**

   The Detail Styles dialog box appears. Another way to open this dialog box is to right-click the time-phased portion of Resource Usage, and then, on the shortcut menu, choose Detail Styles.

2. **In the "Available fields" box, Ctrl-click Budget Cost and Budget Work, and then click Show.**

   Project moves the Budget Cost and Budget Work fields to the "Show these fields" box, as shown in Figure 10-9.

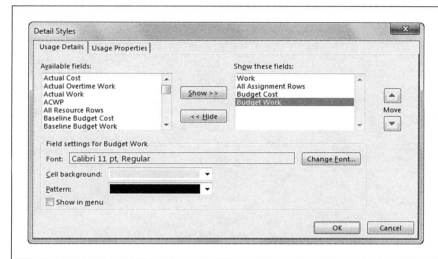

FIGURE 10-9

The order of fields in the "Show these fields" box is the sequence in which Project displays the field's rows. To change this sequence, select a field's name in the "Show these fields" box, and then click the Move buttons until the order is what you want.

3. **Click OK, and then resize the Details column so you can see the new fields.**

   The two fields appear in the time-phased portion of the view, although you can see only part of their names in the Details column. To see their full field names, double-click the right edge of the Details column heading to automatically widen the column to display the longest field name. You can also drag the right edge of the Details column heading further to the right to increase its width.

4. **On the status bar, drag the Zoom slider to display the time period for which you want to enter time-phased budget values. Or adjust the time period in Timeline view, as described on page 620.**

   For example, you can zoom the timescale to show a week, a month, or a quarter at a time. Then you can enter budget amounts per week, per month, or per quarter.

   If you've already entered budget amounts in the table, then those amounts are distributed equally across the project's timespan. You can edit them to the budget values you expect for each time period.

5. **In the cell at the intersection of the row for a budget resource's Budget Cost or Budget Work field and the column for the time period you want, type the budget cost or work amount, as shown in Figure 10-10.**

   You can't edit the Budget Cost and Budget Work cells for nonbudget resource assignments. The box on page 282 tells you where you can enter budget amounts.

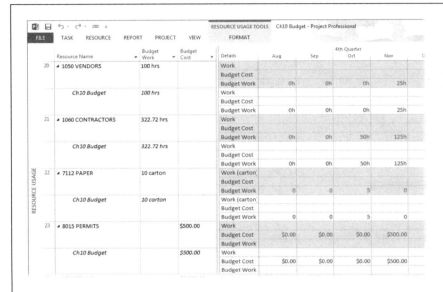

FIGURE 10-10

Even if you enter budget values in the time-phased portion of the view, it's good to keep the Budget Cost and Budget Work columns visible in the table. Those fields show you the overall project totals for each budget category you've created.

FREQUENTLY ASKED QUESTION

Entering Values in Budget Fields

Where can I enter budget amounts in a view?

When you add the Budget Cost and Budget Work fields to a usage view's table or time-phased portion, it's not always clear where you can actually *enter* your budget amounts. No visual cue like shading or hatching indicates areas that are off limits, so the fields seem to be available throughout the entire view. If you try to enter a value and nothing happens, that's your clue that the cell isn't editable.

Project is particular about where you can enter budget amounts. Here are the rules:

1. Enter budget amounts in an assignment field (in Task Usage view, the row with the budget resource's name; in Resource Usage view, the row with the project summary task's name).

2. In a project summary task's Budget Cost or Budget Work cell, enter project-wide budget totals.

3. Enter time-specific amounts in the Budget Cost or Budget work cells in the time-phased portion of the view.

You can't enter budget amounts in assignments for regular resources to regular tasks.

Step 4: Associate Resources with Their Budget Types

Creating budget resources and entering target budget amounts for them in the project summary task is all well and good, but it's only one side of the equation. You also have to set up the other side: the resource costs you want to compare against the budget. This section explains how to connect work, material, and cost resources to cost categories in the budget, whether you want to track all resources against the budget or only a few.

The trick is to use a text field to specify the budget category for each resource you want to track. If you aren't using Resource Sheet view's Group or Code fields, they're both great candidates for your budget categories; they're text fields and are already included in the Entry table for the Resource Sheet. (If you decide to use one of these fields, skip to page 284 to learn how to enter budget types for your resources.) On the other hand, if you're using Group and Code fields for something else, you can set up a custom text field to specify budget categories, as described in the following section.

■ CREATING A CUSTOM RESOURCE TEXT FIELD

If you want to use a custom text field for budget categories, you first have to set it up for that purpose and then add it to the Entry table in Resource Sheet view. Here are the steps:

1. **Display Resource Sheet view (View→Resource Sheet), right-click a table heading, and then choose Insert Column. In the drop-down list, choose the custom text field you want to use, such as Text1 or Text2.**

   Project inserts a new column for the text field to the left of the column you right-clicked.

2. **Right-click the new column's heading and then, on the shortcut menu, choose Custom Fields.**

   The Custom Fields dialog box opens with the Resource option selected at the top of the dialog box and the name of the text field selected in the list below that, which is exactly what you want.

3. **Click Rename and then, in the Rename Field dialog box, type the name you want for this field, such as *Budget Type* or *Budget Item*, and then click OK.**

   When you rename custom fields you use (page 666), Project displays the field's original name in parentheses in the Custom Fields dialog box and in field drop-down lists, so it's easy to tell which fields you've already used.

4. **In the "Calculation for assignment rows" section, select the "Roll down unless manually entered" option. Then click OK.**

   Selecting this option tells Project to distribute the custom field's values across assignments in usage-oriented views unless you manually type a value in a time-phased assignment cell.

Now that the text field is set up, you can designate budget categories for your project's work, material, and cost resources, as described in the next section.

■ CLASSIFYING RESOURCES BY BUDGET CATEGORY

Before you begin typing values in the text field where you're going to store budget categories, decide on the budget category names you want to use. Have a different budget category for each budget resource you've created—for example, Employees, Vendors, Contractors, Permits, and Travel. Here's how:

1. **With your text field (Group, Code, or custom text field) prominently displayed in Resource Sheet view, work your way through the resources, typing the appropriate budget category name for each one, as illustrated in Figure 10-11.**

   Repeat this step for each work, material, and cost resource in the project.

2. **Enter the corresponding budget category value for each budget resources.**

   That's how you connect resource costs and budget costs.

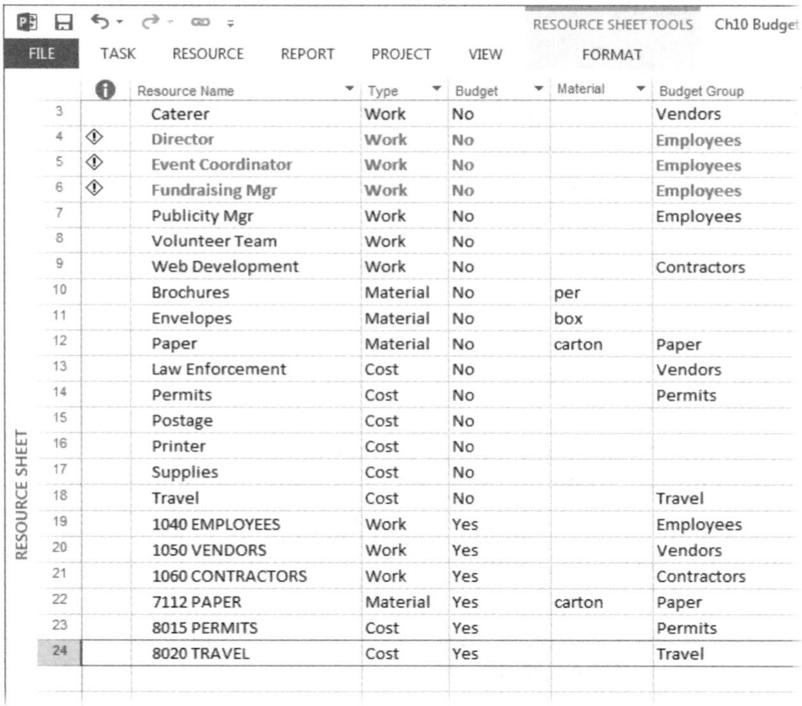

		Resource Name	Type	Budget	Material	Budget Group
	3	Caterer	Work	No		Vendors
	4	Director	Work	No		Employees
	5	Event Coordinator	Work	No		Employees
	6	Fundraising Mgr	Work	No		Employees
	7	Publicity Mgr	Work	No		Employees
	8	Volunteer Team	Work	No		
	9	Web Development	Work	No		Contractors
	10	Brochures	Material	No	per	
	11	Envelopes	Material	No	box	
	12	Paper	Material	No	carton	Paper
	13	Law Enforcement	Cost	No		Vendors
	14	Permits	Cost	No		Permits
	15	Postage	Cost	No		
	16	Printer	Cost	No		
	17	Supplies	Cost	No		
	18	Travel	Cost	No		Travel
	19	1040 EMPLOYEES	Work	Yes		Employees
	20	1050 VENDORS	Work	Yes		Vendors
	21	1060 CONTRACTORS	Work	Yes		Contractors
	22	7112 PAPER	Material	Yes	carton	Paper
	23	8015 PERMITS	Cost	Yes		Permits
	24	8020 TRAVEL	Cost	Yes		Travel

FIGURE 10-11

When you type budget categories into Resource Sheet view, be sure to consistently use exactly the same names with the same spelling. To prevent spurious entries due to typos, set up a custom text field with a lookup table of valid budget categories as described on page 283.

Congratulations! You've completed the daunting task of setting up Project to compare resource costs and work values against your budget.

Step 5: Compare Budget Resource Values

Finally, you're about to reap the harvest of the previous four steps: You're going to compare your project resource cost and work values against the budgeted values from your budget resources. You may find the occasional bad apple if your costs outrun your budgeted values. The good news is that this comparison helps you see potential problems when it's early enough to find solutions.

To compare budget values to planned values, you need a table that shows both budgeted and planned fields. Then you can group the contents of the view by your budget categories. The result is groups of budgeted and planned values for each budget category, and voilà—your budget situation becomes crystal clear. Follow these steps to set up your budget-comparison view:

1. **Switch to Resource Usage view (View→Resource Usage).**

   When you're *entering* budget cost and work values, Task Usage view is better, because it shows the project summary task at the top, with the assigned budget resources just under it. But for *comparing* budget and planned values, Resource Usage view inherits the throne, because you want to group resources by the custom resource text field you set up on page 283, and resource fields aren't available in Task Usage view. Moreover, you want to look at budget values in terms of resources and their assignments.

2. **If they aren't there already, add the Budget Work, Budget Cost, Work, and Cost columns to the table.**

   To add a column, right-click the heading of the column to the right of where you want to insert the new column and then, on the shortcut menu, choose Insert Column. In the Field Name drop-down list, choose the field you want to add. Project displays the new field to the left of the selected column.

3. **To group the resources by the custom resource text field, click the down arrow to the right of the Resource Name column heading and then, on the drop-down menu, choose "Group by"→Custom Group.**

   The Group Definition dialog box appears. See page 656 for the full scoop on creating groups.

4. **In the Group By row, click the down arrow in the Field Name cell, and then, in the drop-down list of resource fields, choose the name of the custom text field for your budget categories (or Group or Code if you used one of those fields instead), and then click Apply.**

   Project groups the resources in your project by the budget categories you set up, as demonstrated in Figure 10-12.

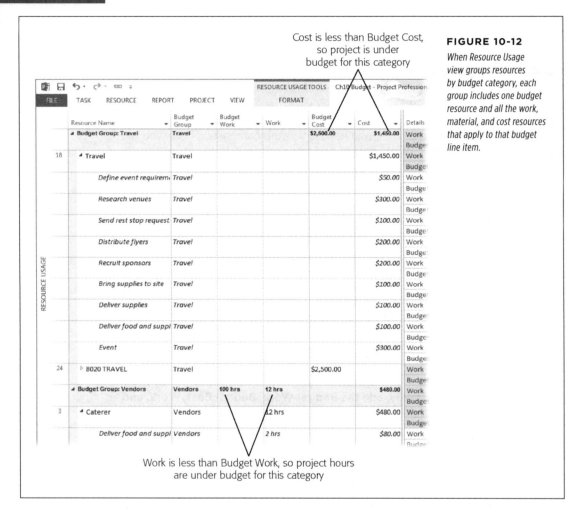

Cost is less than Budget Cost, so project is under budget for this category

Work is less than Budget Work, so project hours are under budget for this category

FIGURE 10-12

When Resource Usage view groups resources by budget category, each group includes one budget resource and all the work, material, and cost resources that apply to that budget line item.

5. **In the group summary rows (which have yellow shading), compare the Budget Cost or Budget Work values to the Cost or Work values, respectively.**

   The Budget Cost or Budget Work cells in the group summary rows show the budget values for each budget resource. For each group, you see a value for Budget Cost or Budget Work, depending on whether the budget resource is a cost resource or a work (or material) resource.

The Cost and Work cells in the group summary rows show the rolled-up cost and rolled-up work for the resources in that particular budgetary group. If the value in a group summary row's Cost cell is higher than the value in its Budget Cost cell, then you've exceeded your budget. If the value in the Work cell is higher than the Budget Work cell, then your work hours are over budget.

TIP If you want to see resources in alphabetical order, click the down arrow to the right of the Resource Name column heading, and then choose Sort A to Z. Project sorts resources within each group in alphabetical order.

6. **To dismantle the groups, click the down arrow to the right of the Resource Name column heading, and then, on the drop-down menu, choose No Group.**

   Resource Usage view returns to its ungrouped state.

TIP Given all the steps needed to fashion a view for comparing budget values, a view with everything already in place can save you time. You want the Budget Cost, Budget Work, Cost, and Work columns side by side, the rows grouped by the text field you used for budget categories, and resources sorted by name. See Chapter 21 to learn how to create a custom view, custom table, and custom group. You can also copy the BudgetComparison view (with its custom table and group) from *ProjectMM_Customizations.mpp* from this book's Missing CD page at *www.missingmanuals.com/cds*.

With your budget fields and values in place, and a custom budget-resource view created, you have everything you need to compare budget values with planned values at any point during the project. See Chapter 14 for more information about monitoring costs during the execution phase.

■ Setting the Project's Fiscal Year

You can set the fiscal year for a project, whether it's the fiscal year your own company uses or the one the project's customer uses. Whether the fiscal year starts in January, July, or October, setting a project's fiscal year can help you communicate project costs to your accounting department in the format it wants.

NOTE You may have heard that Project lets you set up fiscal periods in the project, like 28-day periods, 13-week periods, and so on. This timesheet-related feature is available in the enterprise project-management features of Project Server.

Project handles fiscal years in a rather limited way, and it may cause more confusion than convenience. While Project can show you the fiscal year in the timescale headings of Gantt Chart views and usage-oriented views, Project doesn't change any other dates in the project: The project's start and finish dates, working-time calendar, resource availability dates, and reports all still use the calendar year. If you want to see fiscal year dates in views, here's what you do:

1. **Choose File→Options, and then, on the left side of the Project Options dialog box, choose Schedule.**

   Project displays all the schedule-related settings you can adjust, including fiscal calendar.

2. **If you want this fiscal year setting to apply to all projects from this point forward, in the "Calendar options for this project" drop-down list at the top of the dialog box, choose All New Projects.**

   Do this only if most of your projects work on this fiscal year. Otherwise it's probably best to set the fiscal year individually for each project. If you don't change the setting in the "Calendar options for this project" drop-down list, Project automatically selects the current project.

3. **In the "Fiscal year starts in" box, choose the month in which the fiscal year begins.**

   For example, if your fiscal year runs from June 1 through May 31, choose June.

4. **If your fiscal year is named by the calendar year in which it begins, turn on the "Use starting year for FY numbering" checkbox.**

   With this checkbox turned on, Project sets your fiscal year 2014 dates so they start in 2014: that is, from June 2014 through May 2015. Turn this checkbox off if your fiscal year is named by the calendar year in which it *ends*; for example, if your 2014 fiscal year runs from June 2013 through May 2014.

5. **Click OK.**

   The fiscal year is reflected in the timescale headings of Gantt Chart views and usage-oriented views, as shown in Figure 10-13.

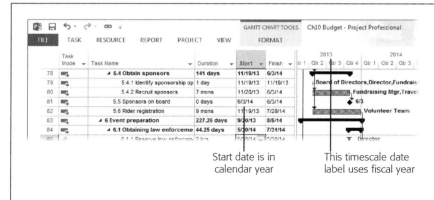

FIGURE 10-13

You can display fiscal year dates in Gantt Chart and usage view timescale headings. However, start and finish dates, as well as any other dates in Project, are still calendar dates. For example, you could see a date like 6/3/14 in a Start cell while seeing Qtr4 2013 in the timescale for the same task.

Start date is in calendar year

This timescale date label uses fiscal year

TIP   If you've set your fiscal year but the timescale headings haven't changed, first check the zoom level of your timescale. If it's zoomed way in to an hour-by-hour basis, Project typically doesn't list the year. In the status bar, drag the Zoom slider until you can see days. If a year appears in the timescale heading and it isn't "fiscal," then right-click anywhere in the timescale heading and choose Timescale. In the Timescale dialog box (page 614), check the tab for each tier that appears (Top Tier, Middle Tier, Bottom Tier) and make sure the "Use fiscal year" checkbox is turned on for the tiers you're using in your project. Also on each tab, check to make sure that the date listed in the Label box includes the year.

Reviewing and Fine-Tuning Your Plan

Balancing a project's scope, schedule, cost, and quality is a bit like juggling eggs: If you don't keep an eye on every element, you'll end up with egg on your face. In the chapters so far, you've built a project schedule based on scope and quality objectives. Now it's time to see whether the schedule and price are right.

To get a schedule to work, you first have to make sure that all elements of your project are based in reality—like task duration, dependencies, and resource assignments. Then you have to make other changes to tasks and assignments to get the equation to balance—for instance, you might shorten task duration, decrease cost, or reduce scope. As you make these tweaks, you have to review the schedule to see if your changes are producing the results you want. Shortening the schedule may increase the project's cost (you'll learn about the technique called *crashing* on page 356), but so can lengthening the schedule.

This chapter starts with examining your project's schedule and cost. You'll learn how to find the best tasks to shorten if the schedule is too long. Because your initial plan is almost guaranteed to need fine-tuning, this chapter also describes several Project features that can help you change the schedule. For example, Project's Task Inspector scans your file for scheduling problems and ways to improve the schedule—flagging scheduling problems with red squiggly lines and opportunities for improvement with green squiggly lines. When you make changes to the schedule, Project highlights all the fields affected by your edits (this feature is called *change highlighting*).

Your review of the schedule starts with taking a look at tasks. Missing or incorrect task dependencies affect when tasks begin and end, so the dates that Project calculates might be too early or too late. In addition, task date constraints and manually scheduled tasks go on the calendar where you tell them to. But if those constraints or dates are wrong—or you accidentally create constraints you don't need—the schedule is both incorrect and less flexible. This chapter tells you how to find and correct task dependencies and inadvertent constraints.

Resource assignments are another weak link. This chapter describes techniques for making a schedule more realistic, including how to handle part-time resources and to take productivity levels into account. Even when you plan with regard to your workers' schedules, you might find that some resources have crushing workloads. You can relieve the pressure by reassigning resources, contouring resource assignments, and leveling assignments to match the time resources have available. This chapter explains all your options.

After you've worked all the kinks out of your tasks and resource assignments, the project's schedule and costs might not be what stakeholders want. Techniques for shortening a schedule start with the same resource-assignment approaches you use to even out workloads. This chapter also describes a few brawnier (though riskier) techniques like *fast-tracking* (vigorously overlapping tasks) and *crashing* (aggressively adding resources or spending more money to shorten duration). Finally, this chapter identifies methods that can help you reduce project cost.

■ Reviewing the Schedule and Cost

The fat lady won't sing until the finish dates in Project meet the project's deadlines *and* the project's cost is right. Your job is to keep fine-tuning the schedule until both the schedule and the cost are in line. This second round of work is also a good time to correct any errors lurking in the schedule, as the box on page 293 describes. In this section, you'll learn how to review dates and costs in your Project file, and how to find the best tasks to change.

Understanding the Critical Path and Slack Time

Stakeholders usually care deeply about when the project is going to finish. The *critical path* determines the project's finish date, which is why it gets a lot of attention during project planning and execution. This section explains why the critical path is critical and how slack time determines which tasks are on the critical path.

The critical path is the longest sequence of tasks in the project schedule. It starts on the project start date and runs to the project finish date. The tasks on the critical path are called *critical tasks*. Why is the critical path critical? Because a delay in *any* of its tasks delays the project's finish date.

Double-Checking the Schedule

Mistakes will always linger in your project schedule, no matter how many times you check it. Moreover, as you refine the schedule, you might introduce mistakes that weren't there before. So it's a good idea to stay on the lookout for errors. For example, you may notice a task scheduled during a period when the assigned resource will be on vacation, or spot the wrong kind of dependency between two tasks. Watch for the following items:

- Task dependencies that shouldn't be there or should be a different type (page 183).

- Tasks with inflexible date constraints (page 188) that they shouldn't have.

- Manually scheduled tasks that should instead be auto-scheduled (page 314).

- Work or duration values that seem too low or too high.

- Work-package tasks without assigned resources.

- Summary tasks *with* assigned resources.

- Overallocated resources (page 327).

- Resource calendars that don't represent people's actual availability (page 214).

In addition, make sure you've included time for often-overlooked types of work, like project-related meetings (including status meetings and project-management meetings) and work reviews. Because several people attend these powwows, the time and expenses add up fast. Even approvals aren't as simple as signing the sign-off sheet. Be sure to include time for people to review documents or other deliverables before they approve them.

NOTE　Project uses the critical path method (CPM) to calculate the start and finish dates for tasks, but Microsoft didn't come up with the concept of the critical path. To learn about the critical path method and its task date calculations, check out Chapter 5 of *Project Planning, Scheduling & Control*, by James P. Lewis (McGraw-Hill).

To understand where the critical path comes from, you need to understand *slack time* (also called float), which is the amount of time that a task can slip without delaying the tasks that follow it (see Figure 11-1). When you link tasks (page 176), predecessor tasks can push (or pull) their successors around. For instance, if a predecessor starts late enough or takes too long for whatever reason, it delays the tasks that follow it. Slack time is the amount of wiggle room a task has. (As you'll see later in this chapter, you can use slack time to help balance people's workloads.)

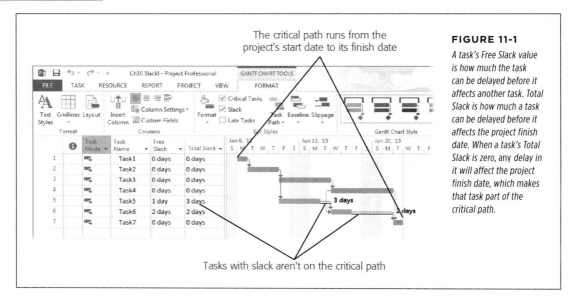

The critical path runs from the
project's start date to its finish date

Tasks with slack aren't on the critical path

FIGURE 11-1

A task's Free Slack value is how much the task can be delayed before it affects another task. Total Slack is how much a task can be delayed before it affects the project finish date. When a task's Total Slack is zero, any delay in it will affect the project finish date, which makes that task part of the critical path.

Driving somewhere is a simple example of a critical path and slack time. Suppose you and your brother are both heading to your elderly Aunt Thelma's for lunch, which starts at noon sharp. You're taking the highway, which takes 65 minutes. Your brother, on the other hand, is driving his sports car over the scenic route, which is 90 minutes of twists and turns. Your brother's drive is the critical path, because it takes the longest. That gives you 25 minutes of slack time before you have to start driving (or you can use the time to stop and pick flowers for your dear auntie).

Project has two fields for slack:

- **Free Slack** represents the amount of time a task can slip before it delays another *task*. For example, Task5 in Figure 11-1 can slip 1 day before it will delay Task6.

- **Total Slack** is the amount of time a task can slip before it delays the *project finish date*. In Figure 11-1, Task6 has 2 days of total slack, because it can delay 2 days before it affects the last task in the schedule. Once a task uses up its total slack, it becomes critical and joins the critical path. (Page 299 explains how tasks can end up with *negative* slack, which can lead to too many tasks on the critical path.)

To add either of these fields to a view's table pane, right-click the table's heading area, choose Insert Column, and then pick the field you want to add.

NOTE The Early Start, Early Finish, Late Start, and Late Finish fields show the earliest and latest dates that a task can start based on the slack of predecessor or successor tasks.

If you look closely at Figure 11-1, you'll notice that the tasks on the critical path (Task1–Task4 and Task7) have one thing in common: Their Total Slack values are *0*—meaning they have no slack whatsoever. When predecessors and successors are linked with no slack at all, as tightly coupled as a freight train's cars, then any delay propagates down the line, delaying the project finish date.

> **TIP** If you want insurance for your project's finish date, you can add buffers to your schedule as described on page 315. That way, if tasks get delayed, they eat into the buffers instead of delaying the finish date.

The critical path's tight coupling has an upside: If a critical task finishes early, its successors can start earlier, too (as long as their assigned resources are available)— which could mean an *earlier* project finish date. So the critical path is the key to success whether you're trying to keep your schedule on track or need to shorten it.

Reviewing the Critical Path

When a project schedule is too long, you want to rein it in with the least amount of disruption to your plan. Because tasks on the critical path directly affect a project's finish date, they're the best candidates for shortening. This section shows you how to see which tasks are on the critical path, so you can focus on the tasks that really make a difference to your schedule.

■ DISPLAYING THE CRITICAL PATH IN PROJECT

Gantt Chart view makes the critical path easy to see. Some built-in views show the critical path out of the box, but it's easy to display it in any Gantt Chart view:

- Standard **Gantt Chart view** doesn't show the critical path or slack time initially—all you see are blue task bars. However, in Project, you can easily format this view to display the critical path and slack time. In the Gantt Chart Tools | Format tab's Bar Styles section, turn on the Critical Tasks checkbox and the Slack checkbox. Once you do that, the view's timescale displays critical tasks in red and slack as thin black bars (they look like underscores) at the right end of task bars (see Figure 11-1).

- **Tracking Gantt view** (in the Task tab's View section, click the down arrow, and then choose Tracking Gantt) shows the critical tasks' bars in red and noncritical tasks' bars in blue. The table area initially displays the Entry table. (If you've set a baseline for your project, as described on page 375, gray task bars represent the baseline schedule.)

- **Detail Gantt view** (in the Task tab's View section, click the down arrow, choose More Views, and then double-click Detail Gantt) also shows critical tasks in red and noncritical tasks in blue. It applies the Delay table so you can evaluate leveling delays.

◼ FILTERING THE TASK LIST TO SHOW CRITICAL TASKS

Filtering the task list to show only critical-path tasks helps you focus on the tasks that need to stay on schedule or finish early. When you use filters in Project, you have to reapply them regularly, like sunscreen, as the box on page 296 explains. To filter the task list to show only critical-path tasks, do the following:

1. **In the View tab's Data section, click the down arrow next to the filter box, and then choose Critical.**

   Project shows critical path tasks and the summary tasks to which they belong.

2. **To hide the summary tasks, in the Gantt Chart Tools | Format tab's Show/ Hide section, turn off the Summary Tasks checkbox.**

   The summary tasks disappear, so you see only critical work-package tasks.

> **TIP** Grouping tasks by critical status keeps noncritical tasks visible but out of the way. In the table pane of a Gantt Chart view, click the down arrow to the right of the Name column heading. In the drop-down menu, choose "Group by"→Critical. Project lists all the noncritical tasks first (under a summary row with "Critical: No" in its Task Name cell), and then lists critical tasks (under "Critical: Yes"). Revert to the regular order by right-clicking the down arrow to the right of the Name column heading and then choosing No Group.

WORKAROUND WORKSHOP

The Ever-Changing Critical Path

The critical path can be slippery. Sometimes shortening a critical task adds a different task to the critical path that wasn't there before. Conversely, since the critical path shows the longest path from start to finish, shortening a task may actually turn it into a *noncritical* task. To understand how this works, consider two tasks that start on the same day. The critical task takes 10 days, and the noncritical one takes 9 days. If you shorten the critical task to 8 days, it isn't the longest path anymore, so it becomes a noncritical task. In the

meantime, the 9-day task is now the longest and, thus, is now on the critical path.

Because the critical path changes, make sure you're using the *current* critical path to choose the tasks you want to work on. Although the Critical filter initially shows only critical tasks, it doesn't update itself as tasks' critical status changes. To quickly reapply the current filter, press Ctrl+Shift+F3.

◼ SHOWING CRITICAL TASKS IN A GANTT CHART TABLE

Bright red task bars in the timescale make the critical path easy to see. But the tasks in the table area still look exactly the same. Project has formatting features to highlight the critical path in tables as well. If you want to see the critical path even in the Gantt Chart table area, do the following:

1. **To change the appearance of the text of critical tasks, in the Gantt Chart Tools | Format tab's Format section, click Text Styles.**

The Text Styles dialog box opens. The advantage to formatting text *styles* instead of individual textual elements is that Project then applies the style whenever it's appropriate. For example, if you modify the formatting for the critical-task text style, then Project applies or removes the formatting as tasks join or drop off the critical path, making it easier for you to spot these changes.

2. **In the "Item to Change" drop-down list, choose Critical Tasks.**

   Any changes you make to the font or colors will apply to all critical-path tasks.

3. **Adjust the font, font style, and font size.**

   The Font list displays the fonts installed on your computer. The "Font style" list controls whether the text is bold or in italics. The Size list includes the standard font sizes (you can type a number in the box to specify a font size not in the list). Turn on the Underline checkbox if you want the text underlined as well.

TIP Colors other than black can make text hard to read. If you decide to change the text color, opt for dark hues. In addition, remember that colors may not reproduce well when you print in black and white. To change the font color, in the Color drop-down list, choose the one you want (for example, dark red to mimic the red task bar formatting).

---

4. **To highlight cells that use this text style, in the Background Color drop-down list, choose the color you want.**

   For example, you can change the background for critical cells to a light red (see Figure 11-2). As you select options and settings, the Sample box previews the text's appearance.

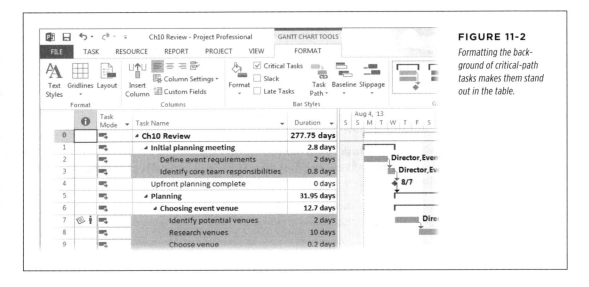

FIGURE 11-2

Formatting the background of critical-path tasks makes them stand out in the table.

NOTE Initially, the Text Styles dialog box's Background Pattern box is set to a solid color. If you prefer, you can change this setting to apply a hatch pattern or to stipple the background, for example, to emphasize critical tasks on a black-and-white printout.

5. **Click OK.**

Cells that use the Critical Tasks text style immediately show the new formatting. The background color (and pattern, if you selected one) apply to all critical-task cells except for the Indicators and Task Mode columns. These changes appear every time you apply the current table. You can also create a custom table (page 638) to show critical tasks in this way.

■ COMPARING FINISH DATES TO DEADLINES

Finish dates are conspicuous in the Gantt Chart timescale because they're where task bars end. The Finish field also appears in the Entry, Schedule, Summary, Usage, and Variance tables, to name a few. But what you really want is to see whether the finish dates come on or before the project's deadlines.

During planning, you can compare the finish dates of the project and key tasks with the deadlines requested by stakeholders. As you learned on page 192, the Deadline field helps track important dates during project planning and execution. You can filter the task list to focus on tasks with deadlines and look for missed-deadline indicators to identify problem areas.

TIP Tasks that finish on time during planning may not stay that way when the work begins. Missed-deadline indicators appear as soon as estimated finish dates are later than their corresponding deadline dates, so it's a good idea to check for missed-deadline indicators regularly.

When you assign a date in a task's Deadline field, a deadline arrow appears at that date in the Gantt Chart timescale (the arrow may be solid green or outlined in black, depending on the view). The task's finish date is late if its task bar ends to the right of the arrow. However, these deadline arrows aren't especially eye-catching. Filtering the task list to show missed deadlines makes them easier to see. The missed-deadline indicator is another hint that the finish date isn't working. Here's how to compare finish dates with deadlines:

1. **To show only tasks with deadlines, in the View tab's Data section, click the down arrow next to the Filter box, and then choose More Filters. In the More Filters dialog box, double-click Tasks With Deadlines.**

    Project shows tasks with deadlines but also shows the summary tasks to which they belong, as you can see in Figure 11-3.

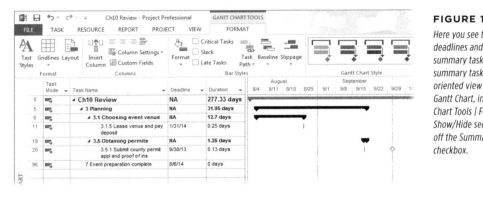

FIGURE 11-3

Here you see tasks with deadlines and their summary tasks. To hide summary tasks, in a task-oriented view like the Gantt Chart, in the Gantt Chart Tools | Format tab's Show/Hide section, turn off the Summary Tasks checkbox.

2. **To find tasks that miss their deadlines, look in the Entry table's Indicators column (the column's heading is an i in a blue circle) for red diamonds with exclamation points inside (see Figure 11-4).**

   If tasks miss their deadlines by a mile, the deadline arrows in the timescale may be a long way from the end of the task bar, so the two may not be visible in the timescale at the same time, depending on the timescale's units. Remember, you can drag the Zoom slider in the status bar to change the time periods that appear in the timescale.

   By scanning the Indicators column for missed deadline indicators, you can identify the tasks to focus on. Of course, if you don't see any missed-deadline indicators, you can move on to checking whether the project's cost works.

■ WHEN TOO MANY TASKS ARE CRITICAL

Project might show some tasks as critical that don't seem critical at all. For example, in the timescale in Figure 11-4, Task5 and Task6 look like they have some wiggle room before they delay the project finish date. However, Task5's Total Slack is 0 days and Task6's Total Slack is negative. To Project, any task with Total Slack equal to or less than zero is a critical task, so it considers Task5 and Task6 critical.

Where does negative slack come from? The solution to this puzzle lies in the *deadline* (page 192) applied to the last task in the schedule (the green downward-pointing arrow below the task bar for Task6). When you apply a deadline (or an inflexible date constraint) to a task, Project uses that deadline or constraint to calculate slack instead of task finish dates. If the deadline or constraint date occurs earlier than the task's calculated finish date, the result is negative slack.

In Project, the Late Finish field is the latest date a task can end without affecting the project finish date, and the Finish field is a task's currently scheduled finish date.

Project's Free Slack field (which Detail Gantt displays) is the length of time between a task's late finish and finish dates. For example, if the late finish date is 10/1/2014 and the finish date is 9/1/2014, then the task's free slack is 30 days.

When you enter a date in a task's Deadline field, Project sets the late finish to the deadline date. So, in the example above, if you set the late finish date to 8/1/2014, that's earlier than the task's finish date (9/1/2014), so you end up with negative slack.

When negative slack adds too many tasks to the critical path, the trick is to focus on the tasks with the lowest slack values. In Figure 11-4, you'd start with the tasks whose Total Slack is –3 days. To finish the project by the deadline date, your goal is to find a way to shorten the schedule by 3 days. (See page 354 and page 356 to learn two methods for shortening project duration.)

> **TIP** Negative slack makes it difficult to see which tasks are *really* critical. Because inflexible date constraints and deadlines can lead to negative slack, it's best to use them sparingly in your Project schedules. (You can see the true slack in your project by removing the deadlines you've set. Then you can add the deadlines back in after the schedule is working. Page 193 tells you how to find tasks with deadlines.) Although deadlines affect Project's critical-path calculations, they don't ignore dependencies between tasks (page 191). If a task finishes later than its deadline, you get a warning when your schedule doesn't meet the deadline, so you can see where the problem is and work to resolve it. Date constraints, in contrast, can overrule task dependencies, which prevents Project from calculating the project schedule for you. For that reason, you're better off applying *deadlines* to tasks instead of inflexible date constraints.

> **TIP** To display negative slack lines as shown in Figure 11-4, in the Gantt Chart Tools | Format tab's Bar styles section, click Format→Bar Styles. In a blank row of the Bar Styles table that appears, add an entry for negative slack. In the row's Show For cell, choose Critical; in its From cell choose Negative Slack; and in its To cell choose Task Start. Then click OK to close the Bar Styles dialog box. (See page 602 for more details on customizing bar styles.)

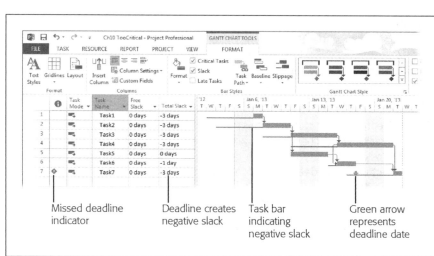

FIGURE 11-4

A deadline or date constraint applied to a task can lead to negative slack, which results in more tasks jumping onto the critical path than you'd expect. Displaying task bars for negative slack is one way to see which tasks you need to focus on. In this example, thin red lines to the left of the task bars represent the tasks' negative slack.

Missed deadline indicator

Deadline creates negative slack

Task bar indicating negative slack

Green arrow represents deadline date

■ WHEN THE CRITICAL PATH IS INCOMPLETE

Every project schedule has a critical path that runs from the project's start date to its finish. But sometimes, the critical path in Project has chunks missing, like a garden hose after it's been run over by a lawnmower. You'll see a series of tasks with red task bars, then a bunch of noncritical tasks, then another set of critical tasks later in the schedule. An incomplete critical path can arise for several reasons. This section explains what can cause gaps in the critical path and what to do about them.

Some missing pieces of critical path are okay. For example, Project doesn't show completed tasks on the critical path, because they're complete and you can't do anything about them. Lag time on the dependencies between critical tasks or nonworking time on a calendar can also produce gaps in the critical path.

Gaps can also arise due to missing task dependencies, date constraints, resource or task calendars, external predecessors, and resource leveling. For example, if a date constraint prevents a critical task from starting right after its predecessor, it's still a critical task, but its Total Slack value is greater than zero.

To fill in the gaps in the critical path, you need to change how Project measures critical tasks. Out of the box, Project considers a task critical if it has Total Slack equal to or less than zero, but you can tell the program to use a different value. First, you need to figure out what the slack value for critical tasks *should* be. Here are the steps to reuniting your project's critical path:

1. **With Gantt Chart view applied, click the Gantt Chart Tools | Format tab. In the Bar Styles section, turn on the Critical Tasks checkbox.**

   The task bars for critical tasks appear in red.

2. **In the view's table pane, right-click the column heading area, choose Insert Column on the shortcut menu, and then choose Total Slack in the dropdown menu.**

   Total Slack tells you which tasks are on the critical path.

3. **Starting at the last task in the schedule (in Figure 11-5, that's Task7), work backward until you find a task that should be critical, but isn't.**

   In Figure 11-5, Task2 is part of the longest path from start to finish, but its Total Slack is greater than zero, so Project doesn't consider it a critical task.

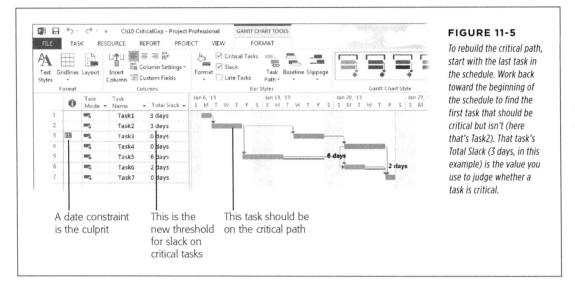

FIGURE 11-5

To rebuild the critical path, start with the last task in the schedule. Work back toward the beginning of the schedule to find the first task that should be critical but isn't (here that's Task2). That task's Total Slack (3 days, in this example) is the value you use to judge whether a task is critical.

A date constraint is the culprit

This is the new threshold for slack on critical tasks

This task should be on the critical path

4. **To change the threshold for critical tasks, click File→Options. On the left side of the Project Options dialog box, choose Advanced and then scroll to the very bottom of the dialog box.**

   The option that controls critical slack is in the "Calculation options for this project" section. Make sure that the project you want appears in the box to the right of the section's label.

TIP The "Calculate multiple critical paths" checkbox resides in the same section of the Project Options dialog box. This setting is turned off initially, which tells Project to display only one critical path—in this case, the overall critical path that affects the project's finish date. However, if you want to see more than one critical path (for example, the critical path for each subproject in a master project or for each project phase), then turn on this checkbox.

---

5. **In the "Tasks are critical if slack is less than or equal to" box, type the value you want to use for critical slack. Then click OK to close the Project Options dialog box.**

   In Figure 11-5, the task that should be critical has a Total Slack value of 3 days. So for this project, you'd type 3 in the box.

   After you change the threshold value, Project adds tasks to the critical path if their Total Slack value is less than or equal to the new threshold you set.

Reviewing Project Costs

By assigning costs to work, material, and cost resources and then assigning resources to tasks—as you learned about in Chapter 8 and Chapter 9—Project can calculate the price tag of your project. You can display costs in many of the program's standard views by applying a table with cost fields. For example, Gantt Chart view shows costs for both the entire project and individual tasks. And applying the Cost table to a usage view shows the cost of individual assignments.

Here are a few ways to review project costs:

- **Review project statistics.** The Project Statistics dialog box (page 269) provides an overview of the project's status. To open it, in the Project tab's Properties section, click Project Information, and then click Statistics at the bottom of the Project Information dialog box. In the Cost column, the Current cell shows the current forecast cost, including any actual cost that's already been incurred.

- **Review total project cost.** Sometimes the total price is the only thing that matters. The project summary task is an easy way to see project-wide cost (page 267). To display the project summary task, in the Gantt Chart Tools | Format tab's Show/Hide section, turn on the Project Summary Task checkbox. Then, in the View tab's Data section, click Tables→Summary. The Cost value for the project summary task represents the total scheduled cost of the project.

- **View costs in the table area.** Apply the Cost table by heading to the View tab's Data section and clicking Tables→More Tables. In the More Tables dialog box, double-click Cost. As shown in Figure 11-6, the Total Cost cell for the project summary task represents the total cost of the project.

- **Display task and assignment costs.** To see task and assignment costs, simply apply the Cost table to the appropriate view (page 267). The Cost table includes columns for planned and actual costs. For example, Baseline shows the cost when you saved the baseline, Actual is the actual cost of the work that's been completed so far, and Variance is the difference between the baseline and the current scheduled cost.

The view you apply depends on which costs you want to see. If you apply the Cost table to task-oriented views, the table area shows task costs. In Task Usage and Resource Usage views, the Cost table shows the total cost by task or resource and assignment, while the timescale shows values for each time period, as shown in Figure 11-7.

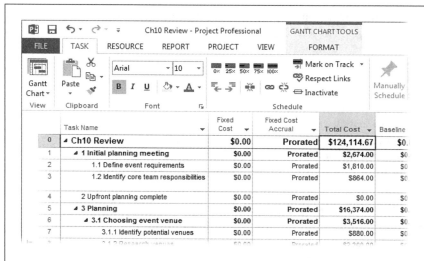

FIGURE 11-6

The Total Cost cell for the project summary task is a rolled-up value of the cost of every task in the project. This includes labor and material costs, other costs you've assigned with cost resources, and any cost you've added as a fixed cost. Project calculates the Total Cost value by adding the actual cost of completed work to the estimated cost for work that hasn't been done.

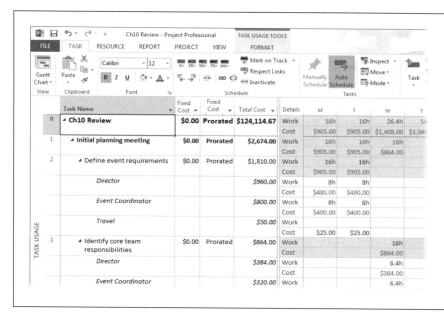

FIGURE 11-7

Initially, usage views show only the Work field in the timescale. To see cost for each time period, right-click anywhere within the timescale and then, on the shortcut menu, choose Cost. Project then adds a second row to each assignment for cost.

TIP If the total cost is too high, you can sort tasks by cost to find the ones that cost the most. To do so, display Gantt Chart view (in the View tab's Task Views section, click Gantt Chart). Then, in the Gantt Chart Tools | Format tab's Show/Hide section, turn off the Summary Tasks checkbox. Next, in the View tab's Data section, click Tables→Cost, and then click Sort→By Cost. After you make these changes, the most expensive task is at the top of the table.

◼ USING PROJECT COST REPORTS

Project includes several reports that show project costs—both the new, graphical reports and visual reports (see page 470 for the differences between them). You can use the following reports to look at cost for tasks and assignments or to evaluate cash flow over time:

- **Cash Flow report.** The graphical Cash Flow report (on the Report tab, click Costs→Cash Flow) shows Total Cost by quarter. A line shows the cumulative cost over time, as you can see in Figure 11-8. The table below the graph shows cost values for the project's top-level tasks. You can change the report's time period or display lower-level tasks.

FIGURE 11-8

You can modify the time periods or fields displayed in the graph by clicking the graph. Then click the Chart Tools | Design tab. In the Show/Hide section, click Chart Data to open the Field List pane. To change the graph's time period, in the Field List pane, click the Edit button, and then choose the period you want. To display different fields in the graph, in the Select Fields list, turn checkboxes on or off.

Name	Remaining Cost	Actual Cost	Cost	ACWP
Initial planning meeting	$2,674.00	$0.00	$2,674.00	$0.00
Upfront planning complete	$0.00	$0.00	$0.00	$0.00
Planning	$16,374.00	$0.00	$16,374.00	$0.00
Planning complete	$0.00	$0.00	$0.00	$0.00
Fundraising	$80,980.00	$0.00	$80,980.00	$0.00

NOTE Chapter 16 provides the full scoop on customizing reports.

- **Resource Cost Overview report.** The graphical Resource Cost Overview report (on the Report tab, click Costs→Resource Cost Overview) includes a graph that shows how much the project spends on each resource. If you need to cut costs, look at the resources that take a big bite of your budget to see if you can replace them with less expensive resources. This report also includes a pie chart that shows how much your project spends on work, material, and cost resources.

- **Task Cost Overview report.** The graphical Task Cost Overview report (on the Report tab, click Costs→Task Cost Overview) shows how much you spend on each top-level task. The table below the graph shows cost values for all top-level tasks.

- **Budget Cost Report visual report.** This report (on the Report tab, click Visual Reports and then choose Budget Cost Report in the "Visual Reports - Create Report" dialog box) displays costs in an Excel pivot table. The Chart1 worksheet contains a Microsoft Excel chart that initially shows cost by quarter. Display the Assignment Usage worksheet to view the data behind the chart and to use pivot table tools to modify the costs you see (page 490).

- **Cash Flow Report visual report.** Project has one Excel-based cash flow visual report and two Microsoft Visio visual reports (one metric and one using U.S. dimensions). Cash Flow Report is an Excel pivot table rendition of project costs (it initially displays them by quarter). To run this report, on the Report tab, click Visual Reports and then choose Cash Flow Report in the "Visual Reports - Create Report" dialog box.

■ Project Tools for Change

As you start changing the schedule in search of steady workloads, shorter project duration, or lower cost, you can put a triumvirate of Project's change-oriented features through their paces:

- **Task Inspector** shows the elements that make tasks start when they do or last as long as they do, so you get some hints about how to fix them. In many cases, the task- or assignment-editing commands you need (Reschedule Task and Team Planner if resources are overallocated) are ready for you, right in the Task Inspector pane.

- **Change highlighting** shades all the cells whose values change in response to an edit you make. You can then review these highlighted cells to see whether the changes you make produce the results you had in mind.

- **Multilevel Undo** lets you undo as many changes as you want. So if you zip through several edits only to find that another strategy is in order, you can undo the changes you made and try a different tack.

This section covers each feature in detail.

See Why Tasks Occur When They Do

Whether you're trying to shorten a project schedule during planning or recover from delays during execution, a typical strategy is to make tasks start or end earlier. A schedule problem in one task often starts somewhere else in your project—in elements that control the task's start date, like predecessors, calendars, or date constraints, to name a few. Task Inspector lists all the factors that affect the task you select, so you can decide what to do. Task Inspector can also help *after* you've begun project execution. If an important task is delayed, you can look at the factors that affect the task to identify which items to change to get back on track. For instance, you might talk to the team leader for the task that's causing the delay, or the manager of a person who's unavailable.

Because Project doesn't calculate dates for manually scheduled tasks, those types of tasks are particularly prone to scheduling problems. In Project, red squiggly lines indicate potential schedule problems, just like the ones for typos in Microsoft Word. When you right-click a cell that has a red squiggly line, you can open Task Inspector to see what the fuss is about or choose the action you want to perform from the shortcut menu.

NOTE   Task Inspector also checks your schedule for potential improvements. For example, if it sees a task that could start earlier, it draws a green squiggly line under the Start Date value. Make decisions about schedule optimizations in the same way you use Task Inspector to correct problems.

To open the Task Inspector pane, click the Task tab. In the Tasks section, click Inspect. The Task Inspector pane appears on the left side of the view and shows the factors that affect the dates for whichever task you select, as shown in Figure 11-9.

If resources are overallocated or task links are a problem, the Task Inspector pane includes repair options. For example, in Figure 11-9, Task Inspector includes Reschedule Task and Team Planner buttons in case you want to remove the overallocation on an overallocated resource.

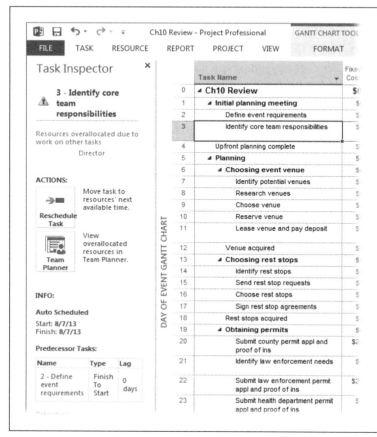

FIGURE 11-9.

The factors that appear in the Task Inspector pane may change as you modify the schedule. For example, if you find another resource to replace the one that's overallocated, the overallocation issue disappears. However, you could then discover that the new resource's calendar or a predecessor task is now the controlling factor.

If you see a red or green squiggly line below a task's value, right-click that cell to display a shortcut menu, as shown in Figure 11-10. Here are some ways you can fix tasks using Task Inspector and the commands on the shortcut menu:

- **Respect Links.** Because manually scheduled tasks start and finish when you specify, those dates may conflict with the task dependencies you've defined. Even with auto-scheduled tasks, date constraints you set can conflict with task dependencies. If you want Project to use task dependencies to determine when to schedule tasks, choose Respect Links on the shortcut menu.

- **Ignore Problems for This Task.** Sometimes a problem that Project finds isn't *really* a problem. Say you schedule a task to occur over a weekend, and the person you've assigned has agreed to that schedule. Sure, you can change the resource's calendar to show that they're available that weekend, but it's easier to simply ignore the problem. In this case, choose "Ignore Problems for This Task" from the shortcut menu, and Project turns off the red squiggly line.

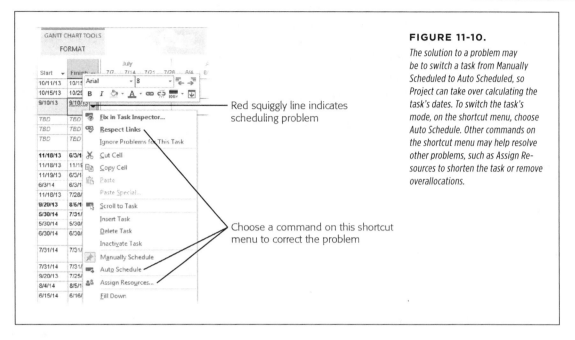

FIGURE 11-10.

The solution to a problem may be to switch a task from Manually Scheduled to Auto Scheduled, so Project can take over calculating the task's dates. To switch the task's mode, on the shortcut menu, choose Auto Schedule. Other commands on the shortcut menu may help resolve other problems, such as Assign Resources to shorten the task or remove overallocations.

Red squiggly line indicates scheduling problem

Choose a command on this shortcut menu to correct the problem

- **Fix in Task Inspector.** If you aren't sure how to resolve a problem, choose "Fix in Task Inspector" to open the Task Inspector pane shown in Figure 11-9. The first section of the pane displays the name of the selected task and the problems Task Inspector identified, such as overallocations, resource calendar issues, predecessor conflicts, and so on. The second section provides commands you can use to correct the problem, like Respect Links and Auto Schedule for task scheduling problems, or Increase Duration and Assign Resources for resource overallocations.

- **Show ignored problems.** After you've fixed a slew of problems, you may decide to take another look at the problems you ignored. To restore problem indicators to the view, in the Task tab's Tasks section, click the down arrow to the right of the word "Inspect" and then, on the drop-down menu, choose Show Ignored Problems. The red squiggly lines reappear for problems you had previously ignored.

TIP   Task Inspector is a good start, but it isn't the be-all and end-all for optimizing schedules. For example, Task Inspector shows task predecessors, but *you* have to dig deeper to discover that a predecessor's duration is caused by a resource who's scheduled for medical leave and that the resolution may be to reassign the predecessor task to someone else. Other sections in this chapter show you how to look at tasks and assignments from every angle.

Seeing What Changes Do

There's no guarantee your changes will correct the problems you're trying to fix. For example, you could assign more resources to shorten a critical path task, only to find out that another task prevents the finish date from changing. Fortunately, Project's *change highlighting* feature shades table cells that have changed due to your last task edit, so you can easily see whether the results are what you want.

Suppose you assign an additional resource to shorten a task's duration. Because the task finishes earlier, its successor tasks start and finish sooner. So change highlighting lights up the successor task's Start and Finish cells with background color, as Figure 11-11 demonstrates. Similarly, if the additional resource increases the task's cost, its Cost field (and its summary task's Cost field) might light up as well.

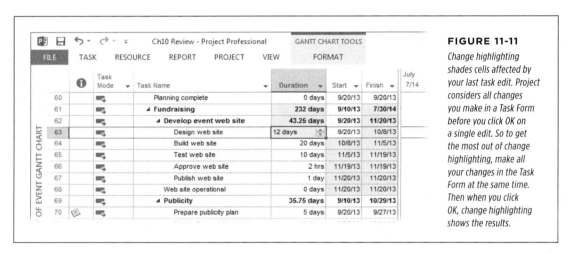

FIGURE 11-11

Change highlighting shades cells affected by your last task edit. Project considers all changes you make in a Task Form before you click OK on a single edit. So to get the most out of change highlighting, make all your changes in the Task Form at the same time. Then when you click OK, change highlighting shows the results.

Happily, modifying your view doesn't wash away change highlighting. You can display a new table, filter the schedule, or group tasks, and *still* see highlighted cells from the last edit. For example, if the Summary table is visible, you can review the changes in dates, duration, and cost. Switching to the Cost table would highlight cost cells affected by the last edit.

When you make another edit, change highlighting shows the effect of this new change. And saving the Project file *erases* any current change highlighting.

TIP It's unlikely, but if you want to turn change highlighting off for some reason, you have to add the Change Highlighting command to a custom group on the ribbon. See page 685 to learn how to customize the ribbon. The Change Highlighting command is in the All Commands group on the "Customize the Ribbon" screen.

Undoing Changes

Some adverse results are obvious, like a delay in a project finish date after you change the duration of a task. In many cases, though, as in a game of chess, you can't tell whether a strategy will pay off until you're a few moves in. Multilevel Undo, introduced in Project 2007, lets you try short what-if games in your current Project file. It lets you backtrack through any number of actions if they don't pan out. (See page 364 to learn how to work on more involved what-if scenarios.) Multilevel Undo can unravel everything a macro does, or reverse changes that other applications make to your Project file.

NOTE You can specify how many actions Multilevel Undo remembers: Choose File→Options. In the Project Options dialog box, choose Advanced. Under General, change the "Undo levels" setting to the number of actions you want to be able to track (up to 99) and then click OK.

Multilevel Undo keeps track of your actions and displays them on a menu so you can select the ones you want to undo. Here's how to put Multilevel Undo to work:

1. **On the Quick Access toolbar, click the tiny down arrow to the right of the Undo button (which looks like a curved arrow pointing to the left).**

   A drop-down menu appears, listing your previous actions with the most recent at the top and the earliest at the bottom. (Project clears this list when you save your Project file or close and reopen it.)

2. **Put your cursor over the earliest action you want to undo.**

   Project highlights every action from the most recent to the one where the pointer is. The last entry in the drop-down menu says "Undo x Actions," where x is the number of actions you've selected, as in Figure 11-12.

   If you're a prolific editor, you may see a few recent actions and a scroll bar on the drop-down menu. Drag the slider until you can see the earliest command you want to undo.

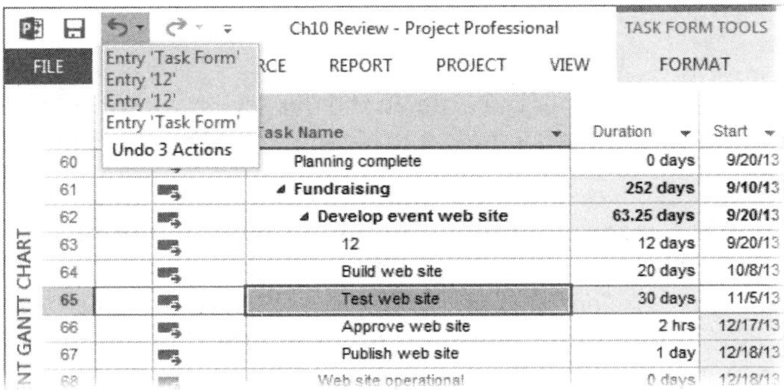

FIGURE 11-12

The entries in the Undo list aren't always as informative as you'd like. For example, if you make changes in the Task Form, the Undo menu simply says "Entry 'Task Form.'" If you can't remember which Task Form edit you want to undo, undo one entry at a time until the erroneous edit is gone.

3. **Click the action your cursor is over to undo the recent commands up to and including the action you clicked.**

■ Making Sure Tasks Are Set Up Correctly

Project can't read your mind. It can't point out missing task dependencies or dependencies that depend on the wrong things. Similarly, Project adds the task constraints you tell it to add. The problem is, seemingly innocuous actions can produce constraints you never intended. So review tasks to make sure you have the dependencies and constraints you want—and *only* those.

What Project *can* do is make it easier to find task dependencies and constraint problems, as this section explains.

Reviewing Task Dependencies

Following the link lines in a Gantt Chart is like trying to untangle a plate of spaghetti. It's hard to trace the lines to see if a task links to the right predecessors and successors, or if the dependencies you've set up are correct. After things get rolling, you might end up with a task-related problem—the assigned programmer is out of commission while she heals from a flambé cooking incident, say. In that case, you might want to see how that task affects the rest of the schedule. This section explains two ways to do that.

■ HIGHLIGHTING TASK PATHS

A welcome new feature in Project 2013 is *task path highlighting*, which makes it easy to review both predecessors and successors to find problems with task dependencies. This section provides a rundown on how it works.

Task path highlighting can emphasize the predecessors and successors of the selected task. Although this feature is turned off initially, once you've built a schedule of linked tasks, it's easy to turn it on to review task dependencies. Here's how:

1. **Display a Gantt Chart view, such as plain ol' Gantt Chart or Detailed Gantt.**

   You can turn on task path highlighting for any view that includes a timescale with task bars.

2. **Click the Gantt Chart Tools | Format tab. In the Bar Styles section, click Task Path, and then choose the items you want to highlight, as shown in Figure 11-13.**

   When you choose Predecessors, the task bars for all predecessors are shown in yellow. If you also choose Driving Predecessors, then the task bars for the predecessors that control when the selected task occurs change to orange. For example, if two tasks are predecessors to the selected task, the one that finishes sooner is a predecessor; the one that determines the selected task's start date is a *driving predecessor*.

   Similarly, choosing Successors highlights successors whose dates aren't directly controlled by the selected task. *Driving predecessors* are successors whose dates are directly controlled by the selected task.

3. **To review the dependencies for a different task, select that task.**

The highlighting shows the predecessors and successors of the task you select.

When you get to the final task or milestone, you're done! When you don't need task path highlighting any more, click the Gantt Chart Tools | Format tab. In the Bar Styles section, click Task Path→Remove Highlighting.

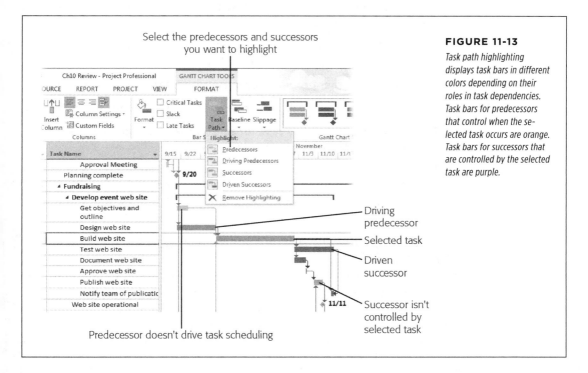

Select the predecessors and successors you want to highlight

Predecessor doesn't drive task scheduling

FIGURE 11-13

Task path highlighting displays task bars in different colors depending on their roles in task dependencies. Task bars for predecessors that control when the selected task occurs are orange. Task bars for successors that are controlled by the selected task are purple.

NOTE If you save your Project file while task path highlighting is turned on, the same highlights appear the next time you open the file.

■ REVIEWING DEPENDENCIES IN TASK FORM VIEW

To check that you've added the right types of dependencies with the correct amount of lag, you can't beat Task Form view. Here are the steps for displaying predecessors and successors in Task Form view, and checking that your dependencies are correct:

1. **With a Gantt Chart view in place, display Task Form view in the Details pane by clicking the View tab, turning on the Details checkbox, and then choosing Task Form in the Details drop-down menu.**

When you select a task in the top view pane, Task Form view displays information about it.

2. **Right-click anywhere in Task Form view and choose Predecessors & Successors.**

   The predecessors to the selected task appear on the left side of Task Form view, and the successors appear on the right side.

3. **Make sure that tasks in the Predecessor Name column are predecessors to the selected task and that the tasks in the Successor Name column are successors to the selected task.**

   If you find links that shouldn't be there, click the erroneous predecessor or successor's row, and then press the Delete key on your keyboard.

4. **Check whether other predecessor or successor tasks aren't listed.**

   If you find missing links, link the two tasks as you would normally (page 180).

5. **Make sure the dependency type for each predecessor and successor is correct, and verify the lag or lead time.**

   Remember, lag time (a delay from one task to the other) is a positive number. If the second task gets an early start, the lag becomes a negative number. (The box on page 315 describes a different kind of buffer—one that many tasks can share in case they require more time.)

Finding and Changing Manually Scheduled Tasks to Auto Scheduled

If some task information was unavailable when you started your project plan, you may have created manually scheduled tasks to record the info you *did* have. Project changes the appearance of task bars to indicate what information is available or missing (see page 61). As you get more information about tasks, you can fill in the missing fields and turn many of those manually scheduled tasks into auto-scheduled ones. (In some cases, you create manually scheduled tasks so you can pin the tasks' dates to the calendar. Those tasks remain manually scheduled for the duration of the project.) Be sure to review all your manually scheduled tasks to confirm that you've filled in missing task information.

Leaving Buffers Between Tasks

Nothing ever runs according to plan, so the reality is that some tasks in your project are going to finish late. If your schedule is tighter than a Hollywood face-lift, the tiniest delay in one task will work its way through the schedule to delay the finish date.

A good way to protect your schedule from delays is to add wiggle room at key points. For example, you can create a task specifically as a buffer between the end of one phase and the beginning of another. Or you can set up a manually scheduled summary task and add the buffer to it. (With a manually scheduled summary task, Project keeps track of the summary task duration you specify *and* the total duration of all the subtasks, so you can see whether the length of the subtasks

remains within the duration of the summary task, as shown in Figure 11-14.) Project managers often add a buffer to each phase of a project that's equivalent to 15 percent of that phase's duration. Then, if a few tasks take longer in an earlier phase, they eat into the buffer instead of your due date.

You don't need buffers between *every* task. Breathing room for phases or key summary tasks is usually good enough. In many projects, tasks that end early may offset tasks that run late, and you don't need the buffer at all. But if a series of tasks adds up to a real delay, you can reduce the buffer by the time that's been lost, and the project finish date will hold fast unless the delay *completely* consumes the buffer.

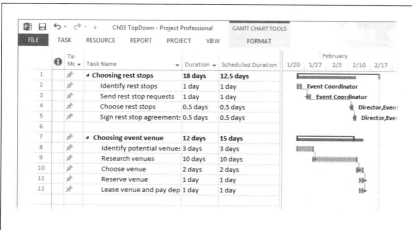

FIGURE 11-14

If subtasks stay within their summary task's duration, the rolled-up summary task bar is teal to indicate that you have extra buffer time. If the subtasks run longer than the summary task's duration, the rolled-up summary task bar turns red. The summary task's Duration field shows the duration you specified, while its Scheduled Duration field shows the duration of its subtasks.

Project's Tasks Without Dates filter (in the View tab's Data section, click the Filter down arrow, choose More Filters, and then double-click Tasks Without Dates) displays tasks without start and finish dates. However, incomplete task info comes in other forms—like tasks with start dates but no finish dates—so that filter doesn't show *all* the tasks you need to see. Filtering your task list to display all manually scheduled tasks is a better place to start. Here's how you can filter your task list and switch tasks to auto-scheduled as you fill in their missing info:

1. **Display the Entry table (in the View tab's Data section, click Tables→Entry).**

   If you use a different table that doesn't include the Task Mode field, right-click the column heading to the right of where you want to insert that field and then choose Insert Column→Task Mode.

2. **To filter your task list to show only manually scheduled tasks, click the down arrow in the Task Mode column heading, as shown in Figure 11-15; turn off the Auto Scheduled checkbox; and then click OK.**

   The task list includes all manually scheduled subtasks and the summary tasks to which they belong. A filter icon appears to the right of the Task Mode column heading to indicate that the list is filtered by that column (this icon is labeled in Figure 11-16).

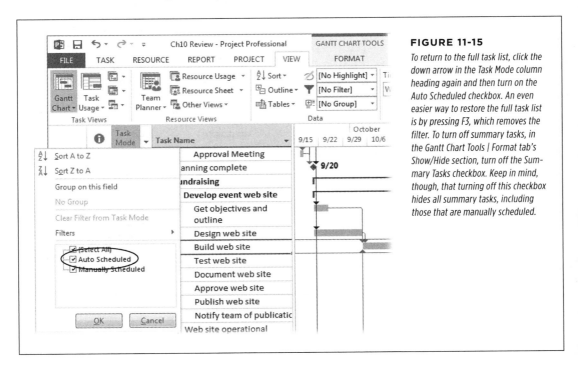

FIGURE 11-15

To return to the full task list, click the down arrow in the Task Mode column heading again and then turn on the Auto Scheduled checkbox. An even easier way to restore the full task list is by pressing F3, which removes the filter. To turn off summary tasks, in the Gantt Chart Tools | Format tab's Show/Hide section, turn off the Summary Tasks checkbox. Keep in mind, though, that turning off this checkbox hides all summary tasks, including those that are manually scheduled.

3. **Review each task in the list, and fill in any missing information.**

   A partially shaded task bar without end-caps means you haven't defined either a start or a finish date for that task. If a task bar has only one end-cap, then the duration or one of the task's dates is missing. To keep the task manually scheduled, fill in the task's Start or Finish fields. You can also switch the task to auto-scheduled, as described in step 4, so Project can use the task's predecessors and successors to calculate its dates.

4. **To switch a task to auto-scheduled, click the task's Task Mode cell, click the down arrow that appears, and then choose Auto Scheduled. Or right-click the task and then choose Auto Scheduled from the shortcut menu.**

   The Task Mode cell switches to the Auto Scheduled icon, and the task bar style in the timescale changes to solid blue (or red if it's critical and the view differentiates critical tasks) to show that the task is auto-scheduled. The newly auto-scheduled task remains in the view. To reapply the Manually Scheduled filter and hide any tasks you've switched to auto-scheduled, simply press Shift+F3.

5. **Repeat steps 3 and 4 until you've filled in all the missing information.**

   When the task list shows only the manually scheduled tasks you created to control task dates, you're done!

Freeing Tasks from Date Constraints

Most schedules originate from a start date, and the project's finish date is calculated from there. When you schedule a Project file from the start date (page 90), Project automatically assigns the flexible As Soon As Possible date constraint to new auto-scheduled tasks, so every task begins on the earliest possible date. (If you work backward from a finish date, Project assigns the As Late As Possible constraint instead.) Other less-flexible date constraints make sense now and then. For example, you can change the assignments for a key resource who's going on sabbatical to a Start No Earlier Than constraint to schedule assignments for when she returns.

Because less-flexible date constraints get in the way of Project doing its job, you're better off using as few of them as possible. Unfortunately, some Project actions create date constraints you don't intend (page 190). For example, typing a specific date in a Start or Finish cell creates a new date constraint for that task. This section tells you how to find and eliminate unwanted date constraints. The box on page 320 describes a few Project settings that control how the program behaves as you edit tasks.

The hunt for unwanted, unintended constraints is a must-do task on every project manager's checklist. Project offers two ways to examine your date constraints: the Constraint Indicator icons, and the Constraint Type field. Here are the steps for finding and fixing date constraints:

1. **Display Gantt Chart view in the primary pane (in the View tab's Task Views section, click Gantt Chart).**

   You can add date constraint fields to the view's table and see the changes to the schedule in the timescale.

2. **In the View tab's Split View section, turn on the Details checkbox, and then choose More Views in the Details drop-down list. In the More Views dialog box, select Task Details Form, and then click Apply.**

   Task Details Form view appears in the Details pane and includes the Constraint Type and Constraint Date fields.

3. **To find tasks with date constraints, first display the Constraint Type column in the view table by right-clicking in the table heading area and then choosing Insert Column→Constraint Type.**

   The Constraint Type column appears in the table.

4. **Filter the task list for constraints other than As Soon As Possible by clicking the down arrow to the right of the Constraint Type column heading, turning off the As Soon As Possible checkbox, and then clicking OK.**

   Project filters the task list to display only tasks that have a constraint type *other* than As Soon As Possible, as you see in Figure 11-16.

TIP You can obtain the DateConstraints custom filter, which hides As Soon As Possible tasks, by downloading the *ProjectMM_Customizations.mpp* file from this book's Missing CD page at *www.missingmanuals.com/cds*. See page 703 to learn how to copy elements from that file to your *global.mpt* file.

---

5. **Select a task with a date constraint so its information appears in the Task Details Form in the bottom pane.**

   The Task Details Form shows both the constraint type and the date, which might jog your memory about why you set a constraint for this task.

6. **If the constraint shouldn't be there, then in Task Details Form view in the Details pane, choose As Soon As Possible from the Constraint Type drop-down list, and then click OK.**

   In Task Details Form view in the Details pane, Project changes the constraint's Date field to NA, and in the Entry table, the Constraint icon disappears from the Indicators column.

Date constraint indicator   Constraint type   Icon indicates filter is applied

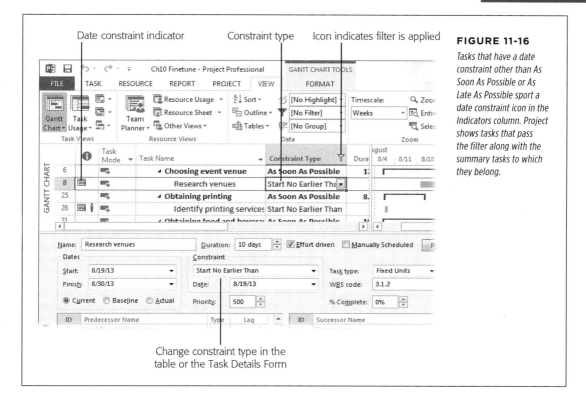

FIGURE 11-16

Tasks that have a date constraint other than As Soon As Possible or As Late As Possible sport a date constraint icon in the Indicators column. Project shows tasks that pass the filter along with the summary tasks to which they belong.

Change constraint type in the
table or the Task Details Form

7. **Repeat steps 5 and 6 to replace date constraints that shouldn't be there. To hide tasks whose constraints you've removed, press Shift+F3 to reapply the Constraint Type filter.**

When you're done, the only date constraints you should see are the ones that are supposed to be there. You can remove the filter by clicking the filter icon in the Constraint Type column heading, turning on the Select All checkbox, and then clicking OK.

Editing Options

When you're busy editing tasks and assignments, you may want Project to behave differently. To make it do that, choose File→Options. Then, on the left side of the Project Options dialog box, click Advanced and scroll to the Edit section. Although the default options are set to the way most people use them, here are the options and how you can change them:

- **Allow cell drag and drop.** This checkbox is turned on initially, so you can drag values from one set of fields or rows to another, which is almost always what you want. If you turn this checkbox off, you can't use your mouse to move or copy values, although you can still use the Cut, Copy, and Paste commands.

- **Ask to update automatic links.** This setting is initially turned on and makes Project ask if you want to update links to other files (page 578) when you open a Project file that contains automatic links to other files.

- **Move selection after enter.** Project turns this checkbox on by default, so when you press Enter, the program automatically selects the field below the current field. That's handy when you're building a task list by typing one task name after another in the Name column of a task table. If you prefer to stay in the same field when you press Enter, so you can see if the results of a change are what you want, turn this checkbox off.

- **Edit directly in cell.** This checkbox is also turned on by default, so you can edit values directly in a table cell. However, if you find that you're editing cell values inadvertently, turn this checkbox off. Then you can edit values only in fields within a dialog box like Task Information or in the Entry bar. (If the Entry bar isn't visible, choose File→Options. On the left side of the Project Options dialog box, click Display and, below the "Show these elements" heading, turn on the "Entry bar" checkbox.)

■ Building Reality into Assignments

A first-draft schedule almost always represents the way projects would go in an ideal world. But you live in the real world, and just as the jeans you buy never look like they do on the catalog model, your real-world project will have a few bumps and wrinkles. Understanding resource units and calendars (page 213) is only half the battle. You also have to figure out how to combine them to handle real-world resourcing situations. This section explains how to make Project's resource features model reality.

Replacing Generic Resources with Real Ones

Sometimes you know the *type* of resource you need, but you don't know exactly who you'll get. In these situations, you may have assigned a resource that represents the role that resource plays, such as website designer, painter, or programmer's muse. Once the powers that be have assigned a real person to your project, you can replace the generic resource with one that represents the flesh-and-blood team member. The Assign Resources dialog box makes it easy:

1. **In a task-oriented view like Gantt Chart, apply the Entry table by heading to the View tab's Data section and clicking Tables→Entry.**

   The Entry table includes the Resource Names field.

2. **Turn off summary tasks by clicking the Gantt Chart Tools | Format tab and, in the Show/Hide section, turning off the Summary Tasks checkbox.**

   Now only subtasks appear in the task list.

3. **Filter the task list to show only tasks assigned to the generic resource you want to replace.**

   Click the down arrow to the right of the Resource Names column heading, and then turn off the Select All checkbox. Turn on the checkbox for the generic resource, such as Fundraising Manager, and then click OK.

4. **Select the tasks that appear in the table by dragging over their ID cells.**

   Project changes the backgrounds of the selected tasks to gray.

5. **In the Resource tab's Assignments section, click Assign Resources.**

   The Assign Resources dialog box opens.

6. **Select the generic resource you want to replace, and then click Replace.**

   The Replace Resource dialog box opens, as shown in Figure 11-17.

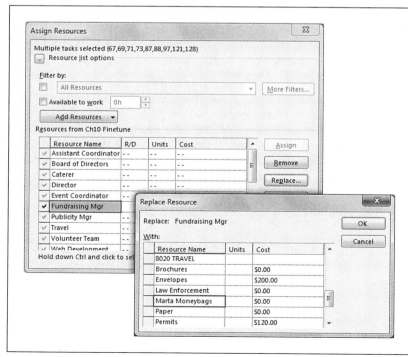

FIGURE 11-17

You can select only one resource in the Replace Resource dialog box. If you want to specify units for the assignment, type the value in the Units cell. When you click OK, Project replaces the generic resource in all selected tasks with the named resource using the units you specified. If you leave the Units cell blank, Project uses the units set for the original resource assigned.

7. **In the Resource Name column, select the named resource you want to use. Optionally, type the units for the assignment, and then click OK.**

   Project replaces the generic resource with the named resource in every selected task. If you filled in the Units cell, the program uses that Units value for every assignment. If you leave the Units cell blank, the program keeps the Units from the generic resource's assignment.

8. **Repeat steps 3–7 for each generic resource in your project.**

   To see whether you've reassigned all your generic resources, display Resource Usage view (in the View tab's Resource Views section, click Resource Usage). The generic resources in the project shouldn't have any tasks listed below their names.

NOTE Project Server includes the "Build Team from Enterprise" feature, which lets you replace a resource in a project with one from the Enterprise Resource list.

Assigning Part-Time Workers

Part-time workers don't work full weeks, so they take longer to finish tasks. For example, someone working half-days takes twice as long, because you get only 4 person-hours a day instead of 8. The best way to model a part-time schedule in Project is to edit the resource's calendar (or create a shift calendar for all the resources that work the same part-time schedule and apply it to the resource, as described on page 120). Then, when you assign part-time resources to tasks, Project automatically doles out time based on the dates and times the people are available. The complete rundown on setting up calendars and work weeks starts on page 107. This section provides an overview of the steps for setting up and assigning resources using a part-time calendar.

Using a part-time calendar works equally well whether part-timers work 5 short days a week, full time a few days a week, or a combination of full-time and part-time days. If you share the person with another project, the best approach is to use a resource pool (page 525) to assign the person to tasks in multiple projects. The box on page 323 explains why changing a resource's Maximum Units value (page 213) *isn't* the ideal way to model a part-time schedule.

Modeling Part-Time Work with Maximum Units

Changing resources' Maximum Units values might *seem* like a simple way to handle part-time work, but it has a couple of limitations.

- It applies only to people who work the same amount of time each standard workday—for example, 4 hours a day Monday through Friday.

- It doesn't reflect a resource's true allocation to an assignment. Suppose you set a part-time worker's Maximum Units to 50% and assign him to a meeting.

Project assumes that resources are available every workday up to the percentage in their Maximum Units cells, so the program automatically assigns the person to the meeting at 50% units. If the meeting is one full day, Project assigns him to the meeting for only 4 hours, even though he will be at the meeting for 8 hours.

Because of these limitations, you're better off using the techniques described in this section instead.

Here's how you handle part-time workers in Project when several resources work the same schedule:

1. **Create a calendar for that part-time shift.**

   In the Project tab's Properties section, click Change Working Time, and then click Create New Calendar. In the Create New Base Calendar dialog box, select the option to copy the calendar you've applied to your project (page 108), and type a name in the Name box that reflects the part-time work week, like Halftime; then click OK. (If only one person works this particular part-time schedule, you can edit that person's resource calendar. In the Change Working Time dialog box's "For calendar" drop-down list, choose the resource whose calendar you want to change. Then proceed to step 2.)

2. **Edit the work week to define the working and non-working times (page 213).**

   In the lower half of the Change Working Time dialog box, click the Work Weeks tab, and then click Details. In the "Details for <work week>" dialog box, specify the working days and working hours, and the nonworking days. With these details in place, Project can schedule tasks for the days and times that the resources are available. When you're done, click OK to close the Change Working Time dialog box.

3. **Assign the new calendar to each person who works that shift.**

   Display Resource Sheet view (in the View tab, click Resource Sheet). Click the resource's Base Calendar cell, click the down arrow that appears, and then choose the shift calendar.

4. **Assign a part-time worker to a task.**

   Assign the part-time worker as you would any resource. Project automatically enters the resource's Maximum Units value (which should be 100% to include all the work hours defined in the part-time calendar) in the assignment's Units field, whether the percentage is 20%, 50%, or 100%. To assign the resource at a lower percentage, type the percentage in the assignment's Units field (page 231).

Project calculates the duration of a task based on the resource units assigned to the task and the resource's calendar. If the resource calendar includes a vacation the first week of June, for example, Project assigns the resource at the assignment units but skips the week that the resource is absent.

> **NOTE** Sometimes, people have different work schedules at different times, such as shorter weeks during the summer or full-time availability only from March through June. Page 216 shows you how to set up varying availability. You can also set a date range for a work week, as described on page 112.

Modeling Productivity in Project

People are usually optimistic about how much they can get done in a given amount of time. (Have you ever had a "5-minute" trip to the grocery store turn into 2 hours?) In the world of project management, a 40-hour work week does *not* necessarily mean people spend 40 hours on their project assignments. Filling out paperwork, attending meetings, and keeping up with gossip can eat into productive time by as much as 25 percent a day. Widely distributed teams—whether they're scattered around the world or throughout a skyscraper—often require more time because of time spent communicating, waiting for someone else to complete a task, or even riding elevators. Working on too many simultaneous tasks also hurts productivity, as the box on page 325 explains.

If you assign resources at 100 percent, one of two outcomes is likely:

- **People have to work longer days to stay on schedule.** Some folks work longer to finish their tasks according to the schedule, but this won't last. Eventually, low morale and exhaustion take their toll, and work starts to slip.

- **The project falls behind.** Expecting 100 percent productivity usually leads to late deliveries. People work the normal workday, but their project work gets only a portion of that day, and durations increase beyond what you estimated. For example, a task that requires 24 person-hours takes 3 days when resources work at 100 percent. Reduce the units to 75 percent, and the duration increases to 4 days, 33 percent longer.

When Multitasking Is Too Much

In Project, you can assign someone to as many simultaneous tasks as you want. Project doesn't complain until the total assigned units exceed the resource's Maximum Units percentage. In the real world, people need time to find where they left off and reacquaint themselves with the work every time they switch from one task to another. Each delay may be small, but they add up until your most productive resource is as slow as a Los Angeles rush hour.

The only way to prevent this problem is to limit the number of concurrent tasks people work on. Some folks can handle more tasks than others, but even those people can handle no more than three or four tasks at a time at most. Project doesn't have any tools specifically for finding multitasking, but you can get help from Resource Usage view (in the View tab's Resource Views section, click Resource Usage). It shows all the assignments that each resource works on. You can scan each time period looking for too many assignments for the same resource. Just keep in mind that several assignments during the same time period isn't *necessarily* a multitasking problem. For example, if you analyze the project week by week, someone could have six tasks, but only one or two a day.

You can tackle the productivity problem in a couple of ways in Project. Either approach provides a more realistic estimate of project duration. Here are the two ways to make a Project schedule reflect your project team's productivity and the pros and cons of each:

- **Shorten the standard Project workday.** If non-project work consumes 25 percent of each day, an 8-hour day contains only 6 productive hours, and a work week is 30 productive hours. The fastest way to come up with realistic task durations is to reset Project's standard 8-hour workday to fewer hours, as shown in Figure 11-18.

  There are two disadvantages to shortening the Project workday. First, the productivity problem is hidden within Project's calculations. Resources look like they're assigned 100%, but Project assigns them only 6 hours of work a day. Second, the work times that you set in Project don't accurately reflect the start and end time of each workday. With a shorter workday in place, the only way you can schedule a task at the end of the real workday is by applying a task calendar (page 193). To keep the workday set to the true start and end time and also make productivity visible, use the next method instead.

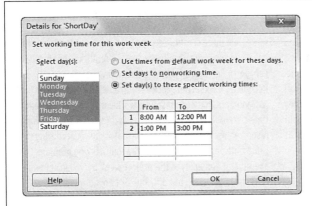

FIGURE 11-18

Shortening the workday takes two steps. First, you change the "Hours per day" and "Hours per week" calendar options (page 105), so Project translates the person-hours into the correct duration in days and weeks. For example, you may change "Hours per day" to 6 and "Hours per week" to 30. You also redefine the standard work week in the project calendar. For example, to snip 2 hours off each day, set each day's end time 2 hours earlier, as shown here.

- **Assign resources at lower units.** To assign resources at their real percentage of productive time, in the Task Form view's Units field (page 233), fill in the lower percentage. For example, to schedule full-time team members for 6 hours of work each day, in the Task Form, set the resource's Units field to 75%. (If you change the Units field for part-time workers to 75%, Project assigns them at 75% of their available hours, such as 3 hours a day if they normally work 4 hours a day.)

NOTE If you use lower assignment units, a stakeholder is bound to ask why people aren't working full time. That's your cue to talk about the drain on productivity and recommend your brilliant plan for increasing productive time. To get some ideas for your plan, read *Slack: Getting Past Burnout, Busywork, and the Myth of Total Efficiency* by Tom DeMarco (Broadway, 2002).

Adjusting Tasks for Resource Capability

Occasionally, you get someone who polishes off work like a dog does an unguarded plate of hamburgers. Other times, you may use trainees who take longer and need more guidance. Most organizations don't reward fast workers by letting them go home early, and you can't make newbies work around the clock to keep up.

The only way to account for people's capability is by changing the person-hours you assign to people (the Work field for an assignment). When you change the task work or duration, Project recalculates the other value (page 251).

If you change work or duration due to people's above- or below-average capabilities, then keep track of your original estimate in case you switch resources again. And consider adding a note to the task to explain the adjustments you made. In a task-oriented view, like Gantt Chart view, right-click the task and then, from the shortcut menu, choose Notes. When the Task Information dialog box opens, the Notes tab is visible. Type your comments, and then click OK.

TIP If potential names for an assignment go back and forth faster than an Olympic table tennis match, consider creating tasks for each potential resource. Activate the task with the current contender and make the other tasks with alternate resources inactive, as described on page 364.

Balancing Workloads

Before you can call a schedule done, you have to balance workloads so your assigned resources (people and equipment) are busy, but not burning out. The first step is recognizing the problem, and Project makes it easy to find assignment peaks and valleys.

Then you have to correct the workload imbalances you find. Project offers several ways to even out workloads. The easiest way to eliminate overallocations is to ask resources if a heavier schedule is OK with them. Pragmatically, you should consider this approach only when overallocations are small and short-lived. The best options are adding more resources and replacing a resource with someone who has more time. Of course, in order to do that, you need to have other resources available with the right skills.

When longer hours or more resources aren't an option, delaying assignments may do the trick. For example, when a resource has two assignments that overlap by a day, delaying one of those assignments by 1 day solves the problem.

This section describes how to spot resource-allocation issues and offers several ways to fix them. If these strategies don't help, you can always look for other available resources, or ask resources to work more.

NOTE When you overload your resources, the project finish date may look good, but it's bogus, because your resources are *overallocated*. In other words, giving people 20 hours' worth of work a day doesn't mean they're going to *do* it. On the other hand, resources who don't have *enough* work cause a whole other set of problems. Besides distracting the people who are working full out, these resources could cost money without delivering results—like the networking consultant who sits idle while your IT staff puts out the fire in the server room. The ideal workload is to assign your resources at exactly—or as close as possible to—the amount of time they have to give.

Finding Resource Over- and Under-Allocations

Assigning resources to tasks is like using a credit card. While you're dealing out time, you don't see the deficit you're running up. Gantt Chart and other task-oriented views that you use when assigning resources show the assignments for the current task but not all the other tasks a resource may work on, so you can't see when you've assigned someone too much time overall. Project's resource- and assignment-oriented views provide a better picture of resource allocation. This section identifies the talents of different views and tools for finding overallocations.

■ FINDING OVERALLOCATED RESOURCES WITH RESOURCE SHEET VIEW

For a sneak peek at the workload balancing ahead, take a look at Resource Sheet view (in the View tab's Resource Views section, click Resource Sheet). If a resource is overallocated at least once during the project, all the text in the resource's row is bold and red, and the Indicators column displays a yellow diamond with an exclamation mark. Because of this, you can quickly spot the resources whose assignments you need to revise. However, this view *doesn't* tell you exactly *when* the resource is overallocated, how much, or on which assignments.

TIP The Overallocated Resources filter is another helpful tool for finding resources with too much work, regardless of which resource view you use (Resource Sheet, Resource Usage, and so on). This filter displays only resources that are overallocated at some point during a project. In the View tab's Data section, click the Filter down arrow, and then choose Overallocated Resources. You can apply this filter to any view, from Resource Sheet to Resource Graph to Resource Allocation view (page 331). To display all resources again, in the Filter drop-down list, choose [No Filter].

■ FINDING OVERALLOCATIONS WITH TEAM PLANNER VIEW

Team Planner view makes it easy to spot overallocated resources (in the View tab's Resource Views section, click Team Planner). The names of overallocated resources appear in red in the Resource Name column, and overallocated assignments in the timescale have red brackets around the portions of assignment bars that contribute to the overallocation. Especially for smaller projects, Team Planner view offers easy ways to remove overallocations. You can reassign a task by dragging it to a resource who doesn't have anything to do, or right-clicking the check and choosing Reassign To on the shortcut menu. Or you can drag a task to a date when the assigned resource isn't busy. Figure 9-10 on page 244 shows what overallocations look like in Team Planner view.

■ VIEWING ASSIGNMENTS WITH RESOURCE USAGE VIEW

To see the assignments that contribute to allocation, turn to Resource Usage view (in the View tab's Resource Views section, click Resource Usage). This view lists all the assignments for each resource in the project, so you can see the hours assigned during any time period. If a resource is overallocated, you can examine the hours for each assignment to come up with ways to balance the workload

The left pane of Resource Usage view lists each resource in your project and displays the tasks to which the resource is assigned underneath the resource's name. The timescale on the right side of the view shows the assigned hours during each time period, as shown in Figure 11-19.

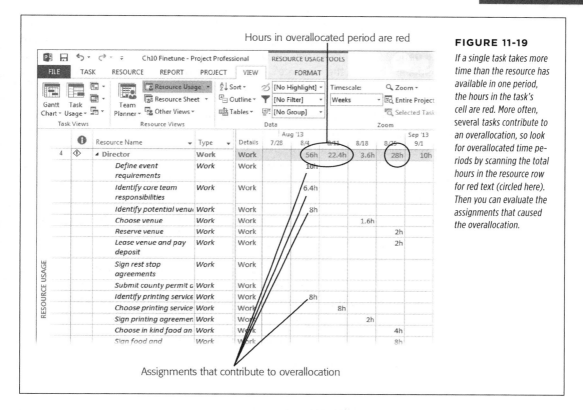

Hours in overallocated period are red

Assignments that contribute to overallocation

FIGURE 11-19

If a single task takes more time than the resource has available in one period, the hours in the task's cell are red. More often, several tasks contribute to an overallocation, so look for overallocated time periods by scanning the total hours in the resource row for red text (circled here). Then you can evaluate the assignments that caused the overallocation.

Like other views, Resource Usage view highlights overallocated resources with bold, red text. In the time-phased grid on the right side of Resource Usage view, hours that exceed the resource's maximum available time appear in red, too. For example, if a single task exceeds the resource's available time in one period, the hours in the cell are written in red. However, if several tasks contribute to the overallocation, the individual task hours may be black, but the total hours in the resource's row are red.

To see overallocations more easily, modify Resource Usage view in the following ways:

- **Show only overallocated resources.** To the right of the Resource Name column heading, click the down arrow and then, in the shortcut menu that appears, choose Filters→Overallocated Resources. Only resources with overallocations appear in the left pane. Alternatively, in the View tab's Data section, click the Filter down arrow, and then choose Overallocated Resources.

- **Display other fields.** Other fields can help you figure out how to correct over-allocations. On the right side of Resource Usage view, right-click anywhere in the Details column. On the shortcut menu, choose the fields you want to see; you can select as many as you want. (Remember, the Assign Resources dialog box lets you look for resources with sufficient time and the right skills, as described on page 235.) For example, the Overallocation field tells you exactly how many hours are beyond the resource's availability. And the Remaining Availability field helps you find resources who have enough time to take over the extra hours.

■ FINDING OVERALLOCATIONS WITH RESOURCE GRAPH VIEW

Resource Graph view plots allocation over time, resource by resource, which is helpful when you want to figure out how to resolve each resource's overallocations. A vertical bar graphically indicates the selected resource's allocation in one time period. When the vertical bar is higher than the resource's availability, Project emphasizes the overallocation by coloring the overallocated portions bright red.

In Resource Graph view, you don't see the assignments for the allocated time. But you can find the problem time periods and then switch to Resource Usage or Resource Allocation view (page 331) to correct the issue.

To open Resource Graph view, in the View tab's Resource Views section, click Other Views→Resource Graph. (Or, to display Resource Graph view in the Details pane, in the View tab's Split View section, turn on the Details checkbox, choose More Views, and then, in the More Views dialog box, double-click Resource Graph.)

Here's how to use Resource Graph view to find overallocations:

- **Choose a resource.** Resource Graph view shows the allocations for just one resource at a time. The current resource appears in the view's left pane with a legend for the information that's displayed in the timescale. Press Page Down to display the next resource, or Page Up to view the previous resource. You can also scroll through your various resources using the horizontal scroll bar below the legend.

- **Change the timescale.** Sometimes, resources are overallocated for 1 or 2 days but have enough time for assignments over the course of a week or so. Before you start rearranging short overallocations, increase Resource Graph view's time period to see whether the overallocations work themselves out. To lengthen the time period, in the status bar, drag the Zoom slider to the left to switch from days to weeks to months, and so on. To shorten the time period, drag the slider to the right. To specify the units for the timescale, in the View tab's Zoom section, click the Timescale down arrow, and then choose the period you want.

- **Graph other values.** Although percentage allocation values make overallocations stand out, Resource Graph view can show other values, such as Work (the hours of assigned work), Overallocation (only the hours beyond the resource's maximum units), Remaining Availability, and so on. For example, after you use

Resource Graph view to find an overallocation, you can switch it to display Remaining Availability to locate someone to take over the extra hours. To do so, right-click the Resource Graph view's timescale, and then, from the shortcut menu, choose the field you want to display in the graph.

■ VIEWING ASSIGNMENTS IN RESOURCE ALLOCATION VIEW

Resource Allocation view displays Resource Usage view in the top pane so you can see the tasks that overallocate a resource, and Leveling Gantt view in the Details pane so you can manually add a leveling delay to resolve overallocations. To use this view, in the View tab's Resource Views section, click Other Views→More Views. In the More Views dialog box, double-click Resource Allocation.

The table in Leveling Gantt view includes the Leveling Delay field, which you can use to delay tasks to remove overallocations. When you make these kinds of edits in Leveling Gantt view, the leveling delay changes the start date for a task, not just the overallocated resource's assignment. See page 337 for instructions on delaying tasks and individual assignments.

> **TIP** If you want a hard copy of Resource Usage view or any other view, print it by choosing File→Print. On the Print page of Backstage view, choose the printer, page range, and dates, as you would for any printout (page 500).

Accepting Overallocations

When a resource is overallocated by a small percentage for a short period of time (for example, no more than 20 percent and 2 weeks), the simplest solution is to leave the assignment exactly as it is—as long as the person is willing to work a few long days. The schedule shows the assignment as an overallocation, but you can add a note to the task (page 156) that documents your agreement with the resource. Just be aware that scheduling longer hours during the planning phase is a risky move. If tasks take more time than you estimated, your resources are already maxed out and you'll have to use other strategies to prevent delays (page 333).

But say you want to formally schedule a resource to work longer days, but you don't want those assignments to show up as overallocations. Don't change the resource's Maximum Units value in the Resource Sheet. Why? Because Maximum Units redefine the number of hours the resource devotes for the *entire* project. Instead, modify the resource's calendar to lengthen specific workdays. For example, if you ask someone to work a few weeks of longer days, you can create a work week to reflect that (page 112). For a few long days, creating a calendar exception is easier.

> **TIP** If resources cost more when they work beyond the normal workday, you can account for the extra cost by assigning work hours specifically as overtime using the Overtime Work field. The cost of overtime is the overtime hours multiplied by the Overtime Rate value. (Working with overtime in Project is tedious, so you should use it *only if* resources cost more after hours and you discover during project execution that you need more hours to finish tasks on time. See page 450 for the full scoop on assigning overtime in Project.)

Eliminating Overallocations with Team Planner

In Team Planner view (in the Views tab's Resource Views section, click Team Planner), you can easily reassign or reschedule tasks to eliminate overallocations. In this view, if two or more concurrent tasks eat up too much of a resource's time, red brackets appear around the parts of assignment bars that contribute to the overallocation. Here's how to remove overallocations in Team Planner:

- **Reassign a task to another resource.** To reassign a task to a resource with available time, drag the assignment bar to the row for the new resource, or right-click the assignment bar and choose Reassign To on the shortcut menu.

- **Reschedule a task to a different date.** In Team Planner view, you can drag each assignment independently. However, if more than one resource is assigned to a task, you usually want to reschedule both assignments. To select all the assignments for a task, right-click one of the task's assignment bars and then, from the shortcut menu, choose "Select All Assignments on This Task." Then drag the assignments to a date where the resources won't be overallocated.

NOTE   If you work in a Project Server environment, Team Planner view shows a resource's assignments on *all* projects, not just the current project, which can be a reminder that you don't have exclusive use of that shared resource.

Rescheduling a Task to Another Day

To move a task into the past or future, in the Task tab's Tasks section, click Move. In the drop-down menu, choose a command for the amount of time you want to move it, as shown in Figure 11-20.

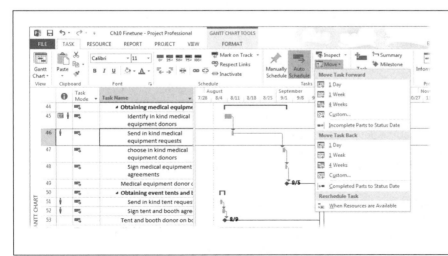

FIGURE 11-20

The Move drop-down menu contains commands for moving tasks by one day, one week, or four weeks. To move a task by any other time span, choose the Custom command under the Move Task Forward or Move Task Back category. This menu also includes commands for rescheduling incomplete work, which you'll learn how to do on page 422.

TIP Dragging a task to a new date is often the easiest way to remove an overallocation when tasks are manually scheduled. However, dragging auto-scheduled tasks in the timeline creates date constraints (page 190), which limit Project's ability to calculate start and finish dates. So take care not to drag auto-scheduled tasks to different dates in Team Planner or in any other view. (Page 317 explains how to find and fix date constraints.)

If a resource works on a hodgepodge of short tasks, finding adjacent time for a longer assignment is almost impossible. Instead, you can tell Project to chop a task up and slide it into a resource's open slots. To do that, select the task you want to reschedule in a task-oriented view like Gantt Chart. Then, in the Task tab's Tasks section, choose Move→When Resources Are Available.

Replacing Resources

Suppose a resource works on two simultaneous tasks on the critical path. You can't delay either one without affecting the project finish date. In this situation, the Assign Resources dialog box (in the Resource tab's Assignments section, click Assign Resources) can help you find someone with similar skills who has more time available. If money is a bigger problem than time, you can replace the person with someone who costs less (assuming that the replacement can get the work done in the same amount of time). And if you have resources who can pinch hit, you can reassign only the overallocated hours or an entire assignment—Project doesn't care which method you choose. You use the Assign Resources dialog box to reassign hours in all three scenarios.

NOTE If you use a custom field like an outline code to identify resources' skills, the Assign Resources dialog box can help you find resources with similar skills (page 236). Also, its "Available to work" checkbox can help you find resources with enough time to complete the work (page 237). (Although Team Planner view lets you drag an assignment from one resource to another [page 244], it *doesn't* help you find resources with similar skills or identify cost implications.)

Here's how you reassign a portion of work with the Assign Resources dialog box:

1. **In the Resource tab's Assignments section, click Assign Resources.**

   The Assign Resources dialog box opens.

2. **In Gantt Chart view (or any other task-oriented view), select the task you want to modify.**

   The resources already assigned to the task appear at the top of the dialog box's Resources table, preceded by a checkmark.

3. **To switch a portion of the work to another resource, in the Assign Resources dialog box, click the assigned resource's Units cell, and then type the new percentage.**

   For example, if the resource's units are 20 percent too high, you can remove that by reducing the units from 80 percent to 60 percent.

4. **Click the Units cell for the resource you want to add to the task, and then type the percentage you're assigning to it. Then press Enter or click outside the Units cell.**

Project updates the existing assignment. The newly assigned resource moves up to the top of the list with the other assigned resources and now has a checkmark to the left of its name.

If you want to replace one resource with another, follow these steps:

1. **With the Assign Resources dialog box open, in the task-oriented view's table, select the task you want to modify.**

The assigned resources for the selected task appear at the top of the dialog box's Resources table, with checkmarks next to them.

2. **In the Resources table, select the assigned resource you want to replace.**

Click the resource's *name*, not the checkmarked cell. You can replace only one resource at a time.

3. **Click Replace.**

The Replace Resource dialog box appears (Figure 11-21). The Replace label at the top of the dialog box shows the resource you want to replace, and the With table lists all the resources in your project.

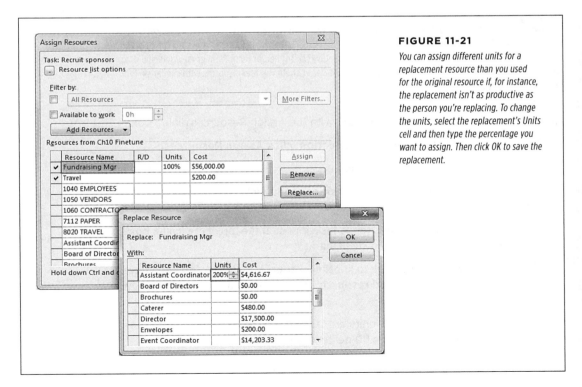

FIGURE 11-21

You can assign different units for a replacement resource than you used for the original resource if, for instance, the replacement isn't as productive as the person you're replacing. To change the units, select the replacement's Units cell and then type the percentage you want to assign. Then click OK to save the replacement.

4. **Select the replacement resource, and then click OK.**

   Project swaps the replacement in for the original resource and assigns the units for the original resource (or the units you typed) to the replacement.

Adjusting Work Contours

Most people don't leap out of bed in the morning raring to go, nor do they work full speed up until the moment they close their eyes at night. Yet Project assumes that resources work at an even pace from the start of every task to the finish—unless you tell it otherwise. To reflect how work *really* gets done, you can apply *work contours* to reshape assignments. Work contours alter the amount of work assigned over the entire duration of assignments. Like people's energy, tasks tend to start slowly, run at their peak in the middle, and then wind down at the end.

> **NOTE** Work contours work only for auto-scheduled tasks, not manually scheduled ones.

Work contours reduce the hours for some time periods (for example, the hours assigned on the first and last days of an assignment), so they extend assignment duration and, in turn, task duration. The Flat contour, which is what Project applies automatically, schedules the same hours of work each day during an assignment, like 8 hours if a resource works 100 percent on the task. Every other contour type has high and low points. The highs schedule the same number of hours in a day as a Flat contour. But because the lows are less than a full schedule, the task ends up taking longer. Figure 11-22 shows how the Bell contour reschedules work hours for a task.

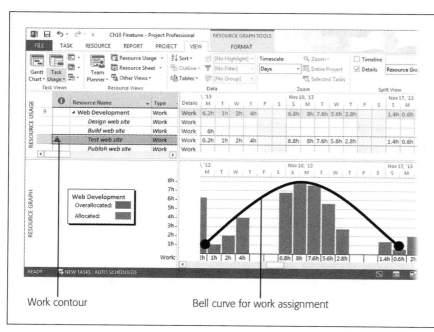

FIGURE 11-22

The original assignment for this web-development team was 40 hours (8 hours a day for 5 days). Applying the Bell contour extends that work to 11 days. When you apply a contour to an assignment, the Indicators column in a view's table displays an icon for the applied contour, such as the Bell contour icon labeled here.

Work contour

Bell curve for work assignment

Table 11-1 describes Project's work contours and what they're good for. The great thing about work contours is that you can assign resources to work on other tasks when other assignments don't demand their full attention. Work contours may be all you need to eliminate some overallocations.

TABLE 11-1 *Work contours and their uses*

CONTOUR NAME	PURPOSE
Flat	Project automatically assigns this constant contour to new tasks.
Back Loaded	This contour starts off slow and increases until the task is complete. If your work hours correspond to your adrenaline level, this contour is perfect.
Front Loaded	This contour starts at full effort and decreases, kind of like unpacking after a move: The first few days you spend all day unpacking boxes, but as time goes on, you unpack less and get back to your life.
Double Peak	This contour looks like the profile of a suspension bridge with a peak near each end and lower hours at the beginning, middle, and end. For example, a debugging task could have an early peak when hundreds of bugs need fixing and a second peak to fix the bugs that stand between you and project acceptance.
Early Peak	This contour starts slowly but quickly peaks and then drops off. This gives you some time to get oriented to a task before really digging in.
Late Peak	Late Peak ramps up to a peak, but has a drop-off at the end for tying up loose ends.
Bell	Bell is like a combination of a Back Loaded contour and a Front Loaded contour: The work continually increases to a peak and then gradually drops off.
Turtle	This contour has low levels at the beginning and the end with fully scheduled resources in the middle. It's probably the closest match to how tasks really proceed.

Here are the steps for applying a work contour to a resource assignment:

1. **Display Task Usage or Resource Usage view (in the View tab's Task Views section, click Task Usage or Resource Usage).**

   Because you apply contours to assignments, you have to open one of these views to see assignments.

2. **In the view, double-click the assignment you want to contour.**

   In Task Usage view, double-click the row for the resource assigned to the task. In Resource Usage view, below the resource's name, double-click the task name for the assignment you want to contour (or select the name and then press Shift+F2). The Assignment Information dialog box appears.

TIP The time-phased portion of the view doesn't automatically show the time periods in which the assignment occurs, so you can't see the results of the contours you pick. To see them, select the task, and then in the Task tab's Editing section, click "Scroll to Task." The time-phased portion of the view jumps to the dates that have work for the selected assignment.

3. **In the Assignment Information dialog box's General tab, in the Work Contour list, choose a contour, and then click OK.**

   Project calculates the new work hours for each day and then applies them to the assignment. Task Usage view and Resource Usage view show the newly contoured hours.

TIP Although you can't define custom contours, you can manually change the hours in Task Usage view's time-phased grid. Simply click an assignment cell and then type the new hours for that period; continue changing cells until you've reassigned all the work hours. This method has a couple of disadvantages, however. First, you have to ensure that the hours you type add up to the original hours. Second, you inherit the responsibility of maintaining that assignment for the life of the project. When you manually edit work hours, you see the Edited Work icon (which looks like a bar chart with a pencil) in the assignment's Indicators cell.

Delaying Assignments

When tasks overlap and overallocate their assigned resources, one solution is to delay some of the tasks so the people assigned can work on the tasks one after the other. If you have a few overallocations to correct, you can manually add delays to tasks and assignments with the help of a few Project views.

NOTE Project has a leveling feature, which can calculate delays and splits *for* you. If your project schedule is rife with resource overallocations, this feature can be a real time-saver, as long as you set up your schedule so leveling can do its job. See page 339 for the full story.

Project offers two types of delays:

- **Leveling delay.** This type of delay applies to tasks; it pushes out the start date for a task and *all* its resource assignments. It's meant specifically for delaying tasks to remove resource overallocations. Using the Leveling Delay field, you can remove all leveling delays in one fell swoop—for instance, if you decide that the leveling delays you add to assignments still aren't doing what you want. If you want to remove leveling delays and start over, in the Resource tab's Level section, choose Clear Leveling.

NOTE A leveling delay isn't the same as lag time. Lag time is the real-world delay that occurs between the end of one task and the start of another—for example, the 7 days it takes concrete to harden after you pour it. Lag time remains in place regardless of resource availability.

- **Assignment delay.** This type of delay applies to a single assignment within a task. Suppose you have a security consultant coming in to help lock down your donation site. However, your employees have prep work to do before the consultant can get started. With an assignment delay, you can assign all your employees to the same "Try hacking into website" task, but delay the consultant's assignment by 2 days.

To delay an entire task using leveling delay, do the following:

1. **In the View tab's Resource Views section, click Other Views→More Views. In the More Views dialog box, double-click Resource Allocation.**

   Resource Usage view appears in the top pane, and Leveling Gantt view appears in the Details pane.

2. **In Resource Usage view's table pane, select the assignment that's causing a problem (click anywhere in the assignment's row).**

   Resource Usage view shows assignments for each resource, whereas Leveling Gantt view shows tasks. When you select an assignment in the top pane, the task to which that assignment belongs appears in the bottom pane.

3. **In Leveling Gantt view's table pane, in the Leveling Delay cell, type the length of time you want to delay the task.**

   To delay the task by 2 days, for example, type *2d*. Project replaces your entry with "2 edays," as shown in Figure 11-23. The "e" at the beginning stands for "elapsed time," because the number of resources or the percentage they're assigned doesn't affect the delay. You want the task to start a specific amount of time later, and elapsed time does just that.

To delay a single assignment within a task, add an assignment delay by doing the following:

1. **In the View tab's Resource Views section, click Other Views→More Views. In the More Views dialog box, double-click Resource Allocation.**

   Resource Usage view appears in the top pane, and Leveling Gantt view appears in the Details pane.

2. **Add the Assignment Delay column to the Resource Usage table.**

   Right-click the table header, and then choose Insert Column→Assignment Delay. The new column appears to the left of the column you right-clicked.

> **NOTE**   If you use Task Details view to work on assignments, you can see the Assignment Delay field by right-clicking the Task Details view's table area and then choosing Schedule. The Delay column represents the Assignment Delay field.

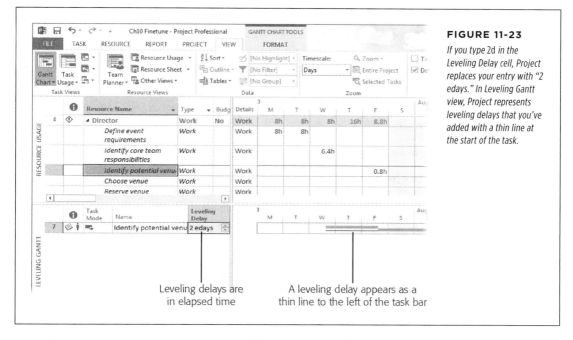

FIGURE 11-23

If you type 2d in the Leveling Delay cell, Project replaces your entry with "2 edays." In Leveling Gantt view, Project represents leveling delays that you've added with a thin line at the start of the task.

3. **Click the Assignment Delay cell for the assignment you want to delay, and then type the length of delay.**

   To delay the task by 2 days, for example, type *2d*. Unlike a leveling delay, an assignment delay is in regular days, not elapsed days, so Project doesn't change the delay you enter to days.

Leveling Assignments

As you learned in the previous section, you can resolve the occasional resource overallocation by delaying tasks and assignments so a resource can work on them in sequence. Project's resource-leveling feature can resolve resource overallocations *for* you by delaying tasks and assignments in the same way. It can also *split* tasks (introduce small gaps in assigned work) so resources can briefly stop what they're doing to crank out a short but more important task. You can use Project's resource leveling to level an entire project, a portion of a project, or the assignments for a resource that's in high demand. Just as with other methods of balancing resources' workloads, leveling tasks and assignments makes them finish later.

TIP Project's resource-leveling feature is a powerful tool in the quest for balanced workloads. However, it can wreak havoc on a schedule if you don't apply it properly. For example, leveling resources without choosing the appropriate settings could push your project finish date out by months. For this reason, it's a good idea to make a copy of your Project file before you level resources. That way, if the results aren't what you want, you can undo the changes or make another copy of the original for additional experiments.

Before you try your hand at automated resource leveling, it's helpful to understand what it can—and can't—do for you:

- **It can balance workloads for Project work resources.** Project's resource-leveling feature can even out workloads for people (generic roles or specific people), equipment, and other resources you've set up using the Work type in Project. But it doesn't do anything with material or cost resources.

- **It can delay or split tasks and assignments.** During leveling, Project looks for resource overallocations. For each one it finds, it locates the offending tasks and decides whether to delay or split them to eliminate the overallocation. Resource leveling only delays or splits tasks (it doesn't assign different resources, adjust resource units, or contour work), but it can balance workloads for both manually and automatically scheduled tasks.

- **It doesn't change the amount of work assigned or who is assigned.** The work hours for tasks and assignments stay the same. Leveling simply reschedules when that work occurs to eliminate resource overallocations. Similarly, the resources assigned to the task stay the same. If you decide to reassign work to someone else, page 333 tells you how to do that.

- **It doesn't change task dependencies.** The dependencies that you've added between tasks remain the same.

NOTE Are you wondering how you delay and split tasks in a project scheduled from the finish date? You can't push the finish date later, so Project adds negative delays to tasks and changes their start dates. The result of leveling a from-finish-date project is that the project's start date moves earlier.

■ PREPPING YOUR SCHEDULE FOR LEVELING

There are a few best scheduling practices that help you get the most out of Project's resource-leveling feature. Here's what you do to prep your schedule for leveling:

- **Don't link tasks to remove overallocations.** People new to project scheduling sometimes add links between tasks—not because the tasks depend on one another, but to schedule the tasks so the assigned resource can work on the tasks one after the other without being overloaded. If you want Project to level resources for you, remove these workload-related task dependencies from your schedule.

- **Set resources' Maximum Units to 100% (fully available).** Although your project might get only half of someone's time, setting that resource's Maximum Units to 50% *isn't* the way to go, as explained in the box on page 323. The better approach is to set resources' Maximum Units value to 100% and then define their working and non-working time in their resource calendars. That way, they're fully engaged in their project tasks when it counts. For example, if your financial expert Priscilla comes in one day a month to review the books, she's dedicated to that review for that day. If you set her Maximum Units value to 5% (one day out of the 20 workdays in a month), Project will assign her at 5% units, and her one day of work will be scheduled for 20 workdays. Instead, you can change her resource calendar to define her workdays on your project. See page 322 for more info on setting up part-time workers.

- **Add project admin time to work tasks.** You can handle administrative tasks in a couple of ways. For resource leveling, the best approach is to add time for project administration (5% or 10%, say) to each work task estimate. For example, if the task estimate is 40 hours, you would enter *44* in the task's Work field. That way, the assigned resource can record time spent on a status report against her work task.

NOTE You can also create recurring tasks for things like status meetings. This approach keeps administrative tasks visible and separately tracks admin time, which might be required by your client's accounting practices. However, all those separate short tasks are tough to manage in Project, and they produce lots of splits in your project work tasks when you use the resource-leveling feature. A third method for dealing with administrative tasks is to create one long administrative task for each phase of the project. However, this approach gives Project's resource-leveling feature heartburn because it has trouble splitting these tasks to schedule project work and admin work. If you find that your project duration has doubled after Project levels resources, a long admin task could be to blame.

- **Use priorities to tell Project what's important.** Project's Priority field is your way of telling the resource-leveling feature which tasks you consider important, so that it places more emphasis on getting those tasks done first when it levels resources. The next section explains how priorities work and how to use them.

■ PRIORITIZING PROJECTS AND TASKS

In the real world, finish dates for some tasks and projects are more important than others—for example, lining up an event venue is more important than getting the signs for the bike race route. But when you use resource leveling, Project has no way of knowing these priorities unless you tell it. The Priority field tells Project which tasks and projects should be completed first, and which ones it can delay to remove overallocations.

NOTE The Priority field comes into play only when you use Project's resource-leveling feature; this field has no effect on your regular scheduling activities. However, you can use the Priority field to focus on key tasks. For example, when you're trying to manage a schedule, you can filter or group the task list by priority to find the tasks to fast-track or *crash* (the project-management term for spending more money to shorten duration; see page 356).

Priority values range from 0 to 1,000. Project automatically assigns new tasks and projects a Priority value of 500 (the middle-of-the-road value). 1,000 is the highest priority, which means that Project doesn't delay projects or tasks with that value. So if you don't want Project to level a task, set its priority to 1,000. You can also change a task's Can Level field to No (you have to insert this field into a table to see it), but that field doesn't appear in any tables automatically (which often produces mystifying leveling behavior, as the box on page 349 explains).

To tell Project to give a task preferential treatment for leveling purposes, set the task's priority to a value like 800, 700, or 600. That way, the program will delay and split lower-priority tasks so that the tasks with higher priority are completed first. For example, it gives tasks with priority of 800 precedence over tasks with priority of 700, and so on.

You're not likely to need all 1,000 of Project's priority levels, no matter how many projects and tasks you want to level. Whether you opt to use three, five, or 20 priority levels, keep 500 as the standard setting. For example, if you use only five levels, you can use 1,000 for high priority (tasks that don't level), 800 for above-average priority, 500 for most tasks, 300 for below-average, and 0 for low priority. (You can use 502, 501, 500, 499, and 498 as well, as long as you don't have to reassign all the tasks with a priority of 500.)

■ CHANGING TASK PRIORITY

The Priority field appears on the Task Information dialog box's General tab, which is fine if you plan to change the priority for only the most important tasks. To assign a new Priority value to a task, in a task-oriented view like Gantt Chart, select the task (click anywhere in its row), and then press Shift+F2. In the Task Information dialog box, select the General tab, and then, in the Priority field, type the number.

However, if you prioritize many tasks, it's easier to add the Priority field to a Gantt Chart table so you can quickly type, copy, and paste priority values to every task, as shown in Figure 11-24. Here's how:

1. **In Gantt Chart view or another task-oriented view, add the Priority field to the table.**

   Right-click the table heading, and then, on the shortcut menu, choose Insert Column→Priority.

2. Click a Priority cell, and then type the new value.

You can copy and paste values from one cell to another using Ctrl+C and Ctrl+V. If several adjacent tasks have the same priority, position the pointer over the first cell's fill handle (page 150). When the cursor changes to a + sign, drag over the other Priority cells.

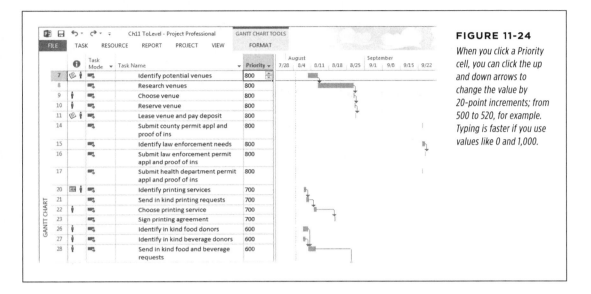

FIGURE 11-24

When you click a Priority cell, you can click the up and down arrows to change the value by 20-point increments; from 500 to 520, for example. Typing is faster if you use values like 0 and 1,000.

■ CHANGING PROJECT PRIORITY

If you have several subprojects in a master project, then entire projects may have a higher priority than the rest, like the presentations for a tradeshow that had better be ready when the show starts. That's why projects have a Priority field, too. Project priority is powerful, so use it sparingly. When you assign priorities to projects and then use resource leveling, Project levels all tasks in lower-priority projects before the lowest-priority tasks in high-priority projects. For example, suppose one project has a Priority value of 800 and another has a Priority value of 500. When you use Project's resource-leveling feature, the program levels a task with Priority 900 in the 500-priority project before it levels a task with Priority 0 in the 800-priority project. (The box on page 345 describes the steps for leveling multiple projects.)

NOTE A priority of 1,000 is sacred, so Project doesn't level tasks set to Priority 1,000 regardless of any priorities their projects have.

To change a project's priority, follow these steps:

1. **Open the project and then, in the Project tab's Properties section, click Project Information.**

   The Project Information dialog box opens.

2. **In the Priority field, type the new priority, and then click OK.**

   The Project Information dialog box closes.

The next time you level projects, Project's resource-leveling feature takes this new priority into account.

■ USING LEVELING GANTT VIEW

Switch to Leveling Gantt view, shown in Figure 11-25, before you level assignments. That way, once you apply resource leveling, you can see the results immediately—and undo them if they aren't what you want. To display this view, in the View tab's Task Views section, click Other Views→More Views, and then, in the More Views dialog box, double-click Leveling Gantt.

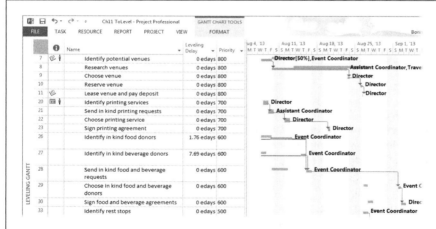

FIGURE 11-25

The upper set of task bars (which are tan in the built-in Leveling Gantt view) show your original schedule. The lower set of task bars (which are blue) show the leveled tasks with any added delays and splits. Leveling delays appear as thin lines at the beginning of task bars.

Leveling Multiple Projects

When you share resources among projects, overallocations from other projects can create delays and splits. But you can change task and project priority and then relevel the assignments to try for better results. The trick is seeing which tasks are causing the problems.

To figure out which tasks are causing trouble, create a master project that contains *all* the projects that share the resources you use (page 518). This master project contains all the tasks that compete for your resources' time, so you can see why the delays and splits are there. To view tasks that share resources with tasks in other projects, follow these steps:

1. Choose File→Open. Choose the location where you store Project files (Computer or Recent Projects, for example), and then open the Project file for your resource pool (page 525).

2. In the Open Resource Pool dialog box, select the "Open resource pool read-write and all other sharer files into a new master project file..." option. Project creates a new master project, which contains the resource pool and all its sharer files.

3. In the View tab's Window section, click Switch Windows→Project 1 to view the new master project.

4. In the View tab's Task Views section, click Other Views→More Views and then, in the More Views dialog box, double-click Leveling Gantt.

5. If necessary, in the View tab's Split View section, turn on the Details checkbox and then, in the Details drop-down list, choose Resource Usage.

6. Select a task that has a questionable split or delay. In the Details pane, Project displays the resources assigned to the task and its assignments from all the sharer projects.

7. In the Task tab's Editing section, click "Scroll to Task."

8. In the Resource Usage pane, examine the competing assignments to see which split or delay should win, and adjust the assignments as necessary.

■ SETTING LEVELING OPTIONS

You can level an entire project, tasks you select, or a single resource. By leveling several tasks that are all vying for the resource—or, alternatively, leveling only the most in-demand resources—you can focus on the problematic portions of your project. Project automatically chooses initial settings in the Resource Leveling dialog box, shown in Figure 11-26, but a few tweaks to these settings might give you better results. You can try one set of settings and then, if you don't like the changes Project makes, undo the leveling and then try different settings. The box on page 349 suggests some things to try if Project doesn't level overallocations. This section describes your leveling options and how to decide which ones to choose.

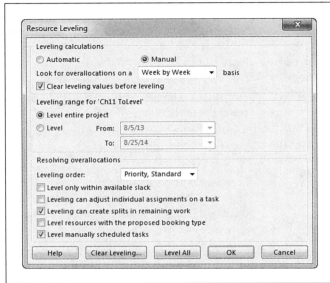

FIGURE 11-26

Project remembers the leveling settings you choose until you change them. After you choose settings, you can level your project by choosing the appropriate commands in the Resource tab's Level section (page 348). If you don't like the result, you can clear the leveling.

To choose leveling options, head to the Resource tab. In the Level section, click Leveling Options to open the Resource Leveling dialog box. When you change the settings in this dialog box, Project uses your settings until you change them. Here's a guide to the options in the Resource Leveling dialog box and how to use them:

- **Automatic or manual calculations.** At the top of the Resource Leveling dialog box, the Manual option is selected initially, and that's almost always what you want. With the Manual option selected, *you* control when Project relevels the schedule. When you want to relevel it, simply choose one of the leveling commands in the Resource tab's Level section (page 348). Then you can review the changes—and undo them if they aren't what you want.

  The Automatic option, on the other hand, tells Project to recalculate your schedule every time you make a change, which tends to slow down the program. In addition, it's hard to see whether the leveling changes that Project makes are what you want.

- **The overallocation time period.** To Project, 1 minute beyond a person's available time is an overallocation. But you know that an overallocation one day often balances out with available time the next day, so longer time periods generally mean fewer overallocations to resolve. In the "Look for overallocations on a __ basis" box, choose "Week by Week" or "Day by Day." These choices usually eliminate overallocations without too much leveling.

- **Remove previous leveling values.** Out of the box, the "Clear leveling values be-fore leveling" checkbox is turned on, which tells Project to remove any previous delays (added by you or by Project) before starting the next round of leveling. If you level the entire project in one fell swoop, starting fresh each time is the best approach, because you can more clearly see the changes Project makes. If you've added leveling delays manually, turn off the "Clear leveling values before leveling" checkbox. Otherwise, Project removes *your* leveling delays as well as any it has added. If you want to clear leveling delays without releveling the schedule, you can click the dialog box's Clear Leveling button (or, in the Resource tab's Level section, click Clear Leveling).

- **How much of the project to level.** The "Leveling range" section's heading includes the project's name to indicate that the option you select here applies only to the current project. Project automatically selects the "Level entire project" option, which means it looks at *every* task as a leveling candidate. By leveling the entire project, you'll be able to see how long the project will take given your team members' availability. To level only the tasks that occur during a specific date range, select the Level option instead and then, in the From and To boxes, choose the start and end dates to level. For example, if a phase runs from October 1 to March 1, level between those dates. (Of course, after leveling, the phase will finish later than March 1.) See page 348 to learn how to level only selected tasks or the assignments for specific resources.

- **How Project decides which tasks to level.** Initially, Project sets the "Leveling order" drop-down list to Standard, which uses predecessor dependencies, slack (how long a task can delay before it affects the end of the project), task dates, task constraints, and task priority to decide which tasks to level. However, the "Priority, Standard" leveling order is the one you want (as long as you assign priorities to tasks as described on page 341). With this leveling order selected, Project weights task priorities first and then the other criteria.

  The reasoning behind Project's ordering of characteristics is that you can delay tasks that don't have successors without affecting other tasks, so they're the best candidates for leveling. When tasks have successors, the ones with the most slack can delay longer without delaying other tasks. Similarly, the later tasks start, the less they affect the project schedule. Task constraints make tasks less flexible schedule-wise, so Project leaves those tasks alone if possible.

  The ID Only leveling order isn't very helpful, because it levels tasks with higher ID numbers *first*, and that's not what you typically want.

- **Level within slack.** Project initially turns off the "Level only within available slack" checkbox, which is usually what you want, because using only slack typi-cally doesn't resolve many overallocations. If you don't want the project finish date to move later, you can turn on this checkbox to level resources as much as possible without changing the project finish date. Then you can use other techniques to shorten the schedule (page 349).

- **Level individual assignments.** Project initially turns on the "Leveling can adjust individual assignments on a task" checkbox, which levels only assignments that overallocate resources. If you assign more than one person to a task, those people usually work together to get the job done. To tell Project to level entire tasks so assigned resources can work together, turn this checkbox off. If leveling tasks doesn't resolve your overallocation issues, then turn this checkbox on and relevel the project.

- **Split remaining work.** The "Leveling can create splits in remaining work" checkbox is turned on initially and that's the setting you want. When this checkbox is turned on, Project levels tasks that haven't started and adds splits to the remaining work for tasks in progress. With this checkbox turned *off*, Project delays assignments only until the resource can complete the work without stopping, which often pushes tasks out for exceedingly long periods of time.

- **Level proposed resources.** Proposed resources are resources you want to use but don't yet have permission for (page 223). If you turn on the "Level resources with the proposed booking type" checkbox, Project levels both committed and proposed resources to show what the project schedule would look like if you get everyone you ask for.

- **Level manually scheduled tasks.** Project turns this checkbox on automatically, which is exactly what you want, because manually scheduled tasks are more prone to overallocating resources than auto-scheduled ones.

TIP Deadlines (page 192) in Project aren't carved in stone. Leveling resources can push a task beyond its deadline, because Project's leveling doesn't pay any attention to task deadlines. To prevent Project from leveling a task with a deadline, change the task's priority to 1,000 (page 342).

■ APPLYING AND CLEARING LEVELING

The commands for applying and clearing leveling are all in the Resource tab's Level section. Here's how to level different parts of your project using these commands:

- **Level an entire project.** Click Level All.

- **Level selected tasks.** Select the tasks you want to level, and then click Level Selection.

- **Level a resource.** Select the resource you want to level, and then click Level Resource.

If you don't like the results you get, the quickest way to remove the leveling is to press Ctrl+Z to undo the leveling command. However, if you've leveled a task here and a resource there, you can remove all delays and splits by heading to the Resource tab and, in the Level section, clicking Clear Leveling.

Leveling Skips Overallocations

After leveling, oftentimes the overallocations you wanted to remove are still there. There can be lots of causes—Project doesn't level tasks and resources for a number of reasons. Check for the following circumstances to see if they're preventing leveling:

- Project doesn't delay tasks that have Must Start On or Must Finish On date constraints. To level these tasks, first change their date constraints to a more flexible type, like As Soon As Possible (page 188).

- When you've scheduled a project from the start date, As Late As Possible date constraints prevent leveling. For projects scheduled from the finish date, As Soon As Possible date constraints inhibit leveling.

- Project doesn't level tasks with a Priority value of 1,000 (page 342). To level a task, change its priority to 999 or less. Conversely, if you manually add delays or splits to a task with a priority of 1,000, then the Clear Leveling command doesn't remove your manual changes.

- Project doesn't delay tasks that have already started, although it might split remaining work if the Resource Leveling dialog box's "Leveling can create splits in remaining work" checkbox is turned on.

- Setting a resource's Can Level field to No prevents Project from leveling that resource's overallocations. If you can't see any obvious reason why leveling isn't working, add the Can Level field to Resource Sheet view (page 633), and then change the value to Yes.

- For tasks, the Level Assignments and Leveling Can Split fields control whether Project levels them. If these fields are set to No, then Project doesn't level the tasks no matter which settings you choose in the Resource Leveling dialog box. Change these values to Yes to allow leveling.

■ Shortening the Schedule

After you rid your project schedule of errors, omissions, and resource overallocations, your next challenge could be that the project finishes later than the customer and other stakeholders want. In addition, once the project is under way, delays often creep in and push the finish date out further than you had planned. Either way, you have to dive back into the schedule to see if you can shorten it. This section starts with a quick overview of options for shortening a schedule and then describes in detail how to apply each one.

There are several shortening methods to choose from, each with its own set of pros and cons:

- **Adjusting resource assignments.** If you have people with spare time, some savvy adjustments to who does what might shorten the schedule. You can also adjust resource assignments to use up any slack in the schedule. This approach is one of the first you should try, because it shortens the schedule without affecting scope, quality, or cost.

- **Splitting tasks into smaller pieces.** Something as simple as breaking long tasks into several shorter ones can sometimes shorten a schedule. You can assign the subtasks to different people, who work on them in tandem, or schedule around other work. This technique also doesn't affect scope, quality, or cost.

- **Overlapping (a.k.a. *fast-tracking*) tasks.** With this approach, you overlap tasks a little instead of working on them in sequence. Fast-tracking works as long as the same resources don't work on both of the fast-tracked tasks. The one downside to fast-tracking is that it increases risk, because changes that occur toward the end of the predecessor task could mess up work that's already complete in the successor.

- **Shortening lag time between tasks.** Some waiting periods between tasks can't be shortened: You can't speed up the time it takes for glue to dry, for instance. However, you might be able to shorten some lag times by, for example, paying for expedited shipping or asking the stakeholders for an emergency approval meeting. Shortening lag time doesn't affect scope or quality, but it might cost more.

- **Crashing the schedule.** The term *crashing* refers to paying more to shorten the schedule (usually by adding more resources). This is one of the last techniques to consider, because it could reduce the quality of your deliverables. And, sadly, it might not shorten the schedule at all (page 357).

- **Reducing scope.** Cutting project scope does shorten the schedule. However, stakeholders must agree to the reduction. And even if the customer and other stakeholders say yes to less scope, there's a risk that they might not be happy with the truncated end result.

Adjusting Resource Assignments

As you schedule your project, you assign some number of resources to tasks, depending on how much help you need (and how many helpers you can manage). After you complete a draft schedule, you often end up fine-tuning some assignments—and that requires finesse, as discussed in the box on page 351. For example, stakeholders may try to throw resources at a problem, only to have learning curves and chaos delay the task even more. Additional resources can increase costs, which may or may not be OK, as you will learn on page 356.

Experienced project managers know that most schedule problems have several solutions. For example, if you find underallocated resources working on critical-path tasks, you can increase their assignment units to shorten task durations. Or you can look for a person with the right skills and more available time. And if you're trying to cut costs, you can look at replacing expensive resources with people who charge lower rates.

After you find assignments to change, the editing techniques are the same ones you learned in Chapter 9. This section identifies Project views that help you find the right assignments to change and reviews your assignment-editing options.

The Fine Art of Assigning Resources

Experienced project managers assign resources carefully, because they know that resource assignments can affect schedule, cost, risk, and quality. Assigning the wrong resources to tasks can increase the risk of delays on the critical path or costs going through the roof. On the other hand, smart assignments can reduce costs or decrease duration—or both.

Because critical tasks are so critical, you can't be too choosy with critical-task assignments. Here are a few resource-assignment strategies to try:

- **Keep resources on critical tasks focused.** When resources have to juggle several tasks at the same time, the potential for delays increases. Although you can tell people to prioritize their critical tasks, one way to prevent delays is to limit the multitasking of resources assigned to critical tasks. Assign those resources to only one or two tasks at a time.

- **Use less expensive resources.** Some tasks use both experienced and inexperienced people, who typically

have different price tags. You can reduce cost by reassigning some or all task work to less expensive, less experienced resources. But offloading work to less expensive resources can be risky, because the people may take longer to do the same work. In addition, newbies on the project may interrupt the experts to the point that no one works productively.

- **Use more expensive resources.** If you need to finish a task quicker or meet quality objectives, you may opt to assign a more expensive, more experienced resource.

- **Use faster resources.** Sometimes, pricier resources are actually *less* expensive in the long run. Say an inexperienced backhoe operator costs $50 an hour and takes 24 hours to do the job ($1,200 total). If an expert operator costs $100 an hour but can finish the excavation in 8 hours, hiring him decreases the cost ($800 total) *and* duration of the task.

■ INCREASING UNITS TO DECREASE DURATION

Before you ask people to work extra hours, look for resources on critical-path tasks who have time available. You can assign them more work to reduce critical task duration. Project doesn't have a dedicated view for this combination of conditions, but you can filter a task-oriented view to show the critical path and alter the Resource Graph to show available time, as illustrated in Figure 11-27.

Selecting a task in the table in the primary pane shows the first resource assigned to that task in Resource Graph view in the Details pane. To see other resources assigned to the task, click the horizontal scroll bar below the resource legend on the left side of the view.

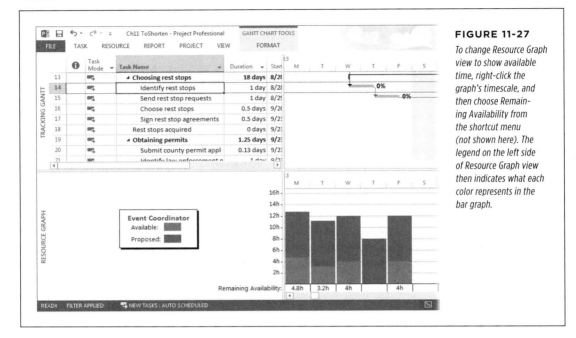

FIGURE 11-27

To change Resource Graph view to show available time, right-click the graph's timescale, and then choose Remaining Availability from the shortcut menu (not shown here). The legend on the left side of Resource Graph view then indicates what each color represents in the bar graph.

To see Tracking Gantt view in the top pane and the Resource Graph in the Details pane, do the following:

1. **In the View tab's Task Views section, click the Gantt Chart down arrow, and then, on the drop-down menu, choose Tracking Gantt.**

    Project displays Tracking Gantt view. (You can use Detail Gantt or Task Entry view instead if you've formatted either view to show critical tasks.)

2. **In the View tab's Split View section, turn on the Details checkbox, and then choose Resource Graph in the Details drop-down list.**

    The Resource Graph appears in the Details pane.

3. **Click the Details pane to make it active.**

    You can tell the Details pane is active when the view's name on the left side of the pane is green.

> **TIP** To obtain a ready-made view like this, download *ProjectMM_Customizations.mpp* from this book's Missing CD page at *www.missingmanuals.com/cds*, and then use the Organizer to copy the Critical Gantt Resources view to your global template (page 703).

You can then add resources to any task you want. The only special view that may help is the one that shows only the critical path (page 295). However, you have to use your judgment to decide whether more resources are going to help or hinder.

■ USING SLACK TIME TO SHORTEN THE SCHEDULE

When a resource works on critical and noncritical tasks at the same time, you can shorten the critical task's duration by assigning more of the resource's time to it. By definition, the noncritical task has slack time (page 294), which means you can delay its finish date without delaying the project. (Page 299 explains why you may not see any slack in your schedule, and how to fix this problem.) Although the noncritical task takes longer, the increase in duration merely consumes some of the task's slack time. See page 295 to learn how to display slack time in the Gantt Chart timescale and in a table.

UP TO SPEED

Shorten Lag Time Between Tasks

If critical-path tasks have lag time between them, shortening that lag time seems like a simple way to shorten the critical path, since you don't have to jockey resources around or pay more for faster results. But remember: Lag time is there for a reason, like the delay you add while you wait for paint to dry. However, sometimes you can streamline processes to cut lag time, like expediting a mortgage approval by having someone carry your paperwork through every step in the process.

In projects, approvals can chew up time, especially if you have to wait until the next meeting of stakeholders or the change control board. When you've shortened the schedule as much as you can with other techniques, you can see whether faster turnaround on approvals is feasible. For example, ask stakeholders if they can meet more often or request that people take 3 days to review documents instead of 5. You can also investigate whether paying extra for faster deliveries from vendors is worthwhile.

Splitting Tasks into Smaller Pieces

Sometimes splitting a long task into several shorter ones can help shorten your schedule. For example, instead of asking one person to carry out one big task, you may be able to assign different people to perform some of the work simultaneously.

Huge, single-handed tasks are rare, as they should be, if you've created a thorough work breakdown structure. However, if a long task sneaked past your WBS work, you can turn the original task into a summary task and create subtasks underneath it. Here are the steps for creating those subtasks:

1. **Select the Task Name cell *below* the original long task, and then press the Insert key to create a new task.**

   A blank row appears underneath the original long task.

2. **Press the Insert key repeatedly until you have enough blank rows for the subtasks you want to create.**

   When you're done, select the blank Task Name cell immediately below the original task.

3. **Type the name of the first subtask, and then press Enter.**

   Project selects the next Task Name cell, so you can repeat this step to fill in the Task Name cells for all the subtasks.

4. **Select all the subtasks you just created, and then in the Task tab's Schedule section, click Indent Task (the green arrow pointing to the right).**

   The original task turns into a summary task with the newly created tasks as its subtasks.

5. **Edit each subtask to define its duration or work, add the resources you want, and then link all the subtasks to one another.**

   Be sure to remove the resources assigned to the original long task, or you'll have *double* the work and cost.

Overlapping (Fast-Tracking) Tasks

Fast-tracking is about getting where you're going faster than usual. Unfortunately, just like applying makeup, drinking coffee, and dialing into conference calls *while* driving to work, fast-tracking projects can also increase risk considerably.

Fast-tracking a project means overlapping tasks that usually follow one another. At its best, fast-tracking shortens a project schedule without increasing cost or sacrificing quality. For example, if you're building a new website for event registrations and donations, you could ask the web team to start working on the site's basics before the planning tasks are complete.

The risk is that work done in a predecessor task won't mix with work that's already been done in an overlapping successor task. Backtracking to recover from these wrong turns can negatively affect your project's time, cost, quality, or scope. In the website example, for instance, changes that the board of directors requests could require redesigning and recoding the site.

■ FINDING TASKS TO FAST-TRACK

Some tasks are more conducive to overlapping than others. For example, tasks that occur earlier in a project are riskier to overlap. Designs tend to change in the early stages, so if you're planning a construction project, you wouldn't want to pour concrete based on early sketches. But once the design is finished and approved, you can overlap plumbing and wiring without too much trouble. You may need to tell each contractor where to start working, but the systems shouldn't interfere as long as everything goes where the architectural plans say it should.

Critical tasks are the tasks to target for fast-tracking, because a shorter critical path means shorter project duration. Long tasks on the critical path are the most effective choices for fast-tracking, because a small percentage of task overlap represents a significant cut in project duration. Moreover, overlapping the longest tasks may shorten the schedule with only a few changes, so you don't have as many risks to monitor. For example, overlapping a 3-month task by 10 percent shortens the critical path by 9 days. If that's the amount you need to shorten the schedule, you have to fast-track only that one task.

Filtering the task list for critical tasks is the easiest way to find tasks to evaluate for fast-tracking. You can then work backward from the finish date looking for critical-path tasks that you can overlap with acceptable risk. To focus on fast-track candidates, do the following:

1. **Hide the summary tasks in the task list by choosing the Format tab, and then in the Show/Hide section turning off the Summary Tasks checkbox.**

   If your project uses several WBS levels, summary tasks can outnumber critical tasks, so hiding summary tasks helps you focus on critical work tasks.

2. **Apply the Critical filter to view only critical-path tasks.**

   Click the down arrow to the right of the Task Name column heading, and then choose Filters→Critical.

3. **Jump to the last task in the task list by pressing Ctrl+End, and then work backward, looking at every pair of linked critical tasks for tasks you can overlap.**

   If you want to look at the longest critical path tasks first, sort tasks by duration from longest to shortest: Click the down arrow to the right of the Duration column heading, and then choose "Sort Largest to Smallest." You see the critical tasks listed with longest durations at the top, as shown in Figure 11-28.

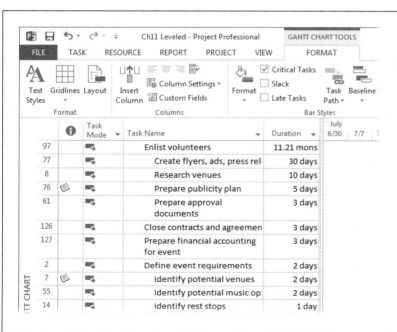

FIGURE 11-28

When you sort tasks by duration, the task ID numbers are as jumbled as the task bars in the timeline. After you've located long tasks to overlap, sort the tasks by ID (in the View tab's Data section, click Sort→"by ID"). If the WBS column is visible, you can also sort by WBS code by clicking the down arrow to the right of the column's heading and choosing "Sort A to Z."

■ MODIFYING TASK DEPENDENCIES TO OVERLAP TASKS

Fast-tracking means starting the next task before its predecessor is complete. For instance, you could tell your accountants to start counting the chickens before all the eggs have hatched. When you identify partial overlaps like these, you create them in Project by adding negative lag to the link between the tasks.

When the link lines in your project look like fishing line in a tackle box, finding the right link line in the timescale is impossible, so don't even try. The Task Information dialog box is the easiest place to add lag. Here are the steps:

1. **In the Gantt Chart table area, double-click the successor task.**

   The Task Information dialog box opens.

2. **Click the Predecessors tab.**

   All the predecessor tasks appear in the list, even those that aren't on the critical path.

3. **Click the Lag cell for the predecessor you want to overlap, and then type a negative number for the overlap.**

   For example, to overlap the tasks by 2 days, type *-2d*. You can also overlap by a percentage of the predecessor task's duration. For instance, if you type *-25%* for a predecessor that takes 8 days, the overlap is 2 days. Keep in mind that a percentage lag's length changes if the predecessor's duration changes.

4. **Click OK.**

   The overlap value appears in the Lag cell, and the task bars overlap in the timescale.

Paying More for Faster Delivery

Spending more money to deliver in less time can make financial sense. A high-tech doodad that will be obsolete in 2 years can't afford a delay getting to market. The extra sales you make could add up to more than the premium you have to pay to finish the project earlier.

Crashing is the term project managers use for shortening a schedule by spending more money—usually by throwing more resources at tasks. To the uninitiated, crashing seems like an easy choice. If two people can build your website in 12 weeks, for example, then four web developers should be able to wrap it up in only 6 weeks. But reality doesn't always work out that way. And sometimes crashing doesn't work at all. The box on page 357 explains several reasons why crashing should be the *last* technique you turn to for shortening a schedule.

It's easy to assume that crashing won't change cost—it looks like you're paying the same rate for the same number of hours. But in reality, there's always a trade-off between time and money. When you crash tasks, you have to choose the tasks that shorten the schedule the amount you need for the least amount of money. That's because every task has a magical duration that results in the minimum cost. If the task runs longer, you spend more money on things like office space, people's salaries and benefits, and keeping the freezer stocked with Cherry Garcia ice cream. Ironically, shorter tasks can cost more, too—for items like additional computers, higher-cost contractors, and managing the larger team it takes to expedite the work. This section explains how to evaluate whether crashing is the right approach for shortening your project.

REALITY CHECK

When Crashing Doesn't Work

Say your project's finish date is fast approaching and it's later than planned. The typical reaction to project delays is to throw people at the problem. But adding more people, especially later in the project, may not deliver the schedule-shortening results you seek. Here are some reasons why:

- If you round up additional resources on short notice, they might not be as good as the people already working on the project. They could be available because they're on the B-list, for example. Using second-string resources might reduce the quality of the work.

- In many cases, adding more resources *increases* duration instead of decreasing it. New people need time to get

up to speed, so they run up the cost while they're less productive than the original team. The problem can be compounded because the original resources sacrifice productivity when they have to help the new people. And more bodies mean more costs for supervision and communication. To learn more about this phenomenon, read *The Mythical Man-Month* (Addison-Wesley, 1995) by Frederick Brooks.

- Sometimes, crashing simply won't work. Some tasks *can't* finish in less time, no matter how many resources you assign. For example, much to the dismay of most pregnant women, you can't assign nine women to have a baby in one month.

■ TIME VS. MONEY

Stakeholders might open the checkbook to crash a project, but they don't want to spend more than they have to. So it's important to remember that shortening tasks that *aren't* on the critical path is a waste of money, because doing so doesn't change the project's duration one bit. Also, keep in mind that crashing doesn't mean shortening *every* task on the critical path. You crash only enough tasks to shorten the project by the amount you need. Like cars, some tasks cost more to crash than others. Your job is to choose the tasks that shorten the schedule for the least amount of money.

Crash tables can help you compare the cost and time you could save by crashing different tasks. For example, one task might cost an additional $50,000 to cut 2 weeks from the schedule, whereas another task may cut 2 weeks for only $25,000. To choose cost-effective tasks, you have to compare apples to apples—that is, how much it costs for each week of duration you eliminate. One way to do this is to build a crash table in an Excel spreadsheet. You can enter the duration you can cut and the cost, and create an Excel formula that calculates the cost per week (or month, or day). The next section explains how to do that.

TIP Long critical tasks are the best candidates for crashing, since you can eliminate longer durations in fewer tasks. Shortening a few long tasks may cost less—and save more time—than crashing a bunch of shorter tasks.

■ USING A SPREADSHEET TO CHOOSE TASKS TO CRASH

The quickest way to identify the tasks to crash is to move task data into an Excel spreadsheet and calculate crash costs there. Finding the perfect combination of tasks to crash can get complicated. One task might offer several weeks' worth of low-cost crashing. However, if shortening that task by 2 weeks takes it off the critical path, then there's no point spending money to shorten it. The most effective approach is to crash one task at a time (by making the crash modifications in Project), and then evaluate the critical path again to see what the next step should be.

Since you start by evaluating the longest tasks and usually crash only a few, start by sorting the critical tasks by duration, and then copy the first several tasks from Project to Excel. Here are the steps for finding critical tasks to crash and then copying them to Excel:

1. **With a task-oriented view (like Gantt Chart) displayed, click the down arrow to the right of the Task Name column heading, and then choose Filters→Critical.**

   To hide summary tasks, head to the Gantt Chart Tools | Format tab. In the Hide/Show section, turn off the Summary Tasks checkbox.

2. **To list the longest critical tasks first, click the down arrow to the right of the Duration column heading, and then choose "Sort Largest to Smallest."**

   The task IDs and task bars show up out of order, but the longest tasks appear at the top of the task list. In addition to copying task names to Excel, Duration and Cost come in handy if you want to sort tasks in Excel by their original durations or costs.

TIP   The Entry table places the Task Name and Duration columns one after the other. To simplify copying the fields you want, insert the Cost column immediately after Duration: Right-click the Start column heading, and then choose Insert Column→Cost.

---

3. **Drag from the Task Name cell of the first critical task to the Cost cell for the last critical task you want to copy, and then press Ctrl+C.**

   Project copies the cells to the Clipboard.

4. **In Excel, click the top-left cell where you want to copy the values, and then press Ctrl+V.**

   Excel pastes the values into worksheet cells starting at the top-left cell and filling in cells to the right and down. (If the values aren't completely visible, widen the columns by dragging the dividers between their headings.)

5. **In the first three blank columns to the right of the copied values, add headings for crash reduction, crash cost, and cost per week (respectively), as shown in Figure 11-29.**

   Fill in each row with the total amount of time you can shorten the task, and how much it costs to do so.

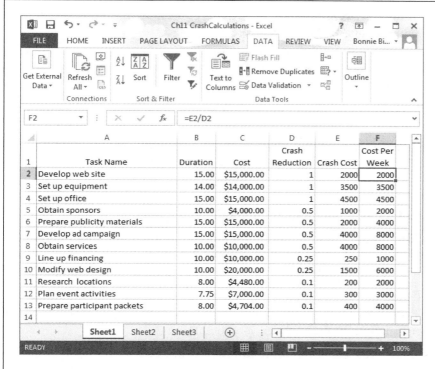

FIGURE 11-29

Project durations include time periods (days, weeks, and so on). If all the units are the same, use Excel's Replace command to remove the units and leave just the numbers: Press Ctrl+H and type the unit in the "Find what" box. Leave the "Replace with" box empty, and then click Replace All. If tasks use different time periods, manually convert each duration to the corresponding number of weeks.

6. **In the first blank Cost Per Week cell, type the formula to divide the crash cost by the crash duration (for instance, *=E2/D2*).**

   You can then point at the fill handle at the bottom right of the cell. When it changes to a + sign, drag over all the other Cost Per Week cells so Excel can calculate their values.

> **TIP** You can obtain the crash-calculation spreadsheet shown in Figure 11-29 by downloading the *Ch11 CrashCalculation.xlsx* file from this book's Missing CD page at *www.missingmanuals.com/cds*.

7. **To find the least expensive tasks to crash, sort the rows first by the amount of schedule reduction and then by the crash cost per week.**

   In Excel, choose Data→Sort. In the Sort dialog box, in the "Sort by" drop-down list, choose Crash Reduction (or the column heading you entered). In the Order drop-down list, choose "Largest to Smallest." Click Add Level to add a second sort criterion. In the "Then by" drop-down list, choose Cost Per Week (or the column heading you entered). In the second Order drop-down list, choose

"Smallest to Largest," and then click OK. The tasks appear with the longest reductions in duration first and the smallest cost per week to the largest, as shown in Figure 11-29.

8. **Switch to Project and make the changes to the first task on the crash spreadsheet to shorten its duration.**

Review the critical path to see whether the results are what you want. For example, if the task is no longer on the critical path, you may want to scale back on how much you crash it.

Repeat this step until the project's duration is the length you want—or the cost prohibits shortening it any further.

At that point, you may need to reduce the project's scope. The section "Inactivating Tasks" on page 452 tells you how to handle that in Project.

■ Reducing Project Costs

You've diligently entered costs into your project plan and either looked at the resulting cost totals as described in "Reviewing Project Costs" on page 303 or compared your planned costs against your budget, as described in "Comparing Costs to Your Budget" on page 273. If your target is $100,000 and your costs are coming out to $130,000, you have to figure out how to trim $30,000 from your planned project costs or heads will roll—most likely yours. How do you go about cutting thousands of dollars from a project? Answer: very carefully.

First, look at your cost assumptions to make sure mistakes haven't sent project costs into the stratosphere. If you're lucky, you can correct a misplaced zero and everything will be hunky-dory. The next line of defense is to reschedule tasks to reduce costs. You can also examine resource assignments to look for ways to cut costs.

NOTE For more information about viewing costs in your project plan, including running cost reports, see pages 303 and 305.

This section discusses each of these cost-cutting techniques. However, if these methods aren't enough to solve your budget crisis, it's time to take a hard look at the budget itself and propose a change to the project's budget, scope, or schedule.

Checking for Cost Errors

When your TV suddenly doesn't turn on or you can't get the channel that's showing world championship bass fishing, you probably don't schedule a technician service call right away. You poke around, hit buttons on the remote, turn things off and on, and see if the picture comes back. If you're really thinking straight, the very first thing you check is whether your dog unplugged the TV cables or power cord again.

The same troubleshooting principle applies when planned project costs don't jibe with your budget. Don't assume that the project is really $30,000 over budget just yet. Look for errors, starting with the simple, most obvious things first. In this section, you'll learn how to systematically scan your project plan for mistakes in cost values or calculations.

Here are cost-related items to check and where to look for them:

- **Task durations.** Review task durations for any that approach the length of geologic eras. An excessive duration could be a mistake, such as a typo in the Duration field or a resource assigned to work only a few minutes a day. Durations affect cost because Project calculates labor costs by multiplying labor rates by the work that contributes to the duration.

- **Costs per use.** In Resource Sheet view, look for values in the Cost Per Use column (page 219). Remember that a cost per use is levied for each task a resource is assigned to. For example, suppose a crane costs $5,000 to get it on site. If you apply the $5,000 as cost per use and then assign the crane to six tasks, your project cost includes $30,000 for crane setup instead of only $5,000. In this situation, a cost resource for getting the crane on site makes more sense than cost per use. On the other hand, a consultant may include a $100 travel fee each time she comes to your office. If a resource has a standard rate combined with a cost per use, make sure they're both legitimate.

- **Resource rates.** Also in Resource Sheet view, review the rates you've assigned to human, equipment, and material resources. If you have a lot of resources, consider sorting the view by standard rate so that excessively high or low rates stand out. (For example, if a janitor comes out higher than an information architect, someone's standard rate is off.) To do so, click the down arrow to the right of the Std. Rate column heading and then, on the drop-down menu, choose Sort Descending. To return the view to its normal order, in the View tab's Data section, click Sort→"by ID."

- **Planned assignment costs.** Apply the Cost table (in the View tab's Data section, click Tables→Cost) to Resource Sheet view, and then check your resources' costs on their assignments. The Cost field shows the total planned cost for a resource for *all* tasks it's assigned to. To see the resources that run the tab up the most, sort the view by the Cost field (click the down arrow to the right of the Cost column heading and then, on the drop-down menu, choose "Sort Largest to Smallest"). Then you can focus on ways to reduce the costs of those resources.

- **Cost resource amounts.** To easily review cost resource amounts, display Resource Usage view (in the View tab's Resource Views section, click Resource Usage), apply the Cost table as explained in the previous bullet point, and then group the view by resource type (click the down arrow to the right of the Resource Name column heading and then, on the drop-down menu, choose "Group by"→Resource Type). Scroll down to the Type: Cost grouping, and the result looks similar to Figure 11-30. To return the view to its normal ungrouped arrangement, click the down arrow to the right of the Resource Name column heading and then, on the drop-down menu, choose No Group.

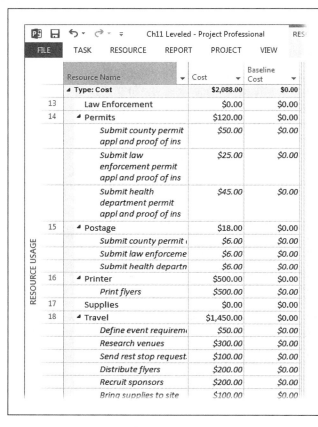

FIGURE 11-30

When you apply the Cost table to Resource Usage view and then group the view by resource type, you see all the cost resources together, the tasks they're assigned to, and the amounts designated for each assignment. If you find an error, you can change it right there in the assignment's row.

- **Fixed costs for tasks.** In Gantt Chart view, check any fixed costs for tasks to see if they have one or two zeroes too many. Apply the Cost table to the view (in the View tab's Data section, click Tables→Cost), and then sort by the Fixed Cost field. (Click the down arrow to the right of the Fixed Cost column heading and then, on the drop-down menu, choose "Sort Largest to Smallest" to see the highest fixed costs at the top of the view.) Make sure you're not using a fixed cost *and* a cost resource for the same expense on the same task.

After you've thoroughly reviewed resource cost assumptions and task information that affects cost, be sure to take a closer look at the budget itself. Rather than being carved into stone by lightning bolts from on high, the budget is prepared by a human being like you. Check the assumptions in the budget, and make sure someone hasn't made any outlandish mistakes there.

Adjusting the Schedule to Reduce Cost

If you've corrected cost mistakes and your planned costs and the budget *still* don't see eye to eye, it's time for Plan B: adjusting the schedule. Here are some ways you can adjust the schedule to reduce costs:

- **Task relationships.** Sometimes by linking tasks more aggressively (in other words, fast-tracking tasks as described on page 354), you can shorten the time you have to pay resources while they wait for their next task to begin.

- **Date constraints.** Any constraints other than As Soon As Possible (or As Late As Possible for a project scheduled from the finish date) are worth a second look (page 317). If a task has a Must Finish On or Start No Earlier Than date constraint applied, resources may be waiting in limbo unnecessarily for the right time to work on tasks. Removing that limbo time can help you cut costs. To look for these issues, add the Constraint Type and Constraint Date fields to a table, and then sort or group by Constraint Type.

Adjusting Assignments to Reduce Cost

If you've adjusted the schedule to optimize your costs but you still have more belt tightening to do, try adjusting resource assignments. Here are a couple of strategies to try:

- **Replace expensive resources with cheaper ones.** Consider having your more experienced (and probably more expensive) resources mentor your less costly resources on tasks for a short time, rather than working entire task durations. Or use cheaper in-house—perhaps borrowed—resources rather than more expensive outside consultants. On the other hand, sometimes hiring temporary contract labor is cheaper than using your in-house employees.

- **Do away with overtime.** If your current schedule involves overtime (and your resources cost more when they work overtime), see if you can adjust assignments to eliminate overtime.

Rethinking Your Budget

If your best efforts on project costs still don't line them up with the project's budget, then it's time for renegotiation. You've checked and rechecked that your costs reflect the project's reality—as you know it so far. The next step is talking to the customer, the project sponsor, or whichever head honcho holds the purse strings. There are two choices in this situation.

- **Increase the budget.** The first and usually most difficult option is trying to get more money appropriated for the project.

- **Cut back on project scope or quality.** Cutting the number of tasks (for example, axing a particular phase), or reducing quality objectives can cut costs—but only if all the stakeholders agree. See page 452 to learn how to inactivate tasks you cut from the project. If the stakeholders find more money and decide to add the scope back in, you can reactivate those tasks in no time.

◾ Playing What-If Games

There's more than one way to skin a cat—or plan a project. The project's stakeholders may ask for the moon—but when they see how much it costs to land on that hunk of rock, they might backpedal and ask for alternative plans. They'll have questions like, "How much less would it cost if we cut this portion of the scope?", "How much longer will it take if we add these change requests to the plan?" and, invariably, "Why can't we do all this extra work in the same timeframe and for the same cost?" In Project, inactive tasks and the Compare Project feature help you evaluate alternatives. This section shows you how to use both.

Inactivating Tasks

If nothing seems to shorten your project's schedule or reduce its budget, a reduction in scope may be in order. As project manager, you can't arbitrarily eliminate scope. Only the stakeholders can redefine the scope, and even then, only if the project's customer approves. Decisions have a way of changing, so making tasks inactive is a great way to cut scope. Should the stakeholders decide to revert to the original plan later on, you can reactivate the inactive tasks without skipping a beat.

> **TIP** Inactive tasks also work well if you want to document nice-to-have work. Create tasks, assign resources to them, and fill in other fields; then make the tasks inactive. That way, their values are visible (and editable) but don't affect your project schedule. If you find that the project has the time and budget for the work, then you can make them active.

Making tasks inactive removes their values from your project's rolled-up schedule and cost. However, the tasks, their resource assignments, and field values remain in the plan, as Figure 11-31 shows, so you have a record of what you cut out. You can edit inactive tasks just as you do active tasks. If you reactivate the tasks, you don't have to re-enter any information.

Changing tasks to inactive is a snap: Select one or more tasks in a task-oriented view and then in the Task tab's Schedule section, click Inactivate. The inactive tasks immediately change to gray with a line drawn through their values in the table area. However, you can edit an inactive task's values by double-clicking it to open the Task Information dialog box or by editing values directly in the table cells.

> **NOTE** Inactivating tasks frees up time that was previously scheduled for assigned resources. If you inactivate tasks to reduce scope, then relevel the assigned resources to see the effect on the schedule. The resources have more time available so their other assignments may finish sooner.

To *reactivate* a task, select it and then, in the Task tab's Schedule section, click Inactivate again.

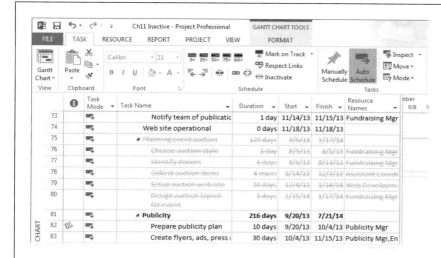

FIGURE 11-31

Inactive tasks are grayed out and have a line through their values. However, you can select an inactive cell in a table and edit its value, or double-click it to open the Task Information dialog box. When you inactivate tasks, their durations and costs don't roll up into summary task values. In addition, inactive resource assignments don't affect the assigned resources' availability.

Comparing Projects

For more involved what-if games, it can be useful to make a second copy of your Project file. With a backup safely in place, you can edit to your heart's content while keeping both the original file and the new one. That way, you can examine both options in detail to see which is better. For example, you may save copies of a Project file at different stages of project execution or to compare changes in the critical path as you shorten it. Or perhaps a colleague sent you a revised copy of the project plan and you want to identify what the differences are between it and the one that you prepared.

Happily, when you want to compare two Project files, you don't have to open the files side by side, planting your left and right index fingers on the computer screen as you scan through the corresponding fields in each file. Project's Compare Projects feature simplifies these types of comparisons. The Compare Projects feature produces a report that compares values from two files side by side along with a column showing the difference between the two. In addition, the timescale includes two sets of task bars, so you can visually compare when tasks start and finish.

Here's how to compare two versions of the same project:

1. **Open the two Project files you want to compare and display the one that's your current version. Then choose Report→Compare Projects.**

   The Compare Project Versions dialog box opens with the "Compare the current project ([project_name]) to this previous version" label at the top, where [project name] is the name of the active project.

2. **In the drop-down list at the top of the dialog box, choose the name of the file you want to compare with the current file (whether it's a previous version or an alternative plan).**

   If the other file isn't open, click Browse and then, in the Open dialog box, choose the file you want to compare.

   NOTE The Compare Projects feature uses the word "current" to identify the values for the first file you selected and "previous" to identify the values for the file you selected in the Compare Project Versions dialog box. That's why it's easier to keep things straight if you select your current file first.

3. **In the Task Table drop-down list, choose the table that contains the fields you want to compare. In the Resource Table drop-down list, choose the table that contains the resource fields you want to compare.**

   The comparison table that Compare Projects builds can become unwieldy because it includes three columns for each field in the original table you selected. To focus on the information you care about most, consider creating a custom table (page 638) that contains only the fields you want to compare. For example, for tasks, you might include Task Name, Duration, Finish Date, and Cost.

4. **Click OK.**

   A message box tells you that Project is creating a comparison report, and windows flicker on and off for a few seconds. When things calm down, you see a Comparison Report pane at the top and the two versions you're comparing at the bottom, as Figure 11-32 shows.

A legend on the left side of the Comparison Report window identifies the symbols it uses:

- Tasks that appear only in the current project include a + sign.

- Tasks that appear only in the previous version include a – sign to indicate that they've been removed in the current version.

- The task bars for the current version are green.

- The task bars for the previous version are blue.

- For each column in the table you selected, the Comparison Report displays three columns. For example, the "Cost: Current" column shows the cost for the first file you selected; "Cost: Previous" shows the cost for the second file you selected; and "Cost: Diff" shows the difference between those two values.

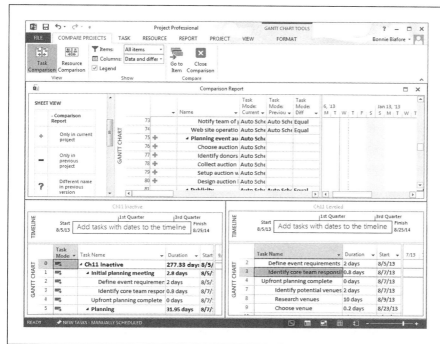

FIGURE 11-32

*When you compare two
versions of a project,
the Comparison Report
window appears at the
top of the main Project
window. Another window
for the current version of
the project appears at the
bottom left, and a third
window for the previous
version appears at the
bottom right.*

While you're looking at the comparison between the two files, the Compare Projects
tab sits between the File tab and the Task tab on the ribbon. On the Compare Projects tab, you can click Task Comparison or Resource Comparison to switch between
the task table and resource table you specified. In the tab's Show section, you can
choose a filter in the box to the right of the Filter icon to examine different aspects
of the comparison. For example, in the drop-down list, choose "Changed items" to
see only the tasks or resources that changed between the two versions. You can also
view items that appear only in the current or previous version. If you want to view a
task in each version, select the task in the Comparison Report window and then, in
the Compare Projects tab's Compare section, click "Go to Item." Project highlights
the task in the windows for each version.

Saving the Project Plan

O nce you obtain the stakeholders' approval, it's time to save an official, approved version of your project plan. This approved plan wears a lot of hats during the life of your project. It's documentation of the agreed-upon scope, schedule, budget, and so on; when questions arise later, you can turn to the approved plan to help sort them out. The project plan also acts as a reference for the project team as they do their work. Finally, the project plan contains the targets you've set for the project. As the team performs the project work, you compare actual performance to the plan to see whether you're on the right track. But first you have a few final planning tasks to complete. A plan is merely a *proposed* plan until the stakeholders accept it and commit their approval in writing.

A project plan covers a lot of ground, and it isn't stored in a single file. Saving a project plan means saving an approved copy of *every* file that contributes to the plan. This chapter talks about setting up a storage system not only for the planning documents, but also for files generated during the rest of the project's life. You'll learn about different ways to store project files and how to structure project information so it's easy to find and manage.

For some types of files, saving a copy is as simple as appending *v1.0* to the end of the filename, but Project files require more attention. This chapter describes how to set a baseline in your Project schedule so you can compare your planned schedule and cost to what you actually achieve. You'll learn how to set baselines at several points during a project to watch for trends over time. Finally, you'll find out how to view baselines in Project, either alone or in comparison to actual performance.

■ Obtaining Approval for the Plan

With the convenience of email distribution lists and shared file storage, you may be tempted to email project stakeholders and ask them to review the plan and email their approvals back to you—without holding a sign-off meeting to make sure everyone understands what they're approving. Unfortunately, the attached plan is likely to sit unread in all those email inboxes. You may receive approvals, but they may get unapologetically revoked later when people realize that the plan doesn't meet their needs.

To obtain approvals that really stick, set up a sign-off meeting to review the plan and snag approvals then and there. (The box on page 370 talks about how to handle another approval issue—starting project execution before the plan is approved.) Here are some tips for a successful sign-off:

1. **Distribute the project plan in advance, and urge the stakeholders to read it before the meeting.**

   You can hand out hard copies, send the plan as an email attachment, or place a copy of the plan online where everyone can access it. The sign-off meeting (described in the next step) provides some motivation for the stakeholders to read the plan beforehand.

2. **At the sign-off meeting, don't assume that the stakeholders have read the plan.**

   Your job as project manager is to present the plan at the meeting, covering its key aspects and pointing out potential conflicts, problems, and risks. Encourage questions and discussion—this is your last chance to hash out issues. To jump-start the discussion, ask stakeholders pointed questions about the areas you see as potential problems.

3. **A nod or a verbal "yes" doesn't constitute approval; circulate the sign-off page and ask everyone to actually sign it.**

REALITY CHECK

Starting Before the Plan Is Approved

Hard deadlines are a fact of life, so some projects start before the project plan is approved—or before the plan is even complete. Beginning work without an approved plan is *absurdly* risky. The team could work hard for weeks, only to have to backtrack and redo it all when the final plan is approved.

If you can, take a stand and persuade stakeholders and management to delay the execution phase until after the plan is approved.

If your persuasive powers don't work, save the plan as it is and begin to execute the project with what you have. At the same time, continue to push—hard—for plan approval. When you get it, save the approved version of the plan and compare performance with the approved version going forward. And don't forget to document any backtracking you have to do, so you can argue against false starts in the future.

■ Storing Project Documents

Even small projects generate an astounding amount of information. Initially, the project plan is a collection of requirements and specification documents, budget spreadsheets, the schedule in Project, and so on. Don't forget the draft documents you generated before you obtained approval, and the emails and memos that flew around as planning progressed. When project execution starts, the amount of information expands exponentially because of project results like design documents, contracts for services, software that's been written, databases, and blueprints. Meanwhile, managing the project produces status reports, change request forms, and so on.

In the good old days, the container for project documentation was called a *project notebook* because it was a three-ring binder (or several) that held paper copies of every project-related document. These days, a project notebook tends to be electronic, with files stored somewhere on a computer. Either way, you need a filing system so everyone can find and access the information they need.

The best project filing system depends on the project: what sort of information it produces, who needs access to that info, any security issues, and the standards your organization follows. The choice boils down to structure and technology. You need a way to track various versions of documents and deliverables—for a construction project, for instance, that includes things like equipment specifications, contracts, architectural design drawings, engineering drawings, construction plans, and as-built drawings. In addition, you may need a system to manage document access and changes. For example, all team members can read the project requirements to see what their tasks are supposed to deliver, but only a few authorized team members can *modify* those requirements.

Regardless of the storage technology you use, you need to structure the information so that finding it isn't an Easter egg hunt. Project information typically falls into a few high-level categories that you can use to build the basic storage structure (as illustrated in Figure 12-1):

- **Project deliverables.** As you learned in Chapter 2, deliverables are the tangible results that a project produces. Because payment often hinges on these deliverables becoming reality, you want them to be easy to find and control. Having separate subfolders within this category for draft and final versions make it even easier to see whether a deliverable is complete.

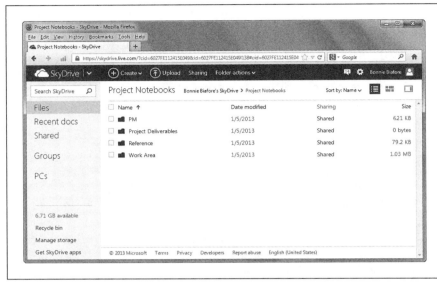

FIGURE 12-1

You can design an information hierarchy with different storage tools. For example, you can build a folder structure on a file server, within a Microsoft SharePoint Server, or on a storage area in the cloud (as shown here, using SkyDrive as an example), as the box on page 373 explains.

- **Project-management deliverables.** Managing a project produces all kinds of intermediate deliverables, like the project plan, status reports, and change request logs. Separate folders for different types of info can forestall information overload. However, the best way to break down this information depends on what makes the most sense to you. For example, you might organize it by project-management phase with folders for planning, execution, control, and closure. Or you may prefer to organize it by project-management activities: planning, communication, finance, risk management, change control, and so on.

- **Reference.** Projects almost always include background information that, although not a deliverable, can be essential. For example, you may need to refer to the charity's promotional materials, but those materials aren't part of your fundraising project.

- **Project work.** All the work products that team members produce have to go somewhere, but (happily) where to store them may not be your problem. For example, software-development projects often store and manage code in source-control systems. In other cases, teams may set up their own work areas and organize their files as they see fit, delivering their work to you when it's complete.

Document Management Options

How you store project documents depends on the technology available to you. If your organization has a document-management system like Documentum, then you can store and manage versions of project documents in high style. Similarly, Microsoft Enterprise Project Management Solutions use SharePoint to provide document libraries and places for tracking issues and risks.

If you don't have these types of power tools, don't despair. Your far-flung project teams can share documents in plenty of other ways:

- **Microsoft SkyDrive.** This cloud storage service is part of Microsoft's Windows Live. People can upload, access, and sync files between a SkyDrive location and their computers and other devices, or through a web browser.

- **Other cloud storage services.** If you use a cloud storage service that's registered with Office 2013, the service appears in the Open and Save As screens of Backstage view (page 93).

- **SharePoint Server.** You don't need Project Server to set up a SharePoint server for sharing documents. For example, if you use Office 365 for midsize businesses, you can store files in an Office 365 SharePoint location. A SharePoint website can carry out workflow processes, such as checking documents in and out, storing multiple versions of a document, or requiring approvals before documents proceed to the next step. You can also set SharePoint permissions to control who can read or write to different areas. Moreover, Project Professional lets you export project files to a SharePoint list (you need SharePoint 2010 Foundation or later), so you can share project information with anyone who's interested.

- **Basecamp.** One of many web-based collaboration packages, Basecamp (*www.basecamphq.com*) provides online folders for storing and sharing documents.

- **Directory structure.** Forgoing fancier tools, you can simply set up folders on a shared network disk drive and use file-naming conventions to track versions of documents. For example, track document versions by appending the date saved to filenames. When a file reaches a milestone, such as Approved, you can add that to the filename as well.

■ Preserving the Original Plan in Project

After stakeholders approve a project plan, they want the project to follow that plan. If it *doesn't*, the stakeholders expect an explanation of the difference between planned and actual performance (called *variance*). Variance is the foundation of a variety of project performance measures (page 441), like earned value and the schedule performance index. To calculate variance, you first have to save the original planned values in your Project schedule.

As you've seen in previous chapters, Project constantly updates fields like dates, duration, work, and cost as you make changes (as long as tasks are set up as automatically scheduled, that is). For example, if you increase the work hours for a task, Project recalculates the task's duration and finish date. When you begin to track progress, Project continues these recalculations; for example, as a delayed predecessor task pushes back the start dates of its successors.

Fortunately, Project has no problem keeping track of both your original plan and the current one. The program stores the original plan in a *baseline*, which is a snapshot of schedule and cost information (you create this snapshot by *setting the baseline*, as explained in the next section). In fact, you can store up to 11 baselines; for example, you can save a baseline after adding a major change request or save several snapshots to evaluate performance trends. At the same time, the schedule you see every time you open Project is the *current* plan, which shows the schedule and cost based on any revisions you've made, as well as the effects of actual performance. As you'll learn in Chapter 14, Project uses baseline values and current values to calculate variances and other performance measures.

A baseline doesn't save *all* the info that resides in a Project file. From hundreds of Project fields, a baseline saves key schedule and cost values for each task, resource, and assignment in the Project file. The following fields show the information stored in Project's primary baseline, appropriately named *Baseline*, but the fields in other baselines (which are named Baseline1 through Baseline10) work the same way:

- **Baseline Start.** Shows the values that were in Start fields for tasks and assignments when you set the baseline. For automatically scheduled tasks, Project calculates these dates; for manually scheduled tasks, it uses the dates you specify.

- **Baseline Estimated Start.** In most cases, when you set a baseline, this field gets filled in with the Scheduled Start date that Project calculates. For automatically scheduled tasks, Baseline Start and Baseline Estimated Start are *always* identical. If you fill in a manually scheduled task's Start field with a date, Project copies that date to Baseline Estimated Start when you set a baseline. However, if you leave a manually scheduled task's Start field blank or type a note in that field, Project copies the Scheduled Start value (the start date that Project recommends for the task) to the Baseline Estimated Start field when you set a baseline.

NOTE With manually scheduled tasks, Scheduled Start and Scheduled Finish fields may not contain values (page 63). The Baseline Estimated Start and Baseline Estimated Finish fields are specifically for manually scheduled tasks *without* specified date values. Project sets these fields to the dates that most closely match where the tasks occur in the project plan. For example, a top-level manually scheduled task without dates or duration has a Baseline Estimated Start date that's the same as the project start date. A manually scheduled subtask without dates has a Baseline Estimated Start date equal to its summary task's start date.

- **Baseline Finish.** Shows the values that were in Finish fields for tasks and assignments when you set the baseline. For automatically scheduled tasks, Baseline Finish represents the dates Project calculates; for manually scheduled tasks, it represents the dates you specify.

- **Baseline Estimated Finish.** When you set a baseline, this field usually copies its values from the Scheduled Finish dates Project calculates. If you type a date in a manually scheduled task's Finish field, Project copies that date to this Baseline Estimated Finish field when you set a baseline. And if you leave a manually scheduled task's Finish field blank or type a note in that field, Project sets the Baseline Estimated Finish field to one day after the task's start date.

- **Baseline Duration.** Represents the planned duration of tasks based on the Baseline Start and Baseline Finish dates.

- **Baseline Estimated Duration.** Shows the duration based on the Baseline Estimated Start and Baseline Estimated Finish dates.

- **Baseline Work.** Contains the planned person-hours for tasks, resources, and assignments. For example, Gantt Chart view's Baseline Work field shows the total planned work for each task when the baseline was set. However, Resource Sheet view's Baseline Work field indicates the hours that were assigned to each resource when you set the baseline. In addition, the Baseline Work field in a time-phased view like Task Usage shows work for each time period.

- **Baseline Cost.** Represents the planned cost of tasks, resources, and assignments when the baseline was set. This field stores time-phased cost, so views like Task Usage and Resource Usage show baseline costs for each time period.

- **Baseline Budget Work.** Saves the budgeted person-hours (page 278) for work resources and budgeted units for material resources. You can compare this field with the Budget Work field to see how actual (or scheduled) budgeted work compares with the baseline budget.

- **Baseline Budget Cost.** Shows the planned budget for project cost resources (page 280).

NOTE If you use the Fixed Cost field to track costs like fixed-price contracts (page 268), the Baseline Fixed Cost field holds your baseline fixed-cost value. The Baseline Fixed Cost Accrual field documents the accrual method you set for your fixed cost. If you're wondering about the Baseline Deliverable Start and Baseline Deliverable Finish fields, these correspond to the planned start and finish dates for the Deliverable feature in Project Server, which lets you publish project deliverables on which other projects may depend.

Setting a Baseline

Project doesn't set baselines automatically, because it has no way of knowing when your plan is ready to be saved for posterity. When stakeholders approve the project plan, one of your very next steps is to set a baseline in Project to save the targets you've committed to. To set the first baseline in Project, do the following:

1. **Open the file you want to set a baseline for, head to the Project tab's Schedule section, and choose Set Baseline→Set Baseline.**

   The Set Baseline dialog box (Figure 12-2) opens.

FIGURE 12-2

The options that Project selects automatically are exactly what you want for the first baseline you set. In fact, you can set up to 11 different baselines, which is a handy way to track trends in performance over time. The information for the other 10 baselines resides in fields whose names begin with Baseline1, Baseline2, and so on.

2. **If this is the first baseline for your project, make sure the "Set baseline" box is set to Baseline and that the "Entire project" option is selected.**

   Whether you plan to set only one baseline or are setting the first of several, save your plan to Baseline this time around. When you first set a baseline, you want to save the values for the entire project. Later on, you may want to save values for selected tasks, like when you add tasks to a project.

3. **Click OK.**

   Project stores the current values for start, finish, duration, work, and costs in the corresponding Baseline fields. The next time you open the Set Baseline dialog box, the "Set baseline" box shows the date you set the baseline.

4. **To save a second copy of the baseline you just created, repeat steps 1–3. In step 2, choose a different baseline in the "Set baseline" box.**

   The box on page 378 explains why it's a good idea to save two copies of your most recent baseline.

■ EDITING A SET BASELINE

Suppose a stakeholder makes a stink about the project plan *after* you've set the baseline. If the other stakeholders acquiesce, you can modify the project plan to address the issues. Once you've made the necessary changes, you'll want to save the edited plan so the baseline reflects your changes.

If a baseline already has values, you usually don't want to overwrite them because you'll lose track of any variances between the original baseline and the actual performance. Here's how to reset just the changed tasks in a baseline that already contains values:

1. **In the Set Baseline dialog box (Project→Set Baseline→Set Baseline), select the name of the baseline you want to reset.**

   If you've saved only one baseline, it appears automatically in the "Set baseline" box.

2. **Select the "Selected tasks" option if the changes affect only a portion of the project.**

   If the changes affect the entire project and you want to replace the baseline completely, select the "Entire project" option instead.

3. **Click OK.**

   A message box warns that you're about to overwrite a saved baseline. Click Yes, and Project overwrites the current baseline values with the new ones and changes the "last saved date" value.

Setting Additional Baselines

Schedule and cost performance can fluctuate when projects continue for months or years. For example, after 3 months, a project is 10 percent behind schedule; at the 6-month mark, it's 20 percent behind schedule; then, at 1 year, your recovery strategy pays off and the project is only 2 percent behind schedule. By setting additional baselines at key points in a project (at the end of each phase or at regular intervals), you can evaluate trends over time.

An additional baseline is also helpful when a project experiences a big change—an interruption to the schedule, a big scope increase, or a spike in the price of materials. Suppose your project is 20 percent complete when a different, high-priority project intervenes. When you resume your project, the original baseline start and finish dates are too old to produce meaningful variances, and costs may have changed significantly. When you recommence work on your project, you need a new baseline that reflects the updated targets. If you don't want to lose the original baseline values, you can save the original to one of the additional 10 that Project provides and save your new baseline to Project's primary baseline fields.

To set another baseline for a project, follow these steps:

1. **In the Project tab's Schedule section, choose Set Baseline→Set Baseline.**

   The Set Baseline dialog box opens with the "Set baseline" box set to Baseline, and the "Entire project" option selected.

2. **In the "Set baseline" box, choose the baseline you want to set, such as Baseline2.**

   Baselines that have already been set have "(last saved on mm/dd/yy)" appended to the end of their names, where mm/dd/yy represents the most recent date you saved the baseline.

3. **Make sure the "Entire project" option is selected.**

   When you save any of the 11 baselines for the first time, you want to save the values for the entire project. Later on, you may want to save values only for selected tasks—for instance, when you add tasks to a project, as described on page 378.

4. **Click OK.**

   Project stores the current values for start, finish, duration, work, and costs in the corresponding Baseline fields, such as Baseline1 Start, Baseline1 Finish, Baseline1 Duration, Baseline1 Work, and Baseline1 Cost. The next time you open the Set Baseline dialog box, the "Set baseline" drop-down list shows the last saved date for the baseline.

   If the selected baseline was saved before, Project warns you that the baseline has already been used and asks if you want to overwrite it. Click Yes to overwrite existing values (if, for example, you've used up the 11 baselines and want to reuse an older one). If you don't want to overwrite it, click No, and then select a different baseline back in the Set Baseline dialog box.

POWER USERS' CLINIC

Viewing Recent Variances

You can make your life easier by using Project's primary baseline (the one named Baseline) to store the most recent values, because that's the one Project uses to calculate variances. By saving your most recent values to the Project baseline named Baseline, it's easy to see the most recent cost and schedule variances. Project calculates Variance field values by subtracting a Baseline field from the current corresponding field value. For example, Cost Variance equals Cost minus Baseline Cost.

Here's how to reserve Baseline for the most recent values as you set additional baselines:

1. When you save your original plan values, set the baseline's name to Baseline.

2. Immediately save the original plan a second time, but this time as Baseline1. That way, your original baseline values are safely stored in Baseline1. And because the original plan is also stored in Baseline, Project variance fields show variances from the original plan.

3. When you set the next baseline, save it as Baseline, so variance fields show variances from the newest baseline.

4. Immediately save the project schedule *again* as Baseline2. This permanently records the second baseline.

5. For each additional baseline, save the project schedule once as Baseline and once as the next empty baseline.

Adding New Tasks to a Baseline

A baseline starts out representing your original plan, but after the plan has been approved, people sometimes ask for changes, which often leads to new tasks in the schedule. For example, a client may make change requests and agree to the extra cost and time. The new finish dates and cost aren't variances from the original plan (because the client is agreeing to *amend* the original plan), so you want the baseline to absorb these additions.

If project execution hasn't started, you can simply reset the entire baseline (page 375). However, when your Project file already includes actual values, you don't want to overwrite baseline values for existing tasks. If you do, Project replaces the original baseline values with current ones, and any variances disappear. Instead, you want to *add* tasks to the baseline, setting the baseline values for only those new tasks and leaving baseline values for other tasks alone.

To add tasks to a baseline that's already set, follow these steps:

1. **In Gantt Chart view or another task-oriented view, select the tasks you want to add to the baseline.**

   You can select any kind of task, including low-level tasks, milestones, or summary tasks. If you want Project to roll up the values for the added tasks into specific summary tasks (see step 5), then be sure to select the summary tasks that you want the baseline to update.

2. **In the Project tab's Schedule section, choose Set Baseline→Set Baseline.**

   The Set Baseline dialog box opens with Baseline and the "Entire project" options selected.

3. **In the "Set baseline" drop-down list, choose the baseline to which you want to add tasks, and then choose the "Selected tasks" option.**

   The checkboxes underneath the "Roll up baselines" label become active, as shown in Figure 12-3. These checkboxes tell Project how you want the added baseline values rolled up into summary tasks.

FIGURE 12-3

Project doesn't automatically update summary task baseline values when you add tasks to a baseline. It assumes that you want to keep original baseline values for summary tasks so you can see how the added tasks affect performance. In effect, the new tasks produce variances in existing summary tasks because they add to duration, work, and cost.

4. **To update all summary tasks with the new task values, turn on the "To all summary tasks" checkbox.**

This checkbox tells Project to update the baseline values for all summary tasks up to the top level, as shown in Figure 12-4.

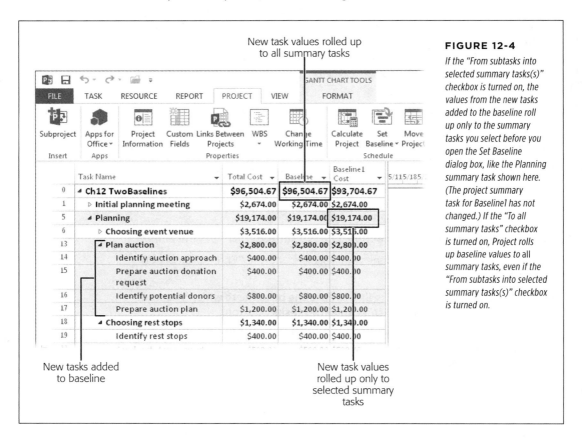

New task values rolled up
to all summary tasks

FIGURE 12-4

If the "From subtasks into selected summary tasks(s)" checkbox is turned on, the values from the new tasks added to the baseline roll up only to the summary tasks you select before you open the Set Baseline dialog box, like the Planning summary task shown here. (The project summary task for Baseline1 has not changed.) If the "To all summary tasks" checkbox is turned on, Project rolls up baseline values to all summary tasks, even if the "From subtasks into selected summary tasks(s)" checkbox is turned on.

New tasks added
to baseline

New task values
rolled up only to
selected summary
tasks

5. **If you want the values for new tasks to update the summary tasks you select (in step 1), turn on the "From subtasks into selected summary task(s)" checkbox.**

This checkbox tells Project to update the baseline values for the summary tasks you select before you open the Set Baseline dialog box with the values from the added tasks. By doing so, you update the baseline for the summary task to which the new tasks belong so you can see their effect. At the same time, you can keep higher-level summary tasks as they were so you can also see the impact of the new tasks on your original schedule and budget.

6. **Click OK.**

Project updates the tasks you specified. If you want to change Project's standard baseline roll-up behavior to match the checkboxes you turned on, click "Set as Default" *before* you click OK.

Saving Sets of Start and Finish Dates

The second option in the Set Baseline dialog box is "Set interim plan." Unlike Project baselines, *interim plans* save only start and finish dates, not duration, cost, and work. If you don't need a full baseline, you can save an interim plan instead. The box on page 382 discusses various uses for interim plans.

To save start and finish dates in an interim plan, follow these steps:

1. **In the Project tab's Schedule section, choose Set Baseline→Set Baseline.**

   The Set Baseline dialog box opens.

2. **Select the "Set interim plan" option.**

   The Copy and Into boxes come to life, waiting for you to tell them the start and finish fields to copy from and to.

3. **In the Copy drop-down list, choose the set of start and finish dates you want to copy.**

   Project automatically selects Scheduled Start/Finish, which copies the current task start and finish dates that Project calculates and is usually what you want. However, if you want to copy dates from a baseline or another interim plan, choose the name of the baseline or interim plan instead. For example, suppose Baseline1 is an old baseline that you want to reuse for more recent information. You can save the baseline dates to an interim plan by choosing Baseline1 in the Copy box and then choosing an interim plan in the Into box.

4. **In the Into drop-down list, choose the fields into which you want to copy the start and finish dates.**

   Project selects Start1/Finish1 here, which means it will copy dates to the first interim plan. However, if you want to save another interim plan, choose Start2/Finish2 for the second interim plan, up to Start10/Finish10 for the 10th interim plan.

   The Into drop-down list also includes the names of baselines. You might wonder why you would copy interim plan dates into a baseline, particularly if the baseline already has values. It turns out that copying from an interim plan to a baseline is how you bring interim plans saved in earlier versions of Project into your Project 2013 baselines. For example, choose Start3/Finish3 in the Copy drop-down list and Baseline3 in the Into drop-down list, and Project copies the interim plan dates into that baseline.

5. **Select either the "Entire project" or "Selected tasks" option, and then click OK.**

Saving values to interim plans works just like saving baselines. You can save the dates for the entire project or save dates for only some tasks, as described on page 379.

Baselines vs. Interim Plans

What should I use interim plans for?

With up to 11 baselines available, you may wonder why Project offers interim plans as well. Interim plans popped up in Project several versions ago, when the program offered only one baseline and project managers clamored for more.

Even now, interim plans have some uses. First, if you import a project schedule from Project 2002 and earlier, any additional baseline information resides in interim plan fields (Start1/Finish1 through Start10/Finish10). You can copy that informa-

tion from interim plan Start and Finish fields (Start2/Finish2, for example) into baseline fields like Baseline2 (page 378).

In addition, if you save additional baselines regularly, 11 baselines may not be enough. As a workaround, you can save interim plans to act as partial baselines in between the full baselines you save. Although interim plans can't track cost and work changes, you can track schedule performance by watching how interim plan task dates change over time.

Clearing a Baseline

When you run out of empty baselines, you can overwrite a previously saved baseline (page 375) with current values. But suppose that you set a baseline by accident or that a set baseline is so obsolete you want to completely eliminate it. Clearing a baseline removes all its values. Here's what you do:

1. **In the Project tab's Schedule section, choose Set Baseline→Clear Baseline.**

The Clear Baseline dialog box appears.

2. **In the Clear Baseline dialog box, make sure the "Clear baseline plan" option is selected.**

If you want to clear an interim plan instead, select the "Clear interim plan" option, and then, in the "Clear interim plan" drop-down list, choose the plan's name.

3. **In the "Clear baseline plan" drop-down list, choose the baseline you want to clear.**

The "Clear baseline plan" drop-down list automatically chooses Project's primary baseline (Baseline), so you must take care to select the baseline you want to clear.

4. **To clear the entire baseline, select the "Entire project" option.**

"Entire project" is what you'll choose most often: You don't often clear values for only some tasks. But, for example, if you want to remove tasks from the baseline because the client has agreed to reduce the project's scope, then you have to select the tasks *before* opening the Clear Baseline dialog box and then choose the "Selected tasks" option.

5. **Click OK.**

Project clears the baseline's values. However, Project doesn't update higher-level summary tasks to reflect the removal of the task baseline values.

Viewing Baselines

When you initially set a baseline, its values are exactly the same as the current Project-calculated field values. As the project team gets to work, the current values begin to stray from the baseline. Evaluating project performance (page 429) involves a lot of reviewing the variances between current and baseline values. You can see baseline values in several places.

For a 30,000-foot view of baseline and current data, head to the Project tab's Properties section and click Project Information. In the Project Information dialog box, click Statistics to open the Project Statistics dialog box, which shows top-level summary information for the whole project, as shown in Figure 12-5.

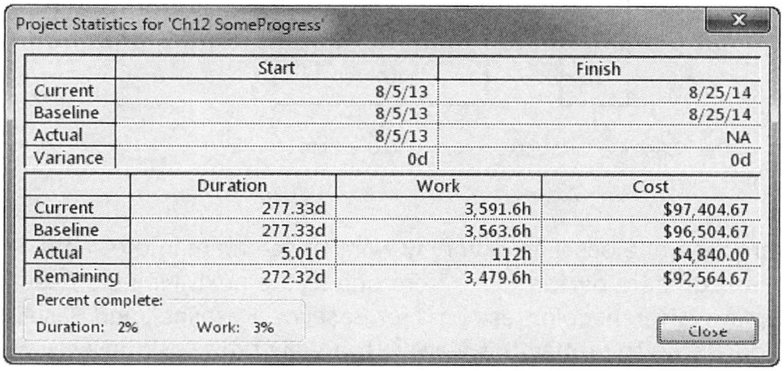

Project Statistics for 'Ch12 SomeProgress'			
	Start		Finish
Current	8/5/13		8/25/14
Baseline	8/5/13		8/25/14
Actual	8/5/13		NA
Variance	0d		0d
	Duration	Work	Cost
Current	277.33d	3,591.6h	$97,404.67
Baseline	277.33d	3,563.6h	$96,504.67
Actual	5.01d	112h	$4,840.00
Remaining	272.32d	3,479.6h	$92,564.67
Percent complete:			
Duration: 2%	Work: 3%		Close

FIGURE 12-5

The Project Statistics dialog box contains current, baseline, and actual values as well as the variance for the project's start date, finish date, duration, total work, and total cost.

■ VIEWING BASELINE AND CURRENT VALUES IN A GANTT CHART VIEW

When you want to compare the baseline schedule with the current status, Tracking Gantt view is perfect. It shows gray task bars for the baseline start and finish dates immediately below task bars for the current schedule. To display Tracking Gantt view, shown in Figure 12-6, in the Task tab's View section, click the Gantt Chart down arrow, and then choose Tracking Gantt. (Or, in the View tab's Task Views section, click the Gantt Chart down arrow, and then choose Tracking Gantt.)

TIP From the ribbon, you can display any baseline you want in any Gantt Chart view. Display the Gantt Chart view you want and then click the Gantt Chart tools | Format tab. In the Bar Styles section, click the Baseline down arrow, and then choose the baseline you want to display.

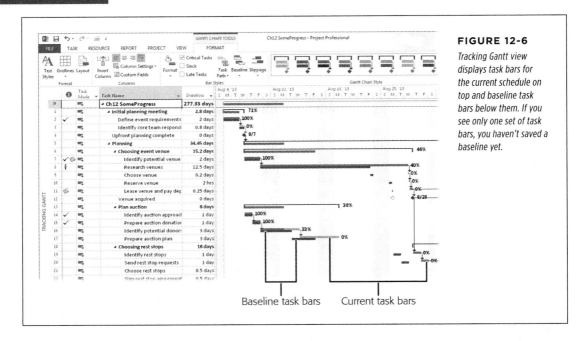

FIGURE 12-6

Tracking Gantt view displays task bars for the current schedule on top and baseline task bars below them. If you see only one set of task bars, you haven't saved a baseline yet.

Baseline task bars   Current task bars

If you save more than one baseline, you may want to see them in the same Gantt Chart so you can compare performance from one to the next. Multiple Baselines Gantt view displays different color task bars for Baseline, Baseline1, and Baseline2, as shown in Figure 12-7. To display this view, in the View tab's Task Views section, choose Other Views→More Views. In the More Views dialog box, double-click Multiple Baselines Gantt.

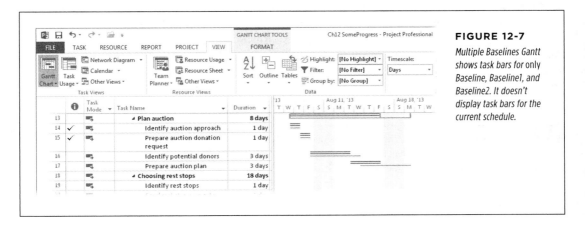

FIGURE 12-7

Multiple Baselines Gantt shows task bars for only Baseline, Baseline1, and Baseline2. It doesn't display task bars for the current schedule.

If you want to show more baselines or different baselines in Multiple Baselines Gantt, you can modify the view to include task bars for other baselines. For example, you may want to see task bars for Baseline1 through Baseline4.

To change the baselines that the task bars represent, do the following:

1. **Copy Multiple Baselines Gantt view and give it a name like FourBaselines.**

   Because swapping task bars requires several steps, it's a good idea to copy the view and then make the changes to the copy (page 598). Then you can copy the customized view to your global template and use it in other Project files. With Multiple Baselines Gantt view displayed, in the View tab's Task Views section, choose Other Views→More Views. In the More Views dialog box, click Copy, type a new name in the Name box, and then click OK. Back in the More Views dialog box, click Close.

2. **On the Gantt Chart Tools | Format tab, in the Bar Styles section, click Format→Bar Styles.**

   The Bar Styles dialog box opens.

3. **Click the cell that contains the first task bar style name you want to replace.**

   For example, click Baseline to edit the normal task bars for Baseline.

4. **Click the same cell a second time to make the name editable, and then type the new baseline number at the end of the name.**

   For example, to change Baseline to Baseline1, make the name editable, and then type *1* at the end. To change Baseline1 to Baseline4, drag over the 1 at the end of the name and then type *4*.

5. **In the From cell in the same row, choose the start date field for the new baseline.**

   For example, to switch the view to show Baseline4, choose Baseline4 Start. This tells Project to draw the beginning of the task bars based on the Baseline4 Start field values.

6. **In the To cell in the same row, choose the finish date field for the new baseline.**

   To complete the task bar style that shows Baseline4, choose Baseline4 Finish. These From and To settings tell Project to draw the task bars for Baseline4 from Baseline4 Start to Baseline4 Finish in the timescale.

7. **Repeat steps 3–6 to modify the Split, Milestone, and Summary task bars to use the same baseline.**

Simply editing the task bar's name isn't enough. The fields you choose for the task bar's start and finish dates are what really matter.

8. **If you want to replace another baseline in the view, repeat steps 3–7.**

Click OK when you're done.

To include an *additional* baseline in the view, you have to insert task bar rows for the baseline's normal, split, milestone, and summary tasks. Here are the steps for inserting the rows:

1. **Open Multiple Baselines Gantt view or a copy you've created.**

Consider copying the Multiple Baselines Gantt view for your new multi-baseline Gantt Chart (step 1 on page 385 explains how). If you copy the customized view to your global template, you can use it in other Project files.

2. **On the Gantt Chart Tools | Format tab, in the Bar Styles section, click Format→Bar Styles.**

The Bar Styles dialog box opens.

3. **Select the row for the task bar you want to duplicate, and then click Cut Row.**

Project removes the row from the table.

4. **Before you do anything else, click Paste Row.**

Project inserts the cut row back where it was originally.

5. **Select the row below where you want to insert the new row, and then click Paste Row again.**

Project inserts another copy of the row immediately above the row you select.

6. **Edit the new row's Name, From, and To cells to match the baseline you want to show.**

To display Baseline4, for example, change the name to include Baseline4, and then, in the From and To cells, choose Baseline4 Start and Baseline4 Finish, respectively.

7. **On the Bars tab in the lower half of the Bar Styles dialog box, choose the shape and color you want for the bar.**

Baseline1, Baseline2, and Baseline3 already use red, blue, and green respectively, so choose a color like teal, orange, or purple. In the Shape box, choose a top, middle, or bottom narrow bar.

8. **If you're including more than three baselines in Multiple Baselines Gantt view, add a second task bar row to the view.**

In Multiple Baselines Gantt view, Project uses narrow task bars so you can display up to three baselines on the same row of the Gantt Chart. But if you want to see more than three baselines, you have to tell Project to add another row to the view. To do that, in the Bar Styles dialog box, head to the new row you created in step 5 and, in that row's Row cell, type 2, as illustrated in Figure 12-8. Doing this tells Project to place the baseline's task bar on a second row in the Gantt Chart.

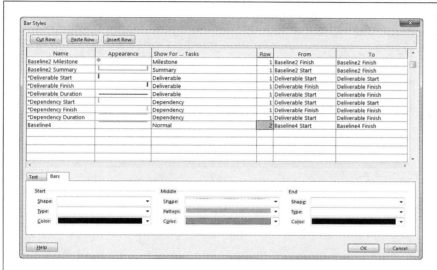

FIGURE 12-8

Multiple Baselines Gantt view includes task bar styles for Deliverable fields. Don't be misled: The Deliverable feature is available only when you use Project Server.

9. **Repeat steps 3–8 to create task bars for split, milestone, and summary tasks for the baseline.**

If you choose the narrow task bars that run at the top, middle, and bottom of a row, you can add three more baselines to the second row of the view, just like Multiple Baselines Gantt view does in the first row.

■ VIEWING BASELINE VALUES IN A TABLE

Although Multiple Baselines Gantt view's timescale shows different task bars for each baseline, you probably want to see baseline costs, duration, and work. The table area of one of the Gantt Chart views is the perfect place to see these values.

Project includes the Baseline table, which displays columns for all the Baseline fields: Baseline Duration, Baseline Start, Baseline Finish, Baseline Work, and Baseline Cost. To display this table, in the View tab's Data section, click the Tables down arrow, and then choose More Tables on the shortcut menu. In the More Tables dialog box, select Baseline, and then click Apply.

TIP When you see values of "0" or "NA" in baseline fields, that's Project's way of telling you that you haven't saved that baseline yet.

If you would rather add baseline fields to another table, you can simply insert columns in the table. To add the Baseline Cost and Baseline Work fields to the Variance table, for example, right-click the table heading area where you want to insert the column. On the shortcut menu, choose Insert Column and then, from the drop-down menu, choose the baseline field you want to add.

NOTE Task Details view can show baseline start and finish dates. Although the form opens initially with the Current option selected, select the Baseline option to see the baseline start and finish dates.

Projects in Action

Tracking Status

After you finish planning a project and get approval from everyone necessary, you save a baseline of the project and give the signal for work to begin. You may then be tempted to sit back at this point and rest on your...ahem...laurels. The hardest part of your job as project manager is done, right?

Wrong. Now that you've stepped over the threshold from planning into execution, plenty of challenges await and you really earn your keep as a project manager: You monitor progress, evaluate performance, make adjustments as necessary, and manage the changes inevitable in projects.

Before you can evaluate project performance and make corrections, you need to know where the project stands. Project status is made up of two components: actual progress and forecasts of what remains to be done. Tracking status is all about information like tasks completed, when tasks actually start and finish, hours worked, and costs incurred. Just as important, you need to find out what's still left to do—that is, the duration or work that team members estimate that it will take to finish. This chapter begins by discussing the merits of different approaches to tracking status and the information you can collect. Then you'll learn about collecting that status data from your team—and several ways to do it.

The next step is updating your Project file with that status info. This chapter describes how to record status data, depending on the information you collect. If you opt for tracking status to a high level of detail, you'll also learn how to update progress at the assignment level, whether task by task or for the entire project.

■ Methods for Tracking Status

The approach you choose to track the progress of your project depends on your organization, the type of project, and the level of detail your stakeholders need. From a practical standpoint, it also depends on how much time you have to gather and incorporate progress data into the project plan. (Collecting detailed status data won't do any good if you don't have time to enter it into Project.) This section starts by describing the difference between updating tasks and updating assignments, and when it makes sense to use each one. Then you'll learn about the specific data you can collect.

Updating Assignments vs. Updating Tasks

The first decision you need to make about status is whether to update tasks or assignments. Updating assignments gives you a more accurate picture of status than updating tasks does, but it also demands more time from you and your team members. If your team members are too busy to submit status updates or you can't keep up with entering the data in your Project file, then your schedule won't reflect what's really happening in your project—and you won't have the information you need to make corrections. For that reason, updating tasks makes more sense for most projects.

NOTE In Project, you can update both assignments and tasks within the same project—but you can't update them both for the same task. If you update assignments on a task, the program rolls the assignment values up to the task level. If you update a task, you can tell Project to distribute the task's values to its assignments.

Here's the lowdown on both approaches:

- **Updating assignments.** With this approach, team members assigned to your project report actual hours for their assignments, as well as their estimates for each assignment's remaining hours. When you enter this data into your schedule, Project rolls up values for a task's assignments to calculate its overall duration, work, and percent complete. The downside is that the volume of data quickly adds up if you have more than a handful of tasks and people. Typically, you'll update at the assignment level if your stakeholders require the detail that updating assignments provides.

NOTE This method is usually feasible only if you have an electronic method for collecting status data from team members *and* an automated method for transferring that data into Project (for example, the timesheet system available in Project Server). Without an automated system, team members might balk at the time it takes to report their statuses, you might not get timesheet data entered in a timely fashion, or errors could creep into your data as it's transcribed from a timesheet into a Project file.

- **Updating tasks.** This approach takes less time than updating assignments, yet it provides a reasonably accurate picture of schedule status. With this method, you typically collect and record actual and remaining durations and actual start and finish dates for project tasks. (You can also collect actual and remaining work hours if you want a more accurate status.) With this approach, Project takes care of allocating actual hours to assignments and time periods.

What Data to Collect

Project offers a variety of fields for recording status information. The good news is that you can update your project accurately using as few as three fields. This section describes the alternatives and when it makes sense to use each one.

For a complete picture of status, you need three types of information about tasks or assignments:

- **Actual start date.** This is the date that a task or assignment actually starts. In Project, you record this info in the Actual Start field.

- **What's been completed.** Depending on the level of detail you choose to track, you can use the actual duration (Actual Duration field), actual work (Actual Work field), or percentage complete (% Complete or % Work Complete) to track what's been completed.

- **What work still remains.** If you track duration, you collect remaining duration (Remaining Duration field) or remaining work (Remaining Work field) information.

> **NOTE** When a task is complete, Project calculates its actual finish date (Actual Finish field). However, you can change this date, if necessary.

Because Project uses values that you enter to calculate other fields, these three types of status information translate into four main methods for collecting status data. Here are your options and the pros and cons of each:

- **Actual and remaining duration.** Asking team members for these two bits of information is the quickest and easiest way to get accurate task status. *Actual duration* is the number of work days someone has already worked on a task, so it's what's been completed. *Remaining duration* is the number of work days the person estimates they'll need to finish the task, so it's a forecast of what remains. You also need to ask for actual start dates, so you know whether tasks start early, late, or right on time. Although Project can calculate the actual finish date from other fields, it's still a good idea to ask people for the actual finish date, because it determines when successor tasks start or finish (page 177). (The box on page 394 explains how Project calculates values for different fields using the data you enter.)

- **Actual and remaining work.** For smaller projects and shorter tasks, getting statuses in terms of days (actual and remaining duration) might be too imprecise. In that case, it's better to ask team members for actual and remaining *work*, instead. *Actual work* is the number of hours someone has already worked on a task, and *remaining work* is the hours they estimate it will take them to finish the task.

You also need actual start and finish dates, as you do when you collect actual and remaining duration, so Project knows when to schedule successor tasks.

> **NOTE** In order to use work fields, you need to have work resources assigned to tasks (page 228).

- **Actual and remaining work at the assignment level.** This method uses actual work and remaining work, just like the previous method. But in this case, you assign values at the individual *assignment* level, rather than for the entire task. For the highest level of detail, you can assign work day by day in the time-phased portion of Task Usage or Resource Usage view, but be forewarned—it's a time-consuming endeavor.

- **Percent complete (% Complete) and remaining duration.** One advantage to this approach is that updating a task's % Complete value is as easy as clicking one of the percent-complete buttons in the Task tab's Schedule section or on the mini-toolbar (page 416). In addition to % Complete data, you also need the task's actual start date and remaining duration.

> **NOTE** If you use % Complete to collect task status, it's essential that you also get an estimate of remaining duration or work from your team members. Without remaining duration, percent complete could mean almost anything: the percentage team members think should be done, what they wish was done, or the percentage they think you want to hear so you'll leave them alone.

POWER USERS' CLINIC

Project's Status Calculations for Tasks

Project calculates values for any of the status fields you don't update directly. That is, when you enter information into one field, Project calculates the values that belong in other associated fields. The following list gives you an "under the hood" look at the relationship between commonly used task-related status fields:

- Actual Start = Scheduled Start unless otherwise entered
- Actual Finish = Scheduled Finish unless otherwise entered
- Duration = Actual Duration + Remaining Duration
- % Complete = (Actual Duration / Duration) × 100
- Work = Actual Work + Remaining Work
- % Work Complete= (Actual Work / Work) × 100

For example, say a team member reports a task's Actual Duration as 3 days and Remaining Duration as 9 days. When you enter that information, Project calculates the task's Duration value as 12 days, and the task's % Complete value as 25%.

In addition, you can rearrange any of these formulas so that Project calculates other fields. For example, Remaining Duration is equal to Duration minus Actual Duration. So if you enter a value in an Actual Duration field, Project calculates Remaining Duration by subtracting Actual Duration from the Duration value.

■ Preparing to Update Your Project

You may be raring to start adding status updates to your Project file, but you need to have a few things in place before you begin. Your file needs to be set up so Project can calculate the schedule and the variance between your plan and what actually occurs. You also need to tell Project how you want it to handle the updates you enter. In addition, you can make your updating job easier by setting up a customized view to go with your progress-tracking method. This section steps through each of these prerequisites.

Setting Tasks to Auto Scheduled Mode

If you've fine-tuned your schedule to make it realistic and to balance resource work-loads (see Chapter 11), your project's tasks are already set to Auto Scheduled mode (page 64). But if any tasks are set to Manually Scheduled mode and should be Auto Scheduled instead, switch them to Auto Scheduled mode before you start entering updates. (See page 60 for reasons why you might create manually scheduled tasks and keep them that way.) That way, Project can recalculate your schedule based on the status updates you enter. For example, if an update shows that a task is going to take longer to complete, the program takes care of rescheduling the task's successors based on the revised finish date. Flip to page 67 to learn how to change a task's mode.

Setting a Baseline

Another important step to perform before recording status updates is to set a baseline for your project (page 375). When you have a baseline saved, Project keeps track of your original planned values as well as the current scheduled values. That way, you can see the variances between your plan and what actually occurs to identify issues that need your attention. (The box on page 396 explains the difference between baseline, scheduled, and actual values.)

Project Settings for Status Updates

Project has several settings related to updating tasks. Some of them are set the way you usually want them right out of the box, but you'll probably want to change others. This section identifies the settings you should choose for status updates and why.

To get to the following settings, start by choosing File→Options to open the Project Options dialog box.

FREQUENTLY ASKED QUESTION

Baseline, Scheduled, and Actual Values

What's the difference between baseline, scheduled, and actual information?

Now that you're about to enter actual values, you may wonder how baseline, scheduled, and actual fields differ. Here's how they work:

- **Baseline fields.** Also known as *planned* information, baseline fields are a snapshot of what your project's Start, Finish, Duration, Work, Cost, Budget Work, and Budget Cost values were when you saved the baseline. You should save a baseline immediately after the project plan has been approved or just before resources begin working on their first tasks. As you and your team work through the project, you can compare baseline values against scheduled or actual values to analyze variances and predict problems. For manually scheduled tasks without dates, the Baseline Estimated Start and Baseline Estimated Finish dates (page 374) show the dates that most closely match where the tasks occur in the schedule.

- **Scheduled fields.** Also known as *current* information, scheduled information encompasses all the fields throughout Project that have anything to do with the schedule. Unlike baseline information, scheduled information is constantly in flux. Whenever you enter actual progress information and forecasts of what remains, Project recalculates task schedules and costs to accommodate the new reality.

- **Actual fields.** Often referred to simply as *actuals*, these fields contain progress information for completed and in-progress tasks. You explicitly enter actuals into the fields you're most concerned about; Project calculates any other actual information based on the formulas defining the relationships between the fields. For example, if you enter dates in a task's Actual Start and Actual Finish fields, then Project calculates the task's Actual Duration as the span between the two dates.

■ SETTINGS IN THE SCHEDULE CATEGORY

On the left side of the Project Options dialog box, click Schedule. Here are the relevant settings in that category and what they do:

- **Split in-progress tasks.** This setting (which lives in the "Scheduling options for this project" section) is turned on initially, which is what you want. With this setting turned on, Project can split tasks to reflect when work occurs—for example, to move the incomplete portion of the task to after the *status date* (the date through which you've collected status information).

- **Updating Task status updates resource status.** This setting is in the "Calculation options for this project" section. If you update tasks (rather than individual assignments), keep this setting turned on. That way, Project distributes task values you enter to the assignment level, calculating the actual and remaining work and cost for associated resource assignments. Turn this setting off if you want to enter updates for individual assignments. In that case, Project rolls up assignment values to calculate the parent task's status.

■ **SETTINGS IN THE ADVANCED CATEGORY**

On the left side of the Project Options dialog box, click Advanced and scroll down to the "Calculation options for this project" section, shown in Figure 13-1. Here are the relevant settings in that category and what they do:

- **Move end of completed parts after status date back to status date.** This setting is turned off initially, but you usually want to turn it on. If you do, Project moves the completed work to before the status date. (The actual duration task bar moves to before the status date, and actual work is recorded in time periods before the status date.) In other words, the program records the completed work as occurring in the past, which is what actually happened.

  For example, say your status date is August 16 and a 4-day task has a start date of August 20. But the task starts early—on August 15. With this setting turned on, when you enter the task's status information (for example, entering actual start date, actual duration, and remaining duration in the Update Tasks dialog box and then clicking OK), Project moves the actual start date to August 15 and sets the percent complete to 50 (because August 15 and 16 are two workdays). However, the remaining work is still scheduled to start on August 22—the date the remaining work was scheduled to occur based on the original start date. In this case, the task is split into two segments: The completed work runs from August 15 to August 16, and the remaining work is scheduled for August 22 to August 23.

  - **And move start of remaining parts back to status date.** If you turn on the "Move end of completed parts after status date back to status date" setting, this setting's checkbox becomes active. It's turned off initially, which means that, when you enter status info for tasks, Project keeps the incomplete portions of tasks on the dates they were originally scheduled to occur. But if people finish some of their work early, chances are good that they're going to keep working on their assignments. That's why you usually want to turn this setting on—so Project moves the incomplete parts of tasks to start as of the status date.

    Using the example from the previous bullet point, if this setting is turned on, Project moves the start of the remaining work to August 19, the first workday after the status date, so the remaining work is scheduled to start immediately after the completed work.

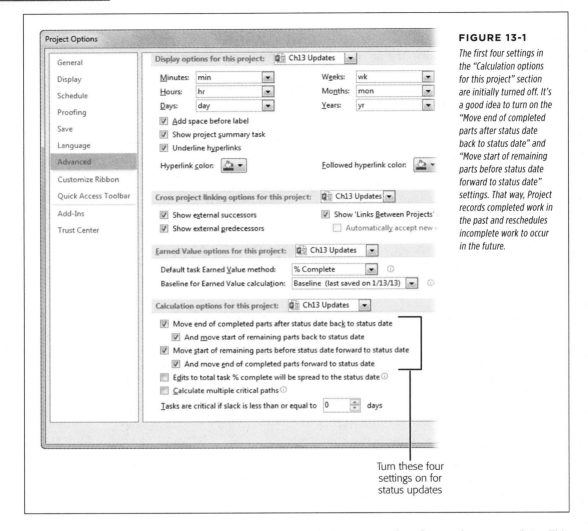

FIGURE 13-1

The first four settings in the "Calculation options for this project" section are initially turned off. It's a good idea to turn on the "Move end of completed parts after status date back to status date" and "Move start of remaining parts before status date forward to status date" settings. That way, Project records completed work in the past and reschedules incomplete work to occur in the future.

Turn these four
settings on for
status updates

- **Move start of remaining parts before status date forward to status date.** This setting is also turned off initially, but you should turn it on. That way, when you enter status info for tasks, Project moves the incomplete part of the task so that it's scheduled to occur in the future (after the status date). That makes sense, because unless you have a time machine, that's when it's going to get done.

Consider a 4-day task with a status date of August 16 that has a scheduled start date of August 8. The task actually starts on August 15, a week late. With this setting turned on, Project leaves that actual start date at August 8 so the completed work shows as occurring on August 8 and 9. However, Project schedules the remaining work to start on August 19, the first workday after the status date. Once again, the task is split in two segments, with the completed work recorded on the original dates and the incomplete work scheduled to start after the status date.

> **NOTE** This setting applies only to tasks that are in progress as of the status date. If a task should have started before the status date but *hasn't*, you'll have to reschedule it to occur in the future.

— **And move end of completed parts forward to status date.** If you turn on the "Move start of remaining parts before status date forward to status date" setting, the checkbox for this setting becomes active. It's turned off initially, which means that, when you enter status info for tasks, Project keeps the completed portions of tasks on their currently scheduled dates. If you turn this setting on, then the task's complete and incomplete portions are contiguous around the status date.

Using the previous example, if this setting is turned on, Project moves the actual start of the completed work to August 15, the day the work really started.

• **Edits to total task % complete will be spread to the status date.** This setting is turned off initially, and there's no reason to turn it on unless you enter values in the % Complete field. In that case, turning this setting on spreads progress evenly up to the status date. For example, if you set a task's % Complete value to 50%, Project divides half the task's work hours evenly over each workday between the task's start date and the status date.

Setting Up a View to Make Updating Easy

As its name implies, Tracking Gantt view helps you track your project's status. It's a good starting point when you're ready to update status values in Project. When you display this view (in the View tab's Task Views section, click the bottom half of the Gantt Chart button, and then choose Tracking Gantt), the timescale includes gray task bars for the project's baseline in the bottom half of each row, as shown in Figure 13-2. The top half of each row displays red and blue task bars for critical and noncritical tasks' current scheduled dates (respectively).

Tracking Gantt view initially displays the Entry table, which doesn't contain the fields that you update for status. The Tracking table (in the View tab's Data section, click Tables→Tracking) contains the right fields, but it doesn't present them in the order that you usually fill them in (as you'll learn shortly). You can drag the columns to reorder them (page 633), but it's easier to download a table with the right fields in the right order. Go to this book's Missing CD page (*www.missingmanuals.com/cds*)

and download the *ProjectMM_Customizations.mpp* file, and then use the Organizer to copy the UpdateDuration and UpdateWork tables into your global template (page 702). Here's what these tables include:

- **The UpdateDuration table,** shown in Figure 13-2, is ideal if you track status with actual and remaining duration. It starts with Task Name and then follows with Actual Start, Actual Duration, Remaining Duration, and Actual Finish. The next two columns are % Complete and Actual Cost, which Project calculates for you. The rest of the fields for updating are at the right side of the table in case you need them (Actual Work, Remaining Work, % Work Complete, and Physical % Complete). (Physical % Complete comes into play when you use earned value analysis to evaluate project performance, as described on page 441.)

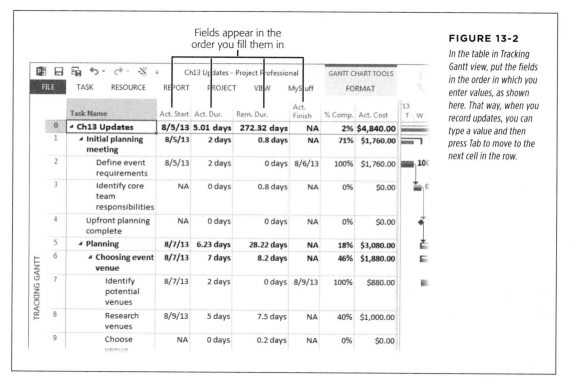

Fields appear in the order you fill them in

FIGURE 13-2

In the table in Tracking Gantt view, put the fields in the order in which you enter values, as shown here. That way, when you record updates, you can type a value and then press Tab to move to the next cell in the row.

	Task Name	Act. Start	Act. Dur.	Rem. Dur.	Act. Finish	% Comp.	Act. Cost
0	◢ **Ch13 Updates**	**8/5/13**	**5.01 days**	**272.32 days**	**NA**	**2%**	**$4,840.00**
1	◢ **Initial planning meeting**	**8/5/13**	**2 days**	**0.8 days**	**NA**	**71%**	**$1,760.00**
2	Define event requirements	8/5/13	2 days	0 days	8/6/13	100%	$1,760.00
3	Identify core team responsibilities	NA	0 days	0.8 days	NA	0%	$0.00
4	Upfront planning complete	NA	0 days	0 days	NA	0%	$0.00
5	◢ **Planning**	**8/7/13**	**6.23 days**	**28.22 days**	**NA**	**18%**	**$3,080.00**
6	◢ **Choosing event venue**	**8/7/13**	**7 days**	**8.2 days**	**NA**	**46%**	**$1,880.00**
7	Identify potential venues	8/7/13	2 days	0 days	8/9/13	100%	$880.00
8	Research venues	8/9/13	5 days	7.5 days	NA	40%	$1,000.00
9	Choose venue	NA	0 days	0.2 days	NA	0%	$0.00

TRACKING GANTT

- **The UpdateWork table** is set up similarly to UpdateDuration. The only difference is that Actual Work and Remaining Work appear between Actual Start and Actual Finish, so it's perfect if you track status with actual and remaining work instead of the duration fields.

TIP Tracking Gantt view displays progress task bars based on the value in the % Complete field, which is in turn based on the Actual Duration of the task. If you update work, you can change the progress task bars to show progress based on the % Work Complete field instead. To do so, in the Gantt Chart Tools | Format tab's Bar Styles section, click Format→Bar Styles. In the Bar Styles dialog box, find the Critical Progress and Task Progress rows. In both these rows, in the To cells on the right side of the dialog box, replace CompleteThrough with % Work Complete.

Once the view and table are set up the way you want, you can save those settings as a new view. Here are the steps:

1. **In the View tab's Task Views section, click the bottom half of the Gantt Chart button, and then choose Save View.**

   The Save View dialog box opens.

2. **If necessary, select the "Save as a New View" option, type a name in the Name box (such as UpdateStatus), and then click OK.**

   Project saves the new view. If you click the bottom half of the Gantt Chart button again, you'll see the view listed under the Custom heading on the drop-down menu.

NOTE To save some time, you can download a ready-made view from this book's Missing CD page at *www.missingmanuals.com/cds*. The *ProjectMM_Customizations.mpp* file contains a view named UpdateStatus, which uses the UpdateDuration table described on page 400. In addition, it's set up to display only work tasks, since you don't need to update summary tasks. After you download the file, use the Organizer to copy the view into your Project *global.mpt* file, as described on page 702.

■ Obtaining Status Data

Once you've chosen your preferred progress-tracking approach and prepped your Project file for updating, the battle has only begun. In this section, you'll learn ways to obtain the progress information you need without pulling team members' teeth.

Collecting Task Status from Team Members

You can get most status information from your team members, although it's not always as easy as it sounds. This section describes some of the best methods for extracting reliable and consistent information from resources.

NOTE If your organization uses Project Server, then team members can submit their progress information through the Project Web App interface. That way, the data is automatically available for you to review and incorporate into your project plan.

■ CREATING AN UPDATE FORM

Whether you intend to ask people for updates in person, via email, or by using some other mechanism, you can simplify data collection by adding the tasks that are under way (or should be) to a form. An Excel spreadsheet is a great option: You can print it out and take it to your status meeting to fill in there or email it to team members. This section shows you how to quickly construct a task-update form.

The first thing you need is a list of the tasks you need to update. It's easy to produce that list in Project and then copy it into an Excel spreadsheet. Here are the steps:

1. **Display UpdateStatus view (if you downloaded it) or the status-update view you created (page 399).**

   To display the view, in the Task tab's Task Views section, click the bottom half of the Gantt Chart button, and then, on the drop-down menu, choose the view's name under the Custom heading.

   You should see only work tasks listed in the table. If summary tasks are visible, in the Gantt Chart Tools | Format tab's Show/Hide section, turn off the Project Summary Task and Summary Tasks checkboxes.

2. **To filter the list to show only the tasks you need to update, in the View tab's Data section, click the Filter down arrow, and then choose More Filters. In the More Filters dialog box, choose Should Start/Finish By, and then click Apply.**

   The Should Start/Finish By dialog box opens. This filter asks for two dates and then filters the list to show tasks that should have started by the first date or finished by the second date.

3. **In the first Should Start/Finish By dialog box, in the "Show tasks that should have started by" box, choose the start date for your status reporting period. Then click OK.**

   This part of the filter looks for all tasks whose Start Date is earlier than or equal to the date you specify.

4. **In the second Should Start/Finish By dialog box, in the "Or tasks that should have finished by" box, choose the last date for the reporting period. Then click OK.**

   This part of the filter looks for tasks whose Finish Date is earlier than or equal to the second date you specify. When you click OK, the view's task list displays only the tasks that pass the filter tests, as shown in Figure 13-3.

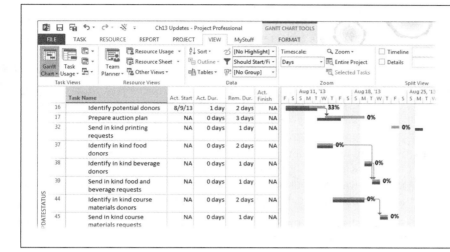

FIGURE 13-3

The Should Start/Finish By filter asks for two dates. To produce a list of tasks for updating, fill in the filter's boxes with the first and last dates of your reporting period (August 9, 2013, to August 23, 2013, in this example). The resulting list shows tasks that should have updates during that period.

5. **Drag over the Task Name cells for the tasks, and then press Ctrl+C to copy the task names to the Clipboard.**

   You can copy and paste task names from Project to cells in an Excel spreadsheet.

6. **Open a blank or existing spreadsheet in Excel.**

   You can download *Ch13_UpdateForm.xlsx*, an Excel spreadsheet with column headings in place, from this book's Missing CD page at *www.missingmanuals. com/cds.*

7. **In Excel, click the first blank cell in the Task Name column (or, if you're using a blank spreadsheet, simply click the first cell in the spreadsheet), and then press Ctrl+V.**

   Excel fills in the cells in the first column starting with the one you clicked. If you started with a blank spreadsheet, insert a row at the top of the grid and type column headings in the cells.

8. **Save the file (choose File→Save). Include the date range in the file's name, such as *Update_20130809_0823.xlsx*.**

   Now you can print it out or email it to team members.

■ GATHERING STATUS UPDATES

There are a few ways to obtain data from team members:

- **Status meetings.** One alternative is to bring the update form to your status meeting and fill it in as team members report statuses. Or, if you're a wiz with Project, you can update task status directly in your Project file. That way, you can discuss any scheduling issues that arise from the updates you made.

> **TIP** Don't underestimate the psychology of competition when going around a table for task progress reports. No one wants to look like a slacker when others are successfully ticking off their tasks one after another. It's counterintuitive, but such status meetings can actually *increase* your team's productivity.

- **Email.** An easy way to request and receive regular status updates is to send email messages (with your update form attached) to team members. Then, when you receive filled-out forms, you can copy and paste the update values into the corresponding fields in your status-update view (page 399).

- **SharePoint tasks list.** If your organization uses SharePoint, synchronizing your Project file with a SharePoint tasks list makes status updates even easier. You initially synchronize your Project file with a SharePoint tasks list so tasks are available on your SharePoint site. But this connection goes both ways. After team members update statuses in the SharePoint tasks list, you can re-synchronize to pull the updated values into your Project file. Then another synchronization pushes the updated schedule back to the SharePoint tasks list for the entire team to see. To learn more about SharePoint tasks lists and Project, download online-only Chapter 25 at this book's Missing CD page (*www.missingmanuals. com/cds*).

■ IMPORTING INFORMATION FROM OTHER TRACKING SYSTEMS

Many organizations ask people to submit timesheet and cost information into specialized tools like an accounting or time-tracking system. If your team members are already entering progress information into another system and the tasks in that system map to your project tasks, then find out if you can obtain that information so they don't have to report progress data twice. Cajole your good buddy in accounting or IT into creating a periodic report of this information in an Excel spreadsheet. Then you can import that data into your project plan, as described on page 541.

If you're bringing information in from another tracking system, designating accounting codes for tasks or resources can help you get data into the right place. For that matter, you may find accounting codes useful if you send information *from* your Project file to another system. If the accounting code is for resources, consider using Project's Code field, which is just a built-in resource text field to use however you wish. Otherwise, you can create a custom text or number field. Page 675 has details about creating a field for an accounting code.

> **TIP** The box on page 405 talks about some of the problems you may face if you try to work with other systems.

Getting Team Members to Submit Status Info

You may be only too aware that getting team members to provide status information is about as easy as herding cats—on a good day. Many team members fork over information when you need it without drama. Others, however, may have concluded that they don't need to do it, they don't want to do it, or it's dumb to do it.

Sometimes, the problem is that people don't want to admit that they dragged their feet getting started. Others may feel they're too busy working on tasks and can't spare the time. Then there's the issue of assigned tasks that don't exactly map to what resources are working on, and they simply don't know *how* to report their time.

The easier and more automated you can make status reporting, the more consistent results you'll get. Take the time to set up a form for reporting status, as explained on page 402. If you use a SharePoint site and synchronize your Project file with a SharePoint tasks list, team members can fill in and submit status updates there.

Sell them on reasons why status updates are so important. Let team members know that accurate status reporting can help do the following:

- Build reality into task duration estimates for future similar projects.

- Convince the customer and other managing stakeholders of the time required to produce quality work.

- Build a case to obtain additional resources, money, and time to implement tasks that result from approved change requests.

- Identify potential problems with the schedule or budget early enough to take corrective action so the team doesn't end up pulling as many all-nighters as they did the last time.

If logic doesn't sway your team, maybe bribery will. Offer a reward for complete progress reporting throughout the project.

Collecting Status Data about Other Resources

Some key resources may be inanimate objects. No, not like George in the corner cubicle, but rather equipment resources, material resources, and cost resources. But just because you can't chat up these types of resources at the water cooler doesn't mean you can ignore status information for them. They often represent significant project costs, and their progress is essential to accurately reflecting status and cost in your Project file.

One way to obtain this information is to have one of the *human* resources report on when equipment resources start working, how many pounds of goop were actually used, or the actual cost of the flight from headquarters to Timbuktu. The people who operate machinery, handle material, or spend money are the logical choices. Even if no one works directly with these inanimate resources, you can still assign status-reporting responsibility to someone or do it yourself. See the box on page 406 for a tip on documenting who owns this reporting responsibility.

Another idea is to check with the bean counters. The organization's general ledger or accounting system may contain time and costs incurred by equipment, material, and cost resources. If so, you may be able to obtain an Excel or Access file of the data to import into Project (page 540).

WORKAROUND WORKSHOP

Designating an Assignment Owner

Just as a designated driver gets inebriated partygoers home safely, a designated assignment owner makes sure that inanimate resources get their progress reported properly. Although Project doesn't include an assignment-owner feature in its non-enterprise version, you can invent it yourself.

Just create a custom text field (page 662) called something like Assignment Owner or Status Reporter. Next, add this field to a

table like Tracking in a task-oriented view or the Work table in a resource-oriented view. Then, for the equipment, material, and cost resources that can't speak for themselves, simply type the name of the person who's responsible for reporting that resource's status into the custom field's cells.

■ Updating Schedule Status in Project

Status information based on what actually happened is usually referred to as project *actuals*. Actuals are made up of data like actual duration, actual start, actual work, and percent complete. (The box on page 396 explains the difference between baseline, scheduled, and actual values in Project.) Keep in mind that, to get a *complete* picture of your project's status, you also need estimates about the remaining duration or work.

In this section, you'll learn how to enter status information into your Project file, including the best methods for each situation. This section covers commonly used methods for tracking status in Project. Some techniques update things from the task's point of view (page 408), and other techniques update things from the resource assignment's point of view (page 417). You'll also learn how to quickly "catch up" to your project if it's gotten stalled for some reason. Finally, you'll learn about the best ways to update cost information in your project.

Setting the Status Date

Before you begin entering updates in Project, it's a good idea to set the *status date*, that is, the date through which you've collected status information. Setting the status date comes in handy if you receive status information from team members on one day, such as the last Friday of the reporting period, but update your schedule on a different day, like the following Monday. This section shows you how to set the status date and display it in the Gantt Chart timescale.

NOTE If you don't set a specific status date, Project uses today's date.

Here are the steps for setting and displaying the status date in a Gantt Chart view:

1. **In the Project tab's Status section, click the calendar icon to the right of the Status Date label.**

   The Status Date dialog box opens.

2. **In the Select Date box, click the down arrow, and then choose the status date on the calendar. Click OK.**

   You can also type the date in the box, such as *8/16/13*. After you set the status date, it appears in the Project tab's Status section, as shown in Figure 13-4.

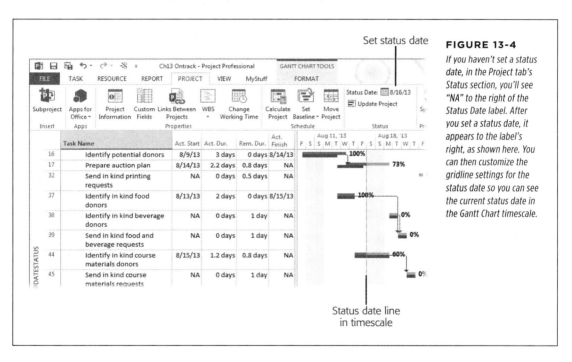

Set status date

Status date line
in timescale

FIGURE 13-4

If you haven't set a status date, in the Project tab's Status section, you'll see "NA" to the right of the Status Date label. After you set a status date, it appears to the label's right, as shown here. You can then customize the gridline settings for the status date so you can see the current status date in the Gantt Chart timescale.

To display the status date in the Gantt Chart timescale, do the following:

1. **In the Gantt Chart Tools | Format tab's Format section, click Gridlines→ Gridlines.**

   The Gridlines dialog box opens.

2. **In the "Line to change" list, click Status Date. In the Type drop-down list, choose a pattern, like a long dashed line. In the Color drop-down list, choose a color that'll stand out, like orange or bright red. Then click OK.**

   A vertical line appears at the status date in the Gantt Chart timescale.

Updating Tasks That Run on Schedule

If tasks run according to plan, you can update them with a single click whether they're complete or in progress. Here's how you update a task as on schedule:

1. **Display the status-update view you created (page 399) or a task view like Gantt Chart.**

   To make it easier to see the tasks you want to update, apply the Should Start/Finish By filter and fill in the start and finish dates for your reporting period, as described on page 402.

2. **Select the tasks that are on schedule by dragging over their Task Name cells or Ctrl-clicking individual Task Name cells.**

   You can simultaneously update several tasks that are complete or in progress, as long as they're all on schedule.

3. **In the Task tab's Schedule section, click "Mark on Track"→"Mark on Track."**

   Progress for the selected tasks is updated as running according to plan, as shown in Figure 13-5. Tasks that should have been completed by the status date are set to 100 percent complete, starting and finishing on their scheduled dates. For tasks scheduled to finish *after* the status date, the Actual Start field value is set to the task's Scheduled Start date, and % Complete is updated as complete through the status date.

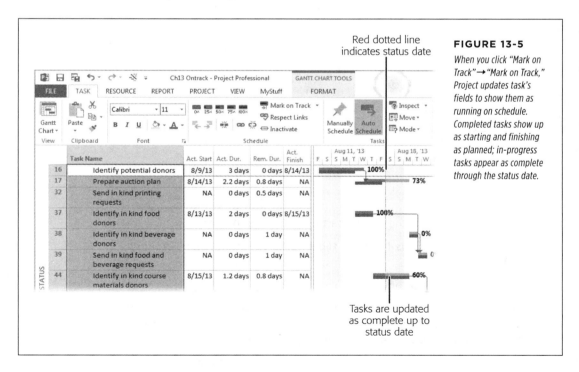

Red dotted line
indicates status date

Tasks are updated
as complete up to
status date

FIGURE 13-5

When you click "Mark on Track"→"Mark on Track," Project updates task's fields to show them as running on schedule. Completed tasks show up as starting and finishing as planned; in-progress tasks appear as complete through the status date.

Updating Completed Tasks That Didn't Run on Schedule

If a task didn't start or finish when it was supposed to but it's now complete, then the actual start and actual finish dates are the best values to enter. (You can set the % Complete field to 100%, but if you do that, then Project assumes that the task started and finished on the *scheduled* dates.) The box on page 411 explains how to update completed tasks whose work is more or less than you planned. Here's how to update completed tasks using actual start and actual finish dates:

1. **In your status-update view (page 399) or a task-oriented view like Gantt Chart view, select the task whose actual start and actual finish dates you want to update.**

   If you have several tasks that share the same actual start and finish dates, you can select them all and then update their dates in one fell swoop.

2. **In the Task tab's Schedule section, click the down arrow to the right of the "Mark on Track" button, and then choose Update Tasks.**

   Project displays the Update Tasks dialog box. If you selected just a single task, then the Current section displays the scheduled start and finish dates. If you selected multiple tasks, then the Current section's boxes are blank.

3. **In the dialog box's Actual section, click the arrow in the Start box, and then choose the actual start date from the calendar drop-down menu, as shown in Figure 13-6. Do the same in the Actual section's Finish box to set the actual finish date.**

   If you look at the fields in the Tracking table (or UpdateDuration table or UpdateWork table if you downloaded them—page 400), you'll see that Project updates not only the task's (or tasks') actual start and finish fields, but also the percent complete, actual duration, and remaining duration fields. If resources are assigned, then it updates the actual work and actual cost fields, as well. If you have change highlighting turned on (page 310), then the ripple effect of delayed tasks appears immediately.

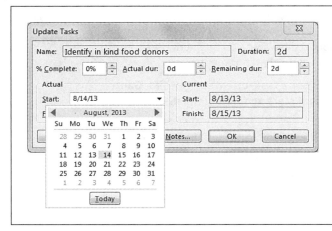

FIGURE 13-6

You can choose a date from this calendar or type a date in the box. The dates in the Actual boxes show "NA" until you enter status information for the task, whether it's percent complete, actual and remaining duration, or actual start and finish. (If you select more than one task in step 1, the boxes in the Update Tasks dialog box are blank instead.)

Updating Tasks That Are in Progress

When you update in-progress tasks, you can run into all kinds of statuses: on time, late starts, interruptions while work is under way, less work completed than planned, more work remaining than planned, and so on. The techniques you use to update tasks depend on the status values you collect and the situation of the task in question. This section describes the different methods you can use to update in-progress tasks.

■ UPDATING ACTUAL AND REMAINING DURATION

With this method, you specify the duration that's complete and forecast the remaining duration. (If the task started since your update, you also specify the actual start date if it's different than the scheduled start.) This approach gives you the opportunity to tell Project that you expect the task to take longer than you originally planned.

To enter task status using actual and remaining durations, follow these steps:

1. **In your status-update view (page 399) or a task-oriented view like Gantt Chart view, select the task you want to update.**

   You can also work in other task-oriented views like Calendar view or Task Usage view.

2. **In the Task tab's Schedule section, click the "Mark on Track" down arrow and choose Update Tasks.**

   Project displays the Update Tasks dialog box, which shows any existing values for actual and remaining duration. The sum of actual and remaining durations is the task's scheduled duration.

Updating Under- and Over-Budget Work

If you track work instead of duration, you can fill in a task's Actual Work field with the number of hours worked to complete the task. When you do this, Project jumps into action and uses the assigned resources' maximum units (page 213) to recalculate the task's Actual Duration. For example, if you type "40 hours" in the task's Actual Work field and the resource works 8-hour workdays, then Project changes the Actual Duration field's value to 5 days. If the task's Actual Work value differs from its Work value (that is, the planned work hours), you have an additional step or two to perform.

Suppose the actual work hours to complete the task are *less than* you estimated. For example, if the task's Work field is set to 40 hours and you type *32 hrs* in the Actual Work field, Project obligingly recalculates the Remaining Work field to 8 hours. (That's because Remaining Work equals Work minus Actual Work.) Because the task was completed in fewer hours, go ahead and type *0 hours* in the Remaining Work field. When you do that, Project changes the task's % Complete value to 100% and its Actual Duration value to 4 days (based on a full-time person working 8 hours a day).

If actual work hours are *more than* the hours in the Work field (say 48 hours, in this example) you fill in the Actual Work field with that value as before. In this case, the value in the task's Remaining Work field changes to zero without any action on your part. And the task's Actual Duration increases based on the number of hours, such as 6 days if the actual work is 48 hours.

But what if the assigned resource worked longer days to complete the task in its original duration, such as working 40 hours in *4 days*? In that case, you can change the person's units in Task Details Form view. Here's how:

1. In the View tab's Split View section, turn on the Details checkbox. In the Details drop-down menu, choose More Views, and then double-click Task Details Form in the Views list.

2. Right-click anywhere within Task Details Form view and then choose Work from the drop-down menu.

3. In the upper pane, select the task you want to update.

4. In Task Details Form view in the Details pane, select the Actual option.

5. Type the actual start date in the Start box, if necessary.

6. In the Task Details Form view's table, in the Units cell, type the percentage that represents the hours the person worked each day, such as 125% for a 10-hour day.

7. In the Actual Work cell, type the actual hours.

8. Click OK to save the task. Project sets the task's Actual Duration to 4 days, as shown in Figure 13-7.

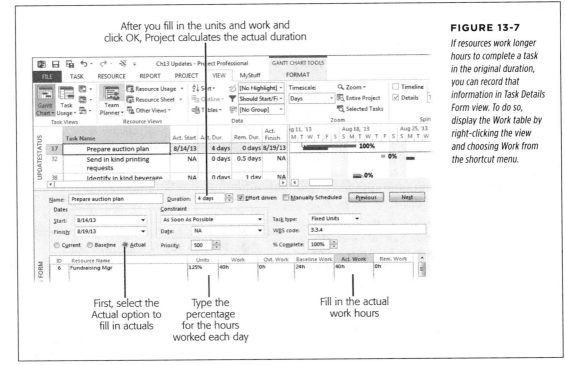

FIGURE 13-7

If resources work longer hours to complete a task in the original duration, you can record that information in Task Details Form view. To do so, display the Work table by right-clicking the view and choosing Work from the shortcut menu.

After you fill in the units and work and click OK, Project calculates the actual duration

First, select the Actual option to fill in actuals

Type the percentage for the hours worked each day

Fill in the actual work hours

TIP If you're not a fan of the Update Tasks dialog box and you're comfortable working directly in tables (and like to watch the change highlighting feature color the table cells), you can also enter actual and remaining values directly in the Tracking table or a table you customized for status updates (page 399).

3. **If the task started since your last update, in the Start box, type the actual start date.**

   Alternatively, click the down arrow to the Start box's right, and then click the date on the calendar. If you don't enter the actual start date, then Project sets it to the task's scheduled start date.

4. **In the "Actual dur" box, enter the actual duration.**

   Use the normal time period abbreviations, like 6h, 2d, or 1w.

5. **If the task is forecast to take more or less time than you planned, then in the "Remaining dur" box, enter the remaining duration for the selected task, and then click OK.**

If you expect the task to be completed in the scheduled duration, you don't have to fill in the "Remaining dur" box. When you enter an actual duration, the values in the "Remaining dur" box, Duration box, and % Complete box don't change immediately. However, Project recalculates the fields in the dialog box when you click OK.

In the Tracking table or your customized status-update table, you can see that Project has updated the task's Actual Start, Actual Duration, Remaining Duration, and % Complete fields based on your duration entries. If resources are assigned to the task, Project also updates its Actual Work field. Likewise, if you set up these resources with cost rates, then Project automatically updates the task's Actual Cost field.

As long as you turned on the settings for moving completed and remaining parts of tasks as described on page 397, Project takes care of recording completed work in the past and moving incomplete work to occur in the future, as shown in Figure 13-8 (top).

If you *didn't* turn on those settings, incomplete work still appears in the past, even though it isn't done yet, as shown in Figure 13-8 (bottom). In that case, you have to manually reschedule incomplete work to occur after the status date. To do that, in the Task tab's Tasks section, choose Move→"Incomplete Parts to Status Date." If you need to record work that was completed early, choose Move→"Completed Parts to Status Date" instead.

TIP If work isn't getting done because the people assigned to do it are busy, you can reschedule a task to when the resources are available. To do that, in the Task tab's Tasks section, choose Move→"When Resources are Available." But be forewarned—if someone works on multiple projects, this command could move a task far into the future.

■ UPDATING ACTUAL AND REMAINING WORK

This method provides a more accurate picture of project status because work is usually specified in hours, compared with duration's days. Similar to updating actual and remaining duration, you specify a start date if the task started since your update, the actual work that's been completed, and a forecast of what remains. You also fill in remaining work if you expect the task to take more or less time than you originally planned.

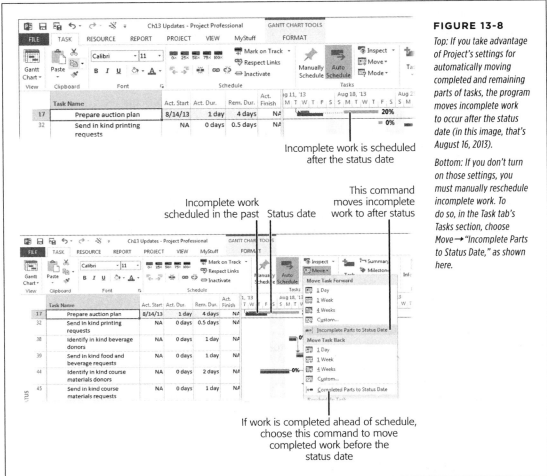

FIGURE 13-8

Top: If you take advantage of Project's settings for automatically moving completed and remaining parts of tasks, the program moves incomplete work to occur after the status date (in this image, that's August 16, 2013).

Bottom: If you don't turn on those settings, you must manually reschedule incomplete work. To do so, in the Task tab's Tasks section, choose Move→"Incomplete Parts to Status Date," as shown here.

Incomplete work is scheduled after the status date

Incomplete work scheduled in the past · Status date · This command moves incomplete work to after status

If work is completed ahead of schedule, choose this command to move completed work before the status date

The Update Tasks dialog box doesn't have fields for actual and remaining work, so you have to enter these values in a table or in Task Details Form view (page 412). Here's how:

1. **Display your status-update view (page 399) or a task-oriented view like Gantt Chart view. In the View tab's Data section, click Tables→More Tables. In the More Tables dialog box, double-click the table you use to update project status (page 399).**

   For example, if you downloaded the UpdateWork table as described on page 400, double-click its name in the Tables list. Then, if necessary, drag the vertical divider bar between the view's table and its timescale to the right to display more columns in the table.

2. **Click the Act. Start cell for the task you want to update, click the down arrow that appears, and then click the task's actual start date.**

You can also type the date in the cell.

3. **Click the Act. Work cell, and type the number of hours that have been worked so far, such as *32h*.**

You can also click the up or down arrow in the cell to increment the value by 1 hour for each click. When you navigate away from the cell by pressing Tab or Enter or by clicking another cell, Project recalculates the value in the Remaining Work field. For example, if the task's Work value is 40 hrs and you type *8h* into the Act. Work cell, the Remaining Work value changes to 32 hrs.

4. **If the estimated work needed to complete the task is more or less than you planned, in the task's Remaining Work cell, type the revised remaining work hours.**

When you navigate away from the cell, Project recalculates the task's other status fields, such as % Complete, % Work Complete, and Remaining Duration.

NOTE If you turned on the settings for moving completed and remaining parts of tasks as described on page 397, then Project takes care of recording completed work in the past and moving incomplete work to occur in the future. See Figure 13-8 (top).

■ UPDATING PERCENT COMPLETE AND REMAINING DURATION

Percent complete is the easiest type of progress to obtain, but it's also the least accurate, as explained on page 394. This method provides reasonably accurate results as long as you update percent complete *and* remaining duration.

Here are the steps for updating task status using percent complete:

1. **Display your status-update view (page 399) or a task-oriented view like Gantt Chart view. In the View tab's Data section, click Tables→Tracking.**

The Tracking table includes most of the fields you need: Actual Start, % Complete, and Remaining Duration. If you want to update Remaining Work, right-click a table heading, and then choose Insert Column→Remaining Work from the shortcut menu.

2. **Select the task you want to update, and then, in the Task tab's Schedule section, click "Mark on Track"→Update Tasks.**

Project displays the Update Tasks dialog box.

3. **If the task started since your last update, in the Start box, type the actual start date.**

Alternatively, click the down arrow to the Start box's right, and then click the date on the calendar. If you don't enter the actual start date, then Project sets it to the task's *scheduled* start date.

4. **In the % Complete box, type the percent complete for the selected task.**

To keep things simple, you may want to limit the values to a few standard percentages like 25%, 50%, 75%, and 100%. If you do that, you can update a task's % Complete field from the task mini-toolbar. Right-click the task and then, on the mini-toolbar, click the 100% down arrow and choose the value you want, as shown in Figure 13-9.

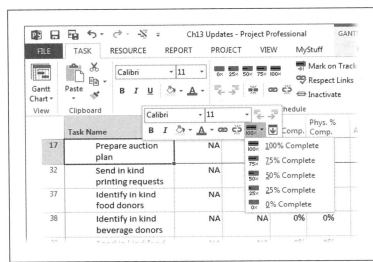

FIGURE 13-9

The mini-toolbar is convenient if you update progress using percent complete. Right-click a task, click the 100% down arrow to get a drop-down list that contains items for 0%, 25%, 50%, 75%, and 100%, and then choose the appropriate percent-complete value.

5. **If the task is forecast to take more or less time than you planned, in the "Remaining dur" box, type the estimated remaining duration, and then click OK.**

When you fill in an actual duration, the values in the "Remaining dur" box and Duration box don't change immediately. Instead, Project recalculates the fields in the dialog box when you click OK. If you type values in the % Complete and "Remaining dur" boxes, the program calculates the Actual Duration (in the "Actual dur" box) and updates the task's duration (see page 394 for the formulas for these fields). For example, suppose you have a 5-day task. If you type *75%* for % Complete and *1d* for "Remaining dur, the value in the "Actual dur" box changes to 3d and the new scheduled duration (Duration) is 4d.

If you want to update percent complete and remaining work, apply your customized status-update table (or the UpdateWork table, if you downloaded it—see page 399) to the task-oriented view. Then you can fill in the Actual Start, Remaining Work, and % Work Complete cells for the task you want to update.

TIP If many tasks have the same percent-complete values, you might find it faster to enter percent complete directly into the view's table. Enter the percent complete in the "% Comp." field for each applicable task. To copy that value to other cells, select the first cell and then put your cursor over the fill handle (the green box at the bottom-right corner of the cell—see page 150). When the cursor changes to a + sign, drag over the other cells.

Updating the Project Using Resource-Assignment Status

When resources are assigned to tasks, you can take status updates to a more detailed level of tracking. Instead of showing status for the task as a whole, you can show status for individual assignments *within* the task. Admittedly, for tasks that have only one resource assigned, you don't see much of a difference. But for tasks that have multiple resources assigned, entering updates at the assignment level provides more detailed status information.

You have to enter more data to update resource assignments this way, but it makes your status information more accurate. Plus, Project uses the values for individual assignments to determine status for the task as a whole. You don't have to resort to guesswork about a task's overall percent complete when, for example, one resource is 100 percent complete, another is 40 percent complete, and the third is 25 percent complete.

This section describes three effective methods for updating resource-assignment status: actual work complete and remaining work, percentage of work complete, and actual work complete by time period. You'll also learn how to create a specialized tracking view that simplifies entering progress information for resource assignments.

▆ ENTERING ACTUAL WORK COMPLETE AND REMAINING WORK

While *duration* refers to the span of time from the beginning of a task until the end, *work* on an assignment refers to the person-hours a resource is assigned to work. Project can calculate work from duration and vice versa, but they don't measure the same thing (see page 162 to get the full story about the difference between duration and work). If your resources report their hours worked, then entering the actual and remaining work provides the most accurate picture of progress and the corresponding labor costs.

Here's how to enter actual work complete and remaining work on an assignment:

1. **In Task Usage or Resource Usage view, select the assignment whose actual and remaining work you want to update.**

   To do this in Task Usage view, select the row containing the assigned resource's name. In Resource Usage view, select the row containing the task's name instead.

TIP If multiple assignments have the same actual and remaining work values, you can select them and update their progress at the same time.

2. **Double-click the selected assignment.**

   Project displays the Assignment Information dialog box.

3. **Click the Tracking tab.**

   The Tracking tab contains several fields you can use to update progress for the individual assignment, as shown in Figure 13-10, including "Actual work," "Remaining work," "Actual start," and "Actual finish." Any existing values appear in the boxes. The value in the Work box is the sum of actual work and remaining work. (In Project, the Work field represents scheduled work—the total of actual work performed and the current estimate of remaining work. To learn more about the difference between baseline, scheduled, and actual values, see the box on page 396.)

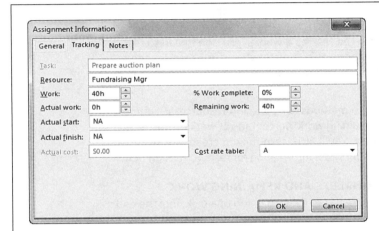

FIGURE 13-10

To update several assignments with the same data, select them all at once, and then open the Assignment Information dialog box to make the change.

4. **If the task started since your last update, in the "Actual start" box, type the actual start date.**

   The box displays NA until you enter a start date (unless you selected multiple assignments, in which case the boxes are blank). If you don't enter the actual start date, then Project sets it to the assignment's scheduled start date.

5. **In the "Actual work" box, enter the actual amount of work that has already been done.**

   Use the normal time-period abbreviations like 8h, 5d, or 2w. When you enter actual work, at first the values in the Work and "Remaining work" boxes don't change. However, after you enter remaining work and click OK, Project recalculates the task's Work value.

6. **In the "Remaining work" box, enter the remaining work hours needed to complete the selected assignment, and then click OK.**

   Project updates the assignment values.

◼ ENTERING PERCENTAGE OF WORK COMPLETE

Percent complete (which is recorded in the % Complete field) refers to completion for a task as a whole, based on duration. Percentage of work complete (recorded in the % Work Complete field), on the other hand, refers to completion based on the number of actual hours worked divided by the scheduled work hours. This section explains how to enter resource-assignment progress using the latter measurement—percentage of work complete. Here's how:

1. **Display Task Usage or Resource Usage view. Then, in the View tab's Data section, click Tables→Work to apply the Work table to the view and see status-related fields for assignments.**

   In Task Usage view, the column you're interested in is titled "% W. Comp." If you don't see this column initially, drag the divider between the view's table and its timescale to the right until you see the column.

   In Resource Usage view, the column is labeled "% Comp."

TIP   To see how actuals affect the schedule when you update progress in a usage view, start by displaying Gantt Chart view in the top pane (choose View→Task Views→Gantt Chart). Then display Task Usage view in the bottom pane by heading to the View tab's Split View section, turning on the Details checkbox, and then choosing Task Usage in the Details drop-down list. That way, as you enter actuals in Task Usage view, you see tasks change (including change highlighting) in Gantt Chart view.

---

2. **Double-click the assignment to open the Assignment Information dialog box.**

   In Task Usage view, Project lists the assigned resources under each task. To select an assignment in Task Usage view, click anywhere in a row that has a resource listed in the Task Name cell (the resource names are indented more than the task names). In Resource Usage view, Project lists the assigned tasks under each resource. To select an assignment in Resource Usage view, click anywhere in a row that has a task's name in the Resource Name cell.

3. **Click the dialog box's Tracking tab.**

   This tab is shown back in Figure 13-10.

4. **In the "% Work complete" box, enter the percentage that represents the progress the resource has made.**

   Remember, enter the percentage that reflects the progress on *this* assignment, not the entire task. Before you click OK, check the assignment's actual start date and remaining work. If you don't enter the actual start date, Project sets the Actual Start field (the "Actual start" box in the dialog box) to the assignment's scheduled start date. If you don't enter a value for remaining work, Project calculates it from the percentage of work complete.

If you enter only percent work complete without actual start or actual finish dates, you can enter percent work complete in the "% W. Comp." field in Task Usage view or the "% Comp." field in Resource Usage view (these headings both represent the % Work Complete field). Remember to enter the value for the *assignment*, not for the task or resource.

NOTE   The percent-complete buttons on the mini-toolbar and the Task tab are grayed out when you select an assignment, because they update tasks, not assignments. However, they become active if you select a task in Task Usage view.

■ ENTERING ACTUAL WORK BY TIME PERIOD

For the ultimate in progress detail and accuracy, you can enter actual work by time period. But be forewarned that this is the most time-consuming method of tracking progress, for you *and* for your resources. Typically, if you need to track this level of detail, you'll use Project Server and Project Web App to automate collecting and recording this information. However, you can enter actual work in the time-phased portion of a usage view, showing how much work was done on an assignment in each time period (day, week, or whatever).

To enter actual work by time period, follow these steps:

1. **Display Task Usage or Resource Usage view. Then, in the View tab's Data section, click Tables→Work.**

   Not only do the usage views show assignment information, but they also show time-phased information, like work or cost values over time.

2. **Display Actual Work in the time-phased portion of the view by heading to the Format tab's Details section and turning on the Actual Work checkbox.**

   Alternatively, you can simply right-click in the time-phased portion of the usage view and then, on the shortcut menu, choose Actual Work. Either way, Project adds a row labeled "Act. Work" to the time-phased portion of the view.

3. **In the time-phased portion of the view, drag the right edge of the Details column to the right so you can see all the text it contains.**

   On the status bar, drag the Zoom slider until the timescale for the usage view shows the level of time detail you want to work with. For example, you can show days, weeks, or months in the timescale. Alternatively, in the View tab's Zoom section, choose the time unit you want in the Timescale drop-down list.

4. **In the table area, select the assignment whose actual work you want to update.**

   You can actually have one assignment selected in the sheet portion, while another assignment is selected in the time-phased portion of the usage view.

5. **To display the cells for the assignment in the time-phased portion of the view, in the Task tab's Editing section, click "Scroll to Task."**

   Project scrolls the time-phased portion of the view to show when work is scheduled to begin on the selected assignment.

6. **In the Act. Work field in the assignment's row, type the actual work values in the appropriate time periods, as shown in Figure 13-11.**

   If a resource tells you more time is needed, update the Remaining Work cell in the table to the value you received. If you don't explicitly enter a value for remaining work, then Project calculates it by subtracting the actual work you just entered from the scheduled amount of work.

TIP   If you want to add a field that's not available on the Format tab or the shortcut menu that appears when you right-click the time-phased portion of the view, in the Format tab's Details section, click Add Details. In the Detail Styles dialog box, select the Usage Details tab. In the "Available fields" box, select the field you want to add, and then click Show. Use the Move arrows to specify the order of fields in the view.

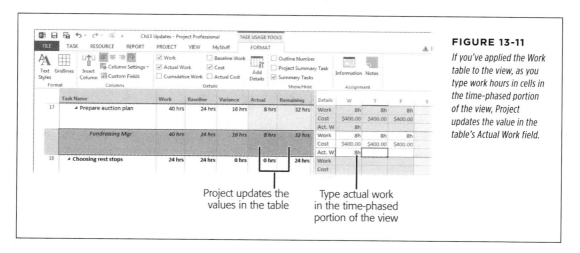

FIGURE 13-11

If you've applied the Work table to the view, as you type work hours in cells in the time-phased portion of the view, Project updates the value in the table's Actual Work field.

Project updates the values in the table

Type actual work in the time-phased portion of the view

Updating the Whole Project

Sometimes, a project goes off kilter and you need a quick way to recover. For example, maybe several months of work was complete when you were told to stop work immediately. Now, a month later, the project is on again. Unfortunately, in the interim, the dates in your Project file marched forward assuming that people were going to do those tasks when they were scheduled.

Or say you were suddenly drafted to handle customer problems onsite. Upon your return, you're relieved to find tasks completed and milestones met. Except...the Project file doesn't have any actual values for the time you were away. The prospect of gathering and incorporating several weeks' worth of actuals into the file is too overwhelming, especially given the other activities you're behind on.

In this section, you'll learn about two quick-fix recovery methods. One method lets you reschedule unfinished work by changing the start dates or resume dates of all tasks to today's date so you can continue from this point forward. Another method is the automatic project-update method, which says, essentially, that all tasks in the project have been done exactly according to plan. This method is kind of like a cat that falls clumsily off the sofa, then walks away acting as if it *meant* to do that all along.

■ RESCHEDULING UNFINISHED WORK IN THE PROJECT

If your project was interrupted midstream and is now resuming, then you have a lot of schedule dates to adjust. Rather than adjust dates manually, it's simpler to have Project reschedule any uncompleted work. Here's how you get the program to do just that:

1. **Display any task-oriented view.**

   The Update Project command you'll use in the next step is available only for task-oriented views.

2. **To reschedule only certain tasks, select them and then, in the Project tab's Status section, click Update Project.**

   The Update Project dialog box appears. If you want to reschedule the entire project, you can tell Project that in step 4.

3. **Select the "Reschedule uncompleted work to start after" option shown in Figure 13-12, and then type the date when work should resume.**

   Any tasks that were in progress when the project was halted resume on that date, as shown in Figure 13-13. It also means that any unstarted tasks scheduled to start before that date now start on this new date instead, and any successors linked to those tasks are rescheduled to follow their predecessors as normal.

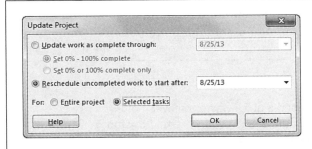

FIGURE 13-12

The Update Project dialog box opens with "Update work as complete through" and "Entire project" selected automatically. If you want to update only certain tasks, be sure to select the tasks before you open the dialog box and then select the "Selected tasks" option instead, as shown here.

4. **To reschedule only the tasks you selected in step 2 (if you did so), select the "Selected tasks" option, and then click OK.**

   Otherwise, with the "Entire Project" option selected, as it is automatically, Project reschedules the entire project.

All uncompleted work in the project now starts after the date you specified, as shown in Figure 13-13. Examine your schedule carefully for issues you need to address. If you created manually scheduled tasks or set date constraints, then reset them as necessary. Check for conflicts between constraints and predecessors (page 307). Also, look at milestone dates and the project finish date to see if you need to shorten the remaining schedule because of the delay. Look at the project costs to see if anything is now going over budget.

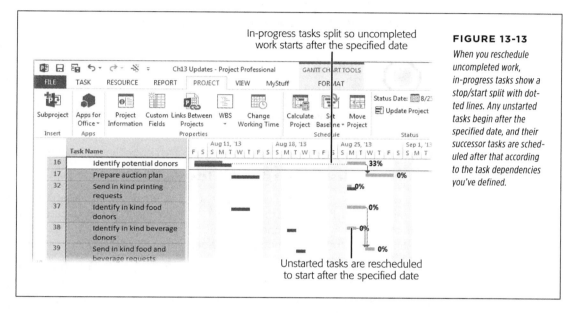

In-progress tasks split so uncompleted work starts after the specified date

Unstarted tasks are rescheduled to start after the specified date

FIGURE 13-13

When you reschedule uncompleted work, in-progress tasks show a stop/start split with dotted lines. Any unstarted tasks begin after the specified date, and their successor tasks are scheduled after that according to the task dependencies you've defined.

If necessary, submit the new schedule to the stakeholders and get their approval again. Once that's done, you may want to save a new baseline. You can either overwrite your original baseline or save a second baseline and work with that as your primary benchmark from now on (page 377).

■ UPDATING THE PROJECT AS SCHEDULED

Anyone who says a project has gone exactly as planned is bound to get some suspicious glances. However, if your project really *has* been progressing with no major mishaps but you've also fallen woefully behind on entering progress updates, you can enter a set of automatic updates that says all work is completed or in progress exactly as scheduled through a specified date.

TIP Keep in mind that updating a project automatically compromises the accuracy of your project data, so you should use it only as a last resort. And if you use project actuals for billing or other accounting purposes, then these automatic updates are no-nos. In that case, you simply have to gather the missing data and update your file.

To globally update work as completed according to the schedule, follow these steps:

1. **Display any task-oriented view.**

   For example, you can choose Detail Gantt view or Calendar view.

2. **If you want to update only certain tasks, select them.**

   Drag across adjacent tasks or Ctrl-click to select nonadjacent tasks. If you don't select any tasks, Project will update every task in your project.

3. **In the Project tab's Status section, click Update Project.**

   The Update Project dialog box appears.

4. **Make sure the "Update work as complete through" option is selected.**

   Project makes the date box to the right of that option available.

5. **In the date box, enter the cutoff date for updating as scheduled.**

   Project will automatically enter progress-update information, such as 100 percent complete, for any tasks scheduled to take place *before* the date you specify.

6. **Indicate which tasks Project should update.**

   If you want Project to update tasks whether they're unstarted, partially finished, or completely finished, select the "Set 0% - 100% complete" option. This option means that some tasks (the ones that are scheduled to start before the cutoff date and finish after it) may update to 50 percent or 75 percent, for example.

   If you want Project to update *only* tasks that should have been 100 percent complete before the cutoff date, then select the "Set 0% or 100% complete only" option instead. When you select this option, tasks that are in progress remain set to 0 percent.

7. **If you want to update only the tasks you selected in step 2 (if you did so), then select the "Selected tasks" option, and then click OK.**

   Otherwise, with the "Entire project" option selected, as it is automatically, Project updates all applicable tasks throughout the entire project.

Updating Project Costs

Projects can have up to five different sources of costs: human resources, equipment, materials, cost resources, and fixed costs for tasks. Each type of cost that applies to your project needs actual cost information before you can see how the project's cost compares to its baseline cost. In this section, you'll learn how to update each of these five cost sources. Project's Cost table is a great starting point, with fields for baseline, scheduled, actual, and remaining costs. You can apply this table to a usage view to see costs for individual assignments as well.

You can also insert cost-related fields like Actual Cost into any table. Just remember that, if you add these fields to a task-oriented table, their values represent *task* costs; if you add these fields to a resource-oriented table, their values relate to resources instead. And when you add these fields to a usage view, you can see values for the individual assignments.

Updating Actual Costs for Work Resources

If you set up resources with standard rates, overtime rates, and costs per use (page 361) and assign the resources to tasks, then Project calculates actual cost as soon as you enter actual work. That means you never have to update actual labor and equipment costs yourself. The box below tells you what you have to do if you want to update resource costs manually.

With equipment resources, the challenge is making sure that actual work time is reported. To solve that problem, designate an assignment owner for equipment resource assignments, as described on page 406.

WORD TO THE WISE

Manually Entering Resource Costs

When you tell Project how much resources cost, assign those resources to tasks, and then enter actual work, Project automatically calculates their actual costs for you. What's not to like? However, Project lets you update resource costs manually—but that doesn't mean it's a good idea. Doing so is cumbersome, tricky, and the results may not be what you expect. But if Project's costs are totally out of whack and you want to report costs in Project anyway, then you can type actual costs into the fields that Project usually calculates. To tell the program to let you do this, choose File→Options; on the left side of the Project Options dialog box, click Schedule; and then

scroll down and turn off the "Actual costs are always calculated by Project" checkbox. With this setting turned off, Project still calculates actual costs, but you can enter total actual costs in tasks' Actual Cost fields.

To manually enter time-phased costs for tasks or resource assignments, display Task Usage view. In the Task Usage Tools | Format tab's Details section, turn on the Actual Cost checkbox to add the Actual Cost row to the time-phased portion of the view. You can then enter actual costs by time period in the Actual Cost field either for the assignment or for the task as a whole.

Updating Actual Costs for Material Resources

With standard rates or costs per use in place for your material resources and the material resources assigned to tasks, Project calculates the actual cost for material resources based on the number of units used or the amount per time period, like 20 jugs of goop at $100 per jug or four jugs of goop per day times a 5-day task duration times $100 per jug (in that case, the actual cost for the material resource is based on the actual duration of the task).

If the actual amount of material used that Project calculates isn't correct, you can change it in the Actual Work field for the material resource assignment. Use Task Usage view, Resource Usage view, or the Tracking tab of the Assignment Information dialog box (double-click an assignment in Task Usage or Resource Usage view to open this dialog box).

Updating Actual Costs for Cost Resources

When you assign a cost resource to a task, you enter the estimated cost (page 248). However, when you enter actual progress for task or resource assignments, Project doesn't include cost resources in its actual cost calculations. Progress information is based on duration or work completed, and cost resources operate independently of time spent on a task. This disconnect means that you could set a task to 100 percent complete, but the cost resource would still show remaining cost, as illustrated in Figure 13-14.

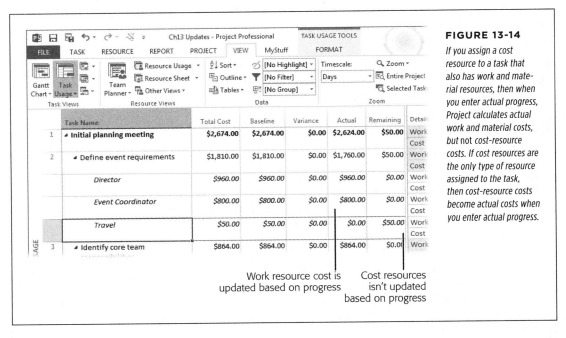

FIGURE 13-14

If you assign a cost resource to a task that also has work and material resources, then when you enter actual progress, Project calculates actual work and material costs, but not cost-resource costs. If cost resources are the only type of resource assigned to the task, then cost-resource costs become actual costs when you enter actual progress.

Work resource cost is updated based on progress

Cost resources isn't updated based on progress

If a task has work and cost resources assigned to it, then you have to explicitly update the actual cost of the cost resources. To enter cost-resource costs as actual costs, follow these steps:

1. **In Task Usage or Resource Usage view, double-click the cost resource assignment for the task.**

   Project displays the Assignment Information dialog box.

2. **Click the Tracking tab.**

   For cost resources, the only fields available are "% Work complete" and "Actual cost."

Check Out Receipt

Lisle Library District
630.971.1675
www.lislelibrary.org

Friday, May 27, 2016 10:54:26 AM
100

Item: 730391000104377
Title: Basics for builders : framing & rou
 carpentry
Call no.: 694.2 SIM
Due: 06/17/2016

Item: 730391005168852
Title: Framing a house
Call no.: 694.2 OSB
Due: 06/17/2016

Item: 730391005789998
Title: Complete book of framing : an illus
trated guide for residential construction
Call no.: 694.2 SIM
Due: 06/17/2016

Item: 730391003935550
Title: Framing floors, walls, and ceilings
Call no.: 694.2 FRA
Due: 06/17/2016

Item: 730391005708244
Title: Microsoft Project 2013 : the missin
 manual
Call no.: 005.369 MICROSOFT PROJECT 2013
Due: 06/17/2016

Total items: 5

****
****
The Library will be closed Sunday
and Monday May 29th and 30th for
Memorial Day. The Library will
re-open Tuesday May 31st at 9:30AM.
****

****

3. **Enter the actual cost of the cost resource.**

Although cost resources are independent of work amount, you can enter a percentage in the "% Work complete" field, and Project calculates an actual cost amount accordingly. For example, suppose you specified $2,420.00 for the Airfare cost resource on a task. If you enter 50% in the "% Work complete" field, then the "Actual cost" field changes to $1,210.00.

You can also simply enter a value in the "Actual cost" field. If it's not the full amount planned, then the remaining amount goes into the Remaining Cost field for the assignment (this field isn't included in the Assignment Information dialog box).

Updating Actual Fixed Costs on Tasks

Fixed costs are primarily used for fixed-cost contracts (page 268). If you use fixed costs, then when you enter actual progress information on a task, Project calculates the actual cost for the fixed cost along with the work and material costs.

For example, if one of your tasks had a fixed cost of $1,500, and you tell Project that this task is now 50 percent complete, Project moves $750 of the fixed cost to the actual cost side of the equation (the Actual Cost field) and leaves the other $750 in the remaining cost side (the Remaining Cost field). The actual cost for the task is the total of these two fixed-cost values and any resource costs on the task.

Unlike most other fields, Project doesn't have a separate field for actual fixed costs. The value in the Fixed Cost field is the total of your estimated fixed costs and actual fixed costs, so be sure to update the Fixed Cost field with the current fixed-cost value. The Cost table includes the Fixed Cost field.

Evaluating and Correcting Project Performance

S mall issues can blow up into project wildfires if you don't douse them early. A delay here, a cost overrun there, and suddenly the finish date, cost, and project objectives are at risk. Regular project performance reviews are a must if you want your daily jolt limited to your double espresso. Comparing the project's current status to baseline schedule and cost can give you early warning of trouble brewing.

Schedule, budget, and other project objectives are interdependent, so where you start your evaluation depends on what's most important. If the project's budget is crucial, you can start by evaluating costs. But in most cases, starting with the schedule makes sense, because delays can affect the finish date *and* the price tag.

This chapter starts by showing you how to evaluate schedule performance, whether you want a quick peek at overall progress or a heads-up about tasks in trouble. You'll learn how to use Project's views, reports, and filters to see high-level and task-by-task progress, as well as to uncover potential problems. You'll also discover ways to find overallocated resources and tasks that are exceeding their work budgets. Likewise, you'll learn about reports and filters for comparing project costs to the baseline cost or a budget. And no chapter on project performance would be complete without a section on earned value analysis. You'll find out how earned value and its related measures help you evaluate performance, and then learn how to use them in Project.

Once you know where your project stands, the next step is usually making adjustments to keep the project on time and within budget. Fortunately, most of the techniques you use during project execution are the same as the ones you use for fine-tuning a project during planning (see Chapter 11). This chapter reviews those techniques and then describes one more option: assigning overtime.

NOTE Evaluating your project's schedule and costs means looking at the project from many directions. This chapter describes some of the ways you may want to customize elements to see performance. *ProjectMM_Customization.mpp* (which you can download from this book's Missing CD page at *www.missingmanuals.com/cds*) contains many of the customized views, filters, and other elements mentioned in this chapter. However, Part Four of this book (which begins with Chapter 18) describes customizing Project elements in detail.

■ Scheduled, Baseline, and Actual Values

During project planning, there's only one set of values to watch—the dates, work amounts, and costs that Project calculates, which are known as *scheduled* or *planned* values. But once a project gets under way, additional types of values suddenly have roles in determining project performance. Before you dive into evaluating performance, it's a good idea to understand the differences among these values and how they contribute to measuring performance. Here are the different types of values that are important during the execution phase and where you find them:

- **Scheduled** values are the forecast values at any point during the project, whether you're putting your plan together or already tracking progress. Scheduled fields like Start, Finish, Work, Cost, and Duration combine actual performance so far with the forecast values for the work that remains. While you're planning, scheduled values are merely forecasts, because no *actual* values exist yet. At the end of the project, scheduled values equal actual values, because there's nothing left to forecast. For example, if you've worked 100 hours so far and you forecast another 200 hours to finish, then the Work field's value is the sum of the two: 300 hours.

- **Baseline** values are what the scheduled dates, work, cost, and duration were when you saved your baseline (page 373), usually after the stakeholders approved your project plan. When you set a baseline, Project copies the values from Start, Finish, Work, Cost, and Duration fields to Baseline Start, Baseline Finish, Baseline Work, Baseline Cost, and Baseline Duration, so you have a snapshot of your schedule's values before you begin tracking status. As you'll learn shortly, the difference between scheduled and baseline values is a *huge* part of evaluating project performance.

- **Actual** values are what actually happened: when tasks really started and finished, how long tasks took, how much work has been done, and how much tasks really cost. The fields for actual values are, unsurprisingly, Actual Start, Actual Finish, Actual Work, Actual Cost, and Actual Duration.

- **Remaining** values are simply the duration, work, and costs that remain. For example, suppose the original forecast work for a task was 120 hours. The assigned resource has completed 60 hours but estimates that it'll take 80 more hours to finish. In this example, the amount of actual work (60 hours) doesn't matter; the Remaining Work value is 80 hours.

- **Variances** are the difference between scheduled and baseline values. In Project, variance fields like Cost Variance and Finish Variance are calculated as scheduled value minus baseline value, like Cost – Baseline Cost. If the scheduled cost is greater than the baseline cost, the positive variance shows that the task is over budget. Likewise, if the scheduled finish date is later than the baseline finish date, the positive variance indicates that the task is behind schedule. In other words, positive variances are bad; negative variances are good. See page 444 to learn how earned value variances, CV (earned value cost variance), and SV (earned value schedule variance) differ from Project's basic variance fields.

> **NOTE** A variance that's equal to zero (0) can mean one of two things: A task is exactly on track—or you forgot to set a baseline. During project execution, tasks that go exactly according to plan produce zero variance. But if *every* task has zero variance, the problem is the absence of a baseline.

■ Is the Project on Time?

Reviewing project dates is usually the first step in evaluating performance, because a project's duration has a way of affecting its price tag, too. This section explains ways to review the schedule, whether at the project level, for day-to-day task management, or to calculate schedule performance metrics. (The box on page 434 describes another way to evaluate performance that doesn't involve Project.)

Because actual progress affects the rest of the project, evaluating performance adds a few techniques to the ones you use to review a schedule during planning (page 292). You keep tabs on the project schedule at several levels:

- **The project finish date.** The bottom line, of course, is whether the project is going to finish when it should, which is what a quick peek at the overall project finish date shows.

- **Tactical task management.** Keeping the overall schedule on track means keeping individual tasks on time. Most project managers check tasks each week to see if any are in trouble or heading that way. Because delays on the critical path mean a late project finish date, critical path tasks are the first ones to examine (page 434). However, you also have to keep an eye on noncritical tasks, because they can *become* critical if they go on too long.

- **Overall schedule performance.** There's more to schedule performance than the finish date. Schedule performance measures like schedule variance (SV) and schedule performance index (SPI), described on page 444, tell you how well you're managing the project's schedule, or whether corrective actions are working. You can compare performance measures from week to week or month to month to look for trends.

The following sections explain how to check your project at each of these levels.

Checking Status at the Project Level

Project-wide status for schedule, cost, and work comes as a package deal in several places within Project. Project-level variances are the first hint of problems. Here are three ways to see overall schedule, cost, and work statuses:

- **Project summary task.** As shown in Figure 14-1, the project summary task is a simple way to see high-level status.

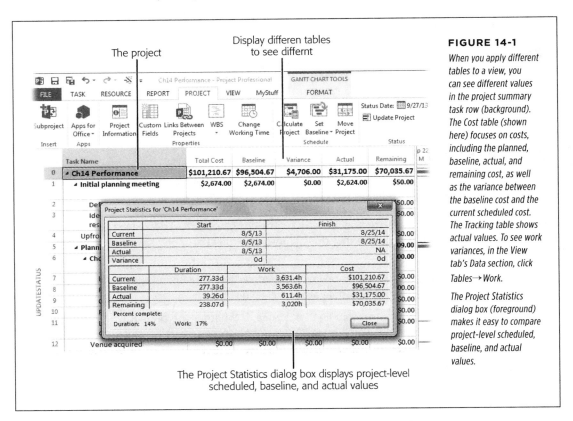

FIGURE 14-1

When you apply different tables to a view, you can see different values in the project summary task row (background). The Cost table (shown here) focuses on costs, including the planned, baseline, actual, and remaining cost, as well as the variance between the baseline cost and the current scheduled cost. The Tracking table shows actual values. To see work variances, in the View tab's Data section, click Tables→Work.

The Project Statistics dialog box (foreground) makes it easy to compare project-level scheduled, baseline, and actual values.

The Project Statistics dialog box displays project-level scheduled, baseline, and actual values

- **Project Statistics dialog box.** This dialog box (Figure 14-1, foreground) shows scheduled, baseline, actual, and remaining values for fields like start and finish dates, duration, work, and cost. To open it, head to the Project tab's Properties section and click Project Information; in the Project Information dialog box, click Project Statistics. At the dialog box' bottom left, the "Percent complete" values can be early warning signs. If the Duration value there is higher than the Work value there, then the project may run late because there's more work to finish than duration to finish it in. However, tasks that schedule more work later in the duration exhibit the same characteristic, so if you know your project includes a lot of back-loaded tasks, then don't be alarmed if that Duration percent complete value is higher than the Work percent complete value.

- **Project Overview report.** This new graphical report provides a high-level view of status and what's coming up. To run it, in the Report tab's View Reports section, click Dashboards→Project Overview. At the report's top left, you see the project's start and finish dates and the percentage of the project's duration that's complete. It also lists milestones that are coming up, the percentage completion for all top-level tasks, and tasks that are past due.

- **Burndown report.** This new graphical report compares baseline, actual, and remaining work so you can see how much work has been completed (or "burned through," which is where the term "burndown" comes from), how much is left, and how that compares to what you planned (see Figure 14-2). To run it, in the Report tab's View Reports section, click Dashboards→Burndown. The chart on the right side of the report shows the number of complete and incomplete tasks.

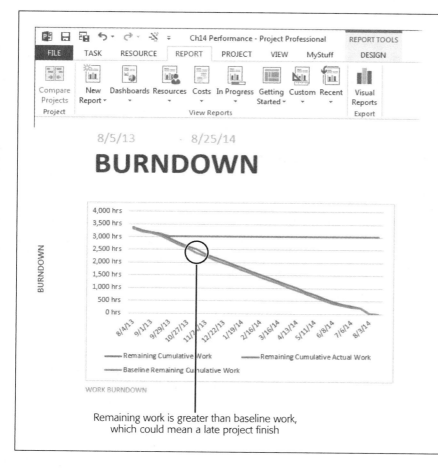

FIGURE 14-2

If the Remaining Cumulative Work line in this report is above the Baseline Remaining Cumulative Work line (as shown here), then you have more work left to complete than you planned, a red flag that the project may finish late.

Remaining work is greater than baseline work, which could mean a late project finish

- **Cost Overview report.** Another new graphical report, this one summarizes the project's cost status. To run it, in the Report tab's View Reports section, click Dashboards→Cost Overview. One of the report's charts compares the percentage complete to the amount of money spent. If the chart's Cost line is above its % Complete line, then the percentage of the total project cost that you've spent is higher than the percentage of duration that's complete, which is a red flag that the project might be over budget. This report also includes a table showing cost status for the project's top-level tasks.

TOOLS OF THE TRADE

What Else Could Go Wrong?

When you plan a project, you put together a risk management plan, which identifies risks and what you'll do if they become reality. During the project's execution, you have to watch for risks that are threatening or explode suddenly. So how do you keep an eye out for potential problems?

Schedule delays and increasing costs can be a sign that a risk has turned into reality, but talking to the team is a more proactive way to track risks. (A risk-management plan may

identify events that foretell imminent risks, like a subcontractor who doesn't report status when progress is slow.) Ask team members if issues have come up—they may need help but are afraid to ask.

If risks *do* become reality, it's time to launch the response you laid out during planning. For example, you may replace a subcontractor, dip into the project's contingency funds, or reduce the project's scope to maintain its schedule and budget.

Keeping Your Eye on Critical Tasks

Tasks on the critical path affect a project's finish date, so it's a good idea to check on them frequently to make sure they aren't delayed. Tracking Gantt view is a good one to use for this, because it displays critical tasks as red task bars (page 383). (Keep in mind that you can display critical tasks in any task-oriented view by heading to the Format tab's Bar Styles section and turning on the Critical Tasks checkbox.) If you want to see *only* the tasks on the critical path, then in the View tab's Data section, click the Filter down arrow and then choose Critical.

See Chapter 11 to learn more about the critical path and various ways to view it.

Looking for Delayed Tasks

Finding tasks whose start dates are delayed can help you correct delays before they get any worse. Delays in noncritical tasks may not affect the project finish date *yet*, but they can if their duration increases. Part of your weekly tactical management routine should be looking for delayed tasks (critical and noncritical alike). Then you can evaluate each delayed task to try to prevent—or at least limit—further delays. This section describes several filters and reports that highlight delayed tasks. The box on page 437 describes other ways to spot troubled tasks quickly.

The first step in a task checkup is looking for tasks that *should* have started but haven't. If you seem to have a lot of late starters, make sure you've entered status values into Project (page 406). Once you've filled in any missing actuals, it's time to find out why the remaining tasks are delayed.

A good way to check for delayed tasks is to use the Should Start By filter. This filter shows tasks that should have started by the date you specify (say, your most recent status date) but haven't. This filter looks for tasks whose Start values are earlier than your Should Start By date but whose Actual Start cells are still empty. Once you've filtered your task list, you can then switch tables in the view to see different task values. Here's how to apply this filter:

1. **In the View tab's Data section, click the Filter down arrow, and then choose More Filters.**

   The More Filters dialog box opens.

2. **Select Should Start By and then click Apply.**

   The Should Start By dialog box opens.

3. **Type your checkup date, and then click OK.**

   The view changes to show only the tasks that should have started before the date you entered but haven't, as shown in Figure 14-3.

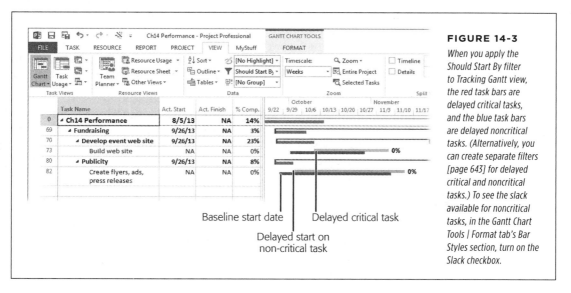

FIGURE 14-3

When you apply the Should Start By filter to Tracking Gantt view, the red task bars are delayed critical tasks, and the blue task bars are delayed noncritical tasks. (Alternatively, you can create separate filters [page 643] for delayed critical and noncritical tasks.) To see the slack available for noncritical tasks, in the Gantt Chart Tools | Format tab's Bar Styles section, turn on the Slack checkbox.

Baseline start date — Delayed critical task

Delayed start on non-critical task

4. **To see work packages without their parent summary tasks, in the Gantt Chart Tools | Format tab's Show/Hide section, turn off the Summary Tasks checkbox.**

   You see only the lowest-level tasks in your project.

Looking for Tasks Heading for Trouble

The next tactic is looking for tasks whose *finish* dates are late—later than their baseline finish dates, that is. These task delays can lead to a late project finish date *and* upset the resource workloads you so carefully balanced during planning, creating new resource overallocations you have to resolve.

Watching for ballooning work hours is another way to spot tasks that are in trouble. Just like time that slips away when attic cleaning turns into reminiscing over old pictures, the time it takes to perform tasks can expand beyond your estimates. These extra hours can produce longer task durations and higher resource costs, so it's especially important to nip these excesses in the bud.

This section shows you how to look for delayed tasks and tasks whose work hours exceed baseline work, even if they haven't yet delayed the finish date. Here are different ways to look for these at-risk tasks:

- **Tasks that are slipping.** The Slipping Tasks filter shows, well, slipping tasks—that is, tasks whose finish dates are later than their baseline finish dates. These tasks may be scheduled to start late, have already started late, or are taking longer than planned. By looking for slipping tasks every week, you may have time to recover from the slip or to prevent it from getting worse. By applying different tables to the current view, you can see dates, variances, work amounts, or costs for the tasks in the filtered list. To apply this filter, in the View tab's Data section, click the Filter down arrow, and then choose More Filters. In the More Filters dialog box, select Slipping Tasks and then click Apply.

- **Tasks that are slipping or falling behind.** The Slipped/Late Progress filter (View→Filter→More Filters→Slipped/Late Progress) looks for slipping tasks *and* checks for tasks whose completed work is less than the amount that should be done. The finish dates of these tasks haven't changed yet, but they're likely to unless you do something.

TIP   To look for schedule trends, sort the Variance table by finish date: On the View tab, click Tables→Variance, and then, in the table's header area, click the triangle next to the Finish heading and choose "Sort Earliest to Latest." That way, tasks appear from the earliest finish date to the latest. If the values in the Finish Variance field grow larger as the finish dates progress, the project is falling further behind over time. On the other hand, if the Finish Variance values are growing smaller, it may be a sign that your corrective actions are working.

- **Assignments that are slipping.** It makes sense that an assignment that slips can turn into a task that slips. The Slipping Assignments filter (View→Filter→More Filters→Slipping Assignments) is a resource filter that you can apply to Resource Usage view to find assignments whose scheduled finish dates are later than their baseline finish dates. One resource with several slipping assignments is a sure sign of someone who could use some help. The problem may be too many tasks at the same time, the wrong skillset, or too many distractions.

Seeing Status

Project offers a couple of features that can help you spot troubled tasks without filtering task lists, which is great because scanning for visual status cues is often easier than wading through numbers. You can customize fields so that they turn red, yellow, or green based on progress. In addition, progress lines show whether tasks are ahead, behind, or right on schedule in the Gantt Chart timescale. Figure 14-4 includes examples of the following status indicators:

- **Custom graphical indicators.** To display graphics based on how late or over budget a task is, you can set up a custom field with graphical indicators like a green happy face if Cost Variance is less than 10 percent of the baseline cost and a red *unhappy* face if Cost Variance is greater than 25 percent of the baseline cost. The custom field "Number4 (Cost Status)" in *ProjectMM_Customizations. mpp* (available from this book's Missing CD page at *www. missingmanuals.com/cds*) does that and more, as long as you've already set a baseline and have some actual

values in your schedule. See the box on page 440 for more information about this custom field.

- **Progress lines.** In the Gantt Chart Tools | Format tab's Format section, choose Gridlines→Progress Lines. In the Progress Line dialog box that appears, turn on the Display checkbox, and then click OK. Voilà—Project displays progress lines in the Gantt Chart timescale. A progress line drops vertically from the project status date in the timescale heading and then points to the progress in each task bar. If the task is on schedule, then the progress line continues its vertical drop. If the task is *behind* schedule, then the progress line points sharply to the left.

If you add a deadline to a task, as described on page 192, you can visually see when that task is due. If the task expands beyond its deadline date, Project displays a missed deadline indicator in the Indicators column of the view's table. See page 298 for the full scoop.

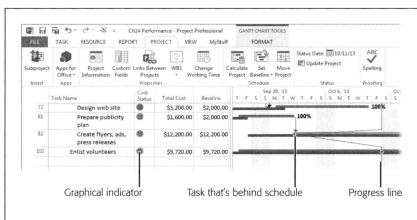

FIGURE 14-4

If you set up custom fields with graphical indicators, you can see status at a glance, like a red unhappy face for over-budget tasks (as shown here). Progress lines show whether tasks are ahead of or behind schedule. If the progress line diverts to the left, a task is behind schedule.

Graphical indicator   Task that's behind schedule   Progress line

Work hours that exceed a task's baseline hours can increase your project's duration and cost. For completed tasks, of course, it's too late to make corrections. Still, it's a good idea to investigate the reason why such overruns occurred, particularly if the same resources are over budget on task after task. You can also check tasks in progress to see if the amount of work you expect is complete. To do that, use one or more of the following Project features:

- **Work table.** The Work table shows several work fields: scheduled, baseline, actual and remaining work, and work variance. It also includes % Work Complete, which is the percentage of the current scheduled work that's done. (The box below explains the difference between % Complete and % Work Complete.) Positive values in the Variance column show tasks whose scheduled work hours are greater than the baseline work hours.

  You can look for tasks that may be falling behind by inserting the % Complete field next to the % Work Complete column in this table. If a task's % Work Complete value is less than its % Complete value, time is passing faster than work is being completed, which is often early warning for future delays.

- **Work Overbudget filter.** The Work Overbudget filter (View→Filter→More Filters→Work Overbudget) shows tasks whose actual work has already exceeded the baseline work, so it's already too late to recover from this overindulgence. However, if several tasks using the same resource are all completed over their work budget, you can try replacing that resource with one who's more productive.

- **Slipped/Late Progress filter.** Although this filter tests for schedule slip, as you learned earlier in this section, it has a work aspect, too. It looks for tasks in which the completed work is less than what you'd planned at this point. To apply it, choose View→Filter→More Filters→Slipped/Late Progress.

UP TO SPEED

How Much Is Complete?

The Tracking table includes columns for actual dates, duration, cost, and work, which are self-explanatory. However, the table's other two columns, % Complete and Physical % Complete, may not be so obvious.

The % Complete field shows the percentage of a task's duration that has passed; it says nothing about how much progress has been made during that time. For example, if 5 days of a 10-day task have passed, the task's % Complete is 50 percent regardless of how much work has been done.

On the other hand, the Physical % Complete field lets you specify how much of the task is complete for earned-value calculations. Project doesn't calculate this field. You have to type values like *20%*, *50%*, and so on to tell Project the amount

of completion to use. For example, suppose you're working on a task to put up signs along the route of the cycling event. You have 100 signs to put up and you've stuck 40 in the ground so far. In that case, Physical % Complete is 40%. (See page 448 to learn more about Physical % Complete and other earned-value fields.)

% Work Complete is yet another field for percentage completion, although it appears initially in the Work table, not the Tracking table. % Work Complete is the percentage of actual work compared with scheduled work. If a task's % Work Complete value is less than its % Complete value, that means the amount of work performed isn't keeping up with the time consumed, meaning the task could be headed for trouble.

▓ Is the Project Within Budget?

Checking cost status isn't as simple as seeing whether there's money in your wallet. When budgeted dollars run out in one place, accounting procedures sometimes grab money from another place. By tracking cost and budget resources in Project, you can follow project money *without* depending on your finance department. And if you work in a relatively simple financial environment, cost variance and other earned value measures may be enough. This section describes different ways to compare cost expenditures to the baseline costs you set.

As you learned earlier, the project summary task shows the cost variance for an entire project—that is, the difference between scheduled and baseline costs. If this variance is positive, then the project is forecasted to be over budget. Unless the project is almost over, you may still have time to reduce costs. (A negative cost variance means the project may come in under budget, although that outcome isn't assured until the project is complete.) This section explains how to dig deeper into your project's cost status if the project summary task shows that costs are over budget.

Comparing Costs Using Views and Filters

Similar to the way they help you look for over-budget work, Project's tables, filters, and reports can help you find expanding costs. The box on page 440 explains how to focus on your project's *biggest* cost overruns. Here are two of Project's built-in elements that show costs:

- **Cost table.** This table (in the View tab's Data section, click Tables→Cost) includes the project's scheduled, baseline, actual, and remaining costs. The Variance column is the Cost Variance field, so you can see whether tasks are forecasted to be over or under budget. (Positive variances mean over budget.) The Total Cost column is really the Cost field, which includes labor costs that Project calculates, cost resources you've assigned to tasks, and fixed costs you've set.

- **Cost Overbudget filter.** To display only tasks whose scheduled cost is greater than the baseline cost, apply this filter. In the View tab's Data section, click the Filter down arrow, and then choose More Filters. In the More Filters dialog box, double-click Cost Overbudget.

Focusing on Big Money Problems

For large projects, going a few dollars over budget on one task can sometimes distract you from the big budget problems on others. Fortunately, custom fields can help you focus on *serious* cost overruns. For example, the "Number4 (Cost Status)" custom field in *ProjectMM_Customizations.mpp* (which you can download from this book's Missing CD page at *www.missing manuals.com/cds*) calculates the percentage of cost variance compared with baseline cost. It displays graphical indicators based on this value, but you can also filter the task list with a field like this. For example, you could create a custom filter (page 643) that shows tasks whose "Number4 (Cost Status)" field is greater than 10 percent.

Another approach is to create a filter that displays tasks whose cost variance is greater than a dollar amount like $5,000. Consider a task whose baseline cost is $200 and cost variance $100. That's a 50 percent overrun, but $100 may mean little in a multimillion-dollar project. As long as you're customizing a filter, you can define it to filter by dollar amount *and* percentage! The BigOverrun filter in *ProjectMM_Customizations.mpp* does just that, although it asks for the cost variance and cost status values you want to use.

Evaluating Costs with Reports

Project has several reports for studying costs. Chapter 16 describes working with Project's reports in detail. Here's a quick intro to reports that help you evaluate cost:

- **Cash Flow.** This new graphical report (Report→Costs→Cash Flow) starts with a banner across the top that shows actual cost, baseline cost, remaining cost, and cost variance. A chart includes bars that represent how much was spent each quarter and a line indicating the cumulative cost over time. And at the bottom is a table with cost status for top-level tasks, although you can change it to display tasks at different outline levels (page 481).

- **Cost Overruns.** This new graphical report (Report→Costs→Cost Overruns) focuses on cost variance by task and resource. The two charts at the top show variance for top-level tasks and all work resources. For example, a resource with a big cost variance could indicate someone who isn't as productive as you expected.

- **Baseline Cost.** You can choose either the Excel or Visio Baseline Cost visual report (see page 489). The Excel Baseline Cost report is a bar graph that compares scheduled cost, baseline cost, and actual cost for top-level summary tasks. If the scheduled cost is greater than the baseline cost, then the summary task is over budget. You can alter the report to compare costs by fiscal quarter or drill down to compare costs task by task (or resource by resource). The Visio Baseline Cost visual report adds icons to task boxes that are over budget for cost or work.

- **Budget.** The Budget Cost visual report is like the Baseline Cost report with budget resource costs added (see page 475). It lets you compare scheduled costs, baseline costs, and the budget line item values so you can see where expenditures are relative to your allotted budget dollars.

> **NOTE** Earned value analysis is such an effective way to evaluate project costs that it gets its own section, which starts below. Project's earned value reports are described there.

Comparing Project Costs to a Budget

Budget resources can represent line items in a financial budget. You can allot budget dollars to budget resources in a Project file and then compare your project costs to the budgeted amounts. Setting up budget resources for this type of comparison takes several steps, explained in detail in Chapter 10 (page 273). If you use budget resources, then you can compare budgeted costs to scheduled costs by category, as shown in Figure 10-12 on page 286.

Budget resources are a type of resource in Project, so you need a resource view like Resource Usage to see them in order to compare budget-resource costs to scheduled costs. With Resource Usage view grouped by budget item, Project creates a summary row for each budget category you track. (The BudgetItem group is available in *ProjectMM_Customizations.mpp*, which you can download from this book's Missing CD page at *www.missingmanuals.com/cds*. In the Organizer, select the Groups tab, and then select the Resource option.) The Budget Cost or Budget Work cells in group summary rows show the budgeted values for each budget category, allowing you to see all the work, material, and cost resources associated with that budget item.

■ Earned Value Analysis

Earned value analysis is like the idea behind that old Smith Barney slogan, "We make money the old fashioned way—we earn it." Earned value analysis measures progress according to how much of your project's value (its cost) you've earned so far by completing work.

Project customers, sponsors, and stakeholders want to know how far along a project is. Earned value alone tells you only how much of the project's cost you've earned—it doesn't say anything about the schedule. Other earned value measures provide a picture of schedule status. If a project has spent half its budget, consumed half its forecast duration, and completed half of its work, you're all set. However, if the budget and duration are half spent, but the work is only 25 percent complete, something is wrong. You have only 50 percent of the budget and duration left to complete 75 percent of the work.

This section explains how to use various earned-value measures to keep tabs on your project.

NOTE Earned value analysis requires a baseline in your Project file, so you have a plan to compare to. If you haven't set a baseline yet (page 374), all the earned value fields are zero. You also have to set a status date and enter actual values as of that date (see Chapter 13) to show what you've accomplished and how much it cost.

Gauging Performance with Earned Value Measures

Earned value analysis uses several calculations to measure schedule and cost status. However, all earned value measures are based on three basic measurements:

- **Planned cost for scheduled work.** In project-management circles, you'll hear *planned value* described as the *budgeted cost of work scheduled* (or BCWS, which is also the name of the corresponding Project field). In English, planned value is the cost you expected to incur for the work scheduled through the status date—that is, the baseline cost for the work that should have been completed as of the status date.

  For example, suppose you're managing a tiger-taming project that's scheduled to tame 24 tigers over 24 months for a total cost of $240,000—$10,000 per tiger. According to that plan, 10 tigers should be tamed at the end of 10 months at a planned value of $100,000.

- **Planned cost for completed work.** This measure is called *earned value* because it represents the baseline cost you've earned by completing work as of the status date. It's also known as *budgeted cost of work performed* or BCWP (the name of the corresponding Project field). For example, if you've tamed six tigers as of the status date, then the earned value is $60,000.

- **Actual cost of completed work.** Actual cost is easy: It's how much you actually spent as of the status date. For example, if you've spent $50,000 through the first 10 months of tiger taming, that's your actual cost of completed work. This measure is sometimes called *actual cost of work performed* or ACWP (again, the name of the Project field).

Analyzing an Earned Value Graph

Because planned value, earned value, and actual cost are all monetary values, you can compare them to evaluate schedule and cost performance. In earned value graphs, the relative positions of the three lines for these measures show whether the project is on schedule and within budget.

Gleaning schedule and cost performance from an earned value graph is easy once you know how to compare planned value, earned value, and actual costs. The Earned Value Report, a new graphical report shown in Figure 14-5, graphs all three measures over time. Here's how you evaluate schedule and cost performance with these three measures:

- **Schedule performance.** The comparison between planned value and earned value is what provides you with a schedule status. Planned value is the baseline cost for the work you *expected* to complete, while earned value is the baseline cost of the work that's *actually* complete. If earned value is less than planned value (like $60,000 versus $100,000 in the tiger-taming project), less work is complete than you expected—thus, the project is behind schedule. If earned value is greater than planned value, then more work is complete than you expected, and the project is ahead of schedule.

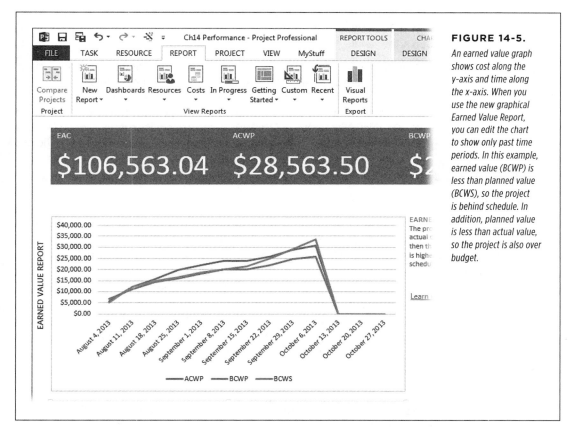

FIGURE 14-5.

An earned value graph shows cost along the y-axis and time along the x-axis. When you use the new graphical Earned Value Report, you can edit the chart to show only past time periods. In this example, earned value (BCWP) is less than planned value (BCWS), so the project is behind schedule. In addition, planned value is less than actual value, so the project is also over budget.

- **Cost performance.** This is the difference between earned value and actual cost. If the earned value is greater than the actual cost, then the work performed cost less than you planned—the project is under budget. For example, the earned value for the tiger taming project is $60,000, while the actual is only $50,000, so it's $10,000 under budget. If earned value is less than the actual cost, then the project is over budget.

Using Additional Earned Value Measures

You can combine a project's planned value, earned value, and actual cost to view project performance from different perspectives. Additional measures show the efficiency of the project or estimated final costs based on performance so far. Here are the additional earned value measures and what they do:

- **Schedule variance** (the SV field in Project) is earned value minus planned value (BCWP – BCWS), the difference between how much work you've completed and how much you planned to complete. If SV is positive, more work is complete than you planned, so you're ahead of schedule. SV for the tiger project is $60,000 minus $100,000, which equals negative $40,000, so the project is behind schedule.

- **Cost variance** (the CV field in Project) is earned value minus the actual cost—in other words, the difference between the baseline and actual cost of the work performed (BCWP – ACWP). If CV is positive, then the baseline cost is greater than the actual cost, so the project is under budget. CV for the tiger project is $60,000 minus $50,000, or $10,000, so the project is under budget. (The box on below explains the difference between Project's Cost Variance and CV fields.)

GEM IN THE ROUGH

Is Positive Variance Good or Bad?

You don't see the Cost Variance and CV fields side by side in any built-in Project tables, which is good because they seem to contradict one another. For example, if the Cost Variance field shows a variance of $1,000, then the CV field shows a variance of ($1,000)—that is, negative $1,000.

With one variance positive and the other negative, it's hard to figure out whether the cost variance is good or bad. The CV field is earned value minus actual cost, which is the *true* arbiter of cost performance. As you've already learned, if earned value is greater than the actual cost, then the project or task is under budget. To help you remember, CV is a positive value when the project or task is under budget, a desirable (that is, positive) result. Keep in mind that the CV field applies only to completed work, because tasks have earned value only for the portion of the task that's complete. (See page 448 to learn how to change the definition of "complete" in Project.)

On the other hand, the Cost Variance field is the Cost field minus the Baseline Cost field, so it's a positive value when the result is *undesirable*—the project or task is over budget.

- **Schedule performance index** (SPI) is the ratio of earned value divided by the planned value (BCWP / BCWS). For example, when the project is on schedule, earned value and planned value are equal, and SPI equals 1.0. An SPI less than 1.0 means earned value is less than planned value, indicating that the project is behind schedule. SPI for the tiger project is $60,000 / $100,000 or 0.6—that is, it's behind schedule.

Because it's a ratio, SPI tells you how good or bad schedule performance is, regardless of the dollars involved. For example, a small project may have SV equal to $5,000, while a large project SV may be $125,000. However, an SPI of 0.6 shows that both projects have earned value that's 60 percent of the planned value.

- **Cost performance index** (CPI) is the ratio of earned value to actual cost (BCWP / ACWP). If the ratio is greater than 1.0, then earned value is greater than actual cost, which means you spent less to complete the work performed than you'd planned—so the project is under budget. For example, CPI of 1.2 means earned value is 20 percent higher than the actual cost. CPI for the tiger project is $60,000 / $50,000 or 1.2. The project is under budget, but *not* by 20 percent! If you remember your algebra, the percentage this sample project is under budget is ($60,000 – $50,000) / $60,000. That's equal to $10,000 / $60,000, or 16.6 percent under budget.

> **NOTE** You might wonder why earned value analysis calculates the cost performance index, instead of the percentage that the project is over or under budget. Because CPI is a simple ratio of earned value to actual cost, you can use it to forecast the cost of the project at completion, as described in the "Estimate at completion" measure described below.

- **Budget at completion** (BAC) is simply the baseline cost. If you look carefully, you'll see that the Baseline Cost and BAC fields are always equal.

- **Estimate at completion** (EAC) is an estimate of how much a task will cost when it's done, based on the performance so far. Here's the formula for EAC:

```
ACWP + ((BAC - BCWP) / CPI)
```

EAC has two components. The first is the actual cost so far (ACWP). The second, (BAC – BCWP) / CPI, is a cost forecast based on the cost performance index. It's the remaining baseline cost (baseline cost minus the earned value) divided by the cost performance index. For example, here's the calculation for the tiger project EAC:

```
Actual cost = $50,000
BAC - BCWP = $240,000 - $60,000 = $180,000
(BAC - BCWP) / CPI = $180,000 / 1.2 = $150,000
EAC = $200,000
```

Because the cost performance index shows that the project is under budget, EAC assumes that trend will continue. That's why project EAC is only $200,000 compared with project BAC of $240,000.

> **NOTE** Project's Cost and EAC fields are not the same. Cost combines actual costs, remaining labor costs (work multiplied to the resource rates), overtime, and other types of cost like those for materials and cost resources. EAC, on the other hand, assumes that the remaining cost will be inflated or decreased by the same amount as the cost so far; it doesn't take remaining work into consideration at all.

- **Variance at completion** (VAC) is the estimated variance when the task or project is done. It's the baseline cost at completion (BAC) minus the estimate at completion (EAC). For example, VAC for the tiger-taming project is $240,000 – $200,000, or $40,000.

• **To complete performance index** (TCPI) is the ratio of the work that remains (expressed in dollars) to remaining available dollars. Here's the formula:

```
(BAC - BCWP) / (BAC - ACWP)
```

The numerator of the ratio is the remaining baseline cost for the remaining work; the denominator is the remaining available dollars. If TCPI is greater than 1.0, then the remaining baseline cost is greater than the remaining dollars—in other words, you don't have enough money left to pay for the remaining work. If the baseline cost for the remaining work is less than the available dollars, then you have a surplus.

TCPI for the tiger project is $180,000 / $190,000 or 0.95, which means the project is under budget.

> **TIP** When you're looking at Project tables and need a quick review of these fields and formulas, position your mouse pointer over the appropriate column's header. When the ScreenTip appears, click the link to the help topic for the column's Project field.

Viewing Earned Value in Project

You can examine earned value measures in several places in Project. To see earned value task by task, nothing beats the program's earned value tables. Project also has a new graphical report that provides a visual status of earned value. And you can run the Earned Value Over Time visual report if you want to analyze earned value in more ways than the graphical Earned Value Report can (page 442). Here's where you can find earned value in Project:

• **Earned Value table.** Apply this table, shown in Figure 14-6, to any task-oriented view (in the View tab's Data section, click Tables, and then choose More Tables. In the More Tables dialog box, double-click Earned Value). This table includes all the basic earned value fields: planned value (BCWS), earned value (BCWP), actual cost (ACWP), SV, CV, EAC, BAC, and VAC.

• **Earned Value Cost Indicators table.** This table focuses on cost performance. It includes basic earned value fields but adds CV% (CV as a percentage of the planned value), CPI, and TCPI.

• **Earned Value Schedule Indicators table.** This table focuses on schedule performance. It includes planned value (BCWS), earned value (BCWP), SV, CV, SV%, and SPI.

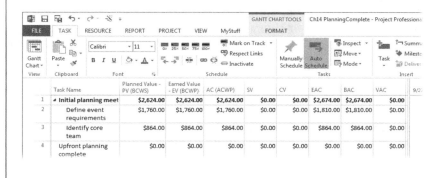

FIGURE 14-6

If you use earned value tables frequently, you can save time by adding them to the Tables drop-down list. In the View tab's Data section, click Tables, and then choose More Tables. In the More Tables dialog box, select the table you're interested in, and then click Edit. In the Table Definition dialog box, turn on the "Show in menu" checkbox, and then click OK. From then on, you can apply the table simply by heading to the View tab's Data section, clicking Tables, and then choosing the table's name.

- **Earned Value Report.** This report initially shows the graph of earned value over time (see Figure 14-5 on page 443). To run this report, in the Report tab's View Report section, click Costs→Earned Value Report.

- **Earned Value Over Time visual report.** This report includes a graph of earned value over time like the graphical Earned Value Report does. As you'll learn in Chapter 16, you can modify this report to show earned value for specific time periods or specific tasks. You can also use this report to export earned value data to another program (page 545). To run this report, in the Report tab's Export section, click Visual Reports. In the "Visual Reports – Create Report" dialog box, select Earned Value Over Time Report, and then click View.

Controlling How Project Calculates Earned Value

Project has a couple of options for calculating earned values. You can specify which saved baseline Project uses as well as which field specifies how complete tasks are.

Initially, Project uses values in the Baseline fields. If you always store your current baseline in the Baseline fields as recommended on page 376, you don't have to change any settings. However, if you want to calculate earned values using Baseline1 through Baseline10 instead, choose File→Options. On the left side of the Project Options dialog box, click Advanced. Under the "Earned Value options for this project" heading, in the "Baseline for Earned Value Calculations" drop-down list, choose the baseline you want.

The PMI's Project Management Body of Knowledge (PMBOK) recommends two possible definitions of "complete" for earned value calculations. But in Project you can choose among *three* ways to define complete:

- **All or nothing.** The conservative approach says a task is complete or it isn't, which means 100 percent complete is the only value that represents complete. Any less than that and the task is incomplete (and not included in earned value calculations). Project uses this approach unless you specifically set up your Project file to use one of the other options in this list. If a task's % Complete field is 100%, then Project calculates its earned value fields. A % Complete value less than 100% means earned value fields are zero.

- **Unstarted, started, or complete.** If a project has very long tasks, the all-or-nothing approach may be too harsh. Another approach is to leave unstarted tasks as 0%, set completed tasks to 100%, and set tasks in progress to 50%.

> **TIP** Another approach is to mimic the values on the task mini-toolbar (right-click a task to see it): 0% for unstarted, 25% for started, 50% for halfway, 75% for almost complete, and 100% for complete.

- **Completed work.** A more accurate approach is to measure completeness by the percentage of work that's complete.

If you want to use the second or third approach, you have to tell Project to use the Physical % Complete field to calculate earned value. Unlike % Complete, which Project calculates, Physical % Complete is a value *you* enter, so you can make it as accurate as you want. For example, you can set Physical % Complete to 0%, 50%, or 100% depending on whether tasks are unstarted, in progress, or complete. Or you can enter the value from the % Work Complete field into the Physical % Complete field.

> **NOTE** Although Project lets you select different earned value methods for different tasks, it's best to use the same method for all tasks. If you use % Complete, then you know that Project calculates the values for you. If you use Physical % Complete, then you have to type in the values.

To use Physical % Complete, choose File→Options. On the left side of the Project Options dialog box, click Advanced. Under "Earned Value options for this project" in the "Default task Earned Value method" drop-down list, choose Physical % Complete.

> **NOTE** Changing the "Default task Earned Value method" option has no effect on *existing* tasks, which are usually the ones you want to evaluate. (The new setting affects only tasks added to the project after the change.) Fortunately, there's an easy way to change the setting for existing tasks: Insert the Earned Value Method field into a table (right-click a table heading and then choose Insert Column→Earned Value Method). Change the value in the first Earned Value Method cell to Physical % Complete, and then drag that value over all the other cells in the column using the fill handle (page 150).

■ Getting Back on Track

One reason project management can be so, ahem, fulfilling is the plethora of choices you have for addressing problems. When your project isn't meeting its schedule or budget, you can choose from several fine-tuning techniques—or a combination of several—to set the project straight. Chapter 11 covered several of these methods, which work as well during execution as they did during planning. This section covers one additional approach that you turn to only during execution: assigning overtime.

A Review of Project-Tuning Techniques

There's no such thing as a free lunch. Techniques that shorten a project's duration may cost more, deliver less, or demand more from resources. Cutting project costs may increase duration, decrease scope, reduce quality, or increase risk. Here's a quick review of the ways you can adjust a schedule to correct course:

- **Increasing resource workloads.** Assigning more of resources' time means more work gets done in a shorter duration (page 351). This approach assumes resources have more time to give, are willing to give it, and remain as productive as they were when they worked a more reasonable schedule. Even then, it works only for extremely short durations.

- **Assigning resources with more availability.** If you have resources who aren't already working around the clock, you can replace busy resources with people who have more available time (page 351). (Don't forget to evaluate the cost of bringing a new person up to speed on the project.)

- **Assigning more resources.** Assigning more resources can shorten duration by providing more work hours every day (page 255). However, the chaos of too many people on one task may actually *increase* duration.

- **Assigning faster or lower-cost resources.** If you're trying to reduce duration, faster resources can help—but often at a higher cost. To save money, you can assign less-expensive resources, possibly increasing duration.

- **Juggle assignments to use existing slack time.** If resources working on non-critical tasks can work on critical tasks instead, then you may be able to shorten the project's critical path (page 353).

- **Shorten lag time.** Reducing lag time (page 353) between tasks can shorten duration. If lag times depend on people's responses, then you have to ask whether they can respond more quickly.

- **Fast-track tasks.** You can shorten duration by overlapping tasks that normally run in sequence (page 354). However, this approach increases the risk of re-work if earlier tasks affect work that's already been done in the successor tasks.

- **Crashing tasks.** *Crashing* (page 356) means spending more money to obtain shorter duration (usually by assigning more resources).

- **Reducing scope.** You can cut duration and cost by reducing the project's scope, as long as the project customer is OK with that change.

- **Reducing quality.** Cutting quality is another compromise, as long as the customer agrees.

- **Using management reserve.** Management reserve is a pool of money or reserved schedule time that management can free up to help a project (see page 169).

Assigning Overtime

Overtime has no place during project planning because it leaves you no room for maneuvering later on. For example, if you create a project plan that has resources working 12-hour days 7 days a week, it's unlikely you can fix a delayed schedule by having resources work *16*-hour days. However, when a project is under way and the schedule slips, overtime can keep task durations from increasing by, in effect, overallocating resources for short periods of time.

Project gives you several ways to represent overtime. You have to resort to the Overtime Work field *only* when resources cost more for overtime hours. Here are two ways to assign extra hours:

- **Increasing work time for a period.** For team members who aren't paid higher overtime rates, you can define longer hours through the resource calendar or the Resource Information dialog box. To specify work hours for a period of time, define a work week or an exception in a resource calendar (page 111). You can set the start and end dates for the period and the start and end times for workdays.

  To change available units for a period of time, in Resource Sheet view, double-click the resource. In the Resource Information dialog box, in the Resource Availability section, specify the start and end date for the extra hours and the units you want to assign during that time.

- **Overtime hours paid at an overtime rate.** When resources are paid more for overtime hours, you have to assign overtime hours in Project (you'll learn how shortly) or the labor costs won't be correct. The box on page 451 explains how Project tracks overtime and calculates overtime cost. You set a resource's overtime rate in Resource Sheet view's aptly named Overtime Rate field.

A customized usage view simplifies assigning overtime and seeing how Project allocates it. Resource Usage view with the Overtime Hours field in the table and time-phased area does the trick. The *ProjectMM_Customizations.mpp* file available from this book's Missing CD page at *www.missingmanuals.com/cds* contains a view called Overtime Usage, which displays Work and Overtime Work. It initially filters the list for overallocated resources, but you can remove that filter by heading to the View tab's Data section, and then, in the filter drop-down list, choosing All Resources.

Overtime Costs

In Project, work hours reside in the Work, Regular Work, and Overtime Work fields. Without overtime, all assigned work hours are regular work hours so the values in the Work and Regular Work fields are equal. If you enter hours in the Overtime Work field, Project subtracts those hours from the Regular Work field; the Work value stays the same. For example, if a task's Work value is 80 hours and you assign 20 hours of overtime, its Overtime Work value changes to 20 hours, while its Regular Work value shrinks to 60 hours.

Project calculates the labor cost for Regular Work hours by multiplying the regular work hours by the standard labor rate (Standard Rate in the Resource Sheet). Overtime labor cost is overtime work hours multiplied by the overtime rate. For example, consider the same 80-hour task. At $50 an hour for regular work, the labor cost is $4,000. If the overtime rate is $60 an hour, then the task's cost changes to $4,200 (60 hours × $50 and 20 hours × $60).

To set up an overtime view of your own, follow these steps:

1. **Copy a new view as a foundation for overtime usage.**

   In the View tab's Task Views section, click the bottom half of the Task Usage button, and then choose More Views. In the More Views dialog box, select Task Usage and then click Copy. In the View Definition dialog box's Name field, type a new view name, like *Overtime Usage*, and then click OK.

2. **If necessary, display the Work table in the view.**

   In the View tab's Data section, click Tables→Work. The Overtime Work column appears to the left of the Work column.

3. **To display Overtime Work in the time-phased area, right-click anywhere in the time-phased grid, and then, on the shortcut menu, click Overtime Work.**

   A checkmark appears to the left of the field's name. Each assignment in the view now includes an additional row for Overtime Work (the label is "Ovt. Work").

To assign overtime work, in the table pane on the left side of the view, select the Overtime Work cell for the assignment you want to modify, and then type the number of overtime hours. Project recalculates the task duration due to the extra hours and allocates the overtime hours over the remaining duration, as shown in Figure 14-7.

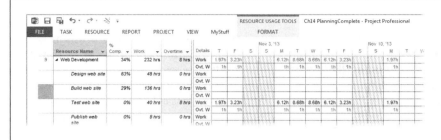

FIGURE 14-7

Although the usage times-cale shows overtime hours allocated day by day, you can't edit the hours in the individual time periods. You can, however, edit the Work hours.

> **TIP** You can also type overtime hours in the Task Form. Right-click the form, and then choose Work from the shortcut menu. Then, in the resource's Overtime Work cell, type the overtime hours.

Reducing Scope by Inactivating Tasks

If nothing seems to shorten the schedule or reduce the budget, a reduction in scope may be in order. *You* don't get to eliminate scope; only the stakeholders can, and even then, only if the project customer approves.

Decisions have a way of changing, so making tasks inactive in your Project file is a great method for cutting scope. Should the stakeholders decide to revert to the original plan, you can reactivate the inactive tasks without skipping a beat.

> **TIP** Inactive tasks also work well if you want to document nice-to-have work. Create tasks, assign resources, and fill in other fields; then make the tasks inactive. Their values are visible (and editable) but don't affect your project schedule. If you find that the project has the time and budget for the work (and the stakeholders approve), you can make the tasks active.

Making tasks inactive removes their values from your project's rolled-up schedule and cost. However, the tasks, their resource assignments, and field values remain in the plan, as Figure 14-8 shows, so you have a record of what you cut out. You can edit inactive tasks as you do active tasks. If you reactivate the tasks, you don't have to re-enter any information.

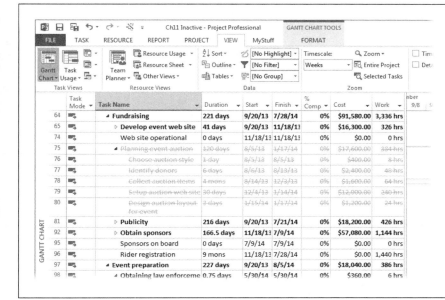

FIGURE 14-8

Inactive tasks are grayed out and have a line drawn through their values. However, you can select an inactive task's cell in a table and edit its value, or double-click the task to open the Task Information dialog box. When you inactivate tasks, their duration and cost don't roll up into summary task values, and their resource assignments don't affect the assigned resources' availability.

Changing tasks to inactive is a snap: Select one or more tasks in a task-oriented view and then, in the Task tab's Schedule section, click Inactivate. The inactive tasks immediately change to gray with a strikethrough line drawn through their values in the table area. You can edit an inactive task's values by double-clicking it to open the Task Information dialog box or by editing directly in the table cells.

To reactivate a task, select it and then, in the Task tab's Schedule section, click Inactivate once again.

Managing Change

N o matter how flawlessly or exhaustively you plan your project, you can't foresee *everything* that might bubble up. Project management is a rich gumbo of
managing time, resources, and costs. You also can't forget to add managing
risks, issues, and change to the project-management pot. In fact, some people say
that managing projects is essentially managing change.

Project changes come in all shapes and sizes. A change can be as small as adding
a single task you overlooked. Cost-cutting measures that eliminate your contract
labor and part-time resources constitute a major change. You can distill all these
changes into two main categories: changes you can address without someone else's
approval and changes you can't. Suppose a task on the critical path takes a few
days longer than planned. In a situation like that, you evaluate your options, such as
fast-tracking or reassigning resources, and choose the one you think is the best for
getting the schedule back on track. However, if a stakeholder asks for a big change
to a deliverable, you probably need approval from the customer or management
team before you jump into action.

This chapter introduces the two major aspects to managing project change: setting
up a change-management system and incorporating changes into your project plan.
A change-management system plays two important roles. First, it helps you prevent
scope creep by identifying changes to the project and then deciding whether or
not to include them. Second, it provides a consistent process for evaluating change
requests and getting them approved (which essentially means getting approval for
the effect of those changes on the project schedule). That process may involve a
change review board—a group of people who have the responsibility and authority
to accept or reject change requests. The chapter also describes ways to track such
requests.

Equally important, you'll learn ways to incorporate changes into your project plan, whether the changes are your solution to a delay or a change request from someone else. The chapter describes ways to add tentative changes to a Project file, so you can determine the impact of a change request before presenting it to the change review board. Finally, you'll learn how to set a new baseline that includes change requests and how to track the progress of change requests.

Setting Up a Change-Management System

When you manage a project, change is unavoidable. You're continually beset on all sides with requests and demands to change some aspect of your project. You also gain a better understanding of the project as time passes. Team members may uncover new information or requirements that seem to be aligned with the project's objectives. The powers that be, who are under considerable pressure to deliver faster results and higher profits, can in turn ask you to bring in the project's finish date or reduce costs—or both.

A significant part of your project manager role is to handle these change requests and incorporate the ones that make sense into the project plan. You need flexibility so you can take advantage of proposed changes, like the one suggested in Figure 15-1. At the same time, you also need a way to ensure that the project's scope, schedule, and budget don't change without the customer's or stakeholders' approval.

A change-management process can deliver that balance between control and flexibility. It provides mechanisms for people to submit change requests, for your team to evaluate submitted requests, and for a change review board to decide the fate of those requests. After change requests are approved, they become part of the project, and you track the work they require as you do the original tasks in your plan.

In this section, you'll learn techniques for controlling project changes like developing a change-request tracking system and forming a change review board for deciding which changes should go into the project plan.

As you learned in Chapter 2, a description of your project's change-control processes is part of the project plan. Publish the processes and forms to a central location so stakeholders and team members know what to do when a change request arises.

TIP There are times when free rein is called for. Suppose you're brainstorming strategies for a project or your team is experimenting with different designs. People need some time to be creative and explore alternatives. Don't bother with change control in situations like these. *After* an alternative is approved by stakeholders, you can place it under change management.

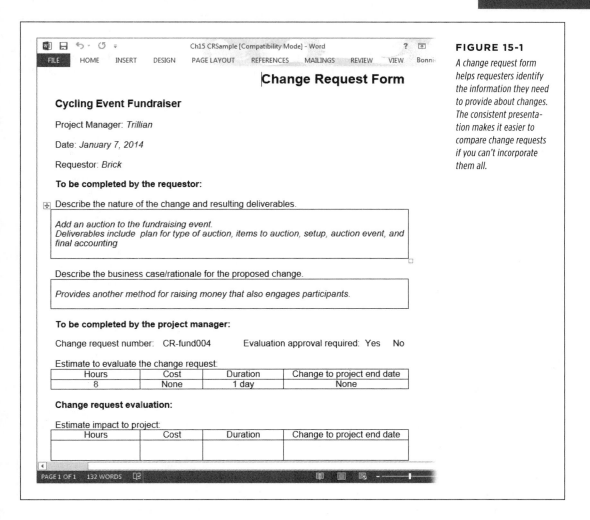

FIGURE 15-1

A change request form helps requesters identify the information they need to provide about changes. The consistent presentation makes it easier to compare change requests if you can't incorporate them all.

Managing Change Requests

You could field change requests by scrawling them on a sticky note when someone stops by with a suggestion, flagging emails containing requests, or just saying no to all demands, like Dilbert's manager. But change requests of any sort of volume make these approaches impractical.

You need a tracking system, which can be as formal or informal as your project or organization itself. A notebook in which you or the requester records the change request may be sufficient. Or people could submit change requests through a change request form posted on a collaboration website (like a SharePoint site) that stores the requests and filters entries depending on their status. The tracking system includes information about each change request, including a unique identification number for each one, the name of the person who requested the change, a description of the change (and why it's needed), estimated hours and cost, and the status of the request.

If you opt for a simple approach like the form shown in Figure 15-1, you can enter and track the status of submitted change requests with an Excel spreadsheet like the one in Figure 15-2. The box below describes some of the features of many change control systems.

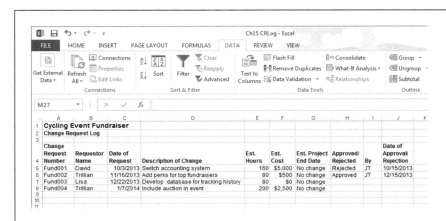

FIGURE 15-2

When you use an Excel spreadsheet to track change requests, you can find change requests more easily if you sort rows or apply an AutoFilter, for example, to display only approved requests. In Excel, in the Data tab's Sort & Filter section, choose either Sort or Filter.

Special Change-Control Situations

The easiest way to develop a change-control system is by using one that already exists, either in your company or in the customer's. If the people who sit on the change review board are already familiar with the processes, change control can be up and running in no time.

If you're developing your own change-control system, be sure to include procedures to handle the following situations:

- **Automatic change request approval.** You could be overwhelmed by the tsunami of change requests that come in. One way to reduce the load is by defining conditions that trigger automatic change request approval, like changes that have no effect on schedule, cost, or scope. You can set thresholds, like a $500 cost limit, for a change request to be automatic.

- **Emergency change requests.** Sometimes a change request needs to be decided on and put into place before the next change review board meeting. The change-control system needs to include a special process for such emergency requests.

- **Documenting changes.** Whether change requests are automatic, emergency, or regular, you need a procedure for documenting the changes and incorporating them into the project plan.

NOTE   You can download a blank change request form, *Ch15_ChangeRequestForm.docx*, from this book's
Missing CD page at *www.missingmanuals.com/cds*. In addition, you can download *Ch15 CRLog.xlsx*, which is the
log shown in Figure 15-2.

The Change Review Board: Deciding on Changes

A change review board evaluates project change requests and gives them a thumbs-
up or a thumbs-down. More importantly, a change review board has the *authority*
to do so.

Consider the composition of your change review board carefully. Stakeholders who
have the authority to approve changes to the project's schedule, cost, or scope are,
of course, essential. But think about including other stakeholders and other team
members, too, like team leaders or resource managers who are familiar with workloads and skillsets. Other candidates are people from departments like accounting,
marketing, and procurement. Another approach is to set up a core change review
board and then invite ad-hoc experts to participate as needed.

Of course you, as project manager, must sit on the change review board. You have
the most intimate knowledge of potential impacts to the project, and the power
to evaluate what-if scenarios (with the help of Project) to help the board make
informed decisions.

As you build your project plan, you decide how often the change review board should
meet, how the meeting should be conducted, and the rules by which changes are
approved or denied. For example, you may facilitate the meetings or delegate that
responsibility to someone else. All these details become the change-management
section of your plan. The box below talks about how to handle the time you spend
on managing changes.

Now that the project is under way, it's time to use your change request tracking
system as the agenda for change review board meetings. The board reviews new
change requests, examines information about requests they're considering, and
follows up on the status of approved requests.

REALITY CHECK

Accounting for Change-Management Work

If you foresee spending many hours attending and preparing
for change review board meetings, don't forget to add tasks
for this work to your Project schedule. You can set up recurring tasks (page 135) for the meetings themselves as well as
the time you spend before and after collecting or distributing
information.

Preparing for these meetings isn't trivial. You may have to
develop and evaluate what-if scenarios for pending change
requests or produce progress reports for approved requests.
Change review board meetings, like status meetings, may not
take as long as the preparation for them, but they require far
more stamina.

Tracking Change Requests

Whenever you leave a change review board meeting, you probably have several action items to attend to. They fall into these three categories:

- **Update the change-tracking system.** You update the change-request log with decisions made during the meeting: changes accepted, changes denied, or changes that need more information.

- **Provide project plan information.** If the change review board asks for more information, your job is to collect that info or delegate the task to someone else. For example, the board may want a cost analysis of a change request, a list of who has the necessary skills and availability for a request, or a Gantt chart showing the new dates if a change is accepted.

- **Update the project plan.** Update the Project schedule with approved changes, as described in the next section. The change in Project may be as simple as replacing one resource with another, or as complex as developing an entire sub-project while still hitting the original project finish date.

■ Managing Changes in Project

The work of the change review board and your work in Project are closely intertwined, both when the board is evaluating changes and after changes have been approved. The board typically compares the benefits of a proposed change with the costs (in dollars or days) and risk. To make that comparison, the board needs to know how a change request affects the project. After approval, the board wants to know how change requests are progressing. Updating progress on change request tasks is no different from updating original project tasks. But you do need a way to distinguish change request tasks from the original work packages.

In this section, you'll learn how to create simple or extensive what-if scenarios based on the level of information the change review board needs. You'll get tips about updating your project plan—including the best ways to use baselines in conjunction with change requests, updating and adjusting information, and checking finish-date and budget targets.

Finding the Effects of a Proposed Change

The change review board may want to know how long the finish date would be delayed or how much more the project would cost if it approves a sizable change request. Project does a great job of number-crunching to come up with this information. However, be sure to preserve the original Project schedule. If the board decides to nix the change, then you want to be able to remove the what-if changes quickly, and you don't want to accidentally leave a remnant of the change request in the project.

Creating a copy of your Project file is one way to play what-if games as much as you want. (Page 365 describes how to compare your original file with the one with your what-if scenario.) Another way to add change requests safely is to add the change-request tasks to your active Project file and then inactivate them until they're approved. This section describes both strategies.

CREATING A WHAT-IF COPY OF A PROJECT

One safe way to play what-if games is simply to copy the Project file and then fiddle with the copy to your heart's content. (See the box below for reasons why using a copy is so important.) Just be sure to clearly name the copy so you don't accidentally use it when you meant to work on the real thing. For example, if your Project filename is "Cycling Event Fundraiser," *don't* name the what-if copy "Cycling Event Fundraiser #2" or "Cycling Event Fundraiser Copy." Instead, include identifying information like the change request ID or change request summary, as in "Cycling Event with Auction."

WORD TO THE WISE

Playing What-If with Your Live Project

You may be tempted to play what-if games with your live project file, rather than creating a copy of it. However, the risk of saving the file without thinking is so likely that the seconds it takes to create a copy are totally worth it and can save hours of backtracking.

Another reason it's important to create a copy is that Project's change highlighting feature (page 310) doesn't tell you *everything* that's changed: Sometimes, change means "remove," and change highlighting can't show that. If you need to remove tasks from the project, consider inactivating them (page 364).

That way, you can easily reactivate them if the schedule and budget take a turn for the better.

For additions and modifications, you can format the altered and affected tasks (in the Task tab's Font section, choose a background or text color) to highlight modified task, resource, or assignment information in a table.

Some changes may include new task dependencies or resource assignments that affect parts of tasks. In this case, add a note to the task (page 156) to describe the change.

SETTING A CHANGE REQUEST BASELINE

If your project is already in progress, you've probably set at least one baseline. If a change request is significant, such as adding an auction to your fundraiser, a new pre-change request baseline makes the effects of the change request scenario stand out. You can compare the updated schedule with this new baseline you save to find changes to the schedule, budget, and resource workloads.

NOTE If task start and finish dates are your only concern, you can save an interim plan (page 381) instead of a baseline. A baseline saves a snapshot of several scheduling fields like Start, Finish, Duration, Work, Cost, and so on. An interim plan saves only the start and finish dates.

The box on page 463 gives tips on creating a what-if scenario on the fly, and Chapter 12 describes saving baselines in detail. Here are the basic steps for saving a pre-change request baseline:

1. **Make sure the what-if change request copy is the active Project file.**

   If you have more than one Project file open, then make sure the what-if copy's filename appears in the main Project window's title bar.

2. **In the Project tab's Schedule section, choose Set Baseline→Set Baseline.**

   The Set Baseline dialog box opens.

3. **In the "Set baseline" drop-down list, choose the baseline you want to use, and then click OK.**

   Baselines you've already saved include the date they were saved to the right of their names.

4. **Modify the what-if Project file with all the alterations the change request entails.**

   Remember, your original Project file is sitting safe and unsullied somewhere else on your computer.

5. **Use your favorite techniques for checking the impact of the proposed change.**

   Chapter 11 describes ways to review effects and compare two Project files. Chapter 14 describes techniques you can use to compare changes to the baselined project. Tracking Gantt view compares the current schedule to the baseline, and Multiple Baselines Gantt view compares several baselines (page 384).

   Be prepared to discuss the effects of the suggested change. If the proposed change affects the schedule, budget, or other characteristics, come up with suggestions for mitigating these effects. The board needs to know all its options and the possible tradeoffs.

6. **Fast-forward to the change review board accepting the change. If you haven't edited the original Project file in any way since you created the what-if copy, then rename the copy to make it your live Project file.**

   Rename your original Project file something like *Cycling Event Fundraiser Original_20140115.mpp*. Then rename the what-if copy to be the live file with the original name, *Cycling Event Fundraiser.mpp*.

NOTE If you manage projects in a Project Server environment, team members may have entered progress updates to your live Project file while you were working on the copy. In this case, recreate the changes you made to the copy in the live Project file so you don't overwrite those progress updates.

Quick-and-Dirty What-If Scenarios

Some proposed changes are relatively simple to make. If you can move around Project quickly and project your computer's screen up on a wall, you can make proposed changes in Project and show the impact to the change review board in real time. Here are the steps:

1. Save the Project file with a different name (page 92).

2. Save an additional baseline (for example, Baseline2 or Baseline3) for later comparison purposes.

3. Make edits to the schedule. Project highlights cells that are affected by the last edit you make, so you can point out the effects of changes.

4. Switch views to answer questions from the board.

5. To backtrack a few steps, on the Quick Access toolbar, click the down arrow next to the Undo button to select the edits you want to undo. Remember, you can undo operations only until the last time you saved the file. (See page 310 for more about Multilevel Undo.)

6. If the board approves the change, you can simply save your file, and much of your work is already done. If the board rejects the proposed change before you save the file, then choose File→Close. In the message box that asks if you want to save your changes, click No. When you open the file again, it's back to its original pristine state.

■ FLAGGING CHANGE REQUESTS IN PROJECT

Suppose an approved change request gives birth to an entirely new set of tasks scattered throughout the project. With changes that have such a large impact, you need a way to identify the resulting tasks so you can track them separately. In addition, keeping them separate is particularly useful should the project sponsor or customer develop a severe case of amnesia about having approved this significant change. Keeping the change impacts visible during management status meetings can also be a gentle reminder of "This is what you asked for."

The previous section described how to use baselines to track the effects of approved changes compared with the original plan. This section describes an effective way to identify all the tasks that represent work required to complete approved change requests in your project, so they're easy to find and review. The solution is to create a custom field to flag such tasks and then filter a view to see all the tasks with that flag. Here are the steps:

1. **Create a custom field for tasks, as described on page 663, and name it (in other words, give it an *alias*) something like CR#.**

   A text or number field is great for flagging tasks by their corresponding change-request identifiers (you'd use a text field for the Change Request Number shown in Figure 15-1 on page 457). That way, you can type the change-request number or name into the custom field.

2. **Insert the custom field into a table in a task-oriented view like Gantt Chart view's Entry table.**

Right-click the table heading, and then choose Insert Column. In the column name drop-down list that appears, choose the custom field name, which looks something like "Number 11 (CR#)." When you rename a custom field, Project lists the field in field drop-down lists twice: once by the built-in custom field name with the alias in parentheses (like so: "Number 11 (CR#)") and once with the alias followed by the custom field name in parentheses (like so: "CR# (Number 11)"). If you type letters to quickly find the fields you want, then Project conveniently searches by the built-in field name and the alias you create. For example, you can type *N* to jump to the Number fields. Or you can type *CR* to find the fields listed as "CR# (Number 11)."

3. **For every task that relates to a change request, type a value in the custom field, as shown in Figure 15-3.**

The value could be something like "Fund004" in a text field or "4" in a number field. Whatever helps you identify which change request this task is related to.

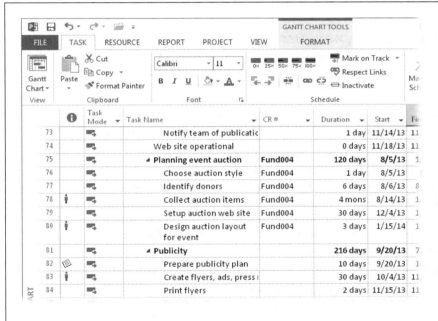

FIGURE 15-3

Insert your custom field into the table (right-click the table heading and then choose Insert Column), and then enter the change-request identifier into that field. If you want to fill multiple adjacent cells with the same change-request identifier—for instance, when a change request creates a summary task with several subtasks—you can drag the value from the first custom field cell over adjacent cells. Select the first cell, and then position the pointer over the fill handle (the small square in the cell's lower-left corner, not shown here). When the pointer changes to a + sign, drag over the other cells.

4. **To filter the custom field, click the down arrow to the right of the custom-field column's heading. In the drop-down menu that appears, turn off the "(Select All)" checkbox and turn on the checkbox for the change request you want.**

   The task list hides all the tasks that don't match the filter. To restore the full list, click the down arrow to the right of the custom-field column's heading, and then turn on the "(Select All)" checkbox.

■ INACTIVATING CHANGE-REQUEST TASKS UNTIL YOU NEED THEM

In many instances, change requests take the form of one or more new tasks in your Project schedule. In such cases, the inactive tasks feature really shines. You can add change-request tasks to your Project schedule to determine their effect. Once you produce the reports you need for the change review board, you can *inactivate* the tasks. You can still see them and even edit their values, but they don't affect your project schedule while they're inactive. If the change review board approves the change request, reactivate the tasks and you're ready to rock and roll.

Here's how to use Project's inactive tasks feature to work with change requests:

1. **Create the tasks you need for a change request, as you would normally.**

   Make them subtasks below summary tasks if you want. Link them to other tasks in your schedule. Assign resources. In short, work with them like any other tasks you create in your project.

2. **Produce the documentation you need to obtain approval for the change request.**

   For example, if cost is the main concern, a report that shows the cost of the change-request tasks may be enough. If schedule is a factor, produce an updated Gantt Chart showing new start and finish dates.

TIP Use formatting tools to highlight the change-request tasks in your documentation. Select all the change-request tasks, and then right-click one of the selected tasks to display the mini-toolbar. Then click the Bold, Italic, or Background Color icon to change the formatting of those tasks.

---

3. **After your change-request documentation is complete, select the relevant tasks in a task-oriented view and then, in the Task tab's Schedule section, choose Inactivate.**

   In the view's table area, the inactive tasks' values immediately change to gray with a strikethrough line drawn through them (see Figure 11-31 on page 365). Despite their appearance, you can edit these values. Double-click an inactive task to open the Task Information dialog box or type a value directly in a table cell.

4. **If the change request is approved, select the tasks for the change request, and then in the Task tab's Schedule section, choose Inactivate to reactivate them.**

   Now the tasks' durations and costs roll up into summary task values, and the tasks' resource assignments affect their assigned resources' availability.

Updating Project with Approved Change Requests

You need to add approved project changes to your Project file for the same reasons you enter actual progress information (page 417): An up-to-date project lets you report quickly about what has already taken place and, more importantly, lets you accurately forecast what will happen in the future.

> **NOTE** If a change request is significant and changes the project scope statement or other project plan documents, be sure to update those documents as well.

If you developed a change request what-if scenario as described in the previous section, most of your work is done. To make the change a permanent part of the project, you may need to add details like accounting codes for added resources or custom fields with more information about new tasks.

How you update the Project file depends on how you want to track the approved change requests you add. Each choice has its pros and cons, so choose the one that fits your needs the best. Here are three options you can use:

- **Adding tasks to a baseline.** If you want to keep track of your original tasks from an older baseline and track new tasks going forward, the best approach is to add tasks to a baseline. Select the tasks you want to add and then, in the Project tab's Schedule section, choose Set Baseline→Set Baseline. In the Set Baseline dialog box, be sure to choose the "Selected tasks" option before you click OK. Project keeps the existing baseline values for existing tasks and adds the current scheduled values for the added tasks to the baseline. You can tell Project whether you want the values from new tasks to roll up into their summary tasks. See page 380 to learn more.

  This approach works fine for new tasks, like when a change request spawns a whole new section of the project. But it falls short for tasks you've modified because of change requests. In that case, you can re-baseline the modified tasks, but future variances will reflect variances from the most recent baseline. You can work around this issue by always creating new tasks for change requests. For example, instead of increasing the work for a task, create a new task with the additional work for the change request.

- **Setting a new baseline.** For a significant change, you can save a new baseline for the entire project. This approach uses the project state *before* you implemented the change as the line in the sand for comparisons. (In the Project tab's Schedule section, choose Set Baseline→Set Baseline.)

  The problem with this approach is that all the original tasks in the Project file have new baseline values. If you compare the current schedule with the baseline, the variances on original tasks represent variances from this more recent baseline. You lose the comparison to your original plan.

- **Saving a data cube instead of a baseline.** If you don't want to use up one of Project's 11 available baselines, you can save your Project file as a *data cube* (page 486), an element of Project's visual reports. A data cube saves a snapshot of Project data into a special kind of database that you can view in Excel or Visio. You can use data cubes to retrieve data by different categories, like when you want to compare the progress for your change requests.

After you decide how you want to track change requests, the techniques you use to enter actual values are the same for original, modified, and new tasks (page 392).

Reporting on Projects

Because communication is such a large part of project management, reports are a mainstay for presenting project information to others. They're also handy when *you* want to see what's going on. During planning, reports show you what your schedule's dates, costs, and resource workloads look like. Once the project is under way, you can use high-level reports to see whether the project is on track. If it isn't, then more detailed reports help you find the problem spots.

Different audiences want different information. For example, teams like to know what tasks lie ahead. Executives, on the other hand, usually want a high-level view of the project's progress and how it compares with the plan. They get concerned if project-related red flags are flying. Coming prepared with reports that show your plan for correcting the project's course can keep status meetings on an even keel.

In Project 2013, *graphical reports* have taken the place of the text-based reports that were available in previous versions of the program. These new reports present project information in ways that are easy to digest. Graphical reports are easy to customize, too.

Project 2013 also offers *visual reports*, which use Excel pivot tables and Visio pivot diagrams to turn heaps of data into meaningful information. Moreover, visual reports can twist data around to show information from different perspectives. For example, from one angle, you may see *tasks* that are in trouble; but by turning the data on its side, you can see whether specific *resources* are having problems. An added advantage of visual reports is that you can use them to export your Project data to other programs.

This chapter begins with an overview of the built-in reports Project offers. You'll learn what each report does, how you might use it, and where to find it. Then you'll learn how to run and customize the new graphical reports. This chapter also describes how visual reports work. Because they use Excel and Visio, you'll learn the key features for manipulating visual report data in both of those programs. In addition to changing the appearance of a visual report, you can also customize templates to modify or create your own visual reports.

■ An Overview of Project's Reports

Although the information in graphical and visual reports overlaps a little, you use each type of report for different reasons. With the program's new graphical reports, you can produce dashboard views of project data to make project status easy to see. Project information can appear in several formats within a single graphical report. For example, the Cost Overview report includes one chart comparing progress and cost, another chart showing actual and remaining cost for top-level tasks, and a table that displays numerical cost values for top-level tasks.

Visual reports, on the other hand, are ideal when you want to look at project performance from different angles. For example, you can run a visual report to check work status month by month, then flip the report to look at work hours by task, and then switch to evaluating work hours by resource. Visual reports can summarize results at the project level, and then drill down to details by task, resource, or time. Visual report tools let you change the fields, resources, and timeframe you see. Visual reports are Excel pivot tables or Visio pivot diagrams that present project information. (To use an Excel or Visio visual report, you need to have Excel or Visio, installed on your computer.)

How you run a report depends on which type it is:

- **To run a graphical report,** head to the Report tab's View Reports section, click a report category (explained below), and then choose the report.

- **To run a visual report,** in the Report tab's Export section, click Visual Reports, and then in the "Visual Reports - Create Report" dialog box, select the report you want and then click View.

Project assigns reports to several categories. For example, visual reports are divided into summary and usage reports, and then into reports that cover tasks, resources, and assignments. Because visual reports can look at data in different ways, it's hard to know whether the Baseline Cost report is a task-summary visual report or a resource-usage report. This section gives some examples of when you might use different built-in graphical and visual reports, and where to find them within Project's report categories.

NOTE Confusingly, some visual reports and graphical reports have the same name, such as the Cash Flow graphical report and Cash Flow visual report.

Overall Status

Several Project reports provide a high-level view of projects. Here are a few reports you can use for a high-level status report:

- **Project Overview.** This new graphical dashboard report (in the Report tab's View Reports section, click Dashboards→Overview) is perfect for a 30,000-foot project view you can attach to a status report. It shows the project's start and finish date, percentage of duration that's complete, percentage complete for top-level tasks, and milestones that are coming up. To help you spot problems that are brewing, it also includes a table of tasks that are late. (The box on page 473 talks about other items to include in a project-status report.)

- **Burndown.** This graphical report (Report→Dashboards→Burndown) displays *burndown status* (in other words, how much of the project you've burned through or completed) in two ways: The Work Burndown chart shows the work that's completed and what's still left to do. The Task Burndown chart also focuses on what's done and what remains, except that it does so by showing the number of completed and remaining tasks. In either chart, your project might be behind schedule if the line for what remains is steeper than the baseline line.

- **Cost Overview.** This graphical dashboard report (Report→Dashboards→Cost Overview), shown in Figure 16-1, summarizes project costs in several ways. At the report's top left, you see the project's start and finish dates, the current scheduled and remaining cost, and % Complete. The Cost Status table displays cost values for top-level tasks, so you can see whether any portions of your project are overrunning their baseline costs. The Progress Versus Cost chart compares % Complete to cumulative cost. If the cumulative cost line is above the % Complete line, your project may be over budget. (However, a project that has high up-front costs will have a Progress Versus Cost chart that looks like that without being over budget.)

- **Work Overview.** Another new graphical dashboard, this report (Report→ Dashboards→Work Overview) presents work status from several perspectives. It starts with the Work Burndown chart, which compares baseline work with remaining work. The next chart shows baseline, actual, and remaining work for each top-level task. Two graphs at the bottom of the report show work and remaining availability by resource, so you can see who has a ton of work to complete and who has time available and might be able to help.

- **Task Status.** This Visio-based visual report initially shows work, cost, and the percentage complete for top-level tasks. As you'll learn shortly, you can include other fields like baseline cost or actual work in this report to see how your project is doing at the top level. If you want to examine parts of your project more closely, you can drill down to lower levels in the task list.

- **Milestone Report.** This graphical report (Report→In Progress→Milestone Report) starts with a list of late milestones, so you can quickly see which parts of the project you need to focus on. The next list is milestones that are coming up. The report also shows completed milestones and includes a chart of completed and remaining tasks.

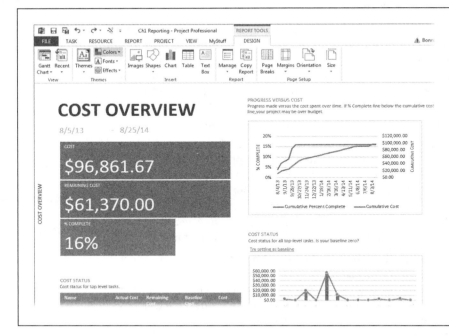

FIGURE 16-1

In the Cost Overview graphical report, the Progress Versus Cost chart at the top right compares % Complete to cumulative cost. If the cumulative cost line is below the % Complete line, as it is here, your project may be under budget, because the percentage of the project that's complete is higher than the percentage of the budget you've spent.

Financial Performance

As you learned in Chapter 14, cost performance is an important part of overall project performance. Several of Project's visual reports and new graphical reports cover different aspects of financial performance. Here are the reports that deal primarily with cost:

- **Cash Flow graphical report.** This report (Report→Costs→Cash Flow) starts with a bar chart of cost by quarter, though you can edit the chart to use different time units. The chart's orange line represents cumulative cost over time. The table at the bottom of the report presents cost and earned value measures for top-level tasks.

- **Cash Flow visual report.** The Excel Cash Flow report looks like the chart in the Cash Flow graphical report. You can expand the time periods to show weekly costs—for instance, to make sure your weekly allowance covers the expenses you incur. The Visio Cash Flow report displays orange exclamation points if the actual cost is over budget. The Cash Flow graphical report is easier to produce than either of these versions, so the Cash Flow visual report makes sense only if you need to look at cash flow from different angles or if you need to export cash flow information to another program.

Reporting Project Status

Typical departmental project-status reports deal mostly with how much work has been done and how much *remains* to be done. But status reports can cover several other topics, including schedule and cost performance, risks, issues, and changes.

How much detail you provide depends on the audience. Small work teams may want to know whether other teams have finished what they've been waiting for. Executives prefer a high-level view. Here are typical topics for a management-level status report:

- **Overall project status.** This section can be a brief description that tells the management team whether the project is on track, slightly off track, or in serious trouble. The rest of the report's sections provide the details.

- **Task status.** This section summarizes completed tasks and provides an update on tasks in progress. The reports described in "Task Management" on page 475 are ideal for gathering this information.

- **Project performance.** Earned values fields like BCWP (budgeted cost of work performed, a.k.a. earned value), CV (cost variance), SV (schedule variance), and EAC (estimate at complete) measure performance compared with the project's baseline. In a status report, you can list the current values and explain any variances. If you present project status to the management team, the Earned Value Report (a new graphical report, described below) provides a chart that compares planned value,

earned value, and actual value. A second chart displays variance over time, so you can see whether corrective actions are helping.

- **Corrective action plan.** Provides an update on any corrective actions you're taking to bring the budget or schedule back in line.

- **Change management.** Provides an update on change requests: requests submitted, requests approved or denied, and progress on change requests that have been added to the project.

- **Risk management.** Summarizes risks that have become reality, and the success of the risk response you've initiated. Also lists risks you're watching that have mercifully remained hypothetical.

- **Issues.** This part of your status report is great for bringing situations to the management team's attention, particularly if you want their help.

- **Items of interest.** Use this section to publicize information, like particularly effective techniques that may be useful to the team.

Alas, Project can't *produce* every portion of a project-status report for you. Project's strengths are task progress and project performance. The other sections of the status report draw upon information you store elsewhere, like Excel spreadsheets, Access databases, or Word documents.

- **Earned Value.** This new graphical report (Report→Costs→Earned Value Report) includes the ever-popular earned value graph, which compares the project's planned value, earned value, and actual value, explained in Chapter 14. (You can see an example of this report in Figure 14-5 on page 443.) This report also includes a chart that shows cost variance and schedule variance over time—perfect for seeing whether your course corrections are bringing the project back on track. The third chart in this report contains lines for schedule performance index (page 444) and cost performance index (page 445) over time.

- **Earned Value Over Time.** This Excel-based visual report looks like the chart in the graphical Earned Value Report.

- **Cost Overruns.** This graphical report (Report→Costs→Cost Overruns) shows cost variance by task and resource, so you can tell which portions of the project are over budget and which resources could be the culprits (see Figure 16-2).

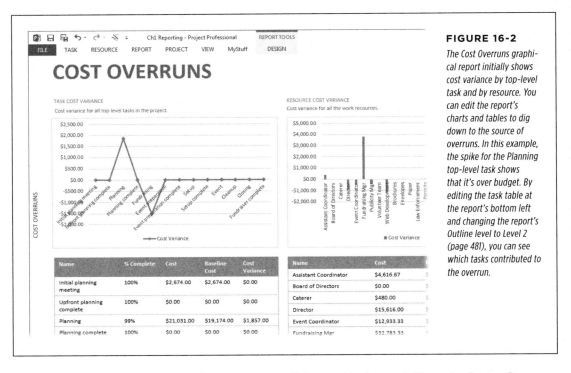

FIGURE 16-2

The Cost Overruns graphical report initially shows cost variance by top-level task and by resource. You can edit the report's charts and tables to dig down to the source of overruns. In this example, the spike for the Planning top-level task shows that it's over budget. By editing the task table at the report's bottom left and changing the report's Outline level to Level 2 (page 481), you can see which tasks contributed to the overrun.

- **Resource Cost Overview.** This graphical report (Report→Costs→Resource Cost Overview) shows baseline, actual, and remaining cost by resource. If a resource's cost bar is higher than the baseline cost line, then you may spend more on that resource than you planned. The report's Cost Details table shows cost info about each resource.

- **Resource Cost Summary.** This Excel-based visual report is a pie chart that shows costs by resource type (work, material, and cost).

- **Task Cost Overview.** This graphical report (Report→Costs→Task Cost Overview) is similar to the Resource Cost Overview report except that it shows cost by task.

- **Baseline.** You can use the Excel and Visio Baseline *Cost* visual reports to compare planned, actual, and baseline costs. With these reports, you can view costs for the entire project, drill down to analyze cost by phase, or switch the report to show cost by fiscal quarter. The Baseline *Work* visual report is a bar graph of baseline, planned, and actual work.

- **Budget.** The Budget Cost and Budget Work visual reports in Excel are graphs of cost or work by quarter. Initially, the bars in the graph show actual, baseline, and budget values, so you can see how actual values compare with the baseline by time period and also compare those values with accounting budget numbers (page 274).

Task Management

Project 2013 introduces several new graphical reports that pinpoint tasks that may need help. For example, in Chapter 11 you learned why critical tasks are important, so reports *about* critical tasks can help you identify what you need to do to keep your project on schedule. Here are the reports best suited for keeping tabs on task scheduling:

- **Critical Tasks.** This graphical report (Reports→In Progress→Critical Tasks) lists incomplete critical tasks with basic 411 like start and finish dates, percentage complete, remaining work, and assigned resources. If you see critical tasks that are just getting started, you might be able to takes steps to shorten their duration to correct a schedule delay.

- **Critical Tasks Status.** This Visio-based visual report shows scheduled work and remaining work for critical tasks. You can display additional fields, like baseline and actual costs, to see whether critical tasks are on track.

- **Upcoming Tasks.** This new graphical report (Report→Dashboards→Upcoming Tasks) shows tasks that are due during the current week and tasks starting during the next week. It's great for identifying tasks that team members should report status on.

- **Late Tasks.** This new graphical report (Reports→In Progress→Late Tasks) includes a table that shows tasks whose finish dates have passed or whose progress on work is behind schedule.

- **Slipping Tasks.** This graphical report (Reports→In Progress→Slipping Tasks) shows tasks that are due to finish after their baseline finish dates (so it works only when you've set a baseline).

Resource Management

Graphical and visual reports both help you manage project resources, whether you're first assigning them or trying to eliminate overallocations. Here are the reports that focus on resources and their assignments:

- **Resource Overview.** This graphical report (Report→Resources→Resource Overview) shows baseline, actual, and remaining work by resource. If a resource's work bar is higher than the baseline work line, then the resource may end up working more hours than you planned. The report's Work Status chart shows the percentage of assigned work that each resource has completed.

- **Overallocated Resources.** This graphical report (Report→Resources→ Overallocated Resources) shows the number of remaining work hours for overallocated resources. The report's Overallocation chart shows the work that unbalanced those resources' workloads and when it occurs. However, Resource Usage view (page 249) and Team Planner view (page 240) are more helpful for finding overallocations than this report. To display Team Planner View, click the Team Planner View link above the Overallocation chart.

- **Resource Work Summary.** This Excel-based visual report shows everything you want to know about resources in work-unit percentages: total capacity, work, remaining availability, and actual work. You can see information for all resources side by side, filter the report to show specific resources, or view work for a specific timeframe.

- **Resource Status.** This Visio-based visual report shows work and cost for each resource. It shades bars darker as resources get closer to finishing their assignments.

- **Resource Work Availability.** This Excel-based visual report is like the Resource Graph on steroids. You can see total capacity, work, and remaining availability over time for work resources.

- **Resource Availability.** This Visio-based visual report shows remaining availability, along with a red flag for overallocated resources.

- **Resource Remaining Work.** This Excel-based visual report shows remaining and actual work for each work resource.

■ Working with Graphical Reports

Project 2013's new graphical reports make it easy to show the information you want. Generating a graphical report is easy, whether it's a built-in report or a custom report you created. If Project doesn't offer the exact graphical report you want, customizing and building your own reports is as easy as dragging and dropping components and choosing settings for what you want to see and how you want to see it.

This section explains how to generate and customize graphical reports.

Generating Graphical Reports

Generating a graphical report takes just a couple of clicks on the Project ribbon. To generate a report, head to the Report tab's View Reports section, click the name of the category that contains the report you want, and then choose the report from the drop-down menu, as shown in Figure 16-3.

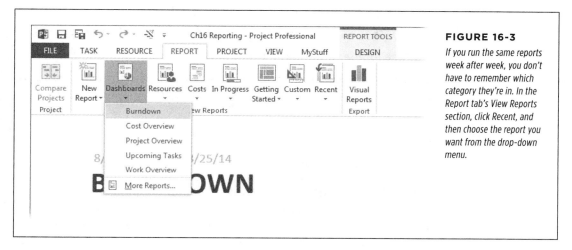

FIGURE 16-3

If you run the same reports week after week, you don't have to remember which category they're in. In the Report tab's View Reports section, click Recent, and then choose the report you want from the drop-down menu.

You can print graphical reports and copy parts of them into a Word document, PowerPoint slide, or other file. If you want to print the report, do the following:

1. **Choose File→Print.**

   The Print screen appears in Backstage view.

2. **Select the number of copies you want (next to the Print button) and, in the Settings section, choose the page range to print.**

   You can also choose a different printer, the paper orientation, and the paper size. To change the page setup (such as margins, headers, and footers), click Page Setup below the Settings section.

   On the right side of the page, you can see a portion of your report. The toolbar at the bottom of the report preview has a few print-preview commands. The left, right, up, and down arrows move one page in the corresponding direction in a multipage report. To zoom in or out, simply click the report itself.

3. **To print the report, click the Print button.**

   That's it!

Suppose you want to include a graphical report in your status report or in a Power-Point presentation. Here's how you copy and paste the report into another program:

1. **Drag over the report elements that you want to copy and paste to select them.**

   For example, you can select a single chart, a table, or the entire report. Selection handles appear at the corners and on the edges of the selected elements.

2. **In the Task tab's Clipboard section, click Copy (or simply press Ctrl+C).**

   Project adds the selected elements to the Clipboard.

3. **Switch to the other program and click where you want to paste the report.**

   For example, click in the PowerPoint slide into which you want to paste the report.

4. **Press Ctrl+V.**

   The report elements appear in the other file.

Customizing Graphical Reports

Although Project 2013 comes with several built-in graphical reports, you may want to change the information that appears in them, or change the *way* that information is displayed. For example, the built-in Cash Flow graphical report shows cash flow by quarter, but you may want to see cash flow by month or see cash flow only for tasks in a specific project phase. Alternatively, you may want to build a new report from the ground up with the data and layout that your stakeholders are used to seeing.

Graphical report customization comes in two flavors. You can use the Field List task pane (page 478) to choose the information you see, like the fields that appear in a table or a chart. You can also apply a filter or group, choose the task outline level to include, or specify the field by which you want to sort results.

For more aesthetic changes, like using a different type of chart or formatting individual table elements, context-sensitive ribbon tabs come to the rescue. You simply click the element you want to customize—like a chart, a table, or a text box—and then head to the Design tab that appears, like the Chart Tools | Design tab, to make your adjustments. The Report Tools | Design tab includes commands for customizing the overall report.

This section describes the various ways you can customize reports and how to create a brand-new report.

■ SPECIFYING WHAT TO DISPLAY

The Field List task pane is command central for specifying the information that you see in a chart or table. You can specify whether you want to see task or resource information, select the fields to include, and choose other settings like the filter to apply.

To customize a report's chart or table, first click it. When you do that, Project displays the Field List task pane on the right side of the window and adds two additional tabs to the ribbon. If you clicked a chart, the tabs are Chart Tools | Design and Chart Tools | Format, as shown in Figure 16-4. If you select a table, you'll see the Table Tools | Design and Table Tools | Format tabs instead.

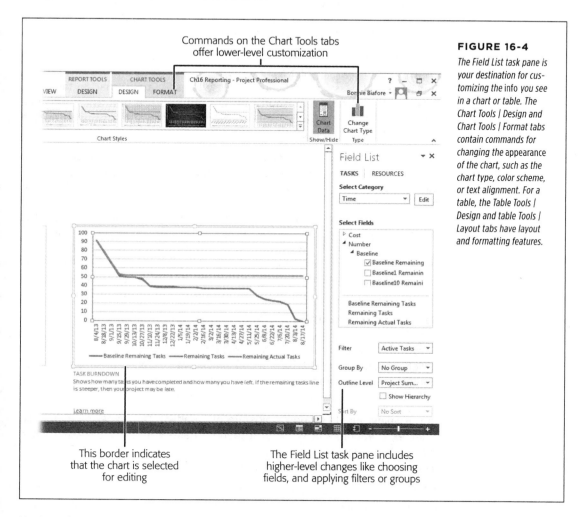

Commands on the Chart Tools tabs offer lower-level customization

This border indicates that the chart is selected for editing

The Field List task pane includes higher-level changes like choosing fields, and applying filters or groups

FIGURE 16-4

The Field List task pane is your destination for customizing the info you see in a chart or table. The Chart Tools | Design and Chart Tools | Format tabs contain commands for changing the appearance of the chart, such as the chart type, color scheme, or text alignment. For a table, the Table Tools | Design and table Tools | Layout tabs have layout and formatting features.

You can display the Field List task pane by clicking a report's chart or table. You can also display (or hide) the Field List task pane by heading to the Chart Tools | Design tab's Show/Hide section and then clicking Chart Data (or the Table Tools | Design tab and clicking Table Data).

Here are the types of changes you can make using the Field List task pane:

- **Choose tasks or resources.** To designate whether the chart or table presents task or resource data, below the Field List heading, click Tasks or Resources. If you're customizing an existing chart or table, it's already set up to display task or resource data, so leave this setting as it is. For example, the built-in Burndown report (Report→Dashboards→Burndown) includes a task Burndown chart. If you click that chart, Tasks is selected in the Field List task pane.

  If you're setting up a new chart or table and click Tasks, the Select Fields list displays task fields, the filters and groups are task filters and groups, and the Outline Level box is active. If you click Resources for a new chart or table, the Select Fields list displays resource fields; the filters and groups are resource filters and groups; and the Outline Level box is grayed out, because outline levels apply only to tasks.

- **Select a category.** If you select a chart, the Select Category box appears in the Field List task pane. The choice you make in this drop-down list specifies the category for the chart's x-axis, like time, task names, resource names, initials, and so on. For example, the built-in Cost Overview report (Report→Dashboards→Cost Overview) includes two charts. If you click its Progress Versus Cost chart, the Select Category box is set to Time, because the chart shows percent complete and cost over time. On the other hand, if you click the report's Cost Status chart, the Select Category box is set to Name, because the chart shows cost by top-level tasks. If you choose time for the x-axis category, click the Edit button to change the timescale settings, like time units, date format, and date range.

- **Select fields.** Turn on field checkboxes in the pane's Select Fields section to specify which fields you want to include in the chart or table. For example, the Cost Overview report's Progress Versus Cost chart, described in the previous bullet point, has two fields turned on: Cumulative Cost and Cumulative Percent Complete. Click an empty checkbox to add that field to the chart or table. Click a checkbox with a checkmark to remove that field from the chart or table.

  In the Select Fields section, fields are grouped by data type, such as Cost, Number, Duration, and Work. To expand a data-type group, click the white triangle to the left of the data type's name. The triangle turns black. To collapse a data-type group, click its black triangle.

- **Filter.** Similar to filtering a task list (page 642), you can filter the tasks or resources that appear in the chart or table by choosing an option in the Filter drop-down list. For example, the built-in Slipping Tasks report (Report→In Progress→Slipping Tasks) has the Slipping Tasks filter applied, so the table lists only tasks that are slipping. For a task-oriented chart or table, the Filter drop-down list includes all task filters in your Project file and global template. For a task-oriented chart or table, the list contains resource filters.

- **Group.** To group the results, choose a group in the Group By drop-down list.

- **Pick an outline level.** For task-oriented charts or tables, the Outline Level box is active. To see project-wide results, choose Project Summary in this drop-down list. To display results down to a specific level of the task outline, choose the level you want, like Outline Level 3. For example, the Outline Level for the built-in Slipping Tasks report described above is set to All Subtasks, which means that it filters the task list for subtasks at every level of the outline.

- **Sort.** To sort the entries in the chart or table, choose the field you want to sort by in the Sort By drop-down list. For example, you may want to sort a cost table by cost variance.

■ CUSTOMIZING A CHART

In addition to specifying the information you want to see, you can customize a chart to show that information in a specific way—for example, with a bar chart or a line graph. To customize the chart's type and layout, head to the Chart Tools | Design tab. Here are the types of changes you can make from this tab:

- **Add a chart element.** Using the options in the tab's Chart Layouts section, you can add individual chart elements or change their settings—for example, to add a legend or to change the location of data labels. Click Add Chart Element; in the drop-down menu that appears, point to the element you want to customize, and then, on the submenu, choose the setting you want. For example, on the Legend submenu, you can choose None for no legend, or Right, Top, Left, or Bottom to specify where the legend appears. To tweak the chart element even more, choose More [element] Options (where [element] represents something like Data Labels or Axes) at the bottom of the drop-down menu. If you do that, another task pane appears on the right side of the window (see Figure 16-5) with additional settings for things like text alignment.

- **Choose a ready-made chart layout.** Built-in chart layouts make quick work of setting up a chart. These layouts come with chart elements, like titles and legends, already in place. To choose one of these pre-built layouts, in the Chart Tools | Design tab's Chart Layout section, click Quick Layout. The drop-down menu that appears has thumbnails of the different layouts that are available. Click the one you want, and Project applies all the layout's settings to your chart.

- **Apply/adjust chart styles.** Chart styles are similar to the Gantt Chart Styles on the Gantt Chart Tools | Format tab. These styles include chart settings like color schemes and background color. To choose one, in the Chart Tools | Design tab's Chart Styles section, click the style you want. Project applies the style's settings to the chart.

- **Change the chart type.** Charts come in a variety of types, like bar charts, line charts, pie charts, and so on. In addition, each chart type has several variations, such as a side-by-side bar chart and a stacked bar chart (where the bars are stacked on top of one another). To change the type of chart, in the Chart Tools | Design tab's Type section, click Change Chart Type. On the right side of the Change Chart Type dialog box, choose the chart type you want, and then, along the top of the dialog box, click the variation you want.

This task pane includes
settings for customizing all
aspects of a legend and its text

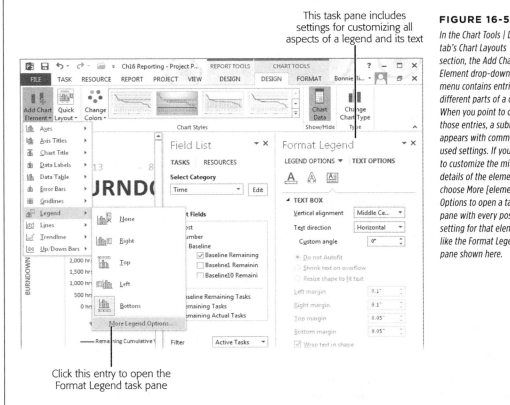

FIGURE 16-5

*In the Chart Tools | Design
tab's Chart Layouts
section, the Add Chart
Element drop-down
menu contains entries for
different parts of a chart.
When you point to one of
those entries, a submenu
appears with commonly
used settings. If you want
to customize the minute
details of the element,
choose More [element]
Options to open a task
pane with every possible
setting for that element,
like the Format Legend
pane shown here.*

Click this entry to open the
Format Legend task pane

To fine-tune your chart's appearance, head to the Chart Tools | Format tab, where you can apply detailed formatting to different chart elements like the fill color for the plot area. If you want to dress up a report, you can insert shapes or use Word Art for text elements. If elements overlap, you can specify whether an element is in the foreground or the background. (To do that, select the element and then, in the tab's Arrange section, click Bring Forward or Send Backward.) In the tab's Size section, type dimensions to specify the size of the chart.

■ CUSTOMIZING A TABLE

To customize a table's layout, head to the Table Tools | Design tab. Here are the types of changes you can make on this tab:

- **Specify table style options.** The tab's Table Style Options section has check-boxes for controlling the appearance of table rows and columns. Turn on the Header Row checkbox to include a header row that shows the field names for each column in the table. Turn on the First Column checkbox to bold the values in the first column. If the last row or last column represents totals, then turn on the Total Row or Last Column checkboxes to emphasize that information. To add gridlines between the rows or columns, turn on the Banded Rows or Banded Columns checkboxes, respectively.

  For example, take a look at the built-in Cost Overview report's Cost Status table (Report→Dashboards→Cost Overview). If you click that table and then head to the Table Tools | Design tab's Table Style Options section, you'll see the Header Row and Banded Rows checkboxes turned on. The Header Row setting tells Project to include the field names in the first table row. The Banded Rows set-ting draws horizontal lines between each row.

- **Apply/adjust table styles.** This section of the tab contains dozens of choices for table color schemes and basic layouts. Simply click the thumbnail for the style you want, and Project applies your choice's style settings to the table.

The Table Tools | Layout tab includes commands for fine-tuning the table's layout, such as the height and width of cells, the alignment of text in cells, and the overall width of the table.

TIP   Tables also work for emphasizing a single project-wide value. To see how this works, look at boxes for project-wide cost, remaining cost, and % Complete at the top left of the built-in Cost Overview report (described earlier in this section). Each entry has the field name in a small font with the value in a large font below it. If you click one of these boxes, the Table Tools tabs appear on the ribbon. That's because each of these project-wide values is in its own table with a header row. In addition, the Outline Level box in the Field List task pane is set to Project Summary, so the value represents a total for the entire project.

■ CUSTOMIZING A TEXT BOX

As you might expect, report text boxes don't have as many options for customiza-tion as charts and tables. When you select a text box in a report, the Drawing Tools | Format tab appears in the ribbon. Here are a few things you can do to customize text boxes using this tab:

- The tab's Insert Shapes section includes commands for inserting additional text boxes, inserting drawing shapes like circles and rectangles, and changing the shape of existing items.

- The tab's Shape Styles section includes styles that boil down to the color of the text box's border, the fill color, and shape effects like shadows.

- Like other elements in a report, you can apply WordArt settings to the text, specify whether the text box is in the foreground or background, or set its height and width. You can also rotate a text box to, for example, include a title that runs vertically along the side of the chart.

■ ORGANIZING REPORT ELEMENTS

In a graphical report, you can position elements wherever you want. If you don't like a report's arrangement, you can move its elements to other locations. Rearranging elements is as simple as selecting the ones you want and then dragging them to their new positions.

Report elements respond to the same selection techniques you use elsewhere in Project and in other programs. Select a single element (like a chart) by clicking it. To select several elements near one another, drag over all the elements you want to select. (You have to drag so that the imaginary box you create *completely* encloses all the elements; elements that aren't completely enclosed won't be selected.) To select several elements that aren't adjacent to one another, Ctrl-click each one.

After you select the elements you want to move, position your cursor within one of the selected elements. When the cursor changes to a four-headed arrow, drag the elements to a new location.

■ REPORT-WIDE CUSTOMIZATION

In addition to the customization you can apply to elements within a report, the Report Tools | Design tab offers a few tools for formatting the *entire* report. Here are your choices:

- **Color scheme.** In the tab's Themes section, click Themes and then select a color scheme for the report. Click Colors to change individual colors, click Fonts to specify the font for the whole report, and click Effects to change the effects applied to the objects in the report.

- **Adding elements to a report.** In the tab's Insert section, click a button to insert a new element. You can insert images, drawing shapes, charts, tables, and text boxes. After you insert an element, you can adjust it using the techniques described in the previous sections.

- **Specify page settings.** The tab's Page Setup section includes all the usual suspects for setting a report up for distribution. You can specify where page breaks occur, the width of page margins, page orientation, and size.

■ CREATING A CUSTOM REPORT FROM AN EXISTING REPORT

The easiest way to customize a graphical report is to copy it and then edit the copy like you do with other elements in Project (page 451). That way, the copy provides a foundation for your new report, and you still have the original report if you need it. Here's how you copy an existing report:

1. **In the Report tab's View Reports section, click the report category, and then choose the report you want to copy from the drop-down menu.**

   The report appears.

2. **In the Report Tools | Design tab's Report section, click Manage→Rename Report.**

   The Rename dialog box opens. The label for the box is "New name for report from [project name]:," which is a hint that you're creating a copy of the report in your Project file.

3. **Type the name for the copy and then click OK.**

   Project adds the report to your custom reports. For example, if you head to the Report tab's View Reports section and click Custom, the report appears on the drop-down menu.

■ CREATING A BRAND-NEW GRAPHICAL REPORT

If the graphical report you want isn't like any of Project's built-in reports or other custom reports you've created, you can start from scratch. Project helps you get started by adding a few elements to your creation. Here's how to create a new report:

1. **In the Report tab's View Reports section, click New Report, and then choose the type of report you want to create from the drop-down menu.**

   Choosing Blank tells Project you want a report with nothing but a text box for the report's title. Choosing Chart creates a report with a text box for the report's title and an empty chart. Table creates a report with a title box and an empty table. And Comparison creates a report with a title box and two empty charts.

2. **In the Report Name dialog box, type a name and then click OK.**

   Project creates the new report. The report name you typed appears in the title text box. If you chose a report type that inserts other elements, they appear in the report, too.

Now you can call on your creative juices and set up the new report using the customization techniques described in the previous sections.

■ Working with Visual Reports

The questions that stakeholders ask in status meetings shift like quicksand: "When did costs start exceeding the budget? How are employees doing compared with contractors? Who's available to help bail out troubled tasks?" Although graphical reports are easy to edit and provide lots of options for displaying information, Project's *visual* reports use Excel pivot charts and Visio pivot diagrams so you can change them on the fly, whether to respond to questions or to drill down in several directions to unearth problems.

The ability to slice and dice data in different ways sets these reports apart from other reports, whether you use the graphical reports in Project or you generate reports from a high-powered reporting tool. For example, you may start with a visual report that shows costs by fiscal quarter, but one quick change and the report can show costs by phase or resource instead. It's just as easy to change the report's graph from cost to work, examine a few time periods in detail while summarizing others, or look at specific tasks and resources. The box below explains what makes visual reports tick.

Project gets you started with several built-in visual reports (see below), whose initial presentation is like the serving suggestions you see on cracker boxes. You can modify the report in real time until it's the way you want.

This section starts with the easy part: generating a visual report. Your options for massaging the report multiply once the report is open in Excel or Visio. The Pivot tools in Excel and Visio are a little different, so this chapter describes how to use both. You'll also learn how to modify or create visual report templates to produce custom visual reports.

> **NOTE** Excel-based visual reports show information in bar graphs, pie charts, or line graphs. These reports work best when you want to compare values side by side or to look for trends. Visio-based visual reports break information down in a hierarchy, like a work breakdown structure. You can drill down level by level, and use icons to highlight good, bad, and indifferent values. (You see Excel-based or Visio-based reports listed in the "Visual Reports – Create Report" dialog box only if you have those programs installed on your machine.)

UP TO SPEED

Changing Your Perspective

Visual reports take advantage of the *pivot table* concept, so named because you can turn the data in different directions—pivoting it to gain a new perspective. For example, you may want to see your project phase by phase, and then twist it around to see overall performance quarter by quarter.

To make these contortions look easy, a visual report builds a specialized database called an OLAP (online analytical processing) cube on your computer, and then connects it to an Excel pivot table or Visio pivot diagram. A *data cube* (which has a *.cub* file extension) stores data in a format that makes it easy to

retrieve data by different categories. For example, in a marketing department, you may want to find customers by household income, hobbies, or Zip code. Each OLAP cube category is like one dimension of a real-world cube, except that OLAP cubes can go beyond three dimensions. In Project visual reports, tasks, resources, and time are the most common dimensions.

After a visual report creates its data cube, it hooks the cube up to a pivot table or pivot diagram. At that point, it's your turn to use the tools in Excel and Visio to model the data into the presentation you want.

Generating a Visual Report

Generating a visual report is easy: Select the visual report template you want, and off you go. The template takes care of gathering the data for the report's cube (see the box above) and setting up the initial pivot table or pivot diagram. Here's how to generate a visual report from an existing template:

1. **In the Report tab's Export section, click Visual Reports.**

   The "Visual Reports - Create Report" dialog box opens, as shown in Figure 16-6. Although the All tab is selected initially, you can click a tab to see specific types of visual reports. Summary reports show overall results and don't include time-phased data. For example, the Resource Summary visual report totals values for resources, such as actual work or remaining work. Usage visual reports, like their Usage view counterparts, *do* include time-phased data. The Assignment visual reports are the most useful because they include time-phased data about both tasks and resources, so you can look at your project from every angle.

   When you start developing custom visual report templates, the All tab may fill up. You can look for more specific reports by selecting a tab like Task Summary. For example, the built-in Cash Flow Report is on the Task Usage tab because it focuses on task costs over time. The Critical Tasks Report is on the Task Summary tab because it looks at total results for critical tasks.

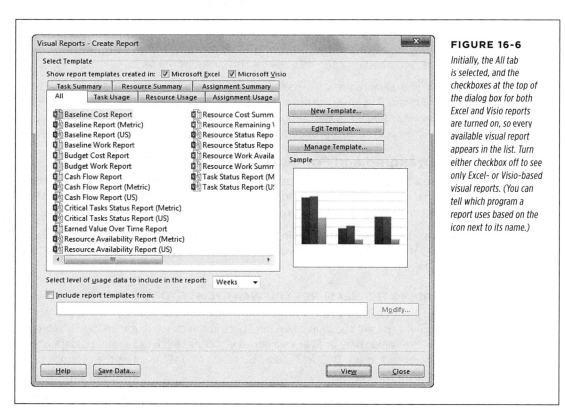

FIGURE 16-6

Initially, the All tab is selected, and the checkboxes at the top of the dialog box for both Excel and Visio reports are turned on, so every available visual report appears in the list. Turn either checkbox off to see only Excel- or Visio-based visual reports. (You can tell which program a report uses based on the icon next to its name.)

2. **Click the name of the visual report you want to use.**

   On the right side of the dialog box, check out the preview to see if the report's general format (bar graph, pie chart, or tree) is what you want. To *truly* tell whether a visual report is what you want, you need to generate the report.

3. **Choose the time period for usage data.**

   In the "Select level of usage data to include in the report" drop-down list, choose Days, Weeks, Months, Quarters, or Years. Days or Weeks are better for shorter projects. For longer projects, choose the shortest period you're likely to evaluate, like Weeks or Months. Keep in mind that collecting too much usage data can slow the visual report's performance to a crawl.

4. **Click View.**

   If you selected an Excel-based visual report, then Excel starts and then sets up an Excel file with the data cube attached to it. The Excel spreadsheet has two worksheets. The Chart1 worksheet is a *pivot chart*—a graph that displays the data. The second worksheet is a *pivot table*, which contains the cube data (see the box on page 486). As you expand, collapse, and reorient the pivot table, as described on page 493, the pivot chart does the same.

   If you selected a Visio-based report, then Visio starts and creates a pivot diagram. The Visio file usually contains two drawing pages. The drawing page named "Page-1" is the diagram itself; if the VBackground-1 page is present, it's simply a Visio background page for adding graphics like your corporate logo.

Rearranging and Formatting Excel Visual Reports

The real fun begins after you create an Excel-based visual report. Excel's pivot chart tools let you knead the report into the shape you want. This section describes the different ways you can configure an Excel-based visual report.

When you open a visual report in Excel, you may see only the pivot chart. To display the pivot chart tools and the PivotChart Fields task pane, shown in Figure 16-7, click anywhere in the graph.

■ ADDING THE MEASURES YOU WANT TO SEE TO THE GRAPH

In the pivot chart, the fields you care about (like cost, hours of work, availability, and so on) usually show up as vertical bars in the chart. If you change the type of chart, the values may appear as a series of connected line segments, data points, 3-D bars, and so on. The fields that you select also show up as the columns in the pivot table worksheet.

Although a visual report gathers data into its OLAP cube, the pivot chart doesn't display *every* field in the cube. When the visual report is open in Excel, you can add, remove, or change the fields that appear in the pivot chart.

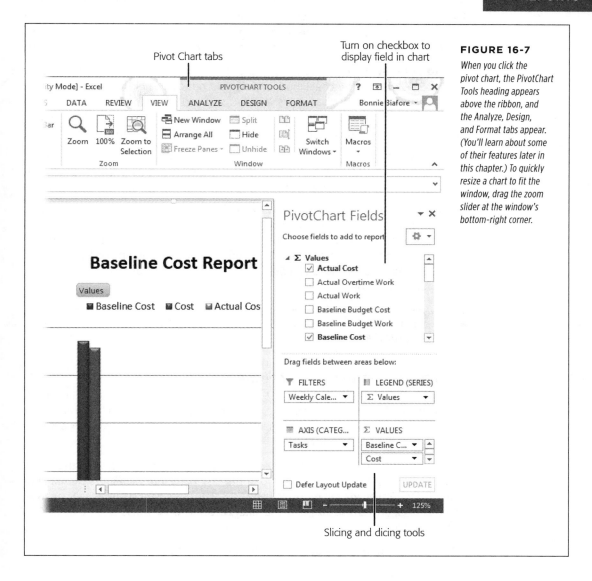

Pivot Chart tabs

Turn on checkbox to
display field in chart

Slicing and dicing tools

FIGURE 16-7

*When you click the
pivot chart, the PivotChart
Tools heading appears
above the ribbon, and
the Analyze, Design,
and Format tabs appear.
(You'll learn about some
of their features later in
this chapter.) To quickly
resize a chart to fit the
window, drag the zoom
slider at the window's
bottom-right corner.*

The PivotChart Fields task pane to the right of the pivot chart, shown in Figure 16-7, lets you change what appears in the chart. Visual report templates start with a few fields turned on; you can tell which one they are because, in the task pane, they're identified by checkmarks in the checkboxes to the left of the names, which are also bolded. Use the following methods to add and rearrange the fields in the pivot chart:

- **Add or remove fields.** To include another field in the pivot chart, simply click its checkbox so the checkmark appears. To remove a field, click its checkbox, and the checkmark disappears. You can also add a field by dragging the field's name from the Σ Values list at the top of the task pane into the Σ Values section (not on the section's heading) at the bottom of the task pane.

- **Reorder fields.** In the Σ Values section at the bottom of the task pane, drag a field to a new location in the list. Although the fields in the Σ Values section appear one below the other, they are ordered from left to right in the pivot chart.

- **Change the field's calculation.** In the Σ Values section at the bottom of the task pane, click the field, and then choose Value Field Settings. In the Value Field Settings dialog box, click the Summarize Values By tab. In the "Summarize value field by" list, select the calculation you want. Depending on the field, you can choose calculations like Sum, Average, Minimum Value, Maximum Value, Count, and so on.

NOTE If the PivotChart Fields task pane isn't visible, then head to the PivotChart Tools | Analyze tab's Show/Hide section and click Field List.

■ FILTERING THE DATA THAT APPEARS

Like filtering in Project, you can filter the information that appears in a visual report. For example, if costs and delays have cropped up recently, you can filter the report to show data for only the current fiscal quarter. Likewise, you could filter a report to show only specific resources.

To use a field as a report filter, in the PivotChart Fields task pane, drag the field's name from the Σ Values list at the top of the task pane into the Filters section. For example, the Baseline Cost report initially uses time as its filter (you can tell because, in the PivotChart Fields task pane, the Filters drop-down menu is set to Weekly Calendar). To filter that report by another category, such as tasks, follow these steps:

1. **Make the pivot table active by clicking its worksheet tab.**

   The worksheet tab's name is based on the visual report category to which it belongs, such as Assignment Usage for the Baseline Cost Report. You can tell you're looking at the pivot table because the task pane's label reads "Pivot*Table* Fields" instead of "Pivot*Chart* Fields."

2. **To switch the report to task filtering, for example, in the task pane, drag Tasks from the Rows section into the Filters section.**

Now the report is set up to filter by tasks but still shows all tasks. When the pivot table is active, the label for the bottom-left section of the PivotTable Fields pane is Rows. When the pivot *chart* is active, the label for the bottom-left section of the PivotChart Fields pane is "Axis (Categories)".

TIP If you have trouble reading any of the labels in the PivotTable Fields task pane, you can make the task pane wider by putting your cursor over the dividing line between it and the pivot table; when the cursor turns into a double-headed arrow, drag the dividing line to the left.

3. **To select specific tasks to display, in the pivot table, click the Tasks down arrow, shown in Figure 16-8.**

Initially, this drop-down list shows only the top-level category. When the pivot table is sorted by tasks, you see the name of the project (in Figure 16-8, that's "Ch16 Reporting"). If you filter by time instead, you see calendar years listed in this drop-down menu.

4. **To select a specific task as the filter, like one phase of the project, click the + signs in the drop-down menu to expand the tasks until the one you want is visible. Select it, and then click OK.**

After you select a task to filter by, the name of the task appears in the filter cell to the right of the Tasks cell. When a filter is in place, the down arrow in the filter cell changes to the filter icon (a funnel with a down arrow below it). You may notice down arrows to the right of the other fields in the pivot table—for example to the right of the Year cell. You can filter within those categories, too, by clicking the down arrow and then choosing a filter to apply. For example, if you use resources as a category, then select the resources you want to evaluate more closely.

TIP If you're looking at the pivot *chart* worksheet tab, you can apply filters by opening a shortcut menu (click one of the buttons at the bottom of the chart, which represent the categories displayed along the pivot chart's horizontal axis). You'll see these buttons for each category in the "Axis (Categories)" section at the bottom of the PivotChart Fields task pane. For example, to filter by resources, click the Resources button and then turn checkboxes on or off.

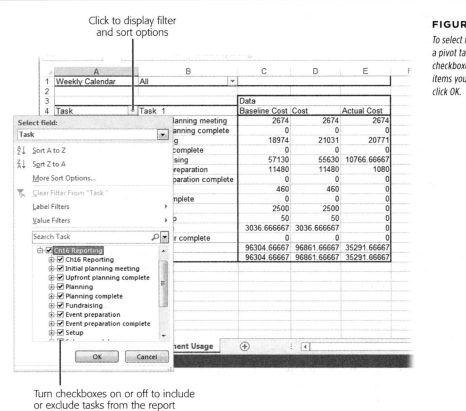

Click to display filter
and sort options

Turn checkboxes on or off to include
or exclude tasks from the report

FIGURE 16-8

To select multiple items in a pivot table, turn off the checkboxes for all but the items you want, and then click OK.

■ CATEGORIZING INFORMATION

The rows in a pivot table typically represent tasks, resources, or time. For example, the Baseline Cost report initially opens a pivot table with a row for the entire project. You can expand that row to show additional rows for each top-level task (like project phases). Changing the category for rows is how you examine data from different perspectives—for example, to show costs over time or by resource. You can also add categories to break down values further, to do things like evaluate cost per phase broken down to each resource working on a phase.

These categories group information on the pivot chart's x-axis like the top-level tasks in the standard Baseline Cost report. Each top-level task has its own set of field bars. You add or remove categories by adding or removing fields in the PivotTable Fields task pane's Rows section (called "Axis (Categories)" if the pivot chart is active). For example, to break down the Baseline Cost report by time periods, drag the Weekly Calendar drop-down list from the task pane's Filters section into the Rows section.

A pivot chart can slice up your project even further—just add another category to the Rows section. For example, to analyze cost by time period and then by resource, as shown in Figure 16-9, drag the Resources field from the list at the top of the PivotTable Fields task pane into the Rows section, and then drop it below the Weekly Calendar drop-down list. By doing so, each resource who works during a time period has his own set of field bars. For example, the resources in Figure 16-9 have field bars for weeks 32 and 33.

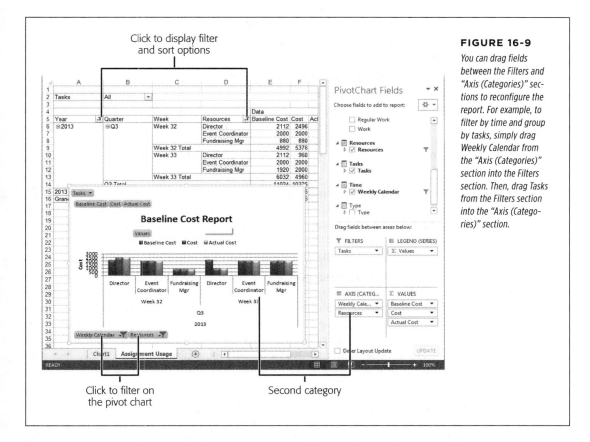

FIGURE 16-9

You can drag fields between the Filters and "Axis (Categories)" sections to reconfigure the report. For example, to filter by time and group by tasks, simply drag Weekly Calendar from the "Axis (Categories)" section into the Filters section. Then, drag Tasks from the Filters section into the "Axis (Categories)" section.

Click to display filter
and sort options

Click to filter on
the pivot chart

Second category

TIP In Figure 16-9, a copy of the pivot chart is pasted onto the pivot table worksheet. That way, you can preview the pivot chart as you tweak settings on the pivot table. When the pivot chart looks good, you can print the one on the Chart1 worksheet, or copy and paste it into a Word document or a PowerPoint presentation.

■ SUMMARIZING AND DRILLING DOWN

Drilling down into details or soaring up to summary views is almost effortless in visual reports. Simply click expand buttons (+) or collapse buttons (–) on the pivot table worksheet. Whatever you can see in the pivot table is what you see in the pivot chart, as Figure 16-9 also illustrates.

For example, the Baseline Cost report in Figure 16-9 is set up to show costs for resources by week. To collapse the chart to show each quarter, click the – sign to the left of Q3. Then, if you want to expand a quarter to show costs by week, click the + button to the left of the quarter's name (Q3, for instance). And note that the entire report doesn't have to be expanded or collapsed to the same level. One section of the report can show weeks while the rest of the report stays summarized.

■ FORMATTING THE CHART

Pivot charts are more muscular than most Excel charts, but you use the same methods for making them look good. For example, you can change the chart type, use a different bar style, and format the labels. Here are a few common formatting tasks:

- **Choose a chart type.** Sometimes, a different type of chart shows information more clearly. For instance, cumulative cost is easier to understand when you draw it as a single line. To switch to a different type of chart, right-click the pivot chart and then choose Change Chart Type. In the Change Chart Type dialog box, select the kind you want, and then select the appearance of the bars or lines. (You can also open the Change Chart Type dialog box from the ribbon: In the PivotChart Tools | Design tab's Type section, click Change Chart Type.)

- **Format labels.** To change the appearance of the chart's labels, in the PivotChart Tools | Format tab's Current Selection section, click the down arrow, and then choose Chart Title, Axis Titles, Legend, Data Labels, and so on. You can also format portions of the chart by right-clicking what you want to format and then, on the shortcut menu, choosing a command like Format Chart Title.

- **Rotate text to remove overlaps.** If the pivot chart contains more than a few resources, tasks, or time periods, the labels along the x-axis are likely to overlap. To fix this, realign the text vertically. Right-click the overlapping labels on the x-axis, and then choose Format Axis. In the Format Axis task pane that appears, click the Size & Properties icon (a square with arrows inside it and dimension marks outside it). In the "Text direction" box, click the down arrow, and then choose "Rotate all text 90°."

> **TIP** When you right-click the pivot chart, a mini-toolbar and a shortcut menu appear. The last command on the shortcut menu is "Format [pivot chart section]," where [pivot chart section] is the part of the pivot chart you right-clicked. Choose that command to format the selected part of the pivot chart. Then, on the mini-toolbar, choose the formatting you want to apply, like a fill color, outline color, or text style.

Rearranging and Formatting Visio Visual Reports

Visio-based visual reports use Visio pivot diagrams. The top box (called a *node*) in a pivot diagram represents your entire project. You can break the diagram down to additional levels by adding categories. The nodes in a pivot diagram typically show field values, but a Visio visual report is best when you want to display icons to indicate status.

When you open a pivot diagram, tools and settings appear in the PivotDiagram task pane. Similar to their Excel counterparts, Visio pivot diagrams accept additional fields and several levels of categories. The following are several of the more common changes you may want to make to pivot diagrams:

- **Add a new breakdown.** To break down a node into more detail, you add a category to that node. Click the node, and then, in the PivotDiagram task pane to the diagram's left, below the Add Category heading, click the category you want to add: Resources:Resources, Type:Type, or Tasks:Tasks, as shown in Figure 16-10. For example, if the first level of the diagram shows project phases, you can add Tasks as the second level to build the equivalent of a work breakdown structure diagram. If you add Resources instead, then you can see how resources contribute to task values.

  To remove a level, right-click the node to which the level is attached (for example, right-click a task node in the work breakdown structure diagram), and then, on the shortcut menu, choose Collapse.

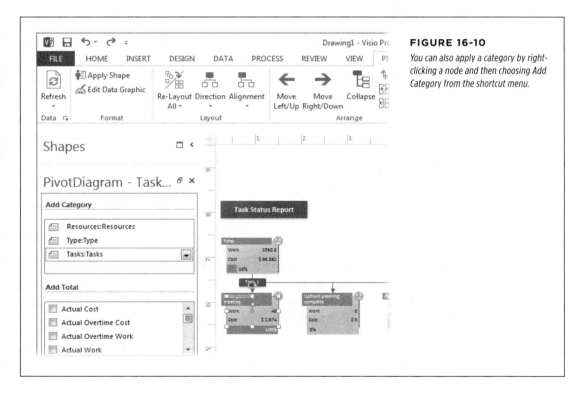

FIGURE 16-10

You can also apply a category by right-clicking a node and then choosing Add Category from the shortcut menu.

- **Change fields in nodes.** Visual report nodes contain some fields, but you can add or remove fields to show exactly what you want. In the PivotDiagram task pane, in the Add Total section, turn on the checkboxes for the fields you want to see. Turn checkboxes off to remove those fields from the nodes.

- **Filter data.** A level in a pivot diagram initially includes OLAP cube data for your entire project, but you can filter a level to show information for just *part* of the project. To do so, right-click the small shape between levels, which contains a category name like Task 1, and then, on the shortcut menu, choose Configure Level. In the Configure Level dialog box, you can define conditions that nodes have to meet. For example, a test that requires that Tasks contains "Food" filters the diagram to show only the project tasks with "Food" in their names.

- **Combine nodes.** You can combine nodes in several ways with the Merge, Promote, and Collapse commands. In the Pivot Diagram tab's Arrange section, click the command you want. For example, to combine two summary tasks, select them and then click Merge. The values in the merged node show the total for both tasks.

- **Change the diagram's background.** Background pages are the place to add your corporate logo or a watermark of some kind. Most Visio visual reports include a Vbackground-1 page for just this purpose (if one exists, you'll see a drawing page tab, labeled "Vbackground-1," at the bottom of the window). If a diagram *doesn't* include a background page, then in the Insert tab's Pages section, click New Page→Background Page. In the Page Setup dialog box, on the Page Properties tab, the Background option is selected automatically. In the Name box, type a name for the page. For example, you can insert the graphic file for your corporate logo by heading to the Insert tab's Illustrations section and clicking Pictures.

- **Quickly format the diagram.** In Visio, *themes* are color-coordinated packages of formatting that help you make your diagrams look good (even if you wear plaids with stripes). To change the appearance of your diagram, in the Design tab's Themes section, click the theme you want; the diagram changes automatically.

Customizing Visual Report Templates

Visual reports are so flexible that customizing them may not even occur to you. But once you realize that you're frequently making the same field, category, and filter changes, you can eliminate this busywork by saving the modified pivot chart or pivot diagram as a *visual report template*. A template saves the visual report's *definition* (that is, the report's layout and the fields it includes), not its actual data. When you use the new report template, it generates a pivot chart or a pivot diagram according to your preferred report settings.

At a lower level, you can also customize the data in a visual report's cube. Cubes come with plenty of fields, but you can add fields you want or remove fields you don't need.

Because visual reports are really Excel pivot charts or Visio pivot diagrams, visual report templates are simply Excel or Visio template files. Whether you copy a built-in template or create one from scratch, you pick the fields to include and the type of cube and then set up the pivot chart or pivot diagram to look the way you want. Here are the details:

1. **In Project, in the Report tab's Export section, click Visual Reports.**

   The "Visual Reports - Create Report" dialog box opens.

2. **Select the built-in visual report whose template is closest to what you want, and then click Edit Template.**

   The "Visual Reports - Field Picker" dialog box appears. Although you're editing an existing template, later on, when you save the template with a new name, you'll have a brand-new template.

TIP   To create a new template from *scratch*, click New Template instead. In the "Visual Reports - New Template" dialog box, select the Excel, Visio (Metric), or Visio (US Units) option to specify the type of visual report. Under Select Data Type, choose the type of cube (Task Summary, Resource Summary, or Assignment Summary for total information; Task Usage, Resource Usage, or Assignment Usage for time-phased data). Click Field Picker, and you're ready for step 3.

---

3. **In the Available Fields list, select the fields you want in the data cube, and then click Add.**

   The Selected Fields list shows fields already tagged for inclusion in the data cube. When you click Add, the fields you picked jump to the Selected Fields list. To remove fields, select them in the Selected Fields list, and then click Remove. As with other list boxes, Ctrl-clicking and Shift-clicking work for selecting several fields.

TIP   A few fields have "(dimension)" after their names, which means they're the categories that the cube uses to organize data—the same categories you use to create additional levels in a Visio pivot diagram or to group and filter data in a pivot chart. Most visual reports use up to three dimension fields. For your own reports, keep the dimension fields to fewer than six, or the report's performance may slow down significantly.

---

4. **In the "Visual Reports - Field Picker" dialog box, click Edit Template.**

   Project builds the OLAP cube with the fields you selected and then starts Excel or Visio (depending on the type of report).

5. **Modify the report so it looks the way you want.**

   Use the techniques described earlier in this chapter to customize the arrangement and formatting of the pivot chart or pivot diagram. If you're building a brand-new pivot table, the Excel worksheet has some guides to help you add fields in the right place, as illustrated in Figure 16-11.

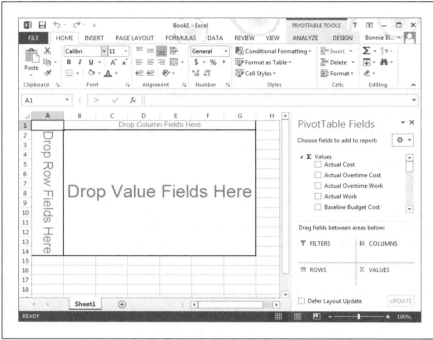

FIGURE 16-11

Excel's PivotTable Fields task pane is exactly the same as the one you see when you're working on a report. You can turn on field checkboxes to add them to the table. Drag fields from the task pane's field list into the labeled areas on the worksheet like Drop Column Fields Here. Or, if the boxes in the task pane make more sense to you, drag fields into the task pane's Filters, Rows, Columns, and Σ Values sections instead.

6. **Save the report as a template.**

   Choose File→Save As. Choose the location and folder where you want to save the template. The Save As dialog box opens.

7. **In the Save As dialog box, in the "Save as type" drop-down list, choose Excel Template for an Excel template, or Template for a Visio template. In the "File name" box, type a new name for the template, and then click Save.**

NOTE To see custom templates in the "Visual Reports - Create Report" dialog box, make sure the "Include report templates from" checkbox is turned on. Click Modify to set the path to your templates folder.

Saving Report Data

When you generate a visual report, Project chugs along for a few seconds (or minutes) as it gathers data into an OLAP cube, like a chipmunk gathering acorns in its cheeks. In addition to fueling the shape-shifting you can do with visual reports, that data can work beyond the report you're generating at the moment. For example, the data cube is a snapshot of project status. And unlike the 11 Project baselines you can save, the number of data cubes is limited only by your disk space. If you wanted to, you could save a data cube every month and open them to look for trends. You can open a cube directly in Excel or Visio and then use the built-in pivot chart and pivot diagram tools to view the information.

Here are the steps for saving project data:

1. **In the "Visual Reports - Create Report" dialog box (Report→Visual Reports), click Save Data.**

   The "Visual Reports - Save Reporting Data" dialog box opens.

2. **In the drop-down list, choose the type of OLAP cube you want to save.**

   Task Summary, Resource Summary, and Assignment Summary cubes contain total work and cost data. Task Usage, Resource Usage, and Assignment Usage cubes include time-phased data like the data in usage views. These options correspond to the tabs at the top of the "Visual Reports - Create Report" dialog box. The data that they represent are described on page 487.

3. **To choose fields other than the ones the cube contains, click Field Picker.**

   Select fields as described on page 497, and then click OK.

4. **Click Save Cube or Save Database.**

   Saving a cube creates a larger database file but makes data based on the cube's dimensions easier to find. Saving a database creates a regular Access database, which you can open using Microsoft Access.

5. **In the Save As dialog box, type a name for the file and click Save.**

   Back in the "Visual Reports - Save Reporting Data" dialog box, click Close.

To open saved report data directly in Excel, do the following:

1. **In Excel, in the Insert tab's Charts section, click PivotChart, and then choose PivotChart or "PivotChart & PivotTable."**

   The Create PivotTable or Create PivotChart dialog box opens. Both dialog boxes have the same settings, but the Create PivotTable one creates only a pivot table. The Create PivotChart one creates *both* a pivot chart and the pivot table that contains the chart's data.

2. **Select the "Use an external data source" option, and then click Choose Connection.**

   In the Existing Connections dialog box, click "Browse for More." In the Select Data Source dialog box, navigate to the folder where you saved the data cube, select the file, and then click Open.

3. **Back in the Create PivotTable or Create PivotChart dialog box, click OK.**

   A new pivot table or pivot chart appears. The PivotTable Field or PivotChart Field task pane displays the fields from the cube or database, and you're ready to use the same pivot tools you've already met.

▇ Printing Views to Report Project Information

A picture is worth a thousand words—and more than a thousand numbers in a view table. In Project, you can print views like Gantt Chart, Task Usage, or Tracking Gantt view to include in the reports you produce for stakeholders, management, and other audiences. (The box on page 502 explains another way to create a document from a view.) Here's how you set up a view to print the way you want:

1. **Display the view you want and make sure the information is presented the way you want it when you print.**

   For example, apply the table you want and, if necessary, insert, remove, or rearrange the columns in the table. For a view with a table and a timescale, drag the vertical divider so you see the amount of table and timescale you want. Adjust the timescale to show the time periods you want.

2. **Choose File→Print.**

   The Print page of Backstage view appears. Printer settings are on the left side, and a preview of the view appears on the right side.

3. **As you would for any other printout, choose the printer, number of copies, page range you want to print, paper orientation, and paper size.**

   If you change the paper orientation or size, the preview changes to show what the printout looks like.

4. **For views that include a timescale, in the Dates boxes, choose the date range you want to display.**

   Fill in the first box with the earliest date in the date range and the second box with the latest date in the range.

5. **To set up the printed page, click the Page Setup link at the bottom of the Print page.**

   The Page Setup dialog box opens with tabs similar to those in other programs. For example, on the Page tab, you can choose the paper orientation and size, adjust the scale of the view, or specify the number of pages to use to print the view. The Margins tab lets you adjust the margins on the page. The Header and Footer tabs are where you specify information to display in the printout's header and footer.

6. **To specify whether the printout includes a legend, in the Page Setup dialog box, click the Legend tab, and then select the option you want.**

Project initially selects the "Every page" option, as shown in Figure 16-12, which means that a legend that identifies the bars appears on every page. To save some trees and show more of your project on each page, select the "Legend page" option instead, which includes one page with a legend.

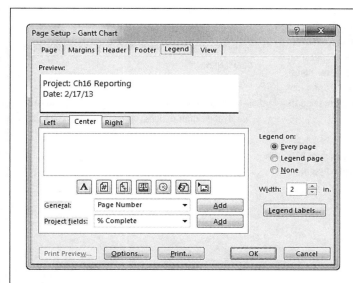

FIGURE 16-12

If you know what the elements in the view represent, on the Legend tab, select the None option. You can also specify the width of the legend by choosing a number of inches in the Width box. If you want to adjust the text formatting for the legend, click Legend Labels.

7. **To fine-tune what appears on the printed page, in the Page Setup dialog box, click the View tab. Then turn on the checkboxes for the elements you want.**

For example, to print all the columns in the table, turn on the "Print all sheet columns" checkbox. To print a specific number of columns on every page of the printout, turn on the "Print first ___ columns on all pages" checkbox and then choose the number of columns. You can also choose to print notes, blank pages, or adjust the timescale to fill the page.

8. **When the settings are the way you want, click Print.**

Project prints the view.

Creating a PDF or XPS Document

Rather than printing a Project view, you can create a copy of your project in PDF or XPS format. These two file formats contain the text data that you save, so you can index the files or copy information out of them. In addition, these formats keep all the formatting, fonts, and graphics that appear on your screen and spit them out looking the same on almost any computer. Anyone can view these documents using free viewers available for download. To create one of these documents, follow these steps:

1. Choose File→Export.
2. On the Export page of Backstage view, choose Create PDF/XPS Document, and then click the Create PDF/XPS button.
3. In the Browse dialog box, navigate to the folder in which you want to save the file.
4. Name the file.
5. In the "Save as type" drop-down list, choose PDF Files or XPS Files.
6. Click OK.
7. In the Document Export Options dialog box that appears, specify the export options you want, and then click OK.

Closing a Project

I f you've ever moved to a new house, you know how additional things to pack seem to appear out of thin air the closer you get to the end. Projects have loose ends to tie up, too. After the project team hands over the last deliverable, the project's scope is complete, but you still have a few project-management tasks to finish. Getting formal project acceptance from the customer is first and foremost—because the project isn't done until the customer says it is.

Once the project is accepted, it's time to write a final report to wrap up the project and document useful information for the future. A *project closeout report* is like a higher-level version of the status reports and other project-related reports you've produced all along. The closeout report summarizes project results, highlighting lessons learned, issues dealt with, and risks that became reality. It should also include a final accounting of schedule and budget—the actual dates and costs and their variances compared with your baseline.

This chapter describes the information you need to gather for closeout reports and which Project reports you can use. It also gives tips on identifying lessons learned without ruffling anyone's feathers.

The final step is storing project information for future reference, using information storage strategies introduced in Chapter 12. In this chapter, you'll learn about different destinations for your final project documents.

■ Obtaining Project Acceptance

Project acceptance is the key to closing a project—and keeping it closed. Unless you get formal acceptance from whomever has the final say, someone could come back later claiming that a deliverable is missing or that the results aren't quite right after all.

The deliverables and success criteria (page 24) you carefully documented in the project plan guided the project team through project execution. They're even *more* important at project acceptance because you and the project customer use them to measure success and finally deem the project complete.

Deliverables tend to be tangible. For example, either the fundraiser reached its goal of raising $1,000,000 or it didn't. But some success criteria can be subjective. The more diligent you are in hashing out clear and quantifiable success criteria during planning, the easier it is to obtain project acceptance at the project's end.

If success criteria aren't completely clear, acceptance may take some time. When you finally get there, it's *essential* to get the customer to sign an acceptance form. Signing a document makes it harder for the customer to renege. Face-to-face meetings seem to give a sign-off more weight, but a conference call to deliver acceptance verbally (followed up with a signed hard copy) is the next best thing.

The acceptance form can be straightforward: The most important part of the document is the John Hancock from whoever has authority to accept the project. You can add other elements like a list of completed deliverables if you want to be very clear about what the customer is accepting. Like other contractual documents, copy the signed document and distribute the copies to the signers and others you need to notify that the project is complete.

■ Tying Up Loose Ends

Transitioning resources is another part of closing a project. What resources do when they finish their work for you may not seem like your problem. However, before everyone starts popping champagne corks and playing Twister, it's in your best interest to make sure that people have completed everything you need for your project, *and* that their managers know when to line up their next assignments. Winning points with resource managers may make it easier for you to get resources on your next project, so managing resource handoffs is a win-win proposition.

If you share resources with other projects, you also need to close out any remaining planned hours in your project schedule. In other words, once the project is complete, the Remaining Work field should equal zero for all resource assignments in the project. To do this, in Task Usage view, display the Work table (in the View tab's Data section, click Tables→Work). Then, in the Task Usage Tools | Format tab's Show/Hide section, turn off the Project Summary Task and Summary Tasks checkboxes. Then, click a Remaining Work cell that's equal to zero, and position your cursor over the fill handle at the cell's bottom right. When the cursor changes to a + sign, drag over all the rows in the table.

> **TIP** After the remaining work hours are set to zero, all your project's tasks *should* have a % Complete value of 100%. To make sure every task is 100% complete, in the View tab's Data section, click Filter→Incomplete Tasks. If any tasks appear in the table, right-click anywhere in the task's row. In the shortcut menu that appears above the row, click 100%, and then choose 100% Complete on the drop-down menu.

Also, you need to close any contracts written for your project (with the project customer, vendors, subcontractors, and so on). Every contract spells out the steps required to close it. Your job is to perform those steps and get sign-offs on all contracts.

Project financial accounting typically doesn't end right away. It's easier to keep the books open for a while so you can handle project expenses that show up later, like support costs, employee expense reports, and so on. On the other hand, take whatever steps you need to with the accounting department so no one can charge additional hours to the project.

■ Producing Project Closeout Reports

A project closeout report is like a status report on steroids. It summarizes project results, risks and issues encountered, and lessons learned. It also presents final performance numbers, including schedule and budget performance, and earned value. This section describes what usually goes into a project closeout report and identifies Project reports you can run to obtain the information you need.

Summarizing a Project

Audiences want to know what's important, and they don't want to spend time digging. A project closeout report summarizes results for quick and easy reading, as the example in Figure 17-1 illustrates. (Folks with a penchant for detail and too much time on their hands can peruse the entire project archive, if they want.)

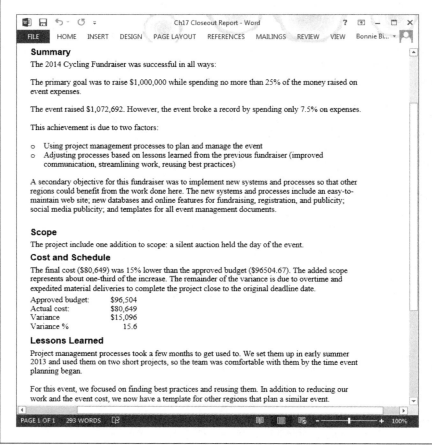

FIGURE 17-1

A closeout report for a small project may be a single page long, like this one. For large projects or those that ran into trouble, you may want to include more detail to answer questions before anyone has a chance to ask.

The closeout report supplements the performance reports described in the next section because it includes an analysis of what happened and a synopsis of the most significant results. These are the main items in a project closeout report:

- **Summary.** This section is like the Letter to Shareholders that a CEO writes for a company's annual report; it's a 30,000-foot view of what the project accomplished and whether the project was a success. State whether the project achieved its goals and objectives. Was it completed on schedule, within budget, and to the required level of quality?

- **Completed scope.** List the completed scope and deliverables. Identify any items from the original scope that weren't completed (and why).

- **Changes.** If the scope changed significantly, briefly describe what was left out or added, as well as other significant changes, like a major redesign to simplify manufacturing. If approved change orders affected the schedule or cost, include a brief summary of the revised dates and change order costs.

- **Explanation of variances.** If the project performance strayed from the baseline, explain why and include recommendations for improving future performance.

- **Lessons learned.** Describe what worked well, what didn't work, and what you would do differently.

- **The effectiveness of risk management.** Identify the risks that turned into issues during the project, the risk response you chose, and whether the risk response successfully reduced the issue's impact. Also describe any issues that arose that weren't identified as risks during initial risk planning.

- **The effectiveness of project management.** Describe the results of the project-management processes you used. If you recommend any changes, describe them.

Reporting Performance

Closeout reports also include quantitative data like cost and schedule variances or project-specific measures like quality-oriented success criteria. You can produce all kinds of schedule and cost reports in Project using visual reports (page 469) or Excel-based reports. Here are some of the project performance measures you may include in a closeout report, along with the Project reports that show them:

■ COST PERFORMANCE

Closeout reports usually compare total actual cost to baseline cost and show the variance between the two. For large projects, you may want to break down costs in other ways, such as by phase or by types of expenses. Here are some of Project's cost-related visual reports:

- The **Budget Cost** report (page 306) is great for slicing and dicing costs by tasks, resources, and types of cost.

- The **Cash Flow** report (page 305) comes in handy when you want to calculate other financial measures, like return on investment or internal rate of return.

- The **Earned Value Report** (page 442) charts cost and schedule performance over the life of the project.

■ SCHEDULE PERFORMANCE

A Gantt Chart view that shows the baseline schedule, like Tracking Gantt, may be the most effective way to compare actual dates to the baseline. The timescale shows the variance visually.

You can also use *earned value* (page 441) to show schedule performance. With earned value, schedule variance is shown in terms of dollars—the actual cost minus the planned cost.

> **NOTE** Cost gives you some idea how your work estimates compared to reality. The Budget Work visual report can show the hours people worked compared with the baseline.

■ QUALITY PERFORMANCE

If quality measures are part of the project success criteria, then include them in your closeout report. The way you present quality performance depends on how you measure quality and where you track that information. For example, if you're measuring the quantity and severity of software defects, you can use your defect-tracking database to produce a graph.

Documenting What You Learned

Most people equate lessons learned with painful or embarrassing experiences. And the alternative term, "postmortem," is even less appealing. All too many work environments focus on finding a scapegoat rather than identifying and learning from mistakes. Yet improving future project performance requires not only avoiding repetition of past mistakes, but also repeating what worked well and coming up with even *better* ways to do things. A first step to making lessons learned more palatable is to call it by a different name: project managers in the know refer to this as the *project implementation review*.

You'd think successes would be easy to find, but they may stay hidden because team members don't realize their significance or don't want to brag. On the other hand, people tend to shy away from admitting mistakes and failures, just as you'd expect. So it takes a light touch *and* an environment of trust to uncover these touchy subjects.

This section explains why lessons learned are so important to future projects. It also gives some hints on coaxing successes, mistakes, and better ideas out of the project team. After you've identified the lessons, they become part of your project closeout report. In addition, you can publicize this information to help other teams learn from your experience.

> **TIP** Lessons aren't learned at the end of a project, so why wait until then to identify them? Collect lessons learned during your status meetings, in status reports, from tracking issues, or by holding specific lessons-learned sessions upon reaching key milestones.

■ DON'T SKIP THIS STEP!

Sure, everyone is eager to finish the project and get on to something else. Before memory fades, though, get the team together and find out what worked, what didn't, and what team members have come up with to do better. If you need some encouragement to perform this step, here are some ways lessons learned can help:

- **Take advantage of successful techniques.** Continuous improvement is what turned circa-1980 cinder block–sized mobile phones into the tiny, feature-packed smartphones of today. Let everyone build on your team's success, whether you discovered an effective way to obtain approvals quickly, stumbled across a remarkable time-saving technique, or developed reusable documents and checklists.

TIP Every project may be unique, but you can recycle a lot of your project-management work by turning documents and Project schedules into templates (page 708).

- **Defuse unrealistic demands.** Executives are renowned for setting dates and budgets before projects are defined or planned. With past performance and lessons learned, you have ammunition to try to persuade stakeholders to change the numbers.

- **Don't make the same mistakes.** Mistakes are costly, so you don't want to pay for them more than once. Analyze mistakes and failures so you can prevent them in the future. For example, suppose you used lower-cost resources to save money but ended up spending more because they worked so slowly. On the next project, you can evaluate cost and productivity to decide whom to use. In the business world, cause-and-effect diagrams (also called *fishbone* diagrams, or Ishikawa diagrams after their inventor) and fault-tree analysis are two ways to identify the origins of failure.

- **Build support for project management.** If your organization is new to project management, the opinion may be that it takes too long and costs too much. Lessons learned are real-life examples of why project management is so important, and the results show how project management—or its absence—affected performance. Suppose your project was swamped with changes that blew the schedule and the budget; that can help you make a case for implementing a change-management system.

■ GATHERING WHAT YOU LEARNED

Without guidance, lessons-learned meetings can alternate between apprehensive silences and finger-pointing melees. Setting up meetings dedicated to lessons learned helps people get in the right mind-set. If you think team members may be hesitant to speak up in front of managers, then set up separate meetings. It's up to you to set a positive tone and run the meetings as effectively as you can. Line up people to perform the following roles, and your meetings will be more productive:

- **Project manager.** You don't have to assign someone to this role if it's yours. In that case, your job is to plan the meeting beforehand as you would any other type of meeting. Prepare an agenda; set a time limit; schedule the meeting; invite the attendees; and distribute materials like status reports and issues beforehand. At the beginning of the meeting, review the agenda and the materials you distributed. (Don't assume people have read them beforehand.) During the meeting, you can ask questions, take notes, clarify misunderstandings, and so on. Afterward, you help prepare a lessons-learned report and follow up on action items.

TIP To make these meetings as nonthreatening as possible, set up ground rules in advance. Print the rules on the agenda, have the facilitator review them at the beginning of the meeting, and remind people if they break them.

- **Facilitator.** You may do double-duty as the facilitator and project manager, but a dedicated facilitator is a boon if the meeting has a cast of thousands. The facilitator spells out the meeting's purpose and ground rules and then gets the discussion started. During the meeting, the facilitator keeps the discussion focused on the agenda and makes everyone follow the rules. (The box below provides some tips for getting discussions going.)

- **Scribe.** Taking notes is a full-time job. Assign someone who's familiar with the project, preferably someone with legible handwriting or speedy keyboarding fingers. To be sure the information you want gets captured, give the scribe a template to fill in, like the one shown in Figure 17-2.

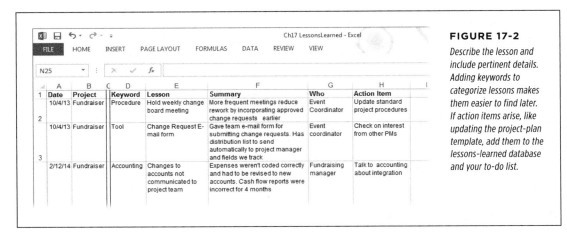

FIGURE 17-2

Describe the lesson and include pertinent details. Adding keywords to categorize lessons makes them easier to find later. If action items arise, like updating the project-plan template, add them to the lessons-learned database and your to-do list.

Get Discussions Going

Discussions in lessons-learned meetings can be hard to start. If you ask a question like, "Did your assignment go well?" the answer may be nothing more than "Yes." The trick is to ask *open-ended* questions—ones that don't invite one-word answers. For example, commonly asked questions include "What went well?" "What didn't go well?" and "What can we improve?" Or you might ask additional questions like "What helped you the most as you worked on your tasks?" "Tell us what you did to deliver your work early," or "What would you do differently next time?"

Before the meeting, review the project and identify tasks that came in early or late, under budget or over budget. Reread the issue and risk logs to see what problems arose, and go through

any lessons learned you've collected already. You can use these materials to put together a few questions to jump-start discussion. Ask each attendee about her experiences.

Jotting down notes on a whiteboard or a flip chart is another way to prompt discussion. As in brainstorming sessions, these notes may trigger ideas in others.

When it comes to discussing mistakes, focus on improvement. Placing blame with a statement like "You didn't tell us that" makes people clam up. Ask questions like "How can we improve our procedures?" "How did you solve the obstacles you encountered?" or "Do you have a suggestion for how to do things differently?"

■ REMEMBERING YOUR LESSONS

The lessons you learn don't do any good if you forget them and no one else finds out about them. Lessons learned are part of the project closeout reports and thus in the project archive, but you need a way to make sure lessons learned get used to improve future projects.

The most effective way to embed lessons learned into the corporate psyche is to add them to existing standard processes and procedures. For example, if a weekly change board meeting improved the turnaround time on change requests, you can update the project-plan template or your project-management guidelines to recommend that schedule. Publishing a project-management newsletter or a company blog are other ways to disseminate significant lessons. And a database of lessons learned can come in handy—as long as it's easy to search (see Figure 17-2).

■ What to Do with Project Information

After you've prepared final project reports, you stick them in the project notebook (page 371), send them to the stakeholders on the report distribution list, and you're done, right? Well, you *could* stop there, but if you plan to reuse the work you've done or share it with other project managers, you also want to archive project information in a way that's easy for people to find and access. The box on page 512 gives you a few more ways to package and share your project information.

All the ways to store project documents and the different types of technology you can use (discussed in Chapter 12) hold true at the end of a project, too. But now that the project is over, consider moving your project archive to a location that more people can access. For example, while the project is in progress, you may want only the project team to access files. When the project is done, those files can be helpful to every project manager in your organization.

> **TIP** You may have hundreds, even *thousands*, of documents by the time a project finishes. At that point, some of them aren't worth the hard-disk space they consume. When you archive project information, take some time to get rid of obsolete documents like individual status reports or the eight draft versions of a document submitted before the client approved the final one.

Handing Off Information

Some projects are like toilet paper stuck to your shoe—you can't shake them off no matter how hard you try. In reality, the project *does* end, but then the ongoing operations kick in. For example, after your fundraiser ends, the membership department steps in and tries to turn donors into ongoing supporters. In these situations, someone else needs information about what was done (and perhaps what's still left to do).

In addition to storing information in an archive, you may have to hand it off to other groups. Here are some typical documents that operations teams need:

- **Final specs, as-built drawings, product documentation, and so on.** This information gets reused as support teams develop maintenance procedures, marketing produces brochures, or manufacturing retools the assembly line. For example, if a fundraiser project developed a website for making donations, the customer service team can use the documentation about the website to resolve donors' transaction problems.

- **Test results.** Read-me files for software programs, for example, usually include a list of existing problems and workarounds developed based on tests that the program didn't completely pass. Product-warranty terms are based on the service and replacements a company expects to provide, and test results are one way to forecast these values.

- **Status and unresolved issues.** If customers purchase software maintenance, unfinished features or unresolved issues may be the beginning of the next software release. Similarly, in construction, a "punch list" lists all the tasks that weren't complete at sign-off.

- **Location of archived project documents.** If the next group in line can access the project archive, then it can obtain any document it needs.

Project Power Tools

Working on More Than One Project

I f you're like most project managers, you juggle several projects at the same time. You may have several smaller projects that are part of a larger effort—like the subprojects for building the different parts of a new airplane. Or you may simply manage several separate projects at once, like several fundraisers for the charity you work for. In almost every case, you have to share resources with others. For organizations with oodles of projects, Microsoft's enterprise project-management software (Project Server and Project Web App, or Project Online) provides tools for managing entire portfolios of projects (page xvii). However, Microsoft Project Standard and Professional also have features for managing smaller numbers of projects.

In Project, a *master project* is the easiest way to work with several projects at the same time. You create a new Project file and then insert other Project files into it to consolidate them into one file. (Although you insert the files into a master project, they still exist as separate Project files.) A master project is great for assembling multiple subprojects in one place, but it works equally well if you're managing a bunch of unrelated projects and want an easy way to keep an eye on all of them at once. This chapter describes how to build a master project from related subprojects and how to consolidate several unrelated projects into one Project file.

Master projects aren't your only option when working with multiple projects, though. Sometimes all you need is a link between a task in one project and a task in another project. Suppose one project in your company has magnanimously funded a new database-management system. One of your projects can use the system, but you don't want to start your database work until the stakeholders have approved the other project's database design. In cases like that, you can create what's called an *external task dependency* (a.k.a. *cross-project dependency*) between the database-design milestone and the start of your project's database work. In this chapter, you'll learn how to create external task dependencies.

Whether you fight over resources with yourself or with other project managers, you eventually have to share the resources you use. Project Server has the niftiest tools for finding and sharing resources, but plain-Jane Project can share resources, too—the program lets you create a file called a *resource pool* to hold information about available resources. In this chapter, you'll learn how to create a resource pool and apply it to your projects. You'll also learn different ways of opening a resource pool and when to use each one.

■ Managing Multiple Projects

If you don't have the option of using Project Server to manage multiple projects, you can insert subprojects into a master project instead, no matter how much or how little the projects have in common. Here are a few situations in which inserting subprojects into a master project can help you manage multiple projects:

- **A large project with subprojects.** Suppose you're managing a project so large that it requires several project managers to handle different parts. For example, a project to build a new airplane may have subprojects for the fuselage, engines, electronics, wiring, and so on. The separate systems progress individually, but they have to come together before the rubber can hit the tarmac. When you set up a master project that contains the separate subprojects, the project managers for the subprojects (whether they're subcontractors or part of your organization) each work on their own Project files. But you can see the big picture of all the subprojects simply by opening the master project.

> **TIP** Master projects and subprojects aren't appropriate for managing humongous projects with casts of thousands, budgets in the millions, hordes of risks and issues, and project interdependencies galore. For a stable of big projects like those, Enterprise Project Management Solutions (which includes Project Server and Project Web App) are what you need to stay on top of everything.

- **Several projects share the same resources.** Say you and another project manager in your company work on different projects, but you both pull your resources from the same pool of employees. After a few hallway tussles over popular resources, you decide to try a better way. The two of you create a resource pool that contains the resources you both share. Then you both link your projects to that resource pool so you can check resources' availability.

- **Several unrelated projects.** If you spend each day juggling several small projects, you'd probably like to keep track of them all within Project. By creating a master project and inserting all your Project files into it, you can open all your projects simply by opening the master file. Even better, you can work on the projects without switching Project windows and create links between tasks in different projects. Similarly, you can produce consolidated views or reports for all your projects. (If you open the same, unrelated projects day after day, using a *workspace* can also save you some time, as the box on page 517 explains.)

TIP When you add subprojects to a master project file, Project calculates a single critical path for all the subprojects. However, if you're using a master project to track *unrelated* projects, you want each project to have its own critical path. To tell the program to calculate separate critical paths for each project, choose File→Options, and then choose Schedule on the left side of the Project Options dialog box. Scroll to the bottom of the dialog box and, in the "Calculation options for this project" section, turn off the "Inserted projects are calculated like summary tasks" checkbox. Then click OK.

- **Reporting on overall progress.** You can insert projects into a master project temporarily to produce consolidated views or reports for several projects.

Opening Several Projects At Once

Say you're working on three small projects that have nothing in common other than having you as the project manager. After a few days of opening one project file after another, a shortcut for opening your files sounds like a good idea. If you don't need the resource-sharing features of a master file, a *workspace file* is just the ticket.

The Save Workspace command isn't on the ribbon, so first you have to make it available. After that, creating and accessing a workspace is a snap. Here's what you do:

1. To add the Save Workspace command to the Quick Access toolbar, click the down arrow to the toolbar's right, and then choose More Commands. In the "Choose commands from" drop-down list, choose "Commands Not in the Ribbon." Scroll down the list, click Save Workspace, click Add, and then click OK.

2. To create a workspace file, first open all the Project files that you want to belong to the workspace. (Close any that you don't want in the workspace.)

3. On the Quick Access toolbar, click the Save Workspace icon.

4. In the Save Workspace As dialog box, navigate to the folder where you want to save the workspace file.

5. In the "File name" box, type something meaningful like *Q1Workspace*. (The file extension is *.mpw* for "Microsoft Project workspace.")

6. Click Save.

Now you can open the workspace file just like you would a regular Project file (page 99). The only difference is that, when you do, *all* the Project files in the workspace open automatically. You still have to close the files one at a time.

Although you can insert a Project file into any *other* Project file (see step 3 on page 518), the best way to keep track of multiple projects is to create a master project—a Project file that contains other projects. Here's how a master project works when you insert Project files into it:

- All the inserted subprojects assemble cheerfully in one Project window, so you can work on and save them all as if they were a single file, even though the individual projects remain separate files.

- The inserted projects look like summary tasks, which you can expand to show all the subtasks, or collapse to see the big picture.

- You can work on subproject tasks as if they belong to the master project—modifying, sorting, filtering, and grouping the aggregated tasks.

- Because a master project is a regular Project file, you can add tasks to it—for example, for the work you do supervising the other project managers.

- A master project maintains continuous contact with its inserted subprojects. If someone modifies information in a subproject, those changes are immediately visible in the master file. Conversely, if you make a change to a subproject in the master project, those changes are immediately visible to anyone looking at the original Project file for that inserted subproject.

Creating a Master Project

Setting up a master project is usually just a matter of creating the master Project file and then inserting the subproject Project files into it. (The less-common alternative is to create a master project when you already have a single large project that you want to break into subprojects. The box on page 521 tells you how to do that.) If you create a master project to supervise several projects managed by others, be sure to store all the files in a shared location that all the project managers can access.

Here's how to create a master project from several individual projects:

1. **Choose File→New, and then on the New page, click Blank Project.**

   Project creates a new, blank file, ready to accept your subprojects. If Project displays the new project in something other than Gantt Chart view, in that Task tab's View section, click the Gantt Chart down arrow, and then choose Gantt Chart.

2. **Select the first blank row.**

   If this is your first time through this list, continue with step 3.

   If this is your second (or third, or fourth...) time through this list, you have some options. If you've created a master project to track several levels of subprojects, then you can insert projects anywhere in the task hierarchy. For example, if a subproject is large enough to have its *own* subprojects, then you can insert Project files underneath the higher-level subproject. To insert a sub-subproject, click the row below which you want to insert it.

   When you insert the subproject in the next step, it appears at the same level as the task immediately above it and pushes the task you selected down one row.)

3. **In the Project tab's Insert section, click Subproject.**

   The Insert Project dialog box appears. Navigate to the folder that contains the first project you want to insert.

4. **Select the project you want to insert, make sure the "Link to project" setting is what you want, and then click Insert.**

In the Insert Project dialog box, Project automatically turns on the "Link to project" checkbox, which tells Project to update the master project whenever the inserted project changes. You almost always want these immediate updates. For example, you'd do this when you decide to turn one large project into a master project as described in the box on page 521. But in some cases, you want subprojects inserted into a master project as read-only entries, as the box on page 522 explains. In such cases, you can turn off the "Link to project" checkbox. For example, you'd do this when you decide to turn one large project into a master project as describe din the box on page 521. In that case, you can unlink all the projects so that their tasks now belong to the master Project file. Of course, when you do this, you should be sure that no one makes changes to the original subproject files.

Project adds a summary task for the inserted project, as shown in Figure 18-1.

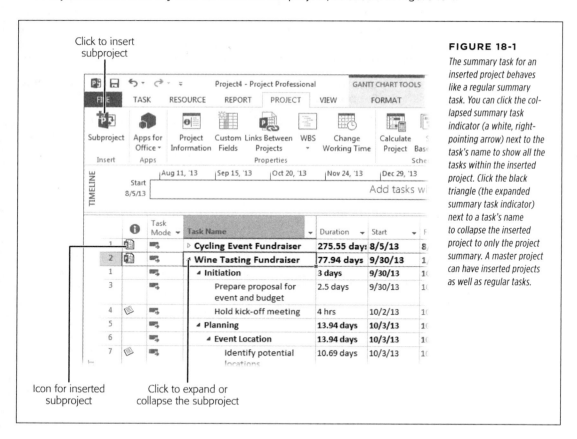

FIGURE 18-1

The summary task for an inserted project behaves like a regular summary task. You can click the collapsed summary task indicator (a white, right-pointing arrow) next to the task's name to show all the tasks within the inserted project. Click the black triangle (the expanded summary task indicator) next to a task's name to collapse the inserted project to only the project summary. A master project can have inserted projects as well as regular tasks.

5. Repeat steps 2–4 to insert additional projects.

Remember, you specify where to insert projects by selecting the row below where you want to insert the project. The project in the row you select shifts down, so the inserted projects don't overwrite what's already there. You can also reorder inserted projects by dragging an inserted project summary task to another position in the task table.

NOTE When you insert projects into a master project, the ID cells for tasks seem to go crazy, as you can see in Figure 18-1. Project assigns sequential ID numbers to each subproject, beginning with 1. However, the tasks that belong to inserted projects have ID numbers that *also* begin with 1. So you're likely to see several tasks with the same ID number. When you work with subprojects, ignore the ID numbers. Instead, refer to the WBS code with a project prefix (see the Note on page 157) to uniquely identify every task.

---

6. Work on the inserted projects as you would regular tasks.

In the Task tab's Schedule section, click Indent Task or Outdent Task (page 144) to move the inserted project to the correct level of the task hierarchy—for example, to include several sub-subprojects underneath a top-level inserted project. You can link tasks within inserted projects to one another *or* to regular tasks in the master project, or you can link one inserted project summary task to another.

7. If you need help identifying tasks and resources from different subprojects, insert the Subproject File column into your Gantt Chart table.

Right-click the Gantt Chart table's heading area, and then choose Insert Column. In the drop-down list, choose Subproject File. Figure 18-2 shows the Subproject File cells with the file paths and names for each inserted project.

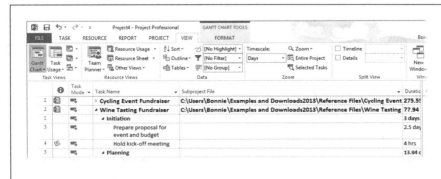

FIGURE 18-2

The Subproject File column contains the full path to the subproject file, which means the column's values are huge, as shown here. Don't widen the column to show the entire path. Instead, you can read the full path simply by putting your mouse pointer over a cell in the column.

Creating a Master Project from One Large Project

You've forged ahead on a massive project, putting all the tasks into one Project file. One day, you realize that this big, awkward file is making it harder for you to manage the project and, more importantly, to delegate subprojects to other project managers. All is not lost—you can turn your gargantuan project into a master project with subprojects without breaking a sweat. Here's how:

1. Create a Project file for each subproject within your large project.

2. In each new file, set the subproject's start date to the start date of the original colossal project and pick the same calendar (page 102) as the original project. (In step 8, you'll link the subprojects so they start on the correct dates.)

3. In the original massive Project file, drag over the ID cells for all the tasks you want to move to the first new subproject file. Then in the Task tab's Clipboard section, choose Copy to copy all the information about the selected tasks to the Clipboard. (If you drag over the Task Name cells instead, Project copies only the tasks' names.)

4. Switch to the corresponding Project file for the new subproject, and then in the Task tab's Clipboard section, click Paste→Paste Special to copy all the tasks from the original Project file. In the Paste Special dialog box's "As:" list, choose Project Data, and then click OK.

5. Save the subproject Project file.

6. Repeat steps 3–5 for each subproject until you've copied all the tasks from the original Project file into subproject files.

7. Create a Project file for the master project, and then insert all the subproject files into it, as described on page 518.

8. Create task dependencies between the subprojects to restore them to the chronological order they had in the original large project (page 176).

TIP If your master project and subprojects contain some of the same resources, Resource Sheet view in the master project contains duplicate entries for those resources, one for each project containing that resource. The problem is you have to select the *correct* resource entry (the one for the subproject) when you assign resources within that subproject. You can tell the resource entries apart by inserting the Project column into Resource Sheet view. But the *best* way to solve the duplicate problem is to set up a *resource pool* for all the projects to share, as described in the box on page 218.

Preventing Changes to Subprojects

Suppose you supervise several newbie project managers and you want an easy way to review all the projects they manage, but you don't want to change those subprojects by mistake. You can insert projects into a master project as read-only. Then you can view the inserted projects from the master project, but you can modify them only by opening their source Project files. To insert projects as read-only, in the Insert Project dialog box, click the down arrow on the Insert button, and then, from the drop-down list, choose Insert Read-Only.

You can also change an inserted project to read-only *after* it's inserted. In a Gantt Chart table, click anywhere in the inserted project's summary task row, and then press Shift+F2 to open the Inserted Project Information dialog box (or in the

Task tab's Properties section, click Information). Select the dialog box's Advanced tab, and then turn on the "Read only" checkbox. To quickly change several subprojects to read-only, insert the Subproject Read Only field in the Gantt Chart table (right-click in the table's heading area, and then choose Insert Column→Subproject Read Only). To make an inserted project read-only, change the field's value to Yes.

One exception to a subproject's read-only status occurs when you open the subproject and then open the master project while the subproject is still open. In that case, Project changes the read-only subproject file whether you make the change in the master project *or* the subproject source file.

Removing a Project from a Master Project

If you no longer need an inserted project in your master project, then you can delete the inserted project task while keeping the original subproject file. Suppose another project manager takes over one of your projects, so you no longer need to see that project. Simply delete it from your master project. The new project manager then works on the original Project file. That's it.

To remove an inserted project, do the following:

1. **In Gantt Chart view, click the ID cell for the inserted project's summary task.**

   Project selects the entire row.

2. **Press the Delete key on your keyboard, or right-click the task's row and choose Delete Task on the shortcut menu.**

   The Planning Wizard dialog box appears and asks you to confirm that you want to delete a summary task and all its subtasks.

3. **Make sure the Continue option is selected, and then click OK.**

   Project removes the inserted project from the master project but leaves the original subproject file where it is. (If you change your mind, click Cancel instead.)

Linking Tasks in Different Projects

Maybe only a few tasks in one project link to tasks in another project. For example, suppose that planning the cycling fundraiser grabs everyone's attention like a cute puppy, so you don't want to start preparing the proposal for the wine tasting until the planning for the cycling event is complete. In order to indicate this connection in Project, you need to link tasks in different projects to create an *external task dependency*. The easiest way to do this is to insert both projects into a temporary master project and then link them the way you would two tasks in the same Project file.

To create an external task dependency, follow these steps:

1. **Choose File→New, and then, on the New screen, click Blank Project.**

   Project creates a new, blank file that's ready to accept your subprojects.

2. **Select the first blank row, and then, in the Project tab's Insert section, click Subproject.**

   The Insert Project dialog box appears. Navigate to the folder that contains the first project you want to insert.

3. **Select the project you want to insert, make sure the "Link to project" checkbox is turned on, and then click Insert.**

4. **Repeat steps 2 and 3 to insert the second project.**

   The two projects look like summary tasks, except that a Project file icon appears in the indicator column. Click the white triangle next to each project's name to display all the subtasks.

5. **Select the task that acts as the predecessor (click anywhere in its row), and then Ctrl-click the successor task.**

   Be sure to select the predecessor first and the successor second.

6. **In the Task tab's Schedule section, click the "Link the Selected Tasks" icon (it looks like two links of chain).**

   Project draws link lines between the two tasks as if they were in the same project. If you insert the Predecessors column, you'll see that the Predecessors field for the successor task includes the full path to the file that contains the successor task with the task's ID appended at the end, as shown in Figure 18-3.

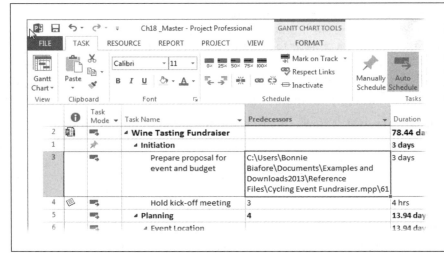

FIGURE 18-3

The Predecessor field shows the full path and filename for the project that contains the predecessor, a backslash (\), and then the task ID of the predecessor.

7. **Choose File→Close. In the first dialog box that asks if you want to save your changes (for the master project), click No. In the second and third dialog boxes that ask if you want to save your changes (for the subprojects), click Yes.**

   By clicking No in the first dialog box, you discard the master project you created. However, the link between the tasks in the two projects is still in place. If you open the file that contains the successor task, the external predecessor appears in the row immediately above the successor task (the text in its row is gray). In the file that contains the predecessor task, the external successor appears in the row immediately below the predecessor task.

> **NOTE** When you open a Project file that contains external task dependencies, the Links Between Projects dialog box might open, which shows all the file's external predecessors and external successors. If you don't see the dialog box or want to open it later on, in the Project tab's Properties section, click Links Between Projects. You can also control the appearance of cross-project links. Choose File→Options. On the left side of the Project Options dialog box, choose Advanced. In the "Cross project linking options for this project" section, you can turn off the "Show external successors" and "Show external predecessors" checkboxes (they're on by default) to hide external tasks. And if you don't want the Links Between Project dialog box to open automatically, then turn off the "Show 'Links Between Project' dialog box on open" checkbox.

■ Sharing Resources Among Projects

People usually work on more than one project for more than one project manager. If each project manager creates a resource to represent the same worker in each Project file, then overallocated resources and resource squabbles will soon follow.

The solution in Project Standard and Professional is a *resource pool*, which is a Project file dedicated to resource information—the pool of resources who work on projects, their cost, availability, and most importantly, how much time they're already allocated to tasks. (A resource pool in Project is based on the same idea as the enterprise resource pool in Project Server, although Project Server includes a few more tools for finding the right resources.)

The beauty of a resource pool is that resource information is in one place. Project managers who use those resources simply link their projects to the resource pool. Assigning resources works exactly as it does when resources are contained in the project file. The only difference is that you can see how much of the resources' time is allocated to tasks from all linked projects.

Creating a Resource Pool

The simplest way to set up a resource pool is to create a new Project file that does nothing but act as a resource pool. Although you *can* use a Project file with tasks in it as the resource pool, you may run into problems if you want to work on the tasks and someone else wants to work on resource information.

TIP If an existing project contains all the shared resources in your organization, you don't have to build a resource pool from scratch. Open the existing project, and then choose File→Save As to save a copy of the project. Open the copy, delete all the tasks in it, and then save the Project file. (To quickly delete all tasks, display Gantt Chart view. Click the Select All cell immediately above the first ID cell to select all tasks, and then press Delete.) Voilà—you have a Project file that can serve as a resource pool.

To create a standalone resource pool, do the following:

1. **Choose File→New→Blank Project.**

   Project opens a blank file.

2. **In the View tab's Resource Views section, click Resource Sheet.**

   Resource Sheet view is home to all the data about your resources (page 79).

3. **Fill in information about your shared resources.**

   Typically, you fill in resource names, their standard charge rates or cost, and the maximum availability for work resources. If you want to include other information like work group, overtime rate, or cost per use, fill in those fields, too.

4. **Choose File→Save.**

   In the Save As page, choose where you want to save the file, such as Computer or SkyDrive, and then choose the folder you want (in the Recent Folders list or by clicking Browse). In the Save As dialog box, name the project something meaningful (like Resource Pool).

   Be sure to save the resource pool in a location that all project managers can access. Saving it to your laptop, for example, won't help other project managers who need to link to the file. So go with a network drive or another shared location instead.

TIP If you have resource information in Microsoft Outlook, Active Directory, or an HR database, then you can import that information into Project, as described on page 211. Or you can copy resources from one Project file and paste them into the resource pool file. (See the box on page 537 for copy and paste steps.)

Connecting a Project to a Resource Pool

Before you can assign resources from a resource pool to project tasks, you have to link the file that contains the tasks to the resource pool. Any Project file that uses a resource pool is known as a *sharer file*. With the project–resource pool connection in place, the resource pool resources act as if they're part of the project file.

To connect a project to the resource pool, do the following:

1. **In Project, open the resource pool file.**

   Since many project managers may share the resource pool, open the resource pool file as read-only so you don't lock anyone out of the file. To do that, in the Open dialog box, select the resource pool file, and then, on the Open button, click the down arrow, and then choose Open Read-Only.

2. **Open the project file that needs to access the resource pool.**

   If you have several projects to share with the resource pool, you can open them all at the same time and then cycle through to connect each one to the resource pool.

3. **With the project file active, in the Resource tab's Assignments section, choose Resource Pool→Share Resources.**

   The Share Resources dialog box opens (Figure 18-4).

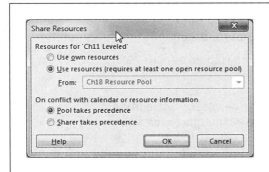

FIGURE 18-4

The Share Resources dialog box includes options to tell Project whether to use resources from the project file itself or from the resource pool. For example, if you want to switch from using the resource pool back to using your own file, select the "Use own resources" option.

4. **Select the "Use resources (requires at least one open resource pool)" option and then, if necessary, in the From drop-down list, choose the resource pool file.**

   If you have several projects open, the From drop-down list shows all open projects that aren't already sharer files.

5. **Under "On conflict with calendar or resource information," select an option to tell Project how you want to resolve resource information discrepancies.**

The best choice is to let the resource pool take precedence (select "Pool takes precedence"), because then the resource pool has the final say about resource information. In that situation, changes made in the resource pool overwrite resource information in the sharer file. For example, suppose someone else opens the resource pool file and updates everyone's standard and overtime rates. When you open a sharer file, the project automatically uses the updated rates. In turn, if you change resource information in your project file, the resource pool is immune to those changes.

If you select "Sharer takes precedence" instead, then resource information you change in your project overwrites information in the resource pool. This approach is fine *if* you use a resource pool for resources dedicated to only your projects. With this option selected, you can change resource information in a project and Project automatically updates the resource pool when you save the project. But if you share the resource pool with several other project managers, the "Sharer takes precedence" option usually leads to unwanted resource changes, as each project manager tries to modify resources.

6. **Click OK.**

The project now obtains its resource information from the resource pool.

Opening and Saving Sharer Projects

When you open a sharer file, Project asks whether you want to open the resource pool (if it's not open), as shown in Figure 18-5. In almost every case, you do indeed want to open the resource pool, because that way you'll see all the resources from the resource pool in your project's Resource Sheet view. All resource assignments (from all sharer files) appear in Resource Usage view, so you can see all the tasks on which a resource works. To open the resource pool, select the "Open resource pool to see assignments across all sharer files" option (see Figure 18-5).

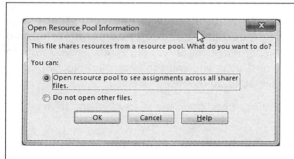

FIGURE 18-5

If you level resources to remove overallocations (page 339), be sure to open the resource pool. When you level resources in one sharer file, the resource pool hears about the modified assignments and passes them on to all sharer files.

TIP Because an open resource pool shows all assignments for a resource, your Resource Usage view is likely to have a lot more tasks than you remember. The problem is you can't tell which assignments are from *your* project and which come from *other* projects. To identify the project an assignment belongs to, right-click the heading row in the Resource Usage table area, and then choose Insert Column→Project. The Project cell for each assignment then shows the sharer file that made the resource assignment.

Opening the resource pool file also means that the resource assignments you make in your project file affect the resource's availability in the resource pool. When you save a sharer file while you have the resource pool file open, Project asks if you want to update the resource pool. To save the resource changes to the resource pool, click OK. (Click Cancel to save the sharer file without updating the resource pool, for example when you're testing what-if scenarios and haven't decided which one you're going to use.)

NOTE If other sharer projects are open, updating the resource pool saves the resource changes from *all* open sharer projects. So before you update the resource pool, be sure to close any sharer files that contain resource changes you don't want in the resource pool just yet. When those sharer files are ready for prime time, open them and the resource pool file, and then save the projects and update the resource pool.

If you select the "Do not open other files" option, then only the resources already assigned to tasks in your project appear in Resource Sheet view. Likewise, you see only the assignments from your project. When you save the sharer file, the resource pool doesn't receive the resource assignments you make.

TIP To make sure you're up to date with the most recent changes in the resource pool, in the Resource tab's Assignments section, choose Resource Pool→Refresh Resource Pool. Project immediately shows the most current information from the resource pool. Similarly, if you've made scads of resource assignments, then you can update the resource pool immediately by choosing Resource Pool→Update Resource Pool.

Detaching a Sharer Project from the Resource Pool

You can disconnect a sharer file from the resource pool, which is perfect if your project gets canned before it gets started. On the other hand, if a project contains a lot of assignment information, keeping the sharer file and the resource pool connected helps you report on all resource assignments at once. For example, if you want to evaluate resource usage for the past year, you want to keep all projects—active, completed, and discontinued—connected to the resource pool.

To remove a project from the resource pool, open the sharer file, and then do the following:

1. **In the Resource tab's Assignments section, choose Resource Pool→Share Resources.**

   The Share Resources dialog box opens.

2. **Select the "Use own resources" option, and then click OK.**

Any resources assigned to tasks remain in the project and appear in Resource Sheet view, but all other resource pool resources disappear from Resource Sheet view. In addition, the assignments from the detached sharer file (which is now just a regular Project file) no longer appear in the resource pool.

Editing Resource Pool Information

Once a resource pool is connected to at least one sharer file, you have three ways to open the pool. Sometimes you just want to see what's in the resource pool. Sometimes you need full read-write access—for example, when you're updating everyone's cost rates or work calendars. Project gives you options for each scenario.

When you open a resource pool file (choose File→Open, and then select the resource pool Project file), the Open Resource Pool dialog box appears with options that win the prize for longest option labels. Here's what your choices are, and when to use each one:

- **Read-only.** The "Open resource pool read-only allowing others to work on projects connected to the pool" option opens the resource pool as read-only. However, even if you choose this option, saving your sharer files updates the resource pool with assignments you've made. The benefit of choosing this option is that everyone else who uses the resource pool can continue to work on their projects at the same time.

- **Read-write.** If you need to make changes to resources in the resource pool, select the "Open resource pool read-write so that you can makes changes to resource information (like pay rates, etc.), although this will lock others out of updating the pool with new information" option. When you select this option, you can modify fields like costs and resource calendars. Of course, you want to use read-write mode for as short a time as possible, because no one else can access the resource pool while you're using it. That means other project managers can't see resource assignments and availability in any of the sharer files connected to this resource pool. If they open their Project files, they have to do so without opening the resource pool.

- **Create master project.** The "Open resource pool read-write and all other sharer files into a new master project file. You can access this new master project file from the View tab, Switch Windows command" option combines the resource pool and all sharer files into a brand-new master project file. If you work on several projects of your own, this is an easy way to build a master project. This master project is also useful when you want to produce reports that span all the projects your organization performs. Remember that the resource pool is read-write, so other project managers can't open their sharer files connected to the resource pool while you have it open.

Exchanging Data Between Programs

Managing projects is much more about communicating with people than tweaking Gantt Charts. Project planning is a collaborative effort among you, the stakeholders, and the rest of the project team. For the duration of the project, people communicate continuously as they complete work, identify and resolve problems, and report statuses.

As you've already seen, Microsoft Project isn't the only program you need for managing projects, especially when it comes to communicating about aspects of your projects: Word documents, Excel spreadsheets, PowerPoint presentations, and other types of files often have better tools. For example, tracking issues and risks is easier in a spreadsheet or a database. (Project Server and Project Online have built-in features for tracking issues and risks.) And PowerPoint is ideal for presenting different views of project information at a status meeting.

Information flows in both directions—from other programs to Project and vice versa. For example, after you hammer out costs and estimates in Excel, you can bring them into your Project schedule. Similarly, looking at change request documents, specifications, or quality control graphs from within Project can save the time it takes to open other files in other programs.

In this chapter, you'll learn how to copy and paste data and pictures between files—the most straightforward way to exchange information. For example, you can copy task names as text or costs as numbers from a Project Gantt Chart table into an Excel spreadsheet, or vice versa.

An Overview of Information Exchange

With the glut of ways to exchange information, it's hard to know which one to choose. This box is a quick guide to the ways you can exchange information between Project and other programs, and when to use each one.

- **Copy.** For small amounts of data and pictures, copying and pasting is the simplest way to get information from one program to the other. You can copy values and then edit them like any other data in the file. In fact, you can't even tell they came from another program and file. You can also copy and paste a picture of a Visio diagram into a Project timescale or copy a picture of your Project schedule into a PowerPoint presentation. Pictures land where you paste them.

- **Import.** Since this book is about Project, the term "importing" refers to transferring data from another program into a Project file. For example, you can import cost estimates from an Excel spreadsheet into Project task fields; once the data is in Project, it acts as if you created it there. Imported data looks and acts like text and numbers you copy and paste into Project. The advantage of importing over copying is you have more control over the data you import and where it goes in your Project file.

- **Export.** Exporting data from Project converts the data into a format that other programs can read. For example, as you learned in Chapter 7, you can export task lists from Project to Excel to build a cost-estimating spreadsheet.

- **Synchronize.** Project 2013 and SharePoint 2013 have a special bond that helps when you want to collaborate with team members on small projects. You can synchronize tasks between these two programs to share project tasks with your team or to obtain status from them. Chapter 25 (available from this book's Missing CD page at *www.missingmanauls.com/cds*) describes how synchronizing tasks works.

- **Link.** When you want changes in one file to appear automatically in other files, linking is the way to go, as you'll learn in detail in Chapter 20. It creates a lasting connection between the source data and its destination, so you can update the source data once and see the changes in every linked object. For example, suppose you use a PowerPoint file to present project status. You can insert a Gantt Chart view into a PowerPoint slide as a linked object to show the current schedule. In the other direction, you might link a risk-tracking spreadsheet to your Project schedule, so you can see where risk responses stand. When you double-click a linked object, the source file opens in the source program, so you *always* modify the original. The drawback to linking is that the links point to the source files, so if those files get moved, then the links break. In addition, links don't work if they point to a computer or network you can't access.

- **Embed.** This method (which is described in detail in Chapter 20) is a middle ground between copying and linking. When you embed an object from one program into another, you insert a package of data along with its source program into the destination file. The data isn't linked to the source file, so you don't see changes made in the original. When you double-click an embedded object, the commands from the source program appear, but you're editing the *copy*. Embedding data is ideal for sending the destination file to someone else. The person who receives the file has everything they need: the destination file, the embedded object, and the program commands for editing the embedded data. The downside to embedded data is that it inflates the destination file's size, sometimes to gargantuan proportions.

Exporting and importing information from one program to another is yet another way to exchange data. For instance, in Chapter 6, you learned how to import a WBS from a Word document into a Project file. This chapter explains the basics of importing and exporting, no matter *which* programs you use to create and receive the data. (The box on page 532 describes the differences among the various methods for exchanging information between programs.)

Copying Information

Copying and pasting moves small amounts of data quickly and easily. It's the way to go when you want to insert a few values from another file, copy a picture into a report, or reference details spelled out in a document. You can copy task data from a Project table and then paste it into Word to create an agenda for a team meeting. Copying numbers from an Excel column into Project table cells works equally well.

Copying Project Data to Other Programs

Copying data from Project tables into another program is blissfully easy; it's like a simple form of exporting. You select the table cells you want in Project and then paste them into the destination file. Copying and pasting between Project and other Office programs brings formatting along with your data, which makes your job easier. For example, if you copy task data from Project to an Outlook email message to show task status, the tasks appear in the email message in a table with the same indenting, highlighting, grouping, and other formatting as the Project table, as shown in Figure 19-1.

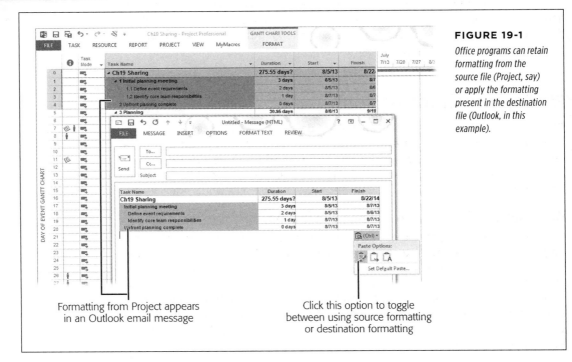

FIGURE 19-1

Office programs can retain formatting from the source file (Project, say) or apply the formatting present in the destination file (Outlook, in this example).

Formatting from Project appears in an Outlook email message

Click this option to toggle between using source formatting or destination formatting

Here are the steps for copying data from a Project table, using Excel as an example destination program:

1. **In Project, display the view and table that contains the fields you want to copy.**

   To copy tasks and their costs to an Excel spreadsheet (or other table-oriented file), display Gantt Chart view. Then in the View tab's Data section, choose Tables→Cost to apply the Cost table, which includes several columns of cost-related fields. (You can also apply a table by right-clicking the Select All cell above the ID column and then, from the drop-down list, choosing the table.)

   TIP If necessary, add the fields you want to copy to the table by right-clicking a column header in the table and then choosing Insert Column from the shortcut menu. To simplify copying nonadjacent columns, drag the columns in the Project table into the order you want, and *then* select the cells or columns you want to copy.

2. **In the table, select the data you want to copy.**

You can select specific cells or entire columns. If the cells are adjacent, drag from the upper-left cell to the bottom-right cell. To select nonadjacent cells—for instance, when you don't want all the columns in the table—Ctrl-drag over each set of cells (in other words, hold the Ctrl key down as you drag over nonadjacent sets of cells). Select entire columns by dragging across their column headings.

3. **Press Ctrl+C or, in the Task tab's Clipboard section, click Copy to copy the selected cells to the Clipboard.**

If you click the Copy down arrow, you can choose Copy to copy data or Copy Picture to copy an *image* of your selection.

4. **Switch to Excel and, in the destination spreadsheet, click the top-left cell of the destination cells.**

The cell you click is the starting point for the data you copy. The data copies from there into cells to the right and below. Even data that's nonadjacent in Project pours into adjacent cells in the destination file.

5. **To paste the data into Excel, press Ctrl+V, or in the Home tab's Clipboard section, click the top half of the Paste button.**

The copied data appears in the destination cells. If you're using Office 2010 and later, column headers from the Project table paste into Excel, even if you don't select them in the Project table.

TIP If you click the bottom half of Excel's Paste button, you can choose between pasting the data using the formatting from the source file or the destination file.

Copying Data from Other Programs into Project

Copying data *into* Project requires more finesse than copying data out of the program because Project is fussy about the type of data that goes into its fields. For example, if you try to copy plain numbers into a Start date cell, Project complains about the mismatch in an error message. To copy data into Project without that kind of drama, take the time to match up the data *before* you start the copy. For example, you may have to rearrange columns so they're the same in both files. Where you rearrange columns doesn't matter; you can rearrange the columns in the Project table or in the external file. Perhaps the easiest approach is to copy each column individually into its Project cousin. (Copying data between Project files works the same way, as the box on page 537 explains.) Otherwise, copying data *into* Project is the same as copying data from it:

1. **In the source program (Word, for example), open the file, and then select the data you want to copy.**

You can copy data from a Word document, an Excel spreadsheet, or a table in an Access database. If necessary, rearrange the columns of data to match the columns in the destination Project table.

2. **Press Ctrl+C or, in the Home tab's Clipboard section, click Copy.**

   Ctrl+C works regardless of which version of Word, Excel, or Project you use.

3. **In Project, open the Project file you want to paste the data into, and then apply the view and table you want.**

   If you didn't rearrange the data before you copied it to the Clipboard, then you can insert, hide, or drag columns in the Project table (page 633) to match the source file's column order.

4. **In the Project view's table area, click the top-left cell where you want to paste the data, and then press Ctrl+V or, in the Task tab's Clipboard section, click the top half of the Paste button.**

   Pasting data into a Project table doesn't insert new blank rows, so the values you paste *overwrite* any existing values in the Project cells, starting from the cell you click to the right and down. If you don't want to overwrite data, then insert enough blank rows to hold the data you're pasting—or paste the data in blank rows at the bottom of the table.

   If the stars are aligned, the data appears in the right cells in Project, with no error messages. If the data from the source file doesn't match the data type in Project, then you see an error message like the one shown in Figure 19-2.

NOTE If you paste content from a Word document or an Outlook email message into Project, Project can transform indents into outline levels, so lines of text automatically turn into summary tasks and subtasks.

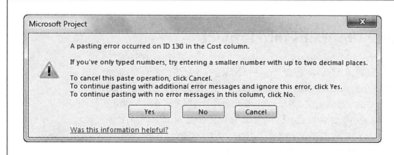

FIGURE 19-2

Project displays an error message for every cell with the wrong type of data. The fastest way to resolve this problem is to click Cancel to stop the paste. Then correct the mismatch by rearranging either the Project columns or the columns in your source file, and then repeat the copy and paste.

TIP Project is happy as long as you paste data into a field with the correct data type. For example, you can paste any kind of text into a text-based field like Task Name. However, values you paste into Start cells had better be dates if tasks are auto-scheduled—otherwise, you'll see an error message. You can also paste data into custom fields, as long as the data types match. For example, values you copy into a custom Project field like Duration1 must be a length of time like 2d.

Copying Data Between Project Files

Copying data from one Project schedule to another is handy when you want to reuse similar tasks from another project—for example, one you completed last year. Copying is the same whether you're copying within the same Project file, from one Project file to another, or from another program into Project. For example, to copy cells from a table in one Project file to a table in another file, select the cells in the source Project file and then, in the Task tab's Clipboard section, click Copy. Then in the destination Project file, select the first cell you want to paste the data into, and then in the Task tab's Clipboard section, click Paste. (Remember, when you copy cells, the paste starts at the first cell you click and continues to the right and down, overwriting any existing data in those cells.)

When you copy data within the same Project file or between two different Project files, you can also copy entire rows in a table. Unlike when you copy and paste cells, Project inserts *new* rows when you paste entire rows. Here are the steps:

1. In the table area, select the rows to copy by dragging over the row ID cells. You can select nonadjacent rows by Ctrl-clicking each ID cell.

2. Press Ctrl+C or, in the Task tab's Clipboard section, click Copy. If you're copying resource rows in Resource Sheet view, you still head to the *Task* tab's Clipboard section and click Copy.

3. To paste the rows in the new location (within the file or in a second Project file), click the ID cell for the row below where you want to copy the data, and then press Ctrl+V (or, in the Task tab's Clipboard section, click Paste).

Creating Pictures of Project Information

From the time you initiate a project until you put the last tasks to bed, you communicate project information to stakeholders and team members. A *picture* of a project schedule shows where a project stands better than row after row of data. Project's Copy Picture command captures all or part of the current view and can create an image fine-tuned for displaying on a computer screen, printing, or publishing on the web. For example, you can create an image of the high-level schedule to publish on your Intranet or a Resource Graph to email to a functional manager (that is, the resource's manager outside the project). After you create the image, you can paste it into any destination you want.

To create a picture of a Project view, follow these steps:

1. **Display the view you want to take a picture of.**

   Views like Gantt Chart, Team Planner, and Resource Graph are good candidates for a picture.

2. **If you want to see specific rows in the view's table, then select them.**

   Select the rows you want by dragging over their ID cells. You can also Ctrl-click the ID cells of nonadjacent rows.

3. **Adjust the view's timescale to show the date range you want in the picture.**

   Partially hidden columns in the view don't appear in the picture, so make sure the last column you want in the picture is displayed completely.

4. **In the Task tab's Clipboard section, click the Copy down arrow, and then choose Copy Picture.**

   The Copy Picture dialog box opens, as shown in Figure 19-3.

5. **In the "Render image" section, choose the option for how you're going to use the picture.**

   Project automatically selects the "For screen" option, which is perfect for a picture you're copying into a program like PowerPoint. Select "For printer" instead if you're creating an image for a report most people will read on paper.

   The "For screen" and "For printer" options both create an image and place it on the Clipboard. To create an image file, select "To GIF image file," and then enter the path and filename. (Click Browse to navigate to the folder where you want to save the file.) For example, a GIF file format is what you need for publishing a picture on a web page.

> **TIP** If you want to save the image in another format, like .jpg or .png, choose the "For screen" option to copy the data, and then paste it into Paint (or another image-editing program). Then you can save the image in the file format you want.

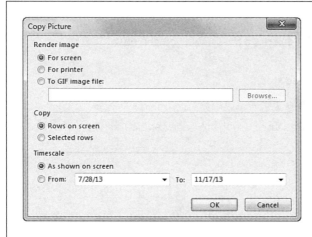

FIGURE 19-3

The options you can select depend on the view that's displayed. For example, for Gantt Chart view and usage views, you can specify the rows and timescale to include. Resource Graph view doesn't have rows, so the row options are grayed out. And Network Diagram view disables the options for rows and timescale.

6. **Choose the option for the rows you want to include.**

   If you haven't selected rows in the table (step 2), Project automatically selects the "Rows on screen" option, which includes only the visible rows. If you want specific rows or all rows in the project, be sure to select those rows *before* you click the Copy Picture command; after you've done that, Project automatically selects the "Selected rows" option.

7. **Choose the option to show the timescale that's visible in the view or a date range you specify.**

   "As shown on screen" includes only the dates visible on the screen. To show a different date range, like the dates from project start to finish or the dates for a phase, select the From option, and then fill in the From and To boxes with the start and finish dates.

8. **Click OK.**

   If you selected the "For screen" or "For printer" option, Project copies the picture to the Clipboard. If you went with the "To GIF image file" option, Project creates the file instead.

9. **In the destination file, click the location where you want to paste the picture, and then press Ctrl+V or, in the Home tab's Clipboard section, click Paste.**

   For a GIF file, use the destination program's command for inserting a picture. For example, with Microsoft programs, in the Insert tab's Illustrations section, click Pictures.

UP TO SPEED

Displaying Pictures in Project

You can copy graphics or pictures into Project to do things like display an Excel graph of bugs reported over time or photos of the customer's employees assigned to the project. Only certain places within Project can host these graphic files:

- A Gantt Chart view's timescale area.

- The Objects box and the Notes box in Task Form view and Resource Form view (in either view, right-click the top of the form, and then, on the shortcut menu, choose Objects or Notes).

- The Notes tab in the Task Information, Resource Information, and Assignment Information dialog boxes.

- The header, footer, or legend of a view or report you print.

Copying a picture into Project is similar to copying picture files in other programs. Here are the steps:

1. To copy an Excel graph as a picture, in Excel, select the graph, and then press Ctrl+C.

2. In Project, display the location where you want to copy the graphic file (or Clipboard graphic).

3. Press Ctrl+V, and Project pastes the graphic at the selected location, as shown in Figure 19-4.

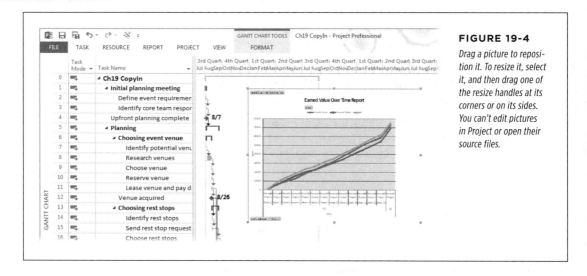

FIGURE 19-4

Drag a picture to reposition it. To resize it, select it, and then drag one of the resize handles at its corners or on its sides. You can't edit pictures in Project or open their source files.

Importing and Exporting Data

Arranging columns in the right order, selecting data, and copying it to the right place can be tedious and error-prone. A more dependable way to get data from one place to another is importing or exporting, depending on which direction the data is headed. In this book, "importing" means pulling data into Project from another program—for instance, importing data from an Excel spreadsheet or an Access database. "Exporting," on the other hand, refers to pushing data out of your Project file to another file format like Excel or XML. Unlike linking and embedding (page 565), importing and exporting convert data from one file format to another, so the data is the same as what you enter directly in the destination program.

The great thing about importing and exporting is the control you have over the data you transfer and where it goes. Because you map fields in one program to fields in the other, you can make sure the right types of data go where you want.

Project provides wizards for importing and exporting data to and from your Project files. The wizards start automatically when you open a file in another format or save to another format (as the box on page 540 explains). For example, if you open an Excel spreadsheet in Project, then the Import Wizard starts up. And if you save a Project file as a text file, the Export Wizard launches.

Maps are sets of settings that match up Project fields with fields or columns in the other program. Project comes with several built-in maps for doing things like exporting cost data, earned values, or basic task information. Because Excel is frequently used as a project-management tool, Excel comes with special templates (page 140) for transferring data to and from Project. For example, one template places all the information about tasks, resources, and assignments on separate worksheets within an Excel spreadsheet. Visio also has special features for exchanging data with Project, as you'll learn on page 552.

as you'll learn on page 552.

UP TO SPEED

File Formats for Importing and Exporting

Project can open different types of Project files, such as Excel files, tab-delimited text files, comma-delimited (CSV) files, and XML files. See Chapter 5 (page 96) for more about the file formats Project works with.

You can save a Project file to other Project file formats, Excel workbooks, text-delimited files, comma-delimited files, and XML. Project doesn't save projects as web pages, because you can use an XML file to generate a web page (as well as for other purposes). Similarly, you can't save a Project file directly to a database format, although you can use a visual report (page 469) to create a database file containing the data for the visual report.

The steps you take to open or save these files vary depending on the format. For example, you can open an earlier Project file format simply by choosing File→Open. However, when you choose File→Open with Excel file formats, comma-delimited files, and so on, the Import Wizard starts. Similarly, when you save files to formats other than the standard Project formats, the Export Wizard starts.

Importing Data into Project

Bringing data from other programs into Project is as easy as opening that file in Project. The Import Wizard guides you through mapping the data to the right Project fields and takes care of transferring the data. Although Project includes a few special tools for importing Excel data, the basic steps for importing any kind of data are the same:

1. **In Project, choose File→Open. In Backstage view's Open page, select the location and folder that contains the file you want to import.**

   The Open dialog box automatically sets the file type box (the unlabeled box to the right of the "File name" box) to Projects (the box says "Projects (*.mpp)" if Windows Explorer is set to display file extensions), so you have to tell Project which type of file you want to import.

2. **In the file type box, click the down arrow, and then choose the file format you want to import—for instance, Excel Workbook, or "CSV (Comma delimited)."**

   In the Open dialog box, the file list shows only the files of the type you selected. So if the file you want is conspicuously absent, it might be a different format than you think.

3. **In the file list, double-click the name of the file whose data you want to import (or click its filename, and then click Open).**

   The Import Wizard starts. Click Next to bypass the welcome screen, which merely explains the process.

4. **On the "Import Wizard - Map" screen, keep the "New map" option selected, and click Next.**

   If an existing map (either a Project built-in map or one you've saved) matches fields the way you want, then select "Use existing map" instead. This option shortens the import process by several steps, as explained on page 547.

5. **On the "Import Wizard - Import Mode" screen, select an option to tell Project where you want to import the data, and then click Next.**

   Project automatically selects the "As a new project" option, which creates a brand-new Project file from the data you're importing.

   The "Append the data to the active project" option is ideal when you want to import several files into the same project—for instance, when you receive WBSs from several team leaders. This option tells Project to insert the appended data in the current Project table after the existing rows.

   The "Merge the data into the active project" option is perfect when you want to import values into existing tasks, like importing estimates into your Project file (page 174). To import values into existing tasks, Project needs a way to match the tasks in each file, as the box below explains.

FREQUENTLY ASKED QUESTION

Importing Data into Existing Rows

How do I import data from another program into the correct tasks or resources in Project?

If you're importing values and merging them into existing tasks or resources, like estimates of task work, Project needs to know how to identify matching tasks or resources. After you map the fields on the Import Wizard's Mapping screen (step 7 on page 543) and then click Next, a message box might appear asking for a *primary key* so Project can merge the imported data. This message means you have to tell Project which fields

are unique identifiers for tasks (or resources). For example, a WBS code is an ideal primary key because every task has one, and each one is different.

On the Mapping screen, in the table of matched fields, select the cell in the "To: Microsoft Project Field" column that represents the primary key, and then click Set Merge Key. Both cells in the row change to include the words "MERGE KEY:" in front of the field name.

---

6. **On the "Import Wizard - Map" Options screen, select the type of data you want to import, as shown in Figure 19-5. Then click Next.**

   First, you have to specify the type of data you want to import: tasks, resources, or assignments. The Tasks and Resources options import data specifically for tasks or resources. The Assignments option imports information about tasks *and* who's assigned to them. (When you exchange data with an Excel spreadsheet, these options turn into checkboxes so you can exchange more than one type of data at a time, as you'll learn on page 550.)

   If the source file's first line or row includes column names, make sure the "Import includes headers" checkbox is turned on. (The "Include Assignment rows in output" checkbox stubbornly remains grayed out no matter what you do, because this checkbox applies only to *exporting.*)

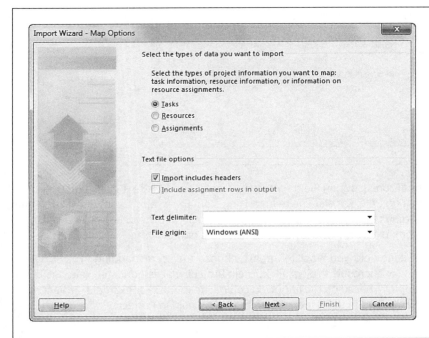

FIGURE 19-5

Project automatically sets options on the "Import Wizard - Map Options" screen depending on the type of file you're importing. For example, importing a text file displays two additional boxes (shown here): the "Text delimiter" checkbox in which you can specify the delimiter as a tab, space, or comma; and the "File origin" option, which you can set to Windows (ANSI), MSDOS, or Unicode.

7. **On the Import Wizard's Mapping screen, map the import fields to their corresponding Project fields, as shown in Figure 19-6.**

   The exact mapping screen that appears depends on the data you selected to import: Task Mapping, Resource Mapping, or Assignments Mapping.

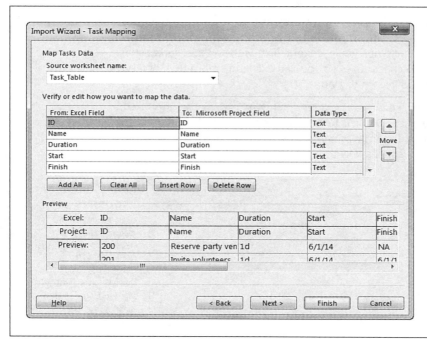

FIGURE 19-6

*You don't have to import
every field in an import
file. Beneath the field table,
click Delete Row to remove
a mapping pair. Click Clear
All to delete all the rows and
start from scratch. Clicking
Add All makes Project read
the import file and insert rows
for each import-file field. The
Insert Row button inserts a
blank row.*

The "From: [source] Field" column (where [source] is Text File if you're import-ing a text file, Excel if you're importing from Excel, and so on) displays column headings from your import file, if they're present. Otherwise, the first cell in the "From: [source] Field" column displays the number 1.

For each field you want to import, choose the corresponding Project field in the "To: Microsoft Project Field" cell. Project makes educated guesses about mappings based on the imported column headings. For example, Project maps a Name field in the import file to the Name field in Project.

The value "(not mapped)" in the "To: Microsoft Project Field" cell is Project's way of saying that you need to tell it which Project field you want. To choose a field, click the down arrow in the "To: Microsoft Project Field" cell, and then choose the field. Leaving the value as "(not mapped)" is one way to tell Project not to import the field. (You can also click in a row and then click Delete Row to remove it from the table, which also removes it from the map.)

The Preview area shows a sample of the import. The first row in the preview shows the names of the selected source fields. The Project row identifies the fields into which the imported data goes. And the Preview rows show several values from that field in the import file, for example, "Reserve party venue" as one task name.

8. **Optionally, to save the map you've defined, click Next.**

The "Import Wizard - End of Map Definition" screen appears with the Save Map button sitting by itself mid–dialog box. Click Save Map to open the Save Map dialog box. In the "Map name" box, type a short but meaningful name for the map, like *Import WBS Tasks*. Clicking Save adds the map to your global template and closes the dialog box.

9. **Click Finish.**

You may see a warning message if you're importing an older file format; click Yes to continue opening the file. Project imports the tasks into your Project file.

Exporting Data from Project

A common reason to export data from Project is so you can work with the data in ways that Project doesn't handle well. For example, you might export comma-delimited data to another program to run Monte Carlo simulations (see the Tip on page 166) on your schedule. Exporting data is also useful when colleagues don't have Project or just want to see the data in another format. "Exporting Project Data to Excel" on page 549 describes the steps for exporting Project data to Excel. This section describes how to export data from Project to file formats *other* than Excel.

The steps in the Export Wizard bear a strong resemblance to those in the Import Wizard, but there are a few key differences. Here's how you export Project data to another format:

1. **Open the Project file you want to export and choose File→Save As. On Backstage view's Save As page, select the location and folder where you want to store the file with exported data.**

The Save As dialog box opens.

2. **In the "Save as type" drop-down list, choose the file format you want to use.**

If you save to one of the Project file formats (Project, Microsoft Project 2007, Microsoft Project 2000-2003, Project Template, or Microsoft Project 2007 Templates), Project opens the Save As dialog box, not the Export Wizard. However, saving to an Excel workbook, a text file, a comma-delimited file, or the XML format all start the Export Wizard.

3. **In the "File name" box, type the name for the file and click Save.**

Project fills in the "File name" box with the Project file's name, but you can rename the export file to whatever you want. Project sets the file extension based on the file format you choose.

If you choose an older file format, such as Excel 97-2003 Workbook or "CSV (Comma delimited)," when you click Save, a message box tells you that the older file format may be less secure than a new file format. If you want to save the file to that format, simply click Yes. To quit, click No, and then repeat steps 1 and 2 to choose a different format. If you see a message box that tells you that you can't save to older file formats, click OK to close the message box. Then Choose File→Options, click Trust Center, and then click the Trust Center Settings button. In the Trust Center dialog box, click Legacy Formats, and then choose the "Prompt when loading files with legacy or non-default file format" option.

4. **When the Export Wizard starts, click Next to bypass the welcome screen.**

5. **On the "Export Wizard - Map" screen, select the "New map" option, and then click Next.**

To use an existing map to match up fields (page 547), select the "Use existing map" option instead.

6. **On the "Export Wizard - Map Options" screen, select the type of data you want to import, and then click Next.**

Your choices are the same as the ones on the "Import Wizard - Map Options" screen (step 6 on page 543), with one exception: The "Include assignment rows in output" checkbox is now active but turned off. If you want to export all the assignment rows for tasks, then turn on this checkbox.

7. **On the Mapping screen, specify the fields you want to export.**

You see the Mapping screen corresponding to the type of data you're exporting (Task Mapping, Resource Mapping, or Assignments Mapping). Compared with the Import Wizard, the Export Wizard's mapping pages have a few additional options, as you can see in Figure 19-7.

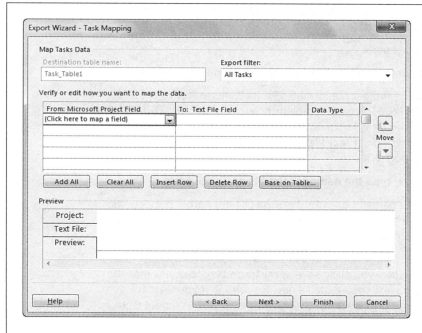

FIGURE 19-7

The "Export filter" box lets you choose the items you want to export. For example, you might choose the Completed Tasks filter to export the final costs for tasks that are done. Click "Base on Table" below the mapping grid to jumpstart field mappings with a Project table.

Because you're exporting to a blank file, Project doesn't fill in the field table for you. Instead of selecting field after field, you can use a Project table like Entry, Cost, or a custom table you create to fill in the field cells. To do so, underneath the field table, click "Base on Table." The "Select Base Table for Field Mapping" dialog box opens, and you can select any table in your project. The granddaddy of all tables is the Export table, which fills in a whopping 84 fields. (If you're exporting tasks, the dialog box displays all the task tables; it lists resource tables if you're exporting resources.) Remember, you can edit the field names in the "To:" column to specify the headings you want in the export file.

TIP   To export exactly the fields you want, use the Add All, Clear All, Insert Row, and Delete Row buttons to build a collection of fields.

The Preview area shows values in your Project by field. The Project and [destination] field names (where [destination] is the destination file format you choose—in Figure 19-7, for example, it's "Text File") are initially identical. To define the field names in your export file to match the needs of the destination program, change the field name in the "To: [destination] Field" cells.

8. **Optionally, to save the map you've defined, click Next.**

   The "Export Wizard - End of Map Definition" page presents the Save Map button, which saves a map exactly like the Import Wizard does.

9. **Click Finish.**

   Project exports the data to the file format you selected, but it doesn't open the file for you.

Using an Existing Map

There's no reason to manually map the same fields every time you import or export them for things like monthly reports you produce. Saving a map and reusing it in future imports and exports is a real timesaver. Bear in mind, though, that using an existing map doesn't bypass any of the pages in the Import or Export Wizard—but at least you don't have to match fields on the Mapping page. Moreover, after you apply an existing map, you can tweak the mapping if it isn't quite right.

Here's how to use an existing map:

1. **When you start either the Import or Export Wizard, follow the steps until you get to the "Import Wizard - Map" page or the "Export Wizard - Map" screen.**

   The wizards' screens vary depending on what you're importing or exporting.

2. **On the "Import Wizard - Map" page or the "Export Wizard - Map" page, select the "Use existing map" option and then click Next.**

   The Map Selection page appears, as shown in Figure 19-8.

3. **Click the name of the map you want to use, and then click Next.**

   If you want to review your settings or make minor adjustments to the map, click Next to step through the remaining wizard screens as described in the previous sections on importing (page 541) and exporting (page 545).

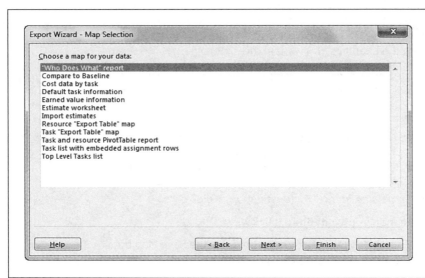

FIGURE 19-8

If you're certain the map is exactly what you want, you can simply click Finish to immediately complete the import or export.

Exchanging Data with Excel

Because Excel spreadsheets can contain more than one worksheet, the settings in the Import and Export Wizards are slightly different from the ones you see when you work with text files. For example, you can import and export tasks, resources, and assignments to Excel all at once. Moreover, when you have both Project and Excel installed on your computer, Excel includes two templates to jump-start your data exchange. When you create an Excel file using either of these templates, the column headings are set up to map to Project fields. To export Excel data without a hitch, see page 97 to learn how to make Project work with older file formats.

> **TIP** You can also exchange data between Project and Excel using visual reports. Chapter 16 has the full scoop on these reports.

■ EXPORTING AN ENTIRE PROJECT TO EXCEL

The Export Wizard contains an option for exporting all the task, resource, and assignment data in a Project file with a minimum of effort. Although the resulting export file doesn't include time-phased data (data that's broken down by time period), you can create an Excel spreadsheet with separate worksheets for tasks, resources, and assignments. Here are the steps:

1. **Open the Project file you want to export to Excel, and then choose File→Save As. Select the location and folder where you want to save the new file.**

   The Save As dialog box opens.

2. **In the Save As dialog box's "Save as type" drop-down list, choose Excel Workbook. In the "File name" box, type a name for the file, and then click Save.**

   Project launches the Export Wizard. Click Next to start the wizard.

3. **On the "Export Wizard - Data" screen, select the Project Excel Template option, and then click Finish.**

   When this book was being written, clicking Finish displayed an error message box that read, "The filter "" cannot be found" (though hopefully that will be fixed by the time you read this). However, Project still exports your project data to an Excel file that contains three worksheets: Task_Table, Resource_Table, and Assignment_Table.

■ EXPORTING PROJECT DATA TO EXCEL

When you want to export specific portions of your Project file to Excel, you can save the Project file as an Excel workbook and use the Export Wizard to specify what gets exported. The steps are *almost* the same as exporting to other types of files. Here's how exporting to an Excel workbook works:

1. **Open the Project file you want to export to Excel.**

   Display the view and table that contains the data you want to export, for instance Gantt Chart view and the Cost table for tasks, Resource Sheet view for resources, or Task Usage view and the Work table for assignments.

2. **In the view's table, select the rows or cells you want to export.**

   You can drag over several ID cells to select multiple rows. Or you can drag over the cells you want to export. Ctrl-click rows or column headings if you want to export nonadjacent rows or columns. To export *all* the data in the table, at the top of the ID column, click the blank Select All cell to select the entire table.

3. **Choose File→Save As. On Backstage view's Save As page, select the location and folder where you want to save the file containing the exported data.**

   The Save As dialog box opens to the folder you selected.

4. **In the "Save as type" drop-down list, choose Excel Workbook. In the "File name" box, type a name for the file, and then click Save.**

   If you have Project's Trust Center setting's set up to prompt you about legacy formats (page 97) and you select Excel 97-2003 Workbook in the "Save as type" drop-down list, when you click Save, a message box warns you that the file may be less secure than a newer file format. Click Yes to save to the older format, or click No to cancel the wizard and go back to step 3.

   Project launches the Export Wizard. Click Next to get going.

5. **On the "Export Wizard - Data" screen, the wizard automatically selects the Selected Data option, which exports the data you selected in the view. Click Next to continue.**

   If you forgot to select data before you started the wizard, click Cancel and jump back to step 1.

6. **On the "Export Wizard - Map" screen, keep the "New map" option selected and click Next.**

   If you already have a map you want to use, select the "Use existing map" option instead, and then select the map as described on page 547.

7. **On the "Export Wizard - Map Options" page, turn on the checkboxes for each type of data you want to export, and then click Next.**

   Because Excel can handle several types of data on separate worksheets, this page includes checkboxes for tasks, resources, and assignments, as you can see in Figure 19-9.

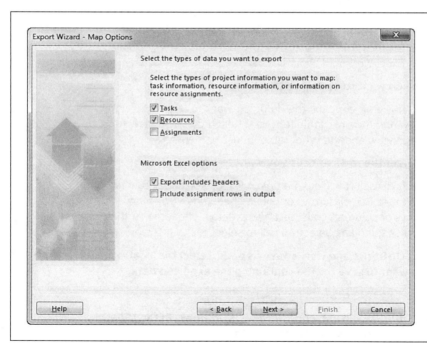

FIGURE 19-9

You can turn on any or all of the data checkboxes. Each type of data lands on its own Excel worksheet. If you selected an existing map, then the wizard initially sets the checkboxes to match the map's definition. The wizard displays a mapping page for each type of data you export.

The wizard automatically turns on the "Export includes headers" checkbox. This setting exports Project field names to column names in Excel, which is usually what you want. If you want to export all the details about resources' assignments, then turn on the "Include assignment rows in output" checkbox.

8. **On the first Mapping screen that appears, in the "Destination worksheet name" box, type a name for the Excel worksheet.**

   The Mapping screen that appears depends on the checkbox(es) you selected on the "Export Wizard - Map Options" page. For example, if you turned on the Tasks checkbox, then the first Mapping screen you see is "Export Wizard - Task Mapping".

   The "Destination worksheet name" box automatically sets the worksheet's name to something like Task_Table1. You can stick with that or change the name to something else.

9. **Set up the field mapping as you would for any other kind of export.**

   You can choose a filter in the "Export filter" box to export specific parts of your Project file—for example, choose the Critical filter to export data about critical tasks to see which ones you can shorten. The rest of the Mapping screen is the same as the one that appears for exporting to a text file or another format (page 545). For instance, you can map fields based on an existing Project table or use the buttons below the table to insert and delete rows.

10. **Repeat steps 8 and 9 for each Mapping screen that appears.**

    The Mapping screens appear in the same order every time: tasks, resources, and then assignments. However, if you aren't exporting a type of data, that Mapping page doesn't show up. The wizard creates a separate worksheet in the Excel file for each type of data you export.

11. **Click Finish.**

    Project exports the tasks into a new workbook (you have to launch Excel and open the file to see it).

    If you saved the exported data to an older Excel format (Excel 97-2003 format, for example) but opened the spreadsheet in a newer version of Excel, then when you try to save it, you may see a message box asking if you want to overwrite the older Excel format with the current format. If you click Yes to update the format, Excel saves the spreadsheet to the version of Excel installed on your computer.

TIP The cells in an Excel export file are set to the General format, which doesn't apply any specific formatting to the values. To display data the way you want or to calculate values, you can change the data types for cells. For example, you can modify cost cells to the Excel Currency format to show dollar signs. To change the data type in Excel, select the column heading. Then, in the Home tab's Cells section, choose Format→Format Cells. In the Format Cells dialog box, choose the appropriate category, such as Number or Currency, and then click OK.

■ IMPORTING DATA FROM EXCEL

Importing data from Excel without a built-in template is almost identical to importing any other kind of data (page 541). In fact, you'll find only two exceptions:

- The "Import Wizard - Map Options" screen has checkboxes for each type of data you want to import, because Excel can create separate worksheets for each type of data.

- On the Mapping screens, Project enters the Excel worksheets' names in the "Source worksheet name" box. If the spreadsheet contains more than one worksheet for a type of data, then choose the appropriate worksheet from the drop-down list.

> **TIP** If you have both Project and Excel installed on your computer, Excel includes two templates whose worksheets and columns are tailored to work perfectly with Project's Import Wizard. The Microsoft Project Task List Import Template is great for importing task lists that your team members give to you. The Microsoft Project Plan Import Export Template helps you import information about tasks, resources, and assignments into Project. See page 137 in Chapter 6 for the full story on the information these templates provide and where to find them on your computer.

Working with Project and Visio

Most of the time, your work with Project and Visio revolves around visual reports, which send Project data to Visio pivot diagrams to dynamically display project information. (See Chapter 16 for more on Visio visual reports.) You can also turn to Visio to produce simpler pictures of your project, akin to the weather maps you see on television compared with the ones that meteorologists analyze. If Project's views are too complicated for your audience, try Visio's Schedule template category, which includes templates for Gantt Charts, timelines, PERT Charts, and calendars:

- **Gantt Chart.** You can export task information from Project into a Visio Gantt Chart to make task bars look more interesting and to weed out the details that executive audiences don't care about. Although most project managers build even the quickest and dirtiest schedules in Project, you can also export any information created in Visio Gantt Charts and import it into Project to jump-start a new schedule.

- **Timeline.** You can produce high-level project views of tasks and milestones along a horizontal bar in both Project and Visio. However, if you want to produce a vertical timeline of your project, your only choice is Visio's Timeline template.

> **TIP** Although Visio includes a PERT Chart template, you're better off using the Project Network Diagram view to show PERT boxes instead. That way, the tasks will be visible in other Project views, as well. The Visio PERT Chart template doesn't import or export data automatically, so it's difficult to display Project data with this type of drawing.

Because data exchange between Visio and Project takes place in Visio, this section switches the meaning of import and export from previous sections. In Visio, "importing" means bringing Project data into a Visio drawing, whereas "exporting" means creating a Project file from Visio data.

Every shape on a Visio Gantt Chart or Timeline drawing has its own sets of options, so you can make the drawing look just the way you want. To learn more about working with Visio schedule drawings, refer to the *Visio 2007 Bible* by Bonnie Biafore (Wiley) or *Microsoft Visio 2013 Step by Step* by Scott Helmers (Microsoft Press).

■ DISPLAYING PROJECT DATA IN A VISIO GANTT CHART

A Project Gantt Chart can show a project summary, but it often contains too much information for most reports and presentations. Visio Gantt Charts are simpler renditions of their Project cousins, so they may be more suitable for audiences less versed in project management.

Project doesn't include tools for pushing its data to Visio, so importing Project data into a Visio Gantt Chart takes place within Visio. Here's how to do it:

1. **In Visio, open an existing Gantt Chart drawing or create a new one.**

   To create a Visio Gantt Chart, choose File→New. In Backstage view's New page, click the Categories heading (below the Search box), click Schedule, and then double-click Gantt Chart. In the Gantt Chart Options dialog box that appears, click OK to accept the settings as they are. You can modify them after you've imported your Project data.

2. **In the Gantt Chart tab's Manage section, click Import Data.**

   The Import Project Data Wizard starts. As a refreshing change, this wizard gets right to business with options on the very first page.

3. **On the screen of the wizard, select the "Information that's already stored in a file" option, and then click Next.**

   Despite the wizard's name, you can actually import data from Excel spreadsheets and text files, as well as Project .mpp and .mpx (an older Project exchange format) files.

4. **On the "Select the format of your project data" screen, leave Microsoft Project File selected, and then click Next.**

   To import from a different type of file, choose the format in the list.

5. **On the "Select the file containing existing project schedule data" screen, open the file you want to import, and then click Next.**

   On the page, click Browse. In the Import Project Data Wizard dialog box that appears, find and select the file you want to import, and then click Open. Back on the wizard screen, you see the path and filename filled in.

6. **On the "Time scale" screen, choose the major and minor timescale units, as well as the time units you use to enter duration. Then click Next.**

   Less robust than the timescale units in Project, Visio timescale units are days, weeks, months, quarters, and years. The duration units come in several variations. For whole numbers, you can choose Weeks, Days, or Hours. To show fractional values, choose Days Hours, Weeks Days, or Weeks Hours.

   Clicking the Advanced button opens a dialog box where you can specify the shapes for the Gantt Chart. However, changing the shapes once the drawing is complete makes it easier to see whether the results are what you want.

7. **On the "Select task types to include" screen, select the category of tasks you want to import, and then click Next.**

   Initially, All is selected, which brings in every task in your Project file. Because you usually turn to a Visio Gantt Chart to produce an overview of your project, one of the other selections may be more appropriate. "Top level tasks only" shows only the highest-level tasks. "Milestones only" shows milestones without any other tasks. "Summary tasks only" includes all levels of summary tasks so only the work-package tasks are eliminated. "Top level tasks and milestones" is a great summary with the highest-level tasks and all milestones.

   NOTE Project tasks with 0 duration come in as milestones. Visio turns tasks designated as milestones that have a duration other than 0 into milestones with 0 duration.

8. **On the last screen, review the settings you've chosen and then click Finish.**

   Visio creates a new Gantt Chart from the imported data, as shown in Figure 19-10. If you import into an existing drawing, Visio creates a new page and then adds the imported Gantt Chart to it.

   To change any import settings, on the last screen, click Back until the appropriate screen appears, and then make the changes you want.

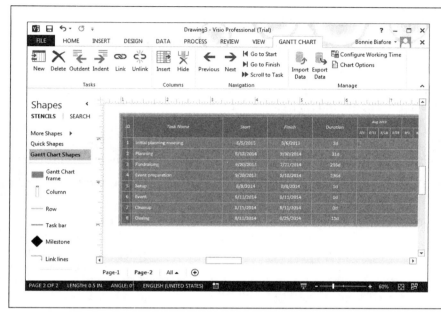

FIGURE 19-10

Visio's Gantt Chart tab helps you find task bars and dates. Click "Go to Start" or "Go to Finish" to move the timescale to the beginning or end of the project. Click Previous or Next to move to the previous or next time period. If you select a task and then click "Scroll to Task," the timescale moves to display the task's task bar.

9. **To change the appearance of the Visio Gantt Chart, in the Gantt Chart tab's Manage section, click Chart Options.**

The Gantt Chart Options dialog box has the same options the wizard presents when you click the Advanced button during the import process (see step 6). You can change the timescale dates, duration units, and timescale units. The dialog box's Format tab lets you choose shapes for task bars, summary bars, and milestones, as well as what the bar labels show.

■ DISPLAYING PROJECT DATA IN A VISIO TIMELINE

Timelines are a great way to show when important events occur and how long phases last. Since Project can produce a timeline (a feature that was introduced in Project 2010), you may not need to import project data into a Visio timeline drawing. However, Visio's timeline tools simplify importing different types of tasks: all tasks in the project or just top-level tasks, summary tasks, and milestones. To import information from Microsoft Project into a Visio timeline, follow these steps:

1. **Make sure the Project file you want to import *isn't* open in Project.**

The Import Timeline Wizard can't read a file that's already open.

2. **In Visio, open an existing timeline drawing or create a new one.**

   To create a Visio Timeline, choose File→New, click the Categories heading, click the Schedule icon, and then double-click Timeline. Visio creates a new drawing and adds the Timeline tab to the Visio ribbon.

3. **In the Timeline tab's Timeline section, click Import Data.**

   The Import Timeline Wizard starts.

4. **On the "Select a Microsoft Project file to import" screen, open the file you want to import and then click Next.**

   Click Browse to open the Import Timeline Wizard dialog box. There, find and select the file you want to import (it has to be a Project *.mpp* file), and then click Open. Back on the wizard screen, the path and filename appear in the box.

5. **On the "Select task types to include" screen, select the category of tasks you want to import, and then click Next.**

   Initially, All is selected, which brings in every task in your Project file. Typically, "Top level tasks and milestones" is best for a summary of the highest-level tasks and all milestones. "Top level tasks only" shows only the highest-level tasks. "Milestones only" shows milestones without any other tasks. "Summary tasks only" includes all levels of summary tasks so only the work-package tasks are eliminated. Project tasks with 0 duration get imported as milestones.

6. **On the "Select shapes for your Visio timeline" screen, review the default shapes, and choose different shapes if you want. Then click Next.**

   The Timeline shape spans the dates for the full project schedule. Project milestones morph into Milestone shapes in Visio, and Project summary tasks become Interval shapes.

7. **On the last screen, review the import properties you've chosen, and then click Finish.**

   Visio creates a new timeline from the imported data, as shown in Figure 19-11. If you imported the data into an existing drawing, then Visio creates a new page and adds the imported timeline to it.

   To change any aspect of the import, click Back until you reach the appropriate page, change the settings you want, and then click Finish.

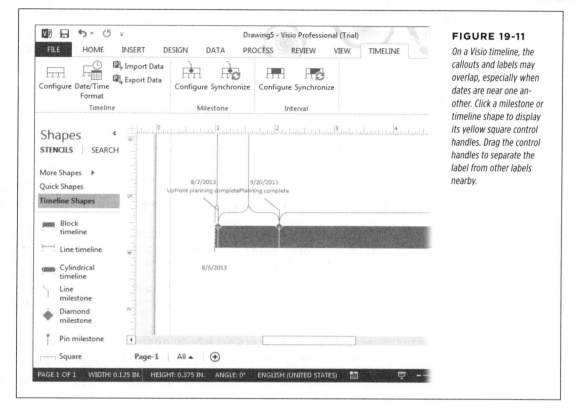

FIGURE 19-11

On a Visio timeline, the callouts and labels may overlap, especially when dates are near one another. Click a milestone or timeline shape to display its yellow square control handles. Drag the control handles to separate the label from other labels nearby.

8. **To change the appearance of the timeline, right-click the shape you want to change and then choose one of the commands from the shortcut menu.**

   To change the time period for the timeline, right-click the timeline shape, and then choose Configure Timeline. You can also choose whether or not to show dates on the timeline. To modify milestones or intervals, right-click the appropriate shape and then choose Configure Milestone or Configure Interval.

   Changing the shape of an element like a timeline shape or milestone shape is as simple as clicking it and then, in the Timeline tab's Timeline, Milestone, or Interval section, clicking Configure. You can also right-click a shape, and then, on the shortcut menu, choose Timeline Type, Set Interval Type, or Set Milestone Type.

■ EXPORTING VISIO GANTT CHARTS TO PROJECT

Suppose you used a Visio Gantt Chart to present a project proposal to the management team for their approval. The information in the Gantt Chart isn't much, but you can export it to Project to jump-start your schedule. When you do that, the tasks in a Visio Gantt Chart turn into tasks in Project with start dates, finish dates, and durations. Similarly, milestones in a Visio Gantt Chart become milestones in Project.

To export a Visio Gantt Chart to Project, follow these steps:

1. **In Visio, open the Gantt Chart drawing you want to export, and select the Gantt Chart frame.**

   Clicking within a Visio Gantt Chart selects individual task bars or task-name text boxes, which are subshapes within the Gantt Chart frame. To select the *frame*, click the very edge of the Gantt Chart. You can tell you've succeeded when selection handles appear at the frame's corners and at the midpoints along each side.

2. **In the Gantt Chart tab's Manage section, click Export Data.**

   The Export Project Data Wizard starts.

3. **On the "Export my project data into the following format" screen, select Microsoft Project File and then click Next.**

   You can also export to Excel files, text files, and Project .mpx files (an older Microsoft Project exchange format). However, you might as well export directly to Project.

4. **On the "Specify the file to enter project schedule data" screen, click Browse and open the folder where you want to save the exported project file.**

   The Export Project Data Wizard dialog box opens. Navigate on your computer or network to the folder you want.

5. **In the "File name" box, type the name for the new Project file and then click Save.**

   The dialog box closes and returns to the wizard, where the "Specify the file to enter project schedule data" box is filled in with the path and filename you specified.

6. **Click Next.**

   The last wizard screen shows that you're exporting a Gantt Chart, and it specifies the file you're creating.

7. **Click Finish.**

   A message box tells you that the data exported. Click OK.

8. **Open the file in Project.**

   You're ready to build a real schedule based on the data you exported from the Visio Gantt Chart. For example, you still have to create task dependencies between the tasks and assign resources.

■ EXPORTING VISIO TIMELINES TO PROJECT

You can also export Visio timeline data to Project. Intervals from a Visio timeline turn into tasks in Project with start dates, finish dates, and durations. Milestones in Visio become milestones in Project. And the Visio timeline shape turns into a task with start, finish, and duration.

To export a Visio timeline to Project, follow these steps:

1. **In Visio, open the timeline file and select the timeline shape.**

   Select the timeline shape by clicking anywhere inside it.

2. **In the Timeline tab's Timeline section, click Export Data.**

   The Export Timeline Data dialog box opens. You can navigate on your computer or network to find the folder you want.

3. **In the "File name" box, type a name for the new Project file, and then click Save.**

   The "Save as type" box is set to Microsoft Project File. When you click Save, a message tells you that the data exported successfully. Click OK.

4. **Open the Project file you created in Project.**

   The timeline data turns into manually scheduled tasks in Project. After you create task dependencies in Project, you can switch these tasks to auto-scheduled (page 78) so Project can do its job.

■ Integrating Project and Outlook

Outlook is Microsoft's email workhorse, but email is only one of the ways that Outlook and Project work as a team. When you're in Project, you can email Project files without jumping over to Outlook to do so. But because both programs can store lists of tasks and names, you can also export Project tasks to Outlook and vice versa. You can even use your Outlook address book to build your resource list in Project. This section explains how to use these features.

Adding Project Tasks to Outlook

If the old saying "Out of sight, out of mind" is all too true in your case, you can keep important Project tasks in sight by adding them (one at a time) to your Outlook Task List. By adding a reminder to these Outlook tasks, you can really stay on top of things. All you need to do is copy and paste. But before you get too attached to this approach, you should know that, when you add Project tasks to Outlook, you have copies of those tasks in two places—and they aren't linked. So if you mark a task as done in Outlook, it *isn't* automatically updated in Project, and vice versa.

If you decide to add tasks to Outlook as reminders, here are the steps:

1. **In a task-oriented view like Gantt Chart, select the Task Name cell for the task you want to copy to Outlook, and then press Ctrl+C. (Or right-click the cell and choose Copy Cell.)**

   You can select only one task at a time. Project copies the task's name to the Clipboard.

2. **In Outlook, display the Tasks list.**

   Click Tasks at the bottom of the Outlook window.

3. **Right-click an empty area of the Tasks list and choose New Task on the shortcut menu. (Or in the Home tab's New section, click New Task.)**

   The task-entry window appears with the heading "Untitled - Task."

4. **Click the Subject box, and then press Ctrl+V.**

   In the Subject box, the name of the task appears. If you want Outlook to remind you about the task's due date, turn on the Reminder checkbox and then choose the date and time you want to be reminded.

5. **On the ribbon, click Save & Close.**

   Repeat steps 1–4 for other tasks you want to add to Outlook.

Importing Tasks from Outlook

Every once in a while, you may create tasks in Outlook that you later realize belong in one of your projects. You can import these tasks into a Project file as a head start. When you import tasks from Outlook, the imported tasks come in with the task names from Outlook and any notes you added. Although these imported tasks come in with the standard duration of "1 day?" (the question mark indicates estimated duration), they have no dependencies, resources, or dates.

To import Outlook tasks, follow these steps:

1. **Open the Project file you want to import the tasks into, display a task-oriented view like Gantt Chart, and then in the Task tab's Insert section, click Task→Import Outlook Tasks.**

   The Import Outlook Tasks dialog box opens. Outlook doesn't have to be running for this command to work, but you must have at least one incomplete task in your Outlook Task list. If you have no tasks in Outlook or they're all complete, a message box tells you there are no tasks to import.

2. **Turn on the checkbox for each task you want to import, as shown in Figure 19-12.**

   Any notes you typed in the Notes box in Outlook appear in the Notes cell in the table.

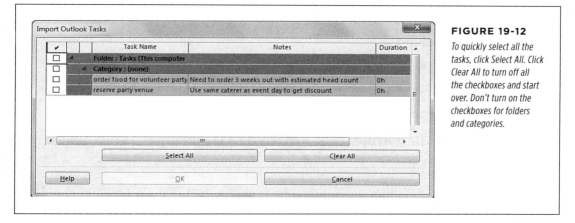

FIGURE 19-12

To quickly select all the tasks, click Select All. Click Clear All to turn off all the checkboxes and start over. Don't turn on the checkboxes for folders and categories.

3. **Click OK.**

    The tasks appear at the end of the list of tasks in your Project file.

Copying Tasks from an Email

If you copy an indented list of tasks from an Outlook email or a Word document, Project is smart enough to turn them into summary tasks and subtasks in your Project Task list. Page 138 in Chapter 6 shows you how to copy tasks from an email and paste them into Project.

Building a Resource List from an Outlook Address Book

If you use Outlook at work, you probably already have information about team members in your Outlook address book or Contacts folder. Rather than retyping all this information in Project, you can import resource names from Outlook into Project. Here are the steps:

1. **In Project, open the file into which you want to import resources.**

    If you use a resource pool (page 218), import the resources into the pool rather than into individual projects. Similarly, if you use Project Server, don't import resources directly into Project; import them into the enterprise resource pool instead.

2. **In the View tab's Resource Views section, click Resource Sheet.**

    Select the row where you want to insert the new resources.

3. **In the Resource tab's Insert section, click Add Resources→Address Book.**

    The Select Resources dialog box appears.

4. **Select the names of people you want to add to your project or resource pool.**

   You can select several resources at a time by Shift-clicking the first name in the group and then the last name in the group. Select nonadjacent names by Ctrl-clicking each name.

5. **Click Add.**

   The names appear in the Add box.

6. **Click OK.**

   Project adds new rows in the Resource Sheet for the selected resources.

Sending Project Information to Others

You've probably emailed thousands of messages with attachments, so the concept of attaching a Project file to an email is nothing new. However, with Project, you can choose to send the whole project or only a few tasks and resources. And if your audience doesn't have Project installed on their computers, you can create a *picture* of the Project information and mail that instead. Project can send files using any MAPI-compliant (Messaging Application Programming Interface) email program.

> **TIP** If your organization uses SharePoint, that's a far easier way to share Project information. Chapter 25 shows you how; download it from this book's Missing CD page at *www.missingmanuals.com/cds*.

When you need approval for a schedule, Outlook's routing mechanism can send the file to reviewers in sequence, so you can get their comments and approvals. While sending attachments tends to clutter email servers with multiple copies of the same file, publishing a Project file to a Microsoft Exchange Public Folder, a Microsoft SharePoint site, or a cloud-storage location like SkyDrive lets everyone look at a single copy (which requires that you use Microsoft Exchange, Microsoft SharePoint, or a cloud-storage service).

■ SENDING PROJECT FILES VIA EMAIL

With the plethora of cloud-storage and collaboration tools available, you might opt to share a file online (for example, in a SkyDrive folder) and send reviewers or collaborators a notification email through the online service. However, sharing a Project file with a few folks via email is easy, whether you send the message from your email program or directly from Project.

In Outlook, simply create a new message, and then, in the "Untitled - Message" window, head to the Insert tab's Include section, and then click Attach File to attach the Project file. (If you use a different email program, simply compose a new message and use the program's equivalent command to attach the Project file.)

On the other hand, if you tend to forget attachments (like most people do), you can create the email message in Project, which *automatically* attaches the file. Here are the steps for sending a Project file from within Project:

1. **In Project, open the Project file you want to send, and then choose File→Share. On Backstage view's Share page, click Email, and then click "Send as Attachment."**

   Your email program starts (if it isn't running already) and opens a new message window with the current Project file already attached. The Subject line contains the filename.

2. **Click the "To:" box, and then, in the Select Names dialog box, choose the names of the recipients.**

   You can also type email addresses directly in the "To:" box.

3. **Edit the Subject box to tell your recipients why you're emailing them this file.**

   In the message area, tell the recipients what you want them to do with the Project file, as shown in Figure 19-13.

4. **Click Send or the equivalent button.**

   The recipients receive your email message with the Project file attached.

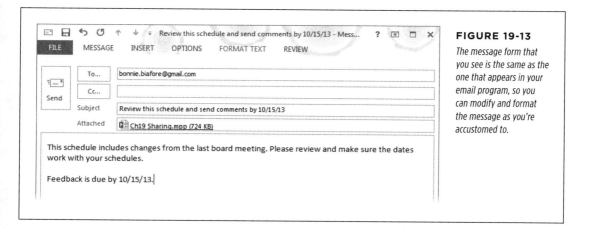

FIGURE 19-13

The message form that you see is the same as the one that appears in your email program, so you can modify and format the message as you're accustomed to.

Linking and Embedding

To manage projects, you usually need several types of information all at the same time. That's why so many project managers have a corkboard plastered with layers of printed pages or a computer screen with a dozen windows open at once. To see information without opening *every* program you own, you can take information created in one program and display an editable copy of it in another program. This exchange goes in either direction: Project data can appear in other programs like Excel and PowerPoint, or information from other programs can appear in Project.

You have three ways to make this happen: copying, linking, and embedding. As you learned on page 533, you can copy data from one program and paste it into another. In a way, copying is a lot like embedding, because you create a copy of the data in the destination program, but embedding does more, as you'll learn shortly. *Linking* means connecting directly to information in one program from another program. For instance, a PowerPoint slide can display a high-level schedule from Project. Then, when you update the schedule in Project, that latest, greatest version of it *automatically* appears in PowerPoint. On the other hand, *embedding* places a *copy* of an object (like a spreadsheet or Visio diagram) from one program into another. The embedded object and the original file aren't linked, so you don't automatically see changes made in the original. But embedded objects are ideal when you want to send self-contained files to colleagues.

The procedures for linking and embedding are usually almost identical—except for turning a Link checkbox on or off. However, a few linking and embedding techniques stray further from the typical path, depending on the type of data and whether you're displaying Project data in other programs, or vice versa. This chapter begins by describing the differences between linking and embedding in detail. Then you'll learn how to link and embed objects between programs, whether you want to place Project data into another program's files or vice versa.

This chapter concludes with another way you can link Project: adding hyperlinks to files, web pages, or other parts of your Project file. You'll learn how to add and modify hyperlinks, regardless of whether you're linking to a location in the same file, to another file, or to a web page.

Understanding Linking and Embedding

Linking and embedding both help you see data from one program in another program. However, these two methods for sharing data have their differences. By understanding what each one does, you'll be able to choose the right approach for what you're trying to do. This section describes the differences between linking and embedding and provides a side-by-side comparison to help you weigh the pros and cons.

Here are the differences between linking and embedding:

- **Linking** means the data remains in the source file, and the destination file merely displays the source file's data. Linked objects get updated automatically, because the data you see in the destination file and the source data are one and the same, so the data in the destination file changes when the source data does.

  When you double-click a linked object, the source program starts and you can edit the source file. For example, suppose you link your Project schedule to a PowerPoint slide, and you spot a schedule change you want to make. Double-click the linked object in the PowerPoint slide, and Project launches and opens the source Project file. Any changes you make are saved in the source Project file *and* appear automatically in the PowerPoint slide.

- **Embedding** means that a separate copy of the source file (called an *embedded object*) becomes part of the destination file. The source file still exists, but the embedded object is independent and doesn't change when the source data changes.

  In most cases, when you double-click an embedded object, the source program doesn't start. Instead, you see the source program's menus in place of the destination program's menus (page 582). For example, double-clicking an embedded Excel spreadsheet in the Project timescale pane replaces Project's menus with Excel's, and you see a hatched border around the object. (The menus revert to the destination program's menus when you deselect the embedded object.) Editing the embedded object doesn't affect the source file. In Project, embedded objects can also behave in another way, which page 582 explains.

TIP Linking and embedding work with any program that supports *Object Linking and Embedding* (OLE), a technology Microsoft developed specifically so that files can contain components created in different programs.

Whether linking or embedding is the better choice depends on what you're trying to do. Bottom line, linking is better if the source data is going to change. Embedding is better when you need to widely distribute the destination file, particularly to recipients who can't access your computers. Table 20-1 shows the pros and cons of each approach.

TABLE 20-1 *The differences between linking and embedding*

FEATURE	LINKING	EMBEDDING
Updating	Linking keeps data up to date in both the source and destination files. You can edit the source file from either program and see the updated information in both places.	The destination file doesn't update along with the source file. If you want to update an embedded object to reflect a change in the source file, then you have to either make the same changes to the embedded object or re-embed the object after making the changes.
Copies of data	Linking means there's only one copy of the data, so you don't have to make the same changes multiple times. The link breaks if you move the source file, but you can repair it (page 581).	An embedded object is a second copy of the data. To show the most recent data in an embedded object, you have to edit the embedded object—or delete it and then re-embed it.
Distributing data	When you distribute a file with links, the recipients see the data *only if* they can access the linked files. If they can't, then the links break and they see an error message instead.	You distribute the destination file with the embedded object in it. The destination file contains everything the recipients need to view and edit the data.
File size	Destination files don't increase in size, because the data remains in the source file.	The size of a destination file increases because it contains the embedded object and all of its data.
Performance	When a file contains multiple links, it takes time to open the links (especially over a network). The file has to examine each source file for updates to the linked objects.	The additional data in embedded objects can make the destination file slower to open and respond.

◼ Linking and Embedding Project Data

Project data comes in handy in lots of other programs. For example, a Project schedule shows project status whether it appears in a PowerPoint slide, a Word-based status report, or an Excel spreadsheet. Similarly, you might embed a Resource Graph into a memo requesting resources. This section describes how to link and embed Project data into other programs. See "Working with Linked and Embedded Objects" on page 578 to learn how to display, select, resize, and edit linked and embedded objects.

Linking Project Files to Other Programs

Sometimes, pictures of Project views aren't enough. For example, you might want to include a Gantt Chart in your status report to show the up-to-date project schedule. When you link a Project file to another program, the linked object initially displays the portion of the view that you copied in Project. Once the linked object is in place, you can edit it to change the view, filter the tasks, and so on (as described on page 579).

> **NOTE**   Office programs can be fussy about linking objects, but the box on page 569 provides some solutions.

Here's how you link a Project file to another program:

1. **Open the Project file and the destination file (a Word document, for example).**

   You can link to a Project view in any program that supports OLE, including Excel, Word, and PowerPoint.

2. **In Project, set up the view the way you want it.**

   Select the view and the table you want. If necessary, insert or hide columns in the table. Filter the view to show only the tasks, resources, or assignments you want.

3. **Select the data you want to link, and then, in the Task tab's Clipboard section, click Copy (or simply press Ctrl+C).**

   Whether you select cells in a table or entire rows by dragging over their ID numbers, the Copy command places what you've selected on the Clipboard.

4. **Switch to the other program and, in the destination file, click where you want to place the linked view.**

   Unlike pasting table cells, a view comes in as one object with its top-left corner at the location you click.

5. **In the Home tab's Clipboard section, click Paste→Paste Special.**

   If you're linking to a non-Microsoft program, the command may be Edit→Paste Special instead.

   The Paste Special dialog box opens.

6. **In the Paste Special dialog box, select the "Paste link" option, as illustrated in Figure 20-1.**

Be sure to select "Paste link," since the Paste option *embeds* the object instead of linking it. If the "Paste link" option is grayed out, be sure to save the Project file, and then recopy and try "Paste link" again.

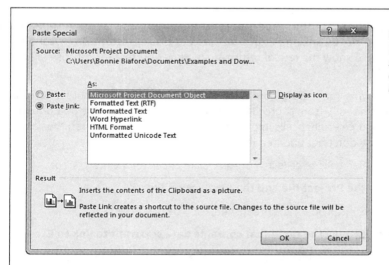

FIGURE 20-1

Turn on the "Display as icon" checkbox to show an icon instead of the entire linked object. When you want to see the linked information, simply double-click the icon.

7. **In the As list, select Microsoft Project Document Object, and then click OK.**

The Project view appears as a single object in the destination file. You can move the linked object around by dragging anywhere in the center of the object. To resize the object, click within it, and then drag the resize handles at the corners and the middle of each side.

TROUBLESHOOTING MOMENT

When Programs Won't Link

If your Office programs like Excel are reluctant to create links, the problem could be your security settings. For example, you've copied Project data to the Clipboard, but in Excel, the Paste Link command (or the Paste Link option in the Paste Special dialog box) is grayed out. Here's how you tell Excel to play well with others:

1. In Excel, choose File→Options.

2. In the Excel Options dialog box, choose Trust Center, and then click Trust Center Settings.

3. In the Trust Center dialog box, choose External Content.

4. Select either the "Enable automatic update for all Workbook links" option or the "Prompt user on automatic update for Workbooks Links" option.

5. Click OK to close the Trust Center dialog box, and then click OK again to close the Excel Options dialog box.

If the "Paste link" option is *still* obstinately grayed out, try saving and reopening your files and then repeating the linking process.

Linking Project Table Data to Other Programs

If the other program's file has cells, such as an Excel spreadsheet, you can create links from portions of Project tables directly to the cells in the other program's file. Any portion of a Project table is fair game: You simply select the data you want (individual cells, groups of cells, entire columns, or entire rows) and then paste a link into the other file. Although the values in the other program *look* just like ones you type directly into that program, they're actually linked to Project cells. So when the Project values change, the linked cells in the other program display the updated values. For example, by linking Project cost cells to Excel, a return-on-investment spreadsheet could show the rate of return at any time—perfect for surprise executive visits.

Linking and copying (page 533) both work with Project table cells, but linked cells get their values directly from source Project cells. Copying pastes the text or numbers from the source Project cells into destination cells, as if you entered the values directly, and they don't get updated if the source data changes.

To link Project table cells to cells in a program like Excel, follow these steps:

1. **Open both the Project file and the destination file.**

   For example, open an Excel spreadsheet.

2. **In Project, display the table that contains data you want to link to Excel.**

   If necessary, display the view you want. (In the View tab's Task Views or Resource Views section, click the name of the view you want to apply.) To change the table, in the View tab's Data section, click Tables, and then choose a table from the drop-down list. (If the table you want doesn't appear on the drop-down list, click More Tables. In the More Tables dialog box, select the table and click Apply.)

3. **Select the data you want to link, and then in the Task tab's Clipboard section, click Copy (or right-click anywhere within the selected cells, and then choose Copy Cell from the shortcut menu, as shown in Figure 20-2).**

   Use any of the usual techniques for selecting data: dragging over column headings to select entire columns, dragging from the top-left to the bottom-right cell of a range, or Shift-clicking cells. The cells you select must be contiguous; if you Ctrl-click or Ctrl-drag to select nonadjacent cells, you can't paste that selection in the other program.

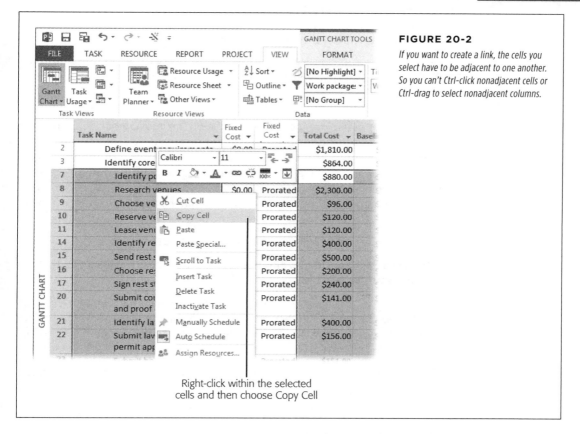

FIGURE 20-2

*If you want to create a link, the cells you
select have to be adjacent to one another.
So you can't Ctrl-click nonadjacent cells or
Ctrl-drag to select nonadjacent columns.*

Right-click within the selected
cells and then choose Copy Cell

4. **In the destination file, click the top-left cell where you want to insert the
linked data.**

When you paste the data (in the next step), it starts at the cell you click, and
then fills in cells to the right and below that cell.

5. **In the destination program, in the Home tab's Clipboard section, click
Paste→Paste Special. In the Paste Special dialog box, select the "Paste link"
option and either HTML or Text, and then click OK.**

The linked data appears in the selected cells. If you can't see the full values,
adjust the column widths in the destination file.

Embedding Project Files in Other Programs

Embedding Project data into another program creates a copy of your project in the destination file. Embedding data creates a self-contained file—for example, for the subcontractors who can't access your computer systems. If you sent them status reports with linked objects, they would see broken links, not data.

> **NOTE**   You can't embed a *portion* of a Project table into another file. You can embed only an entire Project file into another file.

Although you *can* create new objects and embed them into another file all from the same dialog box, as the box on page 574 describes, creating a Project file on the fly to embed in another program is a bad idea, because that Project file is then available *only within* the destination file. If, on the other hand, you create your Project file in Project, then you can work on the original file as you would normally and can also embed the file into another program. Just remember that the embedded Project file won't reflect any changes you make to the original file.

To embed a Project file in another program, follow these steps:

1. **Open the destination file, and then select the location where you want to embed your Project file.**

   Project doesn't have to be running to embed a Project file. Simply launch the destination program, and then put your cursor wherever you want the Project file to go, such as at the top of a new page in a Word document or the first cell in an Excel worksheet.

2. **In a Microsoft Office program, in the Insert tab's Text section, click Object.**

   The Text section is near the right end of the Insert tab. If the entire section isn't visible, click Text and then choose Object on the drop-down menu.

   The Object dialog box opens.

3. **Select the "Create from File" tab, and then select the file you want to embed.**

   To locate the file, click Browse. In the Browse dialog box, navigate to the folder that contains your Project file, click the filename, and then click Insert. The path and filename appear in the "File name" box, as shown in Figure 20-3.

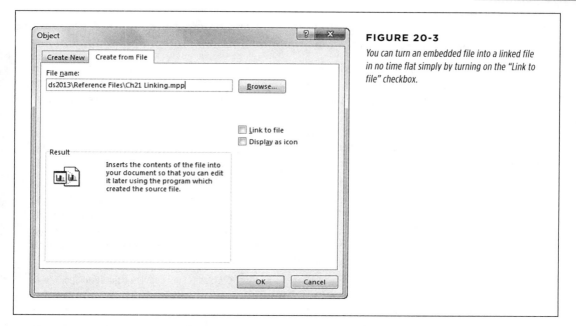

FIGURE 20-3

You can turn an embedded file into a linked file in no time flat simply by turning on the "Link to file" checkbox.

4. **To show an icon until you want to see the Project file, turn on the "Display as icon" checkbox.**

    Turning on this checkbox displays a Change Icon button. Click this button to display the Change Icon dialog box, where you can select the icon and label you want.

5. **Click OK.**

    The embedded file appears at the selected location in the destination file. If you chose to display an icon for the embedded file, then you can open the file by double-clicking its icon.

Creating Objects from Scratch

When you insert an object into a file, the dialog box you use to do so (Object or Insert Object, depending on the program) offers a two-for-one option that lets you create an object *and* embed it in the destination file. Although you can edit this embedded object like any other—for example, to add formulas to a spreadsheet—the only time this approach makes sense is when the information you create is an inseparable part of the destination file. That's because the embedded object you create in this way exists only in that file. So if there's *any* chance you might need the information elsewhere, you should use its source program to create it instead, and then embed the resulting file.

To create a new embedded object, follow these steps:

1. In the destination file (an Excel spreadsheet, for example), select the location where you want the new object to appear.

2. Open the Object or Insert Object dialog box. In Office programs, in the Insert tab's Text section, click Object. If Project is the destination program, you can insert objects into the Task Information dialog box or in the Task Form view's Notes or Objects pane. (To open the Task Information dialog box, select a task and then, in the Task tab's Properties section, click Information. To insert an object in Task Form view, right-click it, and then

choose Notes or Objects on the shortcut menu. To insert the object, above the Notes or Objects field, click the Insert Object button, whose icon looks like a landscape with a cactus.)

3. If the program you're using opens the Object dialog box (like Word or Excel), then select the Create New tab. If the Insert Object dialog box opens instead (like Project), then select the Create New option.

4. In the Object Type list, select the kind of object you want to create. Your choice determines which program menus you see when you double-click the object. For example, to create an Excel workbook, select Microsoft Excel Worksheet.

5. Click OK. A blank object appears in the destination file. (If you create a Microsoft Project document in another file, a distorted Project icon might appear at first. Double-click the icon to edit the object. Then, after you click away from the object, the file's contents should appear.)

6. To add content to the object, make sure it's selected, and then use the program menus that appear.

7. To revert to the destination program's menus, simply click outside the boundaries of the embedded object. To edit the object, double-click it.

■ Linking and Embedding Data into Project

Linking and embedding data goes in either direction. Just as a Project schedule can provide information for a status report or presentation, other files can provide background information for the tasks in your Project schedule. For example, you might link information in a risk log spreadsheet to an at-risk task, so the most recent actions and results appear in the Task Information dialog box. Likewise, you could embed a Visio workflow diagram in the Gantt Chart timescale.

You can link or embed entire files into Project, or link cells from an Excel spreadsheet to Project table cells. In addition, you can embed portions of other files, like Excel charts or Visio drawing pages. This section explains how to link and embed data into Project.

Linking and Embedding Entire Files into Project

Inserting an entire file into Project is one way to get easy access to additional information—for example, a specifications Word document or a change request tracking database. To see more of the file, simply drag the boundaries of the inserted object. To see a different part of the file, select the object and then edit it, as described on page 579. (Another way to access other files is by adding a hyperlink to the file within Project, as described on page 583.)

When you work with entire files, the linking and embedding steps are almost identical:

1. **Open your Project file, and then select the location where you want to insert the other file.**

   Only some areas of a Project file accept inserted objects: the Gantt Chart timescale, the Notes or Objects boxes in Task Form and Resource Form views, and the Notes tab in the Task Information, Resource Information, and Assignment Information dialog boxes. For this exercise, let's assume you're using one of the Information dialog boxes.

   NOTE   If you want to insert objects in the Gantt Chart timescale, you have to customize the ribbon to add the Object command to a custom group (see Chapter 22 for details). In the "Choose commands from" list, choose All Commands, and scroll until you see the Object command.

   ---

2. **On the Notes tab of one of the Information dialog boxes, click the Insert Object button immediately above the Notes area.**

   The Insert Object dialog box opens.

3. **Select the "Create from File" option, and then choose the file you want to link or embed.**

   Click Browse to navigate to the folder that contains the file you want. Double-click the filename, and the path and filename appear in the "File" box.

4. **To *link* to the file, turn on the Link checkbox. To *embed* the file instead, leave this checkbox turned off.**

   What you do in this step is the only difference between linking and embedding; the rest of the process is identical.

5. **To display the file as an icon until you want to see it, turn on the Display As Icon checkbox.**

   After you insert the link or embed the file in Project, you will be able to open it by double-clicking it.

6. **Click OK.**

   The object appears at the location you selected in your Project file.

Embedding Parts of Files in Project

With some programs, you can embed portions of a file into Project. A chart from an Excel spreadsheet, a slide from a PowerPoint presentation, and a drawing page from a Visio document are all candidates for inserting into a Project file. Although the embedded object represents only that portion of the file, the object still increases the destination file's size. And remember that the embedded object doesn't update to reflect any changes to the original file.

NOTE You can't *link* a part of a file. If you copy an Excel chart, PowerPoint slide, or Visio drawing page, and then use the Paste Special command in Project, the "Paste link" option remains grayed out.

To embed a part of a file into your Project file, follow these steps:

1. **In the source program, open the file and select what you want to show in your Project schedule.**

   For example, in Visio, drag across the shapes you want to embed in Project. (If you want to embed an *entire* Visio drawing page, make sure *no* shapes are selected.) For an Excel chart, click inside the chart.

2. **Press Ctrl+C to copy the selection to the Clipboard.**

   Alternatively, in Microsoft Office programs, in the Home tab's Clipboard section, click Copy.

3. **In your Project file, right-click the location where you want to place the object, and then choose Paste Special.**

   If you want to insert these partial objects in the Notes tab of the Information dialog boxes (see step 1 in the previous list for a full list of them), you have to right-click within the Notes area, because the ribbon is inactive while the dialog box is open. You can also insert partial objects in the Objects box in Task Form or Resource Form view. (To display the Objects box in a form, right-click the top part of the form, and then, in the shortcut menu, choose Objects.)

   Project selects the Paste option, which embeds the object. The Paste Link option is grayed out, telling you that you can't link a part of another file.

4. **In the As box, select the type of object you want to paste in.**

   The choices vary depending on what you copied to the Clipboard.

5. **Click OK.**

   The object appears in Project at the location you selected.

Linking Tabular Data in Project

Just as you can link to Project table cells in other programs, you can also bring data from other programs into Project's table cells. When you link data to Project cells, the values look as if you typed them directly into Project, but they're actually linked to the source file and change when the source data changes.

Project demands the right types of data in some of its fields, so you have to make sure the data types are the same in both places. For example, you can link only dates in Project date cells. When you link tabular data from another program in Project, the links point to specific columns or cells in the source file (like column C or cells C5 through C12 in an Excel spreadsheet). If you rearrange columns or cells in the source file, the links in Project still point to the original linked locations, which could produce a data-type mismatch. The easiest way to keep data types in sync is to link column by column. Here's how:

1. **In Excel or another table-based program, select the first column you want to link by clicking the column's heading, and then press Ctrl+C.**

   Clicking the heading selects the entire column. You can also select several cells in a column that you want to link by dragging over them, and then press Ctrl+C.

2. **In Project, display the view and the table in which you want to link the data. Then click the first cell for the linked data.**

   Select the top-left cell for the linked data; Project will fill in the cells to the right and below it.

3. **In the Task tab's Clipboard section, click Paste→Paste Special, and then select the Paste Link option.**

   If you choose the Paste option, Project simply copies the values into the Project cells as text, numbers, dates, and so on.

4. **In the As box, select Text Data.**

   As you learned on page 575, selecting an object type like Microsoft Office Excel Worksheet inserts a linked object that you double-click to open and edit. By selecting Text Data, Project fills in individual cells with linked values. Each linked cell gets its value from the corresponding cell in the source file.

5. **Click OK.**

   The cells display values from the source file with a gray triangle at each linked cell's lower right, as shown in Figure 20-4. To link other columns in the source file, repeat steps 1–5 for each additional column.

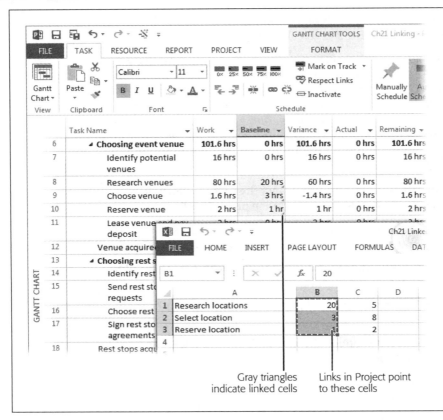

FIGURE 20-4

If you move the linked column or cells in the source file, the links in Project still point to their original location. For example, if you swap columns B and C in the Excel spreadsheet shown here, then Project's linked cell values will change from 20, 3, and 1 to 5, 8 and 2.

Gray triangles indicate linked cells

Links in Project point to these cells

Working with Linked and Embedded Objects

Linking or embedding information into another file is just the beginning. Linked and embedded objects are incredibly versatile, and this section explains all the things you can do with them.

Most of the time, you want the information in linked and embedded objects to be visible at all times, but these objects can just as easily keep a low profile as icons until you want to see what they have to show. Like other elements in files, you can move and resize objects—for instance, to get them out of the way of task bars in a Gantt Chart view or graphics on a Visio diagram. And the whole point of inserting a linked or embedded object instead of a picture is to edit it at some point. To get the most out of linked and embedded objects, you need to know how to manage the objects you insert as well as the links between files. This section explains all that.

Linked and embedded objects work like many other elements in your files. You can select them, move them around, change their size, and delete them. Here's how:

- **Resize an object.** When you select an object by clicking it, resize handles appear at each of its corners and at the middle of each side. You can drag these handles to change the size of the object. To change the object's dimensions while maintaining its proportions, drag a handle at one of the corners (the pointer changes to an angled two-headed arrow). To change the size in only one dimension, drag a handle at the middle of a side (the pointer changes to either a horizontal or vertical two-headed arrow).

- **Move an object.** You can move an object whether or not it's selected by dragging the middle of the object to the new location. The pointer includes a box at its lower right to indicate that you're about to move the object. If you drag too close to one of the object's edges, then you'll resize the object instead.

- **Delete an object.** Select the object, and then press Delete.

- **Display the object as an icon.** When you display an object as an icon, double-clicking the icon brings the full object into view. Dragging the icon moves the object, just as dragging the actual object does.

Editing Linked Objects

Whether you're working in the source program or the destination program when you edit a linked object, you always edit the same source file. Suppose you link an Excel spreadsheet in a task note (page 576). If you edit the spreadsheet in Excel, then your changes show up automatically the next time you open or update your Project file. Alternatively, you can double-click the linked object in Project to start Excel and open the source file for editing.

Editing linked objects works differently from editing embedded objects in that you always edit *the source file*. Here's how it works:

1. **To edit a linked object, double-click it.**

   The source file opens in the source program. For example, double-clicking a linked Excel spreadsheet starts Excel and opens the spreadsheet—as if you'd started Excel yourself and opened the file. (You need to have read-write privileges for the file in order to edit it, just as you would if you opened the file directly. The box on page 580 explains your options if an error message appears when you try to edit a linked object.)

2. **If you see a message box telling you that you're opening an OLE object that could contain viruses and other malicious code and you're *sure* it's safe, click Yes to open the file.**

   If you have any doubts about the file, click No.

3. **When you finish editing, save the file as you would normally, and then close the object's program (Excel in this example).**

Back in the destination Project file, the linked object reflects the changes. If the linked object *isn't* up to date, you can tell the destination program to immediately check for updates, as described in the next section.

Opening Reluctant Links

If an error message appears when you try to edit a linked object (or when you open a file with links), a broken link is the most likely culprit. If the linked file moves to a different location, you have to edit the link to point to the correct file location (page 581).

Another cause of problems editing links could be that the source program isn't installed on your computer. For example, when you edit a linked Visio drawing, Visio starts and opens the file, which means you need to have Visio on your computer.

Managing Linked Objects

Linked objects require ongoing care and feeding. For example, you have to make sure that links can find the files they represent. If links are broken, then you can redirect them to the correct location for the source file. Conversely, you can *intentionally* break the link between an object and the source file to transform the object into an embedded object or picture. Finally, you can update a link immediately and tell the destination program whether you want it to update links automatically or wait for you to say when.

Out of the box, whenever you open a file that contains links, a message box asks if you want to re-establish the links. Click Yes to update the links. If you click No, Project opens the file with the existing values; that is, it doesn't check the source file to see if values have changed.

TIP If you want Project to re-establish links without asking you, choose File→Options. On the left side of the Project Options dialog box, click Advanced. In the Edit section, turn off the "Ask to update automatic links" checkbox, and then click OK.

If you want to perform more specific link-management tasks, you can use the Edit Links command to open the Links dialog box, shown in Figure 20-5. Unfortunately, the Edit Links command isn't on the ribbon, so you have to add it to a custom group (page 689) before you can use it.

NOTE In other Office programs, the dialog box you use to edit links is named Edit Links; in Project, it's simply named Links.

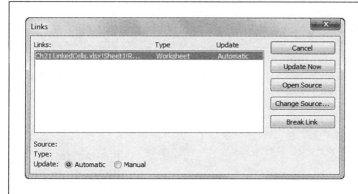

FIGURE 20-5

In Project, you have to customize the ribbon to add the Edit Links command to a custom group (page 689). For other Office programs like Excel, open the Edit Links dialog box by selecting the ribbon's Data tab, and then, in the Connections group, clicking Edit Links.

Here's how to use Project's Links dialog box to keep links in tip-top condition:

- **Review links.** The dialog box lists the links in your file whether they connect to other places in the same file or to different files altogether. Each link shows the source file's name, the type of file, and whether the link is set up to update automatically or manually.

- **Update a link.** To immediately update a link with changes from the source file, select the link, and then click Update Now.

- **Repair a broken link.** You can fix broken links by changing the folder or file that a link looks for. Click Change Source, and then in the Change Source dialog box, click Browse to find the file. Double-click the filename to update the path and name in the Source box. Click OK to save the link.

- **Change a linked object into an embedded object.** Suppose you linked to a document during its development so you always saw the most recent version. Now that the document is approved, you want to embed the object so you can see the document without the baggage of maintaining the link. You can convert a linked object into an embedded object in the Edit Links dialog box by selecting the link and then clicking Break Link. The link disappears from the list in the Links dialog box, but the object remains—and now acts like the embedded object it is.

- **Specify when to update the link.** Initially, Project and other programs create links so they update automatically, which means that the destination program checks source files for changes and updates the objects with any changes it finds. All that checking and updating can slow your computer to a crawl, especially if the source files change frequently or are located on large or complex networks. In this situation, you can control when updates occur by selecting a link and then selecting the Manual option.

Editing Embedded Objects

You double-click embedded objects to edit them, just like you do linked objects. The result depends on where you embedded the object in Project. If you edit an embedded object in the Gantt Chart timescale, the menus for the destination program change to the menus for the embedded object's program. For example, when you double-click a Word document embedded in your Gantt Chart, Word menus appear where the Project menus just were, as illustrated in Figure 20-6. You can then work on the Word object as if you were working directly in Word. When you're done, click somewhere outside the embedded object, and the Project menus reappear. It's like having two programs at your fingertips!

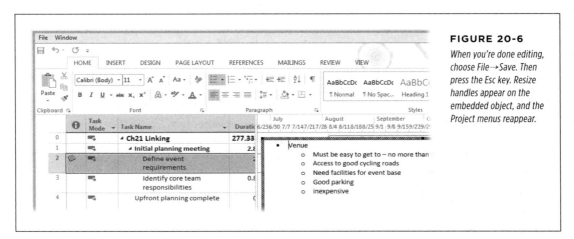

FIGURE 20-6

When you're done editing, choose File→Save. Then press the Esc key. Resize handles appear on the embedded object, and the Project menus reappear.

If you embed an object in a Project task's note (double-click anywhere in the task's row to open the Task Information dialog box, click the Notes tab, and then click the Insert Object icon), double-clicking the embedded object opens the object in its source program. If you can't remember whether an object is linked or embedded, click the File tab in that program. If the title bar says something like "Document in Unnamed - Word," you know you're editing an embedded object, not the source file.

NOTE When you double-click an embedded object, a message box may appear warning you that you're opening an OLE object that could contain viruses and other malicious code. If you're sure the file is safe, click Yes to open it. Otherwise, click No.

Hyperlinking to Information

Managing projects means keeping track of information stored in different places and different types of files. As a project manager, your nose is usually buried in a Project file, so why not access the information you need directly from Project? For example, you can add hyperlinks to tasks to access the corresponding work-package Word documents, an Excel spreadsheet with financial figures, or the web page with your customer's mission statement. Project hyperlinks can also jump to tasks or resources within the Project file. This section explains all your options.

> **NOTE** You can add only one hyperlink to each task, resource, or assignment. However, you can add as many hyperlinks as you want to a *note*. Simply double-click a task, resource, or assignment to open the corresponding Information dialog box, and then click the Notes tab and add the hyperlinks you want in the Notes box.

Creating a Hyperlink to a File or Web Page

Hyperlinks can connect to any kind of file—a Word document, an Excel spreadsheet, a web page, and so on. When you add a hyperlink to a task, resource, or assignment, Project displays a *hyperlink indicator* in that element's Indicators column, which looks like a globe with links of chain. Although the destination file can reside anywhere (anywhere that's accessible to the people who need it, that is), it has to *remain* in that same place. If the destination file moves to another location, the hyperlink can't find the file and becomes what's known as a *broken link*.

To create a hyperlink in a Project file, do the following:

1. **Display the view that shows the task, resource, or assignment to which you want to add a hyperlink.**

   You can insert hyperlinks in any view.

2. **Right-click the task, resource, or assignment, and then choose Hyperlink. (Or click anywhere in the task, resource, or assignment's row, and then press Ctrl+K.)**

   The Insert Hyperlink dialog box opens (Figure 20-7).

3. **In the "Text to display" box, type a brief description of what you're hyperlinking to.**

   The "Text to display" box is initially empty. When you position the mouse over a hyperlink indicator, a pop-up label containing the text from the "Text to display" box appears. If you type a description in this box, Project leaves it in place when you select a destination file. Figure 20-7 explains what happens if you *don't* type a description.

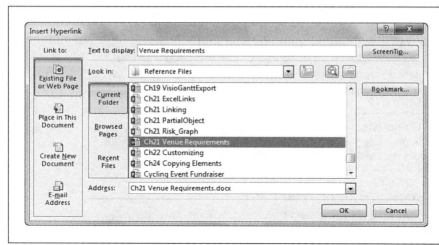

FIGURE 20-7

If you don't type a description in the "Text to display" box, Project fills in the path and filename of the destination file or the URL of the web page.

The Insert Hyperlink dialog box also has a ScreenTip button. When you position your pointer over a hyperlink indicator without clicking, a ScreenTip appears immediately below the description. If you type a meaningful description in the "Text to display" box, you may not need a ScreenTip, but it's handy if you want to see more information about a hyperlink.

4. **In the "Link to" section, select the type of data you want to hyperlink to, like "Existing File or Web Page."**

The left side of the Insert Hyperlink dialog box has two vertical navigation bars for choosing what you want to hyperlink to: "Link to" and "Look in." In the "Link to" navigation bar, the aptly named "Existing File or Web Page" and "Place in This Document" are the most popular types of hyperlinks. (The next section describes the steps for linking to a location in your Project file.) You can also create a hyperlink to an email address, so you can easily email the person assigned to a task.

Although you can simultaneously create a new document and hyperlink to it, creating the document outside Project is more expedient. Outside Project, you can create the document based on a template. Moreover, doing so keeps your multitasking to a minimum.

5. **In the "Look in" section, navigate to the folder that contains the destination file, and then select the filename.**

The "Look in" drop-down list includes all the locations you can reach through Windows Explorer: drives on your computer, network drives, and removable drives. To look for the file you want, click the "Browse for File" button (whose icon is an open file folder) to the right of the "Look in" box. The "Link to File" dialog box opens.

The "Look in" section's navigation bar has three choices for finding files or web pages. Current Folder shows the files in the folder you've selected. Select Browsed Pages or Recent Files instead to hyperlink to files or web pages that you've used recently.

The "Browse the Web" button (its icon is a magnifying glass in front of a globe) to the left of the "Browse for File" button opens a browser window. Surf to the web page you want, select the URL in the browser's address bar, and then press Ctrl+C. Then click the Address box in the Insert Hyperlink dialog box, and then press Ctrl+V to paste the URL.

6. **Click OK.**

A hyperlink indicator appears in the task, resource, or assignment's Indicators column (depending on what type of element you chose in step 1). Click the indicator to open the hyperlinked file with its associated program.

If the Indicators column isn't visible, then you can't tell which elements have hyperlinks. However, if you know a hyperlink exists, you can follow it by right-clicking the task, resource, or assignment, and then, from the shortcut menu, choosing Hyperlink→Open Hyperlink. To insert the Indicators column in the table, right-click a table heading, and then choose Insert Column. In the drop-down menu, choose Indicators.

Modifying Hyperlinks

You can edit and remove hyperlinks to keep your files up to date. For example, if a destination file moves to a new location or a web page's address changes, edit the hyperlink to point to the new location:

- **Modify a hyperlink.** Right-click the hyperlinked task, resource, or assignment, and then, on the shortcut menu, choose Hyperlink→Edit Hyperlink. The Edit Hyperlink dialog box has all the same components as the Insert Hyperlink dialog box. Change the values you want, and then click OK to update the link.

- **Remove a hyperlink.** Right-click the hyperlinked task, resource, or assignment, and then, on the shortcut menu, choose Hyperlink→Clear Hyperlinks (this command is plural even though a task, resource, or assignment can have only one hyperlink at a time). Project deletes the hyperlink, and the hyperlink indicator disappears.

Creating a Hyperlink to a Location in the Project File

Hyperlinking from one place in a Project file to another is a great way to find related tasks or resources. For example, a hyperlink can take you from a work task to the corresponding approval milestone task or to the resource assigned to the task. Although you can add hyperlinks to tasks, resources, and *assignments*, hyperlinks can point only to tasks and resources. Moreover, you need to know the task ID or resource ID that you want to link to *before* you open the Insert Hyperlink dialog box.

To create a hyperlink to another location in the same Project file, do the following:

1. **Right-click the task, resource, or assignment to which you want to add a hyperlink, and then choose Hyperlink.**

   The Insert Hyperlink dialog box opens.

2. **In the "Text to display" box, type a brief description of the hyperlink's destination.**

   Project keeps your description when you select a destination task or resource. If you don't fill in this box, then Project fills it in with the view name and ID that you select, which isn't particularly informative—for instance, "Gantt Chart!20" for task ID 20 in Gantt Chart view.

   You can also add a ScreenTip to a hyperlink to another location. In the Insert Hyperlink dialog box, click the ScreenTip button. In the Set Hyperlink ScreenTip dialog box that appears, type the ScreenTip you want, such as what the hyperlinked location represents, and then click OK. Once you do that, when you position your pointer over a hyperlink indicator without clicking, the ScreenTip appears immediately below the description.

3. **In the "Link to" section, click "Place in This Document."**

   Project replaces the "Look in" area with a box for the task or resource ID you want to link to and a list of views, as shown in Figure 20-8.

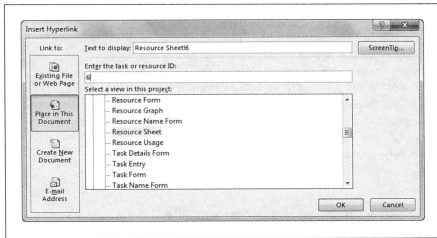

FIGURE 20-8

You need to know the task or resource ID to create a hyperlink to another location. If you don't know the ID, click Cancel, find the ID you want, and then reopen the Insert Hyperlink dialog box.

4. **In the "Enter the task or resource ID" box, type the task or ID you want to link to (the number in the first column of the task's or resource's row in the task or resource table).**

If you haven't filled in the "Text to display" box, then Project inserts the ID number in the "Text to display" box.

Project determines whether the number is a task ID or a resource ID based on the view you select in the next step. For example, it assumes you've entered a task ID when you select a task-oriented view like Gantt Chart; selecting Resource Sheet view, for instance, changes the box to a resource ID.

5. **In the "Select a view in this project" box, select the view you want Project to display when you follow the hyperlink, and then click OK.**

If you haven't filled in the "Text to display" box, then Project inserts the view's name in that box in front of the ID.

A hyperlink indicator appears in the hyperlinked task's, resource's, or assignment's Indicators column. Clicking this indicator switches to the view you chose in the Insert Hyperlink dialog box and selects the task or resource you hyperlinked to.

UP TO SPEED

Reviewing Hyperlinks

Checking that hyperlinks work is a good idea if some time has passed since you added them, as files may find homes in new locations. The ScreenTip pop-up box for hyperlink indicators shows the hyperlink's description, which typically isn't the file or location you're jumping to. If you click a hyperlink indicator, you don't know where the hyperlink goes until Project follows it.

To simplify reviewing hyperlinks, use Project's Hyperlink table, which displays the Task Name, Hyperlink, Address, and SubAddress columns. (If you're using a resource-oriented view, the first column is Resource Name instead.) To apply the Hyperlink table, in the View tab's Data section, click Tables→More Tables. In the More Tables dialog box, choose

Hyperlink, and then click Apply. This table shows hyperlinks for the current file's tasks or resources; if tasks or resources don't have hyperlinks, then only their names are listed in the Hyperlink table.

The Hyperlink table's Hyperlink column shows whatever you (or Project) entered in the hyperlinks "Text to display" box. The Address column represents the Hyperlink Address field and shows the external files or web pages you hyperlinked to. For hyperlinks between locations within the file, the Address cell is empty. Instead, the SubAddress column represents the Hyperlink Subaddress field, which shows the view and ID for internal hyperlinks. All the entries in these cells are "hot," so you can click them to follow their hyperlinks

---

Customizing Project

Viewing What You Want

Just as the tie-dyed T-shirts you wore in school no longer work in a buttoned-down office, what works for one organization may not be right for another. Even if you stay at the same job or on the same project, what you need to see in Project may change as you go along.

Fortunately, Project gives you lots of control over what you view in its window. You can customize or create views to present the right project information in the right way. For example, you can set up Gantt Chart task bars to emphasize the critical path, progress, or at-risk tasks. Most views include a table of information, and these tables are customizable as well. You can add, remove, or rearrange columns and tweak tables in other ways. Of course, text is omnipresent, and its formatting is at your command—whether you want to accommodate the reading-glasses crowd or to make key information stand out. Project can apply formatting to text that falls into a specific category, like critical tasks, or to individual elements like a crucial task bar.

You can also modify or create filters and groups to show particular types of information. By filtering tasks and resources, you can display only what meets the conditions you set, such as tasks with duration longer than two months. Alternatively, you can use groups to shuffle information into categories. Because groups can roll up the values of the items within them, it's easy to see how much you're spending on a particular group of contractors, for instance. Sorting information helps you evaluate your project from every angle—for example, to see tasks listed from longest duration to shortest. You can sort any table you display and/or specify sort order for groups you define.

Although you can't mess with many of Project's built-in fields, like Duration, Start, and Cost, the program offers dozens of fields that you *can* customize. You can set up a formula to calculate a custom field's results, tell Project how to roll up the field's values into summary tasks, specify valid values, or define graphical indicators to make statuses easy to see. This chapter shows you how to do it all.

> **NOTE** You'll find other ways you can make Project your own in the next few chapters. You can customize the ribbon and Quick Access toolbar (Chapter 22), as well as templates (Chapter 23). And if you want to teach Project new tricks, you can write macros (Chapter 24).

■ Creating Your Own Views

When you don't have the information you need, making decisions becomes a matter of luck (just ask someone sitting at a blackjack table in Vegas). Yet too much data can obscure the information you need (as anyone trying to choose an insurance policy can tell you). But the right data shown in the right light exposes flaws, highlights solutions, and generally makes managing projects easier.

Modifying Basic View Contents

In Project, a view is nothing more than a compilation of many elements: fields, tables, filters, groups, and layouts (Microsoft calls these layouts *screens*, as you'll see shortly). To make big, sweeping changes, you can create a new view and choose the screen and other elements you want. For example, you may prefer to have Task Entry view's Details pane display Task Details Form view instead of Task Form view.

Modifying views gets a lot easier when you understand the difference between *single* and *combination* views. As its name implies, a single view is like a picture window that shows one thing, like Resource Sheet or Task Sheet view. A combination view is like a window in which the top and bottom panes slide up and down; it can have one single view on the top and a different single view on the bottom, like Resource Allocation view, which shows Resource Usage view on top and Leveling Gantt view on the bottom.

> **NOTE** Some single views (like Gantt Chart view) include two side-by-side panes: a table on the left and a timescale on the right. These side-by-side panes are features of the screens (page 593) that the views use, which is why a Gantt Chart is still a single view. Combination views are ones that have a top pane and a bottom pane.

Most of Project's built-in views are single views. Gantt Chart, Task Usage, and Network Diagram views are all single views; you can display them in Project's top pane or Details pane. For example, you often see Gantt Chart view and Task Form view together because the built-in Task Entry combination view puts them there.

You get to modify different things in single and combination views. Here's what each one contains:

- **Single views.** In this kind of view, the *screen* is a basic layout of the view's elements (described in a sec). For example, all Gantt Chart views use a Gantt Chart screen with a table on the left and a timescale on the right. You can specify the screen you want to use *only* when you create a *new* view. In other words, you can't change the screen for an existing single view—built-in or custom, although you can change its other settings. In addition, you can choose a table, group, and filter to apply to each single view.

- **Combination views.** A combination view is just a pairing of two single views, so you simply pick the views you want to see in the top and Details panes.

■ SCREEN TYPES

Project comes with many views that present project information in different ways, but they boil down to seven basic screen types. Each single view uses one of these seven screen types. (This chapter describes how to customize each type.) Here are the seven types and what they do:

- **Gantt Chart.** The charts project managers ogle every day are called Gantt Charts because Charles Gantt created a winner. This view lists project tasks and information about them in a table on the left side of the Project window. In the timescale on the right side, task bars visually indicate when tasks occur and how they relate to one another. With additional task bars to show slack time, progress, or delays, Gantt Chart views present a lot of what project managers need to know.

- **Usage.** Gantt Chart views don't show specific assignments or values for each time period, which is why you need usage views like Task Usage or Resource Usage. These views have a table on the left like Gantt Chart views do, showing totals for tasks, resources, and their assignments. But instead of task bars on the right, a usage view has another table, where the columns represent time periods. The rows show assignments with summary rows for each task or resource. Each cell in the timescale contains assignment (or summary) values for that period—for instance, work, baseline work, or cost for a day, week, or month.

- **Timeline.** Timeline view (page 619) distills a project to a simple linear diagram. Out of the box, vertical lines in this view indicate the timeframe that's displayed in the timescale of a Gantt Chart or usage view. Point at either bar and the cursor changes to a two-headed arrow. At that point, you can drag that line to control the dates you see in the timescale (page 613). You can also add tasks to the timeline—for example, to keep project phases, key milestones, or ultra-critical tasks in view at all times.

- **Team Planner.** Team Planner view (available only in Project Professional and described on page 241) includes a row for each project resource and the tasks to which it's assigned, like competitive swimmers lined up in a swimming pool. That's why these rows are referred to as *swim lanes*.

- **Resource Graph.** Resource Graph view shows values for work, cost, and so on in a bar graph. Although Resource *Usage* view shows resource allocation, the colored bars in Resource Graph view let you easily see when resources are overallocated or have time to spare.

- **Network Diagram.** Many project managers use network diagrams to define relationships between tasks and to evaluate the critical path. A network diagram includes a box (or node) for each task and lines for the relationships between them. However, because the diagram isn't drawn to a timescale, each task is the same size, which makes it easier for the eye to focus on task dependencies. In Project, you can build your schedule in the view you prefer and then let Project translate that info into a network diagram.

- **Calendar.** Gantt Charts take getting used to, but everyone understands calendars. This view lets you show tasks as bars spanning the days or weeks the way you mark off your much-needed vacation. Calendar view is great for showing teams what their upcoming schedule looks like.

Depending on the work at hand, you can switch to the view that's most helpful. Within that view, you can change the information you see and how it's displayed. For example, when you're monitoring the critical path, red task bars let you more easily see critical tasks, and variance fields tell you whether progress compared with your plan is good or bad. And if none of the existing views are close to what you want, you can create a view from scratch. The following sections have all the details.

> **TIP**   Project is set up initially to display Gantt Chart view with the timeline above it, which makes it easy to see your project schedule and adjust the date range. However, if you prefer to work with another view—for example, Task Entry view, which includes the Gantt Chart in the top pane and the Task Form in the Details pane—you can change Project's default view. Choose File→Options. In the Project Options dialog box, click General. In the "Default view" drop-down list, choose the view you want Project to apply when you create a new project, and then click OK.

■ MODIFYING A SINGLE VIEW

The View Definition dialog box is command central for choosing settings for the view you're working in. It displays different settings depending on whether the view in question is a single view or a combination view. For a single view, you can choose the view's table, group, or filter. When you choose a table, group, or filter in the View Definition dialog box, the view opens every time with those choices in place, until you choose different elements in the View tab's Data section.

Here's how to customize an existing single view:

1. **If you plan to use a table, group, or filter that doesn't exist, then create it** *before* **you open the View Definitions dialog box.**

   You can't create elements on the fly in the View Definition dialog box. When you modify a view, you tell it the names of the elements to use. Project then applies the table, group, and filter you specified. If you want to create a new table, group, or filter, see "Creating a New Table" on page 638, "Creating and Editing Filters" on page 643, and "Creating a Group" on page 657 for instructions.

2. **In the View tab's Task Views or Resource Views section, click the down arrow next to any view's name and then, on the drop-down menu, choose More Views.**

   The More Views dialog box opens.

3. **In the Views list, select the single view you want to modify, and then click Edit.**

   The View Definition dialog box opens with the single view settings (Figure 21-1). (If the View Definition dialog box opens with combination view settings instead, head to the next section of this chapter.) It lists the view's screen, but you can't edit it. To choose a different screen, you have to create a view from scratch (page 598) or start with a view that uses the screen you want (page 592).

FIGURE 21-1

The View Definition dialog box's heading ends with "in 'Project xyz,'" which tells you that Project stores the modified view in that particular project file. If you want to use the modified view in other projects, you can copy it to the global template with the Organizer (page 702).

4. **In the Table drop-down list, choose the table you want the view to display.**

   The tables you see in the drop-down list depend on whether you're editing a task or resource view. For example, if you edit Gantt Chart or Task Usage view, the drop-down list contains task tables; if you edit views like Resource Sheet and Resource Usage, then you see resource tables instead. For more about Project's various tables, flip to page 632.

5. **In the Group drop-down list, choose the group you want.**

   The section that begins on page 656 explains all about groups in Project. To forgo grouping, simply choose No Group.

6. **In the Filter drop-down list, choose the filter you want to apply.**

   Initially, a filter hides any items that don't pass its tests. (Page 643 explains how to define and edit filters' tests.) But suppose you want a view that shows all tasks or resources but *emphasizes* the ones that pass the tests. In that case, turn on the "Highlight filter" checkbox, which uses blue text in rows that make the cut. To leave the view *unfiltered*, choose All Tasks or All Resources. (You can read all about filters starting on page 642.)

7. **To list the view on drop-down menus for faster access, make sure the "Show in menu" checkbox is turned on.**

   A single click on a view drop-down menu is all it takes to apply a view, including the ones you create yourself, as you can see in Figure 21-2. Because this is so handy, the "Show in menu" checkbox is turned on automatically, so you have to turn it off if for some reason you *don't* want the view in the drop-down menus. If you want to hide built-in views you never use, edit them and then turn off their "Show in menu" checkboxes.

8. **Click OK.**

   The View Definition dialog box closes. To apply the modified view, in the More Views dialog box, click Apply.

TIP   If you make changes to a view as you work—for example, adding a column to a table, applying a group, or filtering the task list—you can quickly save the custom view as a new view or update the current view to include your edits. On the ribbon, click a view button's down arrow (for example, the Gantt Chart button on the Task tab), and then, on the drop-down menu, choose Save View. In the Save View dialog box, make sure the "Save as a New View" option is selected. (If you haven't made any changes to the current view, you won't see this option.) In the Name box, type a name for the view, and then click OK. Project saves the view with the table, fields, filters, and groups you've applied. To update the current view with the changes you've made, select the Update Current View option, and then click OK. (If you haven't made any changes to the current view, you won't see this option.)

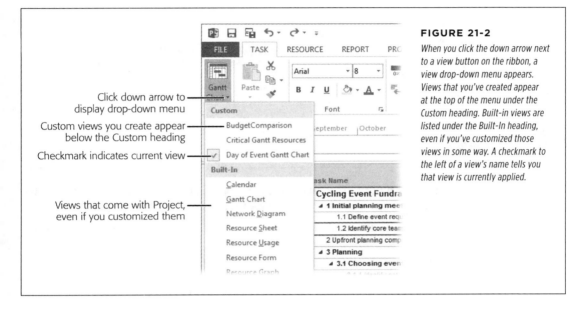

FIGURE 21-2

When you click the down arrow next to a view button on the ribbon, a view drop-down menu appears. Views that you've created appear at the top of the menu under the Custom heading. Built-in views are listed under the Built-In heading, even if you've customized those views in some way. A checkmark to the left of a view's name tells you that view is currently applied.

Click down arrow to display drop-down menu

Custom views you create appear below the Custom heading

Checkmark indicates current view

Views that come with Project, even if you customized them

■ MODIFYING A COMBINATION VIEW

Project has only a few built-in combination views, such as Task Entry and Resource Allocation. Combination views are great because they display the single views you want in both the top and Detail panes. If you create your own combination views (page 593), you can set them up to include the single views you want. (The box on page 57 explains how to change the size of each pane or to hide the Details pane.) Here are the steps for modifying a combination view:

1. **If you plan to use a single view that doesn't exist yet, create it first (as described in the next section).**

   You can't create a new single view from within the View Definition dialog box.

2. **In the View tab's Task Views or Resource Views section, click the down arrow next to any view button, and then, on the drop-down menu, choose More Views.**

   The More Views dialog box opens.

3. **In the Views list, select the combination view you want to modify, and then click Edit.**

   The View Definition dialog box opens with combination view settings, as shown in Figure 21-3.

FIGURE 21-3

When you modify a combination view, the only things you can change are the name of the view, which single views appear in the top and Details panes, and whether the combination view appears on view drop-down menus.

4. **In the Primary View box, choose the view you want in the top pane. In the Details Pane box, choose the view for the bottom (Details) pane.**

   Both drop-down lists include all available views, so you can put any view in either pane.

5. **Click OK.**

   The View Definition dialog box closes, and the view is ready to use.

Creating a New View

Most often, you create a new single view to choose the screen you want, because that's the one element you *can't* change when you edit a view. New combination views come in handy when you prefer a specific combination of views but don't want to touch the ones that Project provides.

The easiest way to create a new view, whether it's a single or a combination view, is by modifying one that already exists. You can tweak the view until it looks exactly the way you want and then save it with a new name. Here's how:

1. **Display a view that's similar to what you want.**

   For example, if you want to create a combination with Gantt Chart and Task Details Form views, click the down arrow on a view button (for example, the Task Usage button in the View tab's Task Views section), and then choose More Views. In the More Views dialog box, select Task Entry, and then click Apply.

2. **Modify the view until it looks the way you want.**

   Apply a different table (page 632), add columns to the table (page 633), apply a group (page 656), or filter the list (page 642).

3. **Click the down arrow on a view button, and then, on the drop-down menu, choose Save View.**

The Save View dialog box opens.

4. **In the Name box, type a name for the view, and then click OK.**

Project saves the view and adds it to the list of custom views in your project. The box below explains how Project saves the views you create.

NOTE If you make additional changes to this view and want to save them, click the down arrow on a view button, and then choose the Save View command again. To save the changes you've made to the current view, in the Save View dialog box, select the Update Current View option and then click OK. If you want to save this modified custom view as yet *another* new view, keep the "Save as a New View" options selected, fill in a new name, and then click OK.

UP TO SPEED

Using New Views in Other Projects

Suppose you format task bars and text in your Gantt Chart view and then save your customizations. Project stores this *modified* view in your Project file, so Gantt Chart view shows your table, formatted task bars, and text each time you open the view. If you want to use this modified Gantt Chart view in *other* Project files, you have to use the Organizer to copy it into your global template (page 702) or into another Project file.

If you want to keep Project's original views in addition to your custom versions, create a new view by copying an existing one *before* you modify it. Then you can use the original or your customized version. Bear in mind that changes in one view don't spill over into other views, which can be good or bad. The advantage to this barrier between views is that you can make scads of changes to a view without worrying about how those changes affect other views. The drawback is that you must repeat formatting in another view if you want to alter it in the same way.

In contrast to how it saves modified views, Project comes set up to automatically copy *new* views you create to the global template (whether you create them from existing views, as described on page 592, or create them from scratch, as explained on page 598), which is perfect when you work solo and don't have to worry about other people sharing your global template. However, if you and dozens of other project managers use the same global template, you may want to keep the new views you create in your file, to keep them from affecting other Project users. To change this setting, choose File→Options. In the Project Options dialog box, click Advanced. Under Display, turn off the "Automatically add new views, tables, filters, and groups to the global" checkbox. Then you have to use the Organizer to manually copy your new views to the *global.mpt* file.

Creating a new view from scratch is easy, too, although you won't see what the view looks like until you apply it. If you want to create a combination view that includes a single view that doesn't exist yet, first create the single view by following these steps once through, and then repeat these steps to create the combination view:

1. **In the View tab's Task Views or Resource Views section, click the down arrow next to any view button, and then, on the drop-down menu, choose More Views. In the More Views dialog box, click New.**

The Define New View dialog box opens.

2. **Select the "Single view" or "Combination view" option, and then click OK.**

   The View Definition dialog box opens with the settings for the type of view you selected. The Name box is filled in with a name like "*View 1.*"

3. **In the Name box, type a new name.**

   In addition to choosing a meaningful name, you can add a keyboard shortcut to open the view from the View menu, although it's quicker to choose a view from one of the ribbon's drop-down view lists. When entering the name, simply type an ampersand (&) before the letter for the shortcut, in the same way that the built-in Gantt Chart view is set to *&Gantt Chart*. For example, if you create a view named *&Critical Gantt Resources*, you can apply the view by pressing Alt to display keyboard shortcuts. Then press W to display the View tab, press G to display the Gantt Chart view drop-down menu, and finally press C (the letter after the ampersand) to display the view, as shown in Figure 21-4. (If another entry uses the same letter for its keyboard shortcut, then you need to press the letter a *second* time to access your view.)

FIGURE 21-4

When you first press the Alt key, the keyboard shortcuts for the ribbon tabs appear, like H for the Task tab and W for the View tab. Once you press a key to choose a tab, the tab keyboard shortcuts disappear, and the keyboard shortcuts for commands on the tab you chose take their place, such as G for the Gantt Chart view drop-down menu and K for the Task Usage view drop-down menu. If you press a key for a command that displays a drop-down menu, shortcut keys appear on the drop-down menu, as shown here.

4. **If you're creating a single view, then in the Screen drop-down list, choose the screen you want.**

   The Screen drop-down list includes names that look familiar: Gantt Chart, Task Usage, Calendar, and so on. Each screen represents a particular layout, like the table and task bar timescale of Gantt Chart view, and the table and tabular time-phased data of Task Usage view. (Alas, you can't create your own screens.)

5. **Choose the other settings for your view.**

From here on, the steps for creating a view are exactly the same as modifying one, as described on page 594 (for a single view) and page 597 (for a combination view). For example, for a single view, you choose the table, filter, and group you want. For a combination view, you select the single views to display in the top and Details panes.

6. **To save the view, click OK.**

Modifying a Gantt Chart View

A Gantt Chart view is a fertile field for customization. In the table area, you can apply various tables, which include columns of Project fields. The timescale displays task bars to show when tasks occur and how they relate to one another. Every component of a Gantt Chart view has its own customizing and formatting features:

- **Table.** The most obvious change is choosing a different table on the left side of the view. Within a table, you can add, remove, or rearrange columns; moreover, the columns' widths, titles, and alignments are at your command. "Changing Tables" on page 632 is your guide to all these customizations.

- **Timescale.** The timescale on the right side of the view chops the project up into time periods, which you can change to fit the length of your project or what you want to focus on. Short projects may use days, whereas months may be better for multiyear projects. You can change the timescale's units, labels, and how many different units the timescale heading holds. See "Customizing the Timescale" on page 619 for instructions. If you want to change a Gantt Chart view's timescale and Timeline view is also open (in the View tab's Split View section, turn on the Timeline checkbox), you can simply drag one of the vertical bars in Timeline view to change the date range or timescale units (page 619). Dragging the Zoom slider (page 56) when a Gantt Chart view is active also changes the timescale's date range and units.

- **Text.** Text is everywhere. You can modify text's appearance to highlight different information, like summary tasks or task bar text. You can also format only selected text. See "Formatting Text" on page 639 to learn how.

- **Task bars.** Changing formatting on different types of task bars emphasizes information. For example, you can show critical task bars in red and noncritical task bars in blue. Or perhaps you want to display different types of task bars for each baseline you've set. You can modify the appearance of a whole category of task bars or just the task bars you select. Link lines and gridlines are customizable, too. The following sections explain how to change the appearance of task bars and other lines in the timescale.

TIP With the Gantt Chart Style gallery, one click is all it takes to change the colors of tasks set to Auto Scheduled and Manually Scheduled mode. When a Gantt Chart view is active, head to the Gantt Chart Tools | Format tab's Gantt Chart Style section and click one of the color combination buttons. The top task bar on the button represents manually scheduled tasks; the bottom task bar on the button shows the color for auto-scheduled tasks. The Gantt Chart Style section displays only a few buttons at a time (the exact number depends on the size of your monitor), but you can scroll to see additional color options.

■ CHANGING THE WAY TYPES OF TASK BARS LOOK

Task bars' color, fill pattern, and shape are all customizable, like the solid red fill for critical tasks, the dotted lines you see for splits in tasks, and the narrow bars that indicate progress. Task bars can also have marks at one or both ends, like the diamond for milestone tasks and the brackets at the ends of a manually scheduled task with defined dates.

Project has two categories of task bar formatting. You can specify bar styles to format *all* task bars in a specific category, like external tasks from other projects; this section describes the steps for formatting categories of task bars. On the other hand, you might want to highlight individual tasks that have special importance, like tasks whose completion trigger payments. In that situation, you can apply formatting only to the bars you select; the next section explains how to do that (see page 604).

TIP When a Gantt Chart view is displayed, several changes to task bar appearance are available right on the ribbon. Head to the Gantt Chart Tools | Format tab's Bar Styles section, and then turn on a checkbox like Critical Tasks, Slack, or Late Tasks. If you want to choose a different set of color-coordinated task bars for auto-scheduled and manually scheduled tasks, choose the color theme you want in the Gantt Chart Style section (see the previous Tip for details).

Formatting a category of task bars is efficient because Project keeps track of the categories tasks fall into and changes their formatting if their category status changes. For example, when you're trying to shorten the schedule, you may want critical tasks' bars to appear in bright red with stars at the end. If a task falls off the critical path, the stars disappear and the color changes to that of a noncritical task. To change the look of a category of task bars, do the following:

1. **Display the Gantt Chart view whose task bars you want to format.**

   Bar styles apply only to the active view in the active project. (You can use a customized view in other projects if you copy the view to the global template, as described on page 701.) If you want task bars in another view to use the same formatting, then you have to repeat these steps for that view.

2. **In the Gantt Chart Tools | Format tab's Bar Styles section, click Format→Bar Styles. (Or double-click any working time period in the background of the Gantt Chart timescale—that is, anywhere in the timescale except on a task bar or a link line.)**

The Bar Styles dialog box opens, as shown in Figure 21-5. (If you double-click nonworking time in the timescale—for example, the gray vertical bars that represent weekend days when the timescale shows individual days—the Timescale dialog box opens to the "Non-working time" tab, presumably so you can format the appearance of nonworking time.)

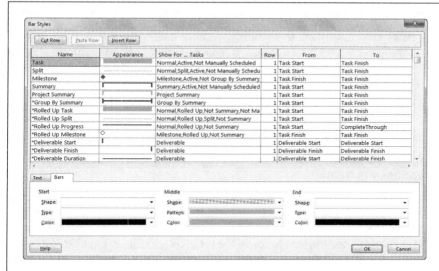

FIGURE 21-5

The table in the Bar Styles dialog box includes a row for each type of task bar in the active view. You may be surprised by the number of rows until you see that auto-scheduled tasks, manually scheduled tasks, critical tasks, progress bars, milestones, summary tasks, and so on each have their own look.

3. **In the table, select the type of task bar you want to modify, and then, in the bottom half of the dialog box, click the Bars tab.**

   The Bars tab has three sections: Start, Middle, and End. The Start and End sections define the marks that appear at the beginning and end of a task bar. You can choose a shape, color, and whether the mark is solid or outlined. The Middle section sets the appearance of the bar itself.

4. **To format the mark at one of the task bar's ends, in the Shape drop-down list (in either the Start or End section), select a shape.**

   Your choices include some exciting geometric shapes: the familiar milestone diamond, various arrows, and even a star. The Shape drop-down list includes shapes for manually scheduled tasks, like the brackets that indicate that a task has a start or a finish date and the shaded ends that depict missing dates. Task bars don't *have* to have marks at the ends, so you can leave the Start and End boxes empty. To remove a mark, at the top of the Shape drop-down list, select the empty entry.

If you choose a mark, Project initially fills in the Type box with Solid, which is usually the best choice, because it makes small marks more visible. You can also choose Dashed or Framed. If you want a color other than black, you can choose it from the Color drop-down list. Try several colors until you find one that looks good. Darker colors are better, because bright colors like lime and yellow disappear into the white background.

5. **To format the bar, in the Middle section, choose the bar shape you want.**

    Bars can be wide, medium, or narrow, just like men's ties. When bars aren't full height, you can choose a position at the top, middle, or bottom of the task bar row. For example, regular and critical tasks are usually full height, progress bars are narrow bars in the middle, and slack is a narrow bar at the bottom.

    Because narrow task bars take up less space, you can display more than one in the same task row. That's how the Multiple Baselines Gantt view (page 384) shows three baselines in the same row.

6. **To apply a pattern and/or color to a bar, in the Middle section, choose the options you want.**

    Most task bars start with a solid pattern, although some tasks bar styles use other patterns, like the vertical hatching for splits in tasks. To emphasize task bars or to print a schedule on a black-and-white printer, use crosshatch patterns. Test colors to see how they look in the timescale. In the dialog box's table, the Appearance cell to the right of the task bar's name previews your masterpiece.

7. **To format a different type of task bar, select it in the table, and then repeat steps 4–6. When you're done, click OK.**

    The dialog box closes, and the new formatting appears in the view.

■ CHANGING THE WAY SELECTED TASK BARS LOOK

To change the look of individual task bars (for example, to change several sign-off meetings to purple bars), you format the *bars themselves*, not bar *styles*. Here's how:

1. **Select the tasks whose bars you want to format, and then in the Gantt Chart Tools | Format tab's Bar Styles section, choose Format→Bar. To format a single bar, double-click it in the timescale.**

    The Format Bar dialog box opens to the Bar Shape tab, which has the familiar Start, Middle, and End sections with the same options that are available for bar styles (page 602).

2. **Pick the shapes, styles, pattern, and colors you want.**

    The preview appears at the bottom of the dialog box. (The background isn't white, though, so you can't accurately judge colors until you see them in the view.)

3. **Click OK.**

    The dialog box closes, and the selected bars sport their new look.

TIP If all you want to change about a task bar is its color, you can do that from the task bar mini-toolbar. Right-click the task bar you want to change. On the mini-toolbar that appears above the task bar, click the Bar Color down arrow, and then choose the color you want. Attractive color-coordinated shades appear under the Theme Colors heading; basic colors appear in a row under the Standard Colors heading—or click More Colors to pick the exact hue you want.

■ CHANGING TASK BAR TEXT

Project lets you attach fields to task bars so you can see key information right in the timescale. For example, displaying the initials of people assigned to tasks lets you see resources without checking the form in the Details pane. And adding dates to milestones emphasizes key dates.

Working with text on task bars is similar to working with the task bars themselves. You can specify the fields to display for a whole category of task bars, or assign fields to selected task bars. Actually, you can customize a task bar *and* its text at the same time, because the two tabs in the Bar Styles (and Format Bar) dialog box offer bar and text formatting options.

To display fields as text for a category of task bars, follow these steps:

1. **Display the Gantt Chart view whose task bars you want to format.**

   Bar styles that you customize or create apply only to the active view in the active project. If you want task bars in another view to use the same formatting, then you have to repeat these steps for that view.

2. **Go to the Gantt Chart Tools | Format tab's Bar Styles section, and choose Format→Bar Styles or double-click any working time period in the background of the Gantt Chart timescale (that is, anywhere in the timescale *except* on a task bar or a link line).**

   The Bar Styles dialog box opens.

3. **In the Bar Styles dialog box's table, click anywhere in the row for the type of task bar you want to work on, like Critical, and then click the Text tab.**

   The Text tab displays fields already associated with the selected task bar type. Task bars have five places for text (although using them all makes the bars almost unreadable): left, right, top, bottom, and inside the bar.

4. **Click the cell to the right of a position label, like the cell next to the Right label to add the finish date to the right end of the task bar. Click the cell's down arrow, and then choose the field to display at that position, as shown in Figure 21-6.**

   Repeat this step to add fields at other positions. To remove a field, select the position box (Left, Right, or whatever), and then press Backspace.

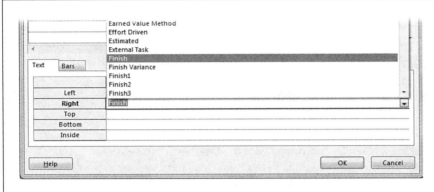

FIGURE 21-6

The Start field obviously belongs on the left end of a task bar, and the Finish field belongs on the right. A field like % Complete or % Work Complete could go on the top, bottom, or even inside the bar, because the central position conveys progress.

5. **To add fields to another type of task bar, repeat steps 3 and 4. When you're done, click OK.**

    The Bar Styles dialog box closes, and task bars that fall in the categories you changed now show values.

> **TIP** You may want to add fields to *individual* task bars—for example, to show the finish dates for a few key tasks. To do that, select the tasks you want to format (Ctrl-click anywhere in their rows in the view's table), and then in the Gantt Chart Tools | Format tab's Bar Styles section, click Format→Bar. On the Text tab, choose the fields you want, and then click OK.

■ DESIGNING YOUR OWN TASK BAR STYLE

Project views usually have several different task bar styles already defined. For example, Detail Gantt view includes task bars for regular tasks, critical tasks, progress, milestones, slack, slippage, summary tasks, and more. But suppose you want a new type of task bar—for example, to highlight tasks added for change requests and flagged with the Flag1 field.

Designing a new task bar style involves more choices than modifying existing ones. You have to tell Project when to use the style and the dates to start and end the bar. To show off your creativity with a custom task bar, follow these steps:

1. **Display the Gantt Chart view whose task bars you want to format.**

    Your task bar work of art applies *only* to the active view in the active project—unless you copy the view to the global template or another file (page 701).

2. **In the Gantt Chart Tools | Format tab's Bar Styles section, click Format→Bar Styles or double-click any working time period in the background of the Gantt Chart timescale.**

The Bar Styles dialog box opens.

3. **Scroll down the dialog box's table, and then, in the first blank row, click the Name cell.**

If you want to base a new style on an existing one, you might be disappointed when you notice there's no Copy Row button. But you can fake it. Select the task bar style you want to copy, and then click Cut Row. The task bar style disappears from the table, but don't worry. Before you do anything else, click Paste Row to insert the row back into the table. Now click anywhere in the row below where you want the copy, and then click Paste Row again. The copied row appears above the row you selected, and you can modify it.

TIP To insert a new task bar style in the middle of the list instead, select the row below where you want to insert the new row, and then click Insert Row. Project adds a blank row above the selected row. (The box on page 609 explains why you might want to do this.)

---

4. **In the Name field, type a name for your task bar style.**

Make the name meaningful. For example, if you're creating a task bar style for change request tasks, you might name it ChangeRequestFlag or simply ChangeRequest.

5. **To tell Project which tasks it should apply the style to, select the style's Show For...Tasks cell.**

Click the cell's down arrow, and then choose the category of task to which this style applies, as illustrated in Figure 21-7. For example, choose Flag1 if the Flag1 field is your change-request indicator. (In this example, Project would use the style for a task bar if the task's Flag1 field equals Yes for both active and inactive tasks.) The Show For...Tasks drop-down menu includes useful choices like Critical, Noncritical, In Progress, Not Started, Not Finished, and so on. And, as Figure 21-7 explains, you can select more than one item in the Show For...Tasks menu to create styles for very specific situations.

A bar style can also apply when a condition *isn't* true. Suppose you create a task bar style for active change requests. The combination "Active, Flag1" tells Project to use the style for *active* tasks with Flag1 set to Yes; the style wouldn't be applied to *inactive* tasks with Flag1 set to Yes. For change-request tasks that have been inactivated (page 364), choose "Not Active, Flag1." (You have to type the *Not* for these combinations.)

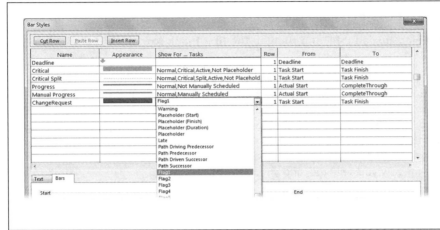

FIGURE 21-7

Sometimes, a style applies to more than one condition in the drop-down list, like active tasks with the change-request flag turned on. To combine multiple conditions, choose the first one in the drop-down list. Without closing the list, type a comma, and then choose the second condition. Rinse and repeat to add more conditions.

6. **In the From and To columns, choose the date fields that specify when the task bar starts and ends.**

   For many task bars, the choices are easy: Choose "Start" in the From cell and "Finish" in the To cell to draw the task bar from the task's start date to its finish date. But other types of task bars use different dates. For example, a progress bar goes from the task's Start date to its Complete Through date. And slippage runs from the task's Baseline Start date to its Start date, to show how far the start has slipped.

7. **On the Bars tab and Text tab, select the settings for the bar style and any fields you want to attach to the task bar.**

   See page 609 and page 639 for formatting bars and fields, respectively.

8. **To add more bar styles, repeat steps 3–7. When you're done, click OK.**

   Custom bar styles have a way of multiplying. For example, if you create a bar style for flagged tasks, you usually want another style for flagged milestones, and possibly flagged critical tasks. Simply repeat the steps in this list to create additional styles.

Task Bars Are Missing

Project draws task bars in the timescale in the order they appear in the Bar Styles dialog box's table. Full-height task bars obscure narrow task bars drawn earlier, so that's why the Progress task bar style follows the Task style in the table. Otherwise, the progress bar would be hidden by the task whose progress it reports.

To make sure you can see all your task bars, you have to order task bar styles in the Bar Styles table with the same amount of care you use for the seating arrangements at a dysfunctional family reunion. To move a task bar style to another location, do the following:

1. Click anywhere in the row you want to move, and then click Cut Row. The row disappears from the table.

2. Select the row below where you want to place the cut row.

3. Click Paste Row. The new row appears above the selected row.

■ STACKING MORE THAN ONE TASK BAR IN THE SAME SPACE

While defining a new task bar style, you may have noticed the Bar Styles dialog box's Row column, which usually contains the number 1. This setting is the key to displaying more than one row in the timescale for each task. For example, Tracking Gantt view uses narrow bars to show the baseline and current task bars in the same row, but if you'd rather use *full-height* task bars for each, then you can include current task bars on the first row and baseline task bars on the second row. Here's how it's done:

1. **Open the Gantt Chart view that you want to modify, and then in the Gantt Chart Tools | Format tab's Bar Styles section, click Format→Bar Styles.**

   The Bar Styles dialog box opens.

2. **To create another task bar style, either insert a new row or copy one of the existing task bar styles.**

   To insert a new row, click anywhere in the row below the new row, and then click Insert Row.

   To copy an existing style, select the row you want to copy, and then click Cut Row. Next, click Paste Row once to reinsert the original style. Then select the row below where you want to copy the row, and click Paste Row again to insert the copy.

3. **In the new or copied row, change the Name field—for example to Task Baseline.**

   Use the Bars tab and Text tab to define the bar's appearance and text that surrounds it. For example, you might use a full-height task bar with blue diagonal lines for the baseline.

4. **In the style's Row cell, type *2*.**

   Project adds a second row to the timescale for each task, as shown in Figure 21-8.

5. **Repeat steps 2–4 to add other rows (up to four), or click OK to close the dialog box.**

   The rows in the table double (or triple, or *quadruple*, depending on your settings) their height, and the new bars appear for the tasks that meet the new task bar style's conditions.

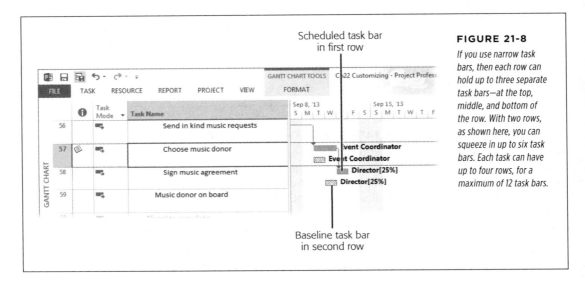

Scheduled task bar
in first row

Baseline task bar
in second row

FIGURE 21-8

If you use narrow task bars, then each row can hold up to three separate task bars—at the top, middle, and bottom of the row. With two rows, as shown here, you can squeeze in up to six task bars. Each task can have up to four rows, for a maximum of 12 task bars.

■ CHANGING THE LAYOUT OF TASK BARS

You've probably struggled to follow link lines between predecessor and successor tasks. Even simple projects can look like a bowl of tangled spaghetti. You can modify the layout of task bars in the timescale to clear up clutter or improve readability. In addition to tweaking the appearance of link lines, you can change the height of task bars, roll up task bars from subtasks to summary tasks, and change the date format. To reach these layout options, in the Gantt Chart Tools | Format tab's Format section, click Layout. Then adjust any or all of the Layout dialog box's settings:

- **Link lines.** The Links section has three link-line options (see Figure 21-9): completely hidden, an S, or an L.

- **Task bar date format.** The "Date format" box sets the date format only for task bars. It's best to choose an abbreviated format (like 1/28), and leave the full dates to table columns.

- **Task bar height.** With bar styles and bar formatting, you can choose task bars that are thin, medium, or full height. "Bar height" defines what that full height is; 12 is the standard. You can vary the height from 6 to 24.

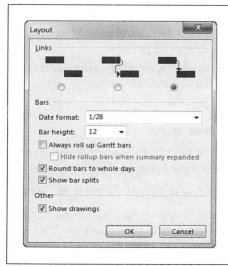

FIGURE 21-9

The S shape is best for visually separating link lines, and the L shape doesn't clutter the diagram as much. For the cleanest look, hide the links completely by selecting the first Links option.

- **Roll up task bars to summary tasks.** You know that summary tasks roll up field values like cost and work. The "Always roll up Gantt bars" checkbox is different; turning it on shows subtasks and milestones on summary task bars. But these roll-ups get messy fast. That's why, when the "Always roll up Gantt bars" checkbox is turned on, you can also turn on the "Hide rollup bars when summary expanded" checkbox. This hides the roll-up bars whenever the subtasks are visible and shows roll-up bars only when subtasks are hidden.

- **Round bars to whole days.** Initially, Project draws task bars that represent the task's *exact* duration, so very short tasks practically disappear when the timescale is set to weeks or months. Turn on the "Round bars to whole days" checkbox to round out durations in the timescale to whole days. (Project still keeps durations in the *table area* exact.)

- **Show splits.** Project chops up task bars into pieces if they contain *splits* (small delays between working times). Most of the time, you want to see splits. But if they become too distracting, then turn off the "Show bar splits" checkbox, and Project draws the task bars as solid lines.

- **Show drawing shapes.** If you use Drawing commands (click the down arrow in the Gantt Chart Tools | Format tab's Drawing section) to add shapes or text to the timescale, you can hide those shapes by turning off the "Show drawings" checkbox.

■ CHANGING HOW GRIDLINES LOOK

Even the gridlines that separate table, timescale, and column-heading elements are customizable. For example, you can change the color of the lines that show the project's start date and the current date. And although the timescale doesn't draw lines between task bar rows initially, you can add them to make it easier to correlate bars to rows in the table. To format gridlines, follow these steps:

1. **Display the Gantt Chart view you want to modify, and then in the Gantt Chart Tools | Format tab's Format section, click Gridlines→Gridlines.**

   The Gridlines dialog box opens.

2. **In the "Line to change" list, choose a type of line.**

   The "Line to change" list includes categories like Sheet Rows and Sheet Columns for the table, and categories like Gantt Rows and Current Date for the timescale.

3. **In the Type drop-down list, choose the line style and the color you want.**

   For example, to show the current date as a bright-blue line, in the "Line to change" drop-down list, select Current Date. Next, in the Type drop-down list, choose the solid line, and then, in the Color drop-down list, choose blue. You can choose from solid, dotted, short-dashed, and long-dashed lines. To remove a line, choose the white entry at the top of the list.

4. **To draw lines at intervals—for instance, after every third row in the table—in the "At interval" section, select the option you want.**

   If the interval is larger than 4, select the Other option, and then type the number in the box. When you use intervals, select the line style and color for the intervals.

5. **If you want to format another gridline, repeat steps 2–4.**

   When you're done, click OK.

■ FAST FORMATTING WITH THE GANTT CHART WIZARD

Project puts the commands for common formatting tweaks right on the ribbon—like the Critical Tasks checkbox, which automatically changes critical tasks to red. When you want to format the Gantt Chart to exacting specifications, you can work through the Bar Styles, Text Styles, and Layout dialog boxes one by one. But if you're looking for a quick way to apply *several* types of basic Gantt Chart formatting, the Gantt Chart Wizard could be the answer.

The Gantt Chart Wizard lets you do things like show the critical path or baseline information, display text on task bars, and hide or show link lines. Here's how to use it:

1. **Display the Gantt Chart view you want to format.**

   The Gantt Chart Wizard makes changes to the view definition (page 594) as if you were doing the work yourself. To keep the current view definition, make a copy of the view (page 385) before starting the wizard, and make your changes to the copy rather than the original.

2. **Add the Gantt Chart Wizard to the Quick Access toolbar.**

Click the down arrow to the right of the Quick Access toolbar, and then choose More Commands. In the Project Options dialog box, in the "Choose commands from" drop-down list, choose "Commands Not in the Ribbon." Then, in the list below that, select Gantt Chart Wizard, and then click Add. Click OK to close the Project Options dialog box.

3. **In the Quick Access toolbar, click the Gantt Chart Wizard icon (it looks like some task bars with a wizard's wand above them). On the wizard's first screen, click Next.**

The first screen simply describes what the wizard does.

4. **Select the option corresponding to the task bars you want to see and what you want them to look like, and then click Next.**

Standard is selected initially, and it shows blue task bars. "Critical path" changes critical tasks to red. The Baseline option shows the baseline as a narrow gray bar with the current schedule as a narrow blue bar below it. The Other option lets you pick alternative bar styles. If you select the Custom Gantt Chart option, the wizard steps you through several additional screens so you can specify formatting for critical tasks, noncritical tasks, summary tasks, milestones, and additional task bars like baseline or slack.

5. **Select the option for the fields you want on the task bars, and then click Next.**

You can show no text at all, dates, resources, or both. Select the None option, and the wizard removes all the fields from the types of task bars you selected in the previous step. If you select the "Custom task information" option, then the wizard lets you pick the fields you want.

6. **Keep the Yes option selected to show link lines, or choose No to hide them. Then click Next or Finish (they both take you to the Format It screen).**

7. **On the last page, click Format It, and then click Exit Wizard.**

The box on the left side of the screen is a preview of what your Gantt Chart will look like. If it's not what you want, click Back to get to the appropriate page, and then select different options.

When you exit the wizard, the view shows the new formatting.

Customizing the Timescale

Views like Gantt Chart view and Task Usage view have a timescale on the right side, which shows information over time. Because of this timescale, Gantt Chart task bars lengthen or shorten depending on their duration. In a usage view, each column of the grid is a time period, so you can see work or cost per day, per week, and so on.

NOTE Like other view customizations, timescale modifications apply only to the active view. They appear every time you use the view, but you have to repeat the changes to see them in other views.

Time units are the part of the timescale you change most frequently. For long projects, units like weeks or months squeeze more onto the screen. For short projects, units like days are better so the task bars don't look scrawny. And sometimes you might switch from months to weeks to focus on issues in part of a long project. You can customize other aspects of the timescale—for example, choosing the time period labels and their alignment, or shrinking or expanding columns to specific dimensions. A view can show up to three tiers of units in the heading area—for instance, to show the year on the top, then months, and finally weeks; or to show the fiscal year, and then fiscal quarters.

TIP To change time units quickly, drag the Zoom slider on the status bar at the bottom right of the window. Or, in the View tab's Zoom section, click the down arrow to the right of the Timescale box, and then choose the time units you want to display, which range from hours up to years.

To format the timescale, follow these steps:

1. **Display a view like a Gantt Chart view, usage view, or Resource Graph view.**

   The view displays a timescale on the right side.

2. **Double-click the timescale heading (or right-click the timescale heading, and then, on the shortcut menu, choose Timescale).**

   Either way, the Timescale dialog box opens, as shown in Figure 21-10.

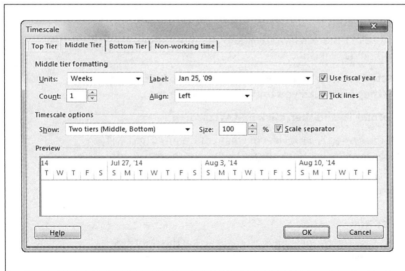

FIGURE 21-10

The Timescale dialog box has four tabs: one for each tier of units that can be displayed at the top of the timescale, and the fourth for non-working time. The Middle Tier tab is selected initially. To change the number of tiers, under "Timescale options," choose a number in the Show drop-down list. When you choose two tiers, the timescale show the middle and bottom tier; if you choose one tier, it shows only the middle tier.

3. **Select the tab for the tier you want to format.**

   The top, middle, and bottom tiers have the same settings: units, unit label, alignment, and so on.

The "Non-working time" tab controls how nonworking time *looks* on the timescale; it doesn't change the nonworking time itself. (See page 113 to learn about defining working and nonworking time in project and resource calendars.) Nonworking time starts as gray shading behind task bars. You can change that color and pattern, which calendar the nonworking time comes from, and whether to hide nonworking time or to draw it in front of task bars.

4. **In the Units box, choose the time unit you want to use for the selected tier.**

   For the middle tier, typical units are weeks or months. The top tier may be months or years, while the bottom tier may be days or weeks. Choose units that work with the length of your project. Keep in mind that the units for a lower tier must be shorter than the units of the tier above it. So if the bottom tier is days, for example, the middle tier must be at least weeks.

   If you track your project by an interval other than a single time unit, choose the number in the Count box. For example, a Count equal to 2 and units set to weeks would change the timescale units to 2-week intervals.

5. **Change how the tier label looks by choosing one of the formats in the Label box.**

   The formats you see depend on the units you choose. For example, formats for weeks include the robust "Sun January 23, 2009" as well as the most concise "23" (which is the first day of that week). Don't worry about the sample format showing a year in the past; the actual timescale labels show the correct year. Quarter formats include "1st Quarter," "Q1," and "Q1, Q2, Q3, Q4,...(From Start)," which numbers quarters sequentially from the project's start date.

6. **To position the label within its tier, in the Align drop-down list, choose Left, Center, or Right.**

   When the "Tick lines" checkbox is turned on, vertical lines appear between each period in a timescale tier.

7. **To display the *fiscal year* instead of the calendar year, turn on the "Use fiscal year" checkbox.**

   You set the fiscal year in the Project Options dialog box (page 687). For example, if the starting month is June and the calendar year in which the fiscal year *starts* denotes the fiscal year, then June 2013 is fiscal year 2013. However, if the fiscal year is based on the *ending* calendar year, June 2013 represents the beginning of fiscal year 2014, because the fiscal year ends in calendar year 2014.

8. **If you use more than one tier, repeat steps 3–7 to format the other tiers.**

9. **If necessary, adjust the settings in the "Timescale options" section.**

   Although the "Timescale options" section is below the tier-formatting section, the timescale options apply to all tiers, so you have to adjust them on only one tab.

If the headings in the Preview section are scrunched up (check the preview at the bottom of the dialog box), then increase the percentage in the Size box. The Size box is like zooming: Increasing the percentage from 75% to 100% stretches each time unit out, which is helpful when task bars are too skinny. If you see pound symbols (#) instead of values in a usage view, increase the percentage until the values appear. Decreasing the percentage squeezes the periods together to fit more duration on the screen.

Keep the "Scale separator" checkbox turned on to draw horizontal lines between each tier.

10. **When you're finished, click OK.**

    The dialog box closes, and your changes appear in the timescale.

Changing a Usage View's Appearance

Usage views like Task Usage and Resource Usage have a table on the left and a timescale on the right, both of which you can customize. Unlike the timescale in a Gantt Chart view, the usage timescale is a grid in which each column represents one time unit, like a day or week, and each row represents an assignment or a summary row. This presentation is known as *time-phased data*.

NOTE This section describes how to choose which fields appear in a usage view's timescale and how to format their values. The box on page 619 describes a shortcut for changing the width of columns in the usage timescale. See other sections in this chapter for info on customizing usage views' table (page 632), text (page 639), and timescale settings (page 613).

To choose fields to show in a usage view, follow these steps:

1. **Display a usage view like Task Usage or Resource Usage.**

    Remember, the changes you make apply only to the active view in the active project unless you copy the custom view to your global template (page 698).

2. **In the timescale grid, right-click any cell, and then, on the shortcut menu, choose Detail Styles, as shown in Figure 21-11.**

    The Detail Styles dialog box opens. (If you right-click the timescale *heading* instead of the grid, then you see a shortcut menu for formatting the timescale heading and changing working time.)

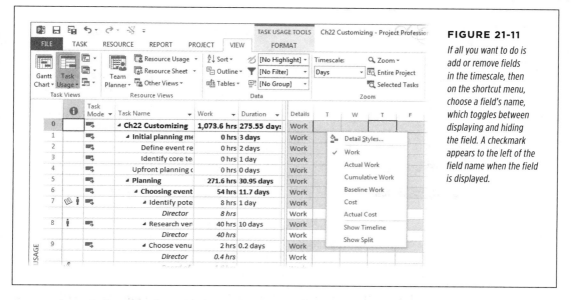

FIGURE 21-11

If all you want to do is add or remove fields in the timescale, then on the shortcut menu, choose a field's name, which toggles between displaying and hiding the field. A checkmark appears to the left of the field name when the field is displayed.

3. **In the Detail Styles dialog box, select the Usage Details tab, if necessary.**

   This tab includes a list of fields you can add to the timescale: work fields, cost fields, allocation, performance measures like CV, and so on.

4. **To add a field to the timescale, in the "Available fields" list, click the field's name, and then click Show.**

   The field jumps to the "Show these fields" list, as illustrated in Figure 21-12, and Project adds a new row for the field to each assignment.

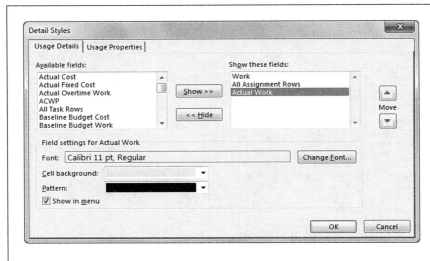

FIGURE 21-12

To add more than one field, Ctrl-click each field's name in the "Available fields list," and then click Show. Remove a field by selecting it in the "Show these fields" list and then clicking Hide. You can rearrange the order of the fields by selecting a field in the "Show these fields" list, and then clicking the Move up or down arrows.

5. **To format the timescale cells for a field, click the field name in the "Show these fields" list, and then change the settings in the dialog box's bottom half.**

   The built-in views use a light-gray background for the task or resource summary rows. The assignment rows have a white background. You can choose a different font, background color, or background pattern. If you want the field to be listed on the shortcut menu that appears when you right-click a cell in the timescale grid, turn on the "Show in menu" checkbox. That way, you can easily turn the field on or off simply by choosing it on the shortcut menu.

6. **If you want to format the view's column headers and detail data, select the Usage Properties tab, and then choose the settings you want.**

   Typically, these settings are fine as they are. The "Align details data" box controls whether values in cells are aligned to the left, center, or right. When "Display details header column" is set to Yes, the timescale starts with a column that shows the field names for each row. (Changing this box to No isn't a good idea, because it means you have to remember which row is which when you type or review values.) The "Repeat details header on all assignment rows" checkbox is turned on initially so that each row has a header. The "Display short detail header names" checkbox is turned on to abbreviate field names so that the first column is as narrow as possible.

7. **Click OK.**

   The dialog box closes, and the changes you made appear in the timescale.

Quickly Change Column Widths

Because usage values often include decimal numbers, the timescale columns may display pound symbols (#) because the numbers don't fit. You can format the timescale to increase the size of the columns (page 631), but it's faster to drag to make the columns wider. Move the pointer between two column headings in the timescale. When the pointer changes to a two-headed arrow, drag to the right until the column is wide enough for values. To make the columns narrower, drag to the left.

If a combination view has timescales in the top and bottom panes, then changing the column width in one pane changes the column width in the other pane, too. For example, if you display Task Usage view in the top pane and Resource Graph view in the Details pane, dragging a column's edge in either pane adjusts the column's width in both so the views stay in sync.

Customizing the Timeline

Timeline view is a great way to summarize what's going on in a project, whether you want to sum up when project phases start and finish, highlight crucial milestones, or keep an eye on an important task that's delayed. In addition, Timeline view makes it easy to share high-level project information with others, because you can copy what you see in this view to an email message or to another program. And Timeline view can control the timeframe shown in a Gantt Chart view's timescale.

Like other Project views, Timeline view has its own set of customization tools. You can drag its vertical bars to change the timescale dates and scale. By adding tasks to the timeline, you can emphasize key tasks—such as payment milestones or critical tasks—in a simple linear diagram. This section describes how to add tasks to the view's timeline, change how tasks look on it, and adjust the information that appears in them.

To display Timeline view, head to the View tab's Split View section and turn on the Timeline checkbox. To work with or customize the timeline, click the Timeline pane and then click the Timeline Tools | Format tab, shown in Figure 21-13.

TIP After you get the timeline just so, you can copy it to share with others. In the Timeline Tools | Format tab's Copy section, click Copy Timeline, and then choose how you want to share the timeline—for example, by email or pasting it into another program. Project places the timeline on the Clipboard, so you can paste it into an email message, Word document, PowerPoint slide, or another program file.

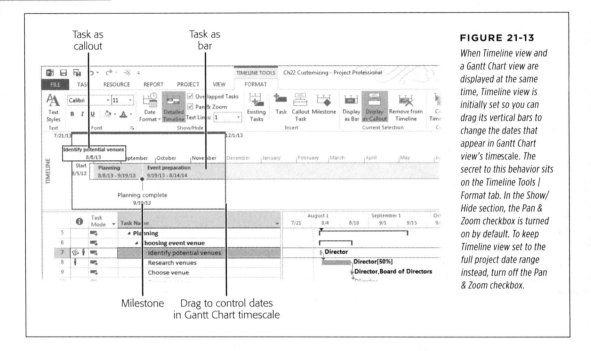

FIGURE 21-13

When Timeline view and a Gantt Chart view are displayed at the same time, Timeline view is initially set so you can drag its vertical bars to change the dates that appear in Gantt Chart view's timescale. The secret to this behavior sits on the Timeline Tools | Format tab. In the Show/Hide section, the Pan & Zoom checkbox is turned on by default. To keep Timeline view set to the full project date range instead, turn off the Pan & Zoom checkbox.

NOTE You have to choose between displaying Timeline view *or* the Details pane (the bottom pane of a combination view). To display Timeline view, in the View tab's Split View section, turn on the Timeline checkbox. If you turn on the Details checkbox there, Project automatically turns *off* the Timeline checkbox, and vice versa.

■ ADDING TASKS TO THE TIMELINE

Work tasks, summary tasks, and milestones are all fair game for Timeline view. You can add tasks to the timeline in several ways:

- **Right-click a task.** In any task-oriented view, like Gantt Chart or Task Usage, right-click a task's Name cell, and then choose "Add to Timeline" on the shortcut menu that appears.

- **Drag a task to the timeline.** In any task-oriented view, click a task's ID cell (in the leftmost column of the table). When the pointer changes to a four-headed arrow, drag it to the timeline.

- **Add existing tasks.** In the Timeline Tools | Format tab's Insert section, click Existing Tasks. In the "Add Tasks to Timeline" dialog box that appears, turn on the checkboxes for the tasks you want to add to the timeline.

- **Insert a new task.** In the Timeline Tools | Format tab's Insert section, click Task to insert a new task as a task bar in Timeline view; click Callout Task to insert a new task as a *callout* (explained in the next section); or click Milestone to insert a new milestone. When you click any of these buttons, the Task Information dialog box opens so you can name the task, set its start and finish dates, or specify other task information.

NOTE Although you can add a manually scheduled task to the timeline, the task appears only if it has at least one specified date. If it has only one date (start or finish), it appears as a milestone; if it has both a start *and* a finish date, it appears as a task bar.

■ CHANGING THE APPEARANCE OF TASKS ON THE TIMELINE

Timeline view can display tasks as task bars or as callouts (Figure 21-13 shows an example of each). Task bars are useful for displaying tasks with long durations, like the summary tasks for project phases. Callouts make it easier to see tasks with short durations' like milestones, and are also helpful for displaying several tasks that occur at the same time.

In addition to choosing between task bars and callouts, you can also customize the appearance of text and dates in the timeline. Here's how to format the appearance of tasks on the timeline:

- **Display a task as a bar or callout.** When you select a task in the timeline, the Timeline Tools | Format tab's Current Selection section highlights the button that represents the task's current appearance: "Display as Bar" or "Display as Callout." To change a task from a bar to a callout, click "Display as Callout"; to change a callout to a bar, click "Display as Bar." (To remove a task from the timeline, choose "Remove from Timeline.")

- **Format text styles.** You can modify the appearance of different categories of timeline text just as you can in other views. In the Timeline Tools | Format tab's Text section, click Text Styles. Page 639 provides the full scoop on formatting text styles.

- **Format text.** Any text in the timeline is fair game for unique formatting. For example, you may want deliverable milestones to stand out with bold green text. Right-click the text you want to format, and then choose formatting commands from the mini-toolbar that appears. Or select the text, and then in the Timeline Tools | Format tab's Font section, click the settings you want to adjust. Either way, you can change the text's font size, color, formatting (bold or italic), and background color (page 639).

■ CUSTOMIZING THE INFO ON THE TIMELINE

You can also control the *amount* of information you see in Timeline view. For example, you might opt to keep the date format short and sweet, or to hide task names and dates. If you add lots of tasks to the timeline, you can choose how many lines of text appear in task bars and whether you want to see tasks that overlap. Your options all reside in the Timeline Tools | Format tab's Show/Hide section:

- **Format dates.** Click the Date Format down arrow, and then choose a date format for the timeline. The choices are the same ones you can choose in Project Options (choose File→Options; in the Project Options dialog box, click General, and then click the "Date format" down arrow). When space is at a premium, use abbreviated formats like 1/28. For more detail, choose a format like Wed Jan 28, '09 (that's right—the format example in Project is based on the year 2009). At the bottom of the Date Format drop-down menu, you can turn the checkmarks on or off to show or hide task dates, today's date, and timescale dates.

- **Show timeline details.** For tasks you add to the timeline, click Detailed Timeline to toggle between showing only bars and showing bars that contain the tasks' names and dates.

- **Show tasks that overlap.** Turn on the Overlapped Tasks checkbox if you want to see *all* the tasks added to the timeline, even if they overlap date-wise (Project adds rows to the timeline to show more tasks on the same dates). If you turn this checkbox off, the timeline shows only the first task for a set of dates.

- **Set the number of text lines in task bars.** In the Text Lines drop-down list, choose the number of lines of text you want to see in tasks you add to the timeline. Initially, only one line of text appears. For longer task names, choose 2 or 3. Although you can choose up to 10 lines of text, keep in mind that larger values mean the timeline takes up more room on the screen.

Customizing Team Planner View

Team Planner view (page 241) is resource-centric: It contains a row (also known as a *swim lane*) for each resource and, in that same row, shows the tasks to which the resource is assigned. To change the appearance of Team Planner view, display the view and then click the Team Planner Tools | Format tab. Many of the formatting options should be familiar: You can format text styles and change the appearance of different types of tasks. However, Team Planner view has a few unique formatting options. Here are your choices on the Team Planner Tools | Format tab:

- **Show parent tasks.** Team Planner view starts out showing *all* subtasks, which means that each bar in the view shows the name of the actual task. To see a summary of your project, in the tab's Format section, click Roll-Up, and then choose the outline level you want to see. That way, instead of the subtask names, bars show the parent task names for the outline level you specify.

- **Format gridlines and text.** In the tab's Format section, click Gridlines, Text Styles, or enter the number of lines of text you want the view to display in task bars. (See page 639 for the lowdown on text styles and page 612 for info on formatting gridlines.)

- **Format task bars.** The Styles section of the tab has commands for formatting categories of tasks. You can change the border color and fill color for auto-scheduled, manually scheduled, external, and late tasks. You can also specify how to display the actual work that's been done.

- **Prevent Overallocations.** Confusingly, the Prevent Overallocations button appears on this tab. When you turn on Prevent Overallocations and assign a task to a resource whose time is already fully allocated for those days, Project automatically moves the task to the resource's next available time. If you turn this setting off and assign a task to a resource who's already fully allocated for those days, Project leaves the task where you placed it and draws red brackets around the overallocated sections of task bars. See the box on page 245 to get the full scoop on the Prevent Overallocations command.

- **Expand resource rows.** This checkbox is turned on initially, which tells Project to expand a resource's row if you assign multiple tasks to the resource during the same timeframe. If you turn the checkbox off, you see only the first assigned task for those days.

- **Show unassigned tasks.** This checkbox is turned on initially, which is what you want. That way, the view's bottom pane shows tasks that aren't assigned to specific resources, so it's easy to see which tasks still need resources.

- **Show unscheduled tasks.** This checkbox is also turned on initially, so that manu-ally scheduled tasks without dates appear in the Unscheduled Tasks column. That makes it easy to see which tasks need additional information.

Customizing Resource Graph View

Resource Graph view (View→Other Views→Resource Graph) is a bar graph of re-source data by time period. Although the bars in Resource Graph view are vertical, the right side of the view is still a timescale with values indicated by the height of the bars. Choosing fields to include in Resource Graph view, shown in Figure 21-14, is similar to choosing fields in a usage view. As in a Gantt Chart view, you can change the appearance of bars and categories of text. The following sections explain your options.

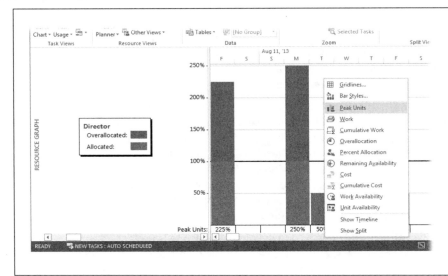

FIGURE 21-14

Resource Graph view has a few formatting limitations. For example, you can't format individual bars and text, and you can pick fields only from the fixed list that Resource Graph view offers.

■ CHOOSING FIELDS TO DISPLAY

To choose fields in Resource Graph view, right-click the background of the view's timescale, and then, on the shortcut menu, choose the field name. (You can also head to the Resource Graph Tools | Format tab and choose the fields in the Graph drop-down list.) Here's what each field represents (listed here in the order they appear in the shortcut menu):

- **Peak Units.** The highest percentage of units assigned to a resource during a period on the graph. Units higher than the resource's maximum units appear as an overallocation (in red by default). See page 253 to learn more about how the Peak field works.

- **Work.** The hours assigned to a resource during a period. If the assigned hours are more than the resource's total available hours (based on maximum units *and* the resource calendar), the excess hours show up as overallocated.

- **Cumulative Work.** The total work assigned to the resource since the beginning of the project.

- **Overallocation.** The hours that the resource is overallocated during the period.

- **Percent Allocation.** The work assigned as a percentage of the resource's available time.

- **Remaining Availability.** The resource's available hours that haven't been as-signed. This field is helpful for finding someone with available time who can pitch in on assignments.

- **Cost.** The total of the labor cost and per-use cost for the resource during the period.

- **Cumulative Cost.** The total cost for the resource since the beginning of the project.

- **Work Availability.** A resource's total available hours based on its maximum units and resource calendar. (Unlike Remaining Availability, this field *doesn't* subtract hours from existing assignments.)

- **Unit Availability.** This field is Work Availability as a percentage.

■ CHANGING THE WAY RESOURCE GRAPH BARS LOOK

The Bar Styles dialog box for Resource Graph view contains boxes for formatting each type of bar, but the information that the bars represent changes depending on the information you choose to display in Resource Graph view itself. For example, if the graph shows a work-related field (like Work), then you can format bar styles for overallocated work, allocated work, and proposed bookings. If Resource Graph view displays cost, the bar styles include resource cost and proposed bookings.

NOTE　Resource Graph view displays different information depending on whether it's in the top pane or the Details pane of a combination view. For example, if Gantt Chart view is in the top pane, Resource Graph view in the Details pane shows data for one resource at a time for the resources assigned to the selected task (you can scroll in Resource Graph view's left pane to see values for other resources). On the other hand, if Resource Graph view is in the top pane, you can tell it to show values for all resources or for a filtered list of resources.

To modify bar styles, double-click the background of Resource Graph view, or right-click the background, and then, on the shortcut menu, choose Bar Styles. In the Bar Styles dialog box, the settings on the left side relate to a larger group of tasks or resources (all tasks or filtered resources, for example); the settings on the right side apply to selected tasks or resources. Resource Graph view draws separate bars for the selected resource and the group of filtered resources so you can compare values. To see bars for only selected resources, be sure to choose Don't Show in the "Show as" menus for all the filtered resources listed on the left side of the dialog box.

For resources that *are* displayed, choose the color and the pattern you want. You can have Project draw values in different ways by choosing one of the following from the "Show as" drop-down list:

- **Bar.** Displays a separate bar for each time period.

- **Area.** Fills in a triangular or trapezoidal area equal to the value, which can span one or more periods.

- **Step.** Instead of separate bars for each period, all adjacent bars are drawn as one filled-in area.

- **Line.** Draws only the boundary of the area you see if you choose the Area option.

- **Step Line.** Draws just the border of the Step filled-in area.

- **Don't Show.** Doesn't show the value on the graph.

TIP If you look at work or allocation in Resource Graph view, in the Bar Styles dialog box, turn on the "Show availability line" checkbox to see a separate line for resource availability. The availability line compared with the height of bars is a great way to see how much work you can still assign. The "Show values" checkbox is turned on by default, and that's usually what you want. With this setting turned on, the graph displays the numerical values that the bars represent below each bar.

Modifying a Network Diagram

A project-management network diagram is a latticework of boxes (called *nodes*) with link lines connecting them. The boxes represent project tasks, and the link lines are the same task dependencies you see in a Gantt Chart view.

Before the dawn of computers and Microsoft Project, a network diagram was where you manually calculated the early start, early finish, late start, and late finish dates that identify the critical path. Happily, you no longer need a network diagram and an abacus to calculate the critical path, because Project does it for you.

Network Diagram view is perfect for working on task dependencies, because it doesn't show time at all. Whether a task takes 1 day or 6 months, its box in the network diagram is the same size, and its successor task is right next door. Because this view doesn't have a table area, task fields appear within each network diagram box. Choosing fields to display in boxes is the most common way to customize this view, but you can also change the appearance of boxes and how Project lays them out. The following sections explain your options.

■ CHOOSING FIELDS AND FORMATTING FOR NETWORK DIAGRAM BOXES

Project's views are simply different ways of looking at the same information. In Network Diagram view, boxes replace the task bars you see in a Gantt Chart view. And just as you can attach fields to each side of a task bar, network diagram boxes can contain several task fields. Before computers, the fields were the early and late start and finish dates, so you could calculate slack and the critical path. But because Project calculates early and late dates, you can pick any fields you want to see and change what the boxes look like.

Like bar styles for a Gantt Chart view, box styles for a network diagram set the content and appearance of boxes within a category, like Critical, Critical Summary, or Noncritical External. To format a category of boxes, follow these steps:

1. **In the Task tab's View section, click the down arrow on the Gantt Chart button, and then, on the drop-down menu, choose Network Diagram.**

   Network Diagram view appears, showing each task in its own box. Every box is the same size, regardless of the duration of the task.

2. **On the Network Diagram Tools | Format tab, click Box Styles (or double-click the background of the network diagram).**

   The Box Styles dialog box opens and lists the box styles for the active view, as shown in Figure 21-15.

TIP To format individual boxes instead of categories, select the boxes you want to format, and then, on the Network Diagram Tools | Format tab, click Box (or double-click the border of a box in the diagram).

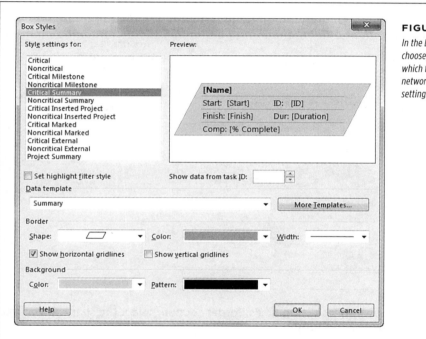

FIGURE 21-15

In the Data Template field, you can choose a template that specifies which task fields appear in each network diagram box and other settings like font and alignment.

3. **In the "Style settings for" list, select the category of box you want to format.**

   The categories for network diagrams focus on critical and noncritical tasks. Most of the categories are a combination of critical or noncritical and another condition like milestone, summary, marked, or external.

4. **To choose the fields that appear in a box, in the "Data template" drop-down list, choose the template you want to apply.**

Data templates define a set of fields and their position in a box. To see which fields a template includes, select it in the drop-down list, and then look at the box in the Preview area. To see what a box looks like with real data, in the "Show data from task ID" box, choose a task ID number.

To choose exactly the fields you want—for instance, to include a custom field, to create a new data template, or to modify an existing one—click More Templates. In the Data Templates dialog box, choose a template, and then click Edit or Copy. (Or click New to start one from scratch.) The Data Template Definition dialog box opens, as shown in Figure 21-16.

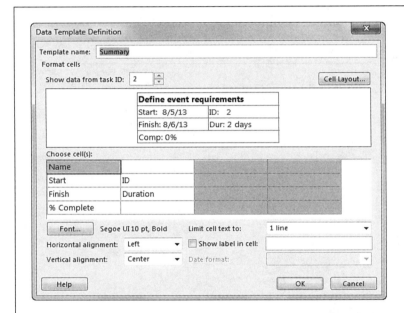

FIGURE 21-16

To pick a field in the data template, in the "Choose cell(s)" section, select a cell. Click the down arrow that appears in the cell, and then, in the drop-down list, choose the field's name. If you want to change the number of rows and columns in a box, click Cell Layout.

5. **In the Box Styles dialog box's Border section, select the shape, color, and width of the box border.**

Turn on the "Show horizontal gridlines" checkbox or "Show vertical gridlines" checkbox to add horizontal or vertical lines between the fields inside a box. To choose a different background color or pattern for the box, use the Background drop-down lists. Check the preview when you choose colors and patterns to make sure the fields are still legible.

6. **To change the formatting for another category, repeat steps 3–5.**

When you're done, click OK to close the Box Styles dialog box.

■ LAYING OUT BOXES

Network Diagram view lays out tasks like a flowchart, with link lines flowing from predecessor tasks to successor tasks. You can change the arrangement of boxes, including the alignment between rows and columns, the spacing between boxes, row height, and column width. You can also draw link lines straight from one box to the next, or use a combination of horizontal and vertical line segments. Your layout choices also include color selections and a host of other options. To make these kinds of changes, on the Network Diagram Tools | Format tab, click Layout to open the Layout dialog box, and then adjust the following settings:

- **Manual or automatic layout.** In the Layout Mode section, the "Automatically position all boxes" is selected initially, which means you entrust positioning to Project. The program uses the "Box layout" settings to arrange and space boxes. When this option is selected, make sure that the "Adjust for page breaks" checkbox is also turned on, so Project doesn't place boxes on top of a page break (which means the box appears on two pages when you print).

  If you can't resist fine-tuning box positions, select the "Allow manual box positioning" option. Project initially lays out the boxes based on the settings in the Box Layout section, but you can also move the boxes by dragging them to new positions.

- **Box layout.** The Box Layout section controls where boxes are and which boxes you see. The Arrangement drop-down list includes layouts like Top Down From Left and "Top Down - Critical First." The Row and Column settings include alignment (Left, Center, or Right), spacing (in pixels) between rows and columns, and box width and height.

  Unlike the organizing influence of summary tasks in a Gantt Chart, summary tasks tend to muddle Network Diagram view, which is why turning off the "Show summary tasks" checkbox is a good idea. Without summary tasks, you can see the relationships among work tasks more clearly. On the other hand, if you link summary tasks to other tasks, then keeping the "Show summary tasks" checkbox turned on shows all your links. The "Keep tasks with their summaries" checkbox tells Project to position subtasks near their summary tasks.

TIP It's easy to change a few network diagram display settings right from the Network Diagram Tools | Format tab. For example, to turn off summary tasks, simply turn off the Summary Tasks and Project Summary Task checkboxes. And to display link lines as straight lines, turn on the Straight Links checkbox.

- **Link line look.** The Link Style section lets you switch link lines from rectilinear (horizontal and vertical segments) to straight from one box to another. The "Show arrows" checkbox is turned on initially, and that's usually what you want. You can also add task dependency text (like "FS" for finish-to-start) on link lines by turning on the "Show link labels" checkbox.

- **Color.** The Link Color section starts with critical links set to red and noncritical links set to blue. If you use other colors for critical and noncritical, choose them in this section.

- **Other options.** The Diagram Options section is a hodgepodge of settings: background color, background pattern, whether page break lines appear in the diagram, whether to show in-progress and completed tasks, and whether to hide all the fields except the ID (perfect when you're concerned only with task dependencies).

Customizing Calendar View

Calendar view is great for showing teams what they're doing during a particular period, as Figure 21-17 shows. The bar styles, text styles, and gridlines are all within your aesthetic control. You can also customize the timescale for bars and change the calendar to show 1 week, several weeks, or whole months.

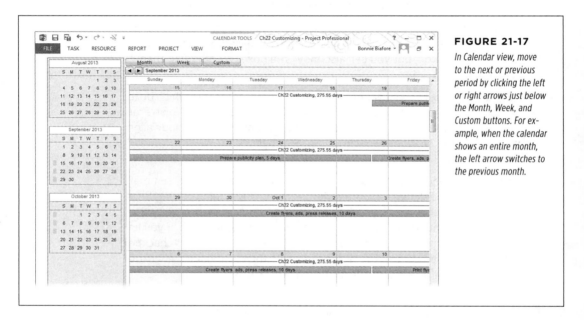

FIGURE 21-17

In Calendar view, move to the next or previous period by clicking the left or right arrows just below the Month, Week, and Custom buttons. For example, when the calendar shows an entire month, the left arrow switches to the previous month.

> **NOTE** Calendar view is different from a project, resource, or task calendar (page 102). It's like the electronic version of an appointment book filled in with project tasks and assignments. Project, resource, and task calendars, on the other hand, are like the shift schedules that workers receive, telling them which days they work or have off, and which shifts they work, but not what work they do during that time.

Here's an overview of Calendar view's settings:

- **Choose a time period.** Calendar view displays 1 month at a time initially, but changing the time period is easy. Above the calendar, click Month, Week, or Custom. If you click Custom, the Zoom dialog box opens so you can set a number of weeks or the specific dates you want to see. Alternatively, you can drag the status bar's Zoom slider to see shorter or longer periods.

- **Add a monthly preview.** Out of the box, Calendar view displays a preview of the previous, current, and next month like many paper calendars do. If you don't want to see these previews, right-click the calendar's background and then, on the shortcut menu, choose Timescale (or simply double-click anywhere in the calendar). In the Timescale dialog box, click the Week Headings tab, and then turn off the "Display month pane" checkbox.

- **Format the timescale.** Right-click the calendar's background, and then choose Timescale (or double-click anywhere in the calendar) to open the Timescale dialog box. Click the Week Headings tab and, in the Monthly, Daily, and Weekly titles drop-down lists, choose titles for months (for instance, January 2009 or 1/09—yes, Project uses examples based on the year 2009), weeks (1/28 or M 28), and days (Monday, Mon, or M). To focus on weekdays, select the "5 days" option. For round-the-clock operations, "7 days" shows every day of the week.

  The Date Boxes tab determines the information that appears at the top and bottom of each calendar box. For example, the day of the month sits at the top right, and the overflow indicator (which tells you there's more information than you can see) at the top left. You can add text at each corner of the box.

  The Date Shading tab controls how working and nonworking time appear. For example, initially, nonworking days on the base calendar are shaded, while working days are white.

- **Customize calendar bar styles.** Calendar bars are different from their Gantt Chart siblings, so their bar style options are different, too. To change the way calendar bar styles look, in the Calendar Tools | Format tab, click Bar Styles. You can use a bar, a line, or just text, and you can set the pattern and color for each type of bar. In the Field(s) box, click the down arrow, and then turn on the checkbox for the field you want to display inside bars. To include more than one field, turn on the checkboxes for additional fields, and then press the Enter key.

- **Layout tasks.** Head to the Calendar Tools | Format tab and click the small arrow at the bottom right of the Layout section to open the Layout dialog box. Initially, the calendar displays tasks based on the sort order that's applied (ID, initially). If you select the "Attempt to fit as many tasks as possible" option, then the calendar sorts tasks by Total Slack and then by Duration. Turn on the "Automatic layout" checkbox to tell Project to reapply the layout options as you add, remove, or sort tasks.

■ Changing Tables

Views like Gantt Chart and Task Usage come with a table of information on the left—each column is a Project field. (Sometimes, the table is the *only* thing in the view, like in Resource Sheet view.) Project comes with several built-in tables, like Entry and Cost, that contain frequently used collections of fields. Like most elements in Project, you can change which table you see, what the table contains, and how data is displayed to suit your needs.

You can easily swap the table you see in a view—for instance, to switch from a summary to a table that shows performance compared with the baseline. But you can also change the columns in a table by temporarily adding columns, or permanently adding, removing, and rearranging columns to reflect how you work. Going a step further, the table's column width, row height, and a few other options are customizable so you can make a table look exactly the way you want.

> **NOTE** Project dutifully records every change you make to a table, so the table shows those changes every time you apply it. Project stores the customized table in your Project file, although it has the same name as the original, built-in table. To use both the original and your custom version, make a copy of the built-in table *first*, and then modify it as described on page 634. If you create a customized table that you want to use in other files, use the Organizer to copy it from your Project file to the global template or another file (page 702).

Switching the Table in a View

Project offers two ways to swap out a table in a view. To choose *any* existing table, the More Views dialog box is the place to go. To choose from just the tables on the Tables menu, there's a shortcut. Here are your options:

- **Never-fails method.** In the View tab's Data section, click Tables→More Tables. In the More Tables dialog box, double-click a table's name. This dialog box lists every table that exists in your global template *and* the current Project file.

- **Fast method.** Right-click the Select All box at the intersection of the row and column headings (above the first ID cell), and then, on the shortcut menu, choose the table you want (or choose More Tables to open the More tables dialog box). You can also head to the View tab's Data section, click Tables, and then choose the table you want. The only difference between these two options is that the Tables drop-down list segregates custom and built-in tables.

Changing a Table's Contents

The easiest way to make changes to a table is to work on it directly in a view. That way, you can see the results immediately and try again until you get it right. Project records your changes in the table's definition, so working in a view changes the table just as working in the Table Definition dialog box (page 634) does. (If you don't want to change the existing table, copy it first and then make your changes. To copy the table, in the view tab's Data section, choose Tables→"Save Fields as a New table.") Here are the techniques for editing tables in a view:

- **Add a column.** Right-click the heading of the column to the right of where you want to add the new column, and then choose Insert Column. In the "Field name" drop-down list, choose the field. To quickly scroll to the field you want, start typing the field's name, and Project selects the first field that matches the letters you've typed. You can also click the Add New Column heading in the last column of the table and then choose the field you want from the drop-down list.

> **NOTE** If you start to type values into the Add New Column cells, Project identifies the type of information you're entering and automatically changes the column to an appropriate custom field. For example, if you type a value like *6/17/2014*, Project changes the column to a custom Date field like Date1.

- **Remove a column.** Right-click the heading of the column you want to remove, and then choose Hide Column. Project removes the column from view *and* from the table's definition. The box on page 634 explains another way to hide columns.

- **Rearrange columns.** If the table has the right columns in the wrong order, you can drag columns into other positions. Simply click the heading of the column you want to move. When the pointer turns into a four-headed arrow, drag the column to its new location. A dark gray vertical line jumps from column edge to edge to show you where the column will settle when you release the mouse button.

- **Edit a column.** Right-click a column's heading and then, on the shortcut menu, choose Field Settings. The Field Settings dialog box opens with the "Field name" box set to the selected field. You can change the column's title, width, and text alignment, and control whether its header text wraps.

- **Fine-tune the column heading.** If you want the column heading to be something besides the field name, open the Field Settings dialog box (see the previous bullet) and in the Title box, type the heading you want. You can align this heading to the Left, Center, or Right using the "Align title" setting. Turn on the Header Text Wrapping checkbox to wrap the words in the title over several lines when the column is narrow.

- **Align data.** In the Field Settings dialog box (see above), the "Align data" setting positions values in the column.

- **Change column width.** Move the pointer between two column headings with the column you want to resize on the left. When the pointer changes into a two-headed arrow, drag to the left or right until the column is the width you want.

> **TIP** When values don't fit in a column, Project replaces them with a series of pound symbols (#), which aren't very informative. Here's a quick way to resize a column to show all its values: Move the pointer to the right edge of the column's heading. When the pointer changes to a two-headed arrow, double-click. Alternatively, in the Field Settings dialog box, click Best Fit to do the same thing.

- **Wrap text in column cells.** Project initially sets some columns like Task Name to wrap text, which means that the program wraps long task names over several lines as you change the column's width. To wrap text in a column, right-click in the column's heading, and then, on the shortcut menu, choose Wrap Text.

- **Change row height.** You can change the height of specific rows in a table. First select the rows whose height you want to change. Then move the pointer to the lower border of one of the selected row's ID numbers, and then drag up or down until the rows are the height you want.

GEM IN THE ROUGH

Where's That Column?

You can hide a column without it losing its place in a table, but finding the column again is another matter. To hide a column without removing it from the table, move the pointer to the right edge of the column's heading cell. When the pointer changes to a two-headed arrow, drag past the column's *left* border. The column disappears, but a look at the table's definition explained below shows the column still there, just with a width of zero.

When you want to restore the column to view, your first challenge is remembering where the column was, because Project doesn't give you any visual clues. Truth be told, a column hidden like this may stay hidden forever—you may even insert the column a second time without realizing that it's already there.

If you're smart enough to remember where the column was before you hid it, move the pointer between the two column headings where the column is hidden, making sure the pointer is slightly to the right of the border line. When the pointer changes into a two-headed arrow, drag to the right until the hidden column stretches into view. You can also open the Table Definition dialog box as explained below and type a value greater than zero for the column's width.

Modifying a Table Definition

If you prefer to do all your table editing in one dialog box, the Table Definition dialog box is for you. You can add, move, remove, rearrange, and modify columns for any table. To edit a table in the Table Definition dialog box, do the following:

1. **In the View tab's Data section, click Tables, and then, in the drop-down list, choose More Tables.**

   The More Tables dialog box opens.

2. **In the More Tables dialog box, select the table you want to work on, and then click Edit. (If you don't see the name of the table you want, try clicking the Task or Resource option at the top of the dialog box.)**

   The Table Definition dialog box opens, with all the customization features you can apply to a table directly when it appears in a view—and a few more besides. The box on page 635 describes the various sections of this dialog box and how to move around in it.

TIP If you want to go back to the current table's original definition, in the View tab's Data section, click Tables→"Reset to Default."

Navigating the Table Definition Dialog Box

The Table Definition dialog box contains a table of its own, so terminology is a challenge. Project doesn't have official names for these elements, so here are the terms used in this section of this chapter:

Figure 21-18 identifies elements in the Table Definition dialog box and a view's table. The Table Definition dialog box's table is called the *grid*. A column in the Table Definition grid is a *property*, while a column in the table you're working on is called the *table column*. A row in the Table Definition grid is called a *row* and represents a Project field within the table you're working on. A row in the table you're working on is called a *table row* and represents a task, resource, or assignment.

Knowing which keys to press in the Table Definition dialog box helps you get to the elements you want to edit. Here's how you move around in the dialog box:

- To move to the next cell in the grid, press the right arrow. (Pressing Enter *doesn't* move to the next cell; it closes the dialog box as if you clicked OK.)

- Tab jumps from one section of the dialog box to the next. For example, if you're in the grid area and you press Tab, Project fills in the rest of the row you were in with standard choices and then jumps to the "Date format" box below the grid.

- To move to the end of a row, press Ctrl+right arrow. To move to the beginning of a row, press Ctrl+left arrow

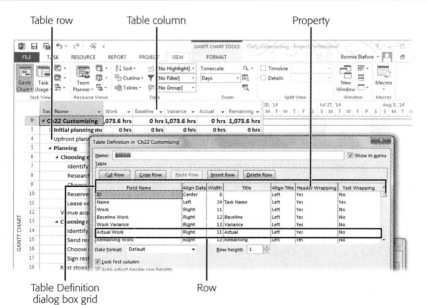

FIGURE 21-18

The Table Definition dialog box lists each table field in a separate row. When you apply the table to a view, the fields listed in the definition from top to bottom appear in table columns from left to right.

Here's how you make changes to a table in the Table Definition dialog box:

- **Display the table in table drop-down menus.** Turn on the "Show in menu" checkbox to tell Project to list the table in table drop-down menus. If you use a table only occasionally, turn *off* this checkbox. Even with this setting turned off, you can still display the table by applying it from within the More Tables dialog box (page 632).

- **Add a table column.** You can insert a table column in any row in the Table Definition grid. To insert a table column at the end of the grid, click the first blank Field Name cell, click the down arrow to the cell's right, and then choose the field you want. Keep in mind that the top row in the grid represents the leftmost table column; the bottom row in the grid is the rightmost table column.

  To add a table column in the middle of the grid, select the row above which you want to add a new row, and then click Insert Row to insert a blank row, as illustrated in Figure 21-19. In the Field Name cell, choose the field you want to use.

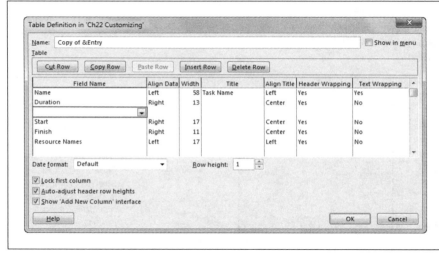

FIGURE 21-19

When you're editing a task-oriented table, the Field Name drop-down list lists only task fields like Task Name. Similarly, you see only resource fields when you work on a resource-oriented table, and only assignment fields when you edit a table in a usage view.

- **Remove a table column.** Select the row containing the field name you want to remove, and then click Delete Row.

- **Rearrange table columns.** Select the field name you want to move, and then click Cut Row. Project places the cut row on the Clipboard. Select the row below where you want to insert the cut field, and then click Paste Row. The cut row slides into its new location.

- **Align values in columns.** To align the values in table cells, select the Align Data cell, and then choose Left, Center, or Right. Left alignment is best for task and resource names. Center is a good choice for columns that include short values like Yes and No. Choose Right for numbers and dates. To align the table column's heading, in the Align Title cell, choose Left, Center, or Right.

- **Change table column width.** Select the Width cell, and then type a number.

- **Change the column title and alignment.** To specify what appears in a table column's heading (like changing "Name" to "Task Name"), type the heading in the Title cell.

- **Wrap text in data cells.** Change the Text Wrapping property to Yes if you want Project to automatically wrap the text in table cells as you change the table column's width.

- **Specify date format.** Below the Table Definition dialog box's grid, in the "Date format" drop-down list, choose the date format you want for date fields in the table. Choosing a table date format here overrides the project-wide date format. (To set the project-wide date format, choose File→Options, click General, and then choose an option in the "Date format" box.)

- **Change table row height.** If you want to adjust the height of all the table rows, then in the Row Height box, type or choose a number. The number is a multiple of the standard height; that is, 2 represents row heights that are twice the standard.

- **Keep the first column visible.** Project turns on the "Lock first column" checkbox, which means the ID column remains visible even if you scroll all the way to the right in the table.

TIP   You can keep task names or resource names in view by making Task Name or Resource Name the first column in the table (by rearranging the grid rows), and then turning on the "Lock first column" checkbox. For example, in the grid's Field Name property column, click the Name cell, and then click Cut Row. Select the first row in the grid, and then click Paste Row to insert the Name field as the first row. Make sure the "Lock first column" checkbox is turned on, and then click OK. In the view, the Task Name column is now in the first column and shaded to show that it's locked. As you scroll, it remains steadfastly in place.

- **Adjust heading row height.** With header wrapping turned on, Project automatically wraps table column headings to fit column width. Project initially turns on the "Auto-adjust header row heights" checkbox, and you should keep it that way. When this setting is turned on, Project adjusts the row height of the table column heading to show the entire heading, increasing the height for narrow columns and decreasing the height as the column widens. With the checkbox turned off, the column heading still wraps, but some of the text disappears at the bottom of the cell.

- **Show "Add New Column."** Out of the box, Project turns on the "Show 'Add New Column' interface" checkbox, which means the rightmost column in the table is Add New Column. Page 633 explains how to use this column to add new fields to a table.

Creating a New Table

You can create a new table from scratch or by copying one that's close to what you want. If you've inserted the fields you want into the current table, you can quickly turn it into a new table by heading to the View tab's Data section and clicking Tables→"Save Fields as a New Table." In the Save Table dialog box, type the name for the table and then click OK.

> **NOTE** When you create a new table, Project automatically copies it to the global template (page 698). If you don't want to share new tables (or other elements like views) that you create, choose File→Options. On the left side of the Project Options dialog box, click Advanced. Under the Display heading, turn off the "Automatically add new views, tables, filters, and groups to the global" checkbox. Then you have to use the Organizer to manually copy your new views to the *global.mpt* file (page 702).

If you want to start from scratch or choose other settings, the More Tables dialog box is the place to start. To create a new table in this way, follow these steps:

1. **In the View tab's Data section, click Tables→More Tables.**

   The More Tables dialog box opens.

2. **To create a table from scratch, select the Task or Resource option to specify the type of table, and then click New. If you want to copy an existing table instead, select it in the list, and then click Copy.**

   Either way, the Table Definition dialog box opens.

3. **In the Name box, type the name for the table.**

   Project initially fills in names like "Table 1" for a new table, and "Copy of [selected table]" for a copied table. Replace Project's name with one that describes the table's contents, like Baseline2 Work or DateSummary.

4. **To include the table in table menus (for instance, when you click Tables in the View tab's Data section), turn on the "Show in menu" checkbox.**

   With this setting turned on, the table also appears when you right-click the Select All box at the intersection of the column headings and row IDs.

5. **Add columns to the table as described on page 633 and page 636.**

■ Formatting Text

Different Gantt Chart views may show the critical path in red or slack time as narrow green lines, but text appears in the same old 8-point Arial font. Happily, Project's *text styles* make it easy to format text for different categories of information, like row and column headings, text for critical tasks, or text at the same position on task bars.

Whether you want to emphasize critical tasks with bold red letters or your tired eyes beg for larger text, you can use text styles to change formatting quickly and keep formatting consistent. Simply choose the type of information to format (headings, milestones, and so on) and the text formatting you want (font, size, style, color, and background color). Or you can reformat a single string of text for special emphasis, like the "Manager of the Year" caption under your boss's picture. This section explains how to do both.

Changing Categories of Text

Project text styles are watered-down versions of their Word cousins: Project doesn't let you change as many text characteristics. Just as a heading style in Word changes all the headings in a document, a text style drapes itself over every occurrence of text in its category. Set the text style for milestone tasks to bold green Verdana font, for example, and the text for every milestone task follows suit. When a task's or resource's values change and it no longer fits the category, Project takes care of changing the text formatting to the style for the task's or resource's new category. Here's how to format text using text styles:

1. **Open the view in which you want to format text.**

    You can use text styles in any kind of view.

TIP When you modify text styles, the changes appear only in the active view in the active project. Sadly, you can't copy these text styles to other views; you have to repeat the text style formatting in each view you want to use it in. On a brighter note, once you modify a view to use attractively formatted text styles, you can use the Organizer (page 702) to copy that view to your global template or to another Project file.

---

2. **Go to the view's contextual Format tab, such as the Task Usage Tools | Format tab. In the tab's Format section, click Text Styles.**

    The Text Styles dialog box opens.

3. **In the "Item to Change" drop-down list, choose the category you want to reformat, as shown in Figure 21-20.**

    The categories you can format are built in, so you can't add your own.

    If you want to format *all* the text in a view—for instance, to enlarge text for your aging stakeholders—select All in the "Item to Change" drop-down list. The formatting changes you make will apply to all text in the active view, including table headings, table text, and task bar text.

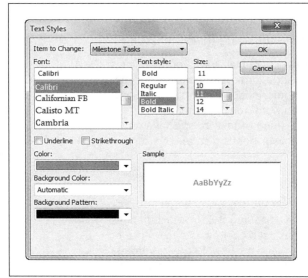

FIGURE 21-20

The last two items in the "Item to Change" drop-down list (which is closed in this image) are Changed Cells and Inactive Tasks. Changed Cells corresponds to Project's change highlighting feature. (Page 310 describes change highlighting in detail.) You can change the text and background color for this category to make changed values stand out. Choosing Inactive Tasks lets you change the appearance of tasks that you set to inactive (page 364).

4. **Choose the font, font style, and font size you want for the category.**

   The Font list displays the fonts installed on your computer. Font Style represents formatting like bold and italic. The Size list includes standard font sizes, but you can type a number in the Size box to pick a size that's not listed. You can also turn on the Underline checkbox to underline text, although underlining gets lost in view tables.

5. **In the Color drop-down list, choose the color you want.**

   Colors other than black can be hard to read, although dark colors are better than light shades. Look at the text after you've formatted it, and maybe print samples in both color and black and white to make sure the colors work.

   > **TIP** If you want Project to take care of choosing text color, background color, and background pattern, then in the Color, Background Color, and Background Pattern drop-down lists, choose Automatic.

6. **To highlight cells that use the text style, in the Background Color drop-down list, choose the color you want.**

   Similar to the shading Project applies to changed cells, you can change the background color for critical tasks, summary tasks, and so on. If you tend to print to black-and-white printers, then it's a good idea to choose a background pattern in the Background Pattern drop-down list instead, because these patterns show up even in black and white. The Sample box shows you what your formatting choices look like.

7. **Click OK.**

The Text Styles dialog box closes. Any text in your selected category displays the new formatting.

TIP A clever extension of background color makes change highlighting possible. In the Text Styles dialog box, the "Item to Change" drop-down list has a Changed Cells entry. If you select this entry, then the Preview area shows the light-blue highlighting that appears when cell values change. If you can't see the light blue due to color blindness, or if you simply prefer a different color, then in the Background Color drop-down list, choose the color you want instead. Once you click OK, cells burst into your favorite color whenever an edit you make changes their values.

Changing Selected Text

Suppose a couple of tasks are on a significant duration-cutting diet, so you want them to stand out from everything else. You can format text that you select down to an individual cell in a table. Formatting selected text is a snap with the mini-toolbar that appears when you right-click a cell, as shown in Figure 21-21. You can apply the same kinds of formatting as with text styles, but the basic steps are a little different:

1. **Select all the cells with the text you want to format, and then right-click one of the selected cells.**

   Select a single cell, several cells, a row, or several rows. The formatting commands format whatever text is selected.

2. **On the mini-toolbar that appears above the shortcut menu selection, click the formatting commands you want.**

   The first line of the toolbar has drop-down lists for fonts and font sizes. The second line has buttons for changing text to bold or italic, choosing a cell background color, and choosing text color. The selected text immediately displays its new formatting.

If you get the bloated tasks you reformatted under control, you have to select their text again to remove the special formatting you applied—there's no way to automatically undo the formatting you added.

TIP Say you apply a special font, font size, text color, and background color to the troubled tasks in your project, and then another task joins the ranks of troubled tasks. Fortunately, you can copy the formatting from an existing troubled task to the new one. To do this, select the text with the formatting you want to copy. Then, in the Task tab's Clipboard Group, click the Format Painter button (shown in Figure 21-21). Finally, click the cell that contains the text to which you want to apply the copied formatting, and Project formats it the same way. If you click a column *header* after clicking the Format Painter button, Project formats all the text in that column, but not the header itself.

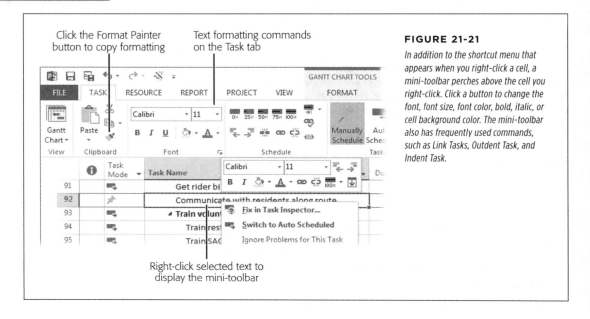

Click the Format Painter
button to copy formatting

Text formatting commands
on the Task tab

Right-click selected text to
display the mini-toolbar

FIGURE 21-21

In addition to the shortcut menu that appears when you right-click a cell, a mini-toolbar perches above the cell you right-click. Click a button to change the font, font size, font color, bold, italic, or cell background color. The mini-toolbar also has frequently used commands, such as Link Tasks, Outdent Task, and Indent Task.

■ Filtering Through Information

Finding project information can be like sifting for gold—lots of project sediment can obscure the scheduling nuggets you're looking for. In Project, filters screen out information you don't care about so you can easily see the info you do want. Project comes with several built-in filters to get you started. For example, the Using Resource filter shows tasks that use resources you specify, and the "Tasks with Estimated Durations" filter shows tasks with question marks in their Duration fields, so you can fill in duration values. If built-in filters don't do what you want, you can copy or edit one of them to create your own. You can also create ad hoc filters with AutoFilter. This section shows you how to work with built-in filters or build your own. (The box on page 645 discusses a few commands that act like filters.)

Built-in filters can act as a tutorial when you want to create your own. They provide examples of combining several tests in one filter, comparing the value of one field with another, and asking for input. For example, you could create a filter to find critical tasks whose dates are slipping by starting with the built-in Slipping Tasks filter and adding a test on the Critical field. Here are some ideas for helpful filters:

- **Critical tasks with overallocated resources.** To find tasks that are at risk, filter for tasks whose Critical and Overallocated fields are both equal to Yes.

- **Incomplete tasks using a resource.** If a resource gets reassigned to another project, you can find all the tasks that person is assigned to that are in progress or haven't started. Then you can work on finding replacements.

- **Work packages.** Create a filter to make Project hide both summary tasks and milestones so the task list shows only work packages.

- **Generic resources.** Display only generic resources so you can see which tasks you still need to staff.

Applying Filters

To apply a filter to the current view, head to the View tab's Data section and pick an item in the Filter drop-down list. The box on page 645 describes another way you can filter tasks in a view.

After you apply a filter, changes you make to a project can affect what should appear in the filtered list—but you have to manually update the filter each time. For example, if you've applied the Critical filter (to display only critical tasks) and then you shorten a task so that it's no longer on the critical path, you'd expect it to disappear from view. But it turns out that Project *doesn't* automatically update the filtered list as you make changes. So to make sure you're seeing the right items, quickly reapply the current filter by pressing Ctrl+F3.

TIP Filters are a great way to confirm that you've made all the changes you need. For example, when you apply the "Tasks with Estimated Durations" filter, the task list displays only tasks with estimated durations. After you change the durations of those tasks, reapply the filter (by pressing Ctrl+F3). When the filtered list is empty, you know you're done.

Creating and Editing Filters

Filters can be as simple as the Critical filter, which just checks whether a task's Critical field is equal to Yes. The AutoFilter feature (page 652) makes quick work of simple filters like these. But filters can also have several nested tests, like the Slipped/Late Project filter. An existing filter makes a great template for creating your own, whether you want filter-building guidance or just a shortcut. For example, to set up a filter that uses both the Critical and Duration fields, you can copy the built-in Critical filter and then modify the copy to add a condition for Duration. This section describes how to create a new filter or to make a copy of an existing one.

The methods for creating filters from scratch or from copies are almost identical. You create the new filter, change the name Project assigns, and then define the filter conditions. Here are the steps:

1. **In the View tab's Data section, click the Filter down arrow and then, on the drop-down menu, choose More Filters.**

   If a task-oriented view is visible, the More Filters dialog box opens with the Task option selected, and the Filters list includes all the task-oriented filters, like Completed Tasks and Milestones. If a resource-oriented view like the Resource Sheet is visible, the Resource option is selected automatically. Select the option for the kind of filter you want to work on (Task or Resource).

2. **To start with an existing filter, in the Filters list, select the filter you want to copy, and then click Copy. To start with a blank slate, click New. To edit an existing filter, select the filter, and then click Edit.**

   You can also start a new filter by going to the View tab's Data section, clicking the Filter down arrow, and then, on the drop-down menu, choosing New Filter.

   The Filter Definition dialog box opens.

3. **In the Name box of the Filter Definition dialog box, type a new name for the filter.**

   Project fills in the Name box with something like "Filter 1" for new filters and "Copy of [filter name]" for copied filters, as shown in Figure 21-22. Replace this name with one that describes what the filter does, like "Work packages."

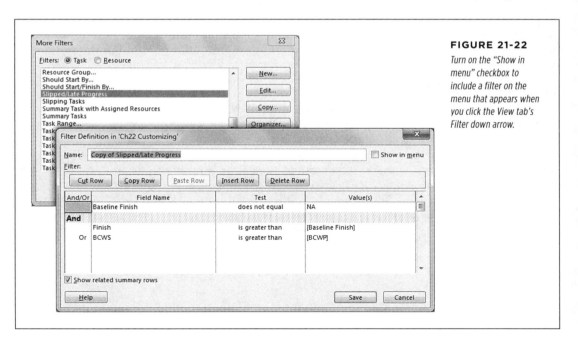

FIGURE 21-22

Turn on the "Show in menu" checkbox to include a filter on the menu that appears when you click the View tab's Filter down arrow.

4. **Add or modify the filter's tests, and then click OK to save the filter.**

The next section explains how to set up filter tests.

Summarizing a Project

Most of the time, you want to see summary tasks *and* their work-package tasks. But when you're working only on work-package tasks—for instance, to find tasks without assigned resources—a task list without summary tasks is better. It's easy to filter out summary tasks in Project:

- **Hide or show summary tasks.** If you want to hide summary tasks to focus on work packages, choose a task view's Format tab (like Gantt Chart Tools | Format). In the tab's Show/Hide section, turn off the Summary Tasks checkbox. To bring the summary tasks back, turn the checkbox back on.

- **Summarize the entire project.** Project can display a top-level task to summarize an entire project. In a task view's Format tab's Show/Hide section, turn on the Project Summary Task checkbox. Project adds a row with ID number 0, which rolls up all the values for *all* tasks in your project. To always show the project-summary tasks for new projects, in the Project Options dialog box, choose Advanced, and then, under "Display options for this project," turn on the "Show project summary task" checkbox.

Defining Filters

Filters are a gauntlet of tests that tasks, resources, or assignments have to pass in order to appear in the current view. For example, the In Progress Tasks filter first tests whether a task has started, and then tests whether it is *not* finished. If a task has started but not finished (that is, it passes both tests), then it appears in the filtered task list because it's in progress. This section describes how to create different types of tests, including the following:

- **Comparing a field with a value.** The simplest tests compare a field with a specific text string, number, or other value, like the Critical filter testing whether the Critical field equals Yes.

- **Comparing two fields.** You can set up a filter to compare the values from two fields. For example, the Cost Overbudget filter tests whether Cost is greater than Baseline Cost.

- **Multiple tests.** Filters are often made up of several tests, like the built-in Should Start/Finish By filter. When you combine more than one test, you have to tell Project whether items must pass all the tests or some combination of them.

- **Interactive tests.** In some cases, you want to filter by a different value each time you apply the filter. For example, say you want to filter tasks by a specific assigned resource depending on whom you're trying to free up. An interactive filter is perfect for this situation because it asks for a value and then uses your answer to filter the list.

You define a filter in the Filter Definition dialog box. The previous section explains how to open this dialog box.

■ COMPARING A FIELD WITH A VALUE

Comparing a field with a value is a good introduction to tests. Many basic filters need only one of these tests—like the perennial favorite Critical filter. Here are the steps to create a test that compares a field with a value, using a filter for critical tasks as an example:

1. **In the Filter Definition dialog box (page 644 explains how to open it), select the Field Name cell, click the down arrow that appears, and then, in the drop-down list, choose the field you want to test (in this example, Outline Level).**

   The field appears in the Field Name cell.

> **TIP** To quickly select a field in the drop-down list, start typing the first few letters of the field's name. When Project selects the field you want, press Enter, and Project inserts that field's name in the Field Name cell.

2. **Select the Test cell, click the down arrow that appears, and then choose the type of test you want to apply, as illustrated in Figure 21-23. For the Outline Level filter, choose "is less than or equal to."**

   Table 21-1 describes the tests that Project offers and gives an example of each one. For example, the Work Overbudget filter uses "is greater than" to see whether actual work hours are greater than baseline work hours.

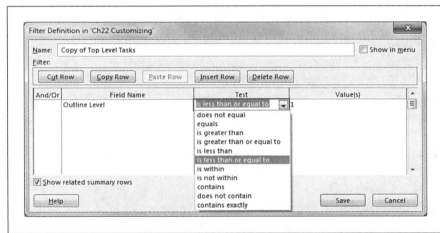

FIGURE 21-23

The "Show related summary rows" checkbox tells Project whether to include the summary rows for tasks that pass the filter's tests. If summary rows outnumber the tasks you're looking for, turn off this checkbox to see only the work tasks that pass the filter.

3. **In the Value(s) cell, type or choose the value to compare with the field.**

   If the field you're testing is a Yes/No field, you can type *Yes* or *No*, or choose the values from the drop-down list. In Figure 21-23, the test checks to see if the outline level is less than or equal to 1.

4. **Click Save to save your new filter, and close the Filter Definition dialog box.**

TABLE 21-1 *Project's filter tests*

TEST	WHAT IT DOES	EXAMPLE
Does not equal	The field value does not equal the test value.	The Incomplete Tasks filter tests whether % Complete does not equal 100%.
Equals	The field and test values must be equal.	The Critical filter tests whether the Critical field equals Yes.
Is greater than	The field value must be greater than the test value.	The Slipping Tasks filter tests whether the Finish field is greater than the Baseline Finish field. (Later dates are greater than earlier dates.)
Is greater than or equal to	The field value must be greater than or equal to the test value.	The Date Range filter tests whether the start date is greater than or equal to the date you specify.
Is less than	The field value must be less than the test value.	The Should Start By filter tests whether the Start field is less than (earlier than) the date you specify.
Is less than or equal to	The field value must be less than or equal to the test value.	The Tasks Due This Week filter tests whether the Finish field is less than or equal to the date you specify for the end of the week.
Is within	The field value must be equal to or between two values you specify.	The Task Range filter tests whether the ID field is within two task ID numbers. In the Value(s) cell, you type the two numbers separated by a comma, like *50,100*.
Is not within	The values must be outside the range you specify.	For example, to find cheap and expensive resources, test whether Standard Rate is not within *25,300*.
Contains	This text-oriented test checks whether the field value contains the text string in the Value(s) cell.	For example, you can see whether the Task Name field contains "Payment" to find all the payment milestones.
Does not contain	This text-oriented test looks for field values that don't contain the text string you specify.	For example, to eliminate all phase two tasks, you can test whether the Task Name field does *not* contain "Phase 2."
Contains exactly	This test looks for exact matches between the field and the test value.	The Using Resource filter tests whether Resource Name contains the exact resource name you type.

TIP The "equals" and "does not equal" tests can compare text field values against strings with wildcard characters; "*" is the wildcard for one or more characters, and "?" replaces just one character. For example, "* Supervisor" finds all the resources with "Supervisor" at the end of their names. On the other hand, "BigDig ???" finds the BigDig 300 backhoe and the BigDig 500, but not the apartment-cleaning BigDig 50.

■ COMPARING TWO FIELDS

The most useful filters seem to be ones that compare two fields. For example, you can create a filter that checks whether the date in the Finish field is greater than the date in the Baseline Finish field; if it is, then you know that the task is due to finish later than you planned.

Setting up a test to compare two fields is similar to comparing a field with a value. Here are the steps:

1. **In the Filter Definition dialog box (page 644), select the Field Name cell, click the down arrow that appears, and then choose the field you want to test (Finish, in this example).**

   The field name appears in the Field Name cell.

2. **Press the right arrow key, click the Test cell's down arrow, and then choose the test you want to apply—"is greater than" in this example.**

   The test you choose appears in the Test cell in the same row.

3. **Press the right arrow key, click the Value(s) cell's down arrow, and then choose the comparison field (Baseline Finish, in this example).**

   In the Value(s) column, Project differentiates fields from text by enclosing the field's name in square brackets ([ ]), as shown in Figure 21-24.

4. **Repeat steps 1–3 to add more tests to the filter.**

   When you've finished adding tests, click OK to save the filter.

■ CREATING COMPOUND FILTERS

In many cases, a filter needs more than one test to do what you want. In those situations, *compound filters* (also known as *multiple-test* filters) are just the ticket. They let you combine tests in lots of different ways. You can set up filters in which items must pass every test or only some of the tests.

Initially, Project evaluates tests in the order they appear in the Filter Definition table, similar to the way a worried mother might ask, "Is he single?" "Is he rich?" and only then, "Is he ready to get married?" The items that pass the first test move on to the next test. Project keeps testing until there are no more tests.

And and *Or* are called Boolean (logic) operators, which you use to specify whether an item has to pass both tests or only one. And and Or work just like they do in real life. If you want items to pass both tests, use And; for instance, "Is he single?" and "Is he ready to get married?" Use Or if the items need to pass only one test, like "Is he rich?" or "Is he smart?"

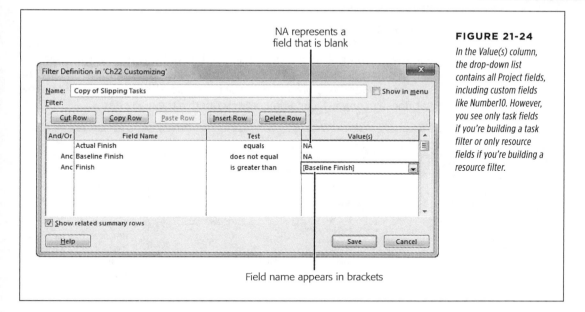

FIGURE 21-24

In the Value(s) column, the drop-down list contains all Project fields, including custom fields like Number10. However, you see only task fields if you're building a task filter or only resource fields if you're building a resource filter.

You (or, in this case, your mother) can use additional Ands or Ors to change the order of tests. For example, he has to be smart or rich; only then does it matter whether he's ready to get married.

The following example creates a filter that finds tasks that have overallocated resources *and* are running late. It first finds baselined tasks with overallocated resources. For those tasks, it checks for delayed finish dates or work that's behind schedule. If a task passes both sets of tests, then it appears in the filtered task list.

Each compound filter is different, but the following steps demonstrate the concept:

1. **In the Filter Definition dialog box's Name field, type a filter name.**

   Because compound filters do so much, build a name from the filter's key features like "Slipped/LateProgress/Overallocated." If you plan to use the filter frequently, turn on the "Show in menu" checkbox. The filter then appears in Project's filter lists—for example, when you click the down arrow in a table column header and then choose Filters.

2. **In the first table row, define the filter condition you want (including field, test, and value).**

   In this example, the first condition checks that the task has a baseline—that is, Baseline Finish does not equal NA. (The Baseline Finish field contains a date if the task is baselined, NA if it isn't.) Type *NA* in the row's Values(s) cell whenever you want to test for a value that's blank (see Figure 21-24).

3. **In the second row's And/Or cell, choose And, and then add the condition in the other cells. Use Or instead if a task or resource has to pass only one of the tests in your filter.**

If you want the condition to become one of several that is evaluated as a set, add a Boolean operator to the row that contains the condition. When you do that, the operator (And or Or) appears on the right side of its cell in unbolded text, as shown in Figure 21-25. On the other hand, if you want to specify the Boolean operator to apply to the sets of tests, add a Boolean operator to a row that doesn't contain a condition, as described in the next step.

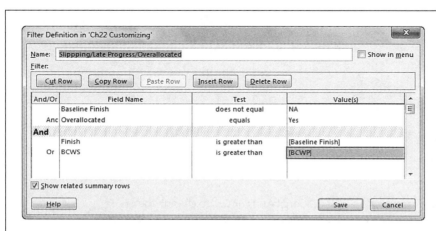

FIGURE 21-25

The test for late progress checks for budgeted cost of work scheduled (page 442) greater than the budgeted cost of work performed. What the test means in English is this: For the duration that has passed, was more work scheduled than has been completed?

4. **To test the previous conditions as a group, in the third row's And/Or cell, choose And, and then click another row.**

As soon as you click any other row, several things happen. Project moves the And you just added to the left side of its cell, bolds the And, and shades its row. This formatting (shown in Figure 21-25) is Project's way of saying that the row acts like the parentheses in a mathematical equation before and after the empty row. For example, with And in the third row, Project evaluates the first two tests as a set and evaluates the tests after the third row as a set, as the following steps show. If you remember how parentheses determine the order in which you evaluate mathematical expressions, you can think of the filter in Figure 21-25 as follows: ((Baseline Finish does not equal NA) And (Overallocated equals Yes)) And ((Finish is greater than [Baseline Finish]) Or (BCWS is greater than [BCWP])).

TIP If you forget to include a test in your filter, you don't have to start from scratch. The box on page 651 explains how to edit a filter to add, remove, and otherwise change condition order.

5. **In the fourth row, bypass the And/Or cell, and then simply add the test for slipped tasks.**

The test for slipped tasks checks whether the Finish field is greater than the Baseline Finish field. You don't have to include an And or an Or, because this test is the first one of the second set.

6. **In the fifth row, choose Or in the And/Or cell, and then add the test for late progress.**

The Or in front of this condition, shown in Figure 21-25, tells Project that a task has to pass either the slipped task test *or* the late progress test. Either situation means the task is in trouble.

7. **Click OK to save the filter.**

When you apply the filter to your task list, Project runs tasks past the first two filter conditions and then checks the tasks that pass the first group of conditions to see whether they pass either of the two tests in the second set.

UP TO SPEED

Inserting, Deleting, and Rearranging Rows

Without planning ahead, chances are good that you'll forget one of your filter conditions. After testing a filter, you may realize that your logic isn't sound. If you find yourself in that situation, you'll find the Filter Definition Dialog box's buttons for inserting, deleting, copying, cutting, and pasting rows quite handy. Here's what each button does:

- **Cut Row.** Select a row, and then click Cut Row to place the row on the Clipboard. The Paste Row button then becomes active so you can paste the row in another location.

- **Copy Row.** Select a row, and then click Copy Row to place the row on the Clipboard. If one row is almost identical to the one you want to add, then copying and pasting an existing row may be easier than defining a condition.

- **Paste Row.** Select the row below where you want to paste the row on the Clipboard, and then click Paste Row. Project inserts the cut or copied row above the selected row.

- **Insert Row.** Select the row where you want to insert a new blank row, and then click Insert Row. The new row appears above the selected row.

- **Delete Row.** If a condition is wrong or unnecessary, select it and then click Delete Row.

■ CREATING CHANGEABLE FILTERS

With some filters, you want to use different values each time you apply them, which is why Project offers *interactive filters*. An interactive filter is one that asks for values to use in tests. For example, when you're trying to find tasks scheduled during people's vacations, you can apply the Using Resource In Date Range filter. Each time you apply this filter, you tell it which resource you're looking for and the beginning and ending dates you're interested in. These values act exactly as though you had placed them in the Filter Definition dialog box in Value(s) cells.

Creating these inquisitive filters is easy once you learn how to define a prompt. Here are the steps:

1. **In the Filter Definition dialog box in the row for the interactive condition, choose the field and the test you want.**

   For example, to filter for tasks to which a specific resource is assigned, choose the Resource Names field, and the "contains exactly" test.

2. **In the Value(s) cell, type the prompt in quotation marks followed by a question mark, as shown in Figure 21-26, top.**

   For example, type a prompt like *"Show tasks assigned to this lucky devil"?* Make sure that the prompt text is enclosed in *double* quotes. The question mark after the quotes tells Project that the filter is interactive.

When you run the filter, Project displays your prompt (as shown in Figure 21-26, bottom) before running through the filter's tests.

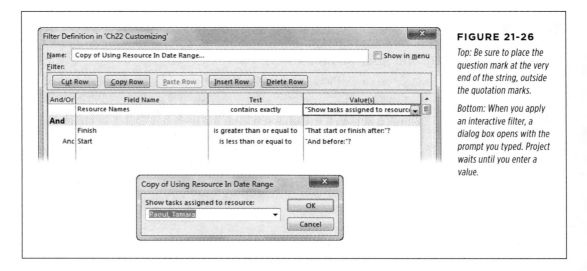

FIGURE 21-26

Top: Be sure to place the question mark at the very end of the string, outside the quotation marks.

Bottom: When you apply an interactive filter, a dialog box opens with the prompt you typed. Project waits until you enter a value.

Quick and Dirty Filtering with AutoFilter

When you have a quick, one-time question, creating and saving a filter doesn't make sense. Instead, turn to Project's AutoFilter feature, which, like its relative in Excel, lets you pick filter fields and values for one field at a time. You can change the fields or the values at will, and combine filters on several fields at the same time. (The box on page 655 shows you how to whip up a custom AutoFilter test, if the filter you want goes beyond the choices on an AutoFilter drop-down menu.)

Here's how to use AutoFilter:

1. **Display the view and table you want to filter.**

    A table must be visible, because AutoFilter works on table columns.

2. **If AutoFilter isn't turned on (down arrows aren't visible to the right of each column heading), then in the View tab's Data section, click the Filter down arrow, and then choose Display AutoFilter.**

    Project comes with AutoFilter turned on. If you want to turn AutoFilter off for new projects, choose File→Options. In the Project Options dialog box, click Advanced, and then, under the General heading, turn off the "Set AutoFilter on for new projects" checkbox.

3. **Click the down arrow in the column you want to filter—for instance, Duration.**

    The AutoFilter drop-down menu includes several filter values based on the data in the column, as illustrated in Figure 21-27.

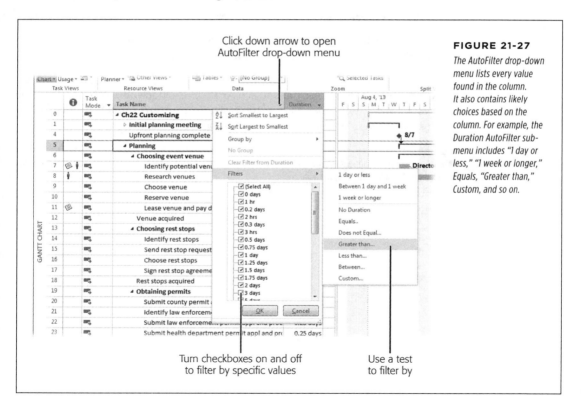

Click down arrow to open
AutoFilter drop-down menu

Turn checkboxes on and off
to filter by specific values

Use a test
to filter by

FIGURE 21-27

The AutoFilter drop-down menu lists every value found in the column. It also contains likely choices based on the column. For example, the Duration AutoFilter submenu includes "1 day or less," "1 week or longer," Equals, "Greater than," Custom, and so on.

4. **To filter by specific values, make sure the AutoFilter checkboxes for the values you want to use are turned on, and turn off all the other AutoFilter checkboxes. Click OK to apply the AutoFilter settings you've selected.**

   For example, to filter by longer durations, you can turn off the checkboxes for shorter Duration values.

5. **To apply a quick AutoFilter test, in the drop-down menu, choose Filters. Then, in the submenu, choose the test or condition you want.**

   For example, to filter for longer durations, choose "Greater than." The Custom AutoFilter dialog box opens. In the value drop-down list, choose the duration to use, such as 10 days, and then click OK. As soon as you apply an AutoFilter to a column, Project filters the list and displays the AutoFilter icon (which looks like a funnel) to the right of the column's heading.

6. **To remove a filter in a column, click the AutoFilter icon (which looks like a funnel) in that column, and then choose "Clear Filter from [column name]."**

   The filtered list updates to show items that pass the AutoFilters still in place.

7. **To add an AutoFilter to another column, click the down arrow in that column's heading row, and then repeat steps 4–6.**

   AutoFilter doesn't have all the options the Filter Definition dialog box provides. Also, AutoFilters on each column act like they're joined with And operators: The results show items that pass *all* the tests. So you can't tell AutoFilter to show items that pass one AutoFilter test or another.

TIP A funnel icon appears to the right of every column with an AutoFilter applied. In addition, the status bar includes the AutoFilter Applied notification.

Building Custom Filters with AutoFilter

Quite often, the filter you have in mind goes a step or two beyond what the AutoFilter drop-down menu offers, but you don't need the full suite of tools from the Filter Definition dialog box. If that's the case, a custom AutoFilter may be the answer. Custom AutoFilters can have one or two conditions joined with an And or an Or. You can even save custom AutoFilters you want to use again and add them to the regular filter list. Here's how to build a custom AutoFilter:

1. Click the down arrow in the column heading for the field you want to filter, choose Filters, and then, on the AutoFilter submenu, choose Custom.

2. In the Custom AutoFilter dialog box, the field is set to the selected column, as shown in Figure 21-28.

3. For the first custom condition, in the drop-down list on the left, choose the test (the same ones you see in the Filter Definition dialog box when you define a filter from scratch, as described on page 644) and then, in the box on the right, choose or type the value.

4. If the custom filter includes a second condition, select the And option if results must pass both conditions. Select the Or option if results must pass only one of the conditions.

5. If the custom filter includes a second condition, then repeat step 3 to define the second condition.

6. To save the custom AutoFilter, click Save. The Filter Definition dialog box opens with all the tests in the test table. All you have to do is type a new name in the Name box and then click OK. If you want to make other changes—for example, to add the filter to the menu or to hide summary tasks—modify the settings in the dialog box before clicking OK.

7. To apply the custom AutoFilter, click OK.

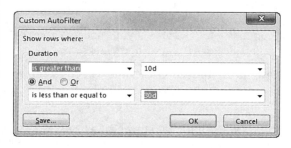

FIGURE 21-28

The Custom AutoFilter dialog box is like a simple version of a filter definition. Project selects the field for you based on the column whose arrow you right-clicked in step 1 (in this example, the field is Duration). You can define two criteria and specify that items meet both or only one of them.

■ Grouping Project Elements

Grouping tasks, resources, and assignments with similar characteristics makes it easy for you to scan and analyze your project information. In Project, the Group feature lets you segregate tasks, resources, or assignments by field values. For example, if you group tasks by schedule variance, troubled tasks will jump right out at you. Or you can group resources by availability to see who can jump in to help burned-out team members. This section explains how to use Project groups.

> **TIP** If you're confused by the different uses of the word "group" in Project, see the box on page 658 for clarification.

Working with Groups

Like filtering and sorting, groups can work with several fields. For example, you can group tasks first by critical and noncritical, and then by duration to find the longest critical tasks for fast-tracking (page 354). Here are a few methods of applying a group:

- **Choose a popular group.** In the View tab's Data section, click the "Group by" down arrow (see Figure 21-29), and then, on the drop-down menu, choose the group you want, like Critical, Milestones, or "Complete and Incomplete Tasks."

- **Choose any group.** In the View tab's Data section, click the Group By down arrow, and then, on the drop-down menu, choose More Groups. In the More Groups dialog box, double-click the group you want.

- **Group by a field.** Click the down arrow to the right of the column heading for the field you want to group by, and then, on the drop-down menu, choose "Group on this field" (for Yes/No fields). For other fields, the drop-down menu may contain the "Group by" command. When you choose that command, a submenu of group options appears—for example, if you choose "Group by" in the Duration field, the submenu includes Duration and Weeks.

To remove groupings, in the View tab's Data section, click the "Group by" down arrow, and then, on the drop-down menu, choose No Group. Or click the down arrow to the right of a column heading and choose No Group on the drop-down menu.

Changes you make to a project can affect the group to which a task, resource, or assignment belongs. For example, if you add resources to shorten task duration, the task should appear in a different Duration subgroup. However, you don't see that happen until you reapply the group.

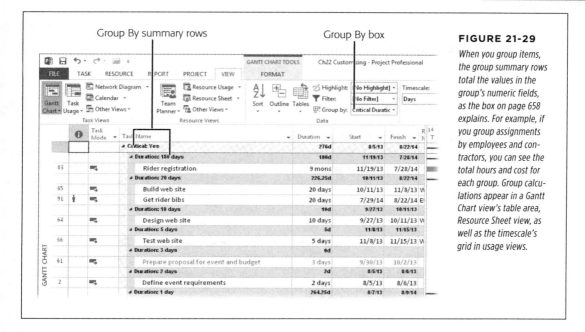

Group By summary rows   Group By box

FIGURE 21-29

When you group items, the group summary rows total the values in the group's numeric fields, as the box on page 658 explains. For example, if you group assignments by employees and contractors, you can see the total hours and cost for each group. Group calculations appear in a Gantt Chart view's table area, Resource Sheet view, as well as the timescale's grid in usage views.

Creating a Group

As with Project tables, the easiest way to create a group is to copy and edit an existing one. That way you keep the original group definition and customize the copy. For example, to set up a group that uses both the Critical and Duration fields, you can copy the built-in Critical group and then add the second condition to the copy. (Basic groups are so simple, though, that there's no problem starting from scratch.)

Groups, Groups, and More Groups

The term "group" is used to describe several features in Project, each of which does something different. Here are the different kinds of groups Project uses, and advice on keeping them straight:

- **Group By command.** In the View tab's Data section, the drop-down list in the "Group by" box (the box initially contains the text [No Group]) lists groups that categorize tasks, resources, or assignments by field values. (You can also click the down arrow to the right of the column heading for the field you want to group by, and then, on the drop-down menu, choose "Group by" or "Group on this field," depending on the field.) For example, the built-in "Complete and Incomplete Tasks" group separates completed tasks from those that aren't finished.

- **Resource group.** In Resource Sheet view, the Group field specifies categories for resources. For example, you could set up group names to associate people with their departments: Sales, Engineering, Fundraising, and so on. Then you could use the Group field to find replacement resources from the same department.

- **Group resource.** A group resource represents several interchangeable resources. Suppose your cycling event team includes 15 volunteers who can do any kind of setup task. In that case, you could create one resource called Volunteers. The Maximum Units for a group resource is the sum of each individual's maximum units, so the Volunteers group resource may have maximum units of 1,500 percent, say. You can then assign the Volunteers resource to tasks and let the team leader worry about who does what. As long as the assignments don't exceed 1,500 percent, your work is done.

- **Ribbon group.** If you customize the ribbon, one of the buttons on the "Customize the Ribbon" page is New Group. This command lets you add a new section to a tab on the ribbon.

Project comes with several groups that apply to tasks and resources, but you can expand the list to analyze your projects in many ways. Here are a few examples:

- **Overallocated resources.** Group tasks by the Overallocated field to find tasks with overallocated resources.

- **Overbudget tasks.** Group tasks by Cost Variance to categorize tasks by how much they're over budget.

- **Critical tasks with overallocated resources.** Critical tasks that use overallocated resources are risking a late project finish date. Group tasks first by the Critical field, and then by the Overallocated field, to see the group of critical tasks broken into overallocated and not-overallocated resources.

- **Internal and external resources.** Group assignments by the Resource Group field to see how much work you've assigned to outside resources.

- **Long critical tasks with little or no work done.** If you're looking for tasks to crash (page 356) to bring a project back on track, critical tasks with longer durations give you the most benefit. If the project is already in progress, tasks that are almost complete won't help. Filter first by Critical, then by % Complete (in ascending order), and finally by Duration (in descending order) so you can see the critical tasks with the least amount of work done and the longest duration.

The steps for creating and copying groups are almost identical. You create the new group (from scratch or by copying), name it, and then define the fields to group by. Here are the steps:

1. **In the View tab's Data section, click the "Group by" down arrow, and then, on the drop-down menu, choose More Groups.**

   If a task-oriented view is active, the More Groups dialog box opens with the Task option selected and task-related groups displayed in the Groups list. To work on a resource-related group (for instance, to group the resources in Resource Sheet view by their standard rates), select the Resource option instead.

2. **To create a copy of an existing group, in the Groups list, select the group you want to copy, and then click Copy. To start a new group from scratch, simply click New.**

   The Group Definition dialog box opens. Copying a group, and then editing the copy, means you'll still have the original group definition in addition to the new one.

> **NOTE**   To make changes to an existing group, in the More Groups dialog box, select the group you want to edit, and then click Edit. The Group Definition dialog box opens with the settings for the existing group. Make the changes you want and then click Save.

3. **In the Name box in the Group Definition dialog box, type a new name for the group.**

   New groups start with a name like "Group 1," whereas copied groups are named "Copy of [group name]." Replace Project's name with one that identifies what the group does, like "Critical/Duration."

> **TIP**   To list a new group on Project's group drop-down menus, be sure to turn on the "Show in menu" checkbox.

4. **To add a new field to group by, select the first blank Field Name cell, click the down arrow, and then choose the field you want to group by.**

   For example, to add the Duration field to the Critical/Duration group, choose Duration in the first Then By row, as shown in Figure 21-30. If you create a group from scratch, start by choosing a field in the Group By row.

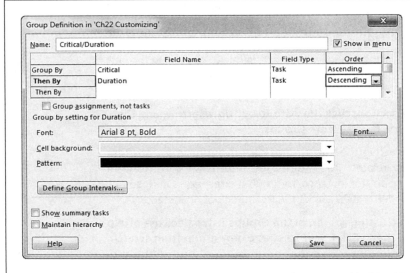

FIGURE 21-30

Project fills in the Field Type cell with Task for a task-related group or Resource for a resource-related group. If you want to group by assignments—for instance, to see which assignments are taking too long—choose Assignments in the Field Type cell and then turn on the "Group assignments, not tasks" checkbox.

5. **In the Order cell, choose Descending or Ascending.**

   For example, to show tasks from the longest duration to the shortest, choose Descending. To show resources from lowest to highest hourly rate, choose Ascending. Ascending shows text fields grouped in alphabetical order. If you group by a Yes/No field like Critical, then choose Descending if you want the fields with Yes to appear first.

6. **To group by assignment instead of by task, turn on the "Group assignments, not tasks" checkbox.**

   In a Task Usage view, you can group by task or by assignment, which determines how Project rolls up values into summary tasks. For example, group by task to see which tasks have the highest schedule variance. If you want to find out which assignments produce those variances, then group by assignments. (For a Resource Usage view, the checkbox label is "Group assignments, not resources.") The box on page 661 explains how group roll-up and other calculations work.

7. **To change the appearance of the group summary rows, change the values in the Font, "Cell background," and Pattern boxes.**

   When Project subtotals groups, it applies a different font to the summary rows and shades the cells. For example, the primary group rows use 8-point Arial, bolded, with a light yellow cell background. To print groups to a black-and-white printer, change the Pattern to cross-hatching, or choose colors that show up as different shades of gray.

NOTE If you want to see summary tasks in the groups, turn on the "Show summary tasks" checkbox. On the other hand, turning on the "Maintain hierarchy" checkbox shows all the levels of summary tasks for subtasks within groups. You can also maintain hierarchy from the ribbon by heading to the View tab's Data section, clicking the Group down arrow, and choosing "Maintain Hierarchy in Current Group."

8. **Click OK.**

The Group Definition dialog box closes. In the More Groups dialog box, click Apply to see the results of your handiwork.

POWER USERS' CLINIC

Calculating Rolled-Up Group Values

Rolled-up values for built-in fields like Cost and Work are simply the sum of values in the group. Other calculations like Maximum, Minimum, and Average are available for group summary rows, but only if you use custom fields (page 662), because you can't tell Project how to roll up built-in fields. If you want to see the average cost of a group of tasks or resources, set up a custom field like Cost1 that's equal to the built-in Cost field, and then set its Rollup value to the calculation you want (Average, in this example).

On the other hand, rolled-up Duration values may just look wrong. For example, a rolled-up Duration might be 63.5 days, while the four tasks in the group are each only 2 days long. That's because Project calculates the group's duration starting from the start date of the earliest task in the group to the finish date of the last task in the group.

Changing Group Intervals

Groups often start out with subgroups for each distinct value in the field you're grouping by. This approach is fine for Yes/No fields like Critical or Milestone. But when you group by cost, duration, and similar fields, the number of unique values could spawn *hundreds* of subgroups, for tasks that cost $3,450, $3,455, and so on.

Setting *group intervals* makes subgroups more meaningful. For example, on a short project, the intervals for the Duration group could be days. Or on a multiyear project, you might modify the Duration group to use 2-week intervals. Here's how you define intervals for a field in a group:

1. **In the Group Definition dialog box (page 659), click the Field Name cell for the field whose interval you want to set, and then click Define Group Intervals.**

   The Define Group Interval dialog box opens, as shown in Figure 21-31. (If the selected field doesn't work with intervals—Yes/No fields are one example—then the Define Group Intervals button is grayed out.)

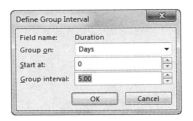

FIGURE 21-31

The name of the field you selected appears at the top. The "Group on" field is set initially to Each Value, which creates a separate subgroup for each unique value. To reduce the number of subgroups, choose an interval measure, such as Days or Weeks for the Duration field. Then, in the "Group interval" box, type a value for the interval size.

2. **To change the interval, in the "Group on" box, click the down arrow, and then choose the units or type of interval you want.**

   The choices in the "Group on" drop-down list vary based on the field you selected. For example, for Duration, the "Group on" choices range from Minutes to Days to Months. % Complete lists typical percentage intervals like "0, 1-99, 100" which groups tasks into unstarted, in progress, and complete. On the other hand, for Cost, choose Interval in the drop-down list to set the interval size (1000 to group on every $1,000, for example).

3. **To start the interval at a specific value, type the number in the "Start at" box.**

   You can group all the rows with tiny values by setting a "Start at" value. For example, if you're grouping on Duration and set the "Start at" value equal to 1 for a 1-day duration, then one group contains all tasks that last less than a day.

4. **To define the interval size, type a number in the "Group interval" box.**

   For example, if "Group on" is set to Days and "Group interval" is set to 5, then the subgroups come in 5-day increments, such as 0 to 5 days, 6 to 10 days, and so on.

5. **Click OK.**

   The Define Group Interval dialog box closes, and you're ready to click Save to save the edited group.

■ Defining Your Own Fields

Project comes with hundreds of built-in fields that track all sorts of information about projects. However, if you want to track performance that Project's built-in fields don't cover, you can modify settings for custom fields and then add those fields to tables in Project views (page 633) just as you would any built-in field. For example, you can create a field that holds the number of lines of code written for each development task. By tracking hours worked and code quantities, you can calculate programming productivity.

You can create custom fields that accept only the values you want by defining *lookup tables*. That way, you or anyone else can pick a valid value from a drop-down list. Custom fields can also contain formulas to calculate results. The usual arithmetic suspects like addition, subtraction, division, and multiplication show up as buttons in the Formula dialog box. But Project offers all sorts of fancy functions that you can combine with any Project field to spit out the answers you're looking for.

Graphical indicators make it easy to see whether a project is on track, going better than expected, or headed for trouble. By customizing fields, you can tell Project to display icons instead of numbers or text.

Outline code fields work like the WBS values that project managers know and love. You can set up outline codes to categorize tasks and resources, and each level of the outline can have its own rules for values and what those values represent. Outline codes can be flexible and let people fill in whatever values they desire, or they can use lookup tables, if you have a specific set of values you allow.

This section explains how to customize fields in all these ways.

Understanding Custom Fields

The field drop-down list that appears when you insert a column into a Project table is proof of how many fields Project has. For built-in fields, your customization options are limited. You can change the title that appears in a table column's heading, its width, and the alignment of its text. But the field's behind-the-scenes calculations and data are set in stone.

Custom fields come in the same data types as Project's built-in fields. For example, you can set up a custom cost field to track early delivery bonuses, a text field to document that custom cost, or an outline code to categorize tasks based on who's footing the bill. Project has one set of customizable fields for tasks and a similarly named set for resources. (To see the custom fields for a specific data type, click the down arrow to the right of the Type box, and then choose the custom field data type you want.) Here are the different types of customizable Project fields:

- **Cost.** Cost1 through Cost10 are currency fields for tracking anything that represents money.

- **Date.** Date1 through Date10 are date fields—for instance, to calculate the date halfway between the start and finish date for a task.

- **Duration.** Duration1 through Duration10 contain units of time. For example, you could create a custom duration field to calculate the time it takes to write one page of documentation.

- **Finish.** Finish1 through Finish10 are date fields. Although these are custom fields, Project stores finish dates for interim plans in Finish1 through Finish10. So if you save interim plans, then leave Finish1 through Finish10 alone and use Date1 through Date10 for your custom dates instead.

- **Flag.** Perfect for tagging tasks or resources, Flag1 through Flag20 are fields that contain either Yes or No. What they say yes or no *to* is up to you.

- **Number.** Because number fields are so versatile—lines of code, lines of code per day, defects reported, and so on—Project provides 20 number fields: Number1 through Number20.

- **Start.** Like their finish date counterparts, Start1 through Start10 are date fields, which Project uses to store start dates for interim plans. If you save interim plans, use Date1 through Date10 for your custom dates instead.

- **Text.** Each of the 30 text fields, Text1 through Text30, can hold up to 255 characters. For short notes, a custom Text field can go right in a table next to another custom field to which it relates—for example, identifying the type of custom cost you've added. Notes (page 156) are another way to annotate tasks and resources, especially when the notes are long or you want to insert pictures or objects.

- **Outline Code.** Outline Code1 through Outline Code10 represent a hierarchy of values, which you set up with a code mask (page 676).

Customizing a Field

Custom fields let you specify how they look and behave. You can change the name of a custom field from, say, Number1 to something more meaningful, like LinesOfCode. You can use a formula to calculate the field's values or create a lookup table to help others pick valid values. How values roll up to summary rows is customizable, too, whether you want a total like other Project fields or another calculation like minimum, maximum, or average. Initially, fields display values, but you can define graphical indicators instead. For example, you can use stoplight colors to indicate whether a measure is on track, on thin ice, or in need of resuscitation.

This section begins with the basics: choosing a field's data type, whether it applies to tasks or resources, and picking the specific custom field you want to work on. From there, you can jump to other sections to learn how to work with lookup tables, formulas, calculations, graphical indicators, and the other available settings. (Because outline codes work a little differently, they warrant their own section, "Coding Tasks and Resources" on page 675.)

No matter which type of custom field you choose, what you can customize remains the same. Here are the basic steps for defining a custom field:

1. **In the Project tab's Properties section, click Custom Fields.**

   The Custom Fields dialog box opens.

2. **Select either the Task option or the Resource option.**

   Project has two sets of custom fields: one for tasks and another for resources. The field names are the same, but the fields are different. For example, you can customize a Number1 task field to store lines of code and a Number1 resource field to store a person's performance rating. When you insert a field into a table, the custom field you get depends on the table. For example, in Resource Sheet view, the Number1 field is the resource field. In a Gantt Chart view, the Number1 field is the task field.

NOTE If you use Project Professional with Project Server, the Custom Fields dialog box's Project option is also available, so you can define project-level custom fields.

---

3. **In the Type drop-down list, choose the type of field, as shown in Figure 21-32.**

   Once you choose a Type option, the Field list displays the fields for the selected data type. (If you've renamed a field, you see the field's name *and* its updated name [a.k.a. alias] in the list.)

FIGURE 21-32

After you select the Task option or Resource option and choose a field type, the Custom Fields dialog box lists the custom fields that correspond to the option and type you selected. For example, if you select the Task option and choose Finish in the Type list, the Custom Fields dialog box lists the Finish1 through Finish10 task fields. To work on a custom outline code, in the Type drop-down list, choose Outline Code, and then go to page 675 for more instructions.

4. **In the Field list, select the field you want to customize, like Number1 or Flag5.**

   You can choose any field in the list. If you decide to customize a field you've already used—for example, to calculate values with a formula—you may see a warning that the calculated values will overwrite any existing data.

5. **To give the custom field a more meaningful name, click Rename.**

   Custom field names start as a combination of the data type and a numeric ID; for instance, Cost3 is the third custom cost field. Whenever you customize a field, rename it so its alias describes what the custom field is for, like "Pages per day" if you're calculating how many pages of documentation the team produces each day.

TIP Although you can change the title in a column heading cell in a table (page 633), the edited title applies only to the current table. Renaming a custom field displays the alias in drop-down lists and every time you insert the field in a table.

---

6. **In the Rename Field dialog box, type a new name for your custom field, and then click OK.**

   The alias and the original field name both appear in the field list, as shown in Figure 21-32.

7. **If you don't want to do any other kind of customization, then click OK.**

   The Custom Field dialog box closes, and you can insert the renamed field in a table.

At this point, the custom field cheerfully accepts any value you enter as long as it's the right data type. For example, if you use a custom number field in a table, Project complains only if you try to type a date, some text, or any other value that isn't a number.

Creating Lists of Valid Values

Some custom fields are cut and dried. Flag fields accept Yes or No; those values appear in a drop-down list in a Flag cell. Similarly, Text fields expect text, but they don't care what that text is. So if you want people to enter correct or at least *consistent* values, it's a good idea to provide some hints about valid values. For example, if the Text1 field is supposed to contain a department name, then you don't want people typing anything they please. Likewise, you wouldn't want one person to type "Manu" for the Manufacturing group and someone else to type "Mfg." You can control the values that a custom field accepts with a *lookup table*—a list of valid values.

You can set up a lookup table to enforce a fixed list of values or to accept additional values not on the list. When a lookup table allows other values, the choices already there act as examples of what's expected. To build a lookup table for a custom field, follow these steps:

1. **In the Project tab's Properties section, click Custom Fields, and then select the custom field you want to work on.**

   You can choose a field you haven't used yet or add a lookup table to a field you've already renamed. If you choose a virgin field, rename it (page 666).

2. **Click Lookup.**

   The "Edit Lookup Table for [field name]" dialog box opens. Project adds the name of the field or its alias to the title bar.

3. **In the Value column, select a blank cell, and then type a value. In the Description cell, type a description of the value.**

   If you enter a value that doesn't match the type of field, Project turns the value red and bolds it. As soon as you correct the discrepancy, the value turns black and unbolded.

   Descriptions are optional, but they can be useful to people filling in values. If you include a description, then the value and the description both appear in a table cell's drop-down list. For example, the description cell can spell out an abbreviation. That way, people know that "Log" means Logistics, not Logging.

4. **Repeat step 3 to add more values to the list.**

   Although you can't copy and paste lookup table values from Excel or the rows in Resource Sheet view, the box on page 669 describes a shortcut to building a lookup table.

   The Edit Lookup Table dialog box has buttons for inserting, removing, copying, and rearranging the values in the lookup table, as Figure 21-33 shows.

Row buttons

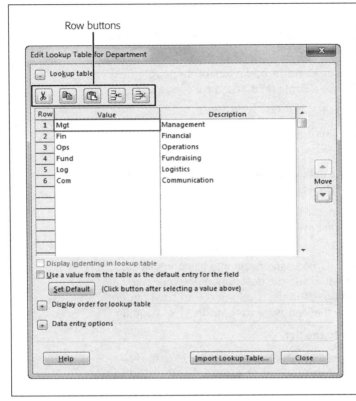

FIGURE 21-33

The first two row buttons, Cut Row and Copy Row, both place the row on the Clipboard so you can then relocate it by clicking Paste Row. To insert or remove rows, click either cell in the row, and then click Insert Row or Delete Row. Another way to rearrange rows is to click either cell in the row and then click the Move up and down arrows to the right of the lookup table.

5. **If you want the custom field to automatically fill in a value, click the cell that contains the default value, and then click Set Default.**

   When you do, Project automatically turns on the "Use a value from the table as the default entry for the field" checkbox and changes the font for the default value to blue and bolded.

   NOTE If you're wondering why the "Display indenting in lookup table" checkbox is grayed out, it's reserved for outline codes (page 675).

6. **To control the order that values appear in a drop-down list, expand the "Display order for lookup table" section (click the + button to the left of the label). Select either the "Sort ascending" or "Sort descending" option, and then click Sort.**

To display lookup values in a drop-down list in the order they appear in the Edit Lookup Table dialog box, keep the "By row number" option selected. This option is ideal when you want to show the more frequently used values at the top of the drop-down list.

When you select a sort order and then click Sort, Project re-sorts the list.

7. **If it's OK for someone to type a value that's not in the lookup table, expand the "Data entry options" section, and then turn on the "Allow additional items to be entered into the fields" checkbox.**

Project turns off this checkbox initially so the field accepts only values in the lookup table. By not allowing other values, you can prevent duplicate values or misspellings. If you *do* allow other values and someone enters a unique value not in the lookup table, then Project automatically adds that value to the lookup table. The other checkbox in this section, "Allow only codes that have no subordinate values," is grayed out because it applies to outline codes (page 675).

8. **Click Close.**

The Edit Lookup Table dialog box closes, and you're back in the Custom Fields dialog box. If you're finished making customizations, then click OK.

GEM IN THE ROUGH

Reusing Lookup Tables

Building lookup tables can take time, especially if the list and descriptions are long. Fortunately, you can bypass this data-entry chore if another custom field already has what you want.

If you know that an existing custom field has everything you want—lookup tables, formulas, and so on—then open the Custom Fields dialog box (page 664) and click Import Field. You choose the Project file, the Task or Resource option, and the field name. Project imports the entire field with *all* of its customizations, not just the lookup table.

But if you want to import *only* the lookup table (a list of departments in your company, for example) into a custom field, here are the steps:

1. If the lookup table belongs to a custom field in another project, open that Project file first.

2. Return to the Project file that you want to import a lookup table into.

3. In the Project tab's Properties section, click Custom Fields.

4. In the Custom Fields dialog box, select the field you want to edit, and then click Lookup.

5. In the Edit Lookup Table dialog box, click Import Lookup Table.

6. If the lookup table is in another project, then in the Project drop-down list, select the filename.

7. Select the option for the type of field (Task, Resource, or Project).

8. In the Field drop-down list, choose the custom field with the lookup table, and then click OK. All the lookup table values appear in the current custom field's table.

Importing a lookup table is the perfect solution if you defined a ginormous lookup table for a custom outline code and then realized that you customized a *task* outline code instead of a *resource* outline code. You can import the lookup table from the task outline code in the same file.

Calculating Field Values

Another way to fill in custom field values is to calculate them. Don't reach for your calculator—Project can do the calculating as long as you give it the formula. A formula can use every Project field, along with typical numeric and logical functions. For example, a "Reg per hour" custom number field could divide the Registrations custom field by the task's Actual Work field to determine the number of registrations completed for each work hour.

> **TIP** If the formula you want already exists in another custom field, then you can import it. First, open the Project file that contains the custom field with the formula you want. Then, back in the Project file with the field you're customizing, in the Project tab's Properties section, click Custom Fields. Select the custom field to which you want to add the formula, and then click Formula. In the Formula dialog box, click Import Formula. In the Import Formula dialog box, fill in the boxes as you do when importing a lookup table (page 669). Unlike most other Project elements, you can't use the Organizer to copy formulas from project to project.

To define a formula to calculate field values, follow these steps:

1. **After selecting the field you want to edit in the Custom Fields dialog box (page 664), click Formula.**

   The "Formula for" dialog box opens with the custom field's name or alias in the title bar.

2. **To add a field to the formula, click Field. In the drop-down list, choose the category and then the field you want to add, as shown in Figure 21-34.**

   The categories are similar to different field data types. IDs and outline codes share a spot in the list, and the Project category contains properties related to the Project file, like the date it was created. When you select a field, Project inserts it into your formula and puts square brackets ([ ]) around the field's name.

3. **To insert a function, click where you want the function in the formula, and then click the appropriate function button.**

   The most commonly used functions have their own buttons, including addition, subtraction, multiplication, and division; equals, parentheses, greater than and less than; and the logical operators AND, OR, and NOT. (The box on page 672 has a tip for building formulas.)

   To find other functions, click Function, choose the category, and then choose the function. Take a few minutes to look at the functions in each category, because you have plenty to choose from. For example, in the Date/Time category, the Weekday function figures out the day of the week based on the date and the first day of the work week. The General category has functions for If-statements (IIf), case statements (Switch), and functions that check for null or numeric values (IsNull and IsNumeric). The Text category has a host of string functions, like Len, Left, and Trim, which are familiar to geeks who've written Visual Basic code.

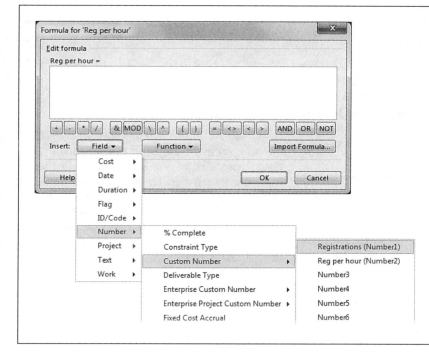

FIGURE 21-34

Within a Field category, Project includes both built-in and customized fields. When the list entry represents several fields (for example, Custom Number, shown here), a right arrow indicates it has a submenu.

If the function you want doesn't have a button, below the text box, click Function, choose the appropriate category, and then choose the function.

4. **To insert a value in the formula, click where you want to insert the value, and then type the number or text.**

   You can also drag to select part of the formula—if you want to delete a field, for example.

5. **To tell Project the order in which to calculate functions, add parentheses to the formula.**

   Click where you want to insert a parenthesis, and then type it (or click the button for the left or right parenthesis character).

6. **When you've finished the formula, click OK. If you're done customizing the field, click OK in the Custom Fields dialog box, too.**

   If the field already contains values, a message box warns you that any data in the field will be replaced by the formula's calculations. If you want to overwrite existing data, click OK. Otherwise click Cancel and use a different field.

TIP When you use a formula, be sure to set up several test cases to make sure the formula does what you want.

Feeding Formulas Values

Suppose you define a formula only to see the custom field cells in a table awash with the dreaded value #ERROR. Dividing by zero is one cause of #ERROR; it's a no-no in Project formulas, as it is in any programming language. To prevent Project from squawking, you can set up formulas to perform calculations only if fields have values, which is where the IIf function comes in.

The IIf function works like an If statement in other programming languages. The function tests a condition, and then does one thing if the condition is true and another if the condition is false. For example, you could create a "Pages per day" custom number field with the basic formula [Number1] / [Actual Work]. You don't want to calculate the formula unless Actual Work field has a value other than zero. (Notice that formulas use *actual* field names, not the aliases you use to rename custom fields.) In this situation, the formula should calculate the result if Actual Work is not equal to zero, and otherwise return zero. Here's what the enhanced formula looks like:

```
IIf([Actual Work]<>0,[Number1]/[Actual
Work],0)
```

(In math speak, the less than sign followed by the greater than sign (<>) translates to "is not equal to.")

Unfortunately, this formula still doesn't deliver the result you'd expect. For example, if Number1 equals 2 and Actual Work equals 1h (one hour), the result is 0.03, because of another Project formula idiosyncrasy. Even third-graders know that 2 divided by 1 equals 2. The reason for this numerical discrepancy is that Project converts any time value into minutes. Therefore, the formula is actually dividing Number1 by 60 minutes (1 hour multiplied by 60 minutes). To get the correct answer in days, you have to add a conversion to your formula. The final formula looks like this:

```
IIf([Actual Work]<>0,[Number1]/([Actual
Work]/60), 0)
```

Calculating Values in Summary Rows

Custom fields don't automatically come with roll-up calculations, but you can control the calculation a custom field uses. The calculation options are in the Custom Fields dialog box's "Calculation for task and group summary rows" section. The simplest option is "Use formula," which calculates roll-ups using the same formula the field uses. You can also tell the program how to distribute values to assignments, as described in the box on page 673.

> **TIP** For built-in fields, Project rolls up values into summary tasks and group summary rows—you don't have a choice in the matter. One way to work around this limitation is to create a custom field equal to the built-in field you want to roll up in a different way. Then simply choose the roll-up calculation you want for the custom field.

In the Custom Fields dialog box, when you select the Rollup option for a numerical field like a cost, date, duration, or number field, the Rollup drop-down list comes to life with several built-in calculations. Here are your choices:

- **And.** For custom flag fields, this choice sets the summary flag to No if at least one lower-level item is No. The value is Yes only if all lower-level values are Yes.

- **Or.** For custom flag fields, this choice sets the summary flag to No only if *all* lower-level values are No. The value is Yes if at least one lower-level item is Yes, like the built-in Critical field does with summary tasks.

- **Average.** For cost, duration, and number fields, this calculation determines the average of all nonsummary values belonging to a summary task or within a set of grouped tasks or resources. For example, you could calculate the average productivity for all work tasks assigned to a specific group.

- **Average First Sublevel.** For cost, duration, and number fields, this choice calculates the average of task values one level below the summary task (including summary and nonsummary tasks) or group.

- **Count All.** For number fields, Count All counts the number of items below a summary task or group (including summary and nonsummary tasks or resources).

- **Count First Sublevel.** For number fields, this choice counts the number of items one level below the summary task or group.

- **Count Nonsummaries.** For number fields, this calculation counts the number of nonsummary items below the summary task or group—for example, to count the number of resources that are overallocated.

- **Maximum.** For all types of fields *except* Flag, Text, and Outline Code, this option sets the summary value to the largest value underneath the summary or group.

- **Minimum.** For all types of fields *except* Flag, Text, and Outline Code, this option sets the summary value to the smallest value underneath the summary or group.

- **Sum.** For cost, duration, and number fields, this totals the nonsummary values below the summary task or group.

UP TO SPEED

Distributing Task Values to Assignments

In the Custom Fields dialog box, the "Calculation for assignment rows" section is where you tell Project how to distribute the value of a custom field to a task's or resource's assignments. For example, suppose you set up a custom field to track the number of event registrations recorded. If you want to divvy up the total number of registrations among each registration resource's assignment, select the "Roll down unless manually entered" option. If you type values into the custom field for each assignment, then you can use those values to calculate individuals' productivity. Otherwise, Project divides the pages written evenly across all assignments.

If you don't want the value distributed to assignments, select None. Project selects this option initially for all custom fields.

Displaying Values Graphically

Displaying pictures instead of values makes it easier to see what's going on, just like an Excel line graph can spotlight the growth rate from a worksheet of numbers. For example, many project managers use traffic-light icons to present project performance: A green light means a task is on schedule, a yellow light means a little behind schedule (for example, 2 days), and a red light means an unacceptable delay (5 days, say). You can set up a custom field to display a graphic instead of a number and specify the conditions under which each graphic should appear.

In the "Values to display" section of the Custom Fields dialog box, Project initially selects the Data option, which simply shows field values. To use graphical indicators instead, follow these steps:

1. **In the Custom Fields dialog box, after selecting the field you want to edit, in the "Values to display" section, click the Graphical Indicators button.**

   The Graphical Indicators dialog box opens. The custom field's name or alias appears in the title bar so you know which field you're working on.

2. **In the "Indicator criteria for" section, select an option to tell Project whether you're defining graphical indicators for summary tasks or nonsummary tasks.**

   Project selects the "Nonsummary rows" option initially. If you define indicators only for nonsummary rows, then summary rows and the project summary row both use those same conditions to determine the indicator to display. In the traffic-light example, the summary tasks and project summary task would both show red lights if they were delayed by more than 5 days.

   But you may want to use different conditions for summary rows—for example, to decrease the delay thresholds because you hope that delays and early deliveries will balance each other out (it could happen). In that case, select the "Summary rows" option and then turn off the "Summary rows inherit criteria from nonsummary rows" checkbox. That way, you can define a separate set of conditions and indicators—for example, to display a red light if summary tasks are delayed by 2 days.

   If you want different conditions for the project-summary row, select the "Project summary" option, turn off the "Project summary inherits criteria from summary rows" checkbox, and then define the conditions for the project-summary row.

3. **To set up a graphical indicator, select the first empty "Test for" cell, click the down arrow that appears, and then choose the test you want.**

   The tests are almost identical to the ones for filters (page 646). The only additional test is "is any value," which displays the indicator as long as the field isn't empty. You can use the "is any value" test as the last condition to ensure that the field always shows a graphical indicator.

4. **In the Values(s) cell in the same row, type the value.**

   Similar to filters, you can type a number or text, or choose a field in the drop-down list to compare the custom field to another field. Say you want to define an indicator for productivity and a value of 1 or less is poor. In the Test cell, choose "is less than or equal to," and then, in the Value(s) cell, type *1*. Or you could compare a custom Finish field to the Baseline Finish field and display a red light when Finish is greater than Baseline Finish.

5. **In the Image cell, click the down arrow, and then choose the graphic you want Project to display when the condition is true, as shown in Figure 21-35.**

   If you're testing for less than or greater than, be sure to include at least one test containing "equal to" to make sure you cover every value. For example, if you test for values less than 1 and 5, include a test for values less than or equal to 5 and another for greater than 5. Otherwise, the test doesn't cover the value 5.

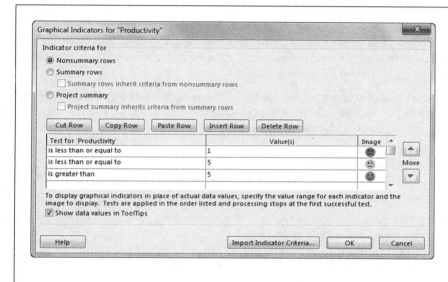

FIGURE 21-35

Project steps through the conditions in order until the field value satisfies a condition, and then it displays the corresponding graphical indicator. The order of tests is important. For example, for "if less than or equal to" tests, test for the smaller value first—less than or equal to 1 before less than or equal to 5, say. If you test for less than or equal to 5 first, 0 passes that test and displays its indicator instead of the indicator for values less than 1.

6. **Repeat steps 3–5 to define another condition and graphical indicator.**

   When you're done, click OK to close the Graphical Indicators dialog box. Click OK in the Custom Fields dialog box if you're finished customizing fields.

> **NOTE** Like other dialog boxes with tables (page 634), the Graphical Indicators dialog box includes Cut Row, Copy Row, Paste Row, Insert Row, and Delete Row buttons, so you can add, remove, or reorder your tests.

Coding Tasks and Resources

In Project, an *outline code* represents a hierarchy of values. The most obvious example of an outline code is the WBS field (page 145), which includes values that correspond to each level in a work breakdown structure. Sometimes you work with other categorization schemes that are examples of outline codes, such as expense codes for the accounting department, job codes that define people's skills, or part numbers for material resources.

You can create up to 10 sets of custom outline codes to categorize tasks and *another* 10 sets to categorize resources. Assigning custom outline codes to tasks and resources is the same as for any other kind of field: You type a value or choose from a drop-down list. And you can use outline codes to filter, group, or sort, just like other types of fields.

The difference between an outline code and any other kind of custom field is its multiple levels of values, each separated by a symbol. Each level can be uppercase or lowercase letters, numbers, or characters. For example, if your organization's accounting codes are a hierarchical structure of levels within levels, create a custom outline code rather than a number or a text field. Then the drop-down list that appears in the custom field cell in a table shows this multilevel outline code, which makes it easier to find the code you need.

Because categorization schemes usually follow rules (similar to the Dewey Decimal System at the library), outline codes typically use a *code mask*, a set of rules that specify the type of characters and the length of each level.

Other than the code mask, customizing an outline code is similar to customizing a text field. For example, you can create a lookup table to help people choose the right values. (You can limit values to what's on the list or let folks add new ones.) And you can sort the values or leave them in the order you placed them in the lookup table.

This section describes how to create a new outline code, set up the format for the code, and create the outline code's lookup table.

■ SELECTING AND NAMING A NEW OUTLINE CODE

Follow these steps to begin creating an outline code:

1. **In the Project tab's Properties section, click Custom Fields.**

   The Custom Fields dialog box appears.

2. **At the top of the dialog box, select either the Task or Resource option as appropriate.**

   If some codes apply to tasks and others apply to resources, you'll have to create two sets of outline codes: one for tasks and the other for resources—you can't combine them.

3. **In the Type drop-down list, choose Outline Code.**

   Although almost all the custom fields let you create a lookup table for them, outline codes are the only type of custom field for which you can create a *multilevel* lookup table.

4. **In the list of fields, select the next available outline code (for example, Outline Code1 or Outline Code10).**

   Because it's a good idea to rename custom fields to indicate what they represent, you can usually tell that a custom field is available if it doesn't include a second name in parentheses.

5. **Click Rename, type the name you want for this field—for example, Account-ing Code—and then click OK.**

The renamed field appears in the list of outline codes with the new name fol-lowed by the original outline code field name in parentheses, such as "Accounting Code (Outline Code1)."

6. **Keep the Custom Fields dialog box open, and continue with step 3 in the next section to set the format for your accounting code.**

■ SETTING UP A TEMPLATE FOR OUTLINE CODE VALUES

A code mask spells out the characters and length for each level of the outline code, as well as the character that separates each level. The Edit Lookup Table dialog box contains an extra section for the code mask. If you create a lookup table with the complete list of valid values, you may think you can skip the code mask entirely. However, when you create a code mask, Project can flag lookup table values you enter that don't match the code mask's specifications.

To set up the code mask, follow these steps:

1. **To customize a custom outline code, in the Project tab's Properties section, click Custom Fields.**

The Custom Fields dialog box opens.

2. **Select either the Task option or Resource option, and then, in the Type drop-down list, choose Outline Code. In the Field list, select the outline code you want to work on (Outline Code1 through Outline Code10).**

Any settings you've specified for the outline code appear in the Custom Fields dialog box.

3. **Click Lookup.**

The Edit Lookup Table dialog box opens. The dialog box's title bar includes the outline-code field's name or the alias you assigned to the outline code.

4. **Expand the "Code mask" section by clicking the + sign to the left of the label, and then click Edit Mask.**

The Code Mask Definition dialog box opens.

5. **In the first Sequence cell, choose the type of characters you want for the top level of the hierarchy, as shown in Figure 21-36.**

Your choices are Numbers, Uppercase Letters, Lowercase Letters, and the no-holds-barred option, Characters, which accepts all three types.

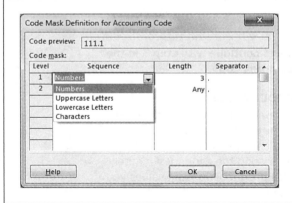

FIGURE 21-36

Project automatically fills in the Separator cell with a period (.). (The separator in the last row of the code mask never appears, since it doesn't need to separate anything.) As you define the code mask, the "Code preview" box at the top of the dialog box shows what an outline code value would look like with the code mask you've defined.

6. **In the first Length cell, choose Any or a number from 1 to 10 for the length of the top level.**

   Project initially selects Any, which means any number of characters is valid. For example, with numbers, you could type *5, 50,* or *5000* without Project balking. Choosing a specific length means the value is fixed at that length. For example, if you choose 3, numbers must have three digits.

7. **In the Separator cell, choose the character that separates the top level from the next level.**

   The separator can be a period (.), a hyphen (-), a plus sign (+), or a slash (/).

8. **Repeat steps 5–7 to add additional levels to the mask.**

   The code mask accepts dozens of levels, but outline code values can be no longer than 255 characters.

9. **When you're done, click OK to close the Code Mask Definition dialog box.**

   Keep the Edit Lookup Table dialog box open and go on to the next section to create the multilevel lookup table for your accounting code.

■ SETTING UP AN OUTLINE-CODE LOOKUP TABLE

Like other fields, outline codes work best when people know the values that are legit. If you set up a code mask and stop there, then *any* value that follows the code mask is valid. To provide examples or to restrict values to a predefined list, build an outline-code lookup table. The steps are the same as the ones for creating a regular lookup table, except that you have to tell Project how to handle the multiple levels. Here are the steps:

1. **In the Edit Lookup Table dialog box below the lookup table itself, turn on the "Display indenting in lookup table" checkbox.**

   This setting indents values in the lookup table based on their level in the outline, as illustrated in Figure 21-37.

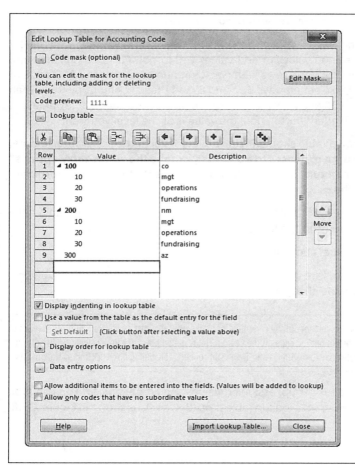

FIGURE 21-37

As you work, you can hide or show outline levels by clicking the triangles to the left of higher-level values. (A black triangle indicates that the higher level is expanded to show lower-level values. A white triangle indicates that lower levels are hidden.) To indent or outdent values to the correct level, click the Indent button (the dark-green right arrow) or the Outdent button (the dark-green left arrow). Click the Show All Subcodes button (the one with two + signs) to display every value in the table for your final quality-control review.

2. **Type a value in the first blank Value cell and a description in the Description cell in the same row.**

The value has to conform to the first level of the code mask. For example, if the first level is supposed to be three numbers and you type a value of *ab* or *12,* Project formats it in bold red text to indicate that that's not an acceptable value. But if you type a legitimate value like *100,* it appears in regular black font.

3. **In the next Value cell, type a value for the second level of the code mask. Click the Indent button (the dark-green right arrow) to push the value to the second level.**

Until you indent the value, it may appear in bold, red text. That's because Project validates the value at the level you place it.

4. **Repeat step 3 to add more outline code values.**

You can use the Cut Row, Copy Row, Paste Row, Insert Row, and Delete Row buttons to rearrange values or add values you forgot. For example, in Figure 21-37, you could copy the rows with two-digit numbers from the 200 code to the 300 code by selecting rows 6, 7, and 8, and then clicking Copy Row. Then click a cell in row 10 and click Paste Rows. To add lookup values at lower levels, simply click the Indent button until the value is at the level you want.

5. **If an outline code value should include every level of the code (for example, to correctly assign expenses to accounts), expand the "Data entry options" section, and then turn on the "Allow only codes that have no subordinate values" checkbox.**

Project initially turns off this checkbox, which means you can enter an outline code with only some of the levels, just like the WBS field works.

6. **When you're done, click Close.**

If the other settings are the way you want, then in the Custom Fields dialog box, click OK to save the changes.

NOTE You can import a custom outline code field or its lookup table just as you can with other types of fields (page 669). To import an outline code, in the Custom Fields dialog box, click Import Field. To import only the lookup table from another custom outline code, in the Edit Lookup Table dialog box, click Import Lookup Table.

After the outline code is set up, assigning values should be familiar. You can type values or choose them from a lookup table drop-down list, as shown in Figure 21-38.

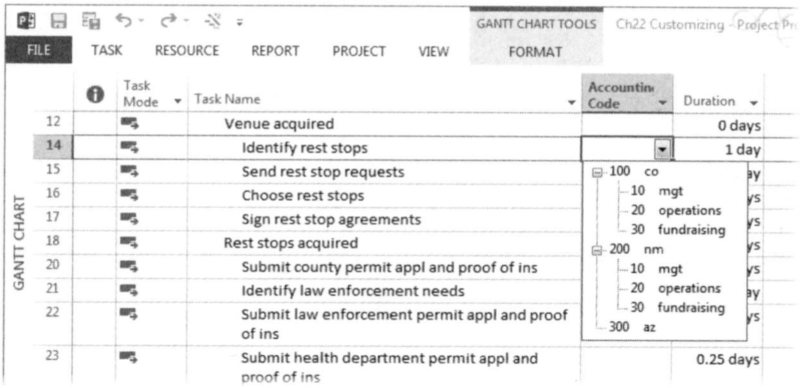

FIGURE 21-38

If you don't create a lookup table for your outline code, you have to type a value and hope for the best. If the value doesn't match the code mask, an error message with the correct format appears. With a lookup table like the one shown here, you simply click the down arrow in the cell and then choose the value you want

Customizing the Ribbon and Quick Access Toolbar

Project 2013's ribbon comes with built-in tabs, each organized in a way that makes project-management tasks easier for most people. After using the program for a while, you may discover that some commands get a lot of exercise, that some starve for attention, and that a few you of your favorites are nowhere to be found. For example, may never click any of the Gantt Chart Style buttons to change the color scheme of your task bars, or you might rather see the Format Painter command on the Format tab. And you frequently use the Edit Links command to update the connections to files you link to your Project schedule, but it's not available as a button on the ribbon. Fortunately, you can customize which commands you see and where they're located.

The Quick Access toolbar sits above the left side of the ribbon. It's always visible and doesn't take up much room, so it's an ideal home for your all-time favorite commands. As the following section explains, adding commands to it is a breeze.

You can also customize the ribbon to suit your needs. You can turn tabs on or off, create your own tabs and groups, add commands to groups, and rearrange the order of elements on the ribbon (tabs, groups, and commands). This chapter shows you how to do all these things. After you get the Quick Access toolbar and the ribbon the way you want, why keep them to yourself? This chapter wraps up by showing you how to share your customizing with your colleagues.

NOTE Project refers to the various sections within tabs as *groups*. The instructions throughout this book, however, refer to ribbon groups as *sections* to differentiate them from other Project features with the word "group" in their names, such as the Group field and the Group By command. In this chapter, the terms "section" and "group" are interchangeable.

Customizing the Quick Access Toolbar

The Quick Access toolbar perches quietly but conveniently above the File and Task tabs. Initially, this toolbar contains only buttons for the Save, Undo, and Redo commands, but you can add any commands you want to it. The Quick Access toolbar doesn't have tabs or groups, so customizing it is fast and easy. You can also move it below the ribbon so it's within easy reach. Here's what you can do:

- **Add a command to the toolbar.** Click the down arrow to the right of the Quick Access toolbar and then choose the command you want to add. A checkmark appears to the left of the commands that are currently on the toolbar, as shown in Figure 22-1. Several popular commands, like New, Open, and Print Preview, are on the drop-down menu, so a quick click is all it takes to add them to the toolbar.

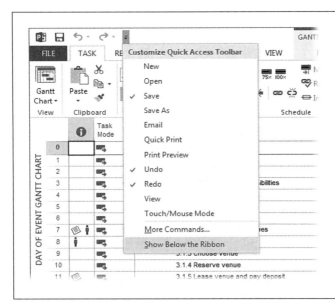

FIGURE 22-1

When you click the Quick Access toolbar's down arrow, this menu appears, which contains several popular commands. Simply click one of the commands to add it to the toolbar. (A checkmark appears to the left of the command's name to indicate that it's on the toolbar.) To remove a command from the toolbar, click its name to turn off its checkmark. To add other commands to the toolbar, choose More Commands to open the Project Options dialog box to its "Customize the Quick Access Toolbar" page.

> **TIP** When you customize the Quick Access toolbar, you can specify whether your changes apply to *all* files you open in Project or just the active one. (Project applies your changes to all documents unless you say otherwise.) To customize the Quick Access toolbar for just the active file, choose File→Options. On the left side of the Project Options dialog box, choose Quick Access Toolbar. In the Customize Quick Access Toolbar box, Project automatically chooses "For all documents (default)," which means the changes you make to the toolbar appear in every file you open. To apply the customized toolbar to only the active file, choose "For <filename>" where <filename> is the name of the active Project file.

- **Quickly add any Project command to the toolbar.** The quickest way to add a command to the Quick Access toolbar is by right-clicking the command on the ribbon and then choosing "Add to Quick Access Toolbar." When you do that, the command's icon takes its place as the rightmost item on the toolbar.

- **Add and organize commands on the toolbar.** Click the down arrow to the right of the Quick Access toolbar and choose More Commands. The Project Options dialog box opens to the "Customize the Quick Access Toolbar" page. You can add or remove commands from the toolbar, and reorder them, using the same steps as for the ribbon (page 689 and page 691).

TIP To quickly remove an item from the Quick Access toolbar, right-click its icon in the toolbar and then choose (you guessed it) "Remove from Quick Access toolbar."

- **Add a ribbon group to the toolbar.** If a group on one of the ribbon's tabs is awash with commands you use all the time, you can add that group to the Quick Access toolbar. Simply right-click the name of the group you want to add to the toolbar, and then choose "Add to Quick Access Toolbar." (Depending on where you right-click, the command that appears on the shortcut menu is either "Add to Quick Access Toolbar" or "Add Group to Quick Access Toolbar.") An icon appears on the toolbar. (The icon's ToolTip is the name of the group.) When you click the icon, the group appears immediately below it.

- **Show the Quick Access toolbar below the ribbon.** If you put your top commands on the Quick Access toolbar, you can reduce the distance you have to move your mouse by putting the toolbar below the ribbon. Click the down arrow to the right of the Quick Access toolbar and then choose "Show Below the Ribbon." The toolbar appears between the ribbon and your Project view. To move it back to the top of the Project window, click the down arrow to the right of the Quick Access toolbar and then choose "Show Above the Ribbon."

TIP Suppose you overdid your Quick Access toolbar customizations and want to revert to the short and sweet version you started with. Restoring the Quick Access toolbar to its original settings is easy: Click the down arrow to the right of the toolbar, and then choose More Commands on the drop-down menu. In the lower-right part of the Project Options dialog box, click the Reset down arrow and then choose "Reset only Quick Access Toolbar." In the message box that appears, click Yes. The Quick Access toolbar switches back to having only Save, Undo, and Redo icons.

■ Customizing the Ribbon

As you've seen throughout this book, the ribbon is made up of several tabs, like Task, Resource, Report, Project, View, and Format. Within each tab, related commands are kept close to one another. For example, the Insert group (a.k.a section) of the Task tab contains commands for inserting tasks, summary tasks, milestones, and deliverables. Some commands reside in a group of one, like the lonely Subproject command in the Project tab's Insert group. The groups are visually separated from one another by vertical lines.

You can customize the ribbon to match how you work, whether you want to create your own tabs and groups; add groups you create to the program's built-in tabs; add commands to groups; reorder tabs, groups, and commands; or remove tabs, groups, and commands you don't use.

You customize the ribbon via the "Customize the Ribbon" page of the Project Options dialog box. The fastest way to reach this page is to right-click the ribbon and then choose "Customize the Ribbon." The long way around is to choose File→Options and then, on the left side of the Project Options dialog box, click Customize Ribbon.

Turning Tabs On and Off

The ribbon comes with several ready-made tabs, most of which are visible when you first launch Project. Whether you use the built-in tabs or build your own, you can turn tabs on when you need them and then turn them off to keep the ribbon tidy the rest of the time. For example, if a rousing session of macro development sounds like fun, you can turn on the built-in Developer tab, which is turned off initially. Then, when your macros are ready for prime time, you can turn off the Developer tab and run your macros from the View tab (page 720) or a custom tab you create (page 687). Here's how to turn tabs on and off:

1. **Right-click the ribbon, and then choose "Customize the Ribbon."**

   The "Customize the Ribbon" page opens in the Project Options dialog box, as shown in Figure 22-2.

2. **On the right side of the page, make sure the "Customize the Ribbon" box is set to Main Tabs.**

   This drop-down list is initially set to Main Tabs, so the list below it shows the built-in tabs (Task, Resource, Report, Project, View, and so on) and any custom tabs you create. If you choose Tool Tabs in the drop-down list, you see the context-sensitive Format tabs for each type of view, such as the Gantt Chart Tools | Format tab and the Team Planner Tools | Format tab.

3. **In the Main Tabs list, turn on a tab's checkbox to make it visible on the ribbon.**

   To hide a tab, turn off its checkbox.

4. **When you're done, click OK to close the Project Options dialog box.**

   The ribbon displays only the tabs whose checkboxes are turned on.

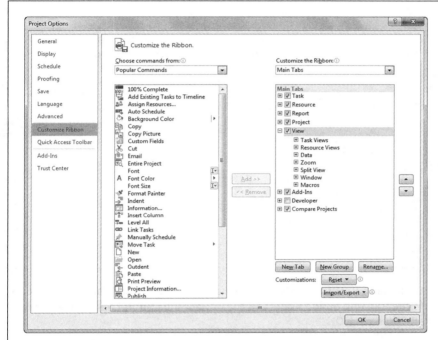

FIGURE 22-2

In the Project Options dialog box, you can choose to customize the ribbon or the Quick Access toolbar. On the left side of the dialog box, click Customize Ribbon to open the "Customize the Ribbon" page. If you click Quick Access Toolbar instead, you see the "Customize the Quick Access Toolbar" page, which is like a simplified version of the "Customize the Ribbon" page, because the Quick Access toolbar doesn't have tabs or groups.

Creating Custom Tabs

When existing tabs won't do, you can blaze a new trail by creating a tab from scratch. Completely new tabs are great when you constantly turn to the same set of commands. To create a new tab, open the "Customize the Ribbon" page (page 686), and then follow these steps:

1. **In the tab list on the right side of the page, select the tab below which you want to add your custom tab.**

   If you forget to select a position in the list before you create the tab, you can move the custom tab to another location later (page 691).

2. **Below the tab list, click New Tab.**

   Project inserts a new custom tab named New Tab (Custom) containing one custom group named New Group (Custom), as shown in Figure 22-3.

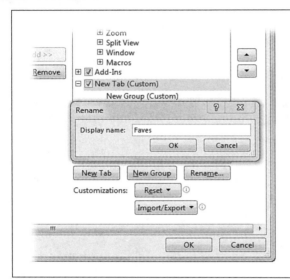

FIGURE 22-3

Project saves you a step by automatically adding a custom group to your new tab. You can add commands only to custom groups, so a custom tab must have at least one custom group. It's a good idea to immediately rename the custom tab and the custom group to indicate what they do. Select the tab's name in the list and then click Rename. Then select the group's name and click Rename.

3. **Click the new custom tab's name in the list to select it, and then click Rename. In the Rename dialog box, type a short but meaningful name, like "Faves," and then click OK.**

   The new name appears in the tab list.

4. **Click the new custom group to select it, and then click Rename.**

   The Rename dialog box opens with dozens of icons to choose from and a box for entering the new name. You don't *have* to choose an icon. But if you do, the icon you select appears if you add the group to the Quick Access toolbar. (If you don't select an icon, Project uses a green circle.)

5. **To display an icon for the group, click the one you want in the Symbol list. In the "Display name" box, type a short but meaningful name, like "MyViews." Then click OK.**

   Your custom tab and group are ready for you to add commands (page 689). See page 689 to learn how to add more groups to a tab. Page 691 explains how to rearrange tabs, groups, and commands.

Creating Custom Groups

If you want to add commands to the ribbon, you have to create custom groups to hold them. (In other words, you can't add commands to Project's built-in groups.) Whether you want to add commands to a built-in tab or a custom tab, you must first create a custom group and then add it to the tab you want. To do so, first open the "Customize the Ribbon" page (page 686), and then do this:

1. **In the tab list on the right side of the page, click the + sign to the left of the tab (built-in or custom) to which you want to add a new group.**

   The tab expands to show the groups it currently includes.

2. **Click the group below which you want to add the new group.**

   If you forget to select a position before you create the group, you can move the custom tab to another location later (page 691).

3. **Below the tab list, click New Group.**

   Project inserts a new custom group named New Group (Custom).

4. **Click the new custom group to select it, and then click Rename. To display an icon for the group, choose one in the Symbol list. In the "Display name" box, type a short but meaningful name, like "Tasks." Then click OK.**

   Your custom group takes its place in the tab, with vertical lines separating it from its neighboring groups.

Adding Commands to Custom Groups

All of Project's commands, as well as the macros you develop (see Chapter 24), are fair game for the ribbon. The "Customize the Ribbon" page (Figure 22-2) includes categories of commands to help you find the ones you want to add to a custom group you've created. You can choose a category like "Commands Not in the Ribbon" to add a command that isn't available in any of Project's built-in tabs.

The steps for adding commands to the ribbon are easy:

1. **Right-click the ribbon and choose "Customize the Ribbon."**

   The "Customize the Ribbon" page opens in the Project Options dialog box.

2. **In the "Choose commands from" drop-down list, select one of the command categories.**

   The categories, shown in Figure 22-4, represent different collections of commands. This drop-down list is set initially to Popular Commands, but you can also choose from all commands, commands on the File tab, and so on. When you select a category, the command list shows the choices within that category. If you don't know which category to choose, select All Commands.

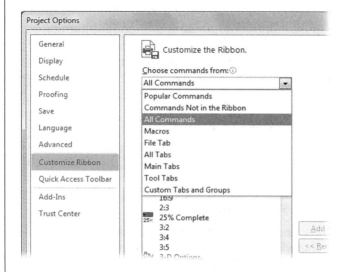

FIGURE 22-4

Unless you know the built-in tabs inside and out, your best bets are the first three categories in this list. Popular Commands are the most frequently used commands. To add a command that isn't on the ribbon, choose "Commands Not in the Ribbon." To make sure you can find the command you want, choose All Commands and then scroll through the list.

3. **In the list of commands below the "Choose commands from" box, select the command you want to add to the ribbon.**

   When you select a command in the list, the Add button becomes active, indicating that you can add it to the ribbon. But don't click Add just yet.

4. **On the right side of the page, expand the tab you want and then select the custom group to which you want to add the command. If other commands are in the group already, select the command below which you want to add the new command.**

   Although you can *select* a built-in group, if you click the + sign next to the group's name, you'll see that all the commands within it are grayed out to indicate that you can't add a new command to that group. If you try to add a command to a built-in group, a message box tells you that you can add commands only to custom groups.

5. **Click Add.**

   The command takes its place in the custom group.

6. **Repeat steps 3–5 to add other commands to the group.**

   When you're done, click OK to close the Project Options dialog box.

Rearranging Tabs and Groups

Although Project is fussy about where you can put commands (only in custom groups), it's happy to let you rearrange tabs and groups in any way you want, regardless of whether the tabs and groups are built-in or custom. For example, if you prefer the View tab to appear to the left of the Task tab, simply open the "Customize the Ribbon" page (page 686) and then, in the Main Tabs list, drag the tab's name where you want it. You can use the same techniques to rearrange groups (built-in and custom) and commands within custom groups (you can't modify the commands within built-in groups).

With the "Customize the Ribbon" page open, simply drag elements (or click the up and down arrows) to move them to another location. Here's how:

1. **Right-click the ribbon and choose "Customize the Ribbon."**

   The "Customize the Ribbon" page opens in the Project Options dialog box.

2. **In the right-hand list, select the tab, group, or command (only commands within custom groups) you want to relocate.**

   You can move only one element at a time.

3. **Drag the element to its new location, or click the up or down arrows to move the element higher or lower in the list.**

   If you drag the element, position the horizontal bar that appears where you want the element to go, as shown in Figure 22-5, and then release the mouse button. Moving an element up in the list moves it to the left in the Project ribbon; moving an element down moves it to the right in the ribbon.

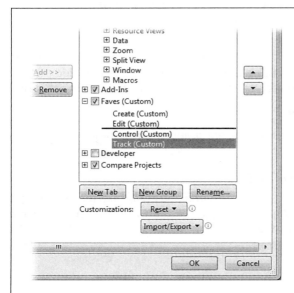

FIGURE 22-5

A horizontal bar shows you where the element goes. If you click the up or down arrow, the element moves up or down one position. Because you can add commands only to custom groups, you might see the up or down arrow grayed out or a No icon (a circle with a diagonal bar through it) indicating you can't relocate the element to the current location (for example, to a built-in group).

Renaming Tabs and Groups

You can also rename any tab or group—built-in or custom. Simply right-click the ribbon and then choose "Customize the Ribbon." In the list on the right side of the page that appears, select the tab or group you want to rename, and then click Rename below the list. In the Rename box, type the new name and then click OK.

NOTE You can rename commands only in the custom groups you create. Page 707 tells you how.

Removing Ribbon Elements

The obvious result of removing elements from the ribbon is that the elements you remove no longer appear on the ribbon. What happens behind the scenes depends on what you remove. Built-in tabs and groups that you remove disappear from the ribbon, but they're still available in the "Choose commands from" list on the left side of the "Customize the Ribbon" page, so you can easily restore them (the next section explains how). On the other hand, removing a custom tab or a custom group from the ribbon deletes that element from Project.

You can remove built-in and custom tabs, built-in and custom groups, and commands you add to custom groups. For example, you can remove the Insert group from the Task tab and replace it with a custom group that has the insert commands you want in the order you want. However, you can't remove commands from built-in groups, like Cut, Copy, and Paste in the Task tab's Clipboard group. The secret to removing elements is the Remove button on the "Customize the Ribbon" page.

Here's how to remove elements from the ribbon:

1. **In the list on the right side of the "Customize the Ribbon" page (page 686), select the element you want to remove by clicking it.**

   You can remove a built-in tab, a custom tab, a built-in group, a custom group, or a command in a custom group. You can tell whether you're allowed to remove the selected element by glancing at the Remove button in the middle of the page: If it's grayed out, you can't remove that element; if it's active, you can.

2. **Click the Remove button.**

   When you click Remove, the selected item disappears from the list, which means it disappears from the ribbon.

Restoring a Built-in Tab or Group

Suppose you removed a built-in tab or group from the ribbon and then realize that you want it back. No worries. Built-in tabs and groups stay in the "Customize the Ribbon" page's "Choose commands from" list, so you can add them back to the ribbon at any time. Here are the steps:

1. **On the "Customize the Ribbon" page (page 686), click the down arrow to the right of the "Choose commands from" box, and then choose All Tabs or Main Tabs.**

   The built-in tabs in that category appear in the list box.

2. **To restore a built-in group, click the + next to the tab that contains the group.**

   The tab expands to show the groups within it.

3. **Click the tab or group you want to restore to the ribbon.**

   If you select a tab in the list box, the Add button in the middle of the page is active even if the tab is already in the "Customize the Ribbon" list on the right side of the page. That means you could add a *second* copy of the tab to the ribbon if you wanted to for some reason.

4. **In the list on the right side of the page, click the item above where you want to restore the tab or group.**

   If you selected a group to restore, the Add button in the middle of the page becomes active as long as the group isn't already in the selected tab or group in the "Customize the Ribbon" list on the right side of the page. If the group *is* in the selected tab or group on the right side of the page, the Add button is grayed out, because the item is already added.

5. **Click the Add button.**

   When you click Add, the item you selected appears in the list on the right. If you didn't add it in the right location, click the up or down button to the right of the list to reposition the tab or group.

Resetting Ribbon Customizations

After you tweak the ribbon, you may decide you want some or all of the tabs back to the way they were when you first installed Project. Rather than finding each change you made and manually changing it back, it's easier to reset them. You can reset the customizations on a single tab or remove all the customizations you've made. Here are the steps:

1. **Right-click the ribbon and choose "Customize the Ribbon."**

   The "Customize the Ribbon" page opens in the Project Options dialog box.

2. **If you want to reset a single tab, in the list on the right side of the page, select the tab.**

   You can reset only built-in tabs. The only way to "reset" a custom tab is to remove it Obviously they are editable, but editing is not "reseting." The original state is it wasn't there at all.

3. **Click Reset and then choose either "Reset only selected Ribbon tab" or "Reset all customizations."**

The "Reset only selected Ribbon tab" option is available only if you select a built-in tab in the list. It removes any customizations you made to that built-in tab. If you select "Reset all customizations," Project removes customizations you made to built-tabs *and* the Quick Access toolbar, *and* deletes all custom tabs.

TIP Before you remove all customizations, export your customizations to a file as explained in the next section. That way, it you want the customizations back, you can import the file.

■ Sharing a Custom Ribbon and Quick Access Toolbar

You may wonder how you can copy your ribbon customization handiwork to other computers, because the ribbon isn't one of the elements you can copy with the Organizer (page 702). To use your ribbon on another computer (or to share it with a fellow project manager), you have to export it to a file. Then you or your compatriot can import that file into Project on another computer. Here's how:

1. **Right-click the ribbon and choose "Customize the Ribbon."**

The Project Options dialog box opens to the "Customize the Ribbon" page.

2. **At the bottom right of the dialog box, click Import/Export and then choose "Export all customizations."**

The File Save dialog box appears, with its "Save as type" box set to "Exported Office UI file."

3. **In the File Save dialog box, navigate to the folder where you want to save the file and type a descriptive name in the "File name" box (something like *MyPrjRibbon*).**

Initially, Project names the file Project Customizations.

4. **Click Save.**

Project saves the UI customization file in the folder you specified.

To import a custom ribbon or Quick Access toolbar, first copy the UI customization file to your computer. Then follow these steps:

1. **In Project, right-click the ribbon and choose "Customize the Ribbon."**

The Project Options dialog box opens to the "Customize the Ribbon" page.

2. **At the bottom right of the dialog box, click Import/Export and then choose "Import customization file."**

The File Open dialog box appears.

3. **In the File Open dialog box, navigate to the folder that contains the file, and then double-click it.**

The drop-down menu to the right of the "File name" box is set to "Exported Office UI file" so the ribbon customization file will appear in the list of files.

4. **A message box asks if you want to replace all existing Ribbon and Quick Access toolbar customizations for Project. Click Yes to load the new customizations, or click No to cancel.**

After the customizations are in place, you can use the techniques described in this chapter to tweak the ribbon or Quick Access toolbar.

Reusing Project Information

A s you use Project 2013 to manage projects, you're bound to make changes to features like views, tables, filters, and reports to help you do your job more effectively. Perhaps you prefer to work with Gantt Chart view in the top pane and Task Details Form view in the Details pane. Or you insert the % Work Complete field to the Summary table. If you go to the trouble of customizing Project, as described in the previous chapters, you probably want to use those customizations in most, if not all, of your projects—or at least show them off to your friends. When you want to reuse your customized elements, you can store them in a special file called the *global template*, so every new project you create can use them.

With each project you manage, you also add to your project-management toolbox. For instance, you might develop a task list and basic schedule for running a fundraiser that you can reuse for next year's event or share with colleagues across the country who are hosting their own events. Part of the closing process for every project is archiving the work you've done, documenting what you learned, and recording that information so others can benefit from it (page 508). Saving the Project file to an archive location at the end of the project accomplishes much of this work. However, if you want to reuse what you learned, you can turn your completed Project file into a *project template* so it's ready to jump-start your next project. These templates are Project files that hold different types of project information, from customized elements to typical tasks with typical durations to Project settings you prefer. Because project templates can hold both customized Project elements and reusable project information, they're ideal for sharing your effort with anyone who needs it for future projects.

This chapter begins by explaining the difference between the global template and individual project templates you can use to create new projects. Once you understand that, you'll see where Project stores elements and settings and how you can keep your customized items in the same place. (You can tell Project to save new customized elements in your current Project file or to automatically copy them to the global template.) You'll also learn to transport and share customized elements using Project's Organizer (a dialog box that helps you manage Project elements like views, tables, calendars, and filters, and copy them between the global template and your Project files). This chapter concludes with an explanation of how to create and use project templates to jump-start your future project endeavors.

■ Understanding the Types of Templates

Project 2013 has two types of templates. Here's what each one does:

- **Global template.** This template acts as a storage facility for built-in and customized Project elements, such as views, tables, groups, filters, and calendars. It also contains the settings for Project options that determine how the program behaves, such as which task mode it uses when you create new tasks. If you customize the ribbon and Quick Access toolbar (Chapter 22), those changes are kept in the global template, too. Project attaches the global template to every new Project file you create. That way, built-in elements, customizations, and settings are available whenever you work on a Project file.

> **NOTE** If you use Microsoft Enterprise Project Management tools (Project Server and Project Professional), you'll also have an *enterprise global template*. This template is like the mother of all global templates—a *global* global template. This template attaches to every Project file that someone checks out, so they get the standards setup by your organization as well as the most up-to-date, enterprise-wide customized Project elements. Once a project is published to Project Server, you must use the elements from the enterprise global template.

- **Project template.** This type of template does double-duty. You can store customized elements in a project template, just like you do in the global template. You can also save some settings, like scheduling options or calculation options, in this type of template. However, a project template can also contain task and resource information—a task list, task links, typical durations, generic resources, and more. For example, once you hold your first fundraiser and find out what it really takes, you can save a project template with all that information. Then, when it's time to start working on next year's event, you don't have to reinvent the wheel.

If you're just getting started with projects, you don't have to create your own templates. Project 2013 offers dozens of templates covering an array of project types. In addition, many companies offer specialized project templates that you can download. Or your colleagues may have templates they're willing to share.

◼ Storing Project Settings and Elements

Project has to keep its settings and built-in elements somewhere, and that somewhere is called the *global template*. It stores settings that tell Project how to behave—like whether you use the Gregorian calendar or want to automatically turn on AutoFilter. All the built-in elements that Project provides are in this file, too—like standard Gantt Chart view, the Standard calendar, and the Entry table. If you customize elements, you can copy them to the global template so they're available to other projects. This section explains what the global template has to offer.

> **NOTE** Ribbon and Quick Access toolbar customizations also reside in the global template. Changes you make to the ribbon apply to Project itself, not just to a particular file, so you see them regardless of which project you work on. See page 694 to learn how to apply Quick Access toolbar customizations to a specific Project file.

The global template is so special that the program attaches it to every Project file you create so your program-wide settings and elements are available. Under the hood, though, the global template is really just a regular project template file called *global.mpt*. If you create a copy of this file, you can open it in Project like any other file. The box on page 701 tells you where to find your global template file after you install Project. The global template stores the following elements:

- Your Project Options settings
- Views
- Tables
- Custom fields
- Calendars
- Filters
- Groups
- Reports
- Import and export maps
- Macros and Visual Basic modules

> **NOTE** Beginning with Project 2010, the program stopped supporting custom forms or toolbars, so you won't find them in the Organizer.

Storing Customized Project Options

If you change a program-wide setting in the Project Options dialog box (choose File→Options), then the global template memorizes that setting and applies that setting to every new Project file you create. In other words, when you create a Project file, it takes on the settings that are in place in the global template at that time. You can tell which settings in the Project Options dialog box apply program-wide because their section headings don't have a box for choosing a project, like the Display heading shown in Figure 23-1.

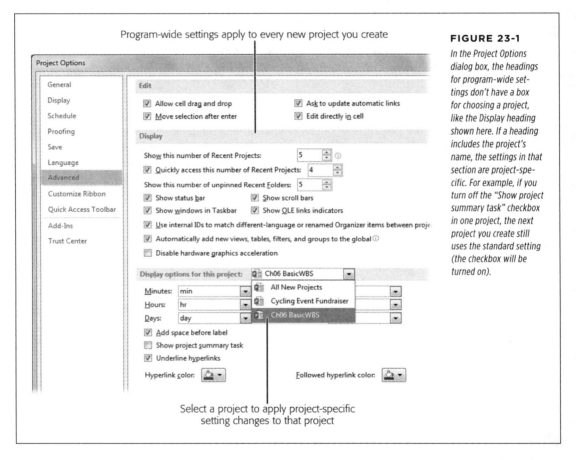

Program-wide settings apply to every new project you create

Select a project to apply project-specific setting changes to that project

FIGURE 23-1

In the Project Options dialog box, the headings for program-wide settings don't have a box for choosing a project, like the Display heading shown here. If a heading includes the project's name, the settings in that section are project-specific. For example, if you turn off the "Show project summary task" checkbox in one project, the next project you create still uses the standard setting (the checkbox will be turned on).

Project also includes project-specific options. When a heading is something like "Display options for this project" and includes a box for choosing a project, you know that the settings in that section are project-specific. Those settings reside in the Project file, not the global template. Although they start out matching what's set in the global template, any changes you make to them remain in your Project file and don't affect other projects. If you want to change a project-specific setting for *all* new projects, then in the "Display options for this project" box, choose All New Projects in the drop-down list (Figure 23-1).

TIP You can also make project-specific settings more global by creating a project template (page 708) with those settings in place. Then, when you create a new project based on that template, the settings you want are already there.

FREQUENTLY ASKED QUESTION

Locating the Global Template

Where do I find Project's global template?

If you want to share your global template with a colleague, you may have trouble tracking it down on your computer. The Organizer dialog box isn't any help, because the label for the "<element> available in" box at the bottom left says only "Global.MPT." You have no way of knowing where that file resides.

When you install Project on a computer running Windows 7 or Windows 8, Project places a copy of *global.mpt* in *C:\ Users\<username>\AppData\Roaming\Microsoft\MS Project\15\1033*, where <username> is the name of the person who installed Project on the computer and 1033 is the language code

for English. (If you install Project using a different language, the number for the folder is set to the code for the installed language.) If you want to use a global template that someone else sends you, replace the *global.mpt* file in this folder.

You may search for *global.mpt* files from the Start menu by choosing Search and never see the one in the AppData folder. Windows initially hides this folder, so it doesn't show up as you browse folders in Windows or use the Windows Search box. To see hidden folders and files in any folder window, in Windows Explorer, choose Organize→"Folder and search options." In the Folder Options dialog box, click the View tab, select the "Show hidden files and folders" option, and then click OK. After that, you can see *global.mpt* and replace it with another copy.

■ Sharing Custom Elements

Project comes with dozens of built-in elements like views, tables, filters, and groups, which you can use as is or customize to suit your needs. When you customize any of these elements, a customized copy is saved in the Project file you're working on, so it initially shows up only when you open that file. (Same goes for project-specific Project Options settings, as shown in Figure 23-1.) Other customized elements like maps go directly into the global template, because Project assumes that you want to use them for every project. Fortunately, the Organizer dialog box makes it easy to propagate customized elements to other Project files or to share them with colleagues. This section tells you how.

TIP It's a good idea to make a backup copy of your global template before you add or remove elements in it. If you want to get rid of elements you added, or retrieve elements you deleted, then you can replace the active global template with the backup copy. The box above tells you where to find the global template on your computer.

The Organizer helps you copy customized elements from the global template to a Project file, from a Project file to the global template, or between two Project files. Here's how the Organizer can help:

- **Using customized elements in new projects.** In many instances, customized elements like views belong to the Project file in which you create them. After you've created customized elements, you can make them available to every new project you create by copying them to the global template (page 703).

- **Sharing customized elements.** Having customized elements in your global template is great when you're working on your computer. But if you're in a colleague's office and fire up Project there, your customized elements aren't available, because they're back in the global template on your computer. Likewise, folks in other offices are out of luck unless you share what you've done. To share customized elements, you can copy them to a Project file and then send that file to someone else. Then they can copy those elements into their global template.

- **Copying customized elements between Project files.** Sometimes a customized element is important for a specific type of project but not spectacular enough to copy to the global template. The Organizer lets you copy elements from one Project file to another (when both files are open).

- **Creating copies and renaming elements.** You can create copies of elements in the Organizer and rename them without opening them in Project.

- **Removing elements from a Project file or template.** The Organizer simplifies file cleanup, too. You can select one or more elements and then delete them at one time.

As you can see in Figure 23-2, the Organizer bristles with tabs, one for every type of element you can customize. (There's no tab for custom formulas, because they belong to custom fields.) When you select a tab, the Organizer displays the elements available in two different Project files: initially, the global template on the left side, and the active Project file on the right. However, on either side of the Organizer, you can select any Project file that's open, which is how you copy elements between files.

To open the Organizer, simply choose File→Info and then click Organizer in Backstage view. Some dialog boxes, like More Views, More Tables, and More Filters, also include an Organizer button that opens the Organizer window.

Copying Elements Between Files

The steps for copying elements between files using the Organizer are the same regardless of which type of element you copy and which two files you use. You choose the file with the element that you want to copy, and the file you want to copy it *to*, and then copy the element.

If you create *new* elements like views, tables, filters, and groups, regardless of whether you create them from scratch or by customizing an existing element and saving it with a new name, Project automatically copies them to the global template, which is a great timesaver if you're the only person who uses your copy of Project. Copying new elements to the global template means they're available for every new project you create. However, if you don't want to fill up the global template with lots of your customizations, you can control whether new elements attain global-templatehood. To set this behavior, choose File→Options and, on the left side of the Project Options dialog box, choose Advanced. Under the Display heading, turn off the "Automatically add new views, tables, filters, and groups to the global" checkbox. That way, if you create a new view called AwesomeView, which uses a new table called KitchenSink, Project keeps copies of those elements only in the active Project file. However, even when this checkbox is turned off, you can still *manually* copy customized elements to the global template (page 703).

■ MAKING CUSTOMIZED ELEMENTS AVAILABLE TO NEW PROJECTS

To use a custom element in new projects you create, copy the element from the Project file to the global template. That way, when you create a new Project file, the program grabs the built-in and custom elements from your global template. (Remember, Project stores import/export maps directly in the global template, so you don't have to copy them to make them available to other files.)

Here are the steps for copying elements to the global template:

1. **Open the Project file that contains the customized element. Then choose File→Info, and then click the Organizer button on the Info page.**

    The Organizer dialog box opens. It contains several tabs to cover all the elements it handles, as illustrated in Figure 23-2.

If you forgot to make the project with the customized element active before you opened the Organizer window, don't worry. In the "[element] available in" drop-down list on the right, simply choose the project (it must already be open in Project), where [element] is the name of the tab you've selected. For example, if the Groups tab is selected, then the label is "Groups available in."

2. **Select the tab for the type of element you want to copy, like Views.**

    The elements stored in the global template appear in the list on the left. The elements in the active project appear in the list on the right.

3. **In the list on the right, select the element you want to copy to the global template, such as Day of Event Gantt Chart in Figure 23-2, and then click Copy.**

    If the global template contains the same type of element with the same name, Project asks if you want to replace what's in the global template. Click Yes if you want to overwrite the one in the global template.

    To keep the one that's in the global template, click No. Then, with the element on the right side selected, click Rename, type a new name, and then click OK. Now you can copy the element without a conflict.

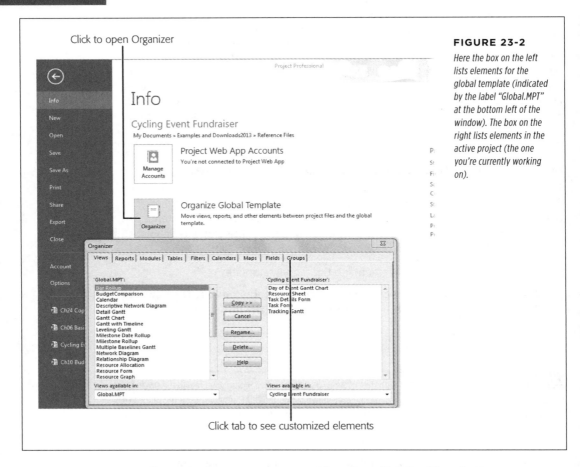

Click to open Organizer

Click tab to see customized elements

4. **If you don't want to copy anything else, click the Close button.**

   The custom element you copied (the "Day of Event Gantt Chart" view, in this example) is now available to all your Project files.

■ SHARING A CUSTOMIZED ELEMENT WITH SOMEONE ELSE

For most types of elements, you can share customizations simply by sending someone the Project file in which you created them, because that's where customized elements are stored. However, maps don't work the same way. Project stores them directly in the global template, so you have to copy them to another file to share them. Then you or the colleague with whom you share the file can copy elements directly from one Project file to another. Here are the steps for both situations:

1. **Open the Project file you plan to use to transfer customized elements. If the customized elements are in a Project file rather than the global template, then open that file, too.**

   Consider creating a new Project file specifically for transferring elements. Name it something like "MyCustomizations" so you and the recipient both know what it's for.

2. **Choose File→Info, click the Organizer button, and then select the tab for the type of element you want to copy.**

   The list on the right side of the Organizer dialog box is either empty or contains a few basic elements, unless you've used this transfer file before, as you can see in Figure 23-3.

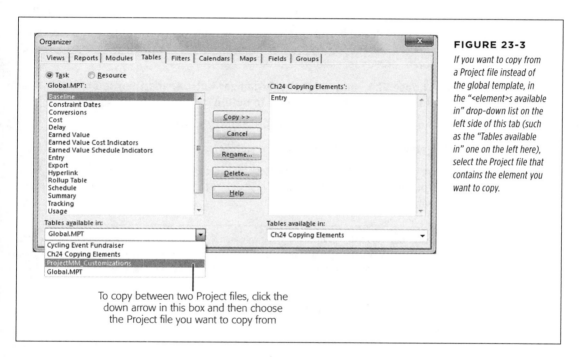

FIGURE 23-3

If you want to copy from a Project file instead of the global template, in the "<element>s available in" drop-down list on the left side of this tab (such as the "Tables available in" one on the left here), select the Project file that contains the element you want to copy.

To copy between two Project files, click the down arrow in this box and then choose the Project file you want to copy from

3. **In the list on the left, select the element you want to share, and then click Copy.**

   If you're feeling generous, you can select several elements in the left-hand list (Ctrl-click to select individual items or Shift-click to select several adjacent items). When you click Copy, Project copies them all to the right at the same time.

4. **If you want to copy other types of elements, select the corresponding tab, and then repeat step 3. When you're done, click the Close button.**

The elements are now stored in the Project file, so you can share those customizations with colleagues by sending them the file.

Removing Customized Elements from Files

Customized elements can be tremendous timesavers, but sometimes you want to get rid of them. For example, after you copy a customized element to the global template, you don't need it in the Project file in which you created it.

Another reason to delete customized elements is to restore what Project came with. For example, suppose you made a dozen formatting changes to Gantt Chart view, and now you want the original version back. When you modify a built-in element, Project creates a customized copy in your Project file. (You can tell because the element shows up in the Organizer, in the box on the right for the active Project file.) To get the original back, in the Organizer, simply delete the customized one.

Deleting customized elements is easy. Just follow these steps:

1. **If you plan to delete a view or a table, first apply a *different* view or table.**

    You can't delete or copy tables and views when they're visible. In the View tab's Task Views section, choose a different view. In the View tab's Data section, click Tables and choose a different table.

2. **Choose File→Info, click the Organizer button, and then select the tab for the type of element you want to delete.**

    The customized elements appear in the box on the right.

3. **Select the element you want to delete, and then click Delete.**

    In the confirmation dialog box, click Yes to delete the element, or click No if you've had second thoughts. The element disappears from the list when you click Yes.

> **WARNING** Be careful about deleting elements from the global template, because you can delete some built-in elements: views, groups, filters, tables, and so on. If you make a habit of deleting elements in the global template, it's a good idea to keep a backup copy in case you want to get something back.

Renaming Customized Elements

The Organizer also lets you rename customized elements, which is helpful if you're trying to copy elements with the same names between files. For example, if you want to copy a customized Gantt Chart view to the global template without over-writing the original Gantt Chart view that comes with Project, you can rename your version before you copy it.

> **NOTE** Some built-in elements are willing to go by a different name, while others aren't. For example, you can rename built-in groups, except for the built-in No Group. And you can't rename custom fields using the Organizer; instead, you have to use the Custom Fields dialog box to do that.

To rename an element, follow these steps:

1. **Open the Project file with the customized elements. Open the Organizer window (choose File→Info→Organizer), and then select the tab for the type of element you want to rename.**

   The customized elements appear in the box on the right.

2. **In the right-hand box, select the element you want to rename, and then click Rename.**

   The Rename dialog box is simple, with a "New name" box and an OK button.

3. **In the "New name" box, type the name, and then click OK.**

   The newly renamed element appears in the list.

4. **When you're done working in the Organizer, click the Close button.**

■ Building Templates for Projects

Despite the differences that make every project unique, many projects have a lot in common. Project gives you several ways to reuse work you've done before. Here are just a few examples:

- **Save time.** Past projects make great starting points for new projects. You've already figured out many of the tasks you need, so why not use them to jump-start new projects? A project template can contain tasks with task dependencies, typical durations, and even resource assignments. Keep anything that stays the same, and change only what's different.

- **Standardize.** Quite often, you learn the hard way what works and what doesn't. You can improve your results by basing new projects on your previous successes, not your past mistakes. By creating templates that reflect your organization's project-management knowledge, everyone can benefit from the lessons learned on each and every project. You can use project templates to define the standards your organization follows. (If your organization uses Microsoft Enterprise Project Management software, the enterprise global template described on page 698 is the repository for your organization's project-management standards.) A template can act like a checklist, with project-management tasks that are part of every project. Or it can contain the views, reports, and customized performance measures that your organization uses to evaluate project status.

  As you've learned, the global template (page 698) stores program-wide settings that apply to every project. You can also make customized elements available to every new project you create by storing them in the global template (page 699).

- **Learn from others.** You don't have to learn everything from the school of hard knocks. Taking advantage of others' expertise can save time and improve your results. Starting with a template built by experts gets a project off on the right foot. You can use templates built by others in your organization or download templates that are available online (page 86).

Creating a Project Template

Whether you want to use a completed project as a basis for new projects or build a standard project that shows off your best project-management practices, a project template can help. Project templates can contain tasks, resources, resource assignments, settings, views, calendars, and more. When you create a new Project file from a project template, the new file inherits everything the template has to offer.

You can save any Project file as a project template. For example, if you completed a project that ran spectacularly well, you can go beyond archiving it for posterity by creating a template from it that includes tasks, resources, assignments, and all its baseline values. When you save a file as a template, the Save As Template dialog box lets you pick the information you want to throw away (and thus the information you want to keep). Here's how to save an existing Project file as a template:

1. **Open the existing project, and then choose File→Save As.**

   The Save As page appears in Backstage view.

2. **Navigate to the location or folder where you want to save your template.**

   If you want the template to show up on the New page in Backstage view, save the template in your personal templates folder (page 88). This folder can be anywhere on your computer, but you have to tell Project where this folder is. For example, if your template folder is on your computer, in the Save As list, click Computer. Then, under the Recent Folders heading on the right side of the page, click the template folder or, if the folder isn't there, click Browse. See page 92 for more details on selecting where you want to save a file.

> **TIP** If you use templates frequently, pinning your templates folder to the folders list makes it easy to access. To do this, in Backstage view, click Open, and then click Computer. On the right side of the Open page, click Browse. In the Open dialog box, navigate to your templates folder, and then double-click it. Click Cancel to close the dialog box and return to the Open page. Now your templates folder appears at the top of the Recent Folders list. Put your pointer over the folder's entry in that list, and then click the pushpin icon that appears on the right side of the page. From then on, your templates folder will always appear at the top of the Recent Folders list, as shown in Figure 23-4.

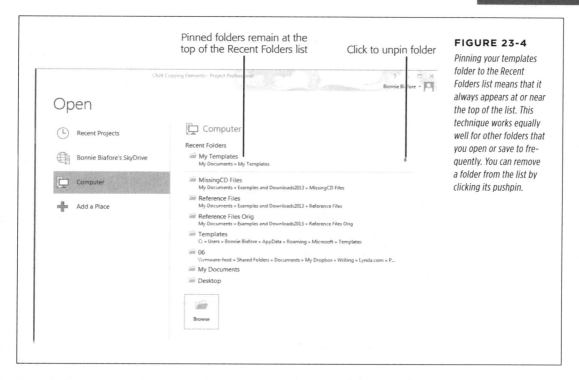

Pinned folders remain at the top of the Recent Folders list

Click to unpin folder

FIGURE 23-4

Pinning your templates folder to the Recent Folders list means that it always appears at or near the top of the list. This technique works equally well for other folders that you open or save to frequently. You can remove a folder from the list by clicking its pushpin.

3. **In the Save As dialog box that appears, in the "Save as type" drop-down list, choose "Project Template." (If you've set up Windows Explorer to display file extensions for all files, the file type appears as "Project Template (*.mpt)" instead.)**

Choosing this option creates a file with the .mpt file extension. (If you forget to change the "Save as type" to Project Template, all you'll do is save the file to a regular .mpp Project file with a different filename.)

4. **In the "File name" box, type a name for the template, and then click Save.**

The Save As Template dialog box (Figure 23-5) opens with checkboxes for specifying the data you *don't* want in the template.

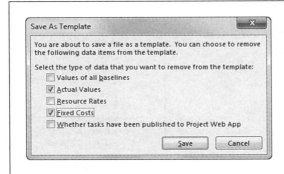

FIGURE 23-5

To keep values that worked in the past, make sure the "Values of all baselines" checkbox is turned off. That way, your baseline values stay in the file. If your baseline values are good to go, turn on the Actual Values checkbox to remove all actual values from the template.

5. **Turn on the checkboxes for the items you want to *remove* from the project.**

   For example, if you want to remove the actual values from the template, turn on the Actual Values checkbox.

6. **Click Save.**

   Project creates a file with an .mpt file extension with only the information you want.

Making Your Templates Easy to Find

After you set up a template with exactly what you want, using it to create a new file is painless—*if* you tell Project where to find the template. Once you tell Project where you store your templates, they're waiting for you each time you go to create a new file. Here's how to tell Project where you store your templates:

1. **Choose File→Options.**

   The Project Options dialog box opens.

2. **On the left side of the Project Options dialog box, click Save.**

   The "Default personal templates location" box is initially empty. If you want to see your templates in Backstage view, you must fill in this box so it points to the folder where you store your templates. You'll do that in the next step.

3. **To change the location of your templates, to the right of the "Default personal templates location" box, click Browse.**

   The Modify Location dialog box appears.

4. **Select the folder that holds your templates, and then click OK.**

When you select a folder in the Modify Location dialog box, the "Folder name" field shows the name of the folder. When you click OK, the Modify Location dialog box closes, and the path to the template folder appears in the "Default user template location" box, as shown in Figure 23-6.

5. **Click OK to close the Project Options dialog box.**

Your templates appear in the New page of Backstage view, described in detail on page 86.

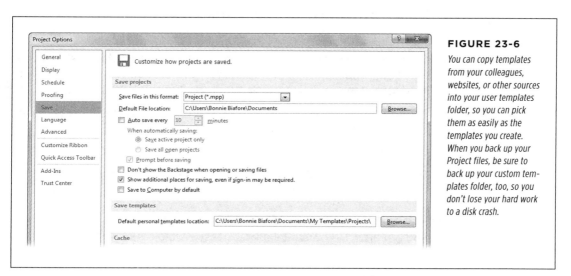

FIGURE 23-6

You can copy templates from your colleagues, websites, or other sources into your user templates folder, so you can pick them as easily as the templates you create. When you back up your Project files, be sure to back up your custom templates folder, too, so you don't lose your hard work to a disk crash.

Editing a Template

If you want to make changes to a project template, you can't open and save it the way you do with regular Project files. If you do, Project saves a copy of the file as a regular Project file with an *.mpp* file extension. That's because Project assumes that you're using the template to start a new Project file—not opening the template in order to edit it. To save template changes in the template file, follow these steps:

1. **Choose File→Open.**

The Open page of Backstage view appears.

2. **Choose the location that contains your templates.**

Page 88 describes how to make the template folder easy to access.

3. **In the Open dialog box, in the drop-down list to the right of the "File name" box, choose Project Templates. (If you've set up Windows Explorer to display file extensions for all files, the file type appears as "Project Template (*.mpt)" instead.)**

Choosing this setting displays only Project templates as you navigate through folders.

4. **Double-click the template you want to tweak.**

Project opens the template for editing. Make the changes you want.

5. **Choose File→Save as if you were creating a new Project file.**

The Save As page appears.

6. **Choose your templates folder, and then in the Save As dialog box's "Save as type" box, choose Project Template (or "Project Template (*.mpt)" if you have file extensions turned on in Windows Explorer). Click Save.**

Because you're trying to save changes to an existing template, a warning appears asking if you want to replace the original file.

7. **Click Yes.**

The Save As Template dialog box opens. Click Save to overwrite the existing template file with the changes you made.

Creating a Project File from a Template

Creating a project file from a template is easy regardless of where you get your template. Here are the steps:

1. **Choose File→New.**

The New page appears in Backstage view.

> **NOTE** If you share templates with other project managers, you want the files in a location that everyone can get to, like a shared network drive. You can create a new Project file from a template simply by double-clicking the template's filename in Windows Explorer.

2. **To use a template you created and stored in your personal templates folder (page 88), below the "Search for online templates" box, click Personal.**

The New page displays the templates in your personal templates folder, as shown in Figure 23-7.

To look for more templates online, click Featured to see popular templates. To find a particular type of template, type keywords in the "Search for online templates" box and then click the magnifying glass icon to the right of the box.

NOTE If your organization uses Project Server, you'll see "Enterprise" instead of "Personal." However, any templates you save in your personal folder show up when you click the Enterprise heading.

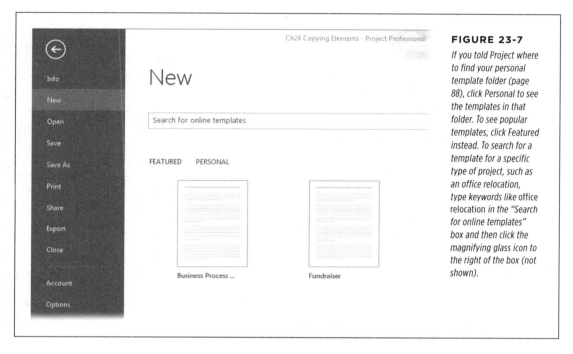

FIGURE 23-7

If you told Project where to find your personal template folder (page 88), click Personal to see the templates in that folder. To see popular templates, click Featured instead. To search for a template for a specific type of project, such as an office relocation, type keywords like office relocation in the "Search for online templates" box and then click the magnifying glass icon to the right of the box (not shown).

3. **Double-click the icon for the template you want to use.**

   Project creates a new file based on the template. The file looks and acts like a regular file.

4. **Before you save the new file, make any changes you need, such as the project start date, and remove any data you don't want.**

   The box on page 714 describes several things you should review and possibly change before you save your new Project file.

5. **After you make the changes you want, choose File→Save.**

   Even though you choose File→Save, Project displays the Save As page since this is the first time you've saved this new file. Once you choose where you want to save the file, the Save As dialog box opens with the "Save as type" box set to "Project" (or "Project (*.mpp)" if Windows Explorer shows files extensions for all files). These settings automatically save a copy of the template as a regular .mpp file, so you don't overwrite the template file.

Adjusting Your New Project File

A template can go a long way toward a new project schedule, but it won't be perfect. Things like the project's start date, resource list, and date constraints are guaranteed to need changing. Here are parts of the file to look at for adjustments you might need to make:

- **Start date.** In the Project tab's Properties section, click Project Information. In the Project Information dialog box, in the "Start date" box, select the date the new project is supposed to start.

- **Task list.** In Gantt Chart view or another task-oriented view, look over the list of tasks. Add tasks that are missing and remove ones you don't need.

- **Task mode.** In Gantt Chart view, display the Entry table. If necessary, switch Manually Scheduled tasks to Auto Scheduled or vice versa.

- **Task estimates.** Durations that end with question marks represent estimated values. Replace these values with

your planned values for the new project. It doesn't hurt to look over all durations and work values to see if they need to be revised.

- **Task dependencies.** Review the links between tasks to see if they still apply for your new project. Modify any task links that need changing.

- **Date constraints.** If you set dates for Manually Scheduled tasks or add date constraints (page 188) to Auto Scheduled tasks, those dates are likely to be obsolete when you create your new project. Modify the dates to reflect your best guess of when those tasks should occur. You can adjust those dates again as you plan the new project.

- **Resources.** Display Resource Sheet view. If you know the people assigned to your new project, add them to the resource list or replace the generic resources on the list with the people who will play those roles.

Saving Time with Macros

Y ou perform many of the same actions in Project day after day (sometimes several times each day). Like doing the dishes, vacuuming the carpet, and washing the cat on the delicate cycle, some repetitive tasks are unavoidable—but timesaving tools sure would help. Instead of hiring a personal assistant to take the drudgery out of your Project work, you can write handy mini-programs called *macros*.

You don't have to be a geek to write your own macros. You can create a macro simply by recording the steps you want the macro to perform. Then you can run the macro to replay the steps again and again. The geeky project managers in the audience can build upon recorded macros by editing them in Visual Basic for Applications (VBA).

This chapter explains macro basics: recording them, running them, adding them to the ribbon, and tying them to keyboard shortcuts. You can even create full-strength custom solutions if you're up for it. And if you're a programmer wannabe, you'll also find resources for learning more about programming in Project.

■ What You Can Do with Macros

A macro does one thing really well—it performs a series of steps each time you run it. For example, you can record a macro that hides summary tasks, turns on the critical path, and then sorts tasks by Duration in descending order. Macros are great timesavers because they can perform the equivalent of dozens of mouse clicks and key presses almost instantaneously. Moreover, macros reduce mistakes because you're not typing and clicking as much.

Any kind of repetitive task is a contender for macrohood. You can create a simple macro that sorts a task list or a sophisticated one that applies a view, filters and sorts the content, runs a report, and then prints it for your stakeholder status report. Since Project's creators couldn't anticipate *every* feature that organizations might need, macros let you create your own Project features, calculating project performance and evaluating your project in various ways. For example, a macro can count the number of on-time and slipping tasks to calculate the percentage of tasks that are headed for trouble.

■ Recording Macros

The best way to get started with macros is to record one. You don't have to write any code or invoke any arcane VBA spells. You simply start the recorder, click the same menus and press the same keys you always do, and then stop the recorder.

Recording a macro is like working a crossword puzzle in pen; your mistakes are indelibly saved along with what you got right. If you make a mistake, you have to rerecord the macro until you get it 100 percent right. So *before* you record a macro, take some time to figure out what you want to record. Then practice the steps a couple of times. (Write up a cheat sheet if you're recording more than a few steps.)

Before you start recording, make sure you perform any preliminary steps that you *don't* want to record in the macro—like opening a specific Project file or applying a view. In addition, the Project file must contain values that let you record all the steps you've planned. For example, if you're recording a macro that sorts tasks by their variances, then the Project file must have a baseline set (page 375).

Now you're ready to record:

1. **In the View tab's Macros section, click Macros→Record Macro.**

   The Record Macro dialog box opens, as shown in Figure 24-1.

2. **In the "Macro name" box, type a short name with no spaces, like *LongCriticalTasks*.**

   You can't include spaces in a macro name. If you want to separate words, insert underscores (_) between them or capitalize the first letter in each word Camel case actually means the first letter of the first word is lowercase, and then each subsequent new word is capitalized.

FIGURE 24-1

Project automatically fills in the "Macro name" box with a name like Macro1, which you can—and should—change to something more meaningful. The program also fills in the Description box with the name of the macro, the date you recorded it, and your name.

3. **In the Description box, fill in detailed information about what the macro does.**

   Briefly describe what the macro does, any conditions that must be in place before you run it (like a selected task or a specific view), and what you end up with when the macro ends (views, filters, sort criteria, and so on). Here's an example of an effective description: "Shows best critical tasks to shorten. No setup required. Applies Detail Gantt. Hides summary tasks. Groups tasks by Critical field. Sorts from longest to shortest duration."

4. **To assign a keyboard shortcut to launch the macro, type a letter (numbers aren't an option) in the "Ctrl+" box.**

   The Ctrl key is the only key that works as a prefix for macro keyboard shortcuts in Project. However, as you can tell from Appendix C, lots of keyboard shortcuts that combine Ctrl with letters of the alphabet are already taken (like the ubiquitous Ctrl+S for Save). Project doesn't give hints about which letters are still up for grabs (but it *does* complain if you try to type numbers or punctuation in the box). A, E, J, L, M, Q, and T are the only letters still available to combine with Ctrl in Project. In addition, if you set up a keyboard shortcut for the macro and then copy the macro to your global template, no other macros can use that keyboard shortcut.

TIP Since you get so few letters to create keyboard shortcuts, save them for the macros you use the most. If you're a prolific macro artiste, create a custom tab or a group on the ribbon (page 685) to store your macros.

---

5. **In the "Store macro in" drop-down list, select the file in which you want to store the macro.**

   Project selects Global File, which stores the macro in your global template (*global.mpt*), so you can run the macro in any Project file you open from now on. To save a macro *only* in the current Project file, choose This Project. (The box on page 719 explains how to choose the best place to store macros.)

6. **If the macro includes moving around in the table area, choose options in the "Row references" and "Column references" sections.**

   Project initially selects the Relative option for row references, which means that it moves the same number of rows from the selected cell when you run the macro. For example, suppose the first Task Name cell is selected, and you select the fourth Task Name cell during recording. Every time you run the macro, Project jumps down four rows from the cell that's selected. The Absolute (ID) option, on the other hand, tells the macro to move to the row with the same ID. So in this example, if you select the row with ID 4 while recording, then the macro always selects the row with ID 4.

   The Relative and Absolute options work similarly for columns. The main difference is that the Absolute (Field) option tells the macro to move to the column that contains the same field, as the name implies. For example, if you select the Cost column, the macro always jumps to the Cost column. Project automatically selects the Absolute (Field) option, which is the typical choice, because it gets you to the right field every time—as long as the field is somewhere in the view's table.

7. **Click OK to start recording.**

   The Record Macro dialog box disappears, and your Project file looks like it did before you created the macro. But the macro recorder is invisibly poised to record your every move.

8. **Choose the commands and perform the actions you want to automate.**

   For example, the steps for the LongCriticalTasks macro begin with going to the View tab's Task Views section, clicking Gantt Chart→More Views, and then double-clicking Detail Gantt. The next step is going to the Gantt Chart Tools | Format tab's Show/Hide section and turning off the Summary Tasks checkbox. The next step is heading to the View tab's Data section and clicking the Group down arrow, and then, in the drop-down list, choosing Critical. Finally, click the down arrow in the Duration column, and choose "Sort Largest to Smallest."

9. **When the steps are complete, in the View tab's Macros section, click Macros→Stop Recording.**

You can't pause recording in Project like you can in Word and some other Microsoft programs—it's all or nothing.

TIP Once you've recorded a macro, you can fine-tune it by editing its VBA code. In fact, the macro recorder can be your programming mentor. Record some macro steps in Project, and presto! The macro recorder dutifully logs the corresponding code. You can then study this code to learn about what you might do when writing macros from scratch. See "Learning More About Programming Project" on page 724 when you're ready for more.

FREQUENTLY ASKED QUESTION

Where to Store Macros

Should I store my macros in the global template or in the project I'm working on?

In most cases, storing macros in the global template (by choosing Global File in the "Store macro in" box) is the best option because you can run the macro whenever you're using Project in whatever Project file is open. In fact, anyone who uses the same global template (basically, anyone using your copy of Project) can use the macro.

On the other hand, storing macros in a specific Project file is useful in two instances:

1. If you need to send the Project file to someone who doesn't use your global template. In that case, storing a macro in the Project file lets your recipient run the macro.

2. If your macro works specifically with one Project file, selecting its unique tasks or resources, for example. In that case, the macro runs only when the correct Project file is open, and if you try to use the macro in any other Project file, it won't work.

■ Running Macros

Project lists all the macros you create in the Macros dialog box (in the View tab's Macros section, click Macro→View Macros). You can run one anytime by selecting it and then clicking Run. But since the whole point of writing macros is to reduce time spent on repetitive tasks, clicking several times to run a macro defeats the purpose.

You can run a macro in any of three ways, each with its pros and cons. In the Macros dialog box, you can select a macro, and then click Run. Adding a macro to the ribbon or to the Quick Access toolbar keeps it close at hand, and a click or two runs it. A keyboard shortcut is another way to run a macro, although the limited number of keyboard shortcuts available makes this method best for only your most popular macros. (Showoffs who edit code in the Visual Basic Editor: You can run a macro there, too, although doing so doesn't count as an everyday method.) This section explains your options.

Running Macros from the Macros Dialog Box

The Macros-dialog-box method requires the most mouse clicks, but it's ideal when you need a refresher course in the macros you have available. Perhaps you've created so many macros that you can't remember them all. Or maybe someone else created the macros, and you want to see what's available. The Macros dialog box lists macros that are available in all open projects. To run a macro from the Macros dialog box, do the following:

1. **In the View tab's Macros section, click Macros→View Macros.**

   The Macros dialog box opens. (If you have spare brain cells for memorization, you can also open this dialog box by pressing Alt+F8.)

2. **In the macro list, select the macro you want to run, and then click Run (or press the F8 key on your keyboard).**

   When you select a macro, the description appears at the bottom of the dialog box, in the Description area, as shown in Figure 24-2. Make sure the macro does what you want and that you've performed any setup the macro requires.

FIGURE 24-2

You can do more than select and run macros in the Macros dialog box. Click Delete, for instance, to remove a hopelessly buggy macro you can't fix. Click Edit to open the Visual Basic Editor (page 722) so you can look at or modify the code directly. Click Step Into if you want to run the macro step by step, which helps you find the problem step when a macro isn't working properly.

Initially, the "Macros in" box is set to All Open Projects, which means you can run any macro stored in your global template or in any open projects. To see only the macros in the global template or in a specific Project file, in the "Macros in" drop-down list, choose Global Template, This Project, or the name of the Project file. The box on page 721 explains security features that make sure you run only the macros you want, not malicious ones that hitched a ride in a Project file.

Setting Security

Project's Trust Center has settings that make it harder for viruses and other malware to infiltrate your computer. The Trust Center lets you designate a list of people you trust so that you can open only files that come from those sources. All other files stay unopened, keeping their malicious code to themselves. The security system also includes a way of creating digital *signatures*, so programs like Project can detect who created a given file. Here's how you set the level of security you want:

1. Choose File→Options.

2. On the left side of the Project Options dialog box, click Trust Center, and then click the Trust Center Settings button.

3. On the left side of the Trust Center dialog box, click Macro Settings.

4. Select the options for the security level you want. Project automatically selects "Disable all macros with notification," which is a good middle ground. It disables all macros but notifies you that it's doing so. (If you select "Disable all macros without notification," Project won't run any macros and doesn't tell you that it's disabled them because of your security setting.) To run macros with digital signatures, select the "Disable all macros except digitally signed macros" option.

Keep in mind that high security doesn't stop you from running macros *you* write. If you want to run a macro from someone else, the default option works well. It lets you tell Project on an individual basis whether or not to run a macro.

Running a Macro from the Ribbon

Buttons on the ribbon are probably the most popular way to run macros. They're quick. You don't have to remember another keyboard combination. You can show the macro name to jog your memory. And you can add as many macros as you want to a custom group on an existing tab, or a custom group on a custom tab (page 685).

Assigning a macro to the ribbon works almost exactly the same as adding other buttons or commands, as described in Chapter 22. You simply choose the macro to add from the Macros category.

To add a button to the ribbon, follow these steps:

1. **Choose File→Options. In the Project Options dialog box, choose Customize Ribbon.**

   The "Customize the Ribbon" page appears.

2. **On the right side of the page, select the tab and group to which you want to add the macro.**

   For example, if you create a custom tab called Favorites, click its + sign to expand the groups it contains, and then select the group you want.

3. **In the "Choose commands from" drop-down list, choose Macros.**

   The available macros appear in the Commands list.

4. **Select the macro and then click Add.**

   The macro appears below the name of the group.

> **TIP** Initially, the macro's name appears on the toolbar or menu (which is one reason to use short macro names). Chapter 22 tells you how to display an icon or different text.

Using Keyboard Shortcuts to Run Macros

If your brain has room to spare after memorizing Project's built-in keyboard shortcuts (Appendix C), you can assign keyboard shortcuts to run macros, too (see step 4 on page 717). After you rule out the keyboard shortcuts that Project already owns, you have only seven letters of the alphabet left to combine with the Ctrl key (A, E, J, L, M, Q, and T). Yet nothing beats a deft two-key shortcut to run a macro you use all the time. To assign a keyboard shortcut, use one of the following two methods:

- **While creating a macro.** In the Record Macro dialog box, in the "Ctrl+" box, type the letter you want to use.

- **When a macro already exists.** In the Macros dialog box, select the macro, and then click Options. In the Macro Options dialog box, in the "Ctrl+" box, type the letter you want to use, and then click OK.

> **NOTE** You can't reuse keyboard shortcuts in the same file. For example, if you assign Ctrl+J to a macro you store in the global template, then no other macro in the global template can use Ctrl+J. However, Ctrl+J *is* still available in individual Project files. In fact, you can assign Ctrl+J to a different macro in every Project file you create by assigning Ctrl+J to a macro and then storing it in the current Project file (page 718). When you press a keyboard shortcut, Project runs the macro assigned to that keyboard shortcut in the file you're working on.

■ Viewing and Editing Macro Code

Learning a programming language like VBA may be the last thing on your mind, but if you create your own macros, it pays to get familiar with—and even edit—some of your macro VBA code. For example, if you recorded a particularly long macro and made one little mistake, a quick edit in the Visual Basic Editor may be easier than rerecording the whole procedure. Similarly, if a macro references a specific name, which has since changed, then a surgical edit to change the name gets your macro working again. (The box on page 724 provides a quick introduction to what Project's VBA code looks like.)

The Visual Basic Editor is the place to look at and edit your macro code. Here's how you open it to inspect your macro:

1. **In the View tab's Macros section, click Macros→View Macros.**

   The Macros dialog box opens.

2. **Select the macro you want to tweak, and then click Edit.**

   The Microsoft Visual Basic window opens, as shown in Figure 24-3. For simple edits, the code window is the only part of the editor you need.

FIGURE 24-3

If you store your macro in the global template, then the module that contains the macro appears on the left side of the window (in the Project Explorer pane) underneath the ProjectGlobal entry. The VBAProject entry for a specific Project file contains macros stored in those Project files. In this example, you can make the macro display a different view simply by changing "Detail Gantt" to, say, "Tracking Gantt."

3. **When you're done editing, choose File→Save Global.MPT.**

   Visual Basic saves your macro to the global template. If you create the macro in a specific Project file, the File menu entry is "Save [Project filename].mpp," where [Project filename] is the file prefix.

4. **To close the VBA window, choose File→"Close and Return to Microsoft Project."**

   The Microsoft Visual Basic window closes.

Learning More About Programming Project

Because this chapter barely scratches the surface of macros, you may want to learn how to do more with VBA and Project. As you'll learn in Appendix B, Project Help doesn't provide much of that information. Instead, try the following resources and websites to get you going.

- **VBA Help.** In the Microsoft Visual Basic window, click Help→"Microsoft Visual Basic for Applications Help." On the left side of the Project 2013 MSDN page, click the "Project 2013 VBA developer reference" link. Click the "Welcome to the Microsoft Project 2013 VBA developer reference" link to read about programming Project with Visual Basic. The first page provides some valuable information, like how to access the Project Developer Reference from within Project, from the MSDN library, or from the Microsoft Download Center.

- **Microsoft Developer Network (MSDN).** To reach the Project Developer Center, go to *http://msdn.microsoft.com/en-us/library/office/fp161358.aspx*. This website is awash with information about programming Project, and the articles get pretty geeky pretty fast.

POWER USERS' CLINIC

A Quick Look at Macro Code

The code required for a macro may be simpler than you think, particularly when you use macros to apply views, filters, and other settings. The steps that a macro performs belong to what programmers call a *subroutine*, like the one shown here. You can find the beginning and end of a macro by looking for the keywords Sub and End Sub:

```
    Sub LongCriticalTasks()
    ' Macro LongCriticalTasks
    ' Macro Recorded 2/4/13 by Bonnie
Biafore.
    '
    ' Shows best tasks for shortening.
    Displays Detail Gantt with no summary
    tasks. Groups by Critical and then
    sorts from longest to shortest
    duration.
```

```
    ViewApplyEx Name:="Detail Gantt",
        ApplyTo:=0
    SummaryTasksShow
    GroupApply Name:="Critical"
    Sort Key1:="Duration", Ascending1:
        =False, Renumber:=False
    End Sub
```

The lines that begin with a single quote (') are comments. Use them liberally to explain what the macro does or why you wrote the code you did. (Project automatically adds whatever you type in the Record Macros dialog box's Description box to your macro's code as comments.) The lines that do the actual work are simple, too. For instance, to apply a view, you use the ViewApplyEx command, and then provide the view's name. Changing a setting in VBA code is incredibly easy. For example, to turn summary tasks back on, you simply add another SummaryTasksShow line to the macro.

Appendixes

Installing Project

Office 2013 and Project 2013 run only on computers that have Windows 7 or Windows 8 installed. As long as your computer passes this operating-system requirement, installing Project 2013 is comfortingly similar to installing other Microsoft programs. If you're installing from scratch, you barely have to tell the wizard anything.

If there's an earlier version of Project already on your computer, you have the option to upgrade the previous version or to keep it in addition to installing Project 2013. (If you already have a 32-bit version installed, the other versions you install must also be 32 bit.) Installing multiple versions of Project offers several benefits. Not only can you use your old favorite features to manage the projects you're already working on, but you can also experiment with Project 2013 to see if it works for you. If it doesn't, you can uninstall it and continue working with your earlier version. *Upgrading*, on the other hand, means that the new version *overwrites* the earlier one, so you would have to reinstall your older version to revert to it.

In this chapter, you'll learn how to install Project 2013 Standard or Professional from a CD or a hard drive. During the installation process, custom options are kept out of the way unless you need them. In this chapter, you'll learn how to find and use them to choose what you want to install, and where. You'll also learn how to install Project Pro for Office 365 if you have a subscription to Office 365.

After installation, you have to activate Project so Microsoft can verify that your copy is legal. Unactivated copies of Project run only for a short grace period and remind you frequently that the software is unlicensed. Fortunately, activation is quick and doesn't divulge any of your personal information. Bottom line: You have to activate Project if you want to use it.

Over time, you may want to change the Project features you installed. And if Project begins to act strangely, repairing the installation often solves that problem. In this chapter, you'll learn how to do both.

Installing Project on Your Computer

The Install Wizard can handle a plain-Jane installation, an upgrade from an earlier version, or a custom installation. But before you get started, make sure your computer has what it takes to run the new version.

> **TIP** The following pages describe how to install Project 2013 on a single PC, but what if your entire team or company is going to use the program? If you need to install Project on many computers at once and keep them up to date, check out the 2013 Office Resource Kit at *http://technet.microsoft.com/en-us/library/cc303401.aspx* to learn about fancy software deployment features.

32-Bit or 64-Bit Project?

Project 2013 comes in both 32-bit and 64-bit versions. If you're like most people, 32-bit software is the way to go. The only time you may need the 64-bit version of Project is if you work with huge amounts of data—for example, files larger than 2 GB or a master project that contains 500 or more subprojects.

> **NOTE** 32-bit and 64-bit refer to the number of bits a computer processor can handle. A 32-bit processor can address about 4 GB of memory, while a 64-bit processor can address more than 16 GB of memory. 64-bit software takes advantage of a 64-bit processor's memory to run faster and to handle larger file sizes.

There are several limitations that might prevent you from running the 64-bit version of Project:

- If your computer runs a 32-bit operating system, you can install only 32-bit programs.

- You can't run 32-bit and 64-bit Office programs on the same computer. So if you already have 32-bit Office programs on your computer—32-bit Office 2010, say—you can't install 64-bit Project. If you need the horsepower and memory of 64-bit, then you have to uninstall any 32-bit Office programs and then install the 64-bit versions of them.

- If you rely on 32-bit add-ins, controls, Visual Basic code, third-party add-ins, and other extensions built on 32-bit programs, those tools might not work with a 64-bit program.

If you download Project 2013, you choose whether to download the 32-bit or 64-bit version. Project DVDs contain both 32-bit and 64-bit versions. Although the name of the folder on the DVD for the 64-bit version includes "x64," the name of the folder for 32-bit software includes "x86," after the Intel chips that computers used to run.

Before You Install

Microsoft recommends a certain amount of computer horsepower for Project to run properly. If you're managing multiple large projects with resource pools, Microsoft's recommendations are likely to be your minimum requirements. These days, the performance you expect often requires *double* the recommended amounts. Table A-1 lists what Microsoft recommends for running Project 2013 Standard or Professional.

TABLE A-1 *Computer resources needed to run Project 2013*

SYSTEM COMPONENT	REQUIRED HORSEPOWER
Processor speed	1 gigahertz (GHz) minimum
Memory	1 gigabyte (GB) minimum for 32-bit; 2 GB minimum for 64-bit
Available hard disk space	3.0 gigabytes (GB) minimum
Media	CD or DVD drive (if you plan to install from a CD or DVD)
Operating system	Windows 7, Windows 8, Windows Server 2008 R2, or Windows Server 2012
Browser	Internet Explorer 8, 9, or 10; Mozilla Firefox 10.x; Apple Safari 5; or Google Chrome 17.x
For importing Outlook tasks	Outlook 2007 or newer
For visual reports	Excel 2007 Visio Professional 2007 or Visio 2010 or 2013
For task list synchronization	SharePoint Foundation 2010 or 2013

NOTE   You initially need the 3 gigabytes of disk space to hold the installation files. After you install Project, you can recover some of that space by deleting the installation files. (However, without the installation files on your hard drive, you'll have to dig out your CD whenever you maintain or repair your installation.)

Installing Project 2013 for the First Time

All you do for a typical installation is click Install Now. Here's how to install Project 2013 without any bells and whistles on a computer that doesn't contain a previous version:

1. **Close any open programs, including your virus-protection software. If you have Project 2013 on a CD or DVD, insert the disc into your CD or DVD drive. If you downloaded the Project 2013 installation file, navigate to the folder where you stored it, and double-click the file.**

   If AutoRun is turned on, then the CD whirs away, the installation wizard starts, and you're on your way. The Setup program takes a few minutes to extract the files it needs, so feel free to refill your coffee.

   If you see a User Account Control dialog box that asks if you want Microsoft Project to make changes to your computer, click Yes.

TIP If Setup doesn't start automatically, the box below tells you what to do.

2. **In the Microsoft Project Professional 2013 dialog box, click Install Now. If you want to install multiple versions of Project or to customize the installation in any way, then click Customize instead (described below).**

   If you click Install Now, a progress bar moves from left to right, which tells you there's time to catch up on phone calls or attain inner peace.

3. **When the installation finishes, click Close.**

   In some cases, you may see a Continue Online button. Clicking it lets you take advantage of online help and other Microsoft Office Online features (page 742).

4. **Choose Start→All Programs→Microsoft Office 2013→Project 2013.**

   Project 2013 launches, and you're ready to go. There are a few more tasks to complete now, as you'll see starting on page 734.

UP TO SPEED

Kick-Starting an Installation

AutoRun is a handy feature that leaps into action as soon as you insert a disc into your CD-ROM or DVD-ROM drive. But the price for convenience can be steep. Because AutoRun starts up immediately, it could run malicious software that's hidden on a disc. AutoRun can also be downright annoying, since it opens a Windows Explorer window every time you insert a photo or music CD in a drive.

If you've turned off AutoRun (in Windows 7 and Windows 8, click Start→Control Panel→"Hardware and Sound," and then

under the AutoPlay heading, click "Change default settings for media and devices") or the installer it doesn't start for whatever reason, then you have to start the Project installation manually:

1. On the Windows task bar, click Start.

2. In the "Search programs and files" box, type *D:\Setup. exe* (replace "D" with the letter for your CD or DVD drive).

3. Press the Enter key. The installation starts (see step 2 above).

Customizing Your Installation

When you install Project, you can specify exactly what you want the program to install and where to install it. On the wizard screen that includes the big Install Now button (see step 2 above), simply click the smaller Customize button instead. Then you can choose exactly the features you want to install, when you want to install them, and where they should be stored. Specifying where to install the software is crucial if your C: drive is packed tighter than a sardine can. Even if you want to specify your name, initials, and organization, you must choose a custom installation.

When you click Customize, three tabs of installation options appear. Here's what you can do on each tab:

- **Installation Options.** To choose the features you want to install and when to install them, expand the section for the relevant product by clicking the + sign to the left of its name. Then click the down arrow to the left of the feature's name (like Microsoft Project Templates), and then choose one of these options (shown in Figure A-1):

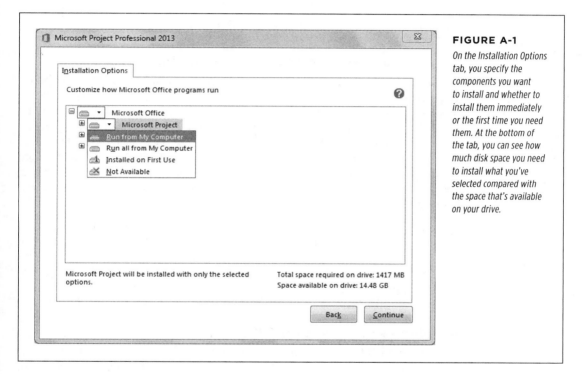

FIGURE A-1

On the Installation Options tab, you specify the components you want to install and whether to install them immediately or the first time you need them. At the bottom of the tab, you can see how much disk space you need to install what you've selected compared with the space that's available on your drive.

- **Run From My Computer** installs the feature on your computer immediately. Choosing this option means that the standard program and all optional features are installed on your computer.

- **Installed on First Use** may *sound* like a good idea, but in reality it's more annoying than helpful. The first time you try to use such a feature, Project prompts you to install it, which means you have to find your Project CD (or get to the installation files, wherever they may be). And you can't do your work until you finish installing the feature.

- **Not Available** skips the feature during installation (but you can install it later, as described in "Adding and Removing Features" on page 735).

The icons you see next to products and features tell you which installation options you've chosen. An icon of a hard drive means the feature will be installed.

An icon of a hard drive with a red X means the feature *won't* be installed. And an icon with a drive and the number 1 means the feature will be installed the first time you use it.

- **File Location.** To install Project somewhere other than the standard spot (*C:\ Program Files\Microsoft Office*), click the File Location tab, and then click Browse. Navigate to the folder you want, and then click OK.

- **User Information.** This tab contains boxes for your name, initials, and organization.

When you're done, click Install Now at the bottom right of the wizard screen.

Upgrading Project from an Earlier Version

Upgrading Project follows the same steps as a fresh installation, except that you have one more decision to make. When you install Project, unless you tell it otherwise, it protects its turf by *removing* previous installations of the program, which may be exactly what you want. But you may want to keep those earlier versions around. For example, if you're putting Project 2013 through its paces, you probably want to keep the previous version around until you decide whether the new version is right for you. If you find some deal-breakers, like the retirement of text-based reports, you can uninstall Project 2013 and continue running the previous version without interruption.

If you want to keep an earlier version of Project on your machine when you install Project 2013, start the installation process by performing step 1 on page 729. When you get to the wizard screen with the Install Now and Customize buttons, click Customize. If the wizard finds any earlier versions, you see an Upgrade tab with options for upgrading. To use multiple versions, select the "Keep all previous versions" option. Then click Install Now to complete the installation as you would normally.

Installing Project Pro for Office 365

If you have an Office 365 account and subscribe to Microsoft Office Professional Plus, you can download and install Office for Windows on up to five computers. With Office Automatic Updates, you can be sure that you always have the latest version of Project and your other Office programs. (Office Automatic Updates does for Office programs what Windows Update does for your Windows operating system.) Before diving into installing Project Pro for Office 365, you have a little setup work to do: Make sure your system has what it takes, sign up for an Office 365 service plan, and log into your Microsoft account.

Here's what you need to get started:

- **A web browser.** Choose your favorite from Internet Explorer 8 or higher, the latest version of Firefox, or the latest version of Chrome.

- **A Microsoft account.** This account used to go by the name Windows Live ID. If you use services like SkyDrive, Hotmail, Messenger, Windows Phone, Xbox Live account, or Outlook.com, you already have a Microsoft account. If you don't, go to *https://signup.live.com*, and then follow the steps to create an account.

Once you've got your Microsoft account, installing Office for Windows (including Project) is easy:

1. **Go to *www.office.com/myaccount* and log in.**

   The My Account page provides account information like how many PCs you've already installed Office on, and the services and products you use (Skydrive, for example). If you sign up for the top Office 365 plan for midsize and enterprise businesses (Plan E3), you can install the subscription version of Office Professional Plus on up to five computers.

2. **To install Office for Windows (including Project Pro for Office 365), click Install.**

   A dialog box opens and asks if you want to save the installation setup file (it's an executable file). Click Save File to download it.

3. **After the download is complete, double-click the setup file, and then click Run.**

   Depending on how your computer is set up, a dialog box might ask if you want the program to make changes to your computer. Click Yes. In the Office status dialog box that appears, a status message at the bottom left tells you how far along the installation is and what it's doing. When a big Office dialog box opens, assuring you that you'll love Office, it connects to your Microsoft account and you're ready to proceed.

4. **Click Next, and then click Accept.**

   The dialog box dances through several screens with smiling faces, a sure indication of the fun that awaits you. Finally, the dialog box welcomes you and asks you how you'd like Office to look.

5. **Click Next a couple more times. When the "We're getting things ready" screen appears, click "No thanks" to finish the installation.**

   When you click "No thanks," a status bar shows you that Office is still wrapping up the installation behind the scenes. If you click "Take a look" instead, you can tour Office's new features while the setup process continues.

6. **To start using Office, choose Start→All Programs→Microsoft Office 2013→Project 2013.**

   Project launches, and you're ready to go.

■ Activating Project

Activation is Microsoft's way of verifying that you're running a legal copy of a Microsoft program. Running Project without activating it turns the program into little more than a viewer, and you can run the program for only a short period of time. (Although Project 2013 runs with reduced functionality before you activate it, Microsoft is starting to eliminate the activation grace period. In Windows 8, you need a product key to install the software.) When you activate Project, Microsoft doesn't ask for personal information, so there's no harm in doing so.

> **NOTE** The Microsoft Office Project Activation Wizard creates a *hardware identifier* for your computer, which means, unfortunately, that you may have to reactivate Project if you rebuild your computer.

The Activation Wizard starts automatically when you run Project for the first time. In the Activate Office dialog box, click "Microsoft account" to sign in with the account associated with your Microsoft products (SkyDrive, Windows Phone, Hotmail, or other Microsoft services). If you have a Microsoft account through work or school, click "Organizational account." Enter your username and password, and then click "Sign in."

> **NOTE** If you have a product key for Project 2013, click the "Enter a product key instead" link. The "Enter your product key" dialog box appears. In the box, type the 25-character product key. If the product key is valid, a green checkmark appears to the right of the text box. Click Install.

When your program is activated, click Close, and you're done.

■ Maintaining and Repairing Project

After you install it, Project requires occasional care and feeding. For example, you may want to add or remove features, or reinstall features that aren't behaving correctly. You can also uninstall the program should you decide to forgo project management and start making origami instead.

If you don't keep installation files on your computer, insert the Project CD in your CD drive, and then start the installation files as if you're installing the software, as described in the box on page 730. If the installation files *are* on your computer, you can use the "Add or Remove Programs" window so you can perform your maintenance tasks. Here are the steps:

1. **If Project is running, exit the program, and then choose Start→Control Panel. In the Control Panel window, click Programs, and then click "Programs and Features."**

   The "Uninstall or change a program" window opens.

2. **In the list of programs, click Microsoft Project Professional 2013 (or Microsoft Project Standard 2013), and then click Change.**

The Project setup wizard starts, as shown in Figure A-2. The following sections explain how to use each option.

The setup wizard lets you change the features you use in Project, repair your Project installation, remove the program entirely, or enter your product key (if you haven't done so already).

Adding and Removing Features

Adding or removing features is like performing a custom installation (page 730). You can change which features are installed or change them to install on first use.

In the setup wizard, select the "Add or Remove Features" option, and then click Continue. The Installation Options tab that appears is identical to the one that appears in a custom installation, shown in Figure A-1. Follow the instructions in "Customizing Your Installation" on page 730. After you've made your changes, click Continue to install or remove the features. When the installation is complete, click Close.

Repairing Your Project Installation

Sometimes Project starts misbehaving. You know this quirky behavior isn't a bug, because the program was working fine a few seconds before. First, try closing and restarting Project. Then try rebooting your computer. If these techniques don't do the trick, then repairing the installation is the next step. Repairing corrects little problems that crop up, like missing files or registry settings gone awry.

In the setup wizard, select the Repair option, and then click Continue. Project analyzes the installation and repairs the problems it finds. As usual, you can tell by the progress bar creeping across the screen that you have time to tackle world hunger—or your own.

TIP If repairing the installation still doesn't fix the problem, uninstall Project (as explained next) and then reinstall it.

Uninstalling Project

In the setup wizard, select the Remove option. When the message box asks you if you want to remove Project, make sure you really want to, and then click Yes.

Getting Help

Microsoft Project 2013 may be your first introduction to project-management concepts like the critical path (page 292) and work breakdown structures (page 123). For you, Project presents a double challenge: learning what the program's commands and checkboxes *do*, and learning what to do *with them*. Or maybe you're a project-management expert and just want the dirt on how to use the program's features to get your work done: scheduling, budgeting, reporting, and keeping your project on course. For you, learning Project is a technical exercise: which features help you with the task at hand, where to find those features, how to get them to do what you want, and how to avoid the program's gotchas and limitations.

Whichever camp you're in, the first place you're likely to look for assistance is within the program itself. Project 2013 Help includes typical help fare like step-by-step instructions for using the program to perform various tasks. Help topics occasionally tell you why a feature is helpful, the best way to put it to use, and even give examples.

Finding the information you need is your biggest challenge. Project 2013 scatters tidbits of assistance throughout the program. For example, if you point to a column heading, a tooltip tells you what the field represents and may even show the formula Project uses to calculate it, as you can see in Figure B-1. Or if you point to an icon like the Insert Summary Task icon on the Task tab, you learn that the command inserts a summary task to help you organize the task list and that any selected tasks become subtasks of the new summary task. If you make changes to tasks and assignments, indicators and option buttons (page 58) help you tell Project what you're trying to accomplish.

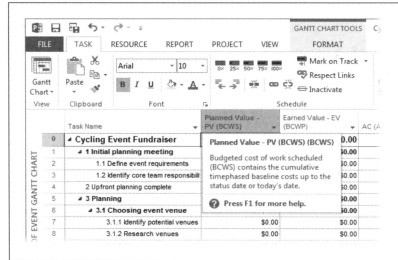

FIGURE B-1

The tooltip for a field provides a brief description of the field and may include the formula Project uses to calculate it. However, the Fields Reference within Project Help provides more information like best uses for the field, examples of how to use it, and so on.

Despite this helpful info, problems can arise when you try to use Project Help to learn the nitty-gritty. Say you aren't sure what the option to show task schedule warnings does. If you type *show task schedule warnings* into Project Help's Search box, you find out that the command is on the Task tab in the Inspect section. Project Help is a work in progress, so clicking Help or pressing F1 may take you to a specific help topic—or not. For example, clicking Help in the Task Information dialog box opens the Project Help window to its top-level help headings, as you can see in Figure B-2—not to the help topic about the field you're interested in.

This chapter explains how to make the best of the help that Project offers. These days, searching by keywords is the mainstay, so this chapter explains where to search for answers and how to ask the right questions. If you prefer scanning a table of contents, it's there, too—if you know where to look.

If Project Help leaves you in the dark, the silver lining may be discovering *other* resources and how helpful they can be. When an enigmatic Project feature is driving you crazy or you want to know how others use Project in the real world, search the Project discussion boards for the answer or post your problem. This chapter also identifies other websites and blogs that provide invaluable Project information.

In Search of Project Help

Naturally, Project Help is the first place you'll likely think to look for answers, and yet, finding them can be maddeningly difficult, as the box on page 740 explains. But because Project Help is right there on your screen, you may still want to start there. This section tells you how.

Regardless of how you access Project Help, you end up in the Project Help window, shown in Figure B-2. Project Help works like a web browser, so you can hop from high-level topics to lower-level ones, or follow links within topics to related information.

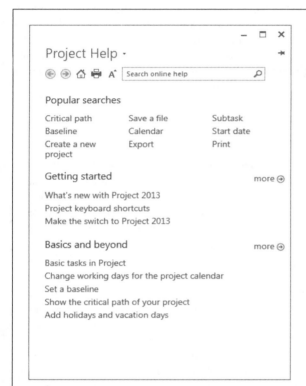

FIGURE B-2

Clicking a category link on the Home page displays the help topics within that category. In turn, Help topic links lead to the nuggets of information each topic holds. You can type new or revised search terms in the Help window's Search box, and then click the search icon (it looks like a magnifying glass) to see what Project Help has to offer.

> **TIP** To get the full scoop on Project fields, type *field reference* in the Search box, and then click the search icon. The Help window displays a list of links that describe all of Project's fields.

The Help window's icon bar includes several commands familiar to veteran web surfers: Back, Forward, Home, and Print. Here's what the Help window's other two icons do:

- **Change font size.** Click the font-size icon (it looks like a capital letter A) to switch between smaller and larger text.

- **Keep on top.** The icon near the top right of the dialog box initially looks like a horizontal pushpin, which means that the Project Help window doesn't stay on top of other windows. Instead, it minimizes when you click the main Project window, which may be just what you want if you work on a small screen and don't have room for the Project window *and* the Help window at the same time. However, if you have screen space to spare, keeping the Help window on top is ideal when you're trying to follow a 20-step process and don't want to switch windows after each step. To tell the Help window to stay on top when you click another window, click the pushpin icon so it changes to "Don't Keep Help on Top" (the icon rotates so it points down).

GEM IN THE ROUGH

Where's the Help?

Although you can access help on your computer (page 739), Microsoft recommends that you use its online help instead. Especially after Microsoft releases a new version of a product, help topics are added and updated frequently, so instructions that are missing initially could show up later. But even up-to-the-minute online Project Help has several issues:

- **Finding the magic keywords or phrases.** Finding the help topic you want means using the right keywords or phrases, just like searching the web. For example, "manual scheduling" retrieves a topic titled "How Project schedules tasks" and then quickly digresses to topics like making the switch to Project 2013 and keyboard shortcuts. However, if you tweak your search slightly by typing "manually scheduled" instead, you see several topics about using manually scheduled tasks. So if you don't find the topic you're looking for, try changing your search terms. See "Searching for Answers" on page 741 for hints on searching help.

- **Missing links.** Sometimes you click a Help link in a dialog box hoping to learn what turning on a checkbox does—but Project Help merely opens to the main Help window. You're left scratching your head over which keywords will give you the answer you seek.

- **Answers for other versions of Project.** Regardless of which Project version you install, help results include topics that apply to both desktop and enterprise project-management versions (Project Server and Project Web Access). Unfortunately, the topics don't explicitly identify the version they apply to, so you may have to try the steps to see if they work in your version of Project.

Whether you find an answer or not, don't ignore the "Did this article help you?" buttons at the bottom of each help topic. Microsoft insiders will tell you that the company takes your votes seriously. Microsoft employees are rated by those responses, so content that no one finds helpful is likely to get an overhaul. If you click No, a text box appears giving you 650 characters to tell Microsoft what you'd like them to change. Clicking Yes opens a text box so you can describe what was helpful. Clicking "Not what I was looking for" opens a text box that asks what you're trying to do—fodder for future help topics.

If the topic you choose isn't *quite* what you want, some topics include a "Related content" section at the bottom of the topic, which may have what you're looking for.

Searching for Answers

The most obvious routes to Project Help lead to a Search box, a big hint that the help system uses keywords. Finding the right keywords can be as delicate as crafting an apology. If one set of keywords doesn't do the trick, try synonyms or related terms; for instance, instead of "layout links," try "layout" or "format bars." Although one keyword usually isn't enough to pinpoint pertinent topics, too many keywords tend to add results that aren't related. Somewhere between two and seven keywords is usually about right.

You can choose from three ways to access Project Help's search feature, two of which you can see in Figure B-3:

- **F1.** Like many programs, Project's response to pressing F1 is opening the Help window to a list of help categories.

- **The Help icon.** The question mark at the top-right corner of the main Project window also opens the Help window.

- **The Help button.** Some dialog boxes have a Help button at their bottom-left corner, which opens the Project Help window. In the past, clicking this button opened the Project Help window to a dialog box reference topic that explained what every field, checkbox, and option in the dialog box did. (If you yearn for the old days of goal-oriented help, see page 743.)

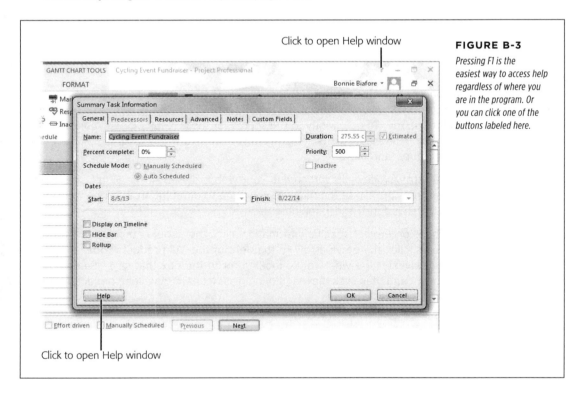

Click to open Help window

FIGURE B-3

Pressing F1 is the easiest way to access help regardless of where you are in the program. Or you can click one of the buttons labeled here.

Click to open Help window

TIP For folks who'd rather experiment than read, Multilevel Undo (page 310) means you can be adventurous. Try a checkbox or an option setting. If you don't like the results, then in the Quick Access toolbar, click Undo, and then backtrack through as many actions as you want.

Online and Offline Help

Out of the box, Project Help jumps online to grab help topics from Microsoft Office Online. Online help is the most up-to-date information, feeding you new and revised topics as Microsoft publishes them. But online help is no help at all if you're stuck in economy class on an overseas flight or without Internet access at your grandparents' house. In situations like these, you can tell Project Help to use its offline resources.

The secret to getting offline help is the down arrow to the right of the Project Help heading at the top of the Project Help window. To go off the grid, click the down arrow, and then choose "Project Help from your computer" on the drop-down menu. After you do that, the word "Offline" appears to the right of the Project Help heading. To go back online, click the down arrow, and then choose "Project Help from Office.com."

NOTE If you forget to switch to offline-help mode when you don't have Internet access, and you run a search, Project automatically searches its offline resources. Just remember to switch to online-help mode when you get back online.

◼ Microsoft Office Online

If you look closely at Project Help results, you see more than help topics. Depending on your keywords, specialized templates or online training courses may appear in the list, too. To go directly to the source for these results, open your browser to Office.com and feast on its help, training courses, downloadable templates, discussion groups, and more.

Type *http://office.microsoft.com* in your web browser. At the Office site, a set of tabs across the top of the page let you jump to different areas of the website, like Products, Support, and Templates.

To focus on Project-specific information, click the Support tab. On the page that appears, click the down arrow to the right of the "All products" box, and choose Project. Next, type what you're looking for in the box that says "Search Project support," and then click the magnifying glass icon. To download project templates, click the Templates tab.

■ Interactive and In-Depth Assistance

Coming up empty-handed in Project Help is depressing. Then again, your problem may not be easily compartmentalized or described in a few keywords. Particularly gnarly problems often need some discussion and brainstorming. Because Project Help focuses on how-to, you may need other resources to learn how to put Project features into practice.

If you're lucky enough to have a Project know-it-all as an officemate, you know how refreshing it is to provide a quick summary and get a quick answer. For those of us who aren't so lucky, the online Project discussion groups are that know-it-all. Speaking of know-it-alls, many of them write *blogs* (web logs) about Project. Although some of the posts may be over your head, blogs are a great resource for learning how features, old and new, really work. This section tells you where to find all these resources.

TIP If Project behaves oddly, you see an enigmatic error message, or you have a gnarly project-management scenario you're trying to resolve with the program, you probably need more assistance than Project Help can give. Sure, you can go to the Microsoft Support website (*http://support.microsoft.com*), but the quickest way to find a solution is to use your favorite search engine: Google, Bing, Yahoo, and so on. In the site's search box, type the error message, error number, or keywords that describe your problem or question. Some of the results will be links to Microsoft's websites, but the answer you need may come from a Microsoft partner's website or someone's blog.

Discuss Among Yourselves

If you like a personal touch, Project forums can be very satisfying. You can search for an answer to your question in previous posts. If you don't find one, you can post a question and get an answer. Some group members are bona fide Project experts, but the answer you need could come from anyone. The two-way communication makes all the difference; you can describe your problem in detail and receive a detailed answer in return. And if you see a question *you* can answer, you can give back by helping out someone else.

Here are a few places you can find Project-related forums:

- **Microsoft Answers.** This site (*http://answers.microsoft.com*) has forums for all of Microsoft's products. To reach the Project forum, on the home page, click Forums, and then click Office. Below the "See answers by topic" heading, click All Topics. In the Office Topic drop-down list, choose Microsoft Office Project.

- **TechNet forums.** Microsoft's TechNet forums (*http://social.technet.microsoft. com/Forums*) are usually a little geekier than other online communities. In many cases, that's exactly what you need. To get to the Project forums, on the TechNet Forums page, type *Project* in the search box, and then click the magnifying glass icon. Developers in the audience have their own Project-oriented forums: *http://social.msdn.microsoft.com/Forums/en-US/category/project*. For support with Project Server or Project Online, try *http://social.technet.microsoft.com/ Forums/en-US/category/project*.

- **Microsoft Project User Group.** This user group (*http://mpug.org*) provides all sorts of support for Project, including forums, webinars, chapter meetings, newsletters, job boards, and so on. Its annual membership fee is well worth it, when you take advantage of everything this group has to offer.

- **LinkedIn Project groups.** If you have an account with LinkedIn (*www.linked.com*), you can find dozens of groups dedicated to Microsoft Project. Click the down arrow to the left of the Search box at the top right of the site's home page, and choose Groups from the drop-down list. Type *Project* in the Search box, and then click the magnifying glass icon.

Project Blogs

Blogs tend to be informal and conversational, but don't let that fool you. They can provide a gold mine of in-depth information, in many cases from Microsoft employees. Go to *http://blogs.office.com/b/project*, which is the official Project team blog. You can find some great places for all kinds of Project info below the More Resources heading on the right of the page. For example, click the Brian Smith link to navigate to the Microsoft Office Project Support Weblog (*http://blogs.msdn.com/b/brismith*). Mr. Smith is an escalation engineer on the Project support team and has a reputation as *the* go-to person for troubleshooting Project and Project Server. Another good blog on all things Project is *http://blogs.technet.com/b/projectsupport*.

Getting Social with Project

If you want to keep up with those in the know, you can connect with Project through its social networking channels:

- **Microsoft Project's Facebook page.** Connect with Microsoft Project and Project folks through Project's Facebook page: *www.facebook.com/msftproject*.

- **Microsoft Project's Twitter handle.** Use @msftProject to connect with the Microsoft Project team. To find all the Project-related tweets, use the hashtag #msproject.

- **Microsoft Project Help writer's Twitter handle.** To see what the people who write Project content for Office.com are tweeting, use @ProjectHelpTeam.

TIP When you find Project gurus who seem to have all the answers and explain things in a way that resonates with you, use social networking to connect with them, too. Follow them on Twitter, like their Facebook pages, or subscribe to their blogs.

Keyboard Shortcuts

Keyboard shortcuts are tremendous timesavers, because your fingers can press a key combination in a fraction of a second compared with the seconds it takes to grasp the mouse and move the pointer to the correct location. Those saved seconds add up when you stick to the keyboard for your most frequent tasks—like saving a file regularly to make sure you don't lose any work or adjusting the position of tasks in the outline.

The only apparent disadvantage to keyboard shortcuts is learning their obscure keystroke combinations. If it takes you 10 seconds to remember that Alt+Shift+* displays all tasks in the project, then you really haven't saved any time. Mercifully, Project shares many keyboard shortcuts with other Microsoft programs, so you may not have to memorize as much as you think. On the other hand, a few minutes spent memorizing vital keyboard shortcuts can add up to *hours* saved down the line.

With Project 2013, you have two ways to use keyboard shortcuts. You can press tried-and-true keyboard combinations like Ctrl+S to save a file just as you could in previous versions of Project. Or you can display KeyTips and press letters to move around the ribbon and choose the command you want. This chapter tells you how to use both methods.

■ How to Use Keyboard Shortcuts

Keyboard shortcuts can be a single key, like F3 to show all tasks or resources. But usually you have to press a combination of Ctrl, Shift, or Alt along with other keys.

If you don't know the keyboard shortcut for something you want to do, you can instead navigate through the ribbon, drop-down menus, and commands with KeyTips (the letters you press to choose a feature). Here's what you do:

1. **To display KeyTips, press Alt.**

   KeyTips appear over each feature in the current tab or menu. For example, if you press Alt and then press H to select the Task tab, you see letters next to each command on the tab, like the G next to the Gantt Chart command (as shown in Figure C-1).

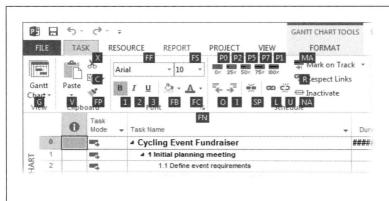

FIGURE C-1

If KeyTips are visible, continue to press letters on the keyboard until you press the letter for the specific feature you want to use. For example, after you press Alt to display KeyTips, press R to display the Project tab, then press B to display the Baseline drop-down menu, and finally press S to set a baseline.

Pressing KeyTip letters to choose features works only when KeyTips are visible. If you turn KeyTips off (by pressing Alt again), then pressing R doesn't display the Project tab—but it does enter an R if the cursor is in a field that accepts letters.

2. **To choose a feature, on the keyboard, press the letter in the feature's KeyTip.**

   As you use KeyTips to switch between tabs and menus, additional KeyTips may show up. For example, if the View tab is visible and you press H, Project switches to the Task tab, which displays the KeyTips shown in Figure C-1.

3. **Repeat step 2 until you press the letter for the command or feature you want.**

   For example, if the Task tab is visible, press G to display the drop-down menu of Project views. Then press M to open the More Views dialog box.

4. **To hide KeyTips, press Alt.**

   When KeyTips are hidden, pressing KeyTip letters doesn't issue commands—it just types letters.

NOTE The keyboard shortcuts in Microsoft Help refer specifically to the US keyboard layout. If you use a keyboard layout for another language, your keyboard shortcuts vary depending on how characters map to the keys on your keyboard. For example, Ctrl+Z is the US keyboard shortcut to undo the previous action. However, the French keyboard layout has W located where Z resides on the US keyboard, so the French keyboard shortcut for Undo is Ctrl+W.

■ Project Keyboard Shortcuts

Some of the keyboard shortcuts in this section apply not only to Project but to every Microsoft Office program, so you can learn them once and then put them to work in all your favorite programs. Project doesn't come with flip cards to help you memorize these esoteric keyboard combinations, but if you memorize the ones for the tasks you perform most, then you can often save time without overtaxing your brain.

> **TIP** If you memorize the shortcuts in this appendix and are still hungry for more, click the question mark (?) at the top right of the Project window's title bar or press F1 on the keyboard. At the top of the Project Help window, in the Search box, type *keyboard shortcuts*, and then click the search icon (it looks like a magnifying glass). The first help topic link should be "Keyboard shortcuts for Project 2013." Click the link to view a complete list of keyboard shortcuts specific to Project, and many that apply to all Microsoft Office programs.

All-Time Keyboard Shortcut Favorites

These favorites apply to all Microsoft Office programs, and they're commands you use all the time. The keyboard shortcuts in Table C-1 should be at the top of your memorization list.

TABLE C-1 *Keyboard shortcuts you're sure to use all the time*

TASK	KEYBOARD SHORTCUT
Create a new file (Project file, Word document, and so on).	Ctrl+N
Open an existing file.	Ctrl+O
Save the active file.	Ctrl+S
Print the current view (such as Gantt Chart).	Ctrl+P
Close the active file.	Ctrl+F4
Undo the last action you performed.	Ctrl+Z
Redo the action you just undid. Ctrl+Y behaves differently in Project than in any other Office program. In Word, Excel, and so on, Ctrl+Y repeats the previous action. In Project, Ctrl+Y redoes the last actions you just *und*id by pressing Ctrl+Z.	Ctrl+Y
Copy a picture of the entire screen to the Clipboard (which you can then paste into a document or file).	Print Screen (might appear as Prnt Scrn or Prt Scr on some keyboards)
Copy a picture of the active window to the Clipboard (for pasting into another file).	Alt+Print Screen

Project Outlining

So much of working with a project schedule is adding tasks and placing them at the proper level in the Project outline. The shortcuts in Table C-2 help you view the outline and indent or outdent tasks.

TABLE C-2 *Outlining without touching the mouse*

TASK	KEYBOARD SHORTCUT
Insert a new task above the selected task.	Insert
Indent the selected tasks.	Alt+Shift+right arrow
Outdent the selected tasks.	Alt+Shift+left arrow
Hide subtasks of the selected summary task.	Alt+Shift+hyphen (or Alt+Shift+minus sign on the numeric keypad)
Show next level of subtasks. Repeat this keyboard shortcut until you can see all the levels you want.	Alt+Shift+= (or Alt+Shift+plus sign on the numeric keypad)
Show all tasks.	Alt+Shift+* (or Alt+Shift+* on the numeric keypad)

Displaying Project Information

Whether you work on one Project file or several, the shortcuts in Table C-3 make it easy to see the information you want.

TABLE C-3 *Displaying Project windows and key dialog boxes*

TASK	KEYBOARD SHORTCUT
Make the next Project file window active (when more than one file is open or when you use View→Window→Switch Windows).	Ctrl+F6
Make the previous Project file window active.	Ctrl+Shift+F6
Maximize all Project file windows within the main Project window.	Ctrl+F10
Open the Task Information dialog box with data for the selected task.	Shift+F2
Open the Resource Information dialog box with data for the selected resource.	Shift+F2
Open the Assignment Information dialog box with data for the selected assignment.	Shift+F2
Open the Field Settings dialog box to add or modify a column.	Alt+F3
Reapply the current filter.	Ctrl+F3
Reset the sort order to sort by ID and turn off grouping.	Shift+F3
Display all tasks or resources.	F3
Display smaller time units in the timescale, for example, switching from weeks to days.	Ctrl+/ (use / on the numeric keypad)
Display larger time units in the timescale, for example, from weeks to months.	Ctrl+* (use * on the numeric keypad)

Moving Around in a Project View

Whether you're setting up, modifying, or monitoring a schedule in Project, you're likely to move around within the table pane or timescale of the Gantt Chart and other Project views. The keyboard shortcuts for moving around in views, shown in Table C-4, are a little easier to remember because they use arrow keys as well as Home and End. For example, to move to the first field in a row, you press Ctrl+left arrow, whereas you press Ctrl+right arrow to move to the last field. The Ctrl key identifies shortcuts for moving within the rows and columns of the table area, and the Alt key applies to the shortcuts for the timescale.

TIP In Project 2013, the Timeline pane is an easy, mouse-driven way to scroll the timescale (page 619).

TABLE C-4 *Moving within views*

TASK	KEYBOARD SHORTCUT
Move to the first row.	Ctrl+up arrow
Move to the last row.	Ctrl+down arrow
Move to the first field in the current row.	Ctrl+left arrow (or Home)
Move to the last field in the current row.	Ctrl+right arrow (or End)
Move to the first field in the first row.	Ctrl+Home
Move to the last field in the last row.	Ctrl+End
Scroll the timescale to the beginning of the project.	Alt+Home
Scroll the timescale to the end of the project.	Alt+End
Scroll the timescale to the left.	Alt+left arrow
Scroll the timescale to the right.	Alt+right arrow
Scroll the timescale left one page.	Alt+Page Up
Scroll the timescale right one page.	Alt+Page Down
Scroll the timescale to display the task selected in the table area.	Ctrl+Shift+F5

Selecting Elements in a Project View Table

After you display the part of the schedule you want, your next step is often to select a field, task, or resource to perform some editing. Selection shortcuts use the arrow, Home, and End keys in similar ways to the shortcuts for moving within a view. The main difference is that selection shortcuts use the Ctrl+Shift combination. For example, moving to the first row is Ctrl+up arrow, whereas selecting from the current selection to the first row is Ctrl+Shift+up arrow. Table C-5 lists the keyboard shortcuts for selecting elements in a Project view.

TABLE C-5. *Selecting within views*

TASK	KEYBOARD SHORTCUT
Expand the current selection to the first row.	Ctrl+Shift+up arrow
Expand the current selection to the last row.	Ctrl+Shift+down arrow
Expand the current selection to the first field in the current row.	Shift+Home
Expand the current selection to the last field in the current row.	Shift+End
Expand the current selection one field to the left.	Shift+left arrow
Expand the current selection one field to the right.	Shift+right arrow
Expand the current selection to the first field in the first row.	Ctrl+Shift+Home
Expand the current selection to the last field in the last row.	Ctrl+Shift+End
Expand the selection up one row.	Shift+up arrow
Expand the selection down one row.	Shift+down arrow

> **NOTE** These selection shortcuts expand the selection based on the fields or rows that are already selected. For example, if a Task Name cell is selected, then expanding to the first row selects all the Task Name cells up to the first row. If the entire row is selected, then expanding the selection to the first row selects all the tasks up to the first row.

Editing Within a View

You're probably familiar with keyboard shortcuts for editing. Ctrl+X, Ctrl+C, and Ctrl+V cut, copy, and paste selected elements in Project, just as they do in Microsoft Word and other programs. But Project includes a few additional keyboard shortcuts for specialized editing, listed in Table C-6.

TABLE C-6. *Keyboard shortcuts for Project editing tasks*

TASK	KEYBOARD SHORTCUT
Create a finish-to-start task dependency between the selected tasks.	Ctrl+F2
Remove all task dependencies from the selected tasks.	Ctrl+Shift+F2
Set the task mode for the selected task to Manually Scheduled.	Ctrl+Shift+M
Set the task mode for the selected task to Auto Scheduled.	Ctrl+Shift+A
Cancel changes without saving.	Esc
Activate a field so you can edit its text.	F2

Navigating Within Dialog Boxes and Forms

Of course, Project has dialog boxes like every other program, and the same keyboard shortcuts for navigating within them. The forms that appear in Project view, such as the Task Entry form, use some additional keyboard shortcuts to navigate within form fields and tables. Table C-7 lists these shortcuts.

TABLE C-7. *Navigating dialog boxes and forms*

TASK	KEYBOARD SHORTCUT
Display the next tab in a dialog box.	Ctrl+Tab
Display the previous tab in a dialog box.	Ctrl+Shift+Tab
Select an option in a dialog box or toggle between turning a checkbox on and off.	Alt+the underlined letter in the option or checkbox
Move to a field in a table within a form (such as the Resources and Predecessors tables in the Task Form).	Up arrow, down arrow, left arrow, and right arrow

Help Shortcuts

You need just a few keyboard shortcuts, listed in Table C-8, to open the Help window and browse help topics.

TABLE C-8. *Keyboard shortcuts for viewing help topics*

TASK	KEYBOARD SHORTCUT
Open the Help window.	F1
Display the previous help topic.	Alt+left arrow
Display the next help topic.	Alt+right arrow

Index

Microsoft Project 2013

THE MISSING CD

There's no CD with this book; you just saved $5.00.

Instead, every single Web address, practice file, and piece of downloadable software mentioned in this book is available at *missingmanuals.com* (click the Missing CD icon). There you'll find a tidy list of links, organized by chapter.

Don't miss a thing!
Sign up for the free Missing Manual email announcement list at missingmanuals.com. We'll let you know when we release new titles, make free sample chapters available, and update the features and articles on the Missing Manual website.